Brown's Guide
TO THE GEORGIA OUTDOORS

Biking, Hiking and Canoeing Trips

Selected from Brown's Guide to Georgia
Edited by John W. English & assisted by Katie Baer

Cherokee Publishing Company
Atlanta, Georgia
1986

Library of Congress Cataloging-in-Publication Data

Brown's guide to Georgia.

   Includes index.
   1. Outdoor recreation—Georgia—Guide-books.
2. Hiking—Georgia—Guide-books. 3. Bicycle touring—Georgia—
Guide-books. 4. Canoes and canoeing—Georgia—Guide-books.
5. Georgia—Description and travel—1981– —Guide-books.
I. English, John Wesley, 1940– . II. Brown's guide to Georgia.
GV191.42.G4B76 1986   917.58   86-26879
ISBN 0-87797-128-5 (pbk.)

This book is printed on acid-free paper which conforms to the American National Standard Z39.48-1984 *Permanence of Paper for Printed
Library Materials*. Paper that conforms to this standard's requirements
for pH, alkaline reserve and freedom from groundwood is anticipated
to last several hundred years without significant deterioration under
normal library use and storage conditions. ∞

Manufactured in the United States of America

ISBN: 0-87797-128-5

Cherokee Publishing Company is an operating division of
The Larlin Corporation, P.O. Box 1523, Marietta, GA 30061

CONTENTS

*Denotes maps enlarged in Appendix.

DEDICATION

To all the writers and editors who contributed to *Brown's Guide* during the 10 years from 1972 to 1982.

*Indicates writers and editors whose writing and ideas helped establish the tone and character of *Brown's Guide* and whose work set a standard for others.

Adcock, George
Aguar, Charles
Alexander, Raymonde
Anderson, William
Baer, Katie
Bailey, Dick
Bassett, Beth
Bernd, Carol
Bledsoe, Christena
Blihovde, Helen
Boardman, Frank
Brown, Lee
Brown, Leon
Bugg, Mary Cobb
Carstarphen, Carol
Champion, Charles
Champion, Patti
Clift, Eleanor
Coram, Robert
Cornelison, Jimmy
Counts, Charles
Crawford, Steve
*Cutler, Bill
Dabney, Joe
DeBacher, Gary
Dickey, Tom
Diefenbach, Robert C.
Dowis, Dick
Dunn, James
Dupree, Nathalie
Earl, John
Edmunds, Emma
Faggart, Maury
Fancher, Betsy
Feldman, Elaine
Feldman, Mitchell
Fore, Troy
Garner, Phil
Goldfarb, Stephen
Greear, Philip F. C.
Greenstein, Jayne

Grey, Farnum
Hall, Wilson
Ham, Margaret Welch
Hargett, G. Forest
Hawie, Sally
Hedgepeth, William
Hester, Conoly
Hill, Lynn
Hoff, P. J.
Holley, Vivian
Humphries, Bob
Hutcheson, Don
*Jacobs, Jon
James, Nathan
Johnson, Kristen
Jolley, Clyde W.
Jones, Randy
Jowers, David
Kay, Terry
Kirby, Martin
Krasel, George
Lewis, Boyd
Mackenzie, Malcolm
Mann, Carolyn Becknell
Marshall, Gerald
Mathews, Earl
Mays, Dennis
McClellan, Mike
McDonald, Bob
*McDonald, Susan
McRae, Barbara
Medford, David
Moll, John
Moore, Gene
Moran, Tim
Mosely, Mark
Mott, Michael
Moye, Falma
Murlless, Dick
Nielsen, Marion
O'Connor, Mary
Obrien, Laurie

Osborne, Margaret Tucker
Parish, Beth Crawford
*Patterson, Tom
Pendley, John
Perry, Whit
Pettigrew, Jim
Philips, Robertine
Phillips, John
Pittman, Wesley
Poort, John
Pope, Jerry
Postag, Ann
Rauscher, Carl
Rock, Maxine
Rymer, Russ
Schemmel, Bill
Scruggs, Carroll Proctor
Shapiro, Charles
Shaw, Russell
Shields, Mitchell
Shister, Neil
Simms, Tina
Smith, Gerald
Smith, Kathy
Smith, Sharon T.
Soules, Terrill Shephard
Steiner, Peter
Stocks, Allan
Sweitzer, Letitia
Talley, Dan
Terhorst, Karen
Terry, Claude
Thomason, Sharon
Tilley, Kathy
Townsend, James L.
Traub, Kit
Turnam, Adeline
*Turrentine, Reece
Warren, Chuck
Williams, Richard
Yarn, Jane

PREFACE

Early in its 10-year history, *Brown's Guide to Georgia* used the tag "The Recreational Magazine You Can Use" to identify itself. It was an apt description throughout its 81 issues from Winter 1972 to October 1982. *Brown's Guide* was, by all standards of journalism, a success. Its utility made it popular with readers, which led to steadily increasing circulation. In mid-1982, it touted itself as the largest monthly magazine in the state with some 60,000 subscribers.

Founder, editor, and publisher Alfred W. Brown made numerous changes in the magazine as he went along. For example, he increased its frequency as revenue dictated, beginning with a quarterly for the first seven issues, switching to bi-monthly for four years, and then, in September 1978, changing to a monthly. Brown also increased the magazine's size, beginning with a 6″ × 9″ page and switching to a standard magazine format of 8½″ × 11″ in March 1979. In addition, the magazine became progressively thicker over the years, growing from 36 pages in Vol. 1, No. 1 to an average of 136 pages in the final two years.

The scope of the magazine's content also expanded over the decade. Brown said he didn't really seek controversy in articles but he didn't avoid it, either. "We're trying to come to grips with the state of Georgia," he said in a 1978 interview. For him, that meant more than writing about old homes. "It has a lot of good and a lot of bad. Sometimes you have to say things people don't want to hear."

Clearly, Brown did not ask his stable of both free lance and staff writers to churn out fluffy promotion pieces for the tourist trade. He let writers roam the state, making discoveries and sharing the results with readers. Although he earned a reputation as a somewhat finicky editor, Brown did get the quality he sought and few could fault him for his standards. To keep writers happy, Brown pushed his payments up to $1,000 for a major piece, the highest in the area. But he also insisted that writers revise their work more than once and expected hard work for top dollar. He gave writers the space if they produced a story he felt was important to understanding the state better, and it was not uncommon for him to use 8,000-word articles, more than three times the conventional length for most magazines.

In virtually every aspect of magazine publishing, *Brown's Guide* became more sophisticated over time. Begun essentially as a family operation, along with advertising manager Don Hutcheson and his wife, Brenda, Brown added staff as needed. Writer-editor Bill Cutler, a mainstay of the magazine, was among the first to sign on. By 1982, the masthead listed a staff of 32.

By publishing industry standards, Brown's style was frugal. He kept the magazine in rambling upstairs offices in unfashionable College Park, out near the Atlanta airport. And he spent little on image. Much of the income was ploughed back into the product, especially in direct mail solicitations to potential subscribers. To keep up with his business competition, Brown did reader surveys and generated demographic data on his audience for his advertisers.

Brown took considerable pride in the magazine's graphic appearance and sought area artists to create an impressive string of covers. The cover art he chose set a tone for the publication, as original paintings, watercolors, and drawings captured the heart of the region. *Brown's Guide* covers, in their way, were as distinctive as those of *The New Yorker*.

Despite all the positive aspects, the magazine didn't quite make it to its 10th anniversary. Media-watchers speculated on the causes of its financial failure; some said the advertising rates were too low (its cost-per-thousand rate was about half of its major competitor, *ATLANTA Magazine*) and didn't keep pace with rising costs of paper, printing, and postage. Brown is still reticent to discuss why he decided to fold the publication at its peak. He acknowledges that he had borrowed funds to expand at the very time interest rates skyrocketed, so loan-maintenance

costs were high. With the prospects for profits appearing dim, Brown's investors refused to keep pumping money in, so there was no alternative but to suspend publication. The October 1982 issue became the last, to the disappointment of the magazine's following.

This guide—an anthology of outdoors articles from the magazine—was conceived at a chance meeting between Fred Brown and this writer one afternoon in 1985 in the parking lot of LeFont's Tara theatre. At the time, Brown was publishing another magazine, called *American Traveller,* for the Days' Inn Corporation, and expressed little interest in reprinting the most useful material from *Brown's Guide*. But he recognized it was a good idea and freely offered reprint rights. The project was born after Ken Boyd of Cherokee Publishing Co. of Marietta gave the go-ahead. Once the project was underway, Brown took active interest in it and assisted in the final selection of the pieces.

The void left by *Brown's Guide* has not to date been filled, so the information created during the magazine's prime is still the only available material of its kind. Its usefulness and value remain high because change in much of the state—especially in relation to nature—moves slowly. Thank God!

Extending the life of this information seemed right from the inception of the idea, but we became even more convinced there was an audience for these reprints after talking to outdoor recreation shop personnel and recognizing that enthusiasm for bicycling, hiking, and canoeing in Georgia continues to be high. We speculated that this guide would find an audience of two distinct types—new readers seeking to reap fresh physical pleasure from this rich state and faithful *Brown's Guide* readers simply wanting guided trips organized between one set of covers. To everyone, we hope the trips around Georgia continue to provide as much satisfaction for readers as they did for their creators.

John W. English
Editor

FOREWORD

Just over two years ago John English and I met by accident in the parking lot of the LeFont's Tara theatre on Cheshire Bridge Road in Atlanta. John is professor of magazine journalism at the University of Georgia, and in years past I had spoken to his classes about *Brown's Guide* and about my narrow view of journalism and writing.

At that chance meeting, he suggested that it would be worthwhile to collect in book form articles that had appeared in the magazine about Georgia out-of-doors. John's idea was that since the subject matter of the book would be mostly guides to the natural features of the state—aspects that don't change very much over the years—the material was of an enduring nature. He also maintained that the editorial approach of the magazine occupied a journalistic niche that had not been duplicated and was worth preserving.

At the time, I had little interest in the project. *Brown's Guide* had not been published for two years. I had been involved in another publishing project and, with some effort, had given little thought to any recycling of the magazine. In fact it was only through the efforts of my wife Ruth that a complete collection of the magazines had been assembled and bound for my bookshelf. John was enthusiastic and insistent, however, and I gave the project my blessing.

John went to work combing through back issues of the magazine and selecting stories that he thought would be useful to readers as guides to Georgia and which, at the same time, reflected the character and style of the publication. Some of his selections went back 10 years to the very first issues.

Some time later he asked me to look over and discuss his selections, and we spent a long summer's day on the screened-in back porch of his Victorian house in Athens doing that. It was during that time that I found myself rediscovering the magazine that I had started and edited for 10 years. I was both pleased and a little awed by the amazing quantities of information about the state of Georgia that was contained in the stories and by the quality of writing. It was as though for a long time I had been too close to the material and lately, too far away.

In putting together the magazine each month, the editors and I had asked writers work hard to pack detail and practical information in each paragraph. We thought nothing about sending a writer back to the top of Rabun Bald to be sure the trail marker pointed south instead of west, or to reride the Cumberland ferry to the Greyfield Inn to check room rates and food. That was a time-consuming and expensive process but it produced reliable information for readers, and the quality has held up over the years. If someone wants *information* about the dirt roads and the rivers and the hiking trails of this state, I can think of no better source than *Brown's Guide*.

Only second in importance to providing good information was providing good writing. I'm not sure whether the *Browns Guide* staff spent more time rehiking trails or rewriting stories about rehiking trails. We believed, with John Keats, that: "Next to good doing, good writing is the top thing in the world," and worked to imbue the magazine with that ethos. The establishment of a journalism scholarship fund at the University of Georgia with the proceeds from the sale of this book will be a tribute to the writers and editors who were a part of the magazine—who were the magazine—for 10 years.

The book is a document filled with affection for this unbelievably resource-rich state. The writers who trudged up and down Blood Mountain, who drove countless miles back and forth on I-16 to and from Savannah, who floated waterways as varied as the rock-strewn rapids of the upper Chattahoochee and the water lily-littered canals of the Okefenokee loved exploring this state and they loved writing about it and it comes across on every page.

My thanks to John English for allowing me to rediscover the work of 10 years, to the writers and editors who did the work, and to the thousands of readers and subscribers whose loyalty and affection for the magazine made it all possible.

Alfred W. Brown

INTRODUCTION

Outdoor recreation is *the* American national pasttime because it consistently fulfills people's need to "get away," keep active, and stay fit. People with an affinity for the outdoors want more than just space to exercise, whether they choose hiking, canoeing, or bicycling. They seek natural beauty and a certain sense of solitude.

Georgia is an especially appealing recreation spot because of its pleasant climate and varied topography.

This guidebook attempts to explore the diversity of the state, from Rabun Gap to Tybee Light. In the northern part of the state, "the highlands," we can traverse steep trails, challenge bold rivers, and explore winding roads. In a band across Georgia's middle, we see and feel an entirely different section, known as "the piedmont." And, in the southern part of the state, below the fall line, which runs from Augusta to Columbus through Macon, lies the "coastal plain."

Georgia is such a beautiful state that it's no wonder moviemakers have found its locations appealing. But our approach here is to go beyond the scenery and to discover each zone in emotional dimensions as well. In the highlands, as one fords mountain streams amid the cool forests, the feeling that there's something eternal and substantial about this terrain is inescapable. It's as calming in its own way as tranquil Lake Rabun or Lake Burton. For excitement, there are two of the last wild rivers in the country—the Jacks and Chattooga.

The rolling piedmont of middle Georgia is more conducive to leisurely strolls and lazy float trips. The productiveness of the farmland—former cotton country, now growing peaches, pecans and soybeans—attests to the fertility of the familiar red soil. Even the piney woods seem to be a crop just waiting for a Georgia-Pacific or Union Camp crew to come slashing in.

The coastal plain has its own feeling as well. The Okefenokee Swamp is the largest wildlife refuge in the Eastern United States, and stretches of wilderness coastline characterize the barrier islands. Spanish moss adds its own mystique to the lushness of the Golden Isles. In much of this part of the state, the expanse of the flatlands appears endless because one can see such distances. This is still plantation country, where bird dogs pursue quail and sunsets seem to last forever.

Each of the three areas offers its own outdoor challenges and pleasures. For example, unquestionably the best known hiking trip in the state is the first (or last, depending on which way you're traveling) 79 miles of the legendary Appalachian Trail, which is located in the highlands region in one of Georgia's two national forests, the Chattahoochee. The other national forest is the Oconee in the piedmont, which also contains miles of less rigorous hiking paths, including parts of the Bartram Trail (named after the 18th Century naturalist who explored the region).

The recreational sites described here are for the most part open all year long (plus a map of state parks and historical sites is included in the book on page 13). Georgia's climate encourages outdoor activity all year-round: the long fall season, relatively mild winter, and pleasant spring are perfect for outdoor activity. So use this book and use the spectacular state of Georgia to replicate the experiences the authors describe here. Or better yet, use those resources to create experiences that are uniquely yours.

J.W.E.

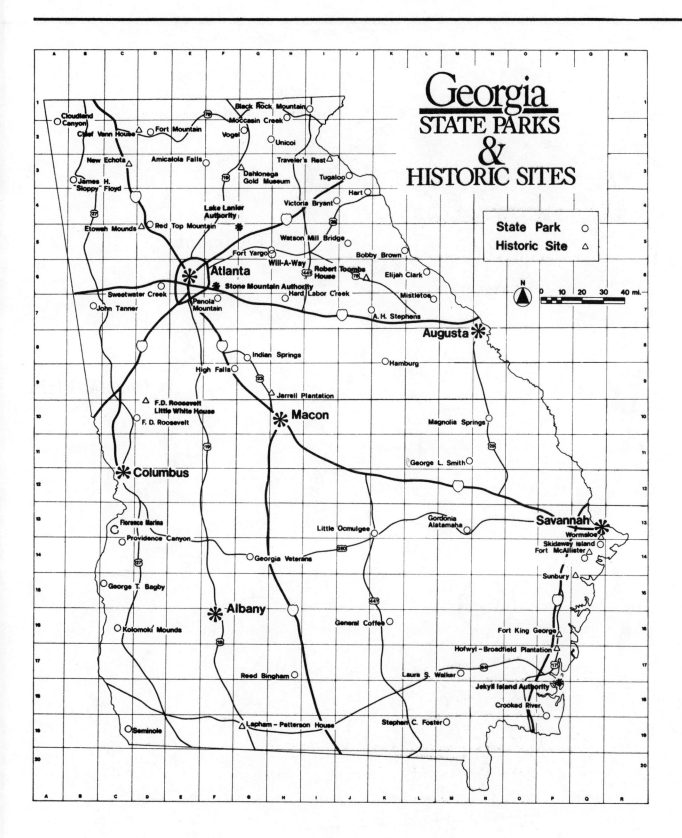

Georgia
STATE PARKS
&
HISTORIC SITES

| State Park | ○ |
| Historic Site | △ |

N   0 10 20 30 40 mi.

Cloudland Canyon
Chief Vann House
Fort Mountain
Black Rock Mountain
Moccasin Creek
Vogel
Unicoi
New Echota
Amicalola Falls
Traveler's Rest
James H. "Sloppy" Floyd
Dahlonega Gold Museum
Tugaloo
Hart
Victoria Bryant
Lake Lanier Authority
Etowah Mounds
Red Top Mountain
Watson Mill Bridge
Bobby Brown
Fort Yargo
Will-A-Way
Robert Toombs House
Elijah Clark
Atlanta
Stone Mountain Authority
Hard Labor Creek
Mistletoe
Sweetwater Creek
Panola Mountain
John Tanner
A. H. Stephens
Augusta
Indian Springs
Hamburg
High Falls
Jarrell Plantation
F.D. Roosevelt Little White House
Macon
F. D. Roosevelt
Magnolia Springs
Columbus
George L. Smith
Florence Marina
Providence Canyon
Little Ocmulgee
Gordonia Alatamaha
Savannah
Wormsloe
Skidaway Island
Fort McAllister
Georgia Veterans
George T. Bagby
Sunbury
Albany
General Coffee
Fort King George
Kolomoki Mounds
Hofwyl – Broadfield Plantation
Reed Bingham
Laura S. Walker
Lapham – Patterson House
Stephen C. Foster
Jekyll Island Authority
Crooked River
Seminole

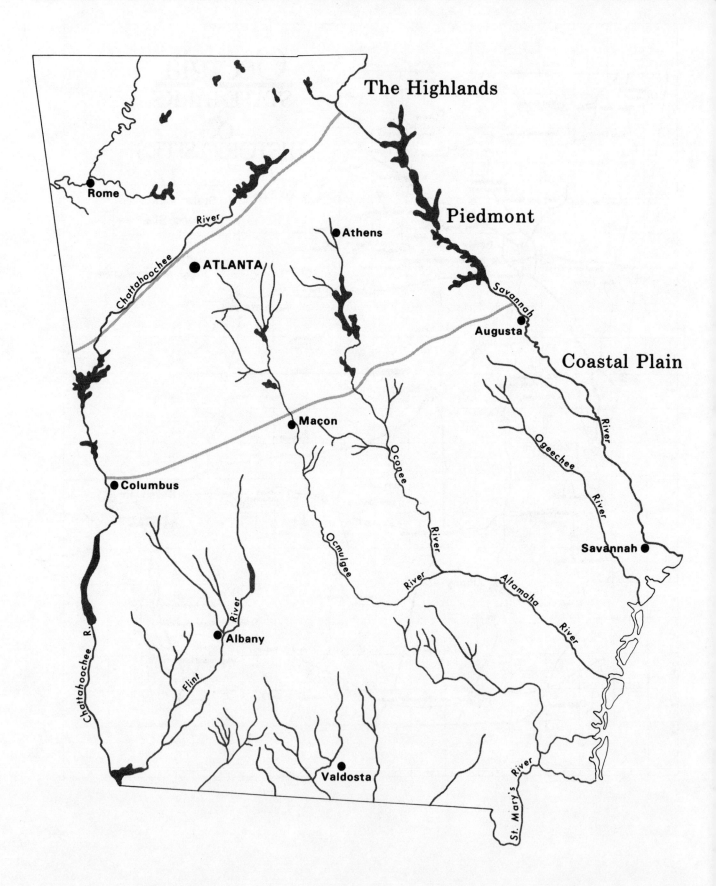

The Highlands

Piedmont

Coastal Plain

Rome

Athens

ATLANTA

Augusta

Chattahoochee River

Savannah

Columbus

Macon

Oconee River

Ogeechee River

Ocmulgee River

Savannah

Albany

Flint River

Altamaha River

Chattahoochee R.

Valdosta

St. Mary's River

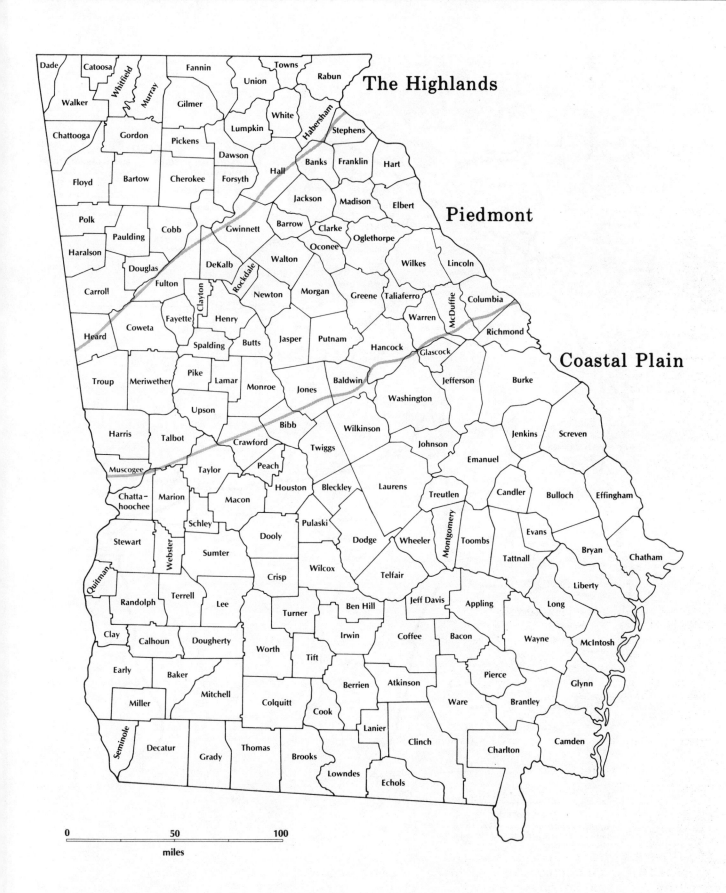

The Highlands

Piedmont

Coastal Plain

Dade	Catoosa	Whitfield	Fannin	Towns	Rabun
Walker	Murray	Gilmer	Union	White	Habersham	Stephens
Chattooga	Gordon	Pickens	Lumpkin	Banks	Franklin	Hart
Floyd	Bartow	Cherokee	Dawson	Forsyth	Hall	Jackson	Madison	Elbert

0   50   100
miles

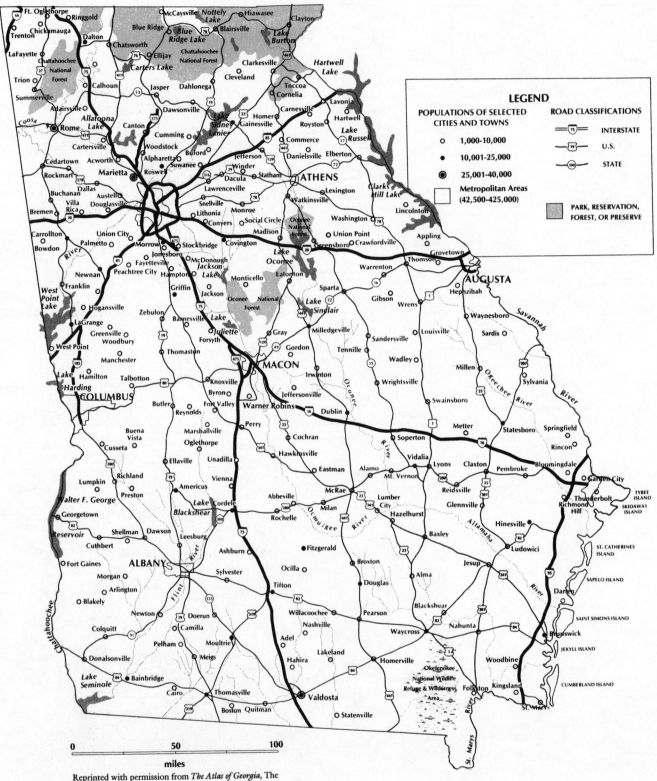

LEGEND

POPULATIONS OF SELECTED CITIES AND TOWNS

○ 1,000-10,000

● 10,001-25,000

◉ 25,001-40,000

□ Metropolitan Areas (42,500-425,000)

ROAD CLASSIFICATIONS

75 INTERSTATE

19 U.S.

300 STATE

PARK, RESERVATION, FOREST, OR PRESERVE

0   50   100

miles

Reprinted with permission from *The Atlas of Georgia*, The Institute of Community and Area Development, The University of Georgia.

Bicycling Trips

CONTENTS

Writing about bicycling in Georgia is virtually synonymous with Bill Cutler, who created the genre at *Brown's Guide to Georgia*. During his tenure, Cutler described and mapped some 60 biking trails for his readers.

His stories exposed bicycling enthusiasts to parts of the state unknown to all but the most-traveled veterans. Cutler not only wrote about new bicycling routes, but also told interesting narratives about the places he visited and profiled the personalities of an area.

For instance, in his cycling trip around Rabun County, in the highlands, Cutler profiled Eliot Wigginton, the editor and guiding light of *Foxfire*. In Cutler's story, Wigginton delves into the issues of North Georgia—the land, development and employment, preserving Appalachian culture—so any bicycling tourist would have a richer understanding of the environment and its people and their concerns.

Sensory details are part of Cutler's passion. On his route through Wolffork Valley, he notes: "You'll not only see up close but smell the cattle grazing in the lush pastureland."

Cutler's candor in his writing endears him to readers. Of another highlands route, he writes: "I love climbing hills better than just about any feature of biking. That's my way of testing myself against the environment without taking anything away from it, unlike most of humankind's methods of measuring self-styled superiority against the natural world. I love North Georgia as cycling terrain precisely *because* of the hills."

Cutler's road trips reflect a love affair with Georgia. Even in a tour of Atlanta, he points out Victorian neighborhoods such as Inman Park and West End and a rare house that survived Sherman's torches more than a century ago. His view of the city where he lives is personal: "This tour takes you into all sorts of urban landscapes—rich, poor, swanky, scruffy, close-knit, haughty, black, white, joyous, and sometimes a little sad." That's a pretty incredible emotional rollercoaster for a 52-mile ride—plus you get a real insider's view of the city to boot.

Cutler's perception is acute and his reporting is exhaustive. For example, in his tour of Warm Springs, he observes: "Walk through the colonnade on the left and look on the ground for the marker (4) identifying the former site of the Meriwether Inn. The fine old Victorian structure, much feared by FDR, was demolished in 1933, as the marker says, 'With regret and relief.'"

Cutler also enlists friends in the cycling fraternity to show him areas he doesn't know, so he almost always shares an insider's view. And he chronicles each experience with absolute honesty. In recounting one conversation in Columbia County a biking companion had with a middle-aged black woman who was doing her house chores, Cutler writes:

"'Got any collards cooked up?' Richard called to her. Food was never far from his thoughts, and we'd have welcomed lunch just then.

"The black woman dismissed Richard's question. 'Naw.'

"'Nothin' I like better'n a big mess of collards cooked up with just a little bit of streak o'lean,' Richard cajoled, unusual warmth and feeling in his voice.

"'Knows what you means,' she replied noncommittally, turning her attention to some object on the porch, as though to signal an end to our conversation."

Often Cutler's trips are true adventures. On a ride through the marsh country of backwoods McIntosh County, he searches for a Revolutionary War fort "that vanished, generations before I learned of its existence." Despite not finding a trace of the fort, he lets his curiosity roam around the Darien area as he relates lots of history he has gathered as clues for his search.

Another Cutler passion—besides history—is roses, so that pursuit becomes an element in his ride through Rose City, Thomasville.

Finally, Cutler takes his readers where his curiosity leads him and it's usually an interesting ride. He deliberately pursues a perspective other tourists rarely get: off-beat, yet romantic; intelligent, yet fun. He meets people easily and makes them part of our lives.

Cutler is also an advocate for the sport of cycling, which he claims is the second most popular physical fitness activity, after jogging. To promote cycling within the state, he established the Trans-Georgia Bicycle Trail, which starts in the southwest corner of the state, follows the Georgia-Alabama border to Providence Canyon state park, then cuts northeast to pass through Atlanta and Gainesville to its conclusion at the Georgia-North Carolina border near Clayton. (For free bike maps, write the Department of Industry and Trade, Tourism Division, P.O. Box 1776, Atlanta, GA 30301. For more detailed county maps of the route, ten different maps can be ordered from the Department of Transportation, Map Sales, No. 2 Capitol Square, Atlanta, GA 30334-1002. The cost is $1.50 each.)

Cutler's articles reprinted here are a model for other cycling guides in that they provide bicycle tourists with concise, accurate information, maps, and a sense of the place and its people. Plus his writing captures the romance and reality of the road, as this passage illustrates:

"After 38 miles of cycling, the beating of my heart felt like it was synchronized with the pumping of my legs on the pedals of my touring bike. A stiff wind blew the perspiration from my eyes as I viewed the wooded landscape along the trail. The trip had begun at the Mt. Pleasant Baptist Church, where my fellow cyclists and I enjoyed a feast prepared by members of the congregation. We had traveled along deserted country roads past tobacco farms, waving back to the field hands who had greeted us like old friends. We had ridden along the Suwannee River, whose dark waters were covered by a canopy of cypress and live-oak trees. Our journey had come to its end at the remains of an old resort, whose weathered tabby walls now enclosed a portion of the tannin-stained Suwannee River. My companions and I dismounted and spent an hour or two swimming or sunning like turtles on a log, allowing our fatigued legs and rumps to recuperate."

J.W.E.

Eliot Wigginton on The Land of Rabun County

by Bill Cutler

He sat hunched over the counter at D's Tavern, a bottle of Miller's in his left hand. Behind him, the pomegranate-red cinderblock walls reflected dully the little light that played across them from the jukebox and a couple of dim overhead bulbs. He saw me enter, advance, and hesitate. To ease my discomfort, he extended his right hand, introduced himself, then went right back to conversation with a broad-backed, chestnut-necked man, whose back rose like a cliff and blocked out my view of Eliot Wigginton, editor and guiding spirit of *Foxfire.*

The broad-backed man got up after awhile to relieve himself, and Eliot Wigginton returned to view. He had the look of a contemplative rabbit. His eyes, behind dark-rimmed glasses, appeared shallow and melancholy. In profile, his chin retreats precipitously from his lower lip, and his front teeth protrude, pushing his upper lip forward. One of his upper left incisors is a fraction of an inch shorter than its neighbor on the right, leaving a horizontal black gap across the front of his open mouth.

Wigginton shook his head in a self-conscious, theatrical gesture. "That guy's story's incredible," he said to me. "This is the first time I've met him. He's a Chicano, worked as a fruit picker for years up and down the East Coast. He came to Rabun County four years ago and put down roots. Got a job as chef at the Dillard House, and he's been here ever since. He's kind of in his cups now, but he's been telling some fantastic stories about his past."

The man lumbered back to his stool. Other patrons came up to Wigginton, shook his hand, engaged in banter, serious talk, business propositions. He sat still, and the men came to him. The broad-backed Chicano left, and Wigginton shook his head again in that same theatrical gesture. "Four years he's been here, and I didn't even know it." His tone was vexed. "I haven't been getting around enough."

We left D's Tavern, bracing ourselves for the cold Mountain City night. Tiny patches of snow were cupped in the lee of cinderblocks, rusted automobile parts, wood remnants that lay around the edges of the parking lot. I backed my van gingerly through the rutted mud and followed Wigginton's green pickup north along the old Indian trail that is now U.S. highway 441 through Rabun Gap toward Dillard, almost at the North Carolina line. The rounded tops of the mountains on left and right cupped the valley we were driving through. My headlights scanned screaming letters at the edge of broad open fields: "Choice Commercial Location. Land For Sale. Land! For Sale!"

We sat down to dinner at the Dillard House. A man from a neighboring table stopped by to congratulate Wigginton on the work of Foxfire. Wigginton received the praise with accepting, impassive gentleness. His long, thin, smooth, pink face, which looked as if a razor had never touched it, was guarded, chary of expression. The corners of his eyes bore witness to the passage of more years than his cheeks testified to. He spoke in a flat monotone, his words carefully spaced, each syllable weighted for effect.

Eliot Wigginton was born near Wheeling, West Virginia, in 1942, the son of a landscape architect. He has been teaching school in Rabun County since 1966, with one year off at Johns Hopkins for graduate work in literature. His English classes—originally at the private, preparatory Rabun Gap-Nacoochee School, now at the public Rabun County High School—have encouraged students to explore and celebrate the traditions and folklore of the mountains. His first class published a magazine called *Foxfire,* containing interviews with older local residents and detailed information about mountain crafts, which was immediately recognized as an invaluable source book on a vanishing culture. More magazines followed, then four books under the Foxfire name, all edited with an introduction by Eliot Wigginton. Today, Foxfire is an institution, a reference point for similar investigations into local customs all over the country, and Eliot Wigginton is a consultant much in demand on art boards, at humanities seminars and colleges throughout Georgia and the U.S. In addition, Foxfire has become a significant locally owned and operated industry inside Rabun County, having expanded from magazine and book publishing to include photography and music collecting and recording.

I asked Wigginton what opportunities existed for his students if they wanted to stay in Rabun County after graduation. I was particularly interested to know if the Foxfire experience had provided young people with opportunities they might not otherwise have had. I got far more by way of an answer than I had bargained for.

"It's incredibly complicated," Wigginton replied, "and where it all gets sticky is the hassle that you have talking about a situation like this. No matter what you say, certain elements in the community are going to hear the opposite of what you said and what you meant. No matter what you say, you're damned."

I watched him with greater interest as he picked his way through minefields, sifting and balancing for audiences visible and invisible. "In terms of the kids that I work with, there are a number of related problems. It gets more and more complicated, because the definition of the problem is dependent on what any particular student wants to do with his or her life. If the goal a student has is to buy a trailer and live on a little plot of land and work in one of the factories here, then that student's got no problem. That option is available.

"If you've got students who want to open a little business, like a little garage or a little beauty shop, then you've got eight problems, one being that there's competition all over these hills, and there's not enough population around to support a second or third or fourth extension of that business. Another problem being that if you had the kind of population in here that would support it—" his voice here slowed almost to a stop, his tone expressed weariness with the roundabout nature of the complexities he pondered, "—then chances are there'd be some pretty expert competition that would knock kids out of it right away because they don't have professional training.

"But now you take one of my kids coming out of high school who may not want to go on to college but who may want to buy thirty or forty acres to put into a dairy farm, and you present him with a piece of bottom land and tell him it's going to cost him four thousand dollars an acre, and see how far he gets. There's not a whole lot of chance that very many of my kids are going to make as much as a-hundred-and-twenty, hundred-and-fifty-thousand dollars in their lifetimes, certainly not working for the new Sangamo Weston plant that's going into Wolffork Valley across the way there." He pointed in the direction of the highway we had driven up, identifiable at night out of the picture windows in the Dillard House dining room by the string of white lights moving north and the string of red lights moving south.

"That's not to say I'm opposed to Sangamo putting food on their tables. But if we're talking about kids wanting to carve out a piece of turf for themselves—if those are the jobs that are open to them, they're not going to get the kind of money they're going to have to have to carve out that piece of turf. So what you're saying is, the local labor pool's going to be relegated to half-acre lots in trailer parks and mobile homes and make enough money to keep the family together, but as far as being able to pass on something to their kids in the form of a homeplace or a heritage, there's not going to be much of that around."

He wanted me to see "The Land," as he called the mountaintop belonging to Foxfire where the Appalachian heritage is taught to students through programs held in log cabins assembled from Rabun and surrounding counties. We agreed to meet the next day at the foot of the mountain and parted for the night. I made my way south on 441, back through Rabun Gap and Mountain City, past D's Tavern, through Clayton to a roadside motel. The check-in counter displayed brochures from local real-estate companies. I leafed through them, wondering if Wigginton had exaggerated the prices his students would have to pay for farmland.

"We have a lot to offer," punned the 24-page booklet from Edwin C. Poss Real Estate. Lots (not acres) in Sky Valley development, Georgia's only skiing resort just north of Dillard, were going for between slightly under $10,000 and over $20,000 each. Land in the Wolffork Valley, soon-to-be-home of the giant Sangamo Weston plant, was being offered at $6000 an acre. Just under 3½ acres of bottom land were being offered for $11,000 along Betty's Creek, where many of the mountain people interviewed in Foxfire publications lived. Under the heading "FARMS-LAND-INVESTMENTS" was the following item: "Valley (said to be an old Indian Village Site). 100 acres. Ideal lake area, water shed for 500 acres which goes through a small rock notch (an easy dam site). Cascading waterfalls with many magnificent home sites. Potential for hydroelectric power to supply many houses. $1250. per acre." Ed West Realty listed 10 to 12 acres in the Betty's Creek area for $3000 per acre "with several beautiful building sites. Owner will divide." Blalock and Griffin Realty offered "RABUN BALD MOUNTAIN. Near the top, 7.87 acres of the most beautiful views. Owner will subdivide. $25,000." In Wolffork

Valley, "32.38-acre farm with a frame 2-story old fashion home and an old barn. Good road frontage and priced at only $2,750 per acre." Quite a steal, apparently.

The next morning, I drove 441 again, north through Clayton, past Edwin C. Poss Real Estate, housed in a long L-shaped contemporary wooden building designed to resemble an old grange. Past Blalock and Griffin Realty, occupying a two-story imitation Swiss Chalet with curlicue decorations along the eaves, Helen-style. Past the Rabun County Welcome Center, set back from the road in an understated wooden structure with a front porch, modeled after simple, back-country mountain homes. It was nearly invisible from the highway, sandwiched in between a red-roofed Pizza Hut and a Bantam Chef.

Eliot Wigginton met me at the foot of his mountain in a four-wheeled-drive vehicle, and drove me up and over a series of washouts and rock slides to The Land. It had snowed, a light dusting, during the night. As we approached his settlement, an intense squall of snow enveloped us. Through the thick curtain of white, I could make out over 20 log cabins of various dimensions scattered across the hillside. We slipped and slid through snow to the cabin housing the Foxfire offices. A middle-aged man and two boys were putting the final touches to a door, hammering, planing, and drilling as we talked. A fire blazed in the stone fireplace. Bookcases held copies of Foxfire magazines and paperbacks. Desks were simple planks. The interior gave off a spruce, scrubbed, stripped-down appearance. The astringent tang of new wood was in the air.

Wigginton needed no priming to continue our discussion. As he talked, I felt I was being carried with him higher and higher into the surrounding mountains and shown an ever more extensive, detailed, complex view of Rabun County. "You've got a hundred points of view represented. That's all part of what makes it so complicated. You have people like my father, for example, who are convinced that one of these days, like it or not, we may be in a situation where raising our own food for the year is going to be one of the few ways we're going to be able to make ends meet. And if you take bottom land and continually pave it over and put up supermarkets and Sangamo Weston plants, then that's one more chunk of potential farming land taken out of circulation.

"You've got another group of people that say that the extent to which that happens is the extent to which the natural beauty and scenery and the real basic attraction of the mountains gets annihilated, and the very reason for wanting to stay here and wanting to live here—i.e. the desire for a basically rural kind of existence—gets axed.

"You've got another group of people, and I—" he sighed, paused, then continued in a descending drawl, like a phonograph record slowed by a child's finger to several rpms below its intended speed, "—I guess I fall into this category, that say that the extent to which you let your chunk of the world become, through development, indistinguishable from any other chunk of the world is the extent to which you've lost a large part of the initial attraction which you once had. If you drive into Clayton, Georgia, expecting to see something unique and unusual, and what you find is a Kentucky Fried Chicken and a Pizza Hut, then why leave home? What was the reason for going?"

His mind had made one complete circle around its subject, always climbing, like a road winding around and up a mountainside. The scenic overlook he now exposed to view took my breath away. "The problems that a region like the Southern Appalachians faces are not nearly as simple as the kinds of things we've been talking about. The core of the problem is two-pronged. One is that you have a number of people in this country who have a healthy income and who have decided that, for whatever reason, a second home is part of their due. People have a right to say—" here his voice became very deliberate, forceful, "—'I and my family are going to spend two months of our lives every year in the country instead of in the city.' So part of the problem is that you can't say, 'We've got this problem, and you've got to stay where you chose to work and not come up here.' We can't just say, 'I want second-home development to go away,' because it's not going to go away. If someone from Atlanta comes to Rabun County and there happens to be land for sale in Rabun County, you can't say, 'You're not allowed to buy this land.' It's for sale. It's for sale to anybody who's got the damned jack. You can't restrict the potential purchasers. You can't say, 'I'm only going to sell to—' you know, '—one-legged Chicanos.' So people who live in the Southern Appalachian region obviously are catching the full force of that problem right in their teeth, because they have the land and people in Atlanta don't and they want it. Understandable—which is what makes it more complicated—and justifiable, which makes it *even* more complicated.

"The second big problem that you've got—the crazy, maybe the biggest one of all—is that the Southern Appalachian region, by and large, is owned by outside corporations, completely. All of the major income-producing industries and corporations in the Southern Appalachian region are owned by outside conglomerates. You can't name one that's not, from the Forest Service, which owns more than sixty percent of Rabun County's land, right through every major coal company in the coal-producing region to every major manufacturing company, whether it be Sangamo Weston—controlled by a European outfit called Schlumberger, pronounced Schlum-berjay—or a major furniture manufacturer or textile mills in Dalton or an alarm-clock plant, whatever it is. Although they pay a certain amount of taxes, the fact of the matter is that the bulk of the profits go outside the region, and the people in the region take home their hourly salary, whatever that happens to be, and if they're not satisfied with that, then it's too damned bad."

A car inched its way up the last feet of the rutted, nearly unquarried mountain road that led to The Land and unloaded three adults and a child. "Damn!" said Wigginton. "How do they know we're here? There's no sign down on the road. Even in weather like this they find their way up here somehow or other." The invaders wandered from cabin to cabin, eventually tracking down the office where we sat. A ruddy-faced, cheerful looking man with stubby grizzled hair greeted Wigginton warmly and introduced his in-laws from Canada. He spoke in the broad, flat drawl of the mountains. Wigginton was clearly glad to see him, a kindred spirit. They exchanged anecdotes of Betty's Creek. The in-laws appeared starry-eyed to have set foot on Foxfire's land.

They left, and we had the hearth to ourselves again, while the carpenters kept on with their work. "The real problem is, of course, that everything is so interlinked," Wigginton said, picking up the narrative. "The problem is the fact that the destiny of the Appalachian region is not in the hands of the Appalachian people. That's the problem, period. There are a lot of folks who would say, 'Well—so what? They're going to have their trailer, they're going to have their little piece of land, they're going to have their regular income—ten, twelve thousand a year, whatever the heck it is—and they're going to survive. They're not going to starve to death. They aren't going to have rickets or beri-beri. They're going to have health care, they're going to have good teeth. What's the problem?'

"Other people are going to say, 'It's always a problem when a region gets taken from its people by outside interests.' Now that's idealistic, philosophical, pie-in-the-sky, whatever you want to call it—it's bleeding-heart, I don't give a damn what you call it. You know, people that think that way suffer from all kinds of unrealistic idealism and misplaced sense of tragedy, but for people that feel that way—as I do—it matters."

Hearing Wigginton talk was like listening to a radio play crowded with characters. I found myself continually caught off guard as he rehearsed the differing points of view, standing outside himself, as he had just done, giving his own position the same objective scrutiny he gave attitudes he did not share.

He had finished his climb now. We were on top of the mountain, high, high above Rabun County and its immediate dilemmas. "Other people are going to say that this region, despite the fact that it is called the Appalachian land for Appalachian people, is in fact a piece of territory that the Appalachian people themselves stole from prior inhabitants, and they've got no more claim to it than anybody else." Wigginton's voice fell into a kind of mechanical, plodding lilt, as though he was reciting stories he didn't put much credit in. "The history of land in this country has been that no one group or collection of people has had a right to call it theirs. And so you've got some people for whom this particular plight doesn't happen to be a tragedy—simply a fact of life. You know, land goes to people who have the power to get it. In the case of the Indians, they didn't have the power to hang onto it. In the case of the Appalachian people now, *they* don't have the power to hang onto it either."

It was time to head for Rabun County High School, where Wigginton for the first time this year teaches his Foxfire classes after 10 years at the private Rabun Gap preparatory school. We inched our way down the mountain, drove south on 441, the main tourist route to the Smokies and the chief cause of Rabun County's rapid growth. "Sometimes in spring and summer I have to wait fifteen or twenty minutes to get out on 441," Wigginton remarked as we passed Clayton's commercial strip. "It's easy to draw a very graphic picture showing *precisely* what this county is gonna look like in twenty years. That's a *snap*. A *third*-grader could do that—" his voice was as crisp and emphatic as I'd yet heard it, "—given the facts."

I had to risk being reduced to second-grade status or lower. "What *is* it going to look like?"

"Well, it would be a combination of—given the current trends—Gatlinburg and Blowing Rock and Boone." He paused, while I looked around at the lovely valley, its soft beauty suddenly fragile and uncertain. "The question is then, given that projection, is that good or bad? For the people that moved into this area because they like a rural kind of situation, it's probably bad, and I and people like me could probably be persuaded to go someplace else, because I'm not crazy about living in a high-intensity center of activity."

Then he balanced the scales of the future again and came up with a different measurement. "For people who have lived in the country all their lives and have had to eke out what's at best a marginal existence and are hungry for some activity and some variety that hasn't been here before, it's probably one of the finest things that could have happened. And I'm going to be the last person in the world to say they're wrong. Certainly the people who make their living off a large number of travelers and a higher percentage of purchasers—I can't say they're wrong."

He paused, the longest pause yet. When he spoke again, I wished I'd been inside the head that studied its own activities as his did and ended up with the judgments he reached about himself. "And just as soon as some crazy like me says, 'I think it's too bad that Rabun County is gonna get built up, and when that does happen, I'm not going to be happy here anymore and I'm going to go someplace else'—as soon as somebody like me says that, there'll be fifty people that will say, 'Well, it's partly because of you that it happened, so what are you bitching about?' Because to a certain extent, the notoriety and popularity this county is enjoying now is a result of Foxfire."

It was hard to talk to Wigginton at the brand-new high school south of Clayton. Kids shadowboxed and hugged him in the halls, and he shadowboxed and hugged them back. His colleagues stopped him for consultations, gossip, nostalgic reminiscences about the passing of mountain ways. The youngsters called him "Wig," his contemporaries mostly "Eliot."

We found a quiet place for a few minutes' conversation before his class began. I asked him whether Rabun Countians expressed much awareness about the loss of their heritage. "As far as a very conscious movement to steal from them everything they have, there's almost no consciousness of that at all. There's a vague feeling, I think, among most people that things are somehow out of whack and out of control. I work constantly with people who come to me either looking for jobs or looking for help or wanting me to co-sign loans, and people are saying, 'I don't know why, but we just can't seem to make things work out financially, we can't seem to put things together to make ends meet.'"

What role did he see Foxfire itself playing in raising the consciousness of local residents, I wanted to know. "We talk about it in class, but I don't know the extent to which that's good. See, you're in the middle of that whole thing now, that's where it's politically touchy and very sensitive. For what reason do you raise the consciousness? Is it wrong or is it right? Is it wrong to make people who might otherwise have been reasonably and comfortably content uncomfortable and discontented? Is it justifiable inside a public school to have kids looking closely at a problem and realizing a problem, if it's a problem they're not going to be able to do anything about 'cause it's bigger than all of us? Really, it's just almost insoluble. I mean, the whole damned thing is almost insoluble."

He turned his head and glared directly at me. I noticed for the first time how long his ears are, how their tops cling to the sides of his head and then how they flare out midway down, with the lobes bellying sideways. I had become used to looking at his right profile with its underslung chin, a contour of roundness and softness and gentleness, an air of infinite patience and sad acknowledgement that hopes for Rabun County's future are as various as the persons who hold them. There was tension in his face now. Diagonal lines crossed his cheeks from the flare of his nose to the corners of his mouth. Gone was the easy joy of the juggler. He was a tightrope-walker, strained in concentration, aware of the danger of falling from heights.

"A number of the people that are actively about the business of—either selling out and getting whatever money they can get from that, selling off the family home, *or* exploiting that in the form of tourist-related businesses—are local people. And, again, you can't say that they're *wrong*. I mean, who the hell am *I* to come in from the outside and say somebody that's been here four generations is wrong for selling their farm when they can't make any money off it? What the hell kind of an argument is that, for God's sake? You know, I *can't*. If we've set this country up in such a way that a man who runs a small farm can't make enough money off it to keep his kids in school, then we've probably set it up so that he hasn't got any choice, and we can't blame him for taking that other option. What the hell you going to do? You can't hang onto it and sit and look at it, you can't take it with you, you can't make it pay. You sell it and try something else. I mean, I can't condemn a man for doing that, for God's sake. But the fact of the matter is that the business of actively selling out and decreasing on a day-to-day basis what little power the Appalachian people already have is by and large being done by Appalachian people. And who am I to say they're wrong?"

We went to Wigginton's classes, two in succession. Students in both saw a film about an outdoors program in North Carolina they were encouraged to take part in that teaches self-reliance and self-discovery. When the classes were over, Wigginton suggested that we go back to D's Tavern for a beer. We drove north on the old Indian trail, 441, past the realtors' offices, the signs for LAND, LAND, LAND, the Pizza Hut, the Colonel's chicken parlor, the Rabun County Chamber of Commerce office in the Welcome Center. It was raining now, a steady, slanting drizzle. Wigginton drove me to my van, and I followed him to the parking lot at D's, even muddier, more treacherous than before. "This is the worst, absolutely the worst, time of year in Rabun County," he remarked, as he picked his way through the wet debris, not to D's Tavern, as I expected, but next door, to Hig's Place.

He ordered a Miller's at the bar, then took a seat at a table in the middle of the nearly empty room. A television set blared noisily in one corner. Two men with slurred speech compared reminiscences of World War II on bar stools at our elbows. A two-year-old child with soiled dress and cheeks caked with crumbs and frosting in a wide ellipse around her mouth snuggled up to Wigginton, flirted, brought him envelopes containing bills and her parents' private correspondence. A gangly boy behind the counter, who had been in Wig's first class that afternoon, rescued the mail and spanked the child. "That was a darned interesting program," he said. "Think I'm going to work it out so I can get in on it this summer."

We drank our beers awhile and talked about the past. Yet the future hung over us, would not loosen its grip on Wigginton's imagination. His voice and face carried a new grimness I had not heard nor seen before as he said, "The people who are making the decisions about Rabun County aren't local people, and the decisions they're making are questionable. The Chamber of Commerce, the realtors, the environmentalists—they're the spokesmen for Rabun County. They're all good people, but they're not from here. I have the impression that the local people defer to them, stay on the sidelines on purpose. But the decisions that are being made in Rabun County are made to benefit the newcomers and protect their investments. By and large, they don't even know the local people." A pause, then an explosion: "It's South Africa, for God's sake!"

His outward demeanor remained casual and deliberate. "The Chamber of Commerce folks will show you graphs of the per-capita income," he said derisively. "But what do they see ahead for these kids here?" He pointed to the gangly boy behind the bar. "A job making three-fifty an hour at the Sangamo Weston plant and a lot in a trailer park." It was palpable, the bitterness and wrath churning deep inside this youthful figure, this Tom Sawyer or Andy Griffith in soft brown boots, new jeans, light tan sweater rolled up to the elbows, his tan hair flopping loose across his right temple.

"If they could spend *one hour* in one of my classes at the high school—*one hour*—they'd never see Rabun County in the same way ever again."

I waited. Nothing. I was going to have to pry the explanation loose. "Why?"

"Because they'd see the powerlessness of those kids. They'd see that by the time the kids get to my classes—ninth, tenth, eleventh grades—they've already been taught not to expect anything better for themselves than their fathers and grandfathers had.

"See that house with the tin roof over there?" He pointed beyond my left shoulder. I turned and saw it, through the smudgy window and the falling rain, on the other side of 441. "A kid from that house is going to be in my class next term. His dad's in the pen. He doesn't feel like he's going anywhere, but we're damned sure going to try to show him some alternatives, what it's like to have some measure of control over your own destiny, how to celebrate certain aspects of this culture that are worth celebrating, to celebrate the capacities that all kids have within themselves to be greater than they think they can ever be." He was talking fast now, as though to machine-gun out of existence by the velocity of his words all the negative, depressing circumstances he'd explored.

"You heard what the kid said about going on the program to North Carolina this summer?" He pointed once again to the gangly boy behind the counter. "That's going to make a difference to that kid. Self-discovery. That's what our program's all about, too. If we can just get them aware of *who they are*—"

The little girl with the smudged face came back and clung to Wigginton briefly, then skipped away. "I don't know what her future is. Her mother works at a factory making two-sixty-five an hour, eighteen years old, has two kids already, miscarried on the third, had her tubes tied. Father's unemployed, grandfather runs this bar." He shook his head. Nothing theatrical

about the gesture this time. "I don't know what the answer is."

I took my leave. At the door I turned back to salute him. Except for the bottles of Miller's, one empty, one half-full, in front of him, he sat, for the first time since I had met him, alone.

1978

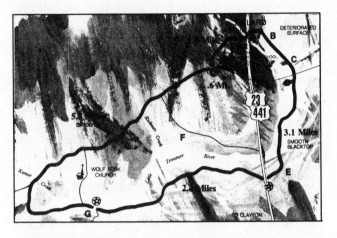

CYCLIST'S ALMANAC*

The Wolffork Valley: Rabun County's Past and Future

Route: A 12.6-mile loop of the loveliest cycling territory I've found in North Georgia: mostly smooth road surfaces, little traffic, moderate terrain (since you're riding in the floodplain of the Little Tennessee River), and lovely, continually changing scenery. You'll not only see up close but smell the cattle grazing in the lush pastureland. The hills closing in the valley on all sides present at times steep, forbidding angles and harsh, bare outcroppings, while in other places they curve gracefully, invitingly to the valley's floor. Giant boulders embedded in the fields remind the casual visitor of the hard work required to cultivate this mountain landscape.

History: Eliot Wigginton's commentary on the Appalachian dilemma echoed in my head as I rode this route. "FOR SALE" signs are everywhere in front of weathered mountain homes, some of them abandoned, some unkempt, others spruce, freshly painted, joyful. I noticed one old home that appeared to be in the process of developing a new personality, since its plain clapboarded roadside self was attached in the rear to a brick ranch-type structure that was nearing completion. I saw that house as a symbol of the area, changing from an exclusively rural to a suburban character. You'll pass large signs for "Sylvan Lake Falls, Rabun County's Oldest Second-Home Community." You'll see individual contemporary residences with fancy cantilevered picture windows, speaking of inhabitants for whom the mountains they look out on are a means of aesthetic satisfaction, not of livelihood. On the other side of 441 you'll pass the giant Burlington Mills complex, one of Rabun County's early industrial developments. Although you won't ride right by it, you may notice signs of the vast Sangamo Weston plant that will soon be transforming the valley which it sits in the middle of.

Points of interest: A. *Rabun Gap-Nacoochee School.* Park in the middle of extensive private-school campus, at the foot of hill leading up to administration building. Scene of Eliot Wigginton's Foxfire classes and publications from their inception in 1966 until last year. **B.** *The Dillard House,* longtime country-cooking mecca and motel run by local family; lovely views out over the valley. **C.** *Wooden plank bridge;* be careful crossing—I dismounted and walked my bike across. **D.** *Burlington Mills Plant,* early industrial development in Rabun County. **E.** *York House,* lovely example of native mountain architecture at its more ornate. **F.** *Sangamo Weston Plant,* not directly on route, but activity at this new giant industrial center may be visible from Wolffork Valley Road. **G.** *Sylvan Lake Falls,* advertised as "Rabun County's Oldest Second-Home Community." Roads inside development not suited for cycling, but you might want to walk your bike a few yards up unpaved surface to see what future is bringing to Rabun County. **H.** *Star-and-semicircle house:* attractive faculty home adjacent to Rabun Gap School; notice decorations in pediment.

The Almost Perfect Mountain Bike Ride

by Bill Cutler

Are you a weekend cyclist who loves the scenery of the Georgia mountains? Do you leave your bike at home every time you visit North Georgia because you assume that any roads you find there will be too challenging for your level of cycling achievement? Change your thinking. Dust off your bike rack, and attach it to the back of your car. Here's a short route through beautiful mountain countryside which is tailor-made for the least experienced pedaler.

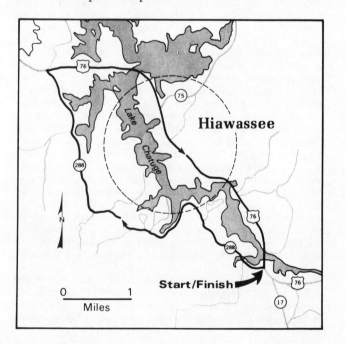

Myself, I love climbing hills better than just about any feature of biking. That's my way of testing myself against the environment without taking anything away from it, unlike most of humankind's methods of measuring its self-styled superiority against the natural world. I love North Georgia as cycling terrain precisely *because* of the hills.

Yet I've found myself frustrated in the search for good roads to ride on there. The ridge-and-valley geography of the mountains necessitates the placing of paved highways in certain narrow, restricted corridors, often very far apart. North Georgia lacks the network of secondary byways that makes cycling in so much of the state easy and enjoyable. The mountain roads that do exist are narrow, highly traveled, and therefore no fun at all for the recreational cyclist. Planning a route around a loop through the mountains on rideable roads is no easy task.

The 10¾-mile loop shown here around Lake Chatuge in Towns County satisfies all my criteria for safe, unhassled cycling. Georgia 288, on which most of the ride is routed, has a fine, smooth blacktop surface (a rarity in the mountains) and does not attract the kind of high-speed, industrial traffic which is a hazard to cyclists. The other road completing the loop, U.S. 76, is the major east-west highway across North Georgia and not recommended for biking on much of its length. Fortunately, however, a wide shoulder provides a natural bike lane from the western intersection of Georgia 288 into the town of Hiawassee, leaving only the short distance from town to the eastern end of the state route to be negotiated in the regular traffic lane. Most of this latter stretch is downhill, permitting the cyclist to move along fairly well in the vehicular traffic, impeding it minimally.

It is important that the route be followed in a clockwise direction, so as to benefit from the wide shoulder and the favorable terrain on U.S. 76. A wide parking area adjoining the eastern intersection of the two routes provides a natural starting and finishing point.

I don't promise you a perfectly flat ride, but the pulls are gentle for the mountains, and every aspect rewards the pedaler with fresh perspectives on Lake Chatuge. I suspect you'll come to feel a special fondness for this intimate body of water, cupped between sweetly sloping hills. I know I did.

1980

The Most %&# Hill in Georgia

Or how the proud cyclist met his match

by Bill Cutler

"Pride goeth before a walk" could be a cyclist's version of the old adage. Some years back, I arranged to pedal from Atlanta to Amicalola Falls State Park to meet friends who were driving up with overnight camping gear. My route took me through the capital city's northern suburbs and over the Chattahoochee by way of several long and tough hills. It was a crisp, bright morning, and I was fresh and full of beans. I charged up those grades like an Olympic champion. I sang and I shouted as I crested slope after slope. "There's not a hill on God's green earth I can't climb" was the refrain that bounced through my head over and over again until at length I jubilantly shouted it aloud.

Fifty-five miles later I reached the visitor's center at Amicalola. The sun had been beating down on me for hours, and I was no longer exerting energy in song and exultant chant. A discreet sign opposite the center stood at the base of the road to the top of the falls. It read, "WARNING: STEEP GRADE. R.V.S. CHECK WITH OFFICE BEFORE ASCENDING." A bicycle could be regarded as an RV, I suppose, but I like to consider mine a business vehicle, a vehicle that means business, that gets me to work, that helps to solve the energy crisis. I charged ahead, still cocky and debonair.

The road began climbing immediately and curved around to the right. Beyond the turn, I could make out a still steeper grade. I was slowing down now, pumping in my very lowest gear. In fact, I was barely making any forward progress at all. What was wrong? I was a veteran mountain cyclist. Why, I had climbed the Richard Russell Scenic Highway. I had made the precipitous ascent from Lake Burton to Tiger in Rabun County at the cost of only a few heavy puffs. But this thing wasn't a mountain. It was a sheer cliff face.

I let the bike veer off the pavement onto the shoulder and deposit me in the grass. I just needed to rest a few moments, I told myself. I'd be all right soon enough. I struggled to my feet and pushed skyward. A yard gained. A couple of feet. Eighteen inches. My thighs hadn't knotted. I wasn't—all—that tired—but—I couldn't—get my ankles—to—ro—tate. I slipped off onto the grass again. Face it, buddy. The only way you gonna get up this unmentionable hill is on foot.

It wasn't all that hard to push the bike, free of camping gear, up the precipice. My chief worry was that I'd be spotted in this ignominious posture by my sag-wagon pals. I was busily plotting some story to regale them with about the hard pull up to the campsite when a voice called out cheerily, "Hey! How about a lift?" It was my friends, smirking away in the comfort of their multi-horsepower vehicle. I refused their offer and doggedly trundled on up to the top of the falls, but I had no need of a fancy story when I reached the camping area.

I returned recently to Amicalola by bike for the first time since that unpropitious day, but I made no plans to try the monster ascent. Indeed, by the time I returned to my starting point at the state park, I was plenty tired out from a succession of smaller but still tough hills along the route shown on the map included here. I was taking an ironic last look at that warning sign to RVs when down the slope hurtled two teenagers on those bikes with frames only a couple of inches off the ground that serious cyclists like myself scorn as unsuited to the human frame. Had they lugged those things to the top of the falls somehow, or had their parents carried the bikes up in

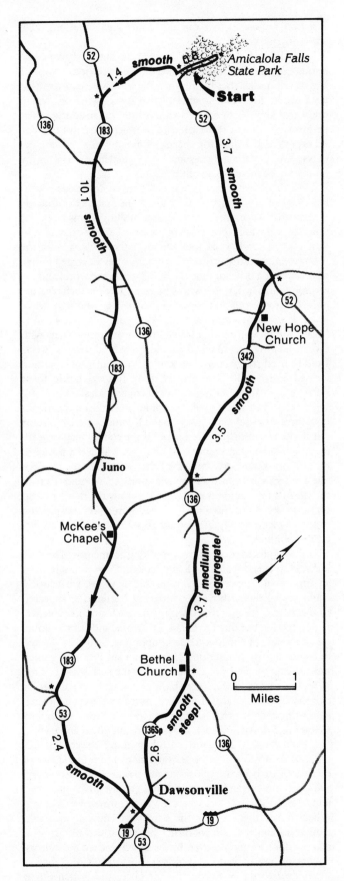

a station wagon so that the kids could enjoy the long (and scary) joyride down?

I didn't ask them. I felt one-upped again by that preposterous geological mistake. That's a childish reaction, I know. I like to tell myself that biking isn't a competitive pastime, that it's a respite from the American fetish for showing off, but in my heart I know better. Cyclists are continually measuring their performance against some standard or other. Why, just that day I'd experienced a dramatic change of mood while pedaling between Amicalola and Dawsonville, a complete reversal in my estimation of myself as an athlete.

All day there'd been a stiff—not to say ferocious—wind blowing out of the northwest, and for the first half of the ride I'd had that force, like a giant hand, pushing at my back. I'd flown over the hills. For much of the time I didn't even need to turn the cranks. I could look out over the fields, admire the postures of the cattle as they grazed, gaze away to jagged purple peaks against a brilliant blue sky, and glory in the world and my relation to it. The farmers whose pastures gave me such pleasure must be prosperous and happy in their tasks, I thought, while I—well, I was a successful Ponce de Leon. The years hadn't placed any burden on me. I could compete in time trials with cyclists half my age. Maybe I should get started the next week. I didn't need to enter any demeaning "veteran's" competition for pedalers over 40. This was my sport. Just watch how those steep grades flatten out under my churning ankles.

I arrived in Dawsonville in a fine lather, like a thoroughbred three-year-old that's just won the Kentucky Derby. A short rest in the town square, a refolding of the county map beneath my plastic handlebar carrier, and off again with a sharp veer to the left, northward. My, how the lather seemed to freeze when the wind struck from over my left shoulder. Another turn to the left in a few hundred yards, and suddenly the flying nomad on his trusty Arabian steed had turned into a powerless victim of the elements struggling toward an oasis that dissolved forever into mirages.

The slightest incline was a mocking tormentor. The sun, hitherto so cheerful and warming, looked down pitilessly from an atmosphere impervious to its rays. The farms, what little I could see of them above the wavering handlebars, appeared hard-scrabble, mean, littered with refuse. What a miserable terrain to try and eke out a living in, I thought, and felt the slopes on either side of the road close in upon me, as if they wanted to engulf this puny interloper. It was Sunday, just after church time, I realized. This was the hour when the parking lots of the shopping centers in St. Petersburg are turned over to senior citizens for tricycle races. I pictured myself in fierce, and losing, competition with octogenarians as I grimly thrust my ankles *for*ward and down and back and *for*ward and down and back.

Even the few and short downhills scarcely served as respites, so hard was it to keep forward momentum in the face of the blast that bent the grasses of the pastures flat against the soil. On and on and on, punishing. At last my mind went numb, and I lost track of where I was and where I was going. When at last the sign for the state park entrance appeared around a bend, I had a moment's hesitation before taking in that my day's agony was over. By the time I reached the visitors' center and my parked car, however, I was exultant. I hadn't succumbed to temptation once, not once, and gotten off to

push up one of those endless hills. I won't promise I could have climbed to the top of the falls without dismounting, but I did just fine. Ain't but *one* hill on God's green earth I can't climb.

1981

CYCLIST'S ALMANAC

Route: Park and begin the ride at the visitors' center in Amicalola Falls State Park. Total distance is 28.4 *hilly* miles over mostly very smooth pavement, 8/10 of a mile of it a reduplicated stretch within the park. Instead of the tough ascent to the top of the falls, this ride includes a much gentler climb to a point at their base where the 729-foot cascade of water (highest in Georgia) may be appreciated. You're on your own if you want to get up to the camping area and the view from above. A mile-long footpath leads from the back of the visitors' center to the summit, and there's always that inviting road. As for the ride to Dawsonville and back, the scenery is breathtaking much of the way, as is, occasionally, the odor from nearby chicken houses.

Hazards: Ga 52 gets some high-speed traffic, but the pavement is wide enough to prevent real discomfort. A minority of Dawson Countians do present something of a problem to cyclists, however. This is a poor county, and some residents resent outsiders. The night I spent in the Amicalola campground was marred by a band of hooligans—their conversation revealed them to be from Dawsonville—terrorizing campers with threats and minor vandalism. Throughout my rest stop in the county seat on my most recent trip, I was scrutinized in a pointedly unfriendly manner by two men in a car. Then, on the return lap, a fellow cyclist who was riding behind me out of my sight was stopped by a middle-aged citizen and told that he wasn't welcome in the county. On the other hand, most of the farmers in battered pickups and unkempt beards waved cheerfully at us as we pedaled along, and so it would seem that the unwelcoming sorts are significantly outnumbered. It might not be a bad idea, nonetheless, to keep your group in sight of each other at all times and not let anyone fall far behind the rest.

We Don't Have A Town, Stilesboro's No Town.

But in a way it is, and so is Euharlee—barely,—and Kingston, towns with a past in search of a future.

by Bill Cutler

Exquisite this turf. In early summer when I cranked my pedals over Etowah Valley's rough and, often, unpaved roads, the Queen Anne's lace and black-eyed Susans paraded in dense ranks at just my helmet's height. I passed fields and meadows in every stage of cultivation—fresh plowed and newly seeded; lying fallow, overgrown with weeds; barely sprouting with the latest crop; just harvested, the hay rough-tumbled into unkempt piles; waist-high with grass—gold, lime, sienna, Kelly green.

Then, suddenly, around a bend and up a grade, and out of sunlit open country into woods cool, moist, and fragrant, where the merest rivulet gave nourishment to roots and ferns. Another curve, a shift of gears to pump uphill again, and—there—the crown upon a slope, an antebellum mansion built of brick, with formal boxwood gardens, imposing porticos and bays—classic, pure, untouched. With all due respect to Georgia's other scenic ecstacies, I have to settle on this spot as the most enticing rural landscape I've found to cycle in so far.

Mightn't Sherman have ridden through a countryside just like this while he was planning the attack on Atlanta and the devastation to the sea? Wrong in details, I know. Cotton was the crop that made the valley rich when Sherman mapped his strategies in Kingston, then its most important town; soybeans are the staple of farmers in the valley now. Yet I cling to my conception that the diversity of land use, the wooded knolls that dot the planted fields, give the valley a 19th-century look.

I didn't just invent, out of some romantic impulse, the antique quality in Etowah's physical face. Both the state and federal governments have recognized the significance of the valley's unspoiled 19th-century towns—Stilesboro, Kingston, Euharlee; the architectural heritage of its remarkable and unique brick manor houses; the ancient Indian archaeological sites that lie beneath its fields and woodlands. Last year the Etowah Valley was officially registered by the U.S. Department of the Interior as Georgia's largest Historic District—40,202 acres of it.

Yet this serene and lovely stretch of Bartow County is close to, and it serves, the industrial heart of Georgia. Smack in the middle of its lushest wind-rippled meadows spreads the vast complex of Georgia Power Company's Plant Bowen—squat concrete storage drums with indented middles like dress forms for monstrously misshapen matrons; frog-green rectangular office buildings; a pair of skyscraping, strobe-lighted smokestacks flashing their sharp stabs of caution at low-flying aircraft.

What a place of contrasts! Giant steel pylons, icon-like symbols of the 20th century, march row after row over a gentle landscape that otherwise looks to the visitor as though he's stumbled through some time chamber back into the 1850s.

The residents of Etowah I met—or most of them—seemed just as out of place in the contemporary world as does Plant Bowen in their landscape. I found them poignant figures, obsessed with history, steeped in yesterday—yet *connected* to one another by that very passion for the past. Their leaves and boughs may tremble in the wind, but they're not going anywhere. They're rooted there, just as their ancestors were for many generations back.

Take the old, old couple rocking on their long-unpainted porch in Stilesboro. I must have cycled past them six or seven times, their arms raised to salute me in the self-same gesture, like Old World figures on a Town Hall clock whose struttings forth denote the passage of the hours. Their house sits on a ridge crest and looks out in two directions on the monuments of past and present, as though their point of vantage were some temporal watershed. Due north two thousand yards, Plant Bowen belches forth and winks and winks and winks. No more than five hundred yards due south a cluster of brick structures and a rough-hewn granite train depot that once served busy travelers wait patiently for kudzu to conceal them from view. My first time through, I stopped to ask them directions to the Stilesboro Academy, one of the valley's most treasured relics. The old lady and I had trouble getting through to one another, even after we'd inched up to within spitting distance. "Is the Academy on the other side of town?" I cried, pointing to the ruins in the foreground. "No, it's on *this* side of town," she called back, motioning off into the far distance. Then, considering my request more carefully, she yelled, "We don't have a town. Stilesboro's no town."

Yet in a way it is. Almost no one lives there anymore, but having lived there once, or having kin who lived there once, creates a tie which is not easily broken. The May Day picnic every year brings family members back from as far away as California, swarms of them. I'd love to share that feast, to see how cows and chickens take the unexpected din of laughing revelers.

I finally found the Stilesboro Academy, the pre-Civil War school house—severe, correct, its unadorned facade upon a knoll rebuking frivolous ostentation. "I am a *temple* of learning," its unbroken lines and precise right angles said to me. "No hopscotch here, please." I pushed its 16-foot-high door to enter, wondering how a child half my height must feel—Alice, thimble-high in Wonderland. Inside, the Lilliput sensation deepened. Walls extended twenty feet from floor to ceiling, while several rows of pupils' desks, unanchored, casually arrayed, might have been pushed aside the day before by youngsters eager to escape their books. Not so—no formal studies have gone on in that old lesson room for several decades.

A local group has been working for years to restore the old school house and I met two of the leading spirits in that effort there. They were sisters, these spruce, trim, old-fashioned ladies whom I should have liked to see in petticoats—Mrs. Rena Beasley and Miss Dorris McCormick. They wanted me to know all there was to know about their shrine. But what would be the very best way of teaching me? There was much fluttering and amiable disagreement. ("Now Dorris, it's not time for *that*." "Well, all right, then, Rena, go ahead.") Finally I was shown a chair, one in a row of old-time pupils' seats, while Mrs. Beasley propped herself against a table right in front and read, with pauses long enough for me to transcribe faithfully, Mrs. Calley Jackson's history of the Academy written for the Stilesboro Improvement Club.

I wrote it all down, too, dwarfed there in that gigantic room whose upper reaches echoed still, to my imagination, with the tedious recitations of last century's Tom Sawyers, desperate for a Becky Thatcher pigtail to dip in ink. *I* had never been to school like this, but I'll bet my father had, just like his dad before him.

The ladies hope to turn the Academy into a museum. "What do you plan to exhibit?" I asked. "Why, we've started already," they said, pointing to several shelves of dusty-looking books against a wall. "Oh, wonderful!" I exclaimed. "Are these the same texts that Academy students read?" "Oh, no!" Their tone was gently condescending. "These books—can you imagine?—were in the Cartersville library and were just going to be dumped last year. *We saved them.*"

Outside, we faced Plant Bowen's busy, smoking, garish bulk. Dorris McCormick pointed to the massive oaks that ring the Academy's grounds and indicated in a reverential tone that each one bore the name of an early president of the Stilesboro Improvement Club. Then, sweeping the full horizon before us, she said, "We have something of everything here—history, slums all around us (it's a shame), a gin, a feed mill, Georgia Power spreading its pollution—why everything's dying at my house. I wish you could see my day lilies." Her sister demurred gently. "They say it's the aphids killing the lilies, not the pollution."

I wish all visitors to the Stilesboro Academy could enjoy a recitation by these ladies. That reading called me back, better than any artifacts in a museum ever could. In some sense, Stilesboro may not be a "town," but these sisters keep its past alive.

I saw the gentle side of Etowah's old-timers, their antiquarian, bookish traits. Everyone I met pressed texts upon me, made me feel that cycling the valley roads could bring me pleasure only after months of careful study in the archives. Well, I didn't read a single one of all the books they felt essential, but that's not meant as any sign of disrespect. I read the Etowah residents' reading and found it full of charm.

There must be something in the valley that attracts the backward-looker, the library dweller. I stopped to visit Mrs. Helen Ayers, a newcomer to the area who, with her husband, former editor of the *Bartow Herald,* is restoring the late-19th-century DeSoto Hotel in Kingston. She runs an antique shop, and books of every size, age, and description lean, lie, and stand among the china and the Chippendales.

She tried to interest me in a very thick and learned dissertation on one of the valley's estates and proudly pulled out of a table drawer a signed first edition of *Gone With the Wind,* among whose pages letters from Margaret Mitchell to her mother lay pressed. Another prized possession was Fanny Howard's Etowah Valley memoirs of the War Between the States, *In and Out of the Lines.*

Mrs. Ayers might have been happier in some previous century herself. She spoke of unsuccessful restoration projects, most poignantly the loss of the fine old train depot that stood directly across the tracks from her hotel. It burned to the ground one summer night two years ago—arson, she's convinced, by people who resented the historical group's plans for preservation. She sees herself and her husband as isolated figures trying to rescue the area's heritage, which the majority of their neighbors care nothing about.

"It's going to take new blood to take care of these houses," Mrs. Ayers believes. "The real old folks don't care. If grandpappy did something one way, that's how they're going to go on doing it." She ticked off some of the historic valley homes that had recently burned or been torn down: "Etowah Cliffs was not being kept up before it burned. One room was full of onions, and cattle roamed about in the family graveyard. The old Harrison house is falling down. They're burning it for kindling."

Kingston does seem left behind, no question of it. The Western and Atlantic Railroad gave the town its prominence before and after the Civil War. In the 1920s there were five or six blacksmiths, three cotton gins, several eating houses plus a hotel. In addition, Kingston was then on the main highway—the Dixie Highway—between Cincinnati and Miami, and cars full of people and all their worldly goods streamed through town on their way to Florida and the big land boom. Remnants of the town's commercial center still line the tracks. Only a couple of the handsome brick structures are occupied today; a few fine residences remain tucked away amid the heavy vegetation.

Yet I wonder if Mrs. Ayers' six years of residency in the valley have given her an accurate assessment of her neighbors' interests. How do you draw the line between being stuck in the mud and working to keep the best of the old traditions alive, between living *in* the past and living *for* the past in the present? No doubt you'll find complacency and inertia and resistance to change in the Etowah valley—these commodities are all too common everywhere. But that's not the whole story.

Certainly not in Euharlee, and Euharlee's less of a town than Kingston, barely a town at all, in fact. Two well-kept churches and a row of sheds that no living painter ever touched and that the weeds and soil seem just about to claim—that's nearly all the slow-moving cyclist will identify as "town." But stop a while, as I did, at the general store and browse among the clippings posted thick upon the bulletin board—proud records of Euharlee's preservation efforts to restore its historic buildings. The man behind the counter may be owner Howard Osborne, mayor of this tiny community, population 168. He accompanied me on a tour of the historic area, center of which is the already restored militia courthouse, where justices of the peace presided until the 1950s, and where Euharlee's city council will meet, starting this fall.

"This whole place down here was so abandoned-looking," Osborne commented. "The courthouse doors were just hanging in their frames; it was utter desolation. Before we started restoring, seemed like everyone just wanted to destroy. But as soon as we got to work, all that just stopped. We could leave our tools and materials around, and they'd never be taken."

The past is a source of energy and enthusiasm in Euharlee. Emmie Nelson, president of the Etowah Valley Historical Society, spearheads the preservation movement in town. Like Howard Osborne, she's sunny-faced, peppy, and in love with the village she grew up in. "You have to live in a community like this to feel its pulse," she asserted with vigor. "Maybe if you're a stranger, it seems just like a sleepy little place, but I'll tell you, there's some *power* underneath. We've got some of *the finest* people here."

With a wicked twinkle, she stared full into my face. "We're going to have a calaboose!" I gaped, considered faking it, then, after much too long a pause, surrendered. "I—can't remember what that is." Not a kind of festival, something to barbecue, or part of a train, a calaboose had a part to play in all small-town courthouses, Miss Nelson explained. It was a retaining jail where the town drunk could dry out. Older residents can remember when Euharlee had one, and it will again, along with a restored public well inside a new 15-acre park, to go with its already standing magnificent covered bridge.

Giant trucks passing to and from nearby Plant Bowen have damaged the bridge badly in recent years, but a new road across the creek will henceforth keep the beautifully designed structure for the use of bicyclists and pedestrians, Emmie Nelson told me. (A nice thought, but I advise my fellow cyclists to push, not ride, their bikes across the splintery, wide-cracked, nail-studded surface. I flatted my rear tire after only a few feet of exposure to the hazards.)

Euharlee seems to know where it wants to go and, more than that, how to get there. I won't claim all of Etowah's residents possess that knowledge. The man who symbolizes for me the complexity of looking backward, the ambiguity of the lessons history teaches, is Henry Tumlin, whose great-grandfather was one of the valley's original white settlers. A bare month or two after the Cherokees were forced to leave their fertile valley homes in 1832, this ancestor took possession of 8000 acres of their land, on some of which *their* ancestral burial mounds are situated. Today, Henry Tumlin runs the Etowah Mounds historic site for the state's Department of Natural Resources.

Tumlin's skin is tanned copper by the sun, his beard a wild, white bush, his eyes and mouth as kindly as the Lord's in the Sistine Ceiling fresco. But behind the eyes and mouth a melancholy lingers, as though the long caring he has done for his beloved valley's past and worry for its future had worn him down a little. I felt the past was painful, bittersweet for him, its secrets just barely out of reach of his imagination.

Great-grandfather lives for Henry Tumlin, casting a long, sharp shadow over his own and Etowah's history. That ancestor roomed with Sherman at West Point and entertained the future general at his home. When war broke out, Sherman prevented Union troops from burning houses he had visited, and so the valley's heritage remains to haunt the visitor today.

"What I would give to speak for half an hour with him! How much he could teach me!" Tumlin exclaimed to me. And then that note of sadness. "There's only myself and a cousin left to care for his tomb. When we're gone—" His voice trailed off. "The vandals and decay—" He spoke in almost identical terms of the Stilesboro Academy and its present guardians, those lovely sisters who had read to me. I found his words about them puzzling, since they seemed so youthful, energetic. "Once they're gone, there won't be anyone left to take a fulltime interest in the Academy. They've devoted years to it. They'll think nothing of spending a whole day at a conference, writing letters, talking up their project. The work at Euharlee has begun to interest a few young people in preservation, but they get easily discouraged if they don't see quick results. Yes, we're going to miss them."

Henry Tumlin's view exactly contradicts the notion of Helen Ayers that new hands are needed to preserve the old. I wonder if Tumlin sees, in an odd way, too far, his vision of history's long sweep resigning him to estimating low what any single generation can achieve. A Cherokee friend of his has painted an inscription in Sequoyah's alphabet around the top of two walls in the Etowah museum's gift shop. Its tone is sorrowful, as Tumlin's is. An obscurely placed plaque carries the moving English translation:

Long ago, Etowah was a sacred city of the people:
The cornfields were abundant,
And the hearts of the people happy.
Now the trails are overgrown, and of the sacred fire of the people,
  only ashes remain.

True—and only partly true. History is cruel, but also comforting. Upon the ashes of one civilization sprouts another. The removal of the Cherokees brought misery and death and exploitation—and also growth and change and beauty.

Today, Plant Bowen towers far above the valley floor. Is it a sentinel, messenger, beacon, warning? The Old Alabama Road south of the river is slated for paving by year's end. Will that open up the valley to development, spur unchecked industrial expansion in this rich, desirable farmland? Are Etowah's residents so obsessed with yesterday that tomorrow will be upon them before they know it?

1976

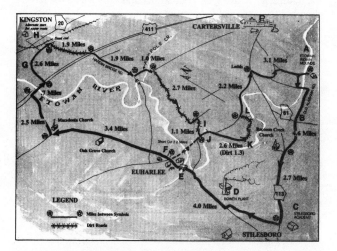

CYCLIST'S ALMANAC*

Routes: Begin and end at Etowah Mounds parking lot. Complete loop 37.7 miles. Divide route in two halves by following dotted line east of Euharlee. Southern half (Mounds-Stilesboro-Euharlee) 22.1 miles; northern half (Kingston and Euharlee—park in Kingston), 20 miles. Very few Bartow County roads carry signs, and landmarks are few, so an odometer on your bike would be a helpful guide to know where to turn.

Cycling conditions: Abysmal. Very few really smooth surfaces. Most pavement is rough aggregate; unpaved stretches treacherous. I used my heavy commuting bike for this trip and was glad of it. Don't try to ride across covered bridges and old trestles—you're just asking for trouble. Old Alabama Road south of the river *may* be paved by fall; if not, by spring '77. Unpaved surfaces north of river likely to remain so. Bring whatever tools you need in case of breakdowns: no repair shops in area, including Cartersville.

Terrain: Rolling; few really steep hills, but when you're on gravel or sand, even slight grades may require a very low gear.

Where To Camp: Red Top Mountain State Park on Lake Allatoona, a few miles southeast of Cartersville, off U.S. 41. For tent campers, some beautifully landscaped sites on the edge of the lake, not accessible to Jetstreams and other monsters. Good bathroom facilities; camp store; swimming and fishing.

Points of interest: (A) *Etowah Mounds Archaeological Area.* Impressive site of Indian settlements between 1000 and 1500 A.D. Museum with displays of artifacts, Indian burial practices, modern archaeological activities. Beautiful picnic spots along Etowah River. Administered by the state's Department of Natural Resources. No admission charge. Open Tues.–Sat. 9–5, Sun. 2:30–5:30; closed Mon. (404) 382-2704. (B) *Ryals Academy,* imposing brick residence built 1853, extensively altered on exterior. Original front facade had delicately detailed front porch spanning full width of house. (C) *Stilesboro Academy,* built 1858–59, not usually open to public. Two original school rooms flank a central auditorium-chapel inside this monumental one-story frame structure in the Classical style, with pedimented gables. Site of state's oldest chrysanthemum show, held annually here since 1912 in early November. Be prepared for vicious dogs: they tried to flat my tires with their teeth. (D) *Plant Bowen,* coalburning Georgia Power plant that towers over the entire valley. (E) *Euharlee Covered Bridge,* built 1886 in the Town Lattice style by a black engineer, name unknown; 116 feet long. Don't miss the ruins of an old mill just downstream from bridge: well worth clambering over. (F) *Euharlee,* nearly intact 19th-century village, part of it in decayed condition. Restored militia-district courthouse, old stores and barns, two handsome churches from the 1850s, Masonic lodge. (G) *Reynolds Plantation,* built c. 1846–50, Classical Revival brick structure with temple-form portico in front composed of two pairs of columns, and a colonnaded porch in rear leading to the kitchen. (H) *Kingston,* happy hunting-ground for nostalgia buffs, once a more important commercial center than Rome. Where Sherman planned his March to the Sea. Lots of historical markers, many well designed houses. (I) *Rose Cottage,* one-story Greek Revival frame cottage from 1850s with boxwood maze in front modeled after pattern at Mt. Vernon. Beautiful pecan groves, enchanting location. (J) *Summerland,* deteriorating 19th-century brick structure on hill overlooking Etowah River. (K) *Malbone,* spectacularly located residence of the Stiles family, overlooking fertile fields. Brick Classical Revival design, dated 1868–70. East facade with front columns two stories high. North facade with triple-arched entrance and two bays, each containing single arched window. (L) *Valley View,* architectural masterpiece of area, but chances are good it will be off limits to visitors.

(Thanks to Marilyn Pennington and Elizabeth Macgregor for detailed information on Etowah Valley architecture and scenic features.)

Looking Out for Lookout Mountain

Uphill and down through the craggy canyon country of Northwest Georgia

by Bill Cutler

Tourists driving south towards Albuquerque, New Mexico, from Santa Fe are startled and perplexed to see a giant, brightly colored billboard emblazoned with the single word "UNDEVELOP." Yet residents of the area understand the message. They know that unplanned growth, mostly in the form of retirement communities, has dangerously lowered the water level in their fragile desert environment and now threatens the existence of unsuspecting newcomer and wary oldtimer alike.

There's no lack of water in the mountains of North Georgia, but the pressures to develop the area as a boom resort region will increase, not abate, in years to come, especially if the national economy continues to strengthen. The closeness of the mountains to Atlanta makes them prime targets for the second-home industry, and, to judge by some of the massive subdivisions that already exist, the frail ecology of hillside, stream, and valley will be disregarded. The consequences of unregulated development in our mountains are subjects every Georgian needs to ponder.

Lookout Mountain in the extreme northwest corner of our state brought the issue home to me, precisely since it is, till now, so little tampered with. I biked its ridges late last March and marveled that this extraordinary natural resource jutting several hundred feet nearly straight into the air should be so sparsely populated. I had the roads to myself and I biked alone, but that was fine. Lookout Mountain invites solitude. The few, unprosperous-looking homes make no demands on the surrounding woods and seem content to crouch in humble spots. I labored up and plummeted down the grades that form Lookout's crest, my exertions rewarded on the peaks by long vistas down into the farmland in the valleys, where, if people walked and worked, I could not see them. I delighted in a landscape of distant fields, houses, roads, of nearly geometrical shapes, of straw-toned yellows and barely budding greens.

Supposing, I thought to myself, the mountain's rims were privately developed, as large stretches of ocean beach have been? Mightn't the day come when the public would be shut out entirely from enjoying these unique vantage-points? Or, conversely, suppose some public or private corporation bought up the entire mountain top and developed it as a resort area, charged admission, putting in expensive rides and attractions, maybe even setting up pinball machines in the choicest locations? Not such a farfetched fantasy—think of what's been done to another very special natural resource in Georgia, Stone Mountain.

Or—yet another "suppose"—I tried to picture the results of a local promoter persuading all the inhabitants of Lookout Mountain to redesign their houses as Japanese temples or Chinese pagodas and then to add clusters of additional Japanese temples or Chinese pagodas as souvenir centers, gift shops, restaurants, and motels. After all, North Georgia already has the example of Helen's redevelopment, which bypassed the natural beauty and restraint of its native Nacoochee Valley architecture in favor of fake Bavarian designs.

Was I just inventing future disasters, or was there some solid reason to suspect that Lookout Mountain might become another Helen or get boostered and promoted out of recognition? Without ever having visited it, I knew that the much-advertised Rock City tourist attraction, complete with bearded dwarfs and other oddities, occupies part of the mountain's northern edge. Might the whole ridge one day be overrun with trolls, gremlins, goblins, and elves?

"We don't want this end of the mountain to develop into Rock City," one of Lookout's most distinguished residents told me when I broached the subject. I stood on the mountain's southern edge overlooking a great rounded bowl called Johnson's Crook with the fine potter Charles Counts, whose studio sits a couple of hundred yards away. The Crook is uninhabited, its sides a great jumble of trees and rocks, while beyond the bowl's farther rim the flatlands stretch for mile on mile to the remote horizon. Off to our right we could see a fertile valley dotted with homes, some clumped together.

Counts is round of face and body, and decisive, pointed, angular of mind. He is something of a poet in words as well as clay, as shown by his feeling for the landscape in which he lives. Sweeping the vast panorama before us, he startled me by saying, "From here you feel the ocean. It's like being on the coast. You stand here and you know there was an inland sea. Then you go down and find fish fossils in the limestone sand rock. The mountain is flat, unlike any other Appalachian peak, because of wind erosion, winds blowing off the water."

Unlike the sea, however, Charles's landscape is attracting human inhabitants, brought by Interstate-59, the new "scar" he pointed to running down the length of the valley to our right. "Our first winter here I could see at most five lights indicating homesteads. Now I see hundreds and expect in a few years to see thousands." Yet all recent changes have not meant a marring of the natural environment. Charles recalls when smog caused by TVA activity poured down from the Chattanooga area along the side of Lookout Mountain and hung over the Crook. Protests by citizens, including the president of nearby Covenant College, have brought about "a marked improvement."

Counts moved to Lookout 13 years ago, "brought by the natural beauty of the place," to escape the urban sprawl of Oak Ridge, Tennessee, and intends to work to keep it "one of the most beautiful parts of Georgia left," free of tourism. He is not alone. We stood on land belonging to his neighbor, internationally known artist Frank Baisden, a member of the Audubon Society, to whom the land is willed. The Crook we were admiring belongs to a Chattanooga doctor, Joseph Johnson, who intends to protect it and keep it natural.

In addition to these individual efforts, a local citizens' organization has recently formed to talk about controlling growth on the mountain. Charles guided me to the house of the Lookout Citizens' Planning Group president, Rosine Raoul. Without his help, I never would have found her. We left the main road and wound down an overgrown track through the woods and past an open gate, with not a dwelling visible. Here we were, in the middle of a modern development called Tucker Branch, Inc., owned by Rosine Raoul and two other family groups, that had been designed so that no two houses were ever in sight of each other.

Charles rang a bell at her contemporary house, constructed of unpainted, weathered wood and landscaped so as not to obtrude from the surrounding terrain, but he happened to be positioned so that she only saw me through her glass doors. Her long, thin, leathery, austere face set in a disapproving grimace, and a voice like a jackhammer stopped me in my tracks. "Yes? What do you want?"

We got through the introductions, with Charles's help, and sat down in a remarkable high-ceilinged living-room, dominated by a gigantic stone chimney, with side walls almost all of glass. Everything about this room, and in it, spoke of money, taste, and character. Clean, straight lines, simplicity, no clutter. I found it hard to pierce Rosine Raoul's wry, gruff, sandpapery demeanor with which she keeps the world at bay. To questions about how Lookout's natural environment could be protected, she replied with fatalistic shrugs, but I sensed that her vagueness about specific future directions masked a deep and troubled concern about the mountain she loved.

She certainly had no overwhelming faith in the ability of the citizens' planning group to arrive at joint decisions to check rampant development. She stressed the organization's youth and its lack of "coherence." Charles and she disagreed as to whether any current zoning regulations applied to the mountain, and I left Rosine Raoul's beautiful home aware that local citizens need more information about ownership of mountain land if they're going to plan ahead. At present they seem to operate more on hunch and rumor than on hard data. Rosine Raoul mentioned "a rumor going around" that Lookout's potentially lucrative coal resources had been bought by Alabama coal people. She feared "that if they don't strip mine it, they'll sell the area to big developers in Atlanta for golf courses."

From the roads I'd biked upon, I had seen no sign that Lookout's ridge is the only place in Georgia containing a significant amount of high-quality coal, but it became clear that these deposits form the center of concern to local environmentalists. Charles Counts described to me the ugly slag heaps left over from earlier mining operations that disfigure the very center of the ridge, and coal preoccupies another member of the planning group with whom I talked, environmental planner and designer Garnet Chapin.

This boyish-looking fellow in his mid-20s occupies a unique position among citizens concerned with Lookout's growth. His great-uncle and namesake, Garnet Carter, developed Rock City, fencing in the wild rocks Rosine Raoul remembers picnicking on as a child. Chapin's father runs the tourist center now, and Garnet himself is involved in a development corporation building condominiums on the mountain. These facts make some members of the planning group uneasy, but Chapin sees himself as occupying a responsible middle position between "Stop everything!" environmentalists and "Full speed ahead!" developers.

"There are ways to accommodate growth, but not if it's scattered all over the place," he told me over lunch at the Rock City restaurant. He himself is working to purchase new park lands that will preserve some areas of the mountain, and he firmly opposes any return to mining on Lookout. "Seven thousand acres on the mountain are owned by a mining operation which has already done extensive drilling. The miners have cut dirt roads into the steep hills, which causes siltation, and the aquatic organisms that fish live on have been killed. Between 1900 and 1940, our native trout population was eliminated by mining. They left spoil piles behind which won't support productive life."

I sensed that Garnet Chapin was struggling to find himself. As an opponent of the war in Vietnam and an ecologist, he is the oddball, the outsider, in a deeply conservative family (his father was Barry Goldwater's local campaign manager 12 years ago). After our lunch together, I watched him interact with the powers-that-be at Rock City and felt they didn't take him very seriously. With his money and commitment, he could become a power in his own right in the movement to shape Lookout's future. His hope is "to create a better link between the decision makers at all levels and the people, so that inhabitants will know what the options are. Compromises will come from airing opposing views." The role he sees for himself is the crucial mediator, "trying to strike a balance between growth and scenic features."

Garnet Chapin is a likeable, engaging young man, but his abstractions made my head spin. I knew, just from the few hours I had spent biking across the top of Lookout, that striking a balance will be no easy task where so unique and exploitable a natural resource as this mountain is concerned. Even the simplest, purest, gentlest activities take on new dimensions here. On my way to Rock City, I pedaled past the best location for hang gliding east of the Mississippi, a spot where the highway runs right along the bluff and the mountain drops away sheer to reveal peaceful farmland hundreds of feet below. It was a Sunday, and the side of the road was thick with cars belonging to the followers of Icarus and those who came to watch the human birds hover and soar silently in mid-air.

The gliders are members of an organization called Tennessee Tree Toppers, one of whose leaders is a tall, thin, intense man of 35 or 40 named Don Guess whom I questioned as he was strapping himself into the complicated apparatus of his $900 kite with its 15-foot wing span. He was rhapsodic about the sport: "It's like ballet, only we're doing what man has wanted to do for centuries. I've actually flown with hawks, hovered with them 30 or 40 feet below me, checking me out. They were in a pretty strong thermal and I joined them. It was the high point of my life."

The Tree Toppers couldn't hope for a better location. A Mrs. Crane has let them use her field in the valley as a landing strip, and a kindly-faced, weathered gentleman named McCardy whom I met chatting with the gliders was happy to let them use his land on the bluff as a take-off site. Lookout's length and steepness divert the wind currents upwards, the farmland below sends off the hot air needed for good soaring, and as a result, gliders have been known to hover in the void for up to five hours at a time.

Great—or is it? Mr. McCardy says he moved to Lookout in 1949 because he "got tired of people." He's a lover of the mountain, having sold 40 of his original 100 acres to "a guy who wanted to keep it natural." Yet now his passion for watching the gliders soar and hang seems to have furnished him with new priorities. The crush of sightseers and aerial acrobats to this unique spot has already created safety hazards for motorists, pedestrians, and spectators. Mr. McCardy talks of leveling some trees across the highway to provide adequate parking facilities.

At the very highest point on the bluff, I watched carpenters hammering together the scaffolding for a concrete ramp that will permit gliders to leap without endangering onlookers as the enormous wing spans sweep toward the brink. I wondered if Mr. McCardy might some day permit an observation tower to be built for better viewing. What about refreshment stands?

Toilet facilities? Will this lovely poetic exercise turn into an uncontrollable nightmare? Can Lookout Mountain escape the curse of its very uniqueness?

And what about Rock City itself, perched at the entrance to the mountain on the north? Oddly enough, it may become one of the most powerful deterrents to unchecked growth, since its wealthy developers are not eager to see competing attractions in the immediate vicinity. For years I had resisted the signs on miniature bird houses and barn roofs all over the Southeast urging motorists to "See Rock City," but my curiosity about the ways in which Lookout's resources should or should not be exploited led me to pump the pedals harder and climb the steep grades faster to find out what made this particular tourist attraction so successful.

My conclusion is that people like having natural phenomena labeled and catalogued for them. I don't. Walking through or around a formation ostentatiously identified as "Needle's Eye," "Mushroom Rock," "Goblin's Underpass," or some other neat and obvious formula diminishes the pleasure I receive from the natural world. If my imagination fancies a resemblance between rock shapes and another shape or experience, I want to feel that *I* discovered it and that my discovery will not interfere with some later onlooker's surprise and recognition at the same spot.

I got to wondering if the mass appeal Rock City enjoys in this country could be imagined anywhere else on earth. The original idea to people the gardens with elves and other scampering critters came from Garnet Carter's wife, a German lover of fairy tales. Yet it was the American Carter, promoter of mini-golf into a gigantic recreation industry, who boostered the attraction and made "See Rock City"—like Burma-Shave signs a few decades ago—as central a feature of the American landscape as "amber waves of grain."

Has hucksterism always been an essential ingredient in our much-vaunted pioneer spirit? Is it possible to separate the vulgarity, the emptiness, with which our imaginations demean our magnificent environment from the vigor, energy, humor, bravery, and even pathos that unquestionably make up the American character? I think not, but I wouldn't be so sure if I hadn't encountered Mr. Clark Byers.

Byers is the Garnet Carter of "Sequoyah Caverns," a vast labyrinth of caves in Alabama not far from Lookout Mountain. He constructed tourist paths through the underground chambers, installed spotlights of every imaginable hue and intensity at strategic spots, and turned promotion of the site over to Rock City's proprietors, thus guaranteeing himself a profitable tourist business.

He's a man I doubt you'd notice on the street—small, compact, middle-aged, coarse and hard of features—but once you heard him speak, you'd not forget him. He guided me and four other tourists through the caves, and I felt myself in the presence of the distilled extract of the American folk character, an amalgam of P. T. Barnum, Mark Twain, Billy Graham, George Wallace, Buford Pusser, and Rube Goldberg. He maintains a steady barrage of commentary from beginning to end of the tour, much of it as fast as an auctioneer's prattle and therefore incomprehensible. His listeners are continually snookered into participating in some verbal practical joke, made the butt of shaggy-dog stories, exposed as city slickers, learned fools. "I wish you was here the day that doctor from the university at Knoxville came through. Why, he said these caves was 10,000 year old. The way he could tell was these here ruberiferous things—" and off he goes on yet another wacky tangent, trailing off, more likely than not, into a new dead-end.

Byers' timing is uncanny. Just as the listener is convinced that *finally* some essential fact about the caves is being explored, the mood is shattered by an obviously preposterous detail—or is it just a slight exaggeration, maybe even the truth? In Byers' monologue everything becomes possible and nothing likely. I'll never know how much—if any—of what he told us he believes himself. I don't have the slightest idea what *I* believe.

I couldn't help admiring Byers' showmanship. His imagination seduced and delighted me. And yet, and yet, I resisted him, too, this sleight-of-hand man with the winking flashlight and the 42nd Street flashing neon displays. His cavern is a hall of mirrors, an endlessly vanishing parade of illusions. Nothing on earth is too sacred to become a sideshow freak. "And here, on your left—yep, right there by that soot mark—you've got your Crucifixion. Now if you'll just step along—don't trip on that snake underfoot, young lady—I'll show you where Sequoyah hid out that time he was writing up his alphybett, I was just a young sprout then, back when those eddicated perfessers in Washington left us country folk alone to run our schools the way God meant us to—"

I learned next day that Byers had unexpectedly lost his young, vigorous son a mere week before, yet here he was, the stalwart trooper, keeping the show on the road. Quite a man, Clark Byers, quite a man.

I was glad to get back on my bicycle seat and continue exploring above ground on Lookout Mountain. The air was full of mist, the colors muted. Redbud flowered all along the mountain's sides. The glossy leaves of rhododendron and the turquoise-greenish splash of mountain streams picked up what light there was and turned it over, played it back.

I'd met good folks on Lookout Mountain, people in whose care its future as a largely untouched area seemed secure. Yet one thing troubled me: its subtle beauty is the beauty of simplicity, and there's something about simplicity that maddens the American mind. Who's to say some tinkering genius won't one day come along to pull this beauty up, install vast batteries of maroon, pink, puce, and lavender footlights in the glens, and turn Lookout Mountain into a shimmering, sophisticated vaudeville theater?

1976

CYCLIST'S ALMANAC

Lookout Mountain

Routes: Round trip between Cloudland Canyon State Park on south and Rock City on north, 41.7 miles. Round trip Cloudland Canyon to intersection of Georgia routes 189 and 157, 31.5 miles. Round trip Rock City to intersection of Georgia routes 189 and 157, 10.2 miles.
Altitude: 1,980′ at Cloudland Canyon, approx. 1,800′ at town of Lookout Mountain; elevation changes every foot or so in between.

Terrain: Steep, steep, steep—almost never flat. Biking country for experienced cyclists only.

History: Dade County, Georgia's northwesternmost, seceded from the Union before the rest of Georgia and was not officially readmitted until 1949. Known locally as "The State of Dade," in part because of its inaccessibility from the rest of Georgia. Until construction of Georgia highway 143 in 1939, county could only be entered by way of Tennessee or Alabama. Area settled by Cherokee Indians between 1720 and 1838 after white settlers forced them out of Smokies. Prehistoric inhabitants not identified. Archaeologists from University of Georgia recently discovered musical instruments from c. 400 A.D. and copper from the Lake Superior region; artifacts taken to Athens, but residents are still awaiting a report on the research.

Points of Interest: *Ruby Falls,* on Tennessee highway 148, ½ mile south of U.S. highways 41, 11, 64 and 72. Most developed of the many spectacular caves underlying Lookout Mountain. Banks of colored lights and labels for the more unusual formations keep visitors in a purely passive relationship to the underground sights. . . . *Rock City,* on Georgia highway 157 (becomes Tennessee 58), in town of Lookout Mountain, Georgia. Dwarf paradise in one of most extraordinary scenic spots on mountain. Magnificent views, great swaying suspension bridge, forlorn herd of deer on a shadeless rock, Mother Goose characters embalmed or perhaps just terminally ill inside underground "Fairyland Caverns." . . . *Sequoyah Caverns,* just off U.S. 11 and I-59, a few miles south of the Alabama-Georgia line, 35 miles south of Chattanooga. Developer Clark Byers (see text) turns what might otherwise be just another garish, over-developed, Disney-like extravaganza into a non-stop, mind-dizzying exploration of our national folk character, complete with warts, beauty spots, wrinkles, comic features, and sublimities. . . . *Covenant College campus,* on Georgia 189 between town of Lookout Mountain and intersection with Georgia 157. Situated on high bluff overlooking scenic valley. Fine views, interesting architecture. . . . *Cloudland Canyon State Park,* off Georgia highway 143 near western edge of mountain. Beautiful, undeveloped natural formations that evolved after a number of consecutive years of torrential rains wearing down the soft sandstone on the mountain's surface. Nicely landscaped trails, deep glens full of rhododendron and other mountain flora, fine waterfalls. . . .

Where to Camp: *Cloudland Canyon State Park* (see above). 50 sites, well landscaped and equipped. A few cottages available but reservations hard to come by.

The Helen-Sautee-Unicoi Loop

A fall foliage bike tour through a beautiful corner of Northeast Georgia

by Bill Cutler

I rode the Helen-Sautee-Unicoi Loop in early summer when the trees were green and full. It was beautiful then, and since this area is the heart of the mountain country that tourists flock to in the autumn our group couldn't help speculating on the scenery cyclists would be treated to in the fall foliage time, when the valleys and hillsides glow with reds and yellows. Regardless of the season, if you've a taste for some good scenic cycling in an area that offers many other attractions and distractions, the Helen-Unicoi-Sautee region ought to satisfy your appetite.

What began for me as a simple bike trip, kept on growing until it turned into a kind of omnibus recreational outing. Eventually, seven of us man, woman and child, took part in some or all of the adventures recorded here.

Our safari began at Atlanta's Brookwood Station where my neighbor Paul Mingo, his friends Karl and Mary Ann Boehmke and I loaded our bikes on a Gainesville bound train at 6:30 A.M. one Saturday morning in early June.

The Gainesville train is a story in itself. You and your bike can take the 60-mile, 60-minute trip from Atlanta's Brookwood Station to Gainesville for $2.22 one way. The train leaves at 7 every morning, but bikes must be checked in by 6:30. You can ride the approximately 60 miles back to Atlanta along peaceful back roads through sleepy little towns like Flowery Branch and Shake Rag, or if you want to pedal through the north Georgia countryside, you can take the train back to Atlanta the next morning.

At the end of the one hour train ride our bikes were handed down to us on the Gainesville platform in perfect condition and we set off on a 40-mile ride to Unicoi State Park. There we joined forces with *Brown's Guide* photographer, Edmund Marshall and two young fishermen, Stephen Hill, 9, and Jeffery Riley, 10. We cyclists relaxed from our exertions in delightfully cool Unicoi Lake while Jeff and Steve fished from the bank. Sunfish were the prey and the fishing was easy.

Edmund and the boys had brought supplies with them in the white Ford van. Dinner was a grand feast . . . chicken and salad and lots of wine followed by watermelon and marshmallows toasted over a fire. We kept the epicurian tradition going at breakfast the next day with eleven fresh sunfish steamed with herbs and butter, a delicious accompaniment to Edmund's plentiful pancakes.

These good eats gave Paul, Karl, Mary Ann and me the energy to set out on our primary mission . . . bike tour of the Helen-Sautee-Unicoi area.

We began by pedaling the short distance from our campsite to Anna Ruby Falls, one of the most imposing natural sights in Georgia. Two streams cascade hundreds of feet down a rocky cliff within a few yards of each other to mingle their waters at the cliff's base. From there, the single stream flows through a beautiful wooded gorge lined with rhododendron, eventually to join the nearby Chattahoochee. The water at the bottom of the falls is as pure and delicious as any I can remember tasting.

The ride back down from the falls to the park entrance was one long delirious swoop, with no dangerous curves or precipitous drops that required braking. But we were brought back to humdrum cycling reality when we hit state route 17 again with its heavy traffic through Helen down to the enchanting settlement of Nacoochee.

If you look closely at the habitations partially hidden in dense foliage along the right-hand slopes of this highway, you'll see some remarkable examples of indigenous North Georgia architecture—long, low structures with front porches across their entire length, some with splendid latticework designs. Once you notice what local builders created to decorate and blend into the lovely valleys of this region, you may well wonder why anyone would have grafted an alien style, pseudo-Swiss ski-lodge onto the simple structures of Helen. No question about it, however, this fabricated kitsch has brought a pile of tourists and their money into the area.

Me, I'll take Nacoochee any day. It's nothing but a converted railroad station, an old mill, a barnlike antique store, a weather-beaten, long-porched hillside percher, and a gorgeous antebellum house with classic lines where Governor Lamartine Griffin Hardman and his family spent their summers. But this heterogeneous collection of buildings evokes a variety of Georgian styles and traditions and ways of life, and brings one into close contact with local history. There's even a reminder of the Cherokee nation that first settled the Nacoochee Valley (Nacoochee was a Cherokee princess) in the burial mound that rises imposingly across state route 17 from the Hardman home. Unfortunately, the governor decorated it with a cupola in the style of his own house, which is an odd way of venerating another people's culture.

We posed for pictures in front of the handsome Crescent Hill Church, just down route 17 from the Nacoochee settlement. Two pleasant young people came out from playing the organ into the bright sun and chatted with us about the area. They told us of a covered bridge we hadn't known about, so Karl, Paul and I pedaled past lovely farms to meet the others there (Mary Ann's ankle had swollen from a fall the day before and was hurting, so she rode in the truck with Edmund and the kids).

The covered bridge turned out not to be one of Georgia's natural wonders, no match for several other such structures we've seen in the state, but our stop there to fish and picnic was one of the memorable moments of this fine outing.

A modern concrete bridge spans the stream (Chickamauga Creek) right next to the old wooden one, and as we dribbled remnants of the previous evening's watermelon into the baked clay on the water's edge, we noticed people congregating on the opposite shore—ladies in long yellow gowns picking their high-heeled way among the tumbled boulders down the slope, gents in starched collars and somber suits. We offered a sharp contrast to this Sunday-go-to-meeting propriety in our bedraggled camping outfits surrounded by our cluttered recreational gear.

We pulled the kids out of the water and hauled in their fishing lines as soon as we realized that the stream was about to become a sacred dunking place where sins are washed away. After the congregation had assembled beneath the modern bridge, the hefty minister took off his shoes and waded into the middle of the stream. Four celebrants huddled in the water with him waiting their turn to be submerged, as the witnesses intoned "Shall We Gather at the River" in a lugubrious and subdued manner.

All in all, it was an oddly joyless ceremony. The newly saved straggled glumly back to shore, and the assembly dispersed with nary a shout nor hallelujah. But all of us, city people with very different roots, felt privileged to have caught a glimpse of a cultural tradition we had only read about before but never witnessed.

By now it was mid-afternoon, and with Paul, Karl, and I pedaled away to finish our tour while the others went back to fishing and wading.

We had a stiff wind to battle much of the way and several fairly rugged hills, but the scenery was so soothing we could find no cause to complain. Just before we had completed the loop back to Unicoi Park, we passed an old farmhouse advertising antiques and curios and stopped to browse. I found an old hand-tooled wooden floor lamp I wanted to buy, and since I couldn't figure out a way to carry it on my bike, we decided to sit on the front porch and rock a spell with the proprietors and wait for the van to pass. We were invited to taste the cool well water drawn right in the front yard, and we recommend it to all passersby who follow our path.

Eventually we rejoined forces with the van and then began the fun of packing bicycles, people, tents, sleeping bags, and other camping gear, and my floor lamp into our one sturdy vehicle. The squeezing done, we drove the short distance to the Sautee Inn where we stuffed ourselves on Mrs. Anthony's very sophisticated country cooking. Seven much plumper and sleepier people crammed themselves back into the van, and our circus vehicle took us valiantly home.

1974

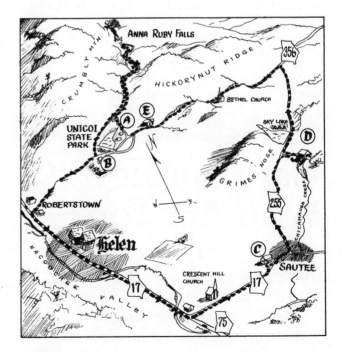

Helen-Sautee-Unicoi Loop

Since this trip is a loop, you can begin it at any point and end up where you started. But if you want to bike to Anna

Ruby Falls (enthusiastically recommended), you'd be well advised to begin in Unicoi State Park and get the short but strenuous climb over with while you're fresh. The total distance of the loop, including falls excursion, is 25 miles.

If you're camping at the park, you can bike to the falls road by taking a poorly paved shortcut now closed to vehicular traffic (A). You'll have to dismount at the north end of this road to get past a barrier built to keep cars out. Otherwise, you can park at the information booth for campers (B) and take the falls road from its intersection with state route 356.

When you complete the round trip to the falls, take a right onto 356 for a long downhill to Robertstown. Watch out for heavy traffic along state route 17 through Helen to the settlement of Nacoochee. Ride single file and keep as close to the right-hand side of the pavement as possible.

Keep on 17 at the intersection by turning left, past the handsome Hardman house and the charming Crescent Hill Church. In a couple of miles you'll pass the Sautee Inn (C) perched on a hill on your left (first-rate country cooking). The settlement of Sautee is centered around the intersection of routes 17 and 255, with the old Sautee General Store its hub. Take 255 off to the left at the store and ride a couple of miles through lovely rolling farm country.

The loop continues up the road marked with a sign to Sky Lake, but you might enjoy a very short detour to see a covered bridge (D) where 255 crosses Chickamauga Creek. If so, retrace your route to the Sky Lake turnoff. The lake itself and the camp that sits on its shores are stunningly beautiful.

The road you're on will deadend after some three miles at Georgia route 356. Take a left and enjoy this roller coaster road for about four miles. After about three miles of this you'll pass the Hex House (E), home of antiques and curios and freshly drawn well water. We stopped and rested in a rocker on the front porch for a few minutes.

If you started the trip in the camping area, take a right at the sign for campsites. Otherwise, keep straight on 356 till you come to the information bureau and parking lot.

Cave Spring, Who Are You?

Mike Burton: "I worried some that I wouldn't find people in the country who shared my interests. The exact opposite was true. I've learned incredibly much about all sorts of things from my neighbors."
Rev. Kim McIntire: "In this town, the only way that you move or you grow is you get someone who's willing to push. And it just wears you out to push." Connor Mobley: "The things our grandpappy and great-grandpappy had, we want to hand them down."

by Bill Cutler

Life in the small northwest Georgia community of Cave Spring near the Alabama border "has turned out to be everything I expected—and less," the town's bicycling Methodist minister, Kim McIntire, remarked to me as we set out on a two-wheeling tour of the area. Kim grew up in the Army and spent his childhood and youth near cosmopolitan centers. Before coming to Cave Spring, he'd served in an urban ministry at Atlanta's Grady Hospital. "That was a round of constant crises," he recalls. "I never got to see again the people I had helped." He wanted a change, a rural ministry where the pace was quieter, the relationships steadier.

Three years ago he moved to the one-time resort area of Cave Spring in beautiful Vann's Valley, a town its residents invariably refer to as "quiet" or "tranquil" or "steady." The peace of its tiny business district, grouped around a triangular greenspace, is broken by the rumble of giant trucks on interstate errands, but otherwise the loudest uproar in downtown Cave Spring comes from the creek that ripples over rapids behind the only supermarket's parking lot. Students from the Georgia School for the Deaf, whose two campuses lie on opposite sides of the central shopping area, flash their signals nimbly to each other as they walk back and forth to class. A cyclist's pace and lack of clangor fit Cave Spring's mood just right.

Kim McIntire isn't always on his bike, of course, and the town's absence of excitement and variety has not quite met his needs. "There's never any, what I would call, major flaps, in terms of upheavals or crises," he told me in his quiet-spoken, reasoning voice. "The folks sometimes consider them major, but in relation to the rest of the world, they're just nothing. The pharmacy is out of Crest toothpaste, or something like that, is major. Folks don't get in too much of a hurry about anything, and they don't really seem interested in anything that I know of."

His clear and barely creased complexion, classically aquiline nose, bright grayish-blue eyes, trim figure, and thickly ringleted brown hair that curls down his neck nearly to his shoulders give Kim the look of a student athlete. He dresses in blue jeans and open-neck shirts, and cycles for business as well as recreation, on visits to parishioners in remote rural areas. Some members of his congregation raise their eyebrows at his unorthodox, casual approach, but the majority accept it without cavil.

Very far from a studious, dry-as-dust theologian, Rev. McIntire, yet his analysis of why he finds Cave Spring deficient is deeply thoughtful, rooted in his training for the ministry. "I think of it from out of the context of theological structures. One of the things that's been hardest for me is to know what is the point of people's lives around here." In other ministries, he said, he knew much better what his congregation wanted, what were their sources of joy and pain, excitement, hope, fear, and anxiety. "But it's *very* undefined for me here."

Perhaps, I suggested, his lack of previous contact with rural people had not equipped him to interpret their lower-keyed expression of feelings. He admitted he was still experiencing "culture shock" in Cave Spring and acknowledged a "whole different way of relating" than he had been used to. "It's important to maintain a certain genteel-ity here," he explained, "for the sake of family relations, public images, and stuff like that, so that there is little open conflict, there's a certain repression, as opposed to dealing with the whole range of emotions. In Cave Spring, the way I experience folks is, you just don't get angry—you just don't do that. A by-product of that is that you don't get happy. If you don't get afraid, you don't get hopeful, and then it becomes a blend, it becomes some grey thing."

Two of Kim's close friends in Cave Spring were the local bank president and the principal at the Georgia School for the Deaf, but both left town after meeting resistance to new ideas. The banker had come over from nearby Cedartown, Kim says, hoping "that this would be a bank to grow with and this would be a place to settle down." He came with what he considered sound business ideas he wanted to implement—expanding services, incentive awards for employees, public relations programs—but "they always met with a constant rebuttal." When he was offered a lateral transfer back to Cedartown, "he would have been a fool not to take it," and he did.

Similarly, the principal came to Cave Spring intending to put into practice new concepts in deaf education to which he'd been exposed, "and again, this wall of resistance, you know—'I will not do that.'" He tried to introduce sex education into the school, but "he couldn't begin to get any of those teachers to consider teaching the children about sex. He was wanting to do it on his time schedule, and they just weren't going to do that. That's not necessarily his fault or their fault, but it certainly isn't very conducive to hanging around very long."

"He was on his way up," Kim continued, explaining why the principal left Cave Spring, "and after two years he was wanting to continue expanding his horizons and working with people who were in the process of expanding theirs. You know, the School for the Deaf was only integrated in 1974. It's ridiculous. And that met with just *unbelievable* resistance on the part of the administration. Then there's the question of what's available for the gifted or even the moderately intelligent deaf students—there's nothing. Until my principal friend came, no one was pushing. In this town, the only way that you move or you grow is you get someone who's willing to push. And it just wears you out to push. It's worn everybody out so far."

Kim made all these points absolutely without bitterness or resentment. He and his family have met many fine people in Cave Spring, he says, who have been "very generous and charitable and loving to us." And life there offers compensations—bicycling, for one. "Whenever I'm feeling really closed in and have to get rid of the cobwebs, a bike ride out into this beautiful valley works miracles," says Kim's wife, Rae Ann.

She accompanied us for a short distance from the brick ranch-style house on the outskirts of town that the Methodist church uses for its parsonage. We rode into a stiff headwind, Rae Ann with three-year-old Kevin in a child's seat on the back of her bike. She turned back after a couple of miles, and Kim

and I continued to explore the little-traveled roads he'd found and enjoyed riding on.

He wanted me to visit a tiny rural community where he preaches two Sundays a month, a place he spoke about with a good deal of admiration. "The folks there do without things the rest of us consider necessary for comfort," he told me as we headed toward Jackson Chapel. "They don't have indoor plumbing or modern appliances or much of anything new. They just keep using over again what they've got."

"Are they poor?" I asked, showing by my question that I assumed people must have an economic reason for such odd behavior.

He paused a long time. I had the impression he'd never considered that possibility. "They're not what you'd call rich, but I don't think they live that way 'cause they have to. They like it that way."

I was intrigued—and skeptical. We turned off a state highway used by pulpwood trucks onto a rough aggregate surface with steep uphill pulls, through country that must once have been cultivated but now scraggled wild. Over the brow of a hill, a loose scattering of home sites and hardscrabble farms came into view.

We stopped before a weatherbeaten frame house whose yard showed years of hard use and poor drainage. The porch floor we stepped onto had buckled and sagged and warped, the screen door Kim knocked on hung precariously in its frame. A young woman came to the door, dressed in her Sunday best, and welcomed Kim enthusiastically. She said the family had just returned from her mother's sister's funeral and her father was changing clothes but would be with us shortly.

We stepped through a dim and sparsely furnished parlor, on one of whose walls was hanging a 1974 calendar with a romanticized picture of a cabin and snow-capped mountain tops bathed in a rosy flush of light. Blanche Mobley, the young woman's mother, was in the high-ceilinged, long-unpainted kitchen, sitting on a counter. She apologized for the room's disarray, and Kim expressed his condolences for the loss of her sister. The plaster in the walls was cracked and coming loose in places, the table in the middle of the room was piled high with provisions and beans and rice already cooked in pots. The old stove threw off a steady and comfortable heat.

In a few minutes, Connor Mobley entered, clothed in neat, clean denim overalls. His ruddy face topped by short-cropped frizzy gray hair gave off the most genial, welcoming glow I can ever recall on any man's features. Here was a contented soul, not given to sulky griping. He greeted Kim with eyes lit up by warmth.

We got around to talking about Jackson Chapel, past and present, and Mr. Mobley beamed even brighter as he spoke of the recent community effort to turn their church around to face the road and spruce it up. "We had the plainest, ruralest church you'd ever want to see, but now we've got it fixed up just as modern."

That was the only time he expressed pleasure in modernity, however. Mainly he talked about the "hand-me-down approach" that "we rural people" had always followed. "The things our grandpappy and great-grandpappy had, we want to hand them down," he said in his soft drawn-out drawl, not making any specific reference or gesture to the well-worn objects that lay around him. He expressed concern that the old values and traditions were passing, that folks in Jackson Chapel seemed ready to throw out what had been good enough for the area's pioneers and early settlers.

He accompanied us out to the front yard and voiced satisfaction in our means of transport, which took him back to his own childhood in Jackson Chapel. His memories made him chuckle. "We used to stuff the tires with cornshucks and cotton seeds, then we'd cover the holes with any old tape we had around. Then we'd walk clear across town to get the pump. Only one family had a pump hereabouts. We were so rural! You'd think we were proud of it!"

As we rode away, I couldn't help but be struck by the number of times he'd used the word "rural." I wouldn't have expected such self-consciousness about life in the country. I told Kim how much I'd liked Connor Mobley, and he echoed my pleasure. "It's sad, though," he added, "how that feeling Connor talked about of holding on to the old ways makes folks out here resent the arrival of new people and new ideas. I talk to them a lot about that and they know it's wrong. But it's just too deep in them to root out."

Kim said he wanted me to meet some other friends who lived out in the country, but in a very different style. We headed east and north, across fertile Vann's Valley watered by Cave Spring's Cedar Creek into rocky, hilly land that looks as inhospitable for productive farming as the stony pastures of New England.

"I've heard folks call the Burtons weird," he said by way of introduction as we neared their property. "Maybe it's partly the wild goat smell you pick up when you get too close to Mike, especially. But, more, it's their life-style that bothers people. They're trying to be completely self-supporting, not needing anything from the outside world, while they want outsiders to need what Mike has to offer. That's hard to manage these days. But I don't consider them weird. They're good friends."

Halfway down the slope of a long hill, I caught a fleeting glimpse through a clearing in the woods of an extraordinary ark or prow made half of weathered wood and half of rough stones, perched on the hillside and jutting toward the sky. "Did you see that?" I yelled to Kim, who was braking to a near-halt ahead of me at the hill's bottom.

"We're here," he yelled back, and turned up a dirt driveway toward the monument. The path curved through trees, past a large barn and a series of small, high, wooden-and-glass structures that looked like a litter of babies spawned by the giant oddity I'd seen from the road. At the end of the drive, we stopped in front of the main building, which I now realized was a house. A short, blonde-headed young woman, a blonde girl of early school age, and a ruggedly built man with bushy dark beard were all on the roof, engaged in laying stones in place for a gigantic chimney.

"Where do you get the stones?" Kim called up, as they continued to labor away.

"Out in the fields, wherever we can find 'em," Mike Burton replied. He had a gentle, musical, humorous quality to his manner, John Keats's soul inside Paul Bunyan's body. His wide, open, generous face is shaped around his strong and pro-

nounced nose. "We pick the ones with the most cow shit on 'em. Gives a good texture, and we don't have any trouble stumbling over 'em up here in the dark. We always know where they are."

Kim took me around the outside of the house, which began as and grew outward from an unadorned old trailer, one narrow side of which is still visible embedded in the larger structure. Glass, stone, and lumber of various sorts are pieced together in eccentric shapes, interspersed with sculptured medallions and carvings. A huge, shaggy dog of indeterminate breed named Thor kept jumping up on me and nearly knocking me over. The bleating of goats carried from the direction of the barn.

In time Mike Burton came down and talked about the home he and his wife Caroline are building. "It grows, organically," he said and laughed, a short, strong spurt of laughter. "I may be working on some wood and like the way it looks, this panel for example,"—he showed me a handsome door notched with carvings like rosettes—"and decide to build it into the house. Then I figure out what I want to go around it and build that."

We went inside, through the low-slung trailer kitchen into an enormous living-room with many windows, heated by a wide stone fireplace. A spiral staircase Mike made of rough wood slats suspended on parachutist's nylon cords appeared to dance and sway on one side of the room. Mike's wall hangings, sculpture, and metal castings animate the interior.

He teaches art at the Georgia School for the Deaf and echoes many of Kim McIntire's concerns about the bureaucratic inertia and timidity there. Yet Mike has taken a special interest in deaf education, become proficient in sign language, and feels a close bond with the students. "Just as there are many blind musicians, I figure many deaf people are potential artists," he says. Despite the frustrations of working within an unresponsive system, Mike finds rich rewards in his job.

His life is satisfying in other respects as well. A native of Floyd County, he traveled out to California to study art before returning to Cave Spring to live. "I worried some that I wouldn't find people in the country who shared my interests and who I could talk art with. The exact opposite was true. I've learned incredibly much about all sorts of things—herbs and crafts and how to get along—from my neighbors. If I'd stayed in California, I might have become a better artist because I'd just have worked at that. But I'm really not into specializing."

Indeed he's not. He and Caroline grow just about everything they eat, milk their own goats, and make their own wine, raise bees, and plan to try experimenting with solar collectors to heat their house more efficiently, in addition to their carpentry and art projects. Mike figures if he ever wanted to give up his job, his family could survive indefinitely on the 50 acres they share with their goats, chickens, guinea hens, and ducks.

The smallness and slowness of Cave Spring are no problems for Mike. He enjoys the old-fashioned pleasure of going into Dewell Lindsey's hardware store, ordering whatever he wants, and settling his bill "once a year, at no interest." He likes a town where he knows just about everyone on the streets, yet

CYCLIST'S ALMANAC

Cave Spring

Routes: Two loops that intersect at the Cave Spring business center, one north to Weiss Lake (17.5 miles), the other south to Cedartown (29.6 miles). You should have no trouble parking and starting right in the heart of Cave Spring.

Terrain: Rolling, with moderate grades. Steepest hill is coming down into Cave Spring from the east. Reversing the direction of southern loop means you will have to climb it.

Road conditions: The Cave Spring-Cedartown Road is extraordinarily scenic and well paved, but narrow, winding, and rather heavily used by high-speed traffic during peak business hours. Expect some very rough pavement on back roads over both loops.

Points of interest: (1) *Dawson Home,* in process of being restored by two of town's newcomers; Diane Dawson is head of the Cave Spring Historical Society. Brick church at corner of Alabama & Fannin is where Kim McIntire ministers. (2) *Presbyterian Church,* built 1866; still being maintained through efforts of a single family. (3) *Depot,* now abandoned, but the city government is contemplating purchasing it for restoration and some future public use. (4) *Elementary School for the Deaf,* formerly the black campus for the school, eventual site of all the institution's facilities. Take a close look at the old rock barn right by the road through campus—beautifully designed; saved from destruction by Mike Burton and individuals in the Cave Spring Historical Society. (5) *J. W. Wesley Home,* one of earliest surviving structures in Cave Spring, built early 1840s of handmade, oversized brick. Brick kitchen in rear 10 or 20 years older, built by Cherokee Indians and home of sub-chief David Vann. (6) *Pettis Home,* lovely one-story Greek Revival cottage built in 1858 from lumber taken from an old Methodist parsonage. (7) *Rolator Park,* favorite gathering-place for family reunions, with its spring-fed pool and creek (don't miss tasting Cave Spring's excellent water) and unused buildings from the old Hearn Academy, now defunct. Historical Society is trying to save the main building, which carries a sign reading "The Park Bench" over former main entrance. (8) *Turner Home,* built mid-1800s, with octagonal tower room; occupied by Union soldiers during Civil War. (9) *Carnes Home,* built mid-1800s with square columns and a hanging balcony; in 1920s, a dormitory for boys attending Hearn Academy. (10) *William Winfrey Peek Home,* built 1843 by Virginia cotton planter who once owned a vast estate north of Cedartown. (11) *Roberts Home,* handsome 19th-century brick birthplace of Mrs. Winfrey Peek, present occupant of (12) *Peek Home Place,* built 1866 by Julius Peek, only son of William Winfrey Peek not killed in Civil War. Handsome though decaying residence contains portrait of William Winfrey Peek with missing left hand destroyed by a Yankee bayonet. (13) *Big Spring Park,* lovely scene of Cedartown's earliest history, site of Indian trading post. (14) *Neel Reid Library,* small brick structure designed by Georgia's most distinguished architect in 1919, being restored by the Cedartown Historical Society for use as a local history museum. (15) *Episcopal church* (on right at intersection), built 1883. Across Bradford St., former Woodland Female College music room, built c. 1855, used as rectory of church c. 1920–65; now threatened with demolition. (16) *Peek Park,* nice place to rest and picnic. (17) *Burton Home* (see text), continually being added to by Mike and Caroline; stop in and say hello. (18) *High School for the Deaf,* formerly campus for white students, eventually to be abandoned. Administration building dates from 1847; facing it, the largest outdoor swimming pool in Georgia, fed by nearby spring; water temperature remains constant at 60° year-round.

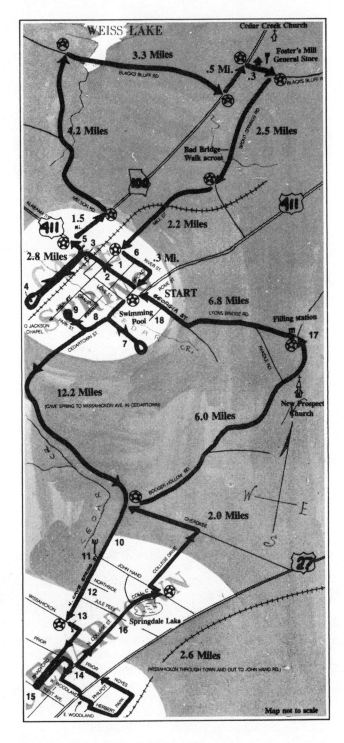

where he doesn't have to live so close to its residents that they're tempting to pry into his business.

Few of us can or even want to be as self-reliant as Mike and Caroline Burton. In their continually evolving house fashioned out of old warehouse timbers and recycled glass doors, they've perfected a kind of "hand-me-down" approach to life, using old recipes and traditional country techniques for survival, that I reckon Connor Mobley would approve of. Simplicity, stripping things down to the nub of necessity—maybe that's the canniest old country recipe of all.

Kim McIntire's three-year stint as minister at Cave Spring will end this summer and he'll be moving on, perhaps back to Atlanta. He's been a temporary walker on Vann Valley's earth and rider of its roads. As an outsider, does he see the town's true character more clearly or more cloudily than its long-time inhabitants, I wonder? I know at least one insider who shares his view that Cave Spring's pokey, lacking push and drive.

Mrs. Jewel Dyer now lives in Cedartown, but she was one of the last students to attend old Hearn Academy at Cave Spring before it closed its doors in the mid-'20s ("I killed it," she said gaily). She later taught at the School for the Deaf before taking over the town's library. She edits the quarterly journal of the North West Georgia Historical and Genealogical Society, of which her husband is immediate past president. Together, they're experts on Cave Spring's history and family lineages, and they enjoy correcting each other.

"There's not another town like it in the world," Jewel Dyer said, rubbing her neck. The afternoon I sat in the Dyers' pretty stone house and chatted with them, her face was heavily powdered, her hair jet-black from dyeing, and she wore a brightly flowered blouse and beige pants. "Cave Spring's just as complacent. God made Sundays. They're contented for things to go along."

"They're not interested for it to grow," her husband commented, taking off his glasses and rubbing his eyes. His voice has a flat, mountain twang, his hair is pure white and shaped in a little flat crown on top of his head. "Why should they bring in a factory?" he challenged.

"I don't want a factory, but I just want them to fix up their houses. A good many have been torn down."

"No, not many," he replied, squinting up his eyes behind their silver-framed lenses.

How does one measure change? And is change growth? A bunch of newcomers to Cave Spring have formed a local historical society to try and save the old homes and school buildings that give the town so much of its charm. *Not* changing, preserving, becomes the surest sign of changing consciousness to these energetic young residents.

The big hotels are gone that once housed summer visitors from Middle Georgia, lured by the famous waters from the spring. The depot sits dusty and deserted. The grand trees that used to arch over every street in town are mostly gone, as is all but one sickly magnolia of a magnificent row that once marched along the creek right in the business heart of town. Great losses, to be sure. Yet Cave Spring still feels intact, whole, comfortable. *Too* comfortable? I'll let you be the judge.

1977

City around the City*

On tree-canopied streets and by collard patches, through beautifully restored neighborhoods and dirt-poor ones, here is a tour that tells about one man's 10-year-long love affair with Atlanta.

by Bill Cutler

Scarcely a building was left standing within a wide radius of the downtown center of Atlanta when Union General William Tecumseh Sherman and his troops pulled out of the destroyed railroad junction in September 1864 on their way toward Savannah and the sea. By the 1870s, however, not only was a thriving commercial center being rebuilt over the ashes of the old, but the business district was beginning to be ringed by handsome dwellings. The remains of Atlanta's Victorian neighborhoods are among the main points of the tour I am about to take you on.

To accommodate the residential needs of the reborn city's business leaders, an engineer and entrepreneur named Joel Hurt laid out a neighborhood east of the downtown center called Inman Park and had a streetcar line run from the central business district to connect residents' homes with their places of employment. Inman Park became one of the most fashionable places for the wealthy to live throughout the last three decades of the 19th century. Mansions decorated with intricate stone parapets and inlaid terra-cotta designs or elaborate wooden scrollwork crowded together along the avenues of the neighborhood. Hurt later sold the development rights in Inman Park to members of the Candler family, who had purchased the patent for an obscure sweet drink from a Dr. Pemberton for $1200 and marketed it into a worldwide craze known as Coca-Cola.

Meanwhile, to the west of downtown other wealthy residents were moving into a community called West End, which existed before Atlanta came into being and which retained its own municipal government until it was absorbed by the city in 1893. Here tended to gather, in addition to merchants and capitalists, distinguished men of letters, such as Clark Howell, the editor of the *Atlanta Journal,* and Joel Chandler Harris, author of the *Uncle Remus* stories and columnist for the *Atlanta Constitution.* Here, as in Inman Park, substantial Victorian homes lined both sides of West End's major streets.

By the turn of the century, the downtown business center was ringed by residential neighborhoods. The wealthy lived not only in West End and Inman Park, but to the north along Peachtree Street and to the south along Washington, Pulliam, Pryor, and Formwalt streets. Meanwhile, middleclass Atlantans, clerks, and office workers were settling Grant Park to the southeast and moving into small homes on side streets in West End. In between the areas settled by white citizens were neighborhoods for Atlanta's black population, east of downtown along and near Auburn Avenue, and north of West End around the growing Atlanta University Center.

Atlantans with money, like their counterparts everywhere in this country, were not satisfied with life in the close-in neighborhoods developed by their parents during the 1880s and '90s. They wanted more space between their houses and more distance between their places of residence and the noise and dirt of the commercial district. Accordingly, the same Joel Hurt who laid out Inman Park began the development of a district called Druid Hills, farther north and east, in the 1910s, later selling out his interests, once again, to the Candlers. Also during the early years of this century, a neighborhood known as Ansley Park was developed north of downtown, laid out with meandering streets and extensive green spaces to simulate a parklike residential setting (Atlantans seem always to have treasured greenery and to have pictured themselves as tamed forest creatures, as the number of their neighborhoods incorporating the word "park" in their names would suggest).

The elite were moving north, following some obscure principle that holds true in many (though by no means all) American cities. After 1900 one address became preeminent for desirability in Atlanta: Peachtree Street. The great mansions that lined both sides of this thoroughfare were the admiration of visitors, and "Atlanta" became synonymous with "Peachtree Street" for tourists and elite residents alike (hence the proliferation of street names with "Peachtree" as part of their titles, to the amazed befuddlement of visitors hunting addresses to this day). Peachtree Street stretches north of downtown, and to the north the trend-setters and parvenus had to move. One can follow their progress by tracing the history of the Victorian playhouse that now sits on the grounds of the Atlanta Historical Society behind the Swan House after having delighted several generations of the city's children. The playhouse was built in the 1890s for a family that lived at 279 Peachtree Street, downtown. Around 1906 it was moved to Inman Park, around 1910 to Ansley Park, in 1926 to Brookwood Hills (a neighborhood close to Brookwood Station, where Interstates 75 and 85 split north of Ansley Park), and in 1932 to Buckhead, which remains a fashionable section today.

As the inexorable march toward the North Star accelerated, the areas south, east, and west of downtown ceased to hold attractions for the well-to-do, and the old neighborhoods fell into neglect. Some of them, like the entire community just south of downtown, disappeared altogether, as did, ironically, all but a couple of those grand houses that gave Peachtree Street such a cachet. Many other communities near downtown (except for Inman Park) have lost their most splendid showplaces, yet the scale and feeling of these Victorian neighborhoods have miraculously survived many decades of neglect and Americans' inveterate determination to replace the tried and true with the new and ticky-tack. The existence of plentiful and cheap land on the outskirts of Atlanta played a role in the preservation of large tracts of turn-of-the-century housing. The land close to downtown was not needed for industrial development (Atlanta has never been a large industrial center), and the Victorian and post-Victorian bungalows of West End and Grant Park and Adair Park were left alone in the mad scramble of moneyed people to get away from their neighbors. Thus, when young professional couples began taking an interest in downtown living some 10 years ago, they found not only attractive and sound housing, but entire neighborhoods, to refurbish, preserve, and care for.

It is the richness and diversity of these older pockets that constitute much of the attraction Atlanta has always held for me. I live in one of these neighborhoods, exactly two miles from City Hall and the heart of downtown, but the morning sun filters into my kitchen window through the branches of 75-foot oak trees, a rooster on the next street west from mine keeps up a lively racket as the nights begin to pale (making me think sometimes as I struggle toward wakefulness from sleep that I'm back on my grandfather's farm), and my neighbors who live in the turn-of-the-century cottages with high ceilings alongside mine know me, watch out for me and my property, create a community of care and concern that I have never known anywhere else and which I cherish deeply.

And so this tour through Atlanta's neighborhoods and parks is meant as a celebration of the features of city life that I love best about Atlanta, a sharing of the funny secret places I have found during the past 10 years of wheeling across and up and down and back and forth along the city's streets. I'll even show you one of the rare houses that survived Sherman's torches 117 years ago. I haven't found Atlanta a pleasant city to walk in—too sprawly and diffuse—but it accommodates itself ideally to the bicycle. This tour, accordingly, takes you into all sorts of urban landscapes—rich, poor, swanky, scruffy, close-knit, haughty, black, white, joyous, and sometimes a little sad. The entire loop is 52.4 miles, and they're tough, hilly miles, so you may not feel like riding the whole distance in one day (the dotted lines on the map indicate possible points where the route may be broken into smaller loops). I urge you, however, to undertake the entire trip at some point or other, even if you have to break it into several sections. The richness of Atlanta's topography and architecture, the wonderful oddity of its people, will only be apparent if you cycle into every quadrant of the city.

You won't see the noted tourist attractions of the city, such as the Peachtree Plaza Hotel, except as distant perspectives looming through the branches of overhanging trees. You'll loop all the way around downtown instead of riding through it, but you'll learn a lot about what and how the city was—and is—by steering clear of the bustling commercial centers. Yes, Atlanta is the trading and financial capital of the Southeast. But it's also a place where people live and play. This is the Other Atlanta. My Atlanta.

The tour may be begun at any point along the route, but I'll orient you from a starting point in *Piedmont Park* (on weekends you'll find Atlanta's most diverse and widely used public park closed to all but pedestrian and bicycle traffic; follow the green "Bike Route" signs along the park's streets). The tour uses the city's only officially marked route for bicycles for approximately 10 miles, but some of the signs have fallen down and not been replaced at crucial intersections, and so you need to keep a close eye on the map included here.

Piedmont Park, originally laid out by landscape architect Frederick Law Olmsted, who also designed New York's Central Park, has accommodated over the years just about every imaginable notion of how urban green space may be enjoyed. Its function continues to change. The extensive greens no longer echo to the smack of golf balls, and ballplayers may soon be banned from the open fields. In place of these activities, city planners would like to return the park to the passive recreational uses originally intended by Olmsted. The hill above the lake is no longer the central meeting place for the city's large hippie and drug communities, as it was nine years ago, but in early May each year the paths on the west side of the lake are jammed with craftsmen's booths and food stalls during the two-week Piedmont Arts Festival. At the top of the steep hill you climb above the tennis courts, you'll see the pretentious entrance to the park's latest attraction, the Atlanta Botanical Garden, composed of several garden settings. Take time to wander among the roses and bonsai plants before setting forth on city streets.

The first neighborhood you visit is *Ansley Park,* laid out in the early years of this century in an intentionally asymmetrical form to simulate a more rural setting. You'll wind along streets that resemble parkways, with houses virtually camouflaged among lush greenery. The tall buildings that rise above the canopy of trees as you climb alongside Winn Park remind you that this cleverly designed enclave of a neighborhood is much smaller than the serpentine roadways make it seem and that the intense development of a major city crowds in upon the edges of Ansley Park. The towers of concrete and glass on the left belong to Colony Square, a development that includes shops, restaurants, condominiums, and offices constructed to provide an entire living environment under roof, similar to the plan of the Omni downtown. Much of Atlanta's public-relations industry is quartered here. The mammoth concrete structure on the right is the new long-distance calling center for American Telephone and Telegraph. To its right, not visible through the trees, is the Atlanta Arts Alliance, home of several arts organizations funded by private donations and by the city government, including the High Museum of Art.

The homes in Ansley Park are primarily conservative and traditional in design, reflecting the tastes of wealthy Americans during the period 1900–1920. You will not find Victorian eccentricities here, but white-columned facades echoing classical longings and square, settled, almost stolid shapes. The distinguished Atlanta architect Neel Reid designed several of the houses here. Look to your right as you pedal along Peachtree Circle between 17th Street and The Prado. The partially obscured building on the hill is an apartment house whose long columned portico once graced the front of the governor's mansion downtown, where Davison's (Macy's) department store is on Peachtree Street. After you pedal around the corner onto The Prado, look to your left just before reaching the intersection of Montgomery Ferry Road and the beginning of a steep descent. The large lot which is considerably overgrown was the site of another governor's mansion before the present pseudo-

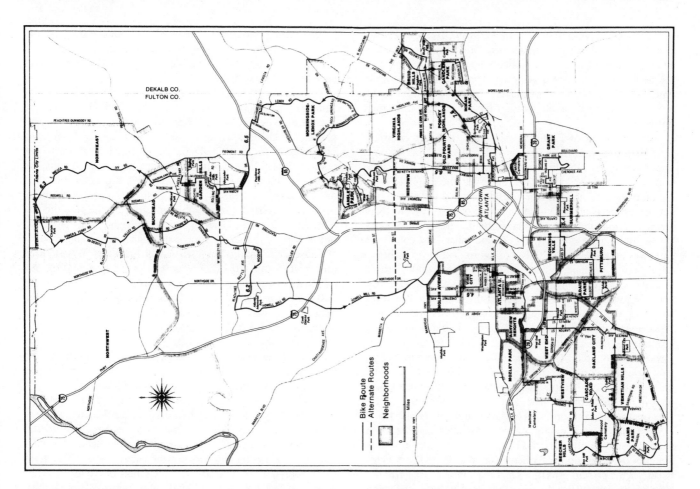

plantation Big House was completed on West Paces Ferry Road in Buckhead in 1968 and first occupied by Governor Lester Maddox.

The moving of the governor's mansion out of Ansley Park reflected a decline in the neighborhood's fortunes during the decades following World War Two. Although the neighborhood's substantial homes remained sound and few commercial intrusions disturbed the residential peace, Atlanta's trendsetters preferred to live farther from downtown, and Ansley Park's property values plummeted. Fifteen years ago, canny investors were able to buy the fine homes for a fraction of their value and began a renovation movement which has reestablished Ansley Park as a desirable address.

As you swoop around several sharp corners and down to the crossing of Peachtree Creek, you'll skirt the residential subdivision of the 1920s known as *Sherwood Forest,* containing quaintsy street names like Robin Hood and Friar Tuck. Past the Ansley Park Golf Club, whose grounds you bisect, you'll enter another residential neighborhood developed after 1920, called *Morningside.* Here the homes are primarily brick, the standard design what might be called Hansel and Gretel Gingerbread. Morningside is a stable community, home to many older people who have lived here for decades as well as to young couples active in business and the professions. The neighborhood lay in the path of a proposed Interstate highway, I-485, which the state Transportation Department had planned to cut through Northeast Atlanta from the Downtown Connector to Georgia

400 north of the perimeter highway, I-285, near Sandy Springs. The neighborhoods affected by the plan banded together to oppose it, hiring expert legal help and succeeding after years of struggle in removing the highway from all area transportation proposals. A large portion of the technical skill needed to coordinate the complicated legal maneuverings required for the transportation battle was provided by residents of Morningside.

You leave the marked bike route at North Highland Avenue. After winding through the increasingly suburban and prosperous-looking streets of Lenox Park, the northern extension of Morningside, you are faced with some difficult biking in the vicinity of I-85 and Piedmont Road, where a paucity of through streets requires you to share the pavement with heavy vehicular traffic. At Acorn, however, you turn off busy Lindbergh (Georgia 236) into the tranquil neighborhood of *Garden Hills,* plentifully endowed with both parts of its name. You'll pass numerous small parks and labor up several steep grades. The homes here are considerably younger than those you passed earlier, reflecting their distance from downtown and the relatively recent development of this area. Even though this is a comparatively affluent section of town, keep your eye out as you struggle up Lookout Place for small gardens where collards are being raised, just as they are in more modest communities close to the urban center.

Garden Hills abuts *Buckhead,* the fashionable shopping area whose business center you skirt while pedaling past several of its fine galleries and restaurants. On the north side of Peachtree Road you leave the section zoned for commerce and enter an exclusive residential area. Notice how the lot sizes increase the farther you get from downtown. The greenish glass monument you see looming above the trees beyond Piedmont Road is Tower Place, a desirable location for accounting and other business firms.

To the north of Piedmont you enter the most exclusive residential region of Atlanta, where the individual lots become impressive and the inhabitants feel no need to give their neighborhoods distinctive names. You have left the neighborhood region of Atlanta, in fact, where residents band together to resist zoning decisions they don't like and other threats to their security. Here, security radiates from the neatly manicured lawns, the curving drives, the gates and pillars and columned entrances on the brows of hills. You won't find much architectural pioneering here, reflective of the Atlanta upper crust's timidity about declaring tastes and preferences that have not been approved in many other places many years ago. Whatever you think about the imitations of baronial estates from all over Western Europe and this country, you're bound to enjoy the grounds and over-arching greenery. The route also passes right through the middle of *Chastain Park,* with the North Fulton Golf Course on one side and a steeply raked picnic area on the other. The Atlanta Symphony presents a series of summer concerts in the amphitheater here, and the Arts and Crafts Center puts on an ambitious program of classes in many disciplines.

The handsomest estates will be found after heading south from Chastain, along Tuxedo, Blackland, and Valley roads. A few blocks to the right of where you cross West Paces Ferry Road lies the present governor's mansion. West Paces Ferry has long been a particularly desirable Buckhead address. Just south of this road lies the grounds of the Atlanta Historical Society. Even if you don't have time or inclination for a ramble through the Society's extensive gallery and house museum, detour a few yards up Andrews Drive from its intersection with Chatham to peer through the gates at the imposing Swan House, Society headquarters. This grand pre-Depression estate with Italianate features and landscaping was built for the Inman family by distinguished local architect Philip Trammell Shutze.

One of the pleasantest sections of this tour is the curving swoop along Peachtree Creek opposite Bobby Jones Golf Course and the Atlanta Memorial Park, which commemorates the Battle of Atlanta (further commemorated by the median-divided thoroughfare which you cross and then circle back to join, Peachtree Battle Avenue). If you feel like envying the owners of the attractive homes that line Woodward Way facing the creek and park lands, you may want to consider that it was a rare spring during the 1970s when the occupants did not have to flee the raging creek waters or bail out their basements and first stories at least once.

The long pull up from Peachtree Creek along Howell Mill Road is extremely gradual and easy, winding through territory that was until recently zoned for single-family residences. Now you see several condominium and apartment developments hacked out of the hillsides and groves, reflecting the proximity of an exit off the Northwest Expressway, I-75. Before you reach the Interstate, the zoning abruptly changes to commercial and strip development. Traffic is heavier here, but the width of the pavement makes bicycling possible at all but the busiest rush hours. From the handsomely landscaped Atlanta Waterworks, you'll get your first (and breathtaking) view of the central business district's skyscrapers.

To this point your tour has passed through sections of Atlanta exclusively or predominately inhabited by whites. At Bankhead Highway (U.S. 78 & 278) the racial nature of the population changes abruptly. The modest homes that crowd both sides of the street make the most of their small yards and porches, which are often jammed with flowers and plants. At Simpson Road you cross into *Vine City,* a neighborhood of mostly lower-class blacks which, despite its lack of financial power, has exerted a remarkable influence on the city, the nation, and the world. The quality of leadership that has come out of Vine City may be appreciated by touring a single block of Sunset Avenue. In a brick house with arches set far back from the street, to the left of 272 Sunset, resides state senator and national political figure Julian Bond. Next door to the left, at 250 Sunset, in the substantial brick house with white trim set back from the street, lives Coretta Scott King in the same place where her husband, Dr. Martin Luther King, Junior, resided throughout the later years of his leadership in the civil-rights struggle. In the large brick apartment house just up the hill on the same side of Sunset just beyond Dunkirk, the former mayor of Atlanta, Maynard Jackson, spent his childhood years.

When you turn east on Magnolia Drive, you can appreciate how close Vine City is to Atlanta's commercial center. Magnolia, in fact, changes its name when it leaves Vine City to the imposing (some might say pretentious) International Boulevard, as it snakes its way between the Georgia World Congress Center (pretension, indeed!) and the Omni International. One might wonder how long a low-density residential community can survive so close to the high-rise intensity of downtown. A community called Lightning, between Vine City and the railroad tracks that form the boundary of the central business district, was largely eradicated when the Omni development was erected less than 10 years ago, and Vine City residents have feared the same result for their community. But the firmness of neighborhood leaders has so far prevented developers and speculators from buying up property or options in Vine City. As you turn south off Magnolia toward the new Vine City rapid-transit station, you'll see some evidence of public commitment to continuing the residential patterns of the neighborhood. The new housing that occupies several acres adjacent to the station was built by MARTA, the rapid-transit agency, to replace housing destroyed for construction of the new rail line. MARTA planners tried to convince neighborhood residents that a more intensive use of the land near their station would be advisable, but when the residents resisted such pressure, MARTA complied with their wishes.

You'll have a steep climb up to Martin Luther King Drive (formerly Hunter Street), which will help you to appreciate even more sharply the extraordinary discovery of the Alonzo Herndon mansion at 587 University Place. Designed in classical Beaux Arts style out of beautifully pastel brick, this was the home of the founder of the Atlanta Life Insurance Company, the second-largest black institution of this sort in the country.

Cynics comment that Herndon placed his grand residence most appropriately, on the brow of a hill overlooking the ghetto homes of his many black brothers and sisters whose nickels and dimes paid for all that pretty brick. Across the street in the low white building at 582 University Place lives Mrs. Grace Hamilton, first black woman elected to the Georgia General Assembly and a direct descendant of Governor George Towns.

Retrace your path down University to Walnut (you run into one-way streets leading you up and down ferocious hills if you continue to the far end of University), and when you cross Martin Luther King, you enter the purviews of *Atlanta University*. You'll pass portions of all six campuses comprising this loosely federated center for black students, in many respects the most important such center in the world. In order, you will pass Morris Brown College, a coeducational undergraduate school; the Interdenominational Theological Center; Atlanta University itself, the center's graduate school; Clark College, a coeducational undergraduate school; Spelman College, an elite undergraduate college for women, heavily endowed by the Rockefellers; and Morehouse College, an elite undergraduate school for men (Julian Bond and Maynard Jackson are two recent graduates).

Look at the small house on the corner of Beckwith and Chestnut (where you turn south). It holds the offices of the Institute of the Black World, a scholarly research center. Here Dr. W. E. B. DuBois, the eminent sociologist and author of, among other works, *The Souls of Black Folk,* had an office while he taught at Atlanta University during the early years of this century. On your right as you pedal down Chestnut is my candidate for ugliest building in Atlanta, the new library for the university. It looks like a gymnasium with eye-hurting red trim.

If you ride to the west end of Greensferry and get on the sidewalk, you'll find a curb cut that allows you access to Westview Drive and a ride past some of the new dormitories of Morehouse. Keeping west on the same street, you'll cross I-20. On your right before you reach the Interstate will be the edge of a middle-class black neighborhood with pleasant streets and homes, many of them built for Atlanta University professors, called *Mozley Park.*

Turning south just after crossing I-20, you enter *Westwood,* the first of several Southwest Atlanta neighborhoods that experienced the traumatizing effects of white flight during the 1960s and '70s. Now predominately black, neighborhoods like this one have kept their tranquil, tree-canopied charm, although unscrupulous real-estate operators panicked former white residents into dumping their property on the market with threats of neighborhood decay and radically lowered property values. The outgoing mayor of Atlanta, Maynard Jackson, recently took up residence in Westwood. South Gordon Street, which you will curve down on your way to John White Golf Course, is one of the loveliest avenues in the city, at points completely overarched by trees.

The farther south and west you travel, the larger the house lots become, generally speaking. You are now seeing the same pattern as you observed on the extreme Northside: houses spaced farther apart as you retreat from downtown. This area was never as exclusive as the regions north of Buckhead, and there is to be seen here even less of a spirit of architectural adventure than one noticed there, but you will enjoy the long curve up Beecher Circle alongside Ben Hill Park in the neighborhood called *Beecher Hills* and, even more, the wide and handsome avenues in the neighborhood called *Adams Park,* named for the large public green space that occupies much of its territory.

Black residents, like their white counterparts, have formed vigorous neighborhood organizations to fight against outside intrusions. In many ways, their task has been harder than the predominately white battle against unwanted freeways on the other side of town. After whites fled Southwest Atlanta, developers began sticking apartment complexes in the middle of previously quiet residential communities, and the new homeowners of Southwest have had a devil of a time asserting their rights with the city's planning and zoning officials. The pattern of zoning in Southwest, accordingly, is less rational, more hodgepodge, than in most of the rest of the city. Black and white neighborhood activists have joined forces in an organization called the Citywide League of Neighborhoods, which endorses candidates for local political office and looks out for the rights of citizens in the organized residential communities.

The pull up from Adams Park to Centra Villa is the toughest of the whole trip (you may have to walk), and Centra Villa itself is like a roller coaster. Sandtown, however, your next road to traverse, runs along the top of a ridge and takes you into the pleasant neighborhood known as *Venetian Hills.* You then swoop down to Avon Avenue, on the left of which is the community called *Cascade Road.* Cascade is to Southwest Atlanta what Peachtree Street once was to the Northside and Paces Ferry Road is now: *the* desirable address.

Avon is another roller-coaster road, leading you into the community called *Oakland City.* Notice, in the vicinity of Oakland Drive, the first evidence on this side of town of architectural distinction. You have left the realm of ranch-style suburbia and re-entered the ring of older communities that surround downtown. Some of these houses along Avon have striking porches and charming roof lines, reflective of turn-of-the-century housing fashions. Oakland City has been the primary beneficiary of an ongoing city-sponsored program to sell run-down older houses for $1 to homeowners who will rehabilitate them at their own expense within a fixed period of time. Known as Urban Homesteading, the program has been put into practice in many places around the country and has so far been used to rehabilitate 140 houses in Oakland City since 1976.

The small streets you take north of Avon were developed later, as you can tell from the modest cottages here that lack the fine features of the homes you have just seen. As you pedal up Donnelly Avenue, you'll notice an industrial park on your right, running in a strip alongside railroad tracks. In the early 1950s, this was carved out of a golf course that used to provide green space for residents of this section of town (now the most deprived region, per acre, with respect to park land).

As you cross the viaduct over the railroad tracks, you enter *West End,* the first of Atlanta's Victorian neighborhoods you will see. A preview of the architectural pleasures to be enjoyed here comes after crossing Mathews Street on Lawton. The second house on the left, with blue trim, sports a cherub's head in the gable, just one of the Victorian frills that show you how much fun our ancestors had designing their homes. The house was recently restored and occupied by Fulton County Commissioner Chuck Williams. The two-story white house adjacent on the left has been recently restored by state Representative Mildred Glover. The cherub's neighbor to the right with the modern glass panels behind which a large arch is visible belongs to city official Percy Harden, director of the Martin Luther King Community Center on Auburn Avenue. This last house shows extensive remodeling of its original Victorian features, a common practice in West End. Many old structures in the neighborhood have adapted with considerably less grace than has the Harden home to their modern additions and changes. The fact that the occupants of these three homes in a row are all elected or public officials and all black shows the degree to which West End has become a coveted address for younger black professionals.

Two blocks north on Lawton you touch the much earlier history of West End. All the property on the right-hand side of Lawton from the alley that bisects the block, Foster Street, until you reach Gordon Street belonged in the late 19th century to Joel Chandler Harris, author of the *Uncle Remus* stories. He built homes for his children facing Lawton (destroyed now, or so modified over the years as to be unrecognizably of the earlier era), while he himself lived a half block away facing Gordon in the "Wren's Nest." It's a wonderfully ornate, dark, rambling structure with lots of latticework gingerbread, sitting far back from the street among large trees (pedal to it and return to Lawton on the sidewalk, since traffic on Gordon is fierce). If you continue just past it to the alley that runs between the Wren's Nest property and the large brick Baptist church on the hill, you can see a small cabin purporting to be Uncle Remus' old slave cabin behind the house and right next to the alley. The church, which used to be known as West End Baptist (all white) and is now called Hunter Street Baptist (a name left over from its earlier location), is presided over by Ralph David Abernathy, second-in-command to Martin Luther King during the civil-rights struggles of the 1960s. The juxtaposition of cabin and impressive church thus provides a pointed visual symbol of the change that has occurred not only in West End but all over the South.

You'll pass turn-of-the-century houses in various shapes and stages of restoration as you continue north on Lawton and then east on Oak. Take another slight detour north on Peeples to look at the last house on the left, a remarkable dark-gray monument with witch's-cap rooflines and intricate gingerbread, abandoned for several years. Finding a restorer for it will be difficult because of its proximity to I-20 and the continual din of traffic. The Interstate, as you see, cuts right through West End, as it does through other previously intact neighborhoods, a fact which complicates present-day residents' efforts to build cohesive community spirit. The vacant land across Peeples from the fine gray house is only one of many evidences of the mis-named "urban renewal" program of the 1960s which blighted West End and many other inner-city neighborhoods in the alleged interest of clearing away slum property and replacing it with sound, new housing. As you see, the demolition was not followed by construction.

The little park on the left of Peeples at the intersection of Gordon is named Clark Howell Park because the house of the influential editor of the *Atlanta Journal* around the turn of the century stood where the park is now. The last house on the right

at the end of the next block on Peeples, at Oglethorpe, was the home of the well known Victorian poet Frank Stanton. With Harris, Howell, and Stanton all living within a couple of blocks of one another, you can picture the role West End played as a haven for prominent and affluent men of letters in the late Victorian period (the captains of industry and commerce, on the other hand, tended to live across town, in Inman Park).

Both sides of Peeples Street between Gordon and Ogle-thorpe are lined with wrought-iron fences and brick pillars, sometimes curving in exaggeratedly stylized forms. These elements are not original to West End and, indeed, are alien to the character of the neighborhood, in which, as in other Southern communities, the houses communicate directly and openly with each other and with the streets they face. The fences and pillars give a sequestered, suspicious feeling to the environment. They were the work of a young white architect named Wade Burns, who moved into West End about 10 years ago and felt the need for security measures. He redesigned almost all the houses you see on both sides of this block and around the corner on Ogle-thorpe, adding woodwork elements to eaves and gables that often have little in common with the scale and feeling of the original Victorian houses. The buildings are now lived in by members of the city's business and political elite, both white and black.

The last few blocks of West End that you traverse return you to the more countrified feel that West End used to have before fences and pillars went up like barricades. On White Street you'll see a little bit of everything, architecturally and socially. West End remains a fascinating melting pot of the tacky and authentic, scruffy and elegant, collapsing and reviving (I live in West End, and I wouldn't live anywhere else).

At the end of White Street you'll see the temporary end of the rapid-transit line's south branch (if federal funding and local taxes permit, the line will be continued to the airport and College Park). The West End station, just north of this point, is scheduled to open late in 1982. After crossing the railroad tracks (notice how often you ride under, far above, or right on top of railroad tracks in the course of this long tour, a reminder that Atlanta was founded and grew because of railroad junctions), you enter the neighborhood of *Adair Park*. This community, with its shaded streets and pre-World War One cottages, is in the midst of transition from a predominately white working-class population to predominately black. It is, therefore, "integrated" (integration in Atlanta being, as one wit put it, the period between the moving in of the first black family and the moving out of the last white family). Elbert Street is one of my favorites, and at the end on the right is one of the great collard patches in existence. The silver-green leaves of the collard plant come into their most luxuriant form after the first frost hits them. Boiled with fatback in a large pot for a long period, the greens are a staple of Southern diet throughout the winter.

Be careful zigzagging across busy Stewart Avenue (U.S. 19 & 41). On its east side lies the neighborhood called *Pittsburg*, a working-class black community with, along its central thoroughfare, McDaniel Street, a delightful row of tiny shops and churches. If you're pedaling through on Sunday (and perhaps at other times as well), you may get to hear some truly ho-o-o-oly rolling from inside one or more of those churches. Don't miss the half-block detour east on Rockwell Street to see the sculpture garden of folk artist E. M. Bailey. John F. Kennedy and Henry Aaron (with a rapt expression on his face and his bat cocked behind his head as he watched #715 sail into the stands) are only two of the figures that sprout from the turnip and collard patch of Mr. Bailey's small front yard (take a close look at his house, as well, ornamented with a medley of materials and textures).

Across yet another set of railroad tracks, you enter the community known as *Mechanicsville,* also a working-class black settlement. Little remains of this once-extensive neighborhood, its entire northern half (above Georgia Avenue) wiped out by various public projects, but Bass Street, which you traverse, shows something of its old-fashioned dignity. Enclaves like this grow smaller and smaller as the big city, only a mile or so to the north, encroaches. Until just a few years ago, a store selling exclusively roots and other home remedies for ailments survived in Mechanicsville. As you turn north onto Pryor, look to your left. Behind overgrown shrubbery you can still discern the outlines of a large pink house, one of the few remnants of the days when Pryor was only one of several fashionable addresses on the near southside of downtown. Prosperous merchants built homes quite the equal of Peachtree Street's along Pulliam and Washington as well as Pryor, but the pull to the north was stronger, and these homes were turned into boardinghouses and rental property. When the Interstate was pushed through south of downtown in the late 1950s, many of the grand relics were pulled down, and the deterioration since has been unremitting and irreversible.

I-75/85 is now the boundary separating Mechanicsville from *Summerhill* to the east. On your left looms the Atlanta-Fulton County Stadium, home of the Braves and Falcons, surrounded by acres of parking lots. Very little remains of Summerhill, thanks to the stadium, the building of which in this location many black citizens saw as a conscious decision by city officials in the 1960s to displace lower-income blacks from their small homes conveniently close to downtown and jobs. The vacant land on the south side of Georgia Avenue once housed the main offices of Atlanta's Model Cities program, a branch of Lyndon Johnson's "Great Society" social-service effort which was as much a waste of time and money in Atlanta as the earlier urban-renewal programs. Model Cities, too, was supposed to replace dilapidated housing with new, sound, up-to-code structures. The vacant land shows you its success.

The small business center of Summerhill east of Capitol Avenue is a somber and unwelcoming (though geographically limited) area. Move on through it rapidly into one of the most diverse and fascinating neighborhoods of Atlanta, *Grant Park.* You'll find just about everything here—noble Victorian castles, hideous modern apartment complexes (more results of bad zoning practices of the past), burned-out hovels, spiffy-looking restored cottages, bizarrely renovated homes which may once have had a claim to style, untouched jewels of houses lived in by the same family for 75 years or more, derelict rooming houses with half of the windows busted out, grand wrecks just beginning to be worked on by ambitious and energetic young people. You'll find an immensely complex sociology here, too. From this neighborhood the Ku Klux Klan used to stage marches to the Capitol back in the 1930s, and there are still

entire blocks here whose property owners have solemnly covenanted with one another not to sell to blacks. Yet black people of all sorts and economic conditions reside in Grant Park alongside whites (of just as many backgrounds). Within a single block you may find an elderly couple tending their lawn, bums, nattily dressed professional people on their way to a social event, and ragtag babies groveling in the dirt. I love it. If I weren't a dyed-in-the-wool West Ender, I'd happily move to Grant Park (*if* I could afford it—property values have risen out of sight in the past five years, as the back-to-the-city movement has gathered momentum).

The route through Grant Park takes you along some characteristic blocks (I recommend extensive prowls on your own, winding back and forth all over this rich turf). Just where you turn off Milledge Avenue onto Broyles Street, look to your left at the modest corner house at 300 Milledge. This was the childhood home of Mayor William B. Hartsfield, after whom the Atlanta airport and the gorilla in the Atlanta Zoo are both named. Hartsfield was mayor longer and during more critical years (the 1930s–1950s) than any other person. In the early decades of this century, political decisions that were not made in City Hall were often made in the grocery stores and barbershops of Grant Park.

You turn east onto St. Paul Avenue off Broyles so that you may pass the most fascinating residential structure still standing in Atlanta—the antebellum L. P. Grant home at 325 St. Paul. It is surrounded by chainlink fences and looks as if it can never regain its majesty, but a determined young man named Dennis Walters has recently come into possession of the great hulk— one of the few antebellum buildings in town—and is trying to stabilize the walls to prevent further decay, with the eventual aim of returning it to its precise 1850s' appearance (he has unearthed enough architectural elements to compose a picture of how the entire original building looked). Colonel L. P. Grant was a railroad magnate who owned all this section of Atlanta, and his house was spared the Yankee torches, reportedly, because he was a Mason, and Sherman had ordered his troops not to burn the homes of Masons. Margaret Mitchell, author of *Gone With the Wind,* took an interest in the run-down structure during the early 1940s, but she was not able to save it from being vandalized, its porches torn off, and the process of deterioration from continuing. How Walters will fare is anyone's guess.

You'll have a lovely long swoop and then hefty, grunty climb through Grant Park itself, a bequest to the city from the Colonel. Here is housed the Atlanta Zoo (say hello to Willie B., the gorilla, who is saved from boredom by watching soap operas on television) and the Cyclorama, a gigantic rendering of the Battle of Atlanta which is expected to reopen in the summer of 1982 after extensive repairs designed to save the mural from mildew and other environmental damage are completed.

You pedal around two sides of the park before heading north on Cherokee. Take a moment to look at the commercial block between Sydney and Glenwood, which contains some beautiful old brick buildings that neighborhood residents are trying to restore for community use. You're still in the neighborhood of Grant Park when you cross I-20, but this small northern section, because of its limited width, is threatened by commercial intrusions and feels cut off from the bulk of the neighborhood. Notice, however, the fine houses along Woodward Avenue and, to the left at the intersection of Grant Street where you turn north, some unusually intricate Victorian embellishments. Another attractive commercial intersection occupied the spot where you turn until a series of mysterious fires wiped it out several years ago (residents suspected that commercial developers had plans for a motel or other Interstate-related business here).

Detour to the right a block at Martin Luther King Drive to take in *Oakland Cemetery*, the oldest burying ground in the city, last resting place of many prominent Atlantans (including Margaret Mitchell), and site from which Union officers watched the progress of the Battle of Atlanta. Just to the right of the dark and primitive tunnel underneath yet another set of railroad tracks stretches the high and impressive rapid-transit station named for Martin Luther King, Junior. The combination of arcs, circles, and loops in concrete is stunning. Here the rapid-transit tracks are set on air rights above the railroad right-of-way.

Past the blocks of the public-housing project known as Capitol Homes, you turn east on Auburn Avenue into the *Martin Luther King Historic District*. On the left at this intersection is the old headquarters building of the Southern Christian Leadership Conference, Dr. King's civil-rights organization. Auburn Avenue was for decades the center of black business activity in Atlanta, christened "Sweet Auburn" by Mayor Maynard Jackson's grandfather, the distinguished preacher John Wesley Dobbs. Following integration, the businesses along Auburn have fallen on hard times, and various public and private efforts to revive the district have not yet shown much success. On the right, at the far corner of Jackson Street, is the church where Dr. King preached many of his most famous sermons, Ebenezer Baptist. Across Auburn is the Martin Luther King Community Center, while adjoining Ebenezer is the multi-million-dollar complex known as the Martin Luther King Center for Social Change, still under construction. Here will be housed a library of materials relating to Dr. King and the civil-rights movement, and here is Dr. King's gravesite, visited by millions of tourists each year. The pretty little firehouse on the right at the far corner of Boulevard was a favorite hangout of the young Martin Luther King, Junior, while just up the street on the same side, at 501 Auburn Avenue, is the small frame house in late Victorian style in which the civil-rights leader was born and passed his early years.

Yet one more crossing of railroad tracks (these are beneath you), and you're in the first of Atlanta's inner-city Victorian neighborhoods to be renovated, *Inman Park* (the sign welcoming you to the community is placed several blocks to the east, at the intersection of Edgewood and Euclid). This section was developed as an exclusive residential suburb in the 1870s and connected to downtown by a streetcar line (note on the right of Edgewood Avenue just before you turn onto Elizabeth Street the long green building with red trim and busted windows; this was the old car barn for that trolley line). The route takes you through Inman Park twice, allowing you to see a great many of the fine ornate mansions built by the Candlers (developers of Coca-Cola) and their pals during the last decades of the 19th century. Like other close-in neighborhoods, this one was abandoned as outlying areas became more fashionable, and 10 years ago the large homes were mostly boardinghouses containing numerous families. Young professional people began buying up the decaying hulks, however, evicting the tenants, and returning the buildings to single-family residences. The process continues, but you will notice more houses in good condition than those that need basic repair work. Banners flying in windows and doorways printed with an emblem of a butterfly identify members of the neighborhood association, Inman Park Restoration.

As you turn up Highland Avenue, you'll notice a change from large, fancy older houses to apartment complexes and cottages from a later era. This is the section known as *Little Five Points*, from its business center two blocks away. The butterfly emblem flies from many houses in this area, also, signifying that the restoration movement has spilled over from the architecturally refined center of Inman Park into a district where property values are less steep. The cleared land you pass through on both sides of Highland near Cleburne Avenue is a reminder of yet another urban expressway defeated by intown residents, this one intended to be called the Stone Mountain Freeway. This road and I-485 (discussed under the tour of Morningside) were to have intersected near here, making Inman Park residents especially sensitive to the negative impacts of major highways through their backyards and streets.

When you turn east on Blue Ridge Avenue, you will once again see the green signs that designate the city's single marked bike route. Remember, again, that not all the signs are in place. Watch the crossing of Moreland Avenue, which is very busy. The road changes its name to Fairview east of Moreland, and the neighborhood is known as *Druid Hills*. You will enjoy the tree-shaded streets and pleasant houses of the 1910s and '20s that you pass here. The Candler family who built large homes in Inman Park were instrumental in turning this area into a fashionable part of town after they moved themselves to be farther away from downtown. Notice, as you circle back south on Oakdale, that the canopy of trees is symmetrical and unbroken. This is because the developers of the area were able to convince the utility companies to run their wires between the backs of the houses, thus leaving the street free for trees to develop to their fullest. As you recross Ponce de Leon Avenue, take note of the wide median and the curve of the road, designed to give a parkway look. The landscaping here and throughout much of Druid Hills was the work of Frederick Law Olmsted, who designed Piedmont Park. The small side road at the edge of the parkland allows residents to reach their homes without interrupting the flow of traffic along the main thoroughfare and also buffers the homes themselves from the noise of traffic.

Crossing North Avenue, you enter the community known as *Candler Park*, after the public green space of that name at its center (one more verbal memory of the great impact the Coca-Cola magnates had upon the city). Here you will find mostly modest homes, built after 1920, but note the great castle on the right at the far corner of Benning Avenue, where you turn east toward the park. Residents of Candler Park have been very active in the neighborhood movement. You come back into

Inman Park by way of Little Five Points itself. If you have time, stop for a while to browse through the small specialty shops that line both sides of Moreland and Euclid avenues near their intersection. The small park you pass over just beyond Elizabeth Street, Springvale Park, was not intended to have Euclid Avenue bisect it and was originally planted with cypresses and other exotic trees. Your route snakes along several streets that give you a sense of the varied architecture and sociology that characterize Inman Park. Like its counterparts among older reviving inner-city neighborhoods, it attracts a splendidly diverse set of individuals as inhabitants.

Once again over railroad tracks and into a corner of a neighborhood still known as *Old Fourth Ward,* a stable community of working-class blacks that has had a significant influence upon the politics of the city. The name is a holdover from an earlier division of the city into wards. You turn north on Parkway and ride over the stub of I-485, formerly intended to blast clear up through Northeast Atlanta to Sandy Springs. The highway's construction occasioned fierce antagonisms and turmoil, but it had the beneficial effect of providing a remarkable view of downtown from this overpass.

North of the Interstate stub, you are in a neighborhood called *Bedford-Pine,* much of which no longer exists. Urban-renewal programs wiped out the western half of the community, also known as Buttermilk Bottom, a poor black section. Now, a consortium of banks and business interests own 78 acres of that land, which they are in the process of developing into housing (mostly expensive), offices, and shops. If you look left as you cross Ralph McGill Boulevard, you can make out some of this construction activity. The blocks north of Ralph McGill will show another side of housing construction funded by public money, and provide a happy note on which to end this tour. The apartment buildings that line both sides of Parkway were in shocking disrepair a decade ago. The entire area looked like the South Bronx in New York City—windows boarded up or jaggedly empty, stoops filthy, yards mere piles of bare dirt, degradation everywhere. As an adjunct to the massive redevelopment of the Bedford-Pine acres by the bankers, these buildings were renovated with government loans, and the results, as you see, are impressive indeed. A single motif for plaques identifying house numbers has been incorporated into the renovation, landscaping has been extensive, and the entire streetscape is among the city's most pleasing and harmonious.

Parkway changes its name to Charles Allen Drive as it crosses Ponce de Leon Avenue and enters the neighborhood known as *Midtown.* Frequently, at the boundaries of areas where black populations changed to white and vice versa, street names in Atlanta were changed so that white residents would not have to suffer the "indignity" of sharing a street address with their black neighbors. You'll be swooping down Charles Allen toward Piedmont Park and your starting point, so you won't have much of a chance to take in the landscape. Midtown has once again become a fashionable and expensive place to live, after years of neglect. The large houses that line the streets parallel to and west of Parkway have, like their counterparts in Inman Park, been returned to single-family (or, in some cases, condominium) ownership after serving as boardinghouses. You'll notice a lot of walls and fences in Midtown—sure sign

that the residents take their property values seriously. They like to think of Piedmont Park as *their* park, but it's also *your* park, so enjoy a few turns around the beautifully landscaped lake before packing it in after such a long and exhausting tour.

1981

LaGrange Callaway

An insider's tour of the city that reflects a family

by Bill Cutler

At last year's dedication ceremonies for LaGrange's new museum in a renovated historic building, LaGrange College art professor John Lawrence compared the museum's and the town's benefactors, the Callaways, to the Medicis, the great family of art patrons in Renaissance Florence. The aptness of the comparison may not be immediately apparent to visitors to LaGrange. Florence, after all, struts the lavish magnificence of Medicean taste in imposing public fountains and piazzas that compel obeisance and respect. Ostentation, however, is not the style of LaGrange, nor of the Callaways. The quiet dignity of this West Georgia town of 26,000 could be matched in placid, white-columned streetscapes in small cities all across the state, and it takes a practiced eye to pick out the telltale marks of Callaway taste and Callaway beneficence scattered throughout the town. Yet no less than the Medicis in Florence have the Callaways imposed a style on their home town, but the style is restrained, subdued, unemphatic.

As you tour LaGrange, watch for brick buildings of plain, rectilinear design with copper roofs, fronted by small limestone porticos whose columns may bear Doric or Ionic capitals, but never showy Corinthian. The pediments of these buildings are often completely unadorned, verging on severe, while others bear simple decorations. Keep your eyes open for the Callaway brick-and-limestone trademark in unlikely places, such as the town's and county's public schools, which have received more than $5,700,000 in grants from the Callaway Foundation, Inc., a religious, charitable, and educational corporation organized 35 years ago by Fuller E. Callaway, Jr. Take note of the Callaway imprint on the large Southern Bell building on Broome Street downtown, with its Doric limestone columns and small Greek-key design over the front door. Then pause in front of its exact but smaller replica next door at 209 Broome. Unless you're equipped with a telescope, you won't be able to read the discreet bronze plaque above the street number identifying this structure as the offices for the Callaway Foundation, Inc.

Inside, full-length portraits of Fuller E. Callaway, Jr., and his older brother, the late Cason Callaway, look down on unpretentious rooms where Foundation officers have administered the disbursement of nearly $67 million and at present watch over the management of $80 million in assets. According to the printed general policies of the Foundation, these funds are usually intended "for the benefit of projects and people in LaGrange and Troup County, Georgia." J. T. "Tommy" Gresham, the president, general manager, and treasurer of the Foundation, explained to me the rationale behind this policy: "The great bulk of the Foundation's resources was raised through the ownership of Callaway Mills Company stock, and the Foundation's trustees feel that since the people in LaGrange actually helped raise the Foundation's money, they should be the main beneficiaries of the income from the fund."

The tour of LaGrange I have mapped out was designed in large part to illuminate the variety of local projects funded by the Callaway Foundation. The only buildings open to the public in LaGrange are open because they benefited, in whole or major part, from Foundation grants. Yet no tour can bring to light the full range of Callaway Foundation gifts to LaGrange. Think, as you travel, of these unobtrusive examples of Callaway donations: dozens of local churches that received grants for permanent improvements; parks, recreation and community centers throughout town that were created and maintained by the Foundation; public-works projects such as bridge enlargements that the corporation paid for; fire and civil-defense equipment bought by the Foundation; even municipal parking lots given the patented Callaway landscaping touch through discreet softening elements.

Add these projects to the endowments for libraries, health programs, and educational facilities of all sorts that are enumerated in the tour description, and you may wonder whether even the Medicis' patronage is an apt analogy for the range of services provided to LaGrange by Callaway money. Certainly knowing about contributions of such magnitude from private sources takes the mystery out of the phenomenally low taxes paid by LaGrange citizens. Yet observant visitors could ride or pedal slowly around the entire route mapped out here and remain ignorant that the Callaways had contributed a penny to the landscape and monuments they enjoy looking at. Only the clearly marked Callaway Science Center on the LaGrange College campus calls attention to Callaway beneficence. That's self-effacement on a scale the flashy, flaunting Medicis couldn't even comprehend.

1979

CYCLIST'S ALMANAC*

LaGrange

Routes: A 14-mile loop on town streets, plus a separate tour of pretty surrounding countryside comprising 14.4 miles. Dotted line shows easiest means to get from one route to the other. Park in high-school lots if cycling only along country route.

Terrain: Hilly, both in and out of town. Bring a cog with a low gear, or strong legs.

Cycling conditions: Better than average in town. Streets kept clear of debris, pavements well maintained. Cameron Mill Road gets very rough north of West Point Lake.

Hazards: Traffic on Vernon Street west of LaGrange College is murderous. Use the bumpy and glass-strewn sidewalks, and keep off the road surface here. (A good sturdy bike with well inflated tires would be useful for negotiating this stretch.) Railroad crossings are rough and numerous (and you may have to wait for several minutes while slow freights lumber through town). Pay close attention to the map: LaGrange's street-marking system is haphazard at best, and you can easily get lost or confused, especially right around the town square.

Points of Interest: (1) Park and start in *Court Square.* At its center is a statue of the Marquis de Lafayette, an exact copy of the statue in Lafayette's home town of Le Puy, France. LaGrange is named for the country place of the Revolutionary War hero, who passed through this section of the state three years before LaGrange was founded and remarked on the similarity of landscape to the terrain of his estate. The statue was erected as a Bicentennial project in 1975 with funds granted by the Callaway Foundation, Inc., which also paid for the enlarging and embellishing of the fountain. The square is presently undergoing extensive remodeling, one feature of which is the widening of the central mall. The east side of the square shows renovation work in progress by individual merchants, who are attempting to withstand the challenge to their businesses by suburban shopping malls (a new one is just now being completed out Greenville Road by I-85). The merchants' greatest ally is the decision by Mansour's, a locally owned department store, not only to remain downtown, but to expand its space so as to encompass the entire western side of the square (building now labeled Rhodes Furniture will become part of the remodeled Mansour's). A Mansour daughter is married to Atlanta architect John Portman's son Jack, and the store's rear buildings along Vernon and Broad Streets show Jack Portman's craftsmanship. The southwestern corner of the square, presently part of Mansour's, was the site of Fuller E. Callaway's Mammoth Department Stores, West Georgia's first such establishment, organized here in 1894 by the 23-year-old founder of the Callaway fortunes. He had started out five years earlier in a cubbyhole called Callaway's Famous Five and Ten Cent Store, and by his 25th year, he was doing business in 36 states. (2) *Bellevue,* massive two-story Greek Revival mansion with Ionic columns on a hill, the home of U. S. Senator Benjamin Harvey Hill, built 1852–53. House was once the center of a 1200-acre estate, entrance to which was through gigantic gates patterned exactly after the gates at the White House (they now belong to LaGrange College). Bellevue was given to the LaGrange Woman's Club in 1943 by the then-newly chartered Callaway Foundation and recently completely restored by the Foundation. Interior contains period furniture, reproductions of Victorian wallpaper, and mammoth, elaborate door frames and other architectural elements. The building, an officially designated National Landmark, is open to the public Tu–Sat 10–12 and Tu–Sun 2–5 (till 6 in Daylight Time); admission $1. (3) *LaGrange College,* founded 1831, oldest independent school in Georgia and second-oldest college (after Franklin College, now the University of Georgia). Formerly a woman's school, became coeducational in 1953; enrollment approximately 800. Eleven of its 16 buildings have been built or acquired since 1958, thanks in large part to grants of over $4 million from the Callaway Foundation, Inc. (4) *Smith Hall,* oldest building on campus, main part built of handmade brick in 1842. Note handsome side facade fronting Broad Street. Smith Parlor, on right as you enter building from campus quadrangle, contains a bust of Lafayette by the French sculptor Houdon, plus a bizarrely amusing collection of paintings done for the Bicentennial by Western artist Charles Hargens, intended to represent scenes in the life of Lafayette. (5) *William and Evelyn Banks Library,* one of four local libraries funded by grants from the Callaway Foundation, Inc. LaGrange is said to have the highest per-capita library use of any town in the

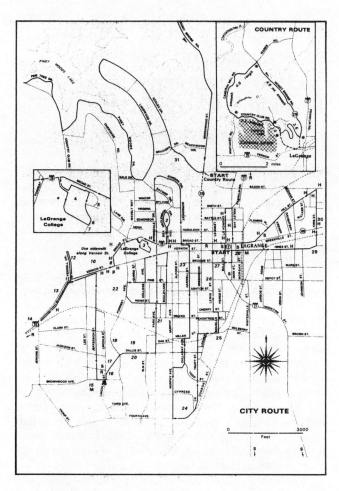

MAP KEY

2 Italicized numbers signify sites associated with the Callaway family or funded by grants from the Callaway Foundation, Inc.

M Plant or building now belonging to Deering Miliken, Inc., which bought the seven Callaway mills in 1968 for more than $50 million in cash.

H House described in detail in an Awareness Tour Map assembled by LaGrange's Ocfuskee Historical Society and available at the LaGrange Chamber of Commerce offices, intersection of Main, Bull, and East Depot Streets.

R Restaurant.

S Interesting shop.

nation. (6) *Methodist Chapel,* built in 1965 with funds from the Callaway Foundation, incorporating elements from the former sanctuary of LaGrange's First Methodist Church (1898), including fine stained-glass windows. Walk all the way around the small building to inspect stones from early religious buildings embedded in the north, east, and south walls with accompanying explanatory plaques. (7) *Callaway Science Center,* third building in a row on eastern end of campus funded by Callaway Foundation, Inc.

Callaway Residences. (View these sights from sidewalks along Vernon Street, beginning on the north side.) (8) *Ivy Oaks,* built in 1922 by distinguished architect Neel Reid for Fuller Callaway's elder son, Cason, the developer of Callaway Gardens, and his bride, the former Virginia Hand of Pelham. Childhood home of Howard "Bo" Callaway, recent Secretary of the Army, Cason's son. (9) *The Oaks* at 1103 Vernon Street, built in 1843. Spectacular Greek Revival building with six fluted Doric columns. The family home of

artist Lamar Dodd, recently purchased by the Callaway Foundation, Inc. Nominated for listing on the National Register of Historic Places. (10) *Hills and Dales,* Italianate mansion designed by Neel Reid in 1916 for Fuller Callaway, Sr. Featured on the cover of *The Architecture of Neel Reid.* Childhood home of Cason Callaway and Fuller Callaway, Jr., now the latter's residence. Center of extensive estate (very much *off limits* to uninvited visitors—trespassers are prosecuted; mansion is obscured by careful landscaping, so grab your first view from near the intersection of Broad and Vernon Streets). Estate's formal gardens were designed in 1841 by Sarah Coleman Ferrell, who assembled trees and shrubs from all over the world and created many curious topiary sculptures in boxwood. All these features have been maintained and elaborated upon by the Callaways. (11) *Callaway-Collier House,* built by Fuller Callaway, Jr., for his wife, the former Alice Hand of Pelham, younger sister of Cason Callaway's wife. Sold by the Callaways when they moved into Hills and Dales following the death of Fuller Callaway, Sr., in 1928. (12) *Offices of Fuller E. Callaway Foundation.* Not to be confused with Callaway Foundation, Inc., whose offices are downtown. This much smaller organization provides scholarship support for nurses at the West Georgia Medical Center and for residents of Troup County to attend any accredited college of their choice. Good spot from which to view the back of Hills and Dales. Across Ferrell Drive is the residence of Mark Callaway, son of the late Fuller E. Callaway, III, grandson of Fuller E. Callaway, Jr. (On returning from tour of Ferrell Drive, cross Vernon Street to sidewalk on south side.) (13) *Boxwood Acres,* pretty Greek Revival cottage with extensive boxwood gardens created by Sarah Ferrell's father and thought to have inspired her in building the great gardens now adorning the Callaway Hills and Dales estate. (14) *West Georgia Medical Center,* largest single beneficiary of Callaway Foundation money, over $7 million. Adjacent but separate is the Enoch Callaway Cancer Clinic, opened in 1975 and fully funded by the Callaway Foundation, Inc., to the amount of almost $4 million. *The Mill Village.* The long ride down Jefferson Street is a joint exercise in geography and sociology. At your back, on high ground, lies the great Callaway estate, Hills and Dales. Ahead of you, at the bottom of the hill, stretches (15) *the former Hillside Mills,* one of the seven branches of the Callaway cotton mills started by Fuller Callaway, Sr., in 1900 at the age of 29. On both sides of you are dotted the modest but sturdy houses built by the Callaways for mill employees, subsequently sold to the residents. (16) *Coleman Library,* a branch of the Callaway Educational Association, an organization established to administer educational, recreational, and entertainment activities for employees of the Callaway mills. Even though the mills have now been sold to Milliken, the Association continues to operate this library—built with funds provided by the Callaway Foundation, Inc.—for its numerous members; it is not open to the public. (17) *Milliken's Customer Information Center,* formerly Callaway Mills headquarters. Now a showroom for Milliken's latest designs and patterns in carpets, many of which are on sale at the nearby Mill Store. Step in if you're in the market for floor coverings; it's an impressive gallery. (18) *Callaway Educational Association offices.* The Association has received over $5 million from the Callaway Foundation, Inc. (19) *Callaway Auditorium,* part of the elaborate Callaway Educational Association physical plant. (20) *Callaway Stadium,* another Association facility, used by local high schools for football games. The Association also operates a swimming pool, tennis courts, and classroom buildings. (21) *Unity School,* in characteristic Callaway brick-and-limestone-with-copper-roof style. Tommy Gresham, the Callaway Foundation's president, describes the money provided by the Foundation to the local school system which has been used to improve the schools' design and appearance as "the icing on the cake." The first of the Callaway mills to be put into operation was called the Unity Cotton Mills. (22) *Price Theater,* the $2-million LaGrange College drama center opened in 1975, a gift from the Callaway Foundation, Inc., along with the five acres on which it sits. Contains a 280-seat auditorium, the most modern audio-visual equipment, and houses the college drama department, which is the resident summer-stock theater company at Callaway Gardens. During regular class hours when college is in session, knock on the front door; department members delight in giving tours. (23) *LaGrange Memorial Library,* handsome stone-and-glass structure partially funded by the Callaway Foundation, Inc. Serves a three-county region. Main reading room contains a model constructed by the Georgia Tech Urban Design Studio of futuristic plans for downtown LaGrange. (Open to the public Mon–Th 10–9, Fri & Sat 10–6, Sun 2–5). (24) *Callaway Memorial Tower,* dedicated July 15, 1929, to the memory of Fuller E. Callaway, Sr., by his associates, friends, and former employees. (25) *Confederate Cemetery and Horace King Grave.* In a grove of cedar trees to the right of the cemetery is the grave of Georgia's master covered-bridge builder, who, because he was black, could not be buried with the Confederate dead and veterans. At one time, Horace King's bridges spanned the Chattahoochee and many smaller streams, but all but one have been destroyed by vandals and demolition experts. They were said to have been so soundly built that dynamite in some instances could not demolish them and fire had to be resorted to. The last known remaining King bridge was moved from Troup County to Callaway Gardens. The covered bridge at Euharlee is thought to have been built by King's son. Harold King's was the first grave to have been marked by the Ocfuskee Historical Society, which is engaged in discovering and marking the burial sites of distinguished LaGrange citizens. (26) *Cary House* at 316 South Lewis Street, built before 1860. Unusually pretty cottage with Italianate columns and intricate Gothic Revival touches. If I could have my choice of any house in LaGrange as a residence, this would be it. (27) *Callaway Foundation offices* at 209 Broome Street. (28) *Chattahoochee Valley Art Association Building* at 112 Hines Street, bought for $51,601 and renovated for $755,000 by the Callaway Foundation, Inc. Built in 1892 as the Troup County jail and later used as a furniture store and newspaper office, the Romanesque Revival building had been abandoned to an uncertain future. Exterior now faithfully restored, while interior imaginatively reshaped into a gallery, studios, offices, and storage space. Very much worth visiting. Atlanta architect Jack Thomas has designed gallery spaces full of interesting and unexpected angles, where the perspective continually changes and where arches and skylights control the sun's illumination. Gallery walls covered with Irish wool, which permits nails for art objects to be driven in between the ribbings. (29) *The Magnolias,* built in 1833 by LaGrange architect Collin Rodgers (1791–1845). Charming Greek Revival 1½-story house with diamond-shaped sidelights and star medallions centering the capitals of the four Ionic columns and two pilasters. (30) *King House,* visible to the right as you cross Greenville Street (covered with pink asbestos shingles). Home of covered-bridge builder Horace King (see tour point #25). (31) *Granger Park,* result of a $200,000 grant from the Callaway Foundation, Inc. The LaGrange Senior High School across Greenwood Street shows evidence of Callaway Foundation design standards and has benefited from grants for recreational facilities.

Keep Out! Welcome!

And other mixed signals rising up from Pine Mountain, as the

State and the Feds maneuver to preserve and pay for a 10,000-acre memorial to Franklin D. Roosevelt.

by Bill Cutler

"This is state property. You say you're not here on official business or to visit a patient, so I'll have to ask you not to ride your bicycle around here again." I stared in bewilderment at the pleasant-faced man in the brown uniform standing near his Department of Human Resources truck. The nameplate on his light-tan shirt read "RUSHING."

I had just completed a bicycle tour of the territory near Pine Mountain which is being proposed for a 10,000-acre national memorial to President Franklin Delano Roosevelt, and I had returned to my starting point in front of Georgia Hall, the imposing admissions building and visual centerpiece of Roosevelt's old Georgia Warm Springs Hospital. Only two days earlier, I had spent two hours at the state Capitol with Tom Perdue, Governor Busbee's executive secretary, who encouraged me enthusiastically to map out the Roosevelt memorial area for cyclists. The chance of increasing tourist traffic to Warm Springs and Pine Mountain was one of the arguments Perdue had been using for more than a year in persuading various state agencies and other groups to stop bickering over their private fiefdoms there and cooperate in unified management of the different properties that had been associated with FDR.

I had seen no signs on the hospital grounds denying visitors access to the public buildings. Yet here was a state employee ordering me off state property. I wanted to make sure I understood the situation. "Is that the policy of this institution?" I asked.

"Yes, it is," Mr. Rushing replied.

Mr. Rushing was in error, I found out the next day when I returned to talk with officials at what is now called the Roosevelt-Warm Springs Institute for Rehabilitation. They assured me that the grounds are wide open and visitors welcome. Yet I cannot guarantee that anyone reading this story and following my lead on a bicycle will not receive a welcome similar to mine. As the director of the Institute, Frank Ruzycki, said to me, "Put a uniform on some of these fellows, and it goes to their heads." State employees, for better and for worse, are trained to follow directions without asking the reasons for them—as they interpret those directions.

Fear or distrust of the state's competence to administer the properties associated with President Roosevelt has characterized events in the Warm Springs area over the past several years. The Little White House, for example, Roosevelt's personally designed home near the Warm Springs Hospital and scene of his death on April 12, 1945, was until July 1 of this year under the management of a special state agency called the Franklin D. Roosevelt Warm Springs Memorial Commission. This agency, established in January, 1946, was composed of 17 friends and associates of Roosevelt's and chartered to be self-perpetuating, self-supporting, and autonomous. It has operated within the context of state government, and yet it has never had to answer to any other branches of government nor to adhere to the rules governing other commissions and agencies. The executive director of the commission for the past 18 years was a confidant and friend of FDR and former mayor of Warm Springs, Frank W. Allcorn, Jr., who died suddenly last April at the age of 88. Although the state's Department of Natural Resources was due to take over administration of the Little White House only two months later and might have been expected to want some say in the naming of a new director, the Commission appointed Allcorn's administrative clerk, Louise Ousley, to succeed him on May 1.

Mrs. Ousley, like many of the other employees hired by the Memorial Commission, had personal ties to FDR. He always bought gas from her mother's Texaco station when he motored in the area, and Mrs. Ousley remembers well the sobbing on the Warm Springs railroad platform as the train bearing the President's coffin to Washington pulled slowly out of the station, its steam pressure carefully built up beforehand so that the engine could glide silently away from the depot. The elderly woman who sells tickets at the entrance gate to the Little White House was a housekeeper at the hospital during the period of Roosevelt's frequent visits and was among the crew brought into the Little White House to tidy up immediately after the President died. Some of the guards, too, who stand about in the rooms of the President's house and the adjacent museum worked for FDR. A few of them are pushing 80, and they recite their little anecdotes mechanically, like windup dolls, and with hesitant quavers. But they're tangible links back to the beloved leader who is still idolized in the South as the Messiah who led his people forth from the Great Depression. As Louise Ousley says, "The atmosphere here will change when a whole generation of the older people is gone. That personal feeling won't be here anymore."

Turning over operations of the Little White House to the state's Department of Natural Resources symbolizes the end of an era. None of the old Rooseveltians presently on the staff will be dismissed, but the final decisions about the property will be made by state bureaucrats, not by persons intimately associated with Roosevelt or their descendants (the present Memorial Commission contains at least three sons of original members, and its chairman, Thomas W. Starlin of Columbus, has served on it since its inception). The departure of the old guard will not occasion universal lamentation in the Warm Springs area, however. At least some local residents associate the management of the Roosevelt legacy by cronies of the late President with arrogant self-advancement and silly obstructionism.

The chief figure to reckon with in the years after FDR died was his onetime law partner, Basil O'Connor, president and treasurer of the Georgia Warm Springs Foundation which administered the hospital and honorary chairman of the Warm Springs Memorial Commission which administered the Little White House. O'Connor was in charge of the nationwide fund drives organized by the Warm Springs Foundation to fight infantile paralysis, or poliomyelitis, the disease that crippled Roosevelt in 1921. Residents of Warm Springs, observing O'Connor's high-handed autocracy, the ostentation of his private automobiles and frequent trips to the West Coast, suspected him of siphoning off polio funds for his personal benefit. He

did not endear himself to the local population when he shut down the public pools at Warm Springs shortly after Roosevelt's death, on the grounds that patients at the hospital were disturbed by the raucous demeanor of the public bathers.

O'Connor died in 1974, and shortly thereafter the Warm Springs Foundation conveyed to the state of Georgia its 956½ acres of land and management of the hospital, contingent upon the state's agreeing to continue its programs for 10 years "in a manner consistent with those of the Georgia Warm Springs Foundation." The announcement last year that the state would close the nearly-empty hospital (the success of the Salk vaccine in treating polio eventually made the specialized treatment apparatus at the hospital unnecessary) was interpreted by the Foundation as a breaking of the 1974 agreement, and the Foundation filed suit against the state to block the closing.

Frantic and complicated negotiations ensued, with many Warm Springs residents expressing their impatience with the Foundation for what they considered pointless nitpicking. A compromise was finally worked out whereby the state would keep the hospital open with a future capacity of 78 inpatients. The old Georgia Warm Springs Hospital has now been merged with the adjacent Georgia Rehabilitation Center, erected by the state in 1964, and the enlarged treatment center is known as the Roosevelt-Warm Springs Institute for Rehabilitation, operated by the Department of Human Resources. The Georgia General Assembly has allocated $6 million to refurbish the old hospital, and the Institute is being touted as a potential national leader in the treatment of handicapped persons, both in terms of job training and in making self-sufficient those invalids who must remain confined to their homes.

Meanwhile, the Little White House has been experiencing troubles of its own. From a peak visitor load of 145,626 in fiscal year 1977, tourist traffic fell off to 139,000 in 1978, 111,480 in 1979, and 97,318 in the fiscal year just ended. The Warm Springs Memorial Commission had always prided itself on meeting operating expenses out of its gate receipts and gift-shop sales, but in order to do so, the admission price had to be continually raised, to its present level of $3 for adults and $1.50 for children 6–12. The state legislature foresaw increased budgetary trouble for the Little White House (they appropriated $128,288 for the fiscal year that began July 1 to cover the difference between anticipated receipts and unusually heavy operating and repair expenses) and, despite vigorous objections from the Memorial Commission, transferred management of the property to the Department of Natural Resources. The Commission will continue to exist, but as its present members die off, they will not be replaced, and, its function now purely symbolic, it will someday vanish forever.

For the first time since shortly after Roosevelt died, the bulk of the property he amassed in Georgia is in the hands of a single owner. In addition to the 4992 acres of the Franklin D. Roosevelt State Park the Department of Natural Resources has been operating for some time, it now controls the 4183 acres connected with the Little White House which were formerly administered by the Warm Springs Memorial Commission (as well as some peripheral property adjacent to the Institute land managed by the Department of Human Resources). These two large tracts are very nearly contiguous, being separated only by a narrow strip of land in private ownership, which the state is considering buying to prevent further commercial strip development on the top of Pine Mountain (see the map for a perspective on how the state's holdings in the region are related).

In order to make the $3 admission price to the Little White House more attractive, the state decided to refurbish the old outdoor treatment pools where Roosevelt found relief from polio. Last July 4, the pools were officially opened to the viewing public (not, however, for recreational or therapeutic use), along with an extensive photographic exhibit showing their functions at different eras. Admission to the pools is included in the entrance fee to the Little White House.

It is too early to tell whether such a move increases tourism sufficiently to keep maintenance of the Roosevelt property from draining the state's coffers. The budget for running the Little White House amounts to nearly nine times the budget for the next most expensive state Historic Site ($441,258, compared to $52,000 to run the Hofwyl-Broadfield Plantation on the coast). State officials are understandably worried about the burdens assumed in running not only the Little White House, with its uncertain income, but a 78-bed hospital with a present patient population of 25 and a future purpose that is at the moment purely theoretical (not to mention a proven difficulty in luring top medical personnel to the remote Warm Springs area).

Where does a state concerned about financial liabilities look for help? The same place Lockheed and the Chrysler Corporation look: the federal government. Governor Busbee wrote Secretary of the Interior Cecil Andrus requesting the appointment of a federal task force to study a Georgia Department of Natural Resources proposal for consolidating the three major Roosevelt properties into a 10,000-acre park. The governor suggested, as one alternative for future management, that the hospital, pools, springs, Little White House, and FDR State Park all be operated by the federal government.

Last June the task force completed its report, which recommended "that the Little White House be designated as *the* Roosevelt Memorial" (instead of some monument or statuary in Washington, D.C., or the Roosevelt family's property in Hyde Park, New York). This was what the governor had hoped for, but the task force's recommendation on future management was far from what state officials had in mind. In a letter to Governor Busbee, Joe Tanner, Commissioner of the Department of Natural Resources, wrote, "I feel strongly that the state should not simply turn over the FDR State Park and the Little White House lands of some 9,000 acres to the National Park Service and in return receive only a National Park Service sign." In essence, the state feels as though the federal government wants to snatch all of the valuable FDR properties and leave the state to shoulder the expense of maintaining them.

Negotiations between the federal and state governments over management of the FDR acreage will continue. The state will try to get officials in Washington to designate all three properties, not just the Little White House, as the official Roosevelt Memorial. Georgia's bureaucrats also hope to secure federal approval for an unprecedented joint management of the park lands, with the state retaining ownership and the federal government paying for much of the maintenance.

What is the future of the FDR region in West Georgia? Its proximity to Callaway Gardens and the unspoiled Flint River increases its attraction as a prime tourist and recreational area.

Franklin Roosevelt knew a good section of the country when he found one, and to an astonishing degree it remains much as he knew it (as contrasted to the surroundings of his Hyde Park estate, which the federal task force calls "an alarming example of undesirable development and commercialization"). Visiting all the sites detailed in the accompanying guided tour provides a fascinating insight into the character and impact of one of this nation's most complex leaders. In addition, the ride along the ridge of Pine Mountain is one of the grandest pleasures for cyclists in the state of Georgia. I just hope that your road to health is not paved with the good intentions of Mr. Rushing and his cohorts in state government.

1980

CYCLIST'S ALMANAC

Distance: The loop comprises just under 35 miles, including tours of the Little White House and Rehabilitation Institute grounds. An additional seven-mile round trip is highly recommended from the Roosevelt Memorial Bridge at the intersection of Ga 190 & 354 to the western terminus of Ga 190 at US 27 and the Callaway Gardens Country Store, then back again. Adding this extra stretch will expose you to the entire ridable section of road along the top of Pine Mountain (designed for this location by FDR himself), with its many fine outlooks and unspoiled woodlands on all sides.
Terrain: Hilly, though if you follow the direction of the arrows in a counter-clockwise pattern, you'll avoid the only grueling climb of the entire route, the long ascent from Warm Springs past the Little White House to Pine Mountain. The swoop down this hill, on the other hand, is one of the state's grand cycling treats. The smaller climbs along the marked route are numerous, however; not to be undertaken by novices.
Hazard: US 27 through the town of Pine Mountain is often heavily traveled, and you may want to cross the railroad tracks and ride on a parallel street through town. This road, unfortunately, dumps you back on 27 before its intersection with Ga 354 when you leave it, but the distance is small.
Points of interest: Park your car in the gravel lot designated for parking which faces Georgia Hall inside the grounds of the Roosevelt-Warm Springs Institute for Rehabilitation. The first part of the tour is on foot, because the sidewalks around the hospital are used by handicapped persons in wheelchairs and on crutches, and cyclists would constitute an unwelcome intrusion. You are free, however, to use all road surfaces shown on this map (Mr. Rushing notwithstanding); avoid all roads marked "Residents Only."

You are now standing at the center of what used to be known as the Georgia Warm Springs Foundation, the only hospital in the country established specifically to treat victims of poliomyelitis. You are in the middle of 265 acres designated by the federal Department of the Interior as a National Historic Landmark.

With your back to Georgia Hall, take note of the two dirt roads leading south, lined by (1) *white-frame Victorian cottages*. The roads remain unpaved because President Roosevelt instructed in his will that the grounds of the property he had bought and loved should remain in a condition as close to natural as possible. Some of the cottages here date from the pre-Roosevelt era in Warm Springs and provide a good visual introduction to the area's history.

For Warm Springs was a place of interest to visitors long before Franklin Roosevelt of New York first landed here in October, 1924. The existence of springs bubbling out of the ground in this vicinity at an unvarying year-round temperature of 88° was apparently known to the Indian tribes dispersed over a wide area, who traveled here from long distances to be healed. In 1832, just as the

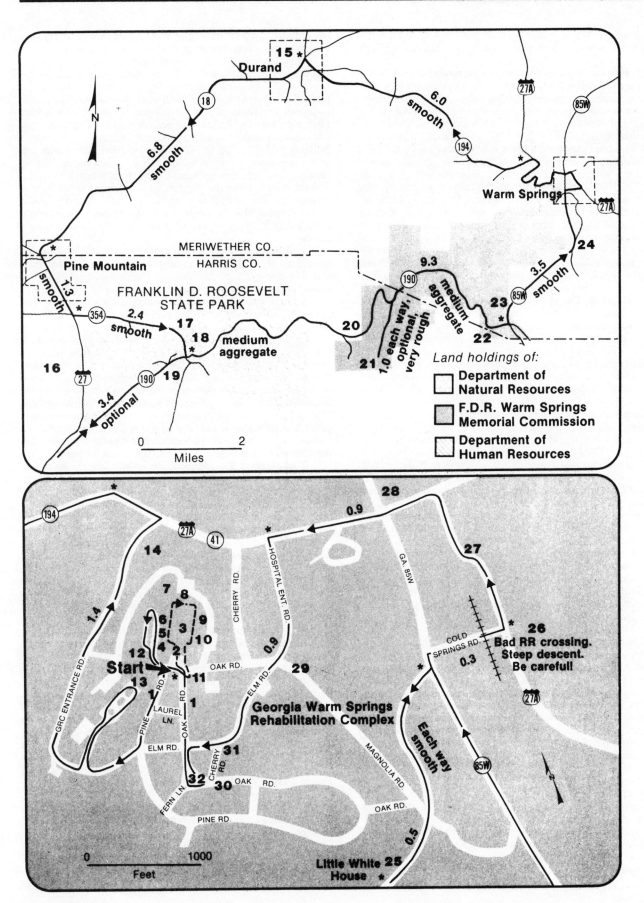

Land holdings of:

☐ Department of Natural Resources

▦ F.D.R. Warm Springs Memorial Commission

▨ Department of Human Resources

26 Bad RR crossing. Steep descent. Be careful!

Georgia Warm Springs Rehabilitation Complex

Little White House 25

Indians were being deported to Oklahoma, the first white man's resort was established here, under the name Meriwether Warm Springs.

In 1896 the town that had grown up around the resort was given the name Bullochville, and during the Gay Nineties it became a favorite summer vacation spot for residents of nearby Columbus. Cottages similar to those you see here dotted the hills near the springs, and short-term guests stayed in a rambling, three-story hotel erected in 1893 with gables, gingerbread, and endless wooden curlicues, known as the Meriwether Inn.

Train service brought crowds to Bullochville. The automobile took them away, to more glamorous resorts farther away from home. By 1920, the Meriwether Inn had closed, and the springs were visited mainly by the local population. An effort to revive the resort at this time attracted the interest of Columbus native George Foster Peabody, a philanthropist and Democratic Party leader, who had moved to New York but remembered fondly the attractions of Bullochville. Peabody invested in the rundown resort and was instrumental in having the village's name changed back to Warm Springs in 1924. That same year he interested his friend Franklin Roosevelt in investigating the curative powers of the springs. Roosevelt had been the Democratic Party's candidate for Vice-President on their losing 1920 ticket, the year before he was stricken by polio, and he had spent three years in a vain search for relief. His first immersion in the unusually buoyant waters of Warm Springs convinced him that he could improve his condition here because of the increased mobility afforded him to stretch and exercise his afflicted legs. That discovery changed the course of American political and social history and altered dramatically the landscape of Warm Springs.

Turn back now to face (2) *Georgia Hall,* one of the earliest structures built under the auspices of the Georgia Warm Springs Foundation, which was incorporated in 1927 by Roosevelt; his law partner, Basil O'Connor; George Foster Peabody; and two other men. The previous year Roosevelt had bought from Peabody 1000 acres of land, some cottages, the old inn, and the baths for $195,000, with the original intention of operating a resort simultaneously with a treatment center for "polios," as victims of poliomyelitis were then called. This idea proved unworkable because the golfers and vacationers were repulsed by the sight of crippled polios and insisted that they be banned from the pools and even from the public dining room, for fear that they would spread the disease. In 1927, thus, the old resort changed its nature, becoming a health spa or a kind of hospital for polios, though without the outward appearance of one. It still looked like a resort or a country club. Construction of buildings to fit the needs of polios began in 1928 with a glass-enclosed patients' pool donated by Mr. and Mrs. Edsel Ford.

Roosevelt was obsessed by dread of fire breaking out in the old Meriwether Inn, and he asked his friend Henry Toombs, a young Georgia architect and descendant of the Confederacy's Secretary of State, Robert Toombs, to draw up blueprints for a building to replace it that would be suitable for handicapped patients. Basil O'Connor intended to raise the money for this structure by appealing to philanthropists around the country, but in March, 1933, an Atlantan named Cator Woolford came up with the idea of soliciting the money from citizens of Georgia. He persuaded textile magnate Cason Callaway of LaGrange to head the fund-raising drive, and he and Callaway put up $100,000 immediately to get the construction started.

It was the height of the Depression, but $100,000 was collected from 60,000 Georgians, and on November 24, 1933, eight months after the campaign began, Georgia Hall was dedicated. Many of the contributions came in the form of nickels and dimes, but every donor, no matter how small, received a certificate of appreciation from the Foundation. Callaway got stuck with $13,000 of the total cost when the fund-raising drive fell short of its goals,

but the magnitude of its success gave O'Connor and others ideas for future nationwide campaigns to benefit the Foundation.

Walk across the newly renovated entrance hall of the building and through the glass doors facing the main portal. Ahead of you lies (3) *Callaway Garden,* dedicated to the memory of Cason Callaway. In preparation for the ceremonies designating the hospital and grounds a National Historic Landmark, the garden was decorated with hanging baskets and beds of begonias by Steve Polk, who landscapes the grounds of the state Capitol for the Georgia Building Authority. The colonnades that surround this garden present a dignified and harmonious ensemble, even though the individual buildings that lie behind them were constructed over a 20-year period. Note the classical restraint of the Greek Revival architecture, first evident in Georgia Hall and carried out here in the colonnades. The effect created is similar to that achieved by the many public buildings erected in nearby LaGrange by the Callaway family.

Walk through the colonnade on the left, and look on the ground for (4) the *marker identifying the former site of the Meriwether Inn.* The fine old Victorian structure, much feared by FDR, was demolished in 1933, as the marker says, "With regret and relief."

Returning to the colonnade, look back toward Georgia Hall. You will notice that its facade facing Callaway Garden is labeled "Columbus Colonnade," to mark the contributions made to the Foundation by citizens of nearby Columbus. Proceeding now away from Georgia Hall, the next building is (5) *Kress Hall,* built as a dormitory in 1935 with funds donated by heirs to the dime-store fortune. The next building is (6) *Founder's Hall* (1957), the most recent of the hospital's structures, containing offices. Notice the frieze of sculpted heads by Edmond R. Amateis, known as the Polio Hall of Fame. It commemorates pioneers in the battle to control polio. The last three figures on the right are, in left-to-right order, Jonas Salk, developer of the vaccine that successfully combatted paralytic polio; Basil O'Connor; and President Roosevelt.

Look through the colonnade when you reach the far corner. To your left is (7) the *Children's Pavilion,* built in 1955, with its octagonal solarium, 30 feet in diameter, completely glass-enclosed. At one time a seven-foot cage containing some 40 parakeets and other tropical birds was suspended in the middle of this structure for the entertainment of child patients. Notice on the solarium's roof the 10 iron silhouettes of birds, very fanciful and decorative, that cling to the roofline like weathervanes. The grounds around the pavilion contain stone statues of owls and other birds.

Turn along the colonnade opposite Georgia Hall. You are passing (8) *the surgical wing,* built in 1939 to save patients trips to Atlanta. During the height of the hospital's use in the 1950s, more than 800 operations a year were performed here. At present the state has no plans for remodeling and using this entire wing.

Turning the corner and heading back toward Georgia Hall, you pass (9) the *east wing,* built in 1946 to bring the hospital's patient capacity to its peak load of 165. The state has recently spent $2.3 million to rehabilitate this wing. The next building is (10) *Roosevelt Hall,* built in 1952–53. The walkway leading up to it, a kind of patio or atrium, contains on its curved walls reliefs sculpted by Edmond Amateis. On the left are represented Anne Sullivan and her patient, Helen Keller, with an inscription from Miss Keller: "While they were saying among themselves, 'It cannot be done,' it was done." On the right are shown FDR and a crippled child beside an inscription taken from the President's first inaugural address in March, 1933: "There is nothing to fear but fear itself."

The interior of Roosevelt Hall, constructed on the site of a dance pavilion dating from Bullochville's heyday as a summer resort, contains an auditorium designed for patients in stretchers and wheelchairs. The walls of the corridors leading to the auditorium are hung with the autographed pictures of entertainment stars of the 1940s and '50s, such as Shirley Temple and Jane Withers, who performed for patients here. Prominent among them is Eddie Cantor, who coined the phrase "March of Dimes" for the most famous of several fund-raising campaigns developed by the Foundation in the 1930s.

Among the most successful of these campaigns was a series of Birthday Balls celebrating the President's date of birth, whose announced purpose was to create a permanent endowment for the Foundation. The first of these events, comprising some 600 balls nationwide, was held on January 30, 1934, and raised over $1 million. The balls continued throughout the decade, bringing in over $2 million by 1939 and resulting in the formation in 1938 of the National Foundation for Infantile Paralysis, headed by Basil O'Connor. One of its avowed purposes was to support research into the causes of poliomyelitis, but when the public discovered that few, if any, of the Foundation's resources during its first year of operations had in fact been used for research, they threatened to boycott future fund-raising efforts. President O'Connor had to curtail some of his more flamboyant activities until public confidence had been restored.

You have now completed the circuit of the Callaway Garden colonnades. Pause at the corner of Georgia Hall to notice the design of the fire escape leading from the auditorium in Roosevelt Hall. It curves gently downward without steps to permit wheelchairs passage to the ground. Take a look inside the dining room that occupies the end of Georgia Hall closest to Roosevelt Hall. Here the first Founder's Day was celebrated at Thanksgiving, 1928, when FDR carved his initial Warm Springs turkey, a tradition that continued in this room throughout his years as President. Notice the three handsome, unostentatious chandeliers.

Walk back through Georgia Hall and across to (11) the *chapel*, built in 1937 from funds donated by Georgia Mustian Wilkins, the great-granddaughter of an early developer of the Warm Springs resort. She inherited most of the property in the area at one time, much of which she sold to Roosevelt, and she remained the President's nearest neighbor after he built his Little White House in 1932. She bequeathed her cottage to the Warm Springs Foundation for use as an FDR museum when she died in 1959, and it was dedicated for that use on April 12, 1961. A visit to the museum is included in the admission to the Little White House. The simple, pretty whitewashed interior of the chapel was the scene of President Roosevelt's last church attendance at Easter on the Sunday before he died in April, 1945.

Now unload your bikes, and continue the tour from the vantage point of your saddles. You'll pass (12) the *school and library*, built in 1939 and operated as an accredited school for children with polio until declining enrollment caused its closing in 1968. The library contained nearly 2000 volumes, just one of the resources that led the Foundation to consider itself, in the words of its brochure published in 1956, "a complete community, a village unto itself." Note once again the serenely restrained Greek Revival architecture of the facade.

Wheel into the parking lot of (13) the *Georgia Rehabilitation Center*, built in 1964, where vocational rehabilitation has been taught. Until recently, the Center and the Hospital, though both run by the state Department of Human Resources, carried on rivalries left over from the days when the Foundation operated the Hospital and intended at one point to erect a fence between its property and the Center's. Each of the two facilities acted as if the other did not exist. Each maintained its own cafeteria for its own staff and refused to share resources. The state has now merged all operations into the Roosevelt-Warm Springs Institute for Rehabilitation and closed one of the cafeterias.

You swoop down alongside the golf course, a remnant from the resort days of Warm Springs and something of a puzzle to the state at present as to how it can serve the needs of the new Institute. The land on the edges of the Institute's property is managed not by the Department of Human Resources, but by Natural Resources, which also maintains (14) the *outdoor treatment pools*.

No more sightseeing for a while. Enjoy some easy and scenic cycling to (15) *Durand*, where guests bound for Meriwether Warm

Springs alighted from the train and boarded a stagecoach in the days before the Georgia Midland Railroad came to Warm Springs itself.

If time permits, take a detour from FDR country to visit (16) *Callaway Gardens* south of the town of Pine Mountain. The winding roads of this developed landscape are ideally suited to bicycling.

Back on the FDR trail, make a stop at (17) the *Liberty Bell Pool* inside Franklin D. Roosevelt State Park. Roosevelt designed the pool with its handsome stone embankments in the shape of—you guessed it. You will see this type of fieldstone, taken from the Pine Mountain area, in structures throughout the park.

The park itself is an outgrowth of programs developed by Roosevelt during the 1930s to try and combat unemployment and poverty generated by the Great Depression. A Civilian Conservation Corps camp was established here as part of an ambitious federal land program which acquired cut-over and farmed-out lands and converted them to public recreational purposes. Massive tree plantings were undertaken here by the Corps, which also built many of the simple log structures still standing in the park (if you want to see them, follow the signs south off Ga 354 to the Trading Post and Lake Delano, but be prepared for some *steep* grades). The 4992 acres of the park make it the second largest in the Georgia park system. Under the proposal submitted by the state Department of Natural Resources to the federal Department of the Interior, the structures and resources of the park will be significantly modified to encourage their use by handicapped persons, thus making the park an important adjunct to the new Institute for Rehabilitation.

When you reach the intersection with Ga 190, pause to admire (18) the *Franklin D. Roosevelt Memorial Bridge*, constructed of the characteristic Pine Mountain fieldstone. A state historic marker nearby credits FDR with the placement of the bridge and the design of what is now Ga 190, the Pine Mountain Scenic Highway, built between 1934 and 1938.

Even if you're not taking the recommended extra leg of this trip to the Callaway Gardens Country Store at the western end of Ga 190, take a short detour to (19) the *Roosevelt Inn*, now the park's visitor center. Sitting high above the road, it commands a remarkable view out over Pine Mountain Valley, where one of the New Deal's least successful programs was attempted. Called a Rural Relocation Homestead Project, it was intended to move indigent people from cities to model farms and new housing. It was an effort to restore self-sufficiency to the countryside through educational programs, loans, and direct assistance and to improve the physical landscape by modern farming methods. The reception room of the Inn contains exhibits relating to FDR's New Deal programs in the area. The arch that supports the fine staircase in this room was designed by Roosevelt. Note again the use of native woods and stone throughout the structure.

You will know when you leave the state park because you immediately enter (20) a *short stretch of commercial development*. It is to prevent more of this sort of thing that the state is considering purchase of the land lying between the park and the old Warm Springs Memorial Commission property attached to the Little White House.

Dedicated Rooseveltians will want to take a detour to (21) *Dowdell's Knob*, the President's favorite picnic spot, with more fine views out over Pine Mountain Valley. The stone barbecue fireplace at the edge of the mountain here was constructed by FDR (its grill area has had to be cemented over because vandals have so badly defaced it). Not-so-dedicated Rooseveltians may want to skip the mile-long and extremely rough road surface to the picnic spot. This road was designed by FDR in the late 1920s.

Just before the intersection with Ga 85W, watch for a state historic marker identifying (22) *Longleaf Pine Planting*. Just south of the marker, Roosevelt planted 5000 longleaf pine seedlings during the winter of 1929–30 on five acres of his farm as a demonstration to local farmers of what could be done with cut-over or burned areas not suitable for agriculture. The project was also intended to suggest techniques for checking erosion. A tornado in 1954 destroyed about half of the original stand of trees.

Immediately after turning onto Ga 85W, look for a state historic marker on the left side of the road identifying (23) *Roosevelt Farm.* No physical evidence of the farm remains, the buildings having been removed in 1959 and replaced with FDR's beloved pine trees, but here stood the center of a 2200-acre tract that Roosevelt assembled between 1926 and 1937. Most of the acreage was in pine and hardwoods, but some 150 acres contained pasture and crop land. The farm was intended as a demonstration project for local residents, embodying the principles of erosion control, reforestation, cover crops, and general soil conservation. Cattle, hogs, and poultry were raised here, along with fruits and vegetables, and these products supplied the Georgia Warm Springs Foundation during the austerities of food rationing during the Second World War. From this description one derives a keen sense of how complete an investment Roosevelt made in the people and countryside of Meriwether County. Here so many of his interests interlocked, which suggests the appropriateness of making this area a memorial to him.

Notice the two rows of concrete foundations on the brow of the mountain (24), the *ruins of the White House Inn.* I took them to be military installations at first, but learned subsequently that they are all that remain of a speculative venture by a group of sports figures in the 1960s, who hoped to develop a fancy resort here (shades of Bullochville!). One member of the group is said to have embezzled the funds.

Your grand swoop down Pine Mountain must be interrupted by a sharp left turn into (25) the *Little White House.* Take note, as you proceed toward the only home FDR built, of the dirt road that runs far below the paved bridge you are riding on. That was FDR's access to his home, leading there from the grounds of the Warm Springs Foundation. He did not have nor want a paved driveway, in keeping with his taste for the natural and simple. His friend Henry Toombs, architect of Georgia Hall, designed the home, which cost, along with the garage, $7350. Roosevelt chose the site himself, having come upon it at the end of an afternoon of tiring horseback riding. At the top of a small hill, he paused and remarked to a companion, "This is where I'll build my house. A little house, flush in front with the ground, but, in back over the ravine, a porch as high as a prow of a ship. Wonderful for sunsets. A home for all the time I'll spend here." Once again you'll note the influence of the Southern Greek Revival architecture which Roosevelt had admired in the towns of the Georgia Piedmont. Its absence of ornamentation and ostentation is in marked contrast to his own birthplace at Hyde Park, no less than to the princely surroundings of certain recent Presidents.

The house is open 9–5 every day and the interior is much as Roosevelt left it. Not in keeping with the spirit of FDR is the rather pretentious avenue of state memorials that leads from the little White House itself to the adjacent museum, lodged in Georgia Mustian Wilkins' old cottage.

Return to Ga 85W, and watch for Cold Springs Rd leading to the right almost immediately. Its name is due to the fact that, indeed, a cold springs used to exist where now is located (26) the *Warm Springs National Fish Hatchery.* On your way into the town of Warm Springs, which retains something of its old resort look and flavor, note at the bend of the road (27) the *Bulloch Home,* perched on a high hill and surrounded by corny signs and red, white, and blue insignia of all types. Remember, this was once Bullochville.

On the right at the main intersection of town stood, until destroyed by the railroad company in 1959, (28) the *Warm Springs depot,* where Roosevelt arrived and departed on his many visits to the area. A plaque marks the exact location.

Reenter the grounds of the Roosevelt-Warm Springs Institute for Rehabilitation. At the first intersection, the paved road to the left is (29) the *old driveway to the Little White House.* Beyond lie (30) the *McCarthy Cottage,* where Roosevelt stayed before the Little

White House was built, and (31) the *LeHand Cottage,* named for FDR's private secretary, who stayed here. Take a short detour on dirt surface to view (32) the *Roosevelt Memorial,* a massive head of the President created by noted sculptor Steffen Thomas of Atlanta. Keep away from the residences of Institute personnel behind the memorial. Return to Georgia Hall and your car.

Biking Through Historic Macon

Macon is a city rich in architectural heritage and the best way to see it is from the seat of a bicycle.

by Bill Cutler

The accompanying bike route is designed to introduce lovers of distinguished urban neighborhoods and buildings to some of the most attractive of Macon's streets that are appropriate for touring by bicycle.

Since parking is hard to come by in Macon, I recommend that you park in the lot behind the new federal building on College Street (accessible from either Georgia or Hardeman Avenue). At Chi-Ches-Ter's College Hill Pharmacy, which faces the lot, you can obtain both the Middle Georgia Historical Society's *A Guide to Macon's Architectural and Historical Heritage* and a brochure on Macon's "Heritage Tour" (free). The former provides an extremely detailed analysis of all the city's valuable buildings as well as photographs of many of them (some of which you will have trouble recognizing in their present dilapidated state). The latter is a handy abbreviated introduction to historic Macon (although its map is inaccurate and not drawn to scale). You will notice markers for the Heritage Tour as you pedal around the bicycle route, but I do not recommend that you follow them because they will take you on heavily traveled streets and up very steep grades.

The architectural tour, marked on our map in a dashed line, is only about six miles in length, designed for frequent stops and close inspection of the city's beauties. It wanders back and forth through the area of Macon called the College Hill district, where most of the city's historic buildings are concentrated. The dotted line indicates an optional trip—also about six miles in length—out to the site of the Ocmulgee Indian Mounds across the Ocmulgee River.

The College Hill loop is intended to introduce you to the variety of Macon's fine architecture—from the awesomely imposing Hay House, which is open to the public and worth a visit, to quaint and modest residential dwellings like the brightly painted orange house on Orange Street. The bicycle

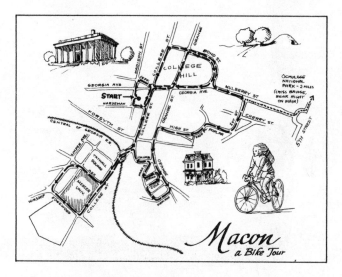

The tour begins in the parking lot of Chi-Ches-Ter's Pharmacy located just behind the new Federal Building on College Street, then wanders back and forth through the area of Macon called the College Hill District. To take the Ocmulgee Indian Mound loop you must brave busy traffic on Mulberry Street and railroad crossings near the Ocmulgee River.

route takes you to a section of the city not included in the Heritage Tour, a neighborhood in transition called Orange Terrace where you can see houses in various stages of disrepair and rejuvenation. Many of these handsome structures are just now being refurbished by enterprising young families. I know of few residential streets in Georgia with the charm of Macon's Cole Street and Highland Terrace.

The heart of the city's architectural interest lies, however, along College Street. From one end to the other of this astonishing avenue you will find almost every building worth close study and admiration. Two other particularly striking thoroughfares are Georgia Avenue—with its great row of handsome mansions—and Mulberry Street, a major commercial artery lined with attractive plantings in the middle and distinguished structures, both public and private, on both sides.

Other points of interest are Mercer University and the birthplace of Sidney Lanier on High Street. Take careful note also of the dwellings that face the Lanier cottage across the small strip of green in the middle of High Street as well as those around the corner on both sides of Orange Street.

To take the Ocmulgee Indian Mounds loop, you must brave busy traffic on Mulberry Street and dangerous railroad crossings near the river. On your way out of town along Mulberry, pause to note the curious yellow structure on the corner of an alley between First and Second Streets, formerly the Macon Library, with its unique corner entrance; and, on the way back, stop to admire the opulent Grand Opera House.

You cross the Ocmulgee River on the busy Fifth Street bridge, but once onto Main beyond the Coliseum (modeled after the Indian Mounds) you'll have a quiet, though uphill, route to the park. Notice the handsome cottage surrounded by a balustraded porch at the corner of Main and Hydrolia Streets on the left. Where Main Street dead-ends near the Emery Highway, you can ride undisturbed on the sidewalk straight to the

park entrance, and you'll find lots of scenic (and hilly) riding inside the park, as well as the fascinating mounds themselves.

A word of caution: although Macon's streets are not marked by the clear hazard of drainage grates like those that catch bicycle tires in some cities, most of them are paved either with brick or with ancient asphalt in very poor condition, both of which are hard on lightweight ten-speed bikes. Ride with extreme care and at a moderate pace.

1973

Bicycling Through Washington and Wilkes County

From the "oldest airport in the world" to a Revolutionary War battle site. Choose a short jaunt around architectural wonders of Washington or ride cross country through historic Wilkes County.

By Bill Cutler

An airport may sound like an odd place to begin and end a bicycle tour of 18th century Georgia. But, then, history-conscious local residents are proud to claim the terminal at Washington-Wilkes County airport as the oldest in the world—a fitting welcome-station to the area its historian, Mrs. Henry Standard, calls "the cradle of Georgia." The structure, located about five miles west of Washington on U.S. highway 78, is a handsome frame house built around 1800. There's plenty of room to park behind it. Take a look upstairs at the attic before setting off on your tour.

You'll have a stretch of 20th century America to negotiate at the outset—narrow U.S. 78 into Washington, with a fair amount of high-speed traffic. Be sure to ride as far to the right as possible and keep up a good rate of speed yourself. About two miles from the airport, follow "Business 78" to the right into town. You'll be on Robert Toombs Avenue (formerly Main Street), the perfect introduction to the extraordinary richness and variety of Washington's architectural heritage. You'll pass, on both sides of the street, white-columned ante-bellum mansions with magnolia-lined walkways, Victorian extravagances with cupolas or gingerbread porches, elegant churches, modest turn-of-the-century cottages with intricately fretted woodwork. As you follow the tour through Washington marked on the accompanying map, you'll also notice some much earlier houses with simpler, more severe lines.

If you're interested in obtaining details about the dates and histories of the houses on the route, head straight for the Washington-Wilkes Historic Museum at 308 East Robert Toombs. There you can pick up a free brochure on the town as well as some feeling for the area you are about to explore.

If you want to cycle only within Washington (about eight miles roundtrip, including loops to the outskirts), you can park behind the museum. Make sure to tour the splendid grounds.

Another building you'll want to visit is the Mary Willis Library on Liberty Street. The stained glass captures the mood of Victorian Gothic admirably.

One final word before leaving Washington to head into the country: if you spend any time in the business district's town square, you'll feel quickly enough how stratified the population is, both racially and economically. Washingtonians are explicit about wanting to maintain a small-town atmosphere, wary of gaudy tourist attractions. This is the Old South you're traversing for sure, with its advantages and its drawbacks—true dignity and grace, and inherent favoritism.

You leave Washington on Georgia Route 44. It's moderately busy, so keep a single line. The road surface is mostly smooth, with intermittent stretches of rough aggregate pavement. About ten miles out of town, you'll pass the Phillips Mill Baptist Church on your right, with two huge grist stones framing the tablet. The church was established in the late 18th century in Mr. Phillips' grist mill.

A little more than a mile beyond the church, take a rough paved road to the right. You'll cross a small creek and as you climb up from the creek bed, you'll pass a three-story brick house on your left very close to the road. This is the Daniel Dillard house, dated variously from 1790 to 1820, and Mrs. George Normandy, a local historian, calls it "the most striking example of Georgian architecture in the whole of the Southeast." ("Georgian" in this context refers to the period, not our state.) The house is being beautifully restored by Mr. and Mrs. David T. Blackburn of Six Flags.

A few yards up the hill on the right lies the Robert Dillard house, far from the road among a grove of trees. It's been renamed "Silvermist Farm" by its present owner, Atlanta dentist Dr. Jim Adcock, who is restoring it. Just beyond the farm, a dirt road to the left sports a yellow marker that reads "Bartram Trail." The sign indicates that the distinguished 18th century naturalist, poet and artist William Bartram passed this way with his Indian guides as he mapped out the lands ceded to the U.S. by Creeks and Cherokees.

Keep jogging along this rough surface for another three or four miles to a little community called Court Ground (no sign). You'll see a number of tiny shacks along this road sagging into the ground, their chimneys still upright and handsome, suggesting that these shed-like structures were once human habitations. Take a sharp right on the only paved cross road in

Take a short (7 miles) scenic tour of the architectural gems of Washington or spin through Wilkes County countryside. Author Bill Cutler narrates both routes in the accompanying story. If the town trip is enough for one day, take Liberty St. to Depot, then turn onto Robert Toombs to complete the loop. The trip is open-ended at highways 47 and 17; ride out these roads as far as you wish then return to town.

Court Ground, and proceed a mile to the Skull Shoals Road marker on your left.

Here you have a choice, depending on your sense of adventure. The stout of heart (or those on trail bikes) can continue straight about two miles and turn left at a rough marker for the Kettle Creek battlefield onto a perfectly terrible dirt road. It clambers up steep grades, staggers in deep ruts down again, and tests the patience of the most rugged cyclist. After 1.1 miles of this torture (you can walk your bike if you don't want to punish it), your reward will be a most curious and melancholy monument.

On top of a high knoll among the woods, a simple stone memorial erected in 1930 informs you that one of the most important battles of the Revolutionary (yes, *not* Civil) War was fought at this spot. Here, you're told, the defeat of the British by a much smaller force of Americans checked the British invasion of Georgia. The site has clearly not been tended for in years; picnic tables lie in fragments in the low scrub, and the few simple graves of men who fought here show signs of being vandalized.

Word is that the federal government intends to restore and improve the site. If you share my taste for historical sites in primitive, unimproved condition, then you'll enjoy Kettle Creek just as it is now. Your imagination will have to do the work of recreating the fierce battle. For my part, I hope the government doesn't turn Kettle Creek into another Gettysburg, with its dioramas, wax museum, and gigantic tourist tower.

You'll have to retrace your path to Skull Shoals Road, where your more timid companions are waiting to continue the ride. Take Skull Shoals a mile to the first paved road on the left, marked Columbus-Granade (note the handsome structure just beyond the intersection to the right). After about two-and-a-half miles, take a right at a stop sign. You'll pass Beaverdam Church, the now-defunct White Rock Church, and a number of handsome cattle farms (cotton began giving way to cattle as the dominant agricultural resource of Wilkes County after a disastrous boll weevil infestation early in this century; now cotton has disappeared entirely).

In about two miles you'll come back to U.S. 78. Its smooth black-top pavement will be welcome after miles of back-country roads with rough surfaces, and its gently rolling grades will be a real change from the steep ups and downs you've just been negotiating. For the two miles you have to travel before the airport comes into view, remember to hug the right-hand side of the road.

I've saved the best for last. Directly across U.S. 78 from the airport lies the Callaway Plantation—original Georgia home of the Callaway family, ensemble of Wilkes County's architectural continuity from 1785 till the middle of the 19th century, repository for agricultural equipment and antiques, working plantation, local rural crafts center—all this and more is embodied here. You can easily spend a full afternoon inspecting all aspects of this fascinating enterprise, as I did. It manages that rarest and most difficult of feats—making a reverence for the past serviceable and life-enriching, rather than quaint, precious, selfish, or escapist, as it so often is.

For this, we have largely Dr. Turner Bryson to thank, though he and his family are quick to insist that Callaway Plantation is a real community effort. Which it is. Local people, upon hearing that old crafts are being practiced once again at the Plantation, volunteer information on lesser-known activities they remember from their own childhood. So it is that you'll find a tar still unobtrusively tucked away in the Plantation's woods—an obscure method of producing pine tar from fat pine. There is no entrance fee to visit the Plantation, but its managers are hoping to make it self-supporting off the sale of products made or grown on the premises.

By the time you return to the airport, you'll have travelled a good thirty miles, not counting the seven or eight needed to see Washington thoroughly.

1974

Biking Morgan County*

Rolling countryside and antebellum houses from Madison to Social Circle and Park's Hill.

by Bill Cutler

Madison, "The Town Sherman Refused to Burn," is the center and highlight of the Morgan County bike routes. When you start exploring Morgan County by bicycle, I think you'll find, as I did, that you can't get enough of this rolling farm country dotted with handsome 19th-century houses and charming, hidden-away towns.

The routes have been planned for riders of varying proficiencies and interests. There's an easy 10-mile loop beginning and ending at Fairplay that remains entirely in the fields and open pastures, while the longer routes pass through towns and contain a few more challenging grades. For the most part, though, you'll find that the terrain gently rises and falls, without sharp drops and climbs. You can combine two or more of these loops if you're looking for more exercise, and a super-cyclist could even undertake all of them in one day and delight in roughly 100 miles of beautiful scenery and paved roads almost free of traffic.

Morgan County is cotton country, and so you might want to plan one of your visits to the area in mid- to late fall, when the cotton balls ripple past you like foam from receding breakers. The gin at Fairplay is no longer in operation, a recent fire having damaged the works too severely to be worth repairing, but you can still get some sense of how the machinery functioned if you poke about in the charred building. You might still see a bedraggled pile of cotton sitting forlornly beside the gin, looking like a soiled snow bank in early spring.

Morgan County is also Civil War country—to be more precise, March-to-the-Sea country—and you'll run across historical markers commemorating Sherman's destructive feat from Social Circle on the west to Swords on the east. In fact, part of the time, you'll be following the line of march of Sherman's left wing, under General Slocum, as it burned its way southeast to join the main force at Eatonton. It was thus actually Slocum, not Sherman himself, who spared Madison for us. As the Union Army approached, one of the town's leading citizens, Senator Joshua Hill, rode out to meet the troops and plead with them not to burn the town. Hill had voted against secession, and his close friendship with Sherman apparently tipped the balance in Madison's favor.

You'll see Hill's fine old home, as well as a host of other pre-Civil War private residences and public buildings. In fact, so little has changed in the part of Madison called Old Town (along Academy Street and Old Post Road) that you can get a clear sense of how a 19th-century Southern town would have looked and felt from riding through it. The streets are extremely narrow, many of the lesser ones still not paved, and the ample gardens and magnificent old trees around the homes provide plentiful roosts for the birds whose chirpings and trillings may be the only sounds you hear. Most surprising of all, in this age of endless suburban sprawl, is the compact, self-contained quality of Old Town. Beyond the rows of shuttered, brightly painted, solid houses to the north there lies a single street where the homes need paint and the weathered wood seems to be gently sagging back into the earth. Beyond these servants' homes stretch open fields—no filling stations, no quickie hamburger stands; just town and country gazing directly at each other as they have for decades.

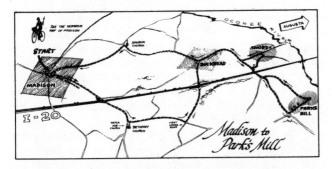

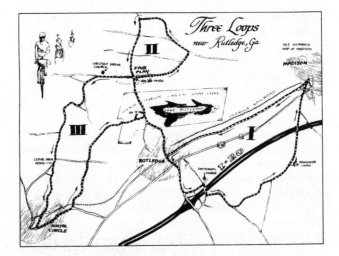

Madison to Park's Mill. *This loop is 35 miles roundtrip. There are a few moderate grades entering and leaving Madison; the rest is gently rolling countryside. You'll pass a lavish plantation a few miles from Madison, visit the quaint towns of Buckhead and Swords, and reach a beautiful old inn on the Oconee River built just after 1800.*

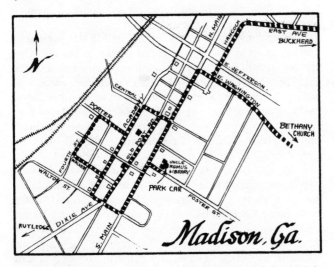

Madison Tour. *Bikes can pedal slowly up and down Main Street, Academy Street, Old Post Road and whatever other lanes and byways seem appealing. The Uncle Remus Library (where you can park) has a brochure with a guide to historic buildings.*

Above all, Morgan County is people country. If you've been dismayed at the discourtesy of drivers on Georgia highways, you'll be delighted at the reception you as a cyclist will get from motorists in this area. Usually, you'll receive a cheerful wave from someone in a passing car, and the horns you'll hear will be honks of greeting, not of anger or derision. The folks you see along the road—playing by a sharecropper's cottage, working in the fields, tending the general store at Fairplay—will make you feel welcome.

One lovely lady I met was Mrs. Lowrey Hunt, the unofficial historian of Morgan County. She must know who's lived on every plot of ground in the county for the past 150 years. She helped me plan my routes by sharing her voluminous knowledge of the back country roads with me. The loop east of Madison I owe entirely to her. She told me of the old inn at Park's Mill beside the Oconee River, built just after 1800, where Jeff Davis stopped on his flight from Federal troops in 1865. She also led me to Swords, the enchanting small com-

Three Loops. *The bike routes shown on this map provide bikers with a variety of riding experiences.*

Madison to Rutledge loop. *Twenty-five miles roundtrip. No difficult grades. Leave your car at the Uncle Remus library on South Main Street in Madison and meander through Old Town and around the town square. Head out of Madison on Dixie Avenue, past some of the area's most elegant ante-bellum houses. Explore sleepy Rutledge, and, if the spirit moves you, take an extra three-mile excursion each way to Hard Labor Creek state park, center for many recreational activities.*

Fairplay loop. *Ten miles. Gently rolling. Park next to the Fairplay general store. Explore the burned-out gin across the street and ride through pastures and cotton fields.*

Hard Labor Creek-Fairplay-Social Circle loop. *Twenty miles. Some moderately steep hills. Cotton fields and the charming late-19th-century town of Social Circle. Explore up Cherokee and Dogwood Roads as well as Hightower Trail. Start and end at the log cabin store in the state park.*

munity tucked into a hollow off the quiet road to Park's Mill. She knows every berry patch and good fishing hole within 40 miles of Madison. When she sees the maps included here, she'll probably be put out with me for not showing a bike route into every cranny and corner of her beloved county.

As you're meandering through Madison, you might have the kind of luck I had to run into a friendly and talkative old-timer. I was admiring a weatherbeaten old cabin whose wooden slats formed interesting patterns, when an elderly gentleman came along carrying some plants he'd just dug up. He told me no one had lived in the cabin for 50 years but he could remember going as a boy to get biscuits—"the best I've ever eaten"—from a woman who lived there. It turned out he is a neighbor of Mrs. Hunt's, and his family has lived in the same house for eight generations. He said there had once been plans to construct a railroad terminus in Madison, but the conservative cotton merchants who had built their elegant homes there didn't want the bustle that would go along with it. So the terminus was placed at Marthasville (its name later changed to Atlanta), and Madison's chance to become a commercial center, maybe even the state capital, went by the board. "They preferred to sit quietly at home with their mint julep—which isn't such a bad idea," my impromptu historian added with a twinkle.

If you choose to start your rides from Madison, park by the Uncle Remus Library on South Main Street. If the library is open, you can pick up a brochure with a guide to the historic buildings there (you can also find one at the drugstore on the town square). It's free. Instead of my providing a detailed tour of the town, I'd suggest just pedalling slowly up and down Main Street, Academy Street, Old Post Road, and whatever other lanes and by-ways appeal to you. Take a spin around the town square, with its handsome brick store fronts. The bike routes east and west will take you out past some of the finest homes just beyond the limits of town, along Washington Street and Dixie Avenue. You might want to drop in at Ye Old Colonial Restaurant on the town square. The bank next to it is now part of the same establishment, the walls of its old vault papered with Confederate money.

An attraction of many of these routes is the lovely state park at Hard Labor Creek. Rutledge and Social Circle are worth exploring, too. Just roam about in these towns as your imagination and wheels lead you. Social Circle contains many fine late-19th-century homes and a handsome downtown center with wide streets and charming storefronts.

The four bicycle loops described provide bikers with a variety of riding experiences.

1973

Invisible Town

Recollections of a linthead

by Bill Cutler, with Frank Smith

For 58 years near the beginning of this century, the small community of Milstead on the outskirts of the Rockdale County seat of Conyers was a company town belonging to the Callaway textile magnates from LaGrange. Milstead had its own water and power supplies, its own four-mile-long railroad which transported very lucrative freight to and from Conyers, and a town plan that accurately reflected the class structure of the mill, as well as the Callaways' interest in social services covering all aspects of their employees' lives. Until the 1940s, Callaway Mills owned around 500 acres of Rockdale County land, and at the time of the mill's closing in 1961, it employed some 900 workers. Although considerably changed today, the community of Milstead still comprises some 260 residences and reveals to an imaginative and interested visitor its original function as a carefully regulated company property. I found Milstead as fascinating a spot to explore as any town in Georgia.

Yet a centennial edition of the *Rockdale Citizen*, published in 1971 and devoted to celebrating the county's history, included no information about the town of Milstead, providing merely two short accounts of churches that remain there. Furthermore, a 214-page *History of Rockdale County*, compiled in 1978, does not even mention Milstead. Pictures of many homes in Conyers are featured, but the architectural features of Milstead—some of them striking indeed—are totally ignored.

Why was Milstead treated as a nonplace inside Rockdale County? I picked the town's historian and Justice of the Peace, Frank Smith, to explain the mystery. He has lived in Milstead since 1924, first as the son of a mill employee and then, at age 15, as a worker himself in the mill's carding room. He's a tall, thin, gaunt man with a great shock of white hair standing high above his brow like a cock's comb.

I said to Smith, "I've been reading a history of Rockdale County, and it's as though people in Conyers didn't even acknowledge the existence of Milstead."

"Right, right. That's right," he agreed.

"They just think they're better?" I asked.

Smith nodded his head. "Yeah," he said and paused. "They had nine grades in the school up here. The company didn't provide any more than nine grades, and I reckon if people back then got nine years of education, they were pretty well educated and ready to go into the mill. They'd be about fifteen, sixteen years old time they finished the ninth grade, and a job'd be provided for 'em here in the mill. But those that wanted to go on and finish high school, the officials' children, the bosses' children, they would be admitted to the Conyers schools. They'd pay a tuition, something like a dollar and a half a month. But only the officials' children were allowed, because we were referred to back then as 'lintheads.'"

Smith went on, "When I finished school up here, they wouldn't let me enroll in Conyers because I was from a poor family. None of my folks were bosses. I wrote a letter to the chairman of the board of the city schools. He wrote me a letter back and said, 'It is the policy of the school of our fair city that we cannot allow people of the Milstead cotton-mill folks to mix and mingle with the children of our fair city. Yours sincerely.'"

Frank Smith was not daunted by this setback, however, and went on to take courses in electrical engineering elsewhere which enabled him to pursue a specialized career with Callaway Mills. He got out of the carding room and eventually became chief electrician for the entire Callaway operation in Milstead. He volunteered to take me on a guided tour of his town, and his observations brought into sharp relief features of it that I had only half-understood riding around on my own. His vivid recollections recreated life for me as Callaway employees had known it during the decades before World War Two.

1981

CYCLIST'S ALMANAC*

Route This 10.7-mile loop (including nearly four miles of circling through Milstead) makes up in hills what it lacks in distance for the cyclist who wants a moderately strenuous outing. Northern Rockdale County lies on a flank of the granite outcroppings that culminate in Stone Mountain, and the terrain is rugged.

Hazards Some of the street surfaces inside and on the way to Milstead are rough and broken in places, and a short stretch of Milstead's New Street is unpaved. Loose gravel here necessitates extreme caution. The highway back into Conyers, Ga 20, attracts a

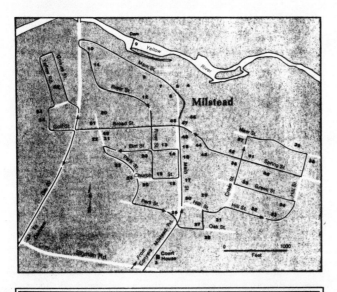

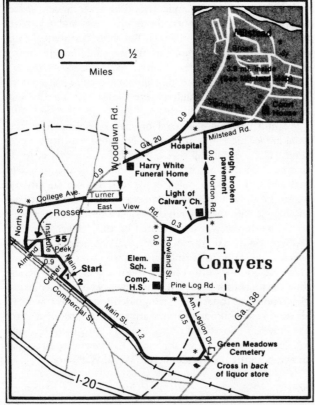

opposite the depot. The drug store contains an amusing collection of antique pharmaceutical supplies, including a still-functioning iron pump that dispenses cod liver oil. Take time to admire the backs of the commercial buildings facing the depot. The local merchants have coordinated efforts to improve the appearance of their businesses, and the signs and brickwork create an harmonious ensemble. The station itself was restored by the local historical society as their headquarters and as space for the Depot Players, who put on several dramatic and musical productions a year inside an arena whose seating can be changed according to the needs of different productions. Before leaving downtown Conyers, look left at the intersection of Main St to observe two of the town's handsomest Victorian homes (2), whose elaborate woodwork is partially obscured by large trees.

The approach to Milstead is marked by no official "City Limits" sign, since Milstead has never been incorporated. As long as Callaway Mills owned the community, the company provided its own security force, a volunteer fire department, and other social services. Now the county is responsible for paving the roads here (a rather haphazard job, as will soon become clear). The small, abandoned building on the right just beyond Sigman Rd (3) bears the imposing title Milstead Court House, but its last official purpose as a polling place was recently given up.

At the intersection of Oak St begins the imposing sweep of Main St downhill toward the mill. Specific features along the street will be pointed out later; for now merely observe the handsome effect still provided by the median green strip and the fine plantings of trees that march along both sides of the pavement, Dutch elms on the right, oaks on the left. In Milstead, as at their home base in LaGrange, the Callaway management expended considerable effort to beautify the physical environment in which their employees lived and worked.

Just after passing Broad St and a modern-looking apartment building on the right, look for a roughly paved track leading off to the right. This leads through a weed-strewn area which used to serve as parking for mill employees to the edge of the bluff overlooking (4) Milstead mill. This side view provides one of the best prospects upon the abandoned mill buildings, because they were built on the side of a hill, with the entrance on the highest level and the actual working areas on lower floors. Including the warehouses that stretch to the left of the actual mill, some five acres are under roof here.

This was not the first mill to occupy this site on the Yellow River. During the 1890s, a paper mill with its own dam and race operated here, at what was then known as Long Shoals. The existence of the dam and race attracted the interest of Frank Milstead, scion of a Baltimore, Maryland, family of cotton manufacturers who were seeking a place to build a cotton mill in Georgia. Milstead looked over the site in 1901 and on January 2, 1902, chartered the Milstead Manufacturing Company. It started out with two spinning frames, two cards, and half a dozen looms, manufacturing at first only spun thread, not woven materials. Frank Smith remembers a conversation he had with a lady named Alice Barnett, who went to work here in 1902 at the age of eight, before there were child-labor laws. The mill employed only three spinners then, and Smith says, "If they played or cut up, like kids would, the bosses'd take a switch and whip 'em. It was very vivid in her memory."

In 1903 management of Milstead Manufacturing Company was taken over by Fuller E. Callaway, Sr., and associates from LaGrange. Three years earlier Callaway had founded what later developed into the Callaway Mills organization with the building of the Unity Cotton Mills at LaGrange. The success of the Milstead and Unity enterprises led to the building of other mills at LaGrange, and in 1932 the various mills were merged in one company under the name Callaway Mills.

Almost as soon as Callaway took over the Milstead plant, its manufacturing capacity was expanded from yarn to the densely woven cotton fabric known as duck. During World War Two the

great deal of high-speed traffic. Fortunately, the road is good and wide throughout the entire long pull out of Milstead, but the pavement narrows inside Conyers, and the seemingly inviting shoulder is almost impossible to ride on, its surface changing every few yards and then periodically disappearing altogether. The route here takes the cyclist off Ga 20 onto residential streets as quickly as feasible.

Points of interest Park and begin the tour at (1) Conyers Depot. To reach the station from I-20, take West Ave (Exit 41) in Conyers north until you cross the railroad tracks, and then follow Railroad St to the right until you see the yellow depot, just past the fourth intersection. Parking is available just behind the station. Refreshments may be obtained at the soda fountain inside Evans Pharmacy mill served a strategic defense function, since heavy duck was used to make tires for trucks. The plant grew to be one of the largest in the area, comprising 10,000 spindles and 500 looms and turning out close to a million pounds of duck a month. During the 1950s the mill manufactured a variety of products, including hose and belt fabrics, filter twills, and fabric used in the construction of tires. Tire companies by this time were moving increasingly toward the use of synthetics in place of cotton, however, and in 1960 Callaway Mills began dismantling the plant, moving the machinery to spinning and twisting rooms in LaGrange.

Since the closing of the mill, a local entrepreneur attempted to use the main building for a giant flea market, but the idea did not catch on, and the plant is at present locked away behind chainlink fences, not open to visitors. The small building with a charred roof and columns directly in front of the mill was (5) the plant office, built in 1909–10. It served recently, before it caught fire, as the office for a local dealer in the native fieldstone used in building chimneys. A pillar on which he advertised his products stands beside the driveway.

To the left as you regain Main St up a steep grade is (6) the former superintendent's house. To its right is the even more imposing (7) former plant manager's house. Note the columns constructed out of local granite. The decision to build this home for the top man at the plant for $5000 led to a split among the board of directors during the 1920s, with director H. Y. McCord selling out his share and starting the Blue Ridge Coffee company in Atlanta. Notice the concave area in front and slightly downhill of a modern house on the left. Now planted in winter vegetables, this is the site of (8) the quarry from which the granite was taken to build the mill.

Down a steep, pebble-strewn bank lies (9) the dam and race on the Yellow River which powered the mill's turbines. It's a picturesque spot for a picnic, but you'd probably better push, rather than ride your bikes down to it. Originally waterwheels and long rope cables transmitted the power to operate the machinery up long rope walks to the plant.

Starting up the steep slope of River St, you enter Old Town, as the residential section on the west side of Main St is still called. Most of the houses here were built before World War One, and although almost all of them have been modified and enlarged since the residences were sold off by Callaway Mills in the late 1940s, certain clues suggest their original floor plans. Compare the house closest to the river on the left (10) with the five that line up alongside it (11). The two doors opening onto the front porch of the former tell you that this was originally a four-room house, whereas the single door on each of its neighbors indicates that these were three-room houses for company employees. The four-room structures could be used to house two families (hence the two doors), but a partition could also be opened up if one family were to occupy the whole house.

The size of the house you were given rent free before World War One by the company depended not only upon the size of your family, but upon the number of family members employed by the mill. As Frank Smith explains the policy, "They liked to have families that had a mother and father and three or four children in the family that was old enough to work. If you wanted a job at the mill and if one person was working in the family and, say, he had five or six children, he wasn't like to get a job because they didn't have housing for him. But, now, if the mother and father both worked and had five children, then they'd warrant a four-room house, and if the company had a four-room house, they'd hire 'em."

The three-room houses were built in an L-shape, with two rooms in front and the kitchen behind the left-hand front room. The adjoining space in the rear contained the back porch, where in summer was stored water from one of the two wells that were placed in each block until 1914, when the town's water tank was built. Each house had a privy in the rear, a "two-holer" for a four-room house, a "one-holer" for a two- or three-room house.

Just beyond the granite outcropping you can see on the left is (12) a row of recent brick houses built on flat rock where once stood the town's mule barn and a row of residences for servants who worked in the nearby superintendent's and plant manager's houses.

Elm St has, unfortunately, lost a number of its elms to the beetles that have caused much destruction all over the country, but a few remain. Milstead has been chosen as the site of a pilot project undertaken by the federal government to arrest Dutch elm disease, and the effort has already met with some success here. The houses on the north side of Elm (13) were considered more desirable than those along River St and were reserved for middle-level employees, above mill hands but below supervisors.

Returning to Main St, notice the empty lot on the right at the corner of Elm (14), with its stone foundation and pile of rubble. This is all that remains of the Milstead Hotel, the last of the town's three hotels to function as a lodging place, where bachelor employees lived at one time. This one also contained a swanky suite for Callaway Mills executives visiting from LaGrange. It burned down five years ago. Across Main is (15) Milstead Recreation Center, created in 1933 by refashioning another of the old hotels, the Martha Washington. The building at one time contained a library, bowling alley, swimming pool, gymnasium with the first indoor basketball courts in the county, TV room, and space for ping-pong, pool, indoor skating, archery, and midget football. Callaway Mills provided even more elaborate recreational opportunities for mill workers in LaGrange.

Main St, because of its attractive median and convenient location, was considered especially classy for residences. The houses alongside the recreation center (16) were lived in by assistant shift foremen and supervisors (known as "second hands" because they were second in command to the foremen, called "bosses" at the plant).

A striking feature of Main St is the placement of (17) the Baptist church and (18) Methodist church directly across from one another. As early as 1904 the mill's board of directors had set aside property for the building of these churches and provided that half the cost of building them would be paid by the company. In addition, during the 1930s the company contributed $12.50 per month to the maintenance costs of each church, an amount that had risen to $75 a month by the time the mill closed.

Despite the modernization and enlarging of most Milstead houses, two shotgun houses remain unchanged, so called because the rooms are lined up one behind another without any kind of hall, giving the impression that one is moving down the barrel of a shotgun. They are (19) 1610 Church St and (20) 1589 Elm St. The other four or five original shotguns in Milstead have been so modified as to be unrecognizable as such today.

Look right at the intersection of Elm and Park streets. The small wooden structure that occupies this block of Park St alone is (21) the last remaining cow stall and feed bin in Milstead. It was Callaway Mills' policy to encourage workers to keep their own cows by providing free pasturage, and they provided a barn for every two families, divided into two stalls. The company would buy the cow and deduct weekly payments from an employee's salary until its cost had been repaid, meanwhile holding a mortgage on the cow. A company pamphlet distributed to potential employees in 1935 spelled out the rationale for this policy, its inducement to economizing and incentive for family self-sufficiency. Families were also encouraged to raise vegetables and keep chickens and hogs. The densely wooded area on the other side of Park St (22) was the location of the community's hog pens, so placed because of the proximity of a creek into which refuse was hosed from the cement surfaces. Workers from as far away as Main St walked down here to feed their hogs from nearby feed bins.

The lower end of Park St (23) was where the company settled what Frank Smith calls "the ne'er-do-well people, the nonchalant type of people. Good workers, dependable workers, but people who didn't try to *be* anybody. They were considered 'poor white trash.' They were the type of people—the houses wasn't kept clean. Yet they were valuable employees to the company, regardless of what their home was. In later years the company hired a nurse, and she'd go around once a week and inspect the homes. If she reported you had a stinkin' house, they'd have the mother or father up to the office and say, 'Look, the nurse has reported that your house is not sanitary clean, health-wise'—see, they was interested in health, too."

This end of Park St must have been a sight in those early years. A spring in the front yard of the house across from the end of Church St (24) sent its water out into the street and thus down the hill. The last house on the far side of Church St (25) was originally one of only two two-room houses built in Milstead. Park St was named for the triangular plot, steeply banked, just below Main St (26) where the company planted shrubbery and colorful floral displays. The dimensions of the park are still clearly evident, although it is no longer maintained. Note that we have returned to the uphill end of Main St where the town was entered, and this park provided a cheerful welcoming spot to the Callaway property.

The water tank (27), still used, was built in 1914 to replace wells as the only source of town water. Oak St was not originally part of the Callaway property. Its southern side (28) was known as "Weenie Row," because it contained a row of shacks at which hot dogs and groceries were sold. Drinking and fighting were strictly forbidden on company land, and the rowdier element came to Weenie Row to blow off steam, safe from Callaway security guards. The row also contained two barber shops where employees could take their Saturday afternoon baths in tubs heated by steam. By the late 1930s the company had bought out the proprietors of the disreputable establishments here and demolished the shacks. Weenie Row was no more. Frank Smith lives and exercises his Justice of the Peace duties in the last house on this deadend street.

Pause when you reach Hill St. Ahead of you stretches (29) the ball park, a center of community life throughout the mill's years. Bleachers seating 500 stood at the far end of the field, and another 500 people would commonly gather on the banks that rise steeply on both sides of the diamond to watch the games, usually held on Wednesday and Saturday afternoons. A first-rate baseball team was a source of considerable pride to mill owners, who went to surprising lengths to secure good players. Mill teams were often stocked with men who had been dropped by the Southern League. Frank Smith, who played outfield for Milstead's team during the 1940s, explains how the system worked. "The company policy was, you had to be on the payroll to play. Say a ballplayer had a good job in Atlanta or somewhere else makin' good money and wanted to play ball with Milstead. Then the company'd hire him and put him on the payroll as a security watch, and they'd let him on some Sunday make *one* round. They had a policy, if you worked one day, they kept you on the payroll for six weeks before you could be discharged, see. Then he wouldn't have to come back for six weeks. He didn't want to work for Callaway, see, but they needed him."

Milstead played other mill teams, like those in Porterdale, Covington, and Buford, as well as the Southern Bag team from Atlanta, during the 1920s and '30s. By the '40s some of those mill teams had disbanded, and Milstead would have to go farther afield to play teams of their caliber. The company would hire a Greyhound bus, and the team and its fans would travel as far as Thomaston, Macon, and Cobbtown in Tattnall County. For home games on Wednesdays, all stores in Conyers would close, and half the town would come out to Milstead to see the "lintheads" play. Says Frank Smith, "Conyers didn't have a good ball field or good clubs. We never did play 'em, unless just for a good workout, see. They weren't in our class. We'd beat 'em, sometimes, 25–1, 25–0. We called it 'battin' practice.'"

On the steep bank closest to Main St (30) the company used to have terraced plantings and greenhouses where employees could buy tomato and potato plants. Occasionally a batted ball would knock out one of the greenhouses' glass panes, but Smith recalls that as an infrequent occurrence. A ball had to land in Main St on the fly to qualify as a home run. If it hit the bank first and then flew across the street, it counted as a ground-rule double.

The present site of the (31) Church of the Lord Jesus Christ, which boasts a 1300-seat auditorium, largest in the county, was the location of Milstead's two-story, nine-room brick schoolhouse. Here Frank Smith and generations of mill children were educated through the ninth grade between its construction in 1914 and 1957, when Rockdale county's schools were consolidated and Milstead children began busing to Conyers. At that point Callaway Mills supported the Conyers schools, distributing large numbers of tools, for example, to the industrial school there.

Proceeding into the residential section of Hill St, we enter New Town, built after the First World War. The first seven houses on the left side were (32) bosses' houses, except for one housing the pastor of the Baptist church. These were five-room residences, and this section of Hill St was one of the most desirable places in town to live. Notice the fine water oaks that line the street unbrokenly. The last house on the left (33) was originally the only other two-room house built in Milstead besides the one at Church and Park (the last digit of its number is missing; only "178" is visible). Here Frank Smith as a carder was lodged immediately after his marriage. As a low-level employee with no children, he was not eligible for a larger or grander house. The building is now owned by Smith's son, who has considerably enlarged it in back.

The desolate appearance of the left side of Green St is due to its trees being cut down before an ordinance was passed protecting the town's trees. As a young man Frank Smith lived in all three of the originally three-room houses on this side of Green closest to Hill St (34). When his parents moved to Milstead in 1924, they were lodged in a four-room house, but because Smith's father was the only family member employed by the mill, he was asked to move to these smaller quarters when the four-room house came into demand. At 1736 Green is (35) one of the town's two six-room houses, built in 1919 as a clinic for the care of patients ravaged by a flu epidemic brought back to this country by soldiers returning from France and Germany. Here ministered a nurse who came to Milstead originally as an employee of the Metropolitan Life Insurance Company. Says Frank Smith, "She came out here to help get the people through these epidemics, because it saved the insurance company money. Every time they saved a life, it saved them paying the insurance out, see." The nurse was later hired by Callaway Mills to continue working for the community. When the clinic was no longer needed, the building was converted into a residence.

The brick house at the corner of Cross and Spring streets (36) was the only nonframe residence in Milstead from the date of its construction, 1958, until 1977, when the row in Old Town were built. Shortly after World War Two, Callaway Mills sold off its residential property in Milstead to the employees for, typically, $3.50 a week over the course of seven years. Total purchase prices ranged from $500 to (rarely) $1500. The company may already have foreseen a shrinking of demand for its product in the postwar period and so wanted to lessen its capital investment in Milstead. In addition, the relatively prosperous war years had brought raised expectations to mill workers, who now wanted indoor plumbing and stoves. Workers' wages in this period had risen to $40–$45 a week; bosses were making perhaps $75 a week.

New St, as its name would indicate, was the last place where the company built homes for workers in the early 1920s. The four-room houses on the two ends of the street (37 and 38) were intended for what Frank Smith calls "the upper class" or "the elite"—not as fancy as bosses' homes on Hill St, but substantial structures for second hands. The gravel path leading off to the north from New St (39) goes to a cemetery·dug out by the company's black yard hands (no blacks worked inside the mill) for victims of the post-World War One flu epidemic. It contains 75–100 graves.

The majority of residences on Spring St were modest three-room houses, but 1775 Spring (40) was a four-room house, Frank Smith's first home in Milstead. This was the place the family had to vacate when the four-room house was needed for a family with more mill employees. Frank Smith recalls the company's policy at the period of his arrival in Milstead: "If you got a job, then they provided you with a house, and you had to pay a small amount of rent, like twenty cents a month per room. If you had a four-room house, you paid eighty cents a month rent. That was a big rent. You was only making—up till 'long about NRA come in [the National Recovery Administration, a Roosevelt New Deal program to regulate workers' hours and wages inaugurated in 1933]—you was only making about ten dollars and a half, ten-eighty, a week for fifty-five hours. When NRA come in, it was forty hours a week, and most people were making twelve dollars and a half a week."

Later, during the Depression, when the mill was only running one or two days a week, the company didn't charge any rent at all. Says Smith, "All you had to pay for was lights. Most people just had one bulb hanging down, didn't have any appliances. You could get by with fifteen, twenty cents a month for lights if you burned small bulbs." Since power was furnished by the company's own power plant, workers' electrical payments went to the mill.

At 1746 Spring is Milstead's only other original six-room house (41), built for a family in which four or five members worked at the mill. Beyond Cross St, the three houses on the right (42) were for "section men," so called because they were responsible for keeping a section of machinery repaired. They were paid better than average mill hands and so could afford the larger houses. The location near the mill was considered desirable.

As the street turns, the house on the left (43) was built for the office manager. During World War Two, when women often took over men's jobs inside the mill, the building was converted into a nursery where the company provided free day care. Its neighbor at 1669 Spring (44) was the supply-room clerk's house. His position was considered part of management.

Look to the right as you start up the grade leading back to Main St. The large white house sitting by itself facing the mill (45), now abandoned and boarded up, was the residence of the "master mechanic" (maintenance supervisor). Pause at the intersection of Main St. Looking left, the house beside the gymnasium (46) contained Milstead's one doctor's office. The doctor was not a company employee. In the empty space between the house and Spring St used to stand a building known as the "pressing-club house," where steam cleaning of clothes was done. A dentist's office and barber shop were upstairs, and some women's groups held meetings in the building, which burned down.

The apartment building on your right (47) used to contain three stories. The basement and ground floor were occupied by what was known as "the company store," even though the mill did not own the business directly. The basement held feed and heavy hardware, while the ground floor contained all the goods usually carried in a country general store, as well as the town post office. The top floor (now gone) was a lodge where, Smith recalls, "the Redmen, Odd Fellows, Pocahantas, Ku Klux Klan, Woodmen of the World, and Masonic Hall all had their meeting place. The Klan had a lot of strength and a lot of authority back in those days." The present location of a service station across the street (48) used to be the site of the town's drug store.

Broad St was, along with Main, a desirable address. The houses here were larger and not built according to a formulaic floor plan. The individual requirements of families were taken into account in the construction. The last house on the left, 1535 Broad (49), looks from the street like two houses set close together, one behind the other, but this is in fact an old farmhouse built around a well between the two lefthand wings.

Look up the hill to the right just before reaching Park St. A modern house set back far from the street marks the site of Milstead's original schoolhouse and Baptist church, dating from the 1890s (50). The pasture just beyond Park St (51) was known as the "bull pen." According to Frank Smith, "Everybody had cows, and the company furnished a big fine Holstein bull, weighed about a thousand, fifteen-hundred pounds. They had one man looked after that bull all week. The company kept it to service all the cows for the Milstead employees. They might have charged fifty cents for his services, or maybe twenty-five cents."

Carefully sequestered from the rest of town across what is now Ga 20 is (52) Milstead's black neighborhood, consisting of Grimes St and Yellow Rd. Here lived the "yard hands" who did the heavy hauling for the mill. They were originally located on Grimes St alone, but as the need for more laborers arose, Yellow St was added parallel to it.

The small, derelict shack next to the road that winds back to Ga 20 (53), once held the clubhouse for Milstead's Riverside Golf Course. Built in the 1930s, the nine-hole course attracted players from as far away as Atlanta. Bosses played here for free, the few town residents who could afford clubs paid 25¢ a round, and out-of-towners paid 50¢ a round. To observe one of its odder features, dismount and walk through the undergrowth some 50 feet to the northwest (54). This is one of the course's "sand greens," still clearly visible, constructed out of granite crushed into a fine sand. An advantage over grass greens was that the cup never had to be moved from the exact center because of heavy traffic.

Returning to the center of Conyers, you zigzag through a residential section of fine Victorian homes. Notice the number of columns and foundations constructed from local granite. The town's most striking granite monument is (55) the Presbyterian church on Main St.

What Is Clinton Anyhow?

A decaying refuge of Georgia aristocracy? A grazing place for Denmark Groover's brindled cow? A museum town?

by Bill Cutler

You'll change Clinton just by cycling through it. You'll set the dogs to howling, and in the racket that attends your turning ankles, you'll miss the special sounds that Clinton whispers to attentive ears: the creak of old house boards adjusting to a change of climate, the sighing of the wind through mulberry and oak and cedar, the scurry and scamper and dash of squirrels chasing each other up tree trunks and scolding in their hoarse, cross chatter, the faint twitter of a sparrow that startles into clarity the deep, full silence.

Ride through Clinton, slowly, just to get a feel for how it fits together, but then take time to walk your bike along the narrow streets that seem to crouch defensively between dense thickets of brier and honeysuckle. Lean your bike against the elegant cast-iron weeping willows that droop symmetrically forever on the fence around the cemetery, and steep yourself in the atmosphere of peace and loss and rest that crowds in upon you here beneath the giant oaks. What a thriving city lies in demure rigidity around you. How many here, how few in the few, plain, weathered houses that butt up against the narrow, vine-infested streets of Clinton.

Try not to wake up Clinton as you walk and ride its paths. Ask your questions softly of this Rip Van Winkle town that looks as if it fell asleep in 1830, shook off its drowsiness some 10 or 15 years ago, and then yawned back into unconsciousness. What's missing here that visitors to all but brand-new Georgia towns just automatically expect to find? The grand white columns, of course, the gingerbread adornments—evidence of preening planters, proud merchants, a leisure class with time and taste for finicky details.

How very restrained and chaste a town is Clinton, its dozen or so frame antebellum houses uniformly white (no bold Victorian splashes here!), their porches simple stoops or two-storied porticoes supported by plain round, fluted columns without capitals. A frontier architecture, functional, unfussy. How startling to see it juxtaposed to structures of contemporary design, equally utilitarian and stripped of ornament. In a large open lot where once the Jones County courthouse stood, flanked on two sides by homes and offices dating back almost to Clinton's founding in 1808, sits a dusty-green-and-cream trailer mounted on cinderblocks. Next to a badly weathered and unlived-in but still dignified two-story house built in 1810 stretches the one-story brick ranch-style home of its owners, looking like a refugee from a subdivision. Across from Clinton's oldest remaining structure, the McCarthy-Pope House—at present a semi-skeleton, a scattering of uprights that stayed upright with the help of braces when years of kudzu vine were pulled away from the roof—squats a large Georgia Power substation, a jungle gym of gleaming metallic pipes fastened together at right angles. In Clinton, very old confronts very new, and nothing intervenes.

Such stark contrasts befit present-day Clinton, which has recently become the focus of impassioned controversy, expressed sometimes openly and bitterly, acknowledged at other times with resignation, sadness, and embarrassment. At one extreme is a group of non-resident antiquarians belonging to a preservation society called the Clinton Foundation. They want Clinton to become a kind of museum town, an educational center comparable to Williamsburg (an analogy Foundation members are fond of drawing). At the other extreme are citizens of Jones and surrounding counties—also not Clinton residents—who look upon the semi-abandoned town as some sort of silly, useless fossil that symbolizes resistance to change and progress. Caught between these opposing forces are the 200-odd inhabitants of Clinton, deeply divided among themselves as to what values their town should represent and whether to form alliances with one side or the other to protect their image of it.

These antagonisms, of outsider against outsider, resident against resident, surfaced at a recent public hearing held in the Jones County courthouse in Gray. The issue under debate was whether or not to widen from two lanes to four lanes a highway that skirts modern Clinton and passes right across important archaeological sites in antebellum Clinton. Yet underlying the discussion were sentiments that have divided citizens of Jones County for over a century.

Setting the tone for the forces of modernity was the young chairman of the Jones County Commission, Butch Moore. Dressed in a pastel leisure suit, his long, bright blond hair meticulously sprayed to stay in place, Moore challenged the Clinton Foundation as obstructionists: "If these people are successful in stopping the four-lane, they deserve to live as Clinton did a hundred years ago, without any telephone, cars, or electricity." The audience—well over 100 people crammed into long rows of seats and overflowing into the aisles of a small courtroom, at least 90% of those present in favor of the highway—cheered enthusiastically. They exulted when R. L. Bibb, a resident along the present two-lane highway more than 70 years, gave Clinton up as a lost cause: "As far as the preservation of old Clinton is concerned, it reminds me of a man who let his horse out of the stable and is locking the door sixty years too late." They hooted and cheered and screamed their appreciation when former state representative Denmark Groover, who owns a filling station along a portion of the two-lane highway being considered for widening, mocked people who would trouble themselves about anything invisible: "Old Clinton died because of its then-citizens' desire to live in the past. In the last fourteen years, I have driven on that road more than ten thousand times, and the only thing I've ever seen on the two historical sites they desire to preserve is a brindled cow."

These and similar remarks that whipped up resentment of preservation efforts occurred in a physical setting that reflects the values of modern Gray, not those of ancient Clinton. The turreted late-Victorian courthouse built of local gray granite is itself the symbol of the political triumph effected in 1905 when the county seat was moved from Clinton to Gray. The retaining wall around the courthouse lawn is composed of blocks taken from the dismantled Clinton jail, still a sore point with residents of the older town. The flamboyant, skyward-reaching design of Gray's most distinctive structure, bustling with non-functional decoration, evokes a spirit dramatically at odds with Clinton's modesty. The contrast is heightened inside the courthouse, where all the original walls have been covered over by inexpensive plywood paneling that jars against the building's architectural style.

As you bike from Gray to Clinton, you'll sense the change in tone and atmosphere and outlook that makes the two miles separating them seem more like 200 years. Residents and friends of Clinton have their own way of describing the difference. They look down their noses at residents of Gray as untutored yokels, boors insensitive to Georgia's heritage, upstarts. It's fashionable for Clintonites to refer to themselves as "aristocrats," while people who settled in and for the newer town are seen as members of a lower class.

Historians might question that assessment as it applies to Clinton's very earliest days. A pioneer town founded on the westernmost edge of the land ceded to white settlers by the Creeks, Clinton was a rough-and-ready place at first, a hard-drinking town known for its taverns. "I've been to Clinton" was a popular saying to explain anything awry or disheveled in one's appearance.

Despite (or because of?) this, Clinton had become by 1820 one of Georgia's largest and most important county seats. The town's healthful location among cedar groves and near seven natural springs made it attractive to adventurers willing to leave the comforts of established settlements. The Clinton Female Seminary, precursor of Macon's Wesleyan College, was a widely respected leader in women's education. Connecticut native Samuel Griswold set up a cotton-gin factory at Clinton which grew into a leading Southern industry. His success led other New England merchants and professional people to follow him south and to build homes that, in many visitors' opinion, give a distinct New England character to this inland Georgia community.

The founding of Macon 12 miles away on the Ocmulgee River in the late 1820s started Clinton's long decline. Without access to river transportation, Clinton simply could not attract new businesses and aspiring entrepreneurs. As a result, when the Greek Revival style of architecture became popular in the late 1830s, Macon, not Clinton, benefitted from the vogue. Clinton's appearance was essentially fixed, frozen, in 1830, which is why the town has such special historic and architectural significance. Nowhere else in Georgia can a visitor find a nearly intact model of the "plantation-plain-style" communities that preceded the grander towns we find throughout the state today.

While distance from a river stopped Clinton's growth, its distance from railroads hastened the process of decline. Samuel Griswold ran his factory in Clinton by steam and sent out his cotton gins on wagons, but, around 1850, when the Central of Georgia rail line connecting Macon and Savannah was completed through southern Jones County, he saw the advantage of moving his operations there to gain easier access to major distribution centers. The resulting loss of population and economic resources to Clinton was considerable. Sherman's army burned down a third of the town, including the buildings that remained from Griswold's factory, during the March to the Sea in November, 1864. Shortly after the Civil War, the town was permanently sealed off from the surrounding countryside when its inhabitants voted against having the Central of Georgia spur from Macon to Monticello pass through Clinton. Accordingly, the railroad line was placed two miles east, and the new town of Gray was incorporated on its path in 1872.

At last summer's highway hearing in Gray, opponents of the Clinton Foundation talked as though modern-day Clinton should be punished because the 19th-century town had chosen not to have the railroad. In return, Foundation members lashed out at the crassness of contemporary commercialism and justified their interest in Clinton as a refuge from what they depicted as the vulgarity and emptiness of present-day life.

One of those who spoke against widening the highway on grounds that it would intrude upon the town's peacefulness was young Macon attorney Bill Cawthon. The hostility of the audience made him nervous, and his speech, which ended with a quotation from Sidney Lanier and an emotional appeal for "Georgians and Southerners" to respect Clinton's uniqueness, seemed incoherent, close to hysterical. It was hard to tell from his presentation why adding to an already existing highway would damage the town.

Away from the pressure of the public hearing, however, Cawthon expressed his feelings to me very clearly. He sees Clinton as more than a settlement containing an unusual number of buildings dating back before 1830. He walked with me to a cleared meadow, site of the Clinton Female Seminary, across the modern highway from what remains of the town. From this particular vantage-point, the highway runs invisibly through a natural depression in the terrain, and Cawthon could demonstrate the appeal of the quiet landscape surrounding the town. "The open spaces all around Clinton are very rare and special," he said, speaking in the languorous, loping cadences to which his voice naturally adjusts itself. "So far, commercial development has not only been kept out of the town, but away from the natural areas where a lot of Clinton's history was made and can still be seen. If we could convince people to give money to secure these open spaces as a part of the town's heritage, Clinton could become a valuable open-space resource for the whole Macon area."

To show further the splendors of Clinton's outskirts, Cawthon led me to another of his favorite natural areas, Jake's Woods, where black stonemason Jake Hutchings worked many years ago, fashioning into steps and hitching posts and foundation stones the giant granite boulders that tumble down the hillside. Bill Cawthon knows the individual faces of the outcroppings as though he and Jake had laid down their tools here just the day before. He showed me where an iron spike was driven into one rock to split it and then, for some reason, never retrieved. He explained the series of shallow rectangular notches that recur along neatly severed edges of many boulders: "Hobson Hardeman, who actually worked with Jake Hutchings when Hobson was a boy, told me that the way they did this, Jake started the hole with an old-fashioned drill and then he would drive a pine peg into the hole. Hobson's job was to carry buckets of water up from the spring below and pour it on the pine pegs and they would swell and burst the rock." At the edge of the woods, Cawthon pointed out a completely dressed block of granite that appeared to be waiting for the oxcart to wheel up through the trees for the journey into Clinton.

Walking through and around Clinton with Bill Cawthon brings the past to life. He knows where the early families kept house, whose niece and great-aunt visited and when, where the old town streets ran, even what the wallpaper looked like in great-grandpa's parlor. The empty lots are composted thick with memories for him.

Three months after the public hearing on the highway, I stood with Cawthon beside the newly bulldozed right-of-way where the additional lanes of traffic will soon run. He opened the trunk of his car and showed me scraps of corroded metal he picked up in the wake of highway machinery dredging the earth around the site of Samuel Griswold's cotton-gin factory. He identified one circular piece as a sawblade used by Griswold employees. We picked our way through upturned soil near where Cawthon believes a well was located at the center of the Griswold manufacturing complex—a potentially rich source of archaeological artifacts, soon to be buried beneath broad strips of asphalt. Here, where Denmark Groover saw his brindled cow, Cawthon unearthed an almost disintegrated metal fragment and carried it back to his car.

Are those rusty bits of metal worth stopping a highway for? There's no way for me to judge. In any case, the question's academic now. The enlarged road is being paved despite objections from the Clinton Foundation. The issue that remains alive is the kind of place Clinton will become, how long-gone Georgia history can best be dramatized in Clinton.

Bill Cawthon believes that the town's present residents could do more to improve its appearance. He and other Foundation members feel that antebellum structures currently endangered by neglect could be saved if inhabitants exerted their influence with the owners to sell to preservationists. Gently, sadly, his tone resigned, his startlingly bright blue eyes clouding slightly in his large, round, youthful face, Bill Cawthon expresses impatience with residents who complain they can't fix up their homes because of lack of funds.

Mrs. Valentine Barron Blair, a fourth-generation native of Clinton, is one resident who feels such pressure from Foundation members. A charter organizer of the residents' Old Clinton Historical Society, she lives in Clinton only half of every year. The front porch of her home, situated on the former courthouse square, has a sagging roof line where columns have been weakened by decades of water damage. When I talked to her last, however, she'd just finished painting the porch floor. Short, stout, graying, Mrs. Blair is not about to let the Foundation nor anyone else push her around.

We sat in her long-unpainted front parlor, whose bold and once-vivid floral patterns on sofas and walls had long since faded. "I do not want all decisions on what happens to Clinton taken away from the natives," she stated firmly but without rancor in her gentle, decorous voice. "I will do anything in the world for Clinton, but I don't like the idea of having a group of dictators tell us what is or is not to be done, because I'm going to do exactly what I'd like to do with the old house or the old place. The Foundation has plans to do all sorts of things up here. I don't think they expect to exclude the Society—we're supposed to work together—but I see the trend very clearly."

The evidence of this "trend" most upsetting to Mrs. Blair is the Foundation's choosing, over her strong objections, to restore Clinton's oldest standing structure, the McCarthy-Pope House, as it was before anyone now living ever saw it. She calls the house "the post office," since that was its function when she first knew it as a girl.

"Fifty to a hundred-thousand dollars they're going to spend restoring the post office, and they're going to take the porch off," she murmured to me in a low voice. "They say it's an addition. Well, there was a porch on that house long as I've known it, and that takes it back a ways. The porch was the making of the house. It breaks my heart. A shed, that's what they'll have when they're through with it. A hundred-thousand-dollar shed."

The Foundation's view, however, is that the porch of the McCarthy-Pope House was added after the first half of the 19th century. Since, their argument runs, Clinton is so special precisely because it visibly carries spectators back to the early decades of Georgia's antebellum period, every effort should be made to recapture the exact appearance of the town in its heyday.

That aim is pure pedantry to Mrs. Blair. She likes the town just as she's always known it, although she had no objection whatever to the highway widening that the Clinton Foundation made such a fuss about. She showed me her back porch, her favorite spot because it looks out on the spacious garden full of family memories. We strolled slowly among the giant magnolias symmetrically placed by her late husband, inhaled the fragrant tea olive, inspected the old tea roses planted by her mother. "I have more serenity of soul here than anywhere on earth. I can come completely worn out and heavy-laden, and the minute I walk through that old front door, it seems to lift. I would never want Clinton to be a place that loses its quiet charm—not I. You can come out in the early morning," she added, her thoughts breaking into disconnected phrases that carried their own inner logic. "I had a hermit thrush here on the lawn the other day. He had the most melodious song."

What *is* Clinton, anyhow? A prime target for commercial strip development along the increasingly busy highway between Macon and Gray? A refuge so precious that it must be protected not only from the outside world but from its own inhabitants? An attractive and very special residential community for people who love old houses and work in Macon or Milledgeville or Monticello? A quietly declining place where Mrs. Blair can hear her hermit thrush, and bicyclists create an uproar just by setting foot on pedal?

The passions over Clinton's future are far from spent. One thing's for sure: the town will change. The town has always changed, appearances aside. Houses change. Porches get added, porches get taken off. We can't recover the past, we just fuss with the present. History? It's now, it's here, it's us. Watch, in Clinton, what we do with it.

1978

CYCLIST'S ALMANAC

Clinton, Gray, & Jones County

Tour of Clinton: As you make your way through Clinton, try to reconstruct the bustling county seat of the 1820s in your imagination, with the help of the map. White squares indicate antebellum structures no longer standing, black squares are existing antebellum structures. Dotted lines indicate the pattern of streets originally laid out for Clinton. 1. *Courthouse, 1818;* used until county seat moved to Gray 1905; roof collapsed during storm in 1928, dismantled few years later. 2. *Three-story brick building,* c. 1820; dismantled 1890. 3. *Winship and Hutchings Store,* 1829. 4. *Tavern;* burned before 1908. 5. *Law office.* 6. *Law office;* turned, so that original front now faces side. 7. *Barron-Blair house,* 1810–20; home of Mrs. Valentine Blair. 8. *Parrish-Billue house,* 1810. 9. *Iverson Law Office,* 1821; apparently connected to Parrish home before Civil War. 10. *Gibson Hotel or Tavern.* 11. *Jane Thigpen's house;* home of Clinton's poetess. 12. *Morgan-Holsenback house,* 1811–12; torn down early 1940s. 13. *Lockett-Hamilton house,* 1830. 14. *First jail.* 15. *Oldest part of cemetery.* 16. *Methodist Church,* 1821. 17. *Town cemetery.* 18. *Jones-Ross house,* 1826; front columns not original. 19. *Clower-Gaultney house,* 1816–19; very much altered. 20. *Jones house.* 21. *McCarthy-Pope house,* 1809–10; oldest standing structure; being restored by Clinton Foundation as Welcome Center. 22. *Jail,* 1843; used until 1905, when torn down and granite blocks used for retaining wall around Gray's new courthouse. 23. *Tavern;* burned before 1908. 24. *Hutchings-Carr house,* 1810–11. 25. *Kingman-Comer house,*

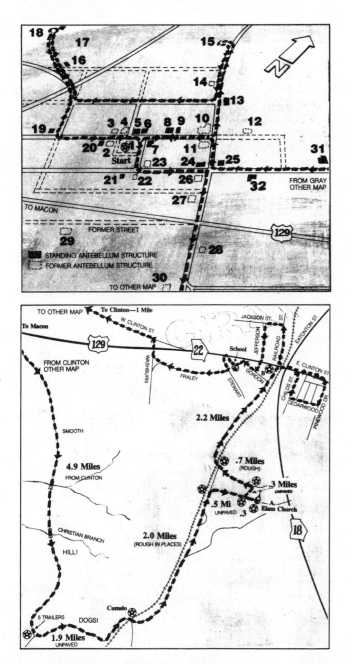

bringing a tough old bike for this tour, since the unpaved surfaces will be hard on delicate frames.

Terrain: You're close to the Fall Line here, so expect to get a good deal of exercise, even though route is short.

Hazard: DOGS! This is the doggiest route I've encountered yet. Fortunately, many of the yapping monsters are close to gnat size and more nuisance than danger, but any furry creature underneath your wheels is a matter of concern, and you'll find plenty that are big and tough.

Points of interest outside Clinton: A. *Elam Church,* established 1808; original baptistery just across dirt road from handsome church building. B. *Jones County courthouse,* scene of tempestuous highway hearing (see text).

Mirrors of Hancock County

"I turned off a paved surface at the store on to a dirt road that led past ragged pasture land where cows strolled among granite pillars, gates, and archways, the sad and solitary relics of substantial buildings, now passageways like giant looking glasses from emptiness to emptiness."

by Bill Cutler

"You *know,*" the neatly dressed lady with a frosted beehive said to me in a hushed, conspiratorial tone, "we're 85 percent."

"*Colored,*" stage-whispered the other, older woman with pinched features, as a black waitress approached.

The lady with the beehive sat at a table in the Jones Coffee Shop in Sparta; the older woman was in a nearby booth, and I stood in the aisle between them. I had joined the conversation after overhearing them discuss how "no one" in Hancock County was going to vote for Jimmy Carter for president. Well, I *had* to butt my nose into that conversation.

"What have Hancock Countians got against Carter?" I asked.

"He let us down," the older lady replied without hesitation. "We had this agitator stirring up the colored people, and we thought the governor would calm things down for us. He came, all right, and we all had our banners and posters. He listened to us, but then he went over to the other side and flew off to Atlanta with the agitator. That's the last we heard from Carter."

The frosted beehive nodded vigorously. "John McCown." She sounded the syllables as if they formed a particularly offensive expletive. "Ten million dollars he got from the government, and what is there to show for it?"

1817; altered. 26. *Winship-Cheatham house;* torn down early in this century. 27. *Lowther Hall,* 1822; Clinton's grandest mansion, probably built by distinguished architect Daniel Pratt; destroyed by fire Thanksgiving Day, 1940. 28. *Jacob Hutchings' house;* home of black stonemason born into slavery who served in Georgia General Assembly during Reconstruction; destroyed by fire early 1960s. 29. *Clinton Female Seminary;* excellent vantage-point for view of Clinton and surroundings; walk your bike through pecan orchard to site. 30. *Gov. McDonald's house,* c. 1818; second story now believed to form first story of another house a short distance north. 31. *Iverson-Edge house,* 1821–26. 32. *Pope-Barron house,* 1818; in summer, almost swallowed up by kudzu.

Distance: An 18.2-mile loop, including tours of Clinton and Gray.

Cycling conditions: Extremely varied. Unpaved surfaces indicated on map; road south from Clinton newly black-topped and excellent, back streets of Clinton rough, road north to Gray from Cumslo adequate, though with many rough places. I'd advise

"We never had any trouble, you know, with race until he came in from outside," the older lady rushed along, her bright eyes dancing.

"Well, how do folks like yourselves feel about life in Sparta now?" I asked.

"We'd all move away tomorrow if we could find someone to buy our houses," the frosted beehive said with determination and, as if to prove the point, stood up and moved to another table closer to the door.

"Who's that?" I asked my one remaining informant.

She sniffed audibly and tossed her head. "Mrs. Lewis. Her husband runs the furniture store down the street. They've never been the slightest help to us in the Sparta Historical Society. Oh, we have *plans*. *We're* not moving out. Looks like we've got some people going to help us restore our beautiful old hotel. Don't you pay any mind to her."

My optimistic friend introduced herself as Mrs. E. A. Reese. On one matter, she and Mrs. Lewis were in perfect agreement and echoed many other whites I talked to in Sparta: they are all bitter about the closing of their county hospital, a disaster they attribute solely to the incompetence of black administrators. Existence in Sparta seems to them precarious, a feeling I heard most poignantly expressed by Miss Sarah Frank Little, owner of the oldest house in town. Walking about with me among fine antiques in nobly proportioned rooms with wide-planked floors, Miss Little spoke, with a slight catch in her voice, of her hopes and fears for Sparta, her family's home for many generations: "If we can just keep Sparta. You see, we're about 50–50 here in town. I don't believe the blacks are interested in restoration, and that's about all we have."

At the heart of white residents' unease is the recognition that while they still control the mayor's and other offices of Sparta city government, all Hancock County positions except for the sheriff's are held by blacks. Every white and black resident of the county knows how that situation was brought about: because the "outside agitator" John McCown came in from South Carolina and registered enough black voters to tip the political balance outside Sparta.

That act alone might have been enough to arouse whites' hatred of McCown, but he influenced Hancock County's life in many other ways as well. He set up the East Central Committee for Opportunity (ECCO), an anti-poverty agency in the small town of Mayfield, near the county's eastern edge. Through the U.S. Office of Economic Opportunity, McCown brought federal funds into the Mayfield area to start a catfish farm and airline, build a large housing project, and launch other programs intended to provide employment for rural blacks.

John McCown recently died in a private plane crash, near Mayfield, at the height of a federal investigation into alleged improper uses of government funds by ECCO. Shortly afterwards, eight of McCown's former associates were indicted by a federal grand jury on charges of conspiring to defraud the government. The indictments allege, among other things, that funds were diverted to improve McCown's personal property.

I had a long talk in Mayfield with McCown's successor as director of ECCO, James Hunt, who also heads the Hancock County school board. Although at first he put a brave face on ECCO's mission, eventually he had to admit that the future looked bleak. The catfish farm is closed, the housing project bankrupt, all of ECCO's other enterprises in a state of limbo.

Efforts to provide local employment for the destitute rural population have failed. Hunt says he knows Hancock residents who commute all the way to Atlanta to work in filling stations. Industries in surrounding counties provide a few jobs, but Hancock does not even begin to support her own citizens.

The full story of John McCown's empire remains to be written. Its collapse has received statewide publicity and has fixed Hancock County in many Georgians' minds as a symbol of race relations at their worst. Yet I was not attracted to the county by reports of failure, but rather in search of a success story little known today, one that 40 years ago proclaimed Hancock County as the bright symbol of hope for rural and urban blacks and, by extension, for rural whites as well.

Near Hancock's northern boundary, 11 sparsely populated miles north and west of Mayfield, lies the community of Springfield. It's not designated as such on state road maps, not marked by so much as a single roadside sign. Even from the seat of a bicycle—the best location I know of from which to read and inwardly digest a landscape—I'd never have remarked its presence without prior guidance. A pretty church and an unkempt general store built of granite blocks were the only signs I saw of communal life there.

I turned off a paved surface at the store on to a dirt road that led past ragged pasture land where cows strolled among granite pillars, gates, and archways, the sad and solitary relics of substantial buildings, now passageways like giant looking glasses from emptiness to emptiness. At the edge of one field I found a cottage sinking back into the ground. Its door stood open, and wisteria grew across the sill and crept along the floor.

Yet amid this desolation one intact monument still stands, a testimonial to the once-thriving community of which it was physical and spiritual heart. The arched wooden entrance to this impressively designed log structure bears the carefully etched words "Camilla-Zack Country Life Center," and a plaque beneath is dedicated to Benjamin Franklin Hubert, "apostle of country life, leader and inspirer of men." By stirring up my imagination and drawing on what I'd read and heard about, I could reanimate these quiet pastures, repopulate the empty road, rebuild the ruined structures, and feel my way delicately back to times when one of Georgia's most extraordinary families gave leadership to Hancock and the nation from this spot.

So here I am in the summer of 1935, facing the Log Cabin Center, as the building was most commonly called. I'd never have known this was the heart of the Depression. Hundreds of people are bustling about in purposeful activity. The men and women with books under their arms are rural teachers from all over Middle Georgia taking part in the summer school program started here by Dr. Ben Hubert in his capacity as president of Georgia State College (later renamed Savannah State). Immediately to my left I see white-jacketed doctors and nurses passing in and out of the Mary Otis Willcox Rural Health Center. In a clearing behind the log cabin, children of the community have gathered for classes on the advantages of rural life taught as a demonstration project in conjunction with the summer school.

I tiptoe inside the log cabin, trying not to disturb the health lecture for teachers and community residents going on in the beautifully proportioned main assembly room. In one corner I find an extensive exhibit of canned products and other farm necessities made by local citizens.

Back outside, I stroll through crowds of people toward the granite store, past teachers' cottages and the hen houses Ben Hubert had built, the first in the area, to show local farmers how to raise chickens scientifically. A little farther on, at the dairy barn, I observe Ben himself with his most prized possessions, some of the Hereford beef cattle he introduced to Middle Georgia five years earlier.

So far, every single soul I've seen has been black, but there, coming out of the community store, is Mrs. Morgan, a white neighbor whose family plays an active part in activities at the Log Cabin Center. She reminds me that, despite segregation, the Louisville Kiwanis Club held its annual meeting there two years before. After all, it's the best facility anywhere around, and local white business people are proud to show their support for Ben Hubert's programs. Why, Ben's always doing favors for them, bringing back crates full of fresh shrimp every time he returns home from Savannah.

Folks are hurrying now toward the dairy barn where Ben's getting ready to show off a prize bull to his good friend Gene Talmadge, the governor, who has driven down specially for the occasion. It riles the white citizens of Hancock some that Gene, who's always preaching segregation and race superiority, can find time to visit with Ben Hubert and never stops to chat with *them*. But there's no taking it away from Ben—he knows how to get things done. Look at all those Northern philanthropists like George Foster Peabody whose money keeps Ben's programs going. Even President Roosevelt has sent letters of commendation, though no government funds have been spent here.

Quite a story, Ben's success. But he didn't start from nothing. His parents Camilla and Zack, in whose memory the Log Cabin Center was built, must have had wills of iron. Zack and two of his brothers were the first blacks to own land in Middle Georgia after the Civil War. Zack married Camilla Hillman in Springfield, and they raised 12 children.

That was accomplishment enough in times when life expectancy was short, but that was just the start. Zack, who had learned to read and write illegally as a slave from his master's son, was determined to send his children to college. Through enormous sacrifice and by juggling their scholastic schedule to accommodate the harvest and planting, all seven sons graduated from Morehouse, four of the five daughters from neighboring Spelman (the youngest daughter was a graduate of Jackson College in Jackson, Mississippi). From there, they went on to more positions of prominence and distinction than all but a few families in the country can boast—to become presidents of colleges, professors, principals of schools, teachers, pastors, the executive secretary of the New York Urban League, and secretary to Mrs. Booker T. Washington.

Even after he'd built the church that still stands at Springfield, Zack Hubert worshipped at the white church in Powelton, and nobody said him nay. The pastor there, Rev. J. H. Kilpatrick, introduced him to advanced agricultural principles, such as rotating and diversifying his crops.

Zack Hubert's farm was entirely self-sufficient. In addition to raising his cash crop, cotton, Zack cut the lumber for his house at his own sawmill, raised all the family's food, made and sharpened his plows at his own blacksmith shop, shoed all of his horses, and respoked his wagon wheels himself. Camilla, meanwhile, made all the family's clothes.

Thus, Ben, the fifth son, had been exposed from infancy to sound, rigorous farming practices. From Morehouse, he went on to graduate work at the Massachusetts Agricultural College in Amherst and then to become director of agriculture at Tuskegee Institute. When Zack and Camilla died in the mid-'20s, their heirs jointly decided that Ben should carry on and extend their work, since he alone among the children had specialized in farming techniques.

Ben turned the Hubert holdings into demonstration projects that taught the most innovative and scientific ideas for improving agricultural production. He was above all an educator. He dreamed of teaching others the satisfactions of farm life and providing an alternative to the urban ghettoes that had lured blacks out of the rural South during and after World War I. School was at the heart of Ben Hubert's vision of the good life.

But where was the school? I found no sign of it anywhere near the Log Cabin Center and so resolved to ask two well weathered men I noticed reclining on the ground just across the unpaved road. One held a roughly handrolled cigarette between his lips, and otherwise the only object I could see inside his mouth was one triangular tooth. His skin might have been stained with nicotine or shoe polish. I had no idea if he was a "black" or "white" man. His companion, I took a flying guess, was white, though, like myself, an off or somewhat grimy white. He wore a CAT cap whose visor kept his eyes in shadow, and several days' stubble covered his jaw and lower lip. He spat almost without stopping and aimed his spittle with unerring accuracy.

"What happened to the school that used to be out here?" I asked by way of introduction.

"They done took it down and carried it to Sparta," said the man with one visible tooth, getting to his feet. "I do believe if Mr. Ben'd been alive, they'd never have done it. Was three–four hundred children could walk to that school at one time. Some of them walked six miles. It hurts a community to lose its school."

"If you folks'd been smart 'n' got some of that money John McCown got over in Mayfield, bet you could have kept it," his companion said. (That tipped me off that the nicotine-stained man must be "black.")

"What happened to all those families with the three or four hundred children?" I wanted to know.

"They give up farmin' and moved to the cities," the one-toothed man replied. "I reckon the gov'ment could save money payin' for them to stay here 'stead of in those cities"—and here he reached out his hand and almost touched me, then winked with stagy emphasis, a gesture equivalent to a nudge from someone else.

Just then a shiny yellow Hancock County school bus drove down the unpaved road past us, a handful of children scattered on its seats.

Why did Hancock Countians give up farming? Cotton is still planted in the surrounding counties, but as I pedaled between Mayfield, Sparta, and Springfield in late October, I noticed no evidence of the harvest there. I pushed past no fields whitened as by a sudden and capricious snowstorm, saw no tag ends of the picking blown about the edges of the roads like stuffing from a mattress that had torn apart at the rough hands of moving men. Where once were cultivated fields are now just pine trees, ridge after ridge of them, in different stages of development, from saplings through skyscrapers to bare stumps just cut. I passed no tractors, mowers, farm rigs, only elongated flat-bed trucks bearing trunks to pulp mills.

The entire county lacks significant agricultural production. Bureau of Census figures show a scant 150 persons 16 years of age or older employed on farms either as laborers or managers in 1970, out of a total Hancock County population of more than 9,000. I asked Red Jernigan, an old white business associate and friend of Ben Hubert's, about the reasons for this dramatic change in the county he's lived in all but four of his 80 years. Jernigan believes the government's farm subsidy program busted a hole in the local economy by paying farmers to keep land out of production. "People don't realize it, but that program ruint this country," he told me in his characteristic "don't contradict me, boy" voice. He speaks out of the side of his mouth, perhaps because the whole bottom part of his head seems to have collapsed, leaving him with no lower jaw.

Red Jernigan sat on the edge of a wide bed in the modest, back-country house he's shared with his wife for 55 years. She rocked vigorously and knitted in a corner, alert to fill in whenever Red's memory groped for a name or place. In pragmatic, country man's terms he contrasted Ben Hubert and John McCown as leaders. "When you worked for Ben, you worked. He didn't throw that money away he got. He really used it right. John was the kind of man—he bought a bunch of cows down there—he didn't have a bit more reason—bought 200 head. I sold him some, Mr. Bertram down here sold him some, Mr. Dickens—and he just carried 'em down and put 'em in that sand pasture and pastured 'em to death and then hauled 'em off and give'm away, carried 'em to public auction. He didn't have no business sense 't all. Ben was right opposite to that."

The Jernigans gave me a new perspective from which to judge John McCown's recent failure. They criticize the whites in Sparta for thinking only of the town's surface appearances instead of the county's economic needs. Community development funds were used to pretty up the sidewalks and storefronts downtown, when, according to the Jernigans, what the town and county really need is an adequate water system. "How you goin' to attract industry if you ain't got no water, boy?" Red asks scornfully. Like everyone else I talked to, he's gloomy about the future of Hancock County: no farming, no jobs, no likelihood of new jobs.

Maybe the deck was hopelessly stacked against McCown from the start, I got to thinking after a talk I had with Rev. R. E. Edwards, a close associate of Ben Hubert's throughout the Log Cabin Community's heydays of the late '30s and early '40s. We sat on Rev. Edwards' scrubbed and tidy front porch, surrounded by brightly blooming sultana plants. A hundred yards to our right stood the Springfield Church where he had served as pastor for many years. Directly across the highway, he told me, in what is now an unkempt field, had stood the imposing, two-story Hubert homestead until it was struck by lightning less than 20 years ago. Rev. Edwards' voice is extremely deep, melodic, his phrases carefully chosen, as though a congregation visible only to himself attended every word. His close-cropped, silver-gray hair frames a large, round, kindly face, his eyes turn aside to scrutinize the past.

I asked him how Ben Hubert might have handled the recent breakdown in communications between white and black residents of the county, and he set his deliberate, cautious judgment to work on the question. "I don't think Dr. Hubert could have completely stopped the movement. With his stabilizing influence, it wouldn't have got out of hand like it did. But you know, that was in the period when Dr. King's movement was attractive, a period of rebellion. And the truth of it is, many injustices had been carried on for so long, and this was a violent reaction when John McCown came in here. Our people just forgot all about, as I see it, a sense of continuity and white friends that had been nice to them over the years. They just went off with McCown."

He paused and then continued. "As you probably know, they run the county now, politically, but the white folks still got the money. In other words, we don't have too much to run." He laughed, a high, long laugh. "It was a most unfortunate situation. I tried to reason with them: 'Whether we want to admit it or not, white people still control the pursestrings, and we don't want to alienate them because we need them to help bring in some industry for our people to work.' But, no, they didn't see that. They thought cursing white folks out was a big thing."

Rev. Edwards' cast of mind was set in the old pre-civil rights days, but he's no Uncle Tom. His son was the first black child to attend Hancock County's integrated school system. I heard no nostalgia in his voice for the period when Ben Hubert planned his successful community by following the advice of Booker T. Washington: "Let down your bucket where you are."

Hubert had not set out to challenge the status quo, as John McCown had done. He was the great conciliator who knew that, to get things done for his people, he needed to curry favor where it would do most good. In Rev. Edwards' view, the soul went out of Ben Hubert—and, hence, out of the Log Cabin Community—when Hubert lost the presidency of Georgia State College. He'd pegged his fortunes too closely to Governor Eugene Talmadge, Edwards believes, so that when Talmadge lost his bid for reelection in 1942, Hubert became a political casualty along with him.

With the rural teachers' summer school program no longer centered at Springfield and with blacks leaving the farm in increasing numbers throughout the '40s, the Log Cabin Community dwindled and eventually died. But supposing, just supposing, that Ben Hubert had succeeded in the hardest, most revolutionary aspect of his program—getting farmers to cooperate rather than to labor separately as competitors. Mightn't the whole sad history of Hancock County have turned out differently, and very much better?

For Ben took the word "community" at its face value. Residents, he intended, were to plan together, working on an ambitious five-year program to improve production. The Log Cabin Center was to be the place, among other things, where decisions affecting the entire community could be collectively hammered out. The granite store was run on a cooperative basis, with profits shared proportionally according to the quantity of customers' purchases. Log Cabin Flour was made from wheat threshed on a cooperatively owned machine.

I asked Rev. Edwards how successful Ben Hubert had been in persuading his fellow farmers to pool their efforts. "Well, I don't know really, suh, Mr. Cutler. It never really got off the ground. You know about farmers. A *few* got the message, but it wasn't overwhelming. A few people who had a little more imagination and foresight than others, they tried to raise cattle like him." How about Dr. Hubert's success in persuading farmers to diversify their crops? "Well, it was spotty."

The day when the individual small farmer could make a living in Hancock County is gone forever, and nothing will ever bring him back. The 27,000 acres of county land that belonged to black owners in 1940 is now mostly in the hands of the big pulpwood companies who grow pines on it, and those pine trees don't bring in jobs for county residents.

So Ben Hubert failed, in one sense. He *didn't* make farm life satisfying to rural blacks over the long haul. Yet in another way of thinking, his associates failed *him*. He had shown them the direction to follow—owning land and businesses cooperatively. With enough small farmers working and trusting each other, combined with a little of that pioneer toughness Zack and Camilla Hubert had so much of, just maybe there wouldn't have been any need or call for John McCown in Hancock County.

1977

CYCLIST'S ALMANAC

Hancock County

Routes: Entire loop comprises 39 miles. Distance may be shortened into a city and county loop by taking the paved road that runs between Culverton on Georgia 16 and Smyrna Church on Georgia 22. Park in front of the courthouse in Sparta or in the large dirt area facing the ECCO office building in Mayfield. The Sparta-Smyrna Church-Culverton loop is 19.2 miles, the Mayfield-Culverton-Springfield loop 28 miles.

Cycling conditions: Fair. Georgia 16 is very smooth, the rest of the surfaces rough aggregate. Unpaved surface less than a mile total from the Springfield store to the Log Cabin Center and back. Try to plan your trip to stay off Georgia 16 during morning and afternoon busy hours. This is the main highway between Warrenton and Milledgeville and attracts a good deal of truck and other commercial traffic.

Terrain: Rolling; seldom flat. One humongous hill outside Mayfield on the way to Georgia 16 (precipitous in both directions—no way to avoid it).

Points of interest inside Sparta: (A) *Hancock County Courthouse,* built 1881–83 by Parkins and Bruce, of which John Linley in *Architecture of Middle Georgia* says, "Not many cities have so interesting a public building; almost none have a grand entrance with such a building as the focal point." Flamboyant and stately; to appreciate it best, look back as you're leaving town at the top of any rise along highway 15-16-22. (B) *Graves House and Barn,* fine examples of

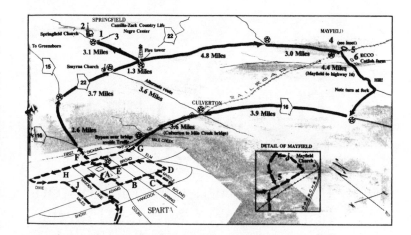

flamboyant Victorian style; notice especially the scalloped scrollwork along the eaves and in the gable ventilator of the barn. (C) *Ethridge-DuBose-Peck House* at 513 Boland Street, dated circa 1853. Unusually fanciful scroll saw work across the porch and along the eaves; Victoriana at its most delightful. (D) *Pomegranate Hall* at 322 Adams Street, dated circa 1830; fine Greek Revival home with beautiful columns, graceful fanlighted door, and handmade brick painted white. (E) *LaFayette Hotel,* formerly the Edwards House and Drummer's Home, built either in 1840 or in the mid-1850s on the site of the old Eagle Tavern where LaFayette was entertained in 1825. Magnificent two-story portico across the whole front of the building. Presently decayed, but local preservationists have hopes of seeing it restored once again for public use. (F) *Terrell-Stone House,* dated circa 1820, remarkable Italianate home of Dr. William Terrell, founder of the University of Georgia's agriculture school. (G) *Harley-Rives House* at 720 Elm Street, dated circa 1850; unobtrusive classical elements. (H) *Rossiter-Little House* at 223 Broad Street, just beyond bike route turnoff onto Miles Street. Built before 1812 and generally believed to be the oldest house in Sparta; remodeled several times. Given by present owner to Hancock County Society for Historical Preservation. Can be visited by appointment only; call (404) 444-5140. (J) *Abercrombie-Skinner-Morris House* at 525 Maiden Lane, circa 1805–1810, one of Sparta's earliest dwellings; note the handmade brick in the great chimneys.

Points of interest outside Sparta: (1) *Former cooperative store* for the Log Cabin Community made of granite blocks; once known as "the cleanest store in the county"; no longer. (2) *Springfield Church* built by Zack Hubert, now being bricked over. Hubert family cemetery to the left side as you face the church, with graves of Ben Hubert and his parents Zack and Camilla (their headstone faces the road instead of away from it like most of the rest). (3) *Log Cabin Center,* also known as Camilla-Zack Country Life Center, built in 1932 of pine logs taken from the surrounding forest and native granite, designed to emphasize its rustic origins. Center of a National Historic District, officially designated by the U.S. Department of the Interior. Inside of the cabin may be visited by applying at caretaker's cottage directly across unpaved road; ask for Mr. Omar Reid. A huge granite fireplace is the focal point of the large central community room, and natural cedar posts are used as supportive columns in the library and on the front porch. Portraits of Northern philanthropists who helped Ben Hubert launch his projects and photographs of leaders in the Association for the Advancement of Negro Country Life on walls of community room. (4) *Housing project* built by John McCown's East Central Committee for Opportunity (ECCO). (5) *ECCO offices* in Mayfield. The large two-story Victorian house to the left as you face the offices was bought by McCown and used as a guest house. (6) *ECCO catfish farm,* now shut down.

Pedaling Through Uncle Remus Country

Putnam County and Eatonton, home of Joel Chandler Harris, Uncle Remus and Brer Rabbit provide the geography for this bicycle tour.

By Bill Cutler

Putnam County adjoins Morgan County to the south, but the two places are worlds apart in atmosphere and appearance. Morgan County's fields are lush, its antebellum houses immaculately trim and prosperous looking. Eatonton and Putnam County, by contrast, have seen better days. The area has been losing population since the First World War, and as you pedal through the countryside, you'll notice abandoned farm houses, some of them nobly proportioned and delicately molded. Town houses, too, are often faded and peeling, their elegance muted but still apparent.

I worked out the route shown here (map) in Putnam County by studying the county map, and discovered in the process some interesting points of reference I wanted to explore. The route I eventually pedaled is a challenging one—roughly forty miles with a couple of hard grades, but almost the entire distance is on well-paved roads practically free of traffic.

The tour is planned to accommodate either day-trippers or weekend campers. You can begin and end the circle in Eatonton (simplest place to park is next to the Putnam County courthouse) or at the campsites fronting Lake Rock Eagle.

The campsites at Lake Rock Eagle are extremely picturesque. You're at the edge of the Oconee National Forest here, and the tall stands of pine throughout the region are magnificent. Fishing is a popular pastime in the lake (rowboats are available for hire at a nearby pavilion), but I believe hunting is prohibited. A doe and her fawn darted across the road near the campsites just in front of me. I like to think they are protected in that beautiful spot.

Camping there may not be so tranquil in the summertime. The state 4-H Club Center, a mammoth establishment, is located just across the lake and the whole area is probably a beehive of activity. But when I was there in late September, I felt, on my nearly-silent bicycle, like a small element in a vast natural scene that had changed little since prehistoric times.

And prehistory is just around the corner. Take the road that loops beside the campsites to the east, away from the 4-H Center. A hundred yards or so uphill you'll notice a spur road off to the right, and at the end of this short lane one of the most astonishing native sights in the state of Georgia awaits you. You have to climb up three flights of wooden steps inside a brick tower to take it all in, but there at your feet lies the gigantic figure of an eagle in full flight formed out of innumerable white quartz rocks of various sizes. Apparently no one knows the purpose or origin of the monument, but people have theorized that it is a ceremonial mound with religious significance. An almost illegible plaque erected by the Georgia Society Colonial Dames specifies the dimensions of this great eagle: 102 feet long, a wingspread of 120 feet, and a depth of breast of eight feet.

Putnam County provides one other, very different link back to an ancient non-western civilization. That link is Joel Chandler Harris, who was born and grew up in the Eatonton area and came in contact with the centuries-old African animal tales that were passed down through generations of American slaves. Our bike route passes Turnwold, a plantation east of town, the home of "Uncle Remus," where Harris lived and worked as a printer's apprentice during the Civil War on what was probably the only newspaper ever printed on a Southern plantation.

As the route enters Eatonton, we turn off state highway 16 past some tennis courts that mark the location of Harris' birthplace. The fact that the home was not preserved (nor his later Eatonton residence, across the street from what is now the Uncle Remus Museum) is preparation for the discovery that Eatonton's recent past has been cherished less tenderly than Harris himself cherished Uncle Remus' folklore.

Yet let us take pleasure in what remains, and it is considerable. Eatonton's Madison Avenue boasts as handsome an array of domestic and commercial structures as any small town can provide. As you approach Madison Avenue along Church Street, you'll see imposing Panola Hall, with its gigantic columns, facing you. According to town legend, the house has been periodically haunted by a ghost named Silvia, who snobbishly appears only to aristocrats.

A block south, on the same side of Madison Avenue, is a magnificent house that seems from the outside to be ripe territory for ghosts. This is the Slade-Harris House, built in 1836, fronted by fine Ionic columns. John Linley, author of *The Architecture of Middle Georgia,* ranks the building "of national importance." At present, however, it's languishing in disrepair. Shutters are hanging loose from their screws, there's a big gap in the iron fence along the sidewalk, shrubs straggle up beside the fence. The splendid proportions are still evident enough, but it's a melancholy splendor.

On a return visit to Eatonton, I stopped at the Slade-Harris House with BROWN'S GUIDE photographer Edmund Marshall to take a picture of the decaying grandeur. Before he could click the shutter, a lady emerged from the interior and pleaded with us not to photograph the house in its present condition. This turned out to be Mrs. Phil Harris, last of a family that had long owned the house. She told us it had just been sold to a young architect, who was planning to restore it. "Take a picture after it's been fixed up," she begged. Of course we honored her request, and we look forward to seeing the house again in a year's time, when once again it does its avenue proud.

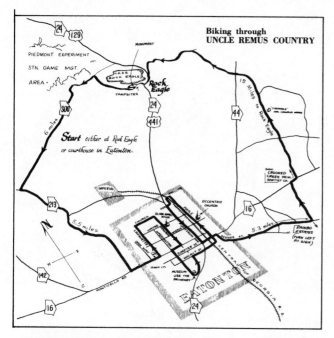

Biking through
UNCLE REMUS COUNTRY

Pedaling Putnam County—*Forty miles round trip with some fairly difficult grades, this is no easy route, but it will provide a rewarding glimpse of town and country.*

Start at either Rock Eagle Park where there are camping facilities or at the county courthouse in Eatonton.

Some readers may elect to divide the map into sections, setting up cars to shuttle bikes and riders back and forth.

Roads are well paved and practically free of traffic.

Madison Avenue contains other notable features—an imposingly gleaming white church with interesting stained glass in its facade; the antebellum Reid-Stubbs House with porches all around, at the corner of Harris Street; and fine rows of brick storefronts in need of restoration as you approach Monticello Road and the town square.

Washington Street is another handsome thoroughfare, not only on account of its pleasant modest houses but because of the arcade of fine trees that line the roadway on both sides. At the foot of Washington Street, on the left, sits the Uncle Remus Museum, an old slave cabin moved to its present site in Eatonton many years ago. A couple of rows of cotton preen picturesquely in front of the cabin—the only cotton I saw in the whole of Putnam County—and an old blacksmith shop invites your curiosity around to the side. Behind the cabin is a facsimile of Brer Rabbit's briar-patch.

Inside the cabin you'll find an array of objects mentioned in the Uncle Remus stories, as well as dioramas depicting many of the most celebrated incidents. You'll enjoy talking to the museum's curator, Mrs. Norma Wiliford, a soft-spoken Southern lady of the old school, still fretting over scalawags and carpetbaggers.

Before leaving Eatonton, you'll pass beside an extremely handsome modern structure, the Peoples Bank, built in 1965, whose curved openings frame banks of indoor plan . Then the route crosses the railroad tracks and parallels them on Maple Street. I think you'll enjoy the very odd facade of the church at Maple and Harris—a hodgepodge of more architectural elements than you're likely to find in five churches, scrunched to-

gether in promiscuous disarray. More fine homes await you when you turn on Phillips to get back to Jefferson Avenue. Then past the rather ridiculous statue of Brer Rabbit in front of the county courthouse, to your car, if you started in Eatonton, or back into open country if you began the round trip at Rock Eagle.

A word of warning: Because Putnam County is so sparsely populated, you'll find no refreshment stands or restaurants anywhere outside Eatonton. There's a coke machine at the dock where boats are rented on Lake Rock Eagle, and that's it. That being the case, you should carry with you whatever food and drink you'll need. For quick energy that won't weigh you down, apples, oranges, and raisins are good to carry along, as are granolas and peanut butter sandwiches.

1973

Plan Your Own Trip With County Highway Maps

If you would enjoy planning your own bike trips on little-traveled back-country roads in Georgia, you should know about the county maps available from the state Department of Transportation. They show all the lanes and byways not indicated on state highway maps, and they also inform you of points of interest you might not otherwise have known about.

Most of the county maps are five–seven years old, and so some of the roads shown as unpaved have been resurfaced in the meantime for good cycling. In rare cases, a road not even shown on the county map will have been recently built, but on the whole you'll find the maps an accurate guide to present road conditions. Maps are $1.50 each. Call 656-5336 for ordering information.

So Long, Cotton; Hello, Hard Times

How Sandersville rode the railroad to prosperity and left Gibson waiting at the station.

by Bill Cutler

"Those hills're just full of chalk," Elvin H. Chalker said, gesturing vaguely in a southerly direction from inside his grocery store in Gibson.

"You mean, kaolin?" I asked.

"I call it 'chalk,'" said Mr. Chalker, the mayor of Gibson

and former chairman of the Glascock County Commission. "Those chalk companies've got options on all that land down there. My son's got twenty-five hundred acres on the Ogeechee, and they've got options on it. I regret it, but they do. What with the chalk companies and the pulpwood companies, there's not much land left in the county for farmin'." Mr. Chalker looked at the clock hanging on the back wall of his store. "Four o'clock on a Saturday afternoon. Time was, you couldn't hardly move around the square for all the people come into town to do their shoppin' Saturday afternoons."

He looked out his front windows on the square, empty now save for a police officer in white shirt and shiny badge sauntering near the police booth that is the only structure inside the square itself. "I can remember when the cotton was piled so high out there," Chalker said, his right hand extended three feet above the ground. "Now I don't suppose there's a hundred acres in the county planted in cotton. They loaded it at the depot here and shipped it out. Funny thing. That little spur of the Georgia and Florida Railroad that came here could've been the line to take all that chalk out. It goes right over to where that chalk is in Washington County. You know, all the profit in railroading comes from shipping merchandise out at the point of origin. Leastways, that's what they tell me. We could've made a heap of money if that old line hadn't been done away with. They send it up from Sandersville on their own little old railroad."

My mind clicked back to the railroad crossing in Sandersville which I had passed over just a few hours before. Sitting on a track near the highway was an engine with the word "SANDERSVILLE" emblazoned in red letters across its side. The Sandersville Railroad owns only four miles of track, but they're four immensely profitable miles. Sandersville flaunts its wealth proudly, too. Block after block of neatly kept, substantial Victorian homes line the main streets, and the countryside is dotted with handsome farms whose fertile fields stretch away symmetrically to the horizon. It's a shock to cross the Ogeechee and enter Glascock County, whose steep hills are covered with scrub undergrowth and ragged stands of pine and whose towns appear close to abandonment. If the kaolin companies start quarrying Glascock's hillsides, will the local economy benefit? Will the chalk in them thar hills turn out to be gold for the citizens of Gibson and the county's other towns or only for investors from other places?

1980

CYCLIST'S ALMANAC

Kaolin Country

This 20-mile triangular route takes in all three of Glascock County's incorporated towns. Most of it traverses the portion of the county rich in kaolin deposits, and you will see little evidence of farming. The road surfaces vary considerably in roughness, and much of the route is hilly, with numerous steep grades. Traffic should present no problems.

Park your car and begin the tour at (1) *former courthouse square* in Gibson. Until about 1915 the courthouse sat in the middle of

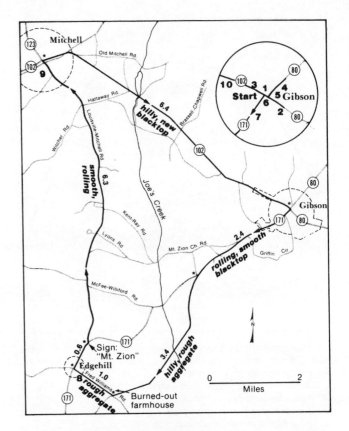

the green space here, as it does in similar settings in other Georgia county seats, but the county commissioners voted to build a *new courthouse* a half block away (2), and the old frame building was bought by a private citizen and moved a half block down the street in the other direction (tour point 10). In the middle of the square stands a plain obelisk monument honoring the memory of Calvin Logue, who gave 20 acres of land as a site for the town of Gibson in 1858. In that same year Logue was the county's first representative in the Georgia legislature, and he served as Gibson's first postmaster before enlisting in the Confederate Army. He was killed at Deep Bottom, Virginia, on August 16, 1864. The monument was erected in 1952.

At one corner of the square stands (3) the *Bank of Gibson*, Glascock County's only financial institution. Catercorner across the square and a short distance up Ga 80 toward Warrenton stands an imposing brick residence with green shutters, the empty *Isom Peebles Home* (4). Peebles (1849–1931) was a prosperous merchant, said to have owned five plantations. He was Gibson's first mayor, serving three terms, a Justice of the Peace, and county treasurer for two years. His widow died several years ago, and the house has been tied up in legal entanglements ever since.

On the same side of the square is Gibson's *Family Opry* (5) an old movie house where gospel singing is performed by local groups Saturday evenings 7–11. Gibson Mayor E. H. Chalker had been interested in renovating the movie house for a town hall some years back, but could not secure the necessary backing. You'll enjoy chatting with the mayor at (6) *E. H. Chalker Store,* one of the few local business still in operation in Gibson. His small stock of goods includes soft drinks. As you head out of town on Ga 171, notice on the left the white frame building with double-story porches close to the road, (7) *Old Swint Hotel,* now a private residence. Here the drummers who sold merchandise to local businesses would stay and eat, in close proximity to the old G & F (Georgia and Florida) depot, also now a residence.

There's not much left of (8) *Edgehill*, whose population is given as 46 on a 1974 map of Glascock County. It was named for a community in Virginia by a native of that state, Mrs. J. C. A. Wilcher, who taught school here. Her husband was the local representative to the Georgia General Assembly, and the community was previously known as the Jule Wilcher Quarters. A little more remains of (9) *Mitchell,* although most of its handsome brick storefronts are abandoned now. The town was incorporated in 1896, having grown up around a depot on the G & F Railroad. It was named in honor of R. M. Mitchell, president of the railroad.

Note as you come back into Gibson an imposing white frame residence with an enormous magnolia tree in front on the right-hand side of the road. This is (10) *Glascock County's former courthouse.* The porch is a modern addition.

Two-wheeling Savannah*

There is no city in the world more ideally suited to sightseeing by bicycle.

by Bill Cutler

As a damned Yankee, I have had an infernal desire since moving to Georgia to imitate Sherman's celebrated feat—to proceed from Atlanta to Savannah in a devastating manner. Now I have done it. I destroyed no crops, burned no towns, killed no one, but by marching to the sea on my bicycle, I managed to devastate a good number of my friends as well as several folks I met up with along the way.

It wasn't even a particularly hard trip—much more downhill than up, with a good stiff tailwind pushing me along most of the way.

After I'd stoked my furnaces at Mrs. Wilkes' legendary boarding house on East Jones Street and replenished the energy expended in pedalling 260 miles in 2½ days, I set out to plan a bike route for Savannah. I suspect there's no city in the world more ideally suited to sightseeing by bicycle than this one. It's completely flat, so you can make your way around it on an old single-speed machine if necessary, and most of the streets are wide enough to accommodate cyclists and motorists together. Distances are too great and the sights too abundant for comfortable walking, but if you try to see everything from the confines of a car, you'll be constantly frustrated by having your perspective cut off. I venture to say that only the patient and adventuresome cyclist can truly measure the scale of Savannah's beauties.

Two words of caution: Several of the one-way streets in town are planned for high-speed traffic, with staggered lights, and are not really suited for cyclists' use. My route was planned almost completely to avoid them. I was not able to avoid, however, the second hazard: rough cobblestone paving on many streets. You might feel more comfortable on a sturdy one- or three-speed bike than on a delicate ten-speed.

The route shown here is meant to supplement, not replace, Savannah's officially marked bike route, which begins at East Broad and Bryan (near the famous Pirate's House). In fact, I strongly urge all cyclists to follow the official trail for a first exposure to Savannah's treasures. A bike route map is available at the Chamber of Commerce. You will see many of the renowned attractions inside the region recently designated an Historic Preservation area (bounded by East and West Broad Streets, the river, and Gwinnett Street on the south). The route I worked out was designed with two chief considerations in mind: to take visitors past as many of the city's lesser-known points of interest as possible, and to show off the stages in Savannah's massive restoration effort.

I was aided in planning my route by Mrs. Donald Stroup, a Philadelphian who moved to Savannah about five years ago and has taken an active role in the refurbishing of the city. She was responsible for restoring Laura's House on East State Street into an early-19th century tea house, and she has turned her own beautiful home at 19 East Gordon Street (you'll pass it on the city's official bike route) into one of the Victorian showplaces of the city.

The preserved area of Savannah stops short of a rich region of late Victorian "gingerbread" mansions, perhaps the densest concentration of such fanciful extravagances in this country. There is at present no protection for the houses in this area, although the recent formation of a Victorian Society means that a number of influential citizens are beginning to take an interest in the architectural wealth of this era. Much of my route meanders through late-Victorian Savannah, in part to stimulate a concern for preserving it. Enterprising readers with a taste for urban restoration are likely to find unmatchable bargains in the great decaying hulks that line block after block of central Savannah's southern edge.

The route begins at what, at time of writing, is merely an idea—the new Chamber of Commerce headquarters on West Broad Street. Presently located in the great Cotton Exchange on Bay Street, the Chamber will soon be moved to a location with plenty of parking near the finest collection of railroad buildings in the country. Take time to wander into the great cobblestoned courtyard to admire the handsomely spaced brick structures, including a splendid roundhouse.

From Broad Street you'll pass beside the handsome new Civic Center and quickly enter an earlier era—the dusty, sleepy decrepitude of Tattnall Street. Then you'll zigzag pass the fronts and backs of a number of Victorian houses in varying states of disrepair and continue south and west through a somewhat desolate neighborhood to Laurel Grove Cemetery. You may want to disembark from your bike here because the paths are chiefly just ruts in the sand, which offer poor traction for your tires. But you'll enjoy the humble, melancholy dignity of this resting-place for Black Savannahians.

On leaving the cemetery, you'll pass in front of some very elegant homes on busy 37th Street and blocks of fine structures, not quite so well kept up, on both sides of tree-lined 36th. Make sure to stop at 36th and Bull to examine one of Savannah's greatest Victorian treasures with the fantastic multiple oval openings in the latticework. It's the sort of house I imagine as the setting for a play by Tennessee Williams or Lillian Hellman.

When you get to Habersham and 31st, you can continue on the Thunderbolt loop (shown on a separate map) that takes you to Bonaventure Cemetery and Savannah State College. The cemetery is one of the area's deservedly famous landmarks, with its luxurious foliage punctuated by hanging strands of Spanish moss. As you pedal along Bonaventure Road, you'll feel you've entered a remote rustic village, so dense is the undergrowth.

Thunderbolt itself is a picturesque fishing village with a rather elegant marina. You'll enjoy pausing along River Road to inspect the yachts and sailboats. The center of Savannah State's campus is extremely handsome, ringed by gigantic live oaks and their everpresent accompaniment, Spanish moss. Be careful as you ride this loop, for traffic is heavy on Skidaway Road as well as Henry and Anderson Streets.

Back on the city loop, slow down as you approach the intersection of Drayton Street and Park Avenue. The houses both to the left and right along Drayton are worth remarking. When you get to the middle of the block between Abercorn and Drayton on Bolton Street, you may be lucky enough still to find a splendid Victorian mansion composed of a delightful variety of asymmetrical elements, complete with a carriage house in the rear. On the other hand, you may find only a parking lot for the Independent Life Insurance Company. The Victorian Society would like to save the mansion, but so far no one has met the insurance people's steep price, so it's likely to be torn down.

When you get to Forsyth Park on Hall Street, cross Drayton and enter the park on a ramp, then follow the wide and level sidewalk around three sides of the park to another ramp at Hall and Whitaker. This will keep you out of the high-speed traffic on Drayton and Whitaker and also allow you to admire from a distance the fine facades that front the park.

After you turn the corner onto Barnard Street from Hall, you'll notice a pair of thin, tall, unpainted Victorian houses with an impressive display of intricate woodwork. Soon you turn onto Gaston Street for the first of a series of lengthy crosstown trips along the same street. The purpose is to show the progress of the restoration under way. Most of Gaston Street has been beautifully refurbished. Indeed, next to Gordon Street, Gaston probably has the most consistently successful abundance of restored townhouses to show in Savannah. When you cross Habersham, however, you'll notice a difference. The houses are now late Victorian, extraordinarily ornate, with towers and cupolas and odd little niches and excrescences, as contrasted to the restrained, rectilinear facades farther west. And many of them are sadly run down—peeling, unpainted, broken up into boarding houses, with some of their gingerbread hanging loose. These are some of my favorite Gothic extravagances in Savannah, and I was interested to see on my last visit that some of them were in the process of being brightly painted and restored.

The next crosstown jaunt is along Jones Street, where the first block you see, between East Broad and Price, is wholly unlike the rest of the street. Here the houses are really cottages, made of wood rather than brick, and older than those in the blocks to the west, which have been very soundly restored. It is hoped that restoration will begin on this block very soon. At the northeast corner of Jones and Habersham you'll notice an unusual and successful contemporary apartment complex—one of many reminders that Savannah's distinguished architectural heritage did not come to an abrupt end before we were born.

As you work your way back east on Charlton Street, pause for a minute in Lafayette Square, where Abercorn crosses Charlton. On the left, at 329 Abercorn, is the imposing Colonial Dames house. On the right, at 119 Charlton Street, is a building with the West Indian design so commonly found in Charleston—two-story side porches, with the main entrance through the side piazza.

After traversing the oldest restored portion of Savannah—around lovely Greene and Washington Squares—note the im-

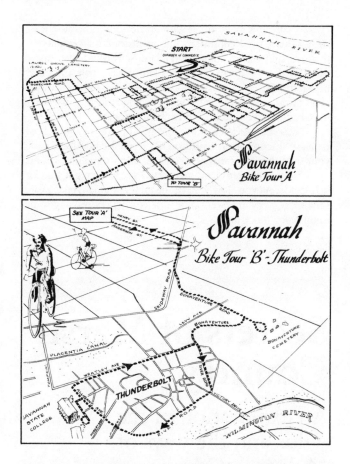

Savannah Bike Tour. *This tour is designed to introduce bicyclists to the many faces and facets of Savannah. It supplements the official bike route which is shorter but provides a good first look at the city. Copies of the official route are available at the Chamber of Commerce. The approximate distance from Anderson Street where tour "B" begins, to Savannah State College is 5 miles.*

posing mansion at the southwest corner of Price and Broughton Streets. This was the first home of William Scarbrough, one of Savannah's most distinguished residents, the builder of the first steamship to cross the Atlantic.

The tour takes you along busy Oglethorpe Street for a few blocks to visit what is at present a parking lot. It's probably the only parking lot in America that will soon be replaced by a copy of an early 19th-century house. At a time when historical landmarks are being replaced by asphalt all over America, it is heartening to know that the process can sometimes be reversed. This lot is at 122 West Oglethorpe, next to a small redbrick Federal house. The parking lot may, by the time you read this, already have begun to be retransformed into the Becu House, which used to occupy this plot. Aaron Burr once stayed here. Now it is slated to house the Savannah offices of one of the country's biggest firms, which is paying to restore it.

Across the street next to the YWCA are two other Federal houses that were reported to be for sale for about $27,000 each.

You see, thus, how the face of Savannah is changing—the old giving way to the new, and the new to the old. The last landmark on our route is on West Broad at the corner of Congress. I passed it many times without noticing it because it's in such a dilapidated condition. But an historic marker tells you this was the second home of William Scarbrough and one of the only three William Jay houses left in Savannah, the others being the Owen Thomas residence and the Juliette Gordon Low birthplace. Perhaps by the time you read this, work will have begun to restore it to its original grandeur.

These are just a few notes to suggest places I've found particularly interesting in Savannah. But you'll enjoy looking on your own, because nearly every block offers some unusual juxtaposition of masonry and greenery, a finely wrought lintel or balustrade. As you slowly pedal through Savannah, take a careful look at every intersection because you may be missing something half a block away.

1973

Secrets of Marsh Country

An exploration of the wilds and the ways of McIntosh County

by Bill Cutler

If I weren't such a fanatic about history, I wouldn't have ended up slipping and sliding along an inhospitable dirt track in backwoods McIntosh County, in search of a Revolutionary War fort that vanished generations before I learned of its existence. I had determined to celebrate the bicentennial on my bicycle and chose the area around Darien, one of the earliest Western settlements in Georgia, because its coastal location promised moderate temperatures for winter riding. I knew from my history books something about the fiercely independent spirit of the Highland Scots who settled Darien and who pushed what was then known as St. Andrew's Parish into rebellious measures against British highhandedness. Yet I was unprepared for the varied sources of interest McIntosh County has to offer a visitor.

I hadn't known, first of all, how beautiful is the early morning light glancing through the marsh grasses and playing off the water. I had had no idea how the marshes alter in appearance as the tides ebb and flow, as the angle of sunlight shifts, as clouds pass and the moon rises. I was totally unprepared for the architectural magnificence of Ridgeville and the quaint charm of Darien itself, with its lines of shrimp boats bobbing at the docks along the Altamaha. And I almost passed out with ecstasy when I discovered I was within easy pedalling distance of Fort Barrington, William Bartram's trail, and the area where Bartram located the mysterious Franklinia Alatamaha!

As you ride around this route, you may find yourself wishing, as I did, that your bike could float. The marshes beckon you from unsuspected vantage-points; ibises pose gracefully on solitary tree stumps in the water, uninhabited islands across the channels promise whole colonies of rare and exotic wild life. To remain landlocked in such an environment is an affront to the senses. Yet sitting perched upon a bicycle has taught me to accept limitations with greater grace and humor than any activity I have undertaken. The ten-speed bicycle is a wondrous machine, to be sure, but what it cannot do and where it cannot take you are at least as intrinsic to its nature as the marvels it performs. In the absence of bike pontoons, I recommend that you take every dirt path, paved surface, and sand spit leading down toward the marshes and wheel right up to the water's edge whenever opportunity offers. Get to feel the special life of the marshes, the delicate balance of forces that coexist among the reeds and water, as fully as your spoked and double-butted mount will permit you.

At the end of one of those tracks leading seaward from Georgia 99 I came upon the unspoiled village of Valona. Inside the community's post office—about the dimensions of a good-sized closet—I met Sam Gore, former saltwater game warden and sailor, now fisherman and leading citizen. "Do you know you're standing on the most unpolluted stretch of coast along the entire Atlantic seaboard?" he asked me by way of introduction.

He led me out onto an old wooden pier with its middle caved in that jutted into the marshes, and from that vantage-point he gave me an expert seaman's guide to the surrounding ocean geography. His arm sweeping the horizon, he named each island hummock and each channel. He pulled out his nautical map for additional details. "See over there?" he asked, pointing slightly to the left. "If you've ever eaten Georgia oysters, that's probably where they come from. Those are the richest oyster beds in the state. McIntosh County is the largest fishing center on the entire coast."

He paused in disgust at the sight of a trawler spilling waste into the marshes. "You used to see a lot more of that sort of thing a few years back," he said. "Today fishermen understand better that pollution is bad for business." As we headed back for shore, he smiled broadly. "You know, I've travelled around the world seven times, and I've never met better people anywhere than my neighbors right here on the Georgia coast. 'Course, you can't say a word against any man hereabouts. All but four of the folks in Valona and Cedar Point [the community immediately north] are related to each other either by blood or marriage, so you're almost sure to be talking to some of their kin. I'm one of the four." He called to his dog Gus, a low-lying hound, to get into his truck, and Gus lept four feet vertically over the side panel of the pick-up, and away they went.

Valona is only one of many little pockets of fishing and boating activity tucked away among the marshes on side roads. Another lovely surprise is Ashantilly, where I came to know a most unusual resident—artist, printer, local historian, former Chamber of Commerce president, and ardent conservationist William G. "Bill" Haynes, Jr. He lives in a handsome, sturdy, antebellum tabby house built by local tycoon Thomas Spalding of Sapelo, who is buried with many of his kinfolk in picturesque nearby St. Andrew's Cemetery.

Haynes talked at length about the problems and prospects of McIntosh County, one of the state's poorer districts. Originally a rice-producing area, it's been in a depressed condition since the Civil War. Impoverished farmers sold their land to giant pulpwood companies back in the '20s and '30s for what looked like substantial cash payments and moved into Darien. As a result, an enormous percentage of McIntosh County belongs to these companies, who, according to Haynes, pay disproportionately small property taxes, plow little revenue back into the county, and get away with ecologically disastrous forestry practices because of lax governmental supervision.

During his presidency of the Chamber, Haynes tried to persuade his fellow citizens that preserving the marshes and swamps—whose qualities few residents had appreciated—benefits the fishing industry. He supports the state's claim to own the marshes for purposes of preservation, a claim, now being adjudicated, that some coastal property owners bitterly dispute. Haynes is currently lobbying for an interpretive center to be built in Darien which would explain to visitors the ecosystems of marsh, swamp, and coast and would involve local citizens in guiding travelers through the channels, thereby helping to educate McIntosh Countians about the value of their marshes.

The poverty of which Bill Haynes spoke will be evident to any cyclist exploring the county's back roads. Many residences are simple box-like structures with few amenities, and local government is apparently not able to afford a reasonable waste-disposal system, since open dumps are to be seen with distressing regularity in woods and clearings beside the roads. Darien itself gives off the poignant sense of a town bypassed—and the completion of I-95 through the area means that little tourist traffic will henceforth enrich local merchants.

Yet interstate travelers hurrying to and from Florida will be missing a very special place. Darien is a town of churches, and its small compass contains more varieties of handsome church architecture than most large metropolitan areas can boast. The town's geography is defined and limited by the marshes, upon which many residents depend for their livelihood. Look just beyond the contemporary brick bungalows and weathered Victorian cottages, glance through the massive overhanging live-oak boughs, and chances are you'll glimpse the golden grasses bending low above the water, as the Altamaha River and Cathead, Darien, and Black Island Creeks curve to nestle the community between their banks.

I expected the town to look older, to reach visibly back into the Revolutionary period. After all, Fort King George on the outskirts of Darien, site of a handsome but sparsely furnished new museum of Colonial Georgia, was, for a brief period, the earliest British settlement in the state, predating Oglethorpe's founding of Savannah by some dozen years. The McIntosh family, after whom the county is named, played a central role in Georgia's early history. Revolutionary General Lachlan McIntosh, who redesigned Darien in 1767, feuded bitterly with Declaration of Independence signer Button Gwinnett and mortally wounded him in a duel at the height of local military activity (it seems a miracle that Georgia *ever* freed herself of the British yoke!).

Yet no trace remains of Darien's early history. The reason is simple: Union troops set the town on fire in 1863 and burned it to the ground. Local historian Bessie Lewis, in her pamphlet

"They Called their Town Darien," sees that tragedy as the fulfilling of a grim prophecy spelled out by the early Scottish settlers of Darien. In 1739, 18 of the town's leaders drafted a petition against the importing of slaves, in which they warned that slaves would be "our Scourge one Day or another for our Sins; and as Freedom to them must be as dear as to us, what a Scene of Horror must it bring about! And the longer it is unexecuted, the bloody Scene must be the greater." A generation later, in 1775, the citizens of Darien passed a resolution supporting the revolutionary activities in Massachusetts and again condemned slavery in strong language. Unfortunately for Darien and the South, the views of these iconoclastic Scots were not widely shared, and Lachlan McIntosh's town went up in flames because of her neighbors' lack of vision.

I felt I derived some faint sense of how Darien might have looked, if not during the Revolution, then in the early 19th century, when I visited nearby Ridgeville. Until recently known just as The Ridge, this was where Darien citizens built their summer homes, apparently believing that residence closer to the sea would help ward off malaria epidemics. Union troops left The Ridge alone, and it remains a remarkably harmonious ensemble of Victorian homes—some antebellum, some later—lining both sides of Georgia 99. As the highway passes through town, it dips and curves to skirt the splendid live oaks that contribute so much to the peaceful atmosphere of this spot.

Frustrated by the absence of Revolutionary mementoes in Darien, I set out for Fort Barrington with high bicentennial expectations. Located at the only fordable place on the Altamaha within many miles, the fort was the strategic key to controlling the southern frontier. Its easy capture by the British in March of 1778 was one of the two or three most significant military events of the war in our state, since it secured passage for the royalists from their safe refuge in Florida to make destructive forays into Georgia. The ease with which the British defended the fort throughout the rest of the war led me to ask Bill Haynes why the Americans had defended it so poorly. "Sheer stupidity at the top" was his wry comment on patriot leadership.

Fort Barrington was clearly no match for Bunker Hill or Valley Forge as scenes of colonial valor, but I was determined to get there. Perhaps I would be lucky enough to register the first official sighting in 173 years of the Franklinia Alatamaha in the wild where William Bartram plucked it on his way to the coast from Fort Barrington. I left the paved road just beyond the tiny railroad hamlet of Cox and began pedalling 3.7 miles of the most inhospitable surface I can remember encountering. It had rained considerably that morning, so the sand my wheels had to ride upon was packed hard enough to give me *some* traction—*some* of the time.

I was heartened by the signs identifying my path as Bartram's trail, but the land I traversed would not have been recognized by the 18th-century naturalist. The original interestingly varied forest had been cut over by pulpwood companies and replanted in monotonous scrub pine. No vestige remained of the rich botanical underbrush that had once flourished there. Two miles or so from Cox I came upon a pulpwood team with tractors and rigs. They had churned the roadbed into a muddy slough, through which I found it necessary to portage my bike on my shoulders.

Skidding, pushing, grunting, I plowed ahead till a steep descent suggested to me that the Altamaha was at hand. I rounded a corner, saw the broad waters of the river in the distance, and in the foreground—no traces of a fort, but a messy, littered landing spot for fishermen with two wild pigs in sole possession of the premises, rooting among the offal. I had trucked through muck and mire to confront history and found, instead, two wild pigs. How Robert Frost would have loved my ironic bewilderment! And how, after a chagrined laugh, *I* loved chasing and being chased by the pigs and futile hunting for Bartram's plant. Who says fun is finding what you set out in search of? I wish you even half as good a time as I had bumbling about McIntosh County on the cold scent of a bicentennial trail that led me in a circle right back to today.

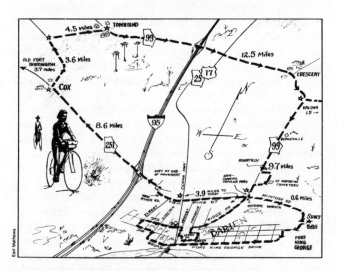

The Bike Trail Darien & McIntosh County*

This route has been planned to keep cyclists off the Coastal Highway U.S. 17. Although Interstate-95 is now complete through McIntosh County and closely parallels 17, the older road still attracts a good deal of high-speed, big-truck traffic, and outside of town the shoulder is not wide enough for comfortable biking. Be very careful crossing the highway inside Darien.

A good point to begin and end your tour is at Fort King George on the outskirts of Darien, site of the oldest English settlement in Georgia. Park cars and unload bikes in the parking area in front of the handsome modern museum.

For the tastes of most recreational cyclists, the stretch of Georgia 99 along the marshes between Valona and Darien contains the greatest concentration of scenic, architectural, and historic points of interest. Unfortunately, if you choose to limit your riding to this stretch, there is no alternative route by which to return to your starting-point; you will have to backtrack on 99 again. It is a smooth blacktop surface with sporadic but manageable traffic. Including the tour of Darien, the roundtrip is approximately 24½miles. Cyclists taking the shorter route will simply continue north on Georgia 99 outside the town limits of Darien instead of turning left onto Pine Street.

Riders in search of more exercise, Revolutionary War fanatics and William Bartram devotees, and eccentrics who enjoy punishing themselves and their bikes in pursuit of uncertain adventures are urged to take on the full 54-mile loop, including 7.4 back-and-forth miles of nearly impassable sand and mud sloughs along the Bartram Trail in search of Fort Barrington (see text). I can't promise you romantic scenery in the backwoods of McIntosh County—the pulpwood companies saw to that by cutting down the richly various original growth and replacing it with the ever-present pine—but the paved surfaces are flat (on a mud or dirt surface, the slightest grade makes for an exciting new set of hazards which I will leave for you to encounter fresh), traffic is virtually non-existent, pavements so-so, and the few human settlements you pass through provide variety.

Darien itself presents some challenges to the bike-route planner. Pavements have a tendency to come to a sudden end, abandoning the cyclist three inches deep in fine sand. Furthermore, the street-signing system in town is wholly haphazard; in some areas, every intersection is carefully identified, while you can ride for blocks in other neighborhoods without the slightest indication of your whereabouts. If you study and follow the map provided here, however, you should experience no difficulty with the street-sign omissions.

The route I eventually planned winds back and forth through town, crossing several times but never using U. S. 17, and puts cyclists on an unpaved surface for only one short stretch at the end of New River Road, before hooking up with Georgia 251. You may prefer to push, rather than pedal, your bike through the deep sand here. Don't miss touring the grounds and museum at old Fort King George. Visitors interested in background information on Darien's history should stop at the Welcome Center on U. S. 17.

Be adventuresome about leaving Georgia 99 to explore side roads leading to the sea. Surfaces are very poor but pleasures many.

1976

I Can Promise You a Rose Garden

A Victorian Ramble through Thomasville and Thomas County

by Bill Cutler

Despite the frequently heard claim that ours is a classless society, almost all American towns, especially in the South and East, reveal clear class distinctions, set social patterns. Yet I had never encountered a community stratified almost in the English sense, presided over by a landed "nobility" that keeps exclusively to itself, until my tires touched the pavements of Thomasville. I wasn't asked to join the hunting set, mind you, nor did I even catch a glimpse of their activities, and you're not likely to, either. But learning about the very special social environment of Thomasville has enlarged my sense of Georgia's heritage and added yet another area of our state to the growing list of places I'll have to keep circling back to, to drop a plumb line in, to probe and pry around in search of further mysteries. And talk about great cycling!

The greatest spot for cycling happens also to be, not surprisingly, the turf where Thomasville's landed gentry take their exercise. I was steered there by Mrs. E. Wade Chastain, whose family runs the new Colonial Oaks restaurant in town. She told me the pavement was dirt, but when I learned I'd be riding through what's supposed to be the most extensive forest of virgin long-leaf pine left in the States, I couldn't be held back. I found the surface hard packed and well graded in late February, and I hope it will be equally satisfactory at other times of year. Banks of azaleas line the roadside beneath the high, straight, elegant, aloof pines, and in late afternoon the light glancing through the corridors of trees seems to condense in mid-air among the trunks like the richest, most luscious and delicate lemon custard.

The finest stands of pine belong to the Greenwood plantation, local home of immensely wealthy huntsman John Hay Whitney, former ambassador to Great Britain and publisher of the *New York Herald Tribune,* but I wouldn't have known the fact if I hadn't been told. I saw nothing but forest—no glimpse of a residence. These plantation owners intend to remain out of sight, and they succeed. They land in private planes at the Thomas County airport, are whisked into a round of exclusive social engagements with their guests and other plantation owners, and depart unobserved by the local populace.

Who are Thomasville's mysterious strangers? I was fortunate to get some insight into their backgrounds when I ran into local historian William Warren Rogers during a visit to the Thomasville-Thomas County Historical Society. Rogers has finished three volumes of a painstaking, authoritative, unusually readable study of Thomas County that brings the chronicle up to the beginning of this century. He's probably the best informed source on any single county in Georgia.

Rogers sketched in a picture of an elite that has little in common with the local residents, a fact that helped me to understand why they remain so aloof from Thomasville's daily life. They're Northerners, mostly, heirs to the vast antebellum agricultural estates started by people from Upper Georgia who imposed a slave economy on a wilderness area that never knew a frontier period. In addition, they're mainly Republicans, carrying on a tradition over 80 years old that attracted national attention when William McKinley came to visit, both as candidate and president, on the invitation of fellow Ohioans wintering in Thomasville (a tradition continued by the arrival of President Eisenhower to hunt and play golf during the 1950s).

The family that throughout the decades has symbolized ruling-class Republican pre-eminence in the area is that of shipping magnate Mark Hanna, Ohio Senator, later McKinley's Secretary of State. One of his descendants married George Humphrey, Eisenhower's Secretary of the Treasury. Another endowed the County Historical Society. The hunters and sportsmen who came together here formed the Georgia-Florida Trial Club, whose membership list still reads today like a Who's Who on Wall Street.

The dirt road I traveled is known, appropriately enough, as Pinetree Boulevard. It developed out of the desire by the plantation set for a pleasurable horseback-riding avenue in the country close to downtown. Individual property owners were encouraged to extend the road along their holdings, until by the 1890s it formed a rough circumferential highway all the way around Thomasville, one of the first perimeter roads in the country. For the last 15 or 20 years it has served as the official city limits.

This rudimentary beltway is not a continuous and connected surface; one must frequently jog a stretch left or right on intersecting roads. Nonetheless, I had the distinct impression that Pinetree Boulevard serves to seal Thomasville off from the surrounding countryside. Beyond the city limits gambol and frolic the financial wizards of our great Northern industrial centers, with bird dogs, guns, and carriages. Beyond those limits, too, stretch the great agricultural enterprises that bring more Georgia produce into Thomasville's Farmers' Market than into any comparable facility in the state (Atlanta's market handles a larger volume of business, but much of the merchandise comes from outside Georgia).

When I visited the produce center at Smith Avenue and Hansell Street, only a few of its many stalls were open for business. I paused to talk with one seller, who assured me that the empty esplanade I had just wheeled across without impediment would be nearly impassable during auction times in late spring, summer, and fall when wholesalers jam the concourse hunting up the best buys.

I had trouble picturing to myself the rough-and-tumble of growing, marketing, and selling the products of the land in this city that gives forth such a genteel, demure air. In other Georgia cities, even wealthy ones, nature always seems to have just barely been beaten back from taking over. In any other town, I'd never be surprised to return after a week's travel and find dust settled thick upon the pavements, the hedges grown unruly after only a few days' absence from the shears, the onion grass rampant, and shrubs, thickets, vines, and creepers reaching up to touch the eaves. So fast does sap flow and greenery sprout in Georgia. But nature doesn't stand a chance in Thomasville. With midwestern or, better, English, fervor, I picture a battalion of gardeners armed with hoes, snippers, trowels, and rakes ready to take on any erring branch or presumptuous tendril that threatens to get out of line.

Self-contained—I guess that's the way I see Thomasville above all. I sensed it in talking to Mrs. Chastain, an eight-year resident who spoke of Pinetree Boulevard as horizon, boundary, outer limit of her world. She knew nothing of the charming communities like Pavo and Boston that dot the landscape of Thomas County. Like Mrs. Davis, hostess at the city Welcome

Center, she was content with the wealth and variety of things she found to see and do inside Thomasville itself.

Civic pride—I enjoy that. Perhaps this cloistered view unconsciously carries over from Thomasville's long history as an isolated and special place. From its beginnings, the area developed closer ties with Florida than with the rest of Georgia. Before the Civil War, its only access to the outside world was by way of the Gulf ports south of Tallahassee, and the absence of a railroad—desperately lobbied for by local planters—effectively cut it off from the north and east.

Thomas County's Whig aristocracy opposed secession because they feared disruption of their profitable mercantile affairs (though when war came, townspeople rallied to the Confederate cause with fervor and more than their share of troops). Union prisoners of war lucky enough to avoid confinement in Andersonville found Thomasville a hospitable and friendly place, and following the conflict, the area never experienced the bitterness of Reconstruction that brought such a long and melancholy legacy of distrust to the rest of the South. Only two lynchings have been recorded in Thomas County between 1865 and 1900, and black citizens appear to have fared, if not well, at least better than their counterparts elsewhere in the region.

A strong strain of Union sentiment throughout the mid-19th century and the development of Republican ties later set Thomas County apart socially and psychologically from its neighbors. Its special status was further enhanced by the odd accident that a railroad link on the Atlantic and Gulf line between Thomasville and Tallahassee was not completed until many decades after it was proposed. This meant that the "Northern Invalids and Pleasure Seekers" whom an 1885 Thomasville map identified as the source of the city's booming winter tourist trade did not discover the sunny attractions of Florida until well into this century. The Atlantic and Gulf ended in Thomasville, and when the lines were finally extended, the pleasure-seekers—or most of them—moved on, too.

The "pine-scented air"—that's what everyone in Thomasville kept alluding to as the source of the town's wealth, strength, appeal. Other resort areas feature mineral springs, mountains, beaches, but those lovely trees I had enjoyed along Pinetree Boulevard were sufficient to make Thomasville *the* winter-resort capital of the nation around the turn of the century, "America's answer to the French Riviera," in the phrase of the Historical Society's archivist, Tom Hill. Its hotels were like palaces, and the grandest of all was the 400-foot-long "Piney Woods."

Was this perception that pine scent brings health one of those Victorian crackpoteries like the vapors, tight corsets, and bustles? I found myself sneezing, choking, and coughing in paroxysms while pedaling among the panaceas—perhaps a reaction to early spring pollens, or a perverse respiratory inclination to dispute the claims of doctors. Never mind. Beneficial or not, visitors perceived (and still perceive) that Thomasville makes them feel good, and perceptions cause realities.

With a society of the ultra-rich established in Thomasville, an entire sub-culture of professional people who cater to their needs—doctors, nurses, hospital administrators, clinical technicians—gravitated toward this salubrious mecca and still account today for much of the town's enormous wealth. I was astonished at the number and variety of health facilities I saw in almost every block of the downtown area, the most imposing of which is the John D. Archbold Hospital, named for a turn-of-the century oil tycoon.

This public facility was endowed by the business magnates of the plantation set originally to serve charity cases alone. The socialites, who might well have treated Thomasville as a playground to be trampled on and abandoned, in the worst "Robber Baron" tradition, fortunately possessed some of that Victorian *noblesse oblige* mentality that motivated Florence Nightingale and Gladstone. They were appalled at the absence of adequate health care for the black citizens of Thomas County and left a monument to their philanthropic concern.

The existence of a large and prosperous professional class provides Thomasville with a middle social level between the fabulously rich plantation owners and the descendants of those charity patients who still manage to scratch out a living in town. Their simple shacks in some cases sit only a hundred yards or so from the immaculate and sturdy residences of doctors, lawyers, and business people, but the invisible line of status and privilege is as clearly drawn here as between those who sport beyond Pinetree Boulevard and those who doctor to them.

To me, Thomasville exudes a more potent, more concentrated sense of what it must have been like to live around the turn of the century than any town in this country. It comes from the feeling that everyone knows "his place," that lines of power have been demarcated and acknowledged for generations. It comes, too, from the Victorian architectural heritage of the town, which many places in Georgia can boast but which conveys something special to me here.

Dawson Street, home of the Historical Society, was one avenue I could not get enough of. I kept inventing reasons to have to cycle back to it and spent an hour late one night, ostensibly to walk my dog, just steeping myself in the breath-catchingly still, stopped solitude of those complacent homes with their clipped and tidy lawns, where lushness held itself in check. They said to me, with the merest edge of wistfulness, "We're just as we've been for the better part of a century. And you—what news do you bring us? Is President McKinley expected again soon?"

I caught those backward tremors even more insistently when I visited the Historical Society. Archivist Tom Hill took me on a long, expansive tour of his domain, which was like traveling in a time machine through a gallery of Victorian manners and morals. Tom's a natural storyteller with an evident love for the foibles and whimsies of his and our ancestors.

The most poignant moment of my visit to the Historical Society came when I walked into a beautifully reconstructed room meant to approximate the sleeping and entertainment quarters of a modest middle-class family in 1877 and felt I had been transported to my own great-grandparents' house. The hilarious family photograph on the wall caught—I swear—the identical dour, long-chinned, slit-eyed, down-at-the-mouth expressions I've seen and feared on the faces of my Scottish Presbyterian ancestors from Tennessee.

This journey backwards into my own and the country's past that Thomasville provided me was brought on, I believe, by my sense that the *spirit* of earlier ways of thinking still resides in its inhabitants, not just that the physical monuments are so well preserved. Take, for instance, my visit to the great Victorian showplace on Dawson Street, the Lapham-Patterson House. It's one of the country's architectural masterpieces, to be sure, but more importantly, its young curator, R. M. Willett, has an uncannily Victorian look and tone to him that made me wonder if he'd been reincarnated from Ruskin or Matthew Arnold—a sort of high earnestness, a passion for hand-carved surfaces, a glowing conviction that he'd been placed in Thomasville for the lofty responsibility of explaining Victorian intentions and achievements to his unenlightened neighbors.

Distinction, separation, discrimination (in more than one sense)—those are the concepts I associate with Thomasville. The town draws distinctions, it is distinguished: unfortunately, we have apparently not yet been able to achieve the latter without doing the former. Yet it's not fair to leave the city without acknowledging an influence that crosses class lines, that defies categories, an influence embodied in the town's slogan, "City of Roses."

I visited briefly with Paul Hjort, the gentle, unassuming man whose grandfather introduced rose-growing to this area. He spoke with quiet pride of the Danish gardener who saw the advantages of Thomasville's soil and climate for rose production, and of the succeeding generations who watched a whole community latch on to the idea and develop the annual Rose Festival in late April that brings all of Thomasville's residents together in a joyous celebration.

My visit to this beautiful and personally haunting place was lucky in many respects—the people I was able to meet, the conversations I held. But I didn't get to see the roses in bloom, reason enough to pedal back there in the next few months. I noted the trim and decorous bushes by the sidewalks, in mini-parks and giant nurseries, all through town, sentinels announcing magnificence to come. Now there's status, there's privilege for you!

1976

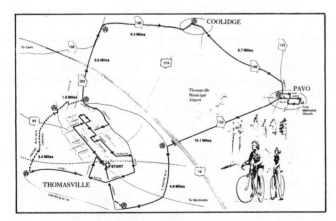

Thomasville Bike Tour*

Only two turnings may present difficulties. There's no sign marking Pinetree off Campbell, but it's the first dirt road to the right after you pass the Rose City Industrial Park. Then, on your way back into town, I've routed you on a dirt road that comes into Pinetree just before Gordon. Take a close look at the first house on your right after the turn. It and its gardens

have been designed in the Japanese fashion, and the result is striking.

Pay careful attention to the map when on Pinetree between U.S. 84 and Georgia 202: you'll have to jog several times on intersecting roads before Pinetree picks up again.

CYCLIST'S ALMANAC

Thomasville and Environs

Elevation: 285'
Population: 18,155 (1970)
Terrain: Gently rolling, no major hills
Temperature Average: January 53.1°, July 80.9°
Average Rainfall: 52"
Blooming Seasons: *Roses,* late April through Thanksgiving; *azaleas,* late February and March; *dogwoods,* March.
Cycling Conditions: *In town:* Good-to-excellent; wide streets, courteous drivers; watch out for a few storm-sewer grates with bars aligned parallel to curbs. *Outside town:* Mostly good; rough aggregate surface on Georgia 188 from intersection with Georgia 202 to Coolidge; excellent black-top on 188 from Coolidge to Pavo; four miles of unpaved surface on Pinetree Boulevard from Campbell Street to Georgia 202, but should present no real problems.
Special Points of Interest Inside Town: *Farmer's Market,* intersection Smith Avenue and Hansell Street. Auctions of Georgia produce late April to October on Mon., Wed., and Fri. afternoons. Friday auctions reported to be especially exciting. . . . *Thomasville Nurseries,* 1842 Smith Avenue. Sam Hjort and son Paul, proprietors. This is the family that pioneered rose gardening in Thomasville, out of which the famous Rose Festival grew. Now one of 26 rose test gardens in country where new rose types are tried out before they're commercially marketed. Fine plantings of day lilies, camellias, azaleas, native azaleas, in addition to roses. . . . *Annual Rose Festival,* late April; parade, rose show, antique show and sale, house tours. . . . *Thomasville-Thomas Co. Historical Society,* 725 N. Dawson Street. Museum full of goodies and surprises (see text), unusually complete collection of county archives. . . . *Lapham-Patterson House,* 626 N. Dawson Street. One of the great Victorian showplaces of the country. Operated by the state as a do-it-yourself museum. . . . *Welcome Center,* 401 S. Broad Street, starting-point for two-hour bus tours of Thomasville's historic homes and nearby plantations (outside visits only). . . . *The Great Oak,* Crawford Street near Monroe, oldest and most spectacular of Thomasville's many live oaks. . . . *Pinetree Boulevard,* nation's first circumferential highway (see text) that on east and south takes you past Glen Arven Country Club, an early and important golf course that is still much admired for its surprisingly steep terrain; Birdwood Junior College, the only Primitive Baptist college in the world, the scene of magnificent plantings; and a number of contemporary condominium developments of the type now as common a feature of the Georgia landscape as the Golden Arches, the Colonel's chicken stands, and used-car lots—developments with enticing names like "Ibis Rise" and "Crystal Brook" that describe not what you will actually find there but what the building of the development itself displaced or destroyed forever.
Special Points of Interest Outside Town: *Coolidge,* sleepy farming town with handsome brick structures, many of them now vacant. . . . *Pavo,* charming and attractive small town with many Victorian homes and a striking First Methodist Church; the sort of place where the roosters make more noise than the people; originally called McDonald after the first settlers, until postmaster discovered there was another McDonald, Georgia; he then tried to change the name to Peacock, after himself, but townspeople ob-

jected, so he got them to accept *Pavo,* though they didn't know this was "Peacock" in Latin.

Where To Camp: Nowhere nearby. *Reed Bingham State Park,* between Moultrie and Adel, and *Seminole State Park* on Lake Seminole, both 40–50 miles away.

Where To Picnic: *Paradise Park,* adjoining Welcome Center, on South Broad Street. Twenty-six densely wooded acres, containing playgrounds, picnic tables, beautiful plantings.

Confessions of A Nostalgia Freak

or: Will the real St. Simons please stand up?

by Bill Cutler

History makes a very faint impression on Georgia's Golden Isles, and no single fact about them could have surprised me more. But had I visited this area more than half a century ago, I might have described it as the Southern Railway did in 1924, as "the shrine of the sea-loving traveller and student of history and tradition." No doubt the rail people romanticized the islands to drum up tourist trade, but perhaps, before St. Simons and Sea Islands were connected by causeways to the mainland, they really were shrines for seekers after history and tradition.

After all, Fort Frederica was Oglethorpe's first settlement in the state. The 18th-century naturalist William Bartram walked from one end of the island to the other, and residents claim they can trace his progress still from the present contours of the landscape. St. Simons and, especially, neighboring Sea Island have been saved from commercial exploitation—no ugly billboards, flashing neon, concrete parking decks. The oaks are gnarled and very beautiful, the beaches clean, the marshes tranquil, bird-infested, and resist intrusion, sea-oats flourish on the dunes and form exquisite sculptures in the sand.

So there's beauty in abundance there, and interest, and variety. It's the elite resort area of our state, where bicycling is welcomed and every other type of leisure-time activity fostered and facilitated. But I didn't get those special backward-pulling twinges of nostalgia which make bicycling in other sections of our state a poignant, sweetly melancholy treat for me.

I sometimes wonder if the act of climbing on my bike seat and pushing round the pedals may not be my way of entering a time machine, traveling backwards to experience the world at a pace and on a scale my grandparents would have recognized and found enjoyable. When I can get that crank to turn at just the speed required to land me back in 1900, give or take a decade, then I'm happiest. That's when the bicycle itself experienced its first public craze and when my parents were on the way to being born.

It doesn't take much to spin the years away—a row of modest frame houses, their porches edged with fretwork; a pattern of alternating crops in open country; old people waiting in their rockers; faded brick storefronts at some deserted crossroads—anything that speaks to me of patience and acceptance and rest from work, of refusal to change for change's sake, of keeping the old and serviceable and trusty in use or ready for some future use.

These qualities are absent on Georgia's Golden Isles. The voices from the past are stilled or muffled or so distorted by distance that the sounds they bring forth barely register as making sense. That doesn't mean a cyclist can't enjoy hours and hours of pleasant recreation. Just don't go there expecting to tap roots.

The absence of visible remains from generations past is due to a number of accidents. The original forests were cut down in the 18th century to provide ships' timbers for the U.S. Navy, since the great live oaks of St. Simons proved tough enough to resist penetration by enemy shot. The cleared and fertile land was then cultivated to grow a special type of cotton plant previously produced in the West Indies known as long-staple cotton, which brought premium prices on English markets. More than a dozen cotton plantations flourished on St. Simons, all of them devastated by Union forces during the Civil War. At the same time, Christ Church was ransacked and nearly demolished. (The present structure was built in 1884.)

On the ashes of the ravaged plantations grew up a new industry after the war, the planing and sawing of timbers cut in the coastal area. Mills were built in two locations on St. Simons, and sailing ships from the Northern U.S., Europe, and South America anchored in the Frederica River while cargoes of lumber were loaded on board. No trace remains today of this important activity, and Rose Cottage, the handsome Gothic home of the mills' superintendents, burned in the mid-1880s.

Toward the end of the last century, St. Simons became a summer resort, whose large hotels accommodating as many as 300 visitors were connected by gangplanks to the piers. The first Hotel St. Simons burned in 1898, the second in 1916. The others, too, are long since gone. Families from Waycross built a community of summer cottages called "Waycross Colony" which was destroyed in an 1898 storm, rebuilt, and burned to the ground in this century.

Thus, even before the building of the bridges that spurred on modern development and led to a transformation of the island's look, St. Simons had lost much of its tangible evidence from the past.

One island place alone stands as a tangible monument to customs and feelings from earlier times. Christ Episcopal Church, on whose property John and Charles Wesley and George Whitfield preached and Oglethorpe worshipped, is one of the very earliest landmarks of Georgia history. Yet today—with its meticulously clipped lawns shaded by moss-hung live oaks, its intensely still cemetery where weathered stones and vegetation seem about to grow together into a single living substance, its punctilious white church building trimmed in black, its gables pointing prayerfully toward heaven—the scene recalls not so much our own colonial period as some tranquil vicarage in a remote, untroubled corner of the British Empire, where tea is punctual at four o'clock, and nothing ever will disrupt the social patterns.

Nearby Fort Frederica was the island's English Colonial center, and the National Park Service, which administers the site, has done its utmost to bring Oglethorpe's stalwart band of pioneers back to life. Employees dressed in rough 18th-century costumes pretend to be engaged in roofpole-raising and musket-loading near the entrance to the fort, and almost every excavated household site displays not just a printed tablet on a slanted box outlining the original settlers' history and occupation, but a button visitors can press to hear what conversations of those inhabitants might have sounded like: "Come quickly, men. Yon hillock hides a warlike Indian, I'll stake my life on it. Move smartly now and . . ."

That ghostly babble goes on elsewhere, too. A few feet off the road I pedaled to and from Fort Frederica, I stopped at another haunting marshside site, where Oglethorpe's men turned back the Spanish once for all and held the colony for England. Bloody Marsh, so tranquil, delicate, wind-brushed as by a lady's lazy fan, so seemingly unsoiled by blood, challenges the imagination to create a scene of panic, frenzy, smoke and soot.

But the imagination doesn't stand a chance. A broken mechanism keeps the pre-recorded history lesson from the slant-topped box droning on and on and on, unwanted. The sound of soldiers' marching feet, the spirited commands of Oglethorpe—you can't escape them. You Are There, in the recording studio.

What *is* this passion to fill up the void, to impose some promoter's pitch upon the silent confrontation each one of us must have with history, with death and loss and victory? The past speaks eloquently, but we must learn to listen, *beneath* the carnival hubbub of the hawkers and concession stands.

I thought I'd hear St. Simons' voices clearest in the undeveloped stretches north of Frederica and Bloody Marsh, where I was farthest from subdivisions and motels. The pavement kept deteriorating as I left civilization behind me, from smooth blacktop to corrugated washboard to nearly uninterrupted pothole to slippery sand and treacherous rut.

I reached land's end at last—a silent, sleepy river scene, baking in the midday sun. A weathered cabin leaned alone amid a field, a two-tiered wooden fishing pier stood at the water's edge, and otherwise all that filled the great hot space were reeds and sky and sun. Squeezed in between the two horizontal levels of the pier was Mr. Ed H. Wright, brick-red of face, his striped shirt large enough to shelter his enormous belly, his overfed and newly castrated bulldog Caesar prone beside him. The two of them looked like the meaty filling of a particularly generous delicatessen sandwich, stretched out there, as Mr. Wright explained, to take advantage of the wind that blew in off the river.

"Fishing's lousy," he remarked, in a gentle, even-tempered voice, pulling himself to his feet. "We've had some real heavy rains that brought in brackish water from the Altamaha." The water curled against the bank, the reeds rustled gently in the wind, I sweated, Mr. Wright sweated, Caesar panted and moved his bloated bulk as gingerly as possible. "This is it," I said to myself. "I've found the *real* St. Simons."

"See that cabin over there?" Mr. Wright interrupted my rhapsody. "Twentieth-Century Fox built it that way for the

movie *Conrack*. They shot it here, you know, and pretended it was South Carolina. That's the way they build them in Carolina. We don't have 'em like that in Georgia."

I thought I'd find a way to penetrate St. Simons' multi-layered artifice by talking to an old black man I'd noticed sitting on a porch just ten feet from an island bike path I had traveled several times. On each occasion he was there, keeping very still and shrouded. What mightn't he have seen through many decades in that spot, or near it? I asked in the village who might remember how the island used to be. "Oh, Mr. Raymond Armstrong, he knows all 'bout them days," they told me, and described the house I'd passed and the quiet old man I'd seen. So, full of hopes, I pushed his gate, which opened on a small and dusty yard presided over by a giant camphor tree. Mr. Armstrong was glad to talk about his island home, where he was born 77 years ago, but I had trouble hearing him. His voice was low, his accent musical, with accentuated pitch, the ends of words got swallowed up, and, to compound my difficulty, the constant roar of passing buses, cars, and trucks so close to where we sat drowned out all but the lovely rise and fall of his intonation. His voice, not what he said, spoke of the sea, of many coasts on several continents and islands near and far.

He remembered St. Simons when it really was an island, unconnected to the shore. His father was a stevedore in Brunswick and came home by boat on weekends only. Had his father been born on the island too? "I guess so. I met him here," he laughed, and I laughed too.

Mr. Armstrong's father had been one of the famous Sea Island Singers who performed until the '40s. Does anyone remember the old music? "I don't know if anyone 'round here used to sing with 'em. I can hardly talk, 'stead of sing," he joked.

What was the island like when he was just a child? "Nothin' but two, three houses, horse and wagon. And that place you call Sea Island, wasn't nothin' there but goats and horses and cows. I come back and find they done build up that. A man used to go over and butcher wild cows. Nobody didn't live over there 't all, nothin' there."

Unlike St. Simons, Sea Island belonged exclusively to single owners until after the building of the causeway to the mainland. After its days as a cotton plantation, it served chiefly as a hunting preserve for private parties, and thus its recorded history was sparse until Howard Coffin, a pioneer in commercial aviation, bought the whole of it in 1925 and '26. Coffin was a founder both of the Hudson automobile company and the Curtis-Wright Aircraft Company, and he saw the possibilities for developing Sea Island into the most exclusive and least commercial resort area on the coast.

The cornerstone of this project was the elaborately designed hotel complex The Cloister, which opened under Coffin's supervision in October, 1928. As adjuncts to this luxurious recreational center, plots of land were for the first time sold to private individuals for development under carefully controlled conditions. From the start, only about 10 tracts a year have been put on the market, and all building plans must be submitted to an architectural board.

Coffin's cousin Alfred Jones took over the Sea Island operations after Coffin lost everything he owned in the Depression. For almost half a century Jones has dedicated himself to protecting Georgia's coastline and offshore islands from Floridization. Sapelo, Cumberland, Jekyll, and Colonel's Islands have all at one time or another benefited from his determination to keep honky tonks, muffler shops, and unplanned residential sprawl from disfiguring the most unspoiled section of our Eastern Seaboard.

I can't help admiring the legacy of Alfred Jones, but I also can't pretend I feel comfortable in it. Sea Island and St. Simons have been domesticated culturally as well as physically. The heritage of plantation life that survived down generations in the rich, evocative songs and spirituals of the famous Sea Island Singers is now gone. What sets the tone of St. Simons today is the village shopping area, with its elegant ice-cream parlor, angularly posturing mannequins in fastidious dress-shop windows, its real-estate office featuring split-level comfort and security for prices in the upper 70s, its painstakingly scrubbed sidewalks—all this could be plucked whole off the island and plunked down in any swanky seaside suburb of Boston, New York, Los Angeles, San Francisco, and no detail would seem inharmonious.

The contemporary housing developments on both islands have a similarly misplaced, anonymous look. The bricked-in impassivity of houses in the Sea Palms subdivision on St. Simons squares so oddly with the subtle, shifting marshes the developers have chosen as their backdrop. Those houses could be duplicated almost anywhere across our land, those marshes almost nowhere. The buildings look like alien transients, come to enjoy the view a year or two, then move on back to Kansas City, the marshes permanent and impenetrable—yet in reality, how fragile, easily penetrated.

Sea Island's homes are grander, but no more appropriate to their environment. They stand like stiff soldiers at attention on both sides of the one paved road running down the narrow middle of the island, inexpressive buildings whose architecture imitates the styles of nearly every Western era. Side by side stand French Provincial, English manor, Spanish ranch, Colonial, Southern tabby, all appearing uninhabited. They seem to hold their breaths and watch each other anxiously, as though some threat to civilization as they understood it lurked just beyond perception in the underbrush.

The values, fears, and tastes of wealthy urban and suburban dwellers have left their mark on Georgia's Golden Isles, rubbing out in the process whatever special character the islands may once have had. What's more, I predict, based on an hour I spent in the Glynn County courthouse investigating recent changes in appraised land values on the coast, that the process of developing and sterilizing these offshore territories will go on at an accelerated pace in the years immediately ahead.

In 1974, the county undertook its first new appraisal in 10 years, and all at once land values jumped dramatically, as much as 800% in some cases. Vacant land belonging to the Sea Island Company on St. Simons' Cannon Point increased in value from $152,700 in 1973 to $1,172,400 in 1975. The entirety of Little St. Simons Island, still in private hands, was appraised at $173,600 in 1973 and $1,324,500 in 1975. The northern, undeveloped end of Sea Island more than doubled in appraised value during the same period, from $1,062,300 to $2,331,300. Can the owners of these undeveloped lands afford *not* to develop them—and fast?

I realize, of course, that development is not an unmixed curse. It brings opportunities in proportion as it takes them off. I know I have to balance my own nostalgic wishes against the health and happiness of residents. A tourist is a sometime thing.

Our past is *not* a sometime thing. It's there, visibly or invisibly, all the time, and we are lessened as we let its vestiges slip away from us. I feel I caught a very faint and poignant glimpse of its heritage at the loveliest spot on Sea Island, a place you're not likely to be privileged to see because it lies beyond a padlocked gate. Two security guards for the Sea Island Company let me explore the narrow beach fronting the Hampton River at the island's northern tip when they learned I was writing a magazine article on the coast.

That beach is breathtaking. Sea oats lean and whisper in the sand with pod ends curved in graceful filigree, like groups of small, thin girls just warming up for practices in ballet class. A row of stumps a bare six inches high protrudes out of the sand—not much of anything to hang a theory on. But the imagination doesn't need much of a boost to get to work, a fact I wish restorers of historic sites would take into account.

I like to think those stumps are what remain of piers where Sea Island's famous cotton was loaded on to ships for transport to foreign mills. Inconsequential as they are, those tiny wooden fragments, in a flattened landscape of sand and brownish water, reeds greenish-yellow along low bluffs, and straw-toned sea oats ever bending in the dance, called forth to me of black men sweating in the sun and cotton baled high and captains counting money, tall-masted ships deep-barnacled, overseers cursing loud, and stevedores with chants and laughter on their lips— the wealth, the meanness, humor, violence, and generosity of the South all tangled up together on that beach, while wind and sun look down on subdivisions eating up the land and never comment from their neutral corners.

1976

CYCLIST'S ALMANAC*

St. Simons and Sea Island

Route: Between 25 and 30 miles, back and forth on all the legs from St. Simons village to Sea Island and Fort Frederica. Trip can obviously be shortened or divided into sections by cycling only one or two legs at a time. A convenient starting point, with plenty of parking, is the St. Simons pier.

Terrain: Completely flat; one- or three-speed bike perfectly adequate. Be prepared for headwinds that may slow you down.

Cycling Conditions: Wretched, surprisingly enough. This center for recreational activity offers poor provisions for two-wheeling. A bike route of sorts parallels Demere Road on St. Simons, but you may prefer to take your chances with the considerable volume of vehicular traffic in the street. The trail disappears into sand several inches deep at most intersections, which makes dismounting advisable. Glass litters the surface, cars park all the way across it, sawtooth palms hang clear across the right-of-way and whip cyclists across their shoulders, the riding surface is very uneven, with poor or, in some cases, no curb cuts. Furthermore, the Demere Road trail dumps cyclists at busy Sea Island Road, where the only choices are turning around on the same trail or plunging onto any of several extremely busy, high-speed roads. A separate Sea Island bike trail picks up just before the causeway over to the island; this one is bumpy and narrow, but adequate. It parallels the one road down the narrow middle of Sea Island.

Points of Interest: (A) *St. Simons Lighthouse and Museum of Coastal History.* Striking tower built in 1872 by noted Savannah architect Charles B. Cluskey, to replace original octagonal tower destroyed during Civil War. Museum, in former lighthouse keeper's residence, focuses on histories of families associated with the lighthouse and on nautical paraphernalia. (B) *Bloody Marsh,* site of decisive battle where Oglethorpe's troops defeated the Spanish and held the colony of Georgia, once for all, for England. Historic marker and recorded history lesson (which, when I was there, unfortunately could not be turned off). (C) *The Cloister,* Georgia's elite resort complex. Main building designed in 1928 by Palm Beach architect Addison Mizner, known for the ornate Spanish motifs—lots of wrought iron, tile, and contorted columns—in the palatial homes he built for Florida's new rich. His main salon at The Cloister definitely worth a visit; very successful at making an enormous room feel comfortable. Cloister grounds landscaped by T. Miesse Baumgardner to make use of existing natural features; in the jocular

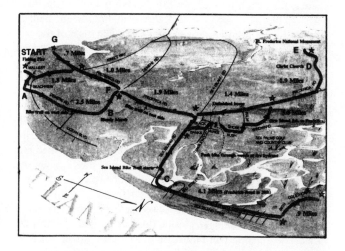

words of Sea Island Company's Sig Kaufmann, "Almost every one of those odd-shaped trees you see, Miesse's designed." (D) *Christ Episcopal Church,* erected in 1884 by Anson Phelps Dodge, Jr., to replace the first church, destroyed during the Civil War. On church property stands the remnant of the famous Wesley Oak, where John and Charles Wesley are said to have held services in 1736. (E) *Fort Frederica,* headquarters for General Oglethorpe's military operations against Spain. Small museum with dioramas and other displays depicting Georgia's colonial history. Film about the town's history shown in auditorium. Spectacular location of earthworks fronting the Frederica River; excavated house sites with recorded history lessons. (F) *Tabby House,* last remaining slave cabin that once housed workers in the cotton fields at Retreat Plantation; now put to rather discordant use as a fancy antique shop, run, very agreeably, by Mrs. Agnes Holt. (G) *Retreat Plantation (now Sea Island Golf Course).* Oak-lined carriage trail leads to ruins of slave hospital and present Club House, built over ruins of plantation's corn barn. Formerly one of the greatest cotton plantations in the South, owned by James Spalding, Major William Page, and Thomas Butler King.

Where the Old's Good as New*

From Fort Gaines to the Chattahoochee to the Kolomoki Mounds

by Bill Cutler

So you'd driven I-75 to and from Florida and thought all of South Georgia was flat and bleak? Well, come bike with me around two loops through Clay and Early Counties, and I'll show you some hills to put your leg muscles to work. I'll also show you the smallest town in Georgia represented on the Bicentennial Commission, some of the country's most spectacular Indian mounds, and a center of the world's richest peanut-producing farmland.

I pedalled this route most recently in late summer, and the fields and air were filled with signs of the transitional season. Caterpillars hunched their way across the pavement, and butterflies flaunted their bright lemon yellows and tiger-stripe oranges against the ripe sorghum spikes. Cornstalks stood brown and brittle at attention, the sumac blazed and glowered by the roadside, and pyracantha berries flamed in unkempt hedges and along neat walks. Rows of dried and dusty near-skeletons marched through some pecan orchards, while neighboring groves held trees still plump and sappy.

I passed fields of melons eerily white on the vine, like dolls' heads of various shapes and sizes with the faces not yet drawn in. Tent caterpillars had spread their destructive mantels in the desiccated tops of trees. The air through which I rode was filled with mysterious pairs of insects, their bodies joined acrobatically together as they flew, in a coupling I imagined to be a defiant denial of the killing weather to come.

Yet the clearest signal of all that summer was at its end lay in the peanut harvest that was just beginning. I stopped to chat with a worker leaning on his pitchfork at one end of the long rows of peanut bushes that bordered my route. A machine that lifted the roots out of the soil and left the peanuts exposed to the sun and wind was making its way toward us. My new friend would heap up the bushes scattered by the turning machine at the field's edge—not a very taxing job, he admitted with a grin.

He described to me how the timing for this operation had to be just right—the peanuts had to be only just formed, not long enough to have become embedded in the soil, whence the machine could not extract them. He recalled without regrets the back-breaking days of laboring in this same field with only a mule to help in turning over the heavy bushes. Then, with the broadest grin yet, he stared up at the sky, thick and dark with rain clouds, and said, "Looks like there won't be any more working today." (Unfortunately for him, however, the clouds that day brought forth just a few random, scattered, splatting drops.)

I pedalled on past fields where the harvesting machines were scooping up the dried nuts and leaving the "hay" behind as eventual winter fodder for cattle. On the outskirts of Fort Gaines an ancient recycled school bus passed me, its back door replaced by a sheet of plywood, its seats ripped out, and its interior filled nearly to the top of the window frames with peanuts.

At the Columbian Peanut Company inside town I saw that bus again, as well as long lines of carts, tractors, trucks, and rigs waiting to have their loads of peanuts weighed and tested. A long metal cylinder suspended from a high platform sampled each load as it entered the company's courtyard by sucking a few peanuts up into a cloth bag. Once the quality of the batch was determined, the load went to be cleaned and dried.

Brown's Guide photographer Edmund Marshall and I talked to Charlie, a worker whose job it was to oversee the dumping of the peanuts into an underground chamber for cleaning. He wore a mask over his mouth and nose to keep the thick peanut dust that hung in the air out of his respiratory system. From his post the peanuts go inside the factory, Charlie told us, to be shelled and eventually made into peanut butter and brittle and every other kind of peanut goodie. Bless George Washington Carver!

We gave Charlie and his co-workers copies of *Brown's Guide* and headed for a tour of Fort Gaines. We'd barely begun savoring the distinctive atmosphere of this very old pioneer town when we were hailed by a worker from the peanut factory who'd followed us in his car. "If you're looking for unusual people in Fort Gaines," he told us, "don't miss Brooksie Brown. She's got a service station full of rare old rocks, and she knows all about our history here."

We followed his directions and found her to be, indeed, a real quarry of information. Brown's service station at 203 North Hancock Street should be the first stop for any visitors to the area who want to feel their way into its history and traditions. Brooksie Brown's great-great-grandfather was a cabinet-maker who moved to Fort Gaines from Connecticut. Her great-grandfather walked home from Atlanta after Appomattox. "He built himself a tent in the back yard so he could take a bath before they let him in the house, he was so covered with lice," she says drily. We met her mother, a gentle, wistful person who lamented the absence of any kind of museum to house the town's historical records and relics. "There just isn't the money," Mrs. Brown moaned.

True, Fort Gaines is not a wealthy town. When the citizens were offered several years ago an intact 19th-century apothecary's collection that had survived generations of downtown drugstore business, they realized that they lacked the funds to keep it open as a showplace. The entire collection was shipped to nearby Lumpkin, where it makes an impressive addition to that community's resurgent courthouse square. Fort Gaines' Washington Street, home of the town's early magnates, is now a forlorn avenue of empty store fronts and disintegrating mansions.

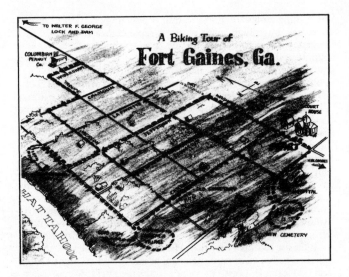

Yet there's no small town in Georgia I love more than Fort Gaines. It's a slightly worn, lived-in kind of place. For the most part, its blocks of modest late Victorian houses are neither showily spruce nor depressingly decrepit. Like most of the rest of us, they're just maintaining themselves, patching up as need occurs, making do. Fort Gaines doesn't have to prove anything to anyone; it's content to be comfortable and open and welcoming.

Take Brooksie Brown again. As soon as she learned we cared about her town's past, she went home to get a hand-drawn self-guided tour of Fort Gaines—with detailed descriptions of points of interest—which she and her mother had put together (be sure and ask to see it when you're there). Then she entertained us with stories and legends of the town's early days.

It was a real outpost back in the 1810s and '20s. Just north of town began Indian territory. Folks came with their cotton to trade and left a contingent inside the fort to guard against attacks. The gigantic Dill House on Washington Street was paid for, so the tale goes, by paper money saved up by General Dill's wife while she was a captive of the Indians. Seems they kept the silver coins received in trades but threw the paper currency away; their enterprising prisoner hid what she considered worthless in her dress. "Another woman was scalped by the Indians but it didn't kill her," Brooksie Brown said matter-of-factly. "She just wore a bonnet the rest of her days."

Later in the 19th century Fort Gaines became a booming metropolis. Merchants came there from Alabama and all around to sell their cotton. The town boasted two or three hotels, two newspapers, and "saloons everywhere." The decline set in with the ominous boll-weevil depression of the 1910s.

We learned about the surrounding countryside from Brooksie Brown as well, in particular the Colonel William Toney house next to the reservoir north of town. The oldest house in Clay County, it is supposed to have lodged the mercurial Aaron Burr, either after his famous duel with Alexander Hamilton in 1804 or in 1807 when General Edmund Gaines (after whom the fort was named) arrested him for treason.

I cycled out to see the house, whose classic—and classy—lines are still visible beneath the modern siding that now covers it. The building had to be displaced when the dam was built, and its two chimneys were removed. Present owners the W. V. Standleys hope to replace them someday. They kindly showed me through the house, whose interior reveals the building's beautiful wide original boards. Weary cyclists will find the Toney House a lovely spot to rest and the Standleys gracious guides to the history-conscious.

The building of the giant Walter F. George lock and dam across the Chattahoochee just north of Fort Gaines displaced more than the Toney house. In Brooksie Brown's service station are displayed cephalopods she claims to be 50 million years old. They are dredged up from 65 feet below the river when dam construction began some 20 years ago. She's got a collection of rocks from 35 states and, best of all, some splendid wood sculptures of her own (not for sale, worse luck). Many of her delightful birds and animals are fashioned from cedar blocks that also came to her from the dam site. Putting the old to new uses—to me that's like an epigraph for Fort Gaines and its presiding spirit, Brooksie Brown.

Of course, one can lose one's perspective in a charming town like Fort Gaines. History didn't begin with Edmund Gaines and Aaron Burr, and it's good of cephalopods to remind us of the fact. In town I'd been hearing about civilization from the perspective of America's European settlers and their descendants. As we prepare for the Bicentennial madness, it seems fitting to conclude with acknowledgement of a civilization in the Fort Gaines area that long predated the arrival of Brooksie Brown's great-great-grandfather.

The starting and finishing point for my cycling explorations was Kolomoki Mounds State Park, site of the largest temple mound east of the Mississippi. Excavations have traced civilizations at this spot back to 800 A.D., with the mounds dated sometime between 1000 and 1300. I tried to visualize what the park's historic brochure said the area had been—a ceremonial center with perhaps as many as two thousand Kolomoki inhabitants at the height of its importance in the 13th century. But the placid lake, the close-cropped green fields, and the groves of sturdy live oaks hung deep with Spanish moss gave off no echoes of that busy time.

Until the summer of 1974 visitors to the park could at least experience what our parents' generation thought ancient Indian civilizations had been like. A park museum contained anthropologists' reconstructions of Indian family and village life through the use of carved wooden figurines. A magnificent pottery exhibit showed what the excavations of the mounds had unearthed.

Yet the destruction of the past which European civilization brought to this continent has not yet come to an end. A year and a half ago the Kolomoki museum was ransacked and all its precious artifacts stolen. The building is now just a shell.

Park Superintendent Cecil Hall is cautiously hopeful that funds allocated by the state for a new museum collection will be released soon, but he doubts that the more "scientific" exhibits being planned will have the public appeal of the old figurines. Try to get to know Mr. Hall when you're visiting the park. He may seem gruff and taciturn at first, but a playful, wry wit, a gentle mocking of present-day accepted wisdom, begins to warm the air the longer you engage him in talk.

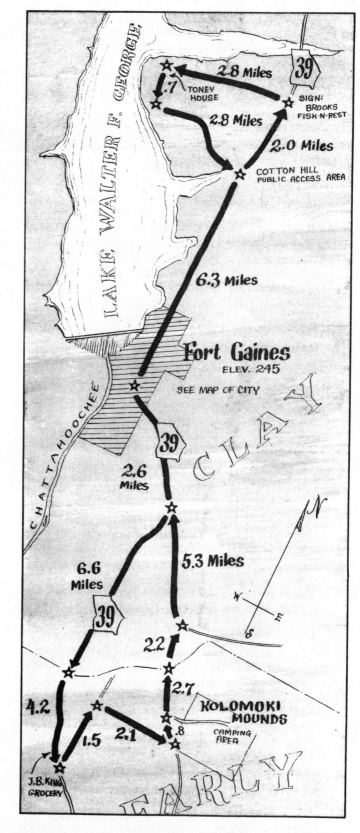

Get to know, above all, this rich, remote corner of Georgia and as many as you can of its quietly eloquent citizens. I know I just scratched the surface in my wheelings and crankings around Clay and a corner of Early Counties. I plan to be back, to dig deeper and deeper yet. Who knows what cephalopods and other treasures lie hidden beneath those melons and those peanuts?

1975

Bike Route Description

Centering in the old frontier town of Fort Gaines, this ride is planned in two loops. The northern end, approximately 21 miles, takes cyclists to the Walter F. George Lock and Dam on the Chattahoochee and to the fine old Colonel William Toney House, described in the text. The southern loop, roughly 30½ miles not including the tour of Fort Gaines, takes in Kolomoki Mounds State Park.

Georgia route 39, the backbone of the trip, offers a splendid blacktop surface. The side roads, especially in Clay County, are composed of an extremely rough aggregate substance which is hard on a biker's nerves. All surfaces are paved, with the exception of those inside Kolomoki park. If you happen to ride there during a prolonged dry spell, you will find the navigating tough indeed, because the dust lies thick and a ten-speed bike's narrow tire will find nothing to grip. In wet weather the surface is sufficiently hard packed to provide decent traction.

Kolomoki's camp sites are handsomely landscaped; they're located 1.9 miles from the access road entrance. In summer a swimming pool near the camp sites is open to the public.

Parking is no problem in Fort Gaines; the county courthouse is a convenient place to start. Moving north on Washington Street, take note of #204, the John Sutlive House, and, a block further, the massive crumbling pile that is listed on the National Register of Historic Places and known as the Dill House. Sutlive and Dill were partners in many local enterprises, including a trading post, during the first half of the 19th century. You'll see the tombs of both men in the picturesque but unkempt Old Cemetery on Carroll Street.

Don't miss the New Cemetery, adjoining the county hospital off Hartford Road. It is also listed on the National Register, as is its central feature, a lovely gazebo or summer house with the inscription "Fort Gaines Improvement Society 1880." It sits upon a small Indian mound. Local legend has it that if you stomp in the middle of the summer house floor and say, "Indian, Indian, what are you doing down there?" he will say nothing.

Fort Gaines' main tourist attraction is a replica of the original 1814 fort called "Frontier Village," situated on a high bluff overlooking the Chattahoochee. Leave the paved road just beyond the "Boy Scout" house, and ride or push your bike across the grass to a path along the top of the bluff. A beautiful flight of modern steps zigzags down the bank. If you look closely, you can make out what used to be the old cotton slide, leading down to where huge river warehouses used to store cotton for shipment in steamboats. Views in both directions along the river are breathtaking.

Hiking Trips

CONTENTS

INTRODUCTION

Hiking enthusiasts have a veritable passion for nature and love to study it up close. Often amateur botanists and zoologists, they thrill at identifying such plants as gaywings and bloodroot or sizing up curious hoof prints or paw tracks near the path. Many hard-core hikers prefer to travel alone so they enjoy the solitude of nature and the beauty of the trail scenery unspoiled by others. Besides, they insist, you're likely to see more wildlife if you follow little-hiked routes, plus you can move at your own pace. Others prefer to stick to well-known trails, so they share the camaraderie of trail and camp-fire.

Veterans of the trail always seem to know about the factors that assure a successful trip. For instance, having good instincts about weather conditions can mean the difference between a pleasant outing or a miserable one. Also, knowing what to wear and what supplies to bring can make a big difference in one's enjoyment of the outdoors.

Veterans, such as Tim Homan, easily share the advice he has picked up over the miles. He'll explain the intricacies of hikers' etiquette:

•Ask others about their trips, so they will later give you the opportunity to describe yours. Never litter the trail and leave the camp area cleaner than you found it. Share trail tips and supplies you have with those who appear to need them. Don't spoil someone else's trip by intruding into their peace and quiet, yet don't hold back companionship from those who want it.

•Have a planned route and realistic check points, so that if you don't show up, someone will be alerted. In other words, hiking is not just wandering around the countryside. Have a plan, whether it's to take an established trail, follow roads or even railroads, or go cross-country when no footpaths exist. Never set off without adequate maps, a guidebook, or thorough knowledge of the trail.

•Set a pace so that you don't have a pounding heart or find yourself gasping for breath. Take a canteen so you don't dehydrate or overheat. Clothing for the trail should protect the hiker primarily from wind, so layering is important. Wool is best because it's lightweight, warm, and dries quickly.

•Camp only in hikers' shelters because it confines the litter, the campfire scars, and other signs of civilization in fewer areas, not spoiling the wilderness character of the countryside.

•Don't be too spartan. It's important to remember that the point of hiking is outdoor recreation, which includes occasional stops in town (if you undertake a long-distance hike) for shopping, laundry, a shower, or a restaurant meal.

Hiking in nature is a timeless experience. The sensations of the forest are no different today than they were 200 years ago, maybe even 2,000 years ago.

The hikers who wrote for *Brown's Guide* had a variety of types of trips. Sometimes they wound up at trail's end. Sometimes they simply got lost, as many hikers do occasionally. Al-

ways, the hiking-writers packed the reader along for the adventure. The descriptive writing of Tom Patterson, Susan McDonald, and Margaret Tucker, among others, captures not only the sights of the trail—scenic vistas and micro-observations—but also often notices the sounds of the area as well, whether it's rushing water, bird calls, or a distant roar of a chainsaw. The writers often relate small personal pleasures, such as discovering a lush thicket of blackberries or sharing moonshine with mountaineers.

In every case, writers sought the best experience to share. Most trips are oriented toward beginners, people who are in good physical condition. Often, stories offer alternative routes to the same destination. For example, three trails up Georgia's highest peak, Brasstown Bald, ranged from 2.2 miles to 15 miles and included trails through forest and dense laurel thickets and along a nearly abandoned country road. During the climb, writer McDonald points out the changing vegetation and animal life that are part of the half-mile change in altitude:

"Trees and bushes are shorter and scrubbier near the mountaintop, where the strong winds and colder temperatures stunt their growth. Flowering shrubs, such as rhododendron and flame azalea, growing near the mountaintop often bloom three weeks later than the same species in the surrounding lower elevations. The summit area is also the home of Georgia's only population of ravens, large blackbirds resembling their smaller cousins, the crows."

In another instance, McDonald charted six autumn hikes to waterfalls along trails that passed through some of the prettiest spots in the highlands, all located in the Chattahoochee National Forest.

A few hikes are unique in being located in and near Atlanta. On a trek along 15 miles of marked trail in the Kennesaw Mountain National Battlefield Park, writer Laurie O'Brien points out the site where General Joseph E. Johnston's Confederate troops dug in to defend Atlanta against the invading forces of Major General William T. Sherman. And she explores Fernbank Forest, that pristine forest in Decatur with its own visiting hours.

Also in the piedmont, writer Leon Brown explores the 100,000 acres of wilderness called Oconee National Forest. "If you wish to camp in an area where you really are camping out, walk on trails that, except for a hunter or two, only wild animals use, and spend several days doing this without ever seeing another person, then the Oconee's the place," he advises, right up front about the primitive nature of the place.

As *Brown's Guide* writers suggest, there is lots to be said for the simplicity of traveling on foot, intimacy with nature, and the satisfaction that comes from spending time being part of the outdoor world. There is also the sense of accomplishment that comes from having walked a tough trail.

J.W.E.

Come On Along the Rough Ridge Trail

by Margaret Tucker

The Cohutta mountains contain some of the wildest country in North Georgia, land so rugged and densely forested that it is prime habitat only for the wild boar and the black bear, an animal which cannot share its territory with large numbers of human intruders. A fifth of the area has a slope steeper than 60 percent. Rainfall is up to 85 inches per year and the tree canopy is so dense that there are few vistas. It's a great place to get away from concrete. It's a place to explore, to enjoy but to enter with respect. It is wilderness.

My first trip into the Cohuttas was to meet friends coming out after an overnight backpack to the Jacks River Falls. Some of them came out. The others we went after and found, trudging up the trail two hours late after a trip up one of the unmarked side trails. One of them had remarked on a lovely, moss-green stump, pointing it out to the others as they walked by. A little later they noticed another one. You guessed it . . . same stump. It's easy to do. There are many unmarked trails up the various creeks and along the Jacks River, particularly at crossings, where the main trail may turn but a fisherman's trail will stay along the river for some distance.

The Jacks River area can be explored by many different trails; from Tennessee via an abandoned road into the river at Beech Bottoms, by a trail the length of the Jacks itself (better left for summer and fall as it makes about two dozen crossings), and by the Rough Ridge and Penitentiary Branch Trails which offer a weekend backpacking trip with an easy shuttle. Going into the river on the Rough Ridge Trail and out on the Penitentiary Branch Trail will give you a taste of both the ridge and the ravine environments and show you a variety of spring wildflowers.

The old roads down Rough Ridge and Penitentiary Branch have been closed and seeded for wildlife. Motor vehicles, even 4-wheel drive and trail bikes, are prohibited, although I've encountered both on the Penitentiary Branch Trail. On Rough Ridge, trees dropped across the trail enforce the ban. It works, but you feel like a Green Beret in training as you struggle over and under them with a 40-pound pack.

A quarter-mile from the start of the Rough Ridge Trail, a small stream running east to Wilson Creek offers one of only two water sources on the ridge trail. I have drunk from the Jacks and many of its tributaries without harm, but none of the water has been tested, so be your own judge.

Oaks dominate the ridge—white oak, northern and southern red oak, chestnut oak. Most are second growth trees, from 30 to 40 years old, as the Cohuttas were timbered in the 1930's.

Many of the steep coves, however, escaped the axe and boast huge hemlocks, beech, maple, tulip poplar, and basswood. About two miles out you will see a few vistas of civilization in the valleys to the east. Ahead and to the west Buckeye Mountain dominates the view.

The old road ends about four miles down the ridge and you're abruptly on a rough, rock-strewn path which plunges down the mountain. This is not a constructed trail and the footing is tricky. Watch carefully for the trail markers, orange metal diamonds.

Saving its best for the last few miles, the trail plummets down an almost impossibly steep slope. It then lulls you with a mile or so of gradual descent before sneaking around the eastern side of a hillside so steep your left ankle is soon in painful revolt.

Then you hear the river. One short, rocky drop and the Rough Ridge Trail joins the Jacks River Trail, as the latter turns west from the river. To this point you have hiked eight miles, probably spending at least 3½ to 4 hours.

The character of the trail changes in the moist gorge. Hemlock needles soften the ground and scent damp air. The area has almost completely recovered from the scars of the logging era. The only traces of the old narrow gauge railroad along the river which hauled out the logs are the green humps a few places on the trail.

When you reach the falls, you'll find plenty of space for sunbathing or picnicking. There's sheltered camping in a grove of pines and poplars above the falls and across the river from the mouth of Beech Creek. The vegetation and temperature change from moist to dry environment are particularly noticeable on Penitentiary Branch Trail. As you walk up the creek you are surrounded by cove hardwoods, hemlocks, and rhododendron thickets. As you ascend, pines become smaller. When you turn east toward Hemp Top Road, oaks, black gum, and hickory predominate, on the dry south-facing slopes and Virginia pines replace the white pines. The road continues to climb up the side of the Jacks gorge for about a mile, then turns almost due east for the last mile and a half, the sound of the river is abruptly cut off. There are good views of Rockwall Branch Ravine on your right as you climb. A gap, one last climb and you reach Hemp Top road, to cover approximately 6½ miles. However, keep your plans flexible. Especially in the spring and after heavy rain, the river may be too high to cross. It's happened to me. A lovely, clear day's hike was followed by evening showers. A nice, gentle sound on my ears changed to a terrible roaring as I awoke in the dark to a downpour with thunder, lightning and wind.

I spent anxious minutes straining to see if the drip I felt came from a pinhole in the tarp, a leaky seam, or the failure of a drip cord. How I wished for one of those wonderful (and expensive) light-weight tents with floor, breathable nylon top and coated, waterproof covering fly. At dawn the wettest of our party shouted, "Pack it up." We did. As organizer of the trip, I got dark looks. It was a record storm. As we hiked out, we encountered as much as two inches of rain in an hour. The trail became a creek. Rough Creek became a river. Our car was too wet to start and we had to push it off. When we got down to the valley, people were being evacuated. So, don't go into the Cohuttas without raingear.

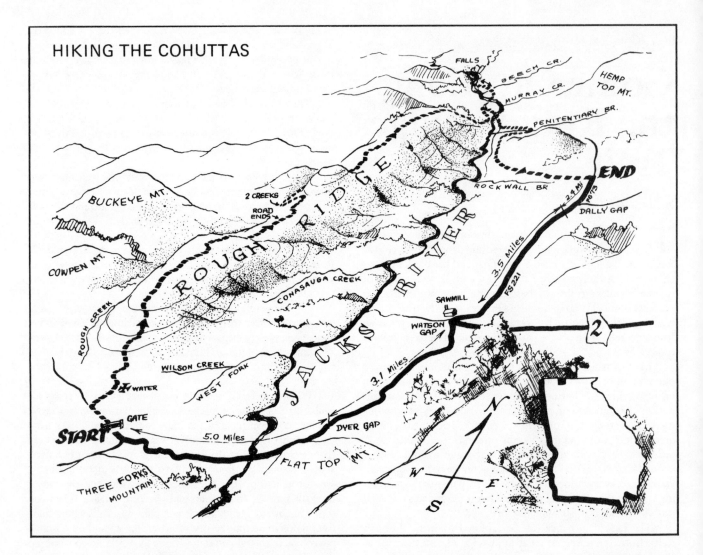

HIKING THE COHUTTAS

Still, with all the rough spots: steep trails, unpredictable weather, evil stares from friends, the Cohuttas provide one of the finest walks in the southeast. This trip combines some good scenery, some physical challenge and some good companionship with fellow hikers to produce an experience that will be long remembered.

HIKING GUIDE

This map traces a hike to Jacks River Falls in the Cohuttas Wilderness. As shown here, this is a two-day hike with an overnight at the falls. Note by the way that the Jacks River flows north, so the first day you will be walking downstream toward the falls.

Easy access to the area is from state highway 5 in the north-central part of the state. Turn onto state highway 2 going west toward Higdon. Near Higdon the pavement ends and you'll be driving on a high quality gravel road. From highway 2 turn right onto Forest Service road 221 at Watson Gap (this road is marked). Go 3.5 miles. At the intersection of Forest Service roads 221, 91

and 73, take 73. Follow 73 for 2.4 miles. At this point look carefully for an older road on your left. It is marked only by a small yellow sign which indicates that motor vehicles are prohibited. This is the terminus of Penitentiary Branch Trail where you will end your hike. Park one car here to set up a shuttle.

To reach the starting point, return to Watson Gap. Go 8.1 miles until you come to a "Y" intersection. The road to the right is blocked by a gate: the road to the left is open. This is the head of the trail. Walk up the gated road toward Cowpen Mountain. After a few minutes, turn right onto an old abandoned road. This older road is marked with a "foot traffic only" sign and several trees have been felled to block motorized traffic.

It is about 9½ miles (5½ to 6 hours) from the start of the hike to the falls and 6½ miles (5 hours) from the falls out to the end of the hike.

A word of caution: even experienced hikers have become lost and confused in the Cohuttas due to the fact that many side trails branch off from the main routes. For that reason some of the trail switching that must be done is outlined in detail here. Note that the trails are marked with orange metal diamonds and you can't go far wrong if you keep an eye out for these signals.

Most of your walking the first day will be along Rough Ridge Trail. Eight miles from the start of the hike, Jacks River Trail intersects. Take Jacks River Trail. You'll be walking downstream toward the falls. You'll follow Jacks River Trail all the way to the falls. It crosses Rough Creek and descends through a tunnel of rhododendron to the river. Cross the river (you must wade) and continue along the trail to a small creek. Just on the other side of the creek, Beech Bottoms Trail enters from the east (right). You continue on Jacks River Trail. An island and rapids tell you you are approaching the falls.

The rocks around the falls make good picnicking and sunbathing spots and you can find a suitable campsite nearby.

On the way out, retrace your steps back up Jacks River Trail. Continue on past the place where Rough Ridge Trail intersects. About ¾ of a mile past the Rough Ridge Trail intersection the trail crosses the river. After crossing the river you'll stay on Jacks River Trail for another quarter mile until you come to Penitentiary Branch. There Penitentiary Branch Trail (an old logging road) turns off to the left up Penitentiary Branch. Take this trail. You'll walk up Penitentiary Branch, cross it and come back downstream. You'll follow this trail on out to the end of the hike.

Remember that it's easy to get turned around in this wilderness. Keep an eye out for the orange blazes that mark the trail.

1974

Hold the Line, Edward Tinney

For Southerner and Northerner alike, a hike through Chickamauga National Park helps answer some questions, questions like, "Where are we coming from?"

by Laurie O'Brien

The heat of the day has not yet hit the battlefield at Chickamauga, but already the history buffs, sightseers, campers, and tourists are beginning to trickle into the park. As they pass through the visitors' center, watching slide shows, looking at battle plans and weapons displays, buying books and postcards, park historian Edward Tinney relaxes in his book-lined office in the back of the building.

"It's a great thing to have people coming here to see this place," says Tinney as he props his feet up on the desk, "but it would be such a shame if it became too commercial. It's the country's oldest military park, and the biggest one, too, and we've got an Act of Congress telling us we have to maintain this place just like it was back when those boys fought here in September, 1863. We want these fields to look the same as they did to those soldiers then, and while we want people today to be able to see their heritage here, we've got to do everything we can to protect this battlefield from the intrusion of man and his modern conveniences."

Tinney—crusty, friendly, an enthusiastic lover of history, and a zealous protector of the past—is the chief historian at Chickamauga. He is gray-haired and gruff, with an ever-present twinkle in his eye. He sometimes appears caught in the middle between his present-day gregariousness and his affection for the past, but he always maintains a blustery cheerfulness to all comers. In between slide shows for the Rotarians and bicycle trips for youth groups, he holds court in his office at the visitors' center, where he imparts history with an enthusiasm rarely encountered in a classroom or library.

"See this young man here," Tinney says, pointing to one of his young assistants. "His granddaddy rode with Nathan Bedford Forrest. Now I don't know how much you know about history, but if everybody who said they rode with Forrest really did, he'd of had the whole Confederate Army right at his side. Sort of like all those beds George Washington slept in, you know. Well anyway," Tinney continues, "this young man's grandfather *really did* ride with Nathan Bedford Forrest."

Tinney nods in satisfaction at having such a near-celebrity in his office, and the young assistant, perched on the edge of a table amid a clutter of books, papers, and slide trays, beams a little sheepishly.

"He's like a lot of young people that are coming to the park these days," Tinney says. "They're looking for their roots. They're asking, 'Where did we come from?' History is our legacy," Tinney continues, "and the person who looks back in time is really seeking his own soul."

For Tinney, history isn't a job. It's his life. He grew up in the Shenandoah Valley of Virginia, taught school in a place called Brandy Station, and took his first park service job as a ranger in Shenandoah.

"I fell in love with the park service ideals and goals, to preserve and protect," Tinney says, "and I really believe in what I'm doing."

From Shenandoah, Tinney transferred to the west Tennessee battleground at Shiloh to be an historian, and from there to Chickamauga.

"You know, you can't say there's anything too unusual about the park service—countries all over the world have park services—but a place like Chickamauga is unique; there's only one of a kind. People hear this place called a park, and they think we ought to have slides and swings and shuffleboard courts and swimming pools, but that's not why we're here. We have an unending responsibility to perpetuate the memory of the 34,000 men who fell here in battle."

Tinney, whose conversation is spiced with gossip from a general's diary or anecdotes from a corporal's letters, takes the care of Chickamauga very seriously. He quotes easily from the writings of Robert E. Lee, but is equally at ease discussing Jane

Fonda or Ramsay Clark. He is gratified by the fact that people these days do seem to be looking a little more closely at the past, but he is also worried about what he sees as a general decline in historical awareness.

"There's no cultivation of the mind any more," Tinney says. "It's a celluloid world, a television world. If people don't like what they see, they can just flip a channel.

"These people who fought here at Chickamauga weren't just pages from a history book. They were human. If you stuck 'em, they bled. Some of them were farmers, and some of them were aristocrats, but they all had a lot of pride and a lot of honor."

Tinney spends much of his time helping people track down relatives who fought at Chickamauga. He has even helped two little old ladies who didn't know each other locate the marker for the regiment in which both their grandfathers fought. He has little patience, however, with people who walk around the park calling themselves "Rebels" and "Yankees."

"They just don't know what they're saying," says Tinney, a first-generation American whose father is Hungarian, mother is seven-eighths Indian, and wife is from Odessa. "We are all of us Americans, and as Abraham Lincoln and the United States Constitution put it, the only real crime is the dissolution of the Union."

Take away the tourists, the stone markers, the occasional green government truck, and you have Chickamauga, one of the bloodiest battlefields in America's history. It is a land of rolling hills and lush forests, quiet streams and small farms, a place where the boys in blue met the lads in gray in a three-day battle that left history's indelible mark forever upon these hills.

The battle between the Union troops of General William Rosecrans and the rebel forces of General Braxton Bragg was joined almost by accident. The two armies, maneuvering for control of the strategic city of Chattanooga, apparently stumbled upon each other as they groped through the tangled brush of the North Georgia countryside.

Sergeant Axel Reed was a soldier in the Second Minnesota Infantry, Company "K," who fought in the battle of Chickamauga.

He began his diary entry on September 17, 1863, ". . . there seems to be a great battle pending with near 100,000 men on each side."

Two days later, Reed wrote of an all-night march, followed by a stop for breakfast, "but did not have time to cook any; got coffee partly cooked and had to go on." By midmorning, Reed's unit was involved in "hard fighting." Reed, who was under arrest for writing a letter to a newspaper critical of army policy, was not armed when the fighting began. He took a gun from a wounded man in his company, and "made the best use of it I could."

Throughout the long day Reed and his company fought, often supporting Union troops that fell back before Confederate charges. At dusk, they took a position along a ridge above the lines of battle and listened to the firing, which continued until long after dark.

The next morning, the sun rose "red and fiery," and Reed and his compatriots began the final day of their stand at Chick-

amauga. It was to be a bloody day, a day filled with suffering and death.

"The sound of cannon and musketry was terrific," Reed wrote. "Shell and shot were flying through the air in all directions with all the hideous sound imaginable. . . . The fire was terrible on us, many shots taking effect. Sgt. Pomeroy of my company lay about six feet from me. I saw him just as a ball struck him in the top of the head. He raised his head a little, gave a groan, and his face dropped on the ground as he lay quivering. I could see that he still breathed. . . .

"It was a horrible sight to look at the men of my own regiment lying in line just as they were shot, on their faces. Sgt. Pomeroy, Corporal Metzger, and little Johnnie Cutting, who had long been my messmate, lay there within ten feet of each other, just as though they were sleeping. Sgt. Pomeroy was still breathing."

The final stand made by Reed's unit was at a place called Snodgrass Hill, just northeast of where the first battle lines had been drawn along the LaFayette Road. In spite of repeated Confederate charges, the Union forces held the hill, and with it the key to their successful retreat after the rebel victory.

"At seven p.m. last evening," wrote Axel Reed, "we were ordered to withdraw from the bloody scene and to keep as quiet as possible. We were the last brigade to leave the field."

The cannons at Chickamauga are quiet now, but they still stand overlooking the battlefields once so desperately fought for by so many men. The few log houses, the rolling hills, the dense forest, all remain unchanged, a quiet memorial to the men who died here over a hundred years ago.

As Edward Tinney puts it, "This place needs to stay unspoiled. Its history is our legacy, and every time you chip away at that legacy, you lose something."

Ed Tinney plans to see that that doesn't happen at Chickamauga.

HIKING GUIDE

Use the seven-mile drive-through tour of Chickamauga as an overview to get your bearings. Then park your car in the lot at the visitors' center at the north entrance to the park and explore some of its 36 miles of hiking trails.

The trails wind through the battlefields of Chickamauga National Military Park, and provide a first-hand feeling of what it might have been like to advance before enemy guns, or retreat under enemy fire. The trails cover a variety of terrain, from open fields, to dense forest, to the lowlands around Chickamauga Creek. There are some little hills, but no major climbs, and the going is never extremely difficult. Although the trails intersect paved park roads from time to time, the hikes still convey a feeling of remoteness and quiet.

The Loop Trail, which is approximately 20 miles long, circles the park and provides a variety of terrain, where the visitor derives the greatest sense of "getting away from it all." The Alabama Trail cuts straight up through the center of the park almost parallel to the LaFayette Road (US 27) and gives you a chance to see many of the monuments and markers that proliferate at Chickamauga.

You can follow either of these trails, which are easily accessible from directly in front of the visitors' center, or you can put together

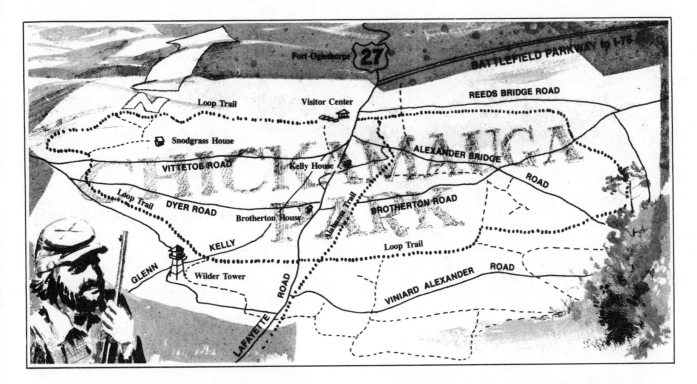

your own Chickamauga hike by studying the map and figuring out which points of interest really interest you.

Cannons and commemorative markers dot the trails and serve as memorials to the men who fought and died in each particular place. There are also battlefield markers which explain just what was happening during the battle at each specific place. If you're a real history buff, you can arm yourself with an inexpensive guide book from the visitors' center and then read the markers as you go. You will probably wind up knowing more about Chickamauga than the generals who led the fighting.

On the other hand, if history is something you left behind in the tenth grade, you can use a hike through Chickamauga simply as a pleasant outdoor experience, with just a little battle information thrown in on the side. Going to Chickamauga without discovering a little of its history is like going to the beach and not getting wet, but it is possible to hit the high points of the battle without getting bogged down in the details.

Basically, the Yankees and the Confederates formed their first battle lines along LaFayette Road. You can stand by the cannons and look out over the fields and get a pretty good idea of how things stood. The battle, which began somewhat accidentally, continued for three days, and included a high degree of mistake-making by both the rebels and the Yanks in command. The Confederate forces did achieve something of a victory—they lost about 2,000 fewer men than the Union Army did—but they failed to follow up their advantage, and the Yankees made a safe retreat north to Chattanooga.

You can fill in on this outline by examining the dioramas in the visitors' center, which include "Mix-up in the Union Command" and "The Confederate Breakthrough," before setting out on your hike.

If your great-grandfather fought with the Tennessee cavalry or the Ohio infantry, you can use a topographical map that is available in the visitors' center to pinpoint the location of the marker for his regiment and plan your hike to include a stop there.

No matter what your inclinations about Chickamauga, you will probably want to include some of the points of interest which are scattered around the park, besides the cannons and the markers.

Snodgrass Hill, in the northwest corner of the park, is the sight of the last Confederate charge, which the Union soldiers repelled. The Snodgrass House still stands as it was then, a small log building, with cannons in its front yard. There is a tiny barn across the road, and the field by the house has been sown with corn and other vegetables. An old hay wagon is parked by the side of the road, and a weathered plow lies at the edge of the field. Several roads and trails come together near here, and you can hike off into the woods to see what the assaulting rebels were up against. The Snodgrass House and its environs also make a good spot to stop for lunch and a rest.

The Kelly House and the Brotherton House, also standing as they were back in 1863, make other interesting stops to include on your hike. You might also try climbing Wilder Tower, in the western part of the park, for a bird's-eye view of Chickamauga.

How To Get There: Go north on I-75 to the battlefield exit, then follow the Battlefield Parkway to US 27, just south of Fort Oglethorpe.

Fort Oglethorpe has restaurants and grocery stores, but only one small motel, so your best bet for overnight accommodations, if you're not camping, is to stay in Chattanooga, which is nine miles north on US 27.

Camping: A primitive camping area is available in the park. You should make reservations by contacting the Superintendent, Chickamauga Battlefield, Fort Oglethorpe, Georgia 30741; (404)866-9241.

In hiking and camping at Chickamauga, you should wear sturdy shoes and carry water and a snakebite kit. Park rangers patrol the area, and the personnel in the visitors' center can help with any problems.

1977

Secret Trails

Walking through the mountains nobody knows

by Tom Patterson

The Armuchee Ranger District, located in Georgia's northwestern corner, is the smallest of the Chattahoochee National Forest's seven ranger districts, encompassing about 64,000 acres—only one twelfth of North Georgia's federally owned forest land. Its relatively small size and the fact that it's located in an area of the state that is often overlooked by hikers and other travelers help to explain why there are so many fewer hiking trails located here than in the other districts of the Chattahoochee National Forest. Slowly but surely, over the past three years, Paul Bullard, the ranger for the Armuchee District, has been trying to change this situation. "For some reason," he says, "nobody has emphasized trail building in this district in the past. Like all U.S. Forest Service programs, we're at the mercy of Congress when it comes to construction and maintenance of hiking trails. It all depends on the availability of funds."

Before 1978 there were no hiking trails at all in Bullard's district, and he says that the three loop trails that have now been built probably wouldn't have been constructed at all except for "a matter of circumstance. A few years back," Bullard says, "we got some Youth Conservation Corps workers through the U.S. Department of Labor, and it was up to us to provide jobs and supervision for those kids. So we used that situation as leverage to get some trail-construction and maintenance funds, and we got those kids to build some trails for us."

Hiking enthusiasts should be grateful to those kids, since the trails that they built make this topographically distinct section of the state easily accessible to foot travel. Before the late 1970s the only way to hike in the Armuchee District was by following the random, unmarked network of old logging roads that crisscross the area, or by bushwhacking, which can be unusually tricky in this region characterized by steep slopes, sheer rock cliffs, and dense underbrush. Georgia's northwestern corner is the only part of the state that includes portions of the Valley and Ridge District of the Appalachian Mountains, a section of long, fairly straight ridges which extends southwestward from eastern Tennessee into southern Alabama. The cliffs are separated from one another by creek and river valleys. You can get a feel for the lay of the land here without a topo map by looking at a Georgia highway map; the roads in this part of the state tend to run along the bottoms of the valleys or, in a few cases, along the tops of the ridges.

Each of the three trails in the Armuchee Ranger District is a loop trail, so there's no need to set up shuttles. The longest of the trails is just over six miles, while each of the others is about two miles long. All three can be hiked in a weekend. If you prefer primitive camping, you'll find some good camping spots along the Chickamauga Trail. Otherwise, you can camp at one of the designated sites at The Pocket Recreation Area. The Keown Falls Recreation Area is the only place included in this guide where camping is not permitted.

If you'd like to obtain more information about the Armuchee District before making your trip, call the district's office: (404) 638-1085.

HIKING GUIDE

Three Trails in the Armuchee Ranger District

CHICKAMAUGA TRAIL (6.2 miles)

Driving Directions: Drive east on Ga 136 from its intersection with US 27 in the center of the LaFayette business district. After 4½ miles Ga 136 briefly joins Ga 151. Drive 1.5 miles north to the point where 136 and 151 split. Turn right here, and follow 136 for another 3.3 miles to a point where it is intersected from the south by a paved road and from the north by a dirt road. Turn left onto the dirt road, and drive .7 mile to a fork. Take the right fork here, and drive 1.8 miles to the end of the dirt road, where the trailhead is marked by a wooden sign.

Hiking Directions: Shortly after beginning your walk, you'll cross a wooden footbridge (1) over a small stream. From here the trail continues up a hill; the route is well marked by white blazes on trees. After a short distance the trail reaches a T intersection (2) where the loop part of the trail begins and ends. Turn right here (note that the painted blazes are now blue). A wooden sign at this point says, "UNRESTRICTED TRAVEL NEXT 3.9 MI.," which means that there's a chance you might encounter equestrians or kids on trail bikes in this vicinity. This first portion of the loop, well marked and easy to follow, leads sometimes eastward, sometimes southward along a series of curves and switchbacks that follow the lower slopes of Dick Ridge.

The trail crosses several small streambeds and passes a number of large rocks. At about a mile from the beginning of the trail is a sharp uphill switchback (3), beyond which the trail heads north for several miles.

A little less than a mile beyond this shift in the trail's direction is a wide clearing (4) that is part of a power-line right-of-way. Just beyond this clearing is the trail's intersection with a one-lane dirt jeep road (5). Turn left onto this road. The trail follows the road for under ½ mile, leading uphill with occasional switchbacks. Ignore forks in the road; the distinctive blue blazes on the trees mark the route clearly. Once the road reaches level ground, watch for the point where the trail leaves it on the left (6).

The trail now heads downhill for a short distance, then climbs to the crest of Dick Ridge (7), where it parallels a cluster of jagged stones on the left. Follow the ridge to the northernmost point of the loop (8), where the trail bends sharply southward (left) and where a narrow, unmarked trail joins it on the right. Stay on the blue-blazed trail here as it begins a gradual descent on the west side of Dick Ridge. A short distance down the hill the trail meets another dirt road (9) and turns left to follow it for a short distance (follow the blue blazes). The blue blazes end at a wooden sign (10) that says, "FOOT TRAVEL ONLY NEXT 2.3 MI." At this sign the trail bears to the left and is marked for the remainder of its length by white blazes. This part of the trail extends through a low-lying area and fords a network of small streams. Before the trail leaves this area, it passes, on the right, a large mound of old sawdust (11); a small sawmill once stood here.

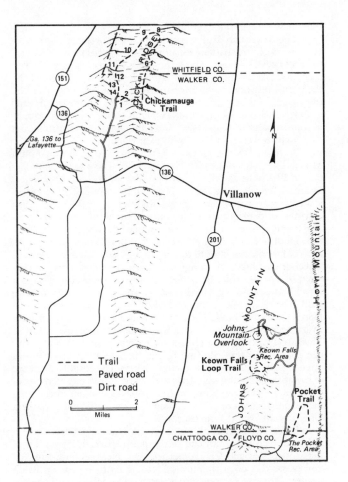

Trail
Paved road
Dirt road

0   2
Miles

Now the trail begins another climb and crosses another dirt road (12), after which it heads downhill. Here it passes a couple of primitive campsites (13) with small stone fire rings and supplies of firewood. Beyond this point is another clearing (14). Just beyond the clearing is the end of the loop (2). Turn right here, and follow the access trail to your car.

KEOWN FALLS LOOP TRAIL (just under 2 miles)

Driving Directions: To reach the other areas included in this hiking guide from the end of the dirt road where the Chickamauga Trail begins and ends, retrace your route 2.5 miles on this dirt road to its intersection with Ga 136. Turn left onto 136, and drive 3.5 miles to Ga 201 at the little community of Villanow. At .4 mile beyond this intersection a paved road marked by a wooden sign indicating Keown Falls and The Pocket recreation areas leaves 136 on the right. Turn right here, and drive 2.3 miles to the point where the road bends sharply to the right and crosses a bridge. The pavement ends on the far side of the bridge. Drive 1.8 miles from the bridge to the turnoff for the Johns Mountain Overlook, marked by a sign on the right side of the road. The overlook area has no hiking trails, but it's worth a brief detour here to take in the expansive view of the long ridges to the west. Turn right at the sign for Johns Mountain Overlook, and follow a winding dirt-and-gravel road for 2.3 miles to the overlook, a wooden platform that juts out over the edge of Johns Ridge and offers a view that includes Taylor Ridge and Lookout Mountain to the west, as well as the valley bisected by Armuchee Creek at the foot of Johns Mountain. This view will provide you with a better sense of the topography of this section of northwest Georgia, where the dominant features are these long ridges and parallel valleys.

Return to the turnoff for Johns Mountain Overlook, turn right, and continue on the dirt road for a mile to a turnoff that leads to Keown Falls, marked by a wooden sign on the right side of the road. Turn right here, and drive .7 mile to the point where the road ends at the parking area for Keown Falls. The beginning of the Keown Falls Loop Trail is clearly marked by a wooden sign at this parking area.

Hiking Directions: The Keown Falls Loop Trail is neatly graded, covered with gravel, and bordered by small stones along its first hundred yards. It leads through the woods on fairly level ground for a short distance and then splits. A wooden signpost here lacked its sign when I hiked this trail in late spring, but I guessed correctly that this is the point where the loop begins and ends. Either fork can be taken here, but this guide will take you on the right fork. The trail, unmarked by blazes on trees but still easy to follow, heads up a fairly steep grade from here to Keown Falls, following switchbacks along the way. As it nears the falls, it passes a series of stone steps with wooden railings. Before you climb, notice the trail that intersects from the left at the bottom of these stairs, which you'll have to follow later in order to complete the loop. The stairs lead to a wooden overlook, similar to the Johns Mountain Overlook, perched over the waterfall itself. From here you'll have a good view not only of Keown Falls, but also of Horn and Mill Creek mountains to the east. The little stream that drops over the rock precipice here to form Keown Falls is clear and clean.

Retrace your steps to the bottom of the stone stairs, and turn right onto the intersecting path mentioned above. This path leads below the falls and along a series of steep rock walls on the right which are usually drenched with spring water that seeps out of the rocks and ornamented with lush ferns and mosses. From here the path leads down an easy mile-long grade to the bare signpost where the loop begins and ends. Follow the access trail back to the parking area.

THE POCKET TRAIL (2.5 miles)

Driving Directions: To reach The Pocket Recreation Area, where you'll find the last of the three hikes included in this guide, leave the Keown Falls parking lot, and return to the dirt road from which you made the turnoff to Keown Falls (note Keown Falls sign). Turn right on this road, and drive 2 miles to the point at which the pavement resumes, where the road enters Floyd County. At .2 mile beyond this point notice the turnoff to The Pocket Recreation Area on the left, marked by a wooden sign. The Pocket is the only designated camping area included in this guide. Each of the 21 campsites here includes a tent platform, a grill, and a picnic table. The sites are clearly numbered on small wooden posts. The gravel road through the area makes a loop through these campsites. Follow this loop about ¾ of the way around, paying attention to the campsite numbers as you pass them. The beginning of The Pocket Trail is located between sites 16 and 17, on the right side of the road.

Hiking Directions: The Pocket gets its name from the fact that it is a low-lying area surrounded on three sides by the steep ridges of Horn Mountain, giving it an inverted U shape, like a pocket, on topo maps. It is often confused with a state-owned area on Pigeon Mountain, about 25 miles to the northwest, which is also called The Pocket.

It's easy to lose your sense of direction on this trail; it is confined for the most part to low-lying streambeds, and it winds this way and that, never permitting much of a view of the surrounding ridges. Don't worry about getting lost, however, since the trail is well defined and clearly marked with white blazes along its entire length. No particularly distinctive natural features, such as waterfalls or overlooks, are on this trail, but it provides a pleasant enough walk. Folks interested in geology should notice that the soil's subsurface in this area, unlike the subsoil in other places included in this guide, is made up of white limestone, which erodes more easily than the rocks which make up the higher elevations of northwestern

Georgia. This easily eroded rock allowed the area to assume its present topographical characteristics. The trail doesn't quite make a complete loop; it ends at the picnic area located just south of the one-way traffic loop where it begins.

1981

Three Paths to The Top of Georgia

by Susan McDonald

From the top of Brasstown Bald, Georgia's highest mountain at 4784 feet, the view takes in four states and, on exceptionally clear days, even the city of Atlanta 80 miles to the south. Hikers who want to see what Georgia looks like from the top have a choice of three foot trails leading up to the mountain's summit. These three vary not only in length but also in trail character, which allows the hiker to plan a route that best matches his or her schedule and outdoor skills.

Possible routes range in length from 2.2 miles to 15 miles and can include trails through forest and dense laurel thickets or along a nearly abandoned country road. All the Brasstown Bald trails have sections with steep grades, but hiking them is well within the capability of people in good physical condition who take the climbs at a pace that feels comfortable to them.

Walking up the mountain gives hikers a first-hand look at the changes in vegetation and animal life that accompany the half-mile change in altitude from the valley below. Trees and bushes are shorter and scrubbier near the mountaintop, where the strong winds and colder temperatures stunt their growth. Flowering shrubs, such as rhododendron and flame azalea, growing near the mountaintop often bloom three weeks later than the same species in the surrounding lower elevations. The summit area is also the home of Georgia's only population of ravens, large black birds resembling their smaller cousins, the crows. These birds normally live in areas much farther north, but feel at home on the mountaintop because its altitude makes the climate seem closer to that of New England than of Georgia. In fact, the highest summer temperature ever recorded on top of Brasstown Bald was a comfortable 84 degrees.

HIKING GUIDE

Brasstown Bald

Here are descriptions and hiking information for the three trails that climb Georgia's highest mountain, plus details on how to combine these trails into longer hikes:

The Arkaquah Trail spans the 5½ miles between Track Rock Gap and the public parking lot atop Brasstown Bald. From the gap, the trail rises 2100 feet, with a very steep climb coming in the first mile or so. At the mountaintop, the trail ends at a path connecting the public restrooms with the parking lot. Blue blazes of paint on tree trunks adjacent to the trail delineate its entire length, and brown wooden signs pinpoint both ends of the trail. Hiking time is approximately 5 hours from Brasstown Bald to the bottom, but 6–7 hours traveling in the opposite direction.

To reach Track Rock Gap, turn south onto a paved road just east of Zion Methodist Church on US 76. This road is 6.2 miles east of Blairsville and 1.3 miles west of Young Harris. The gap is located 2.2 miles along the road and can be identified by an historical marker that speculates on the origin of the prehistoric Indian carvings, or petroglyphs, visible on the boulders a few yards away. The trail entrance is about 75 feet south of the historical marker.

Double Knob Trail referred to locally as Wagon Train Road, is an old roadbed that until recently was used occasionally by four-wheel-drive vehicles. Although it is now becoming too rugged even for this type of vehicular traffic, the road lends itself well to foot travel between Young Harris and the summit area of Brasstown Bald. The north end of the trail begins on the campus of Young Harris College. From US 76, turn onto the street running adjacent to the western boundary of Sharp Memorial Methodist Church. This street turns from asphalt to dirt after about 100 yards. This dirt road is the trail. Be sure to park in a location that will not impede traffic or staff-parking at the college. The 2500-foot change in elevation along the trail occurs at a fairly steady rate along its 6-mile length. The trail skirts Brasstown Bald's summit, intersecting the road that connects the mountain's peak with the public parking lot at a point 75 feet from the lot.

Jack's Knob Trail also blazed with blue paint, stretches 4.5 miles between the south end of the public parking lot on top of Brasstown Bald and Chattahoochee Gap. Near its midpoint, the trail crosses Ga 66 at the turn-off leading up to Brasstown Bald's summit. This intersection conveniently gives hikers the opportunity for a two-hour, 2.2-mile climb up or down Brasstown Bald's south face, which might be just the route to suit novice hikers or those with just a few hours to spare. The wooden sign at the Brasstown Bald Access Road calls this half of the trail "Laurel Corridor," rather than Jack's Knob Trail. South of Ga 66 the trail enters a forest on top of a hill that was partially cut away during road construction. At Chattahoochee Gap the trail dead-ends into the well-traveled Appalachian Trail, which is newly blazed with white paint.

The Appalachian Trail does not cross Brasstown Bald, but its intersection with Jack's Knob Trail provides a way for hikers on the Appalachian to reach a major road without having to backtrack. By adding this section of the Appalachian Trail to the end of their route, hikers beginning at Young Harris or Track Rock Gap can make a rugged two-day (or leisurely three-day), 14- to 15-mile continuous trip that passes over the summit of Georgia's highest mountain. The 4.5 miles of the Appalachian Trail from Chattahoochee Gap to Unicoi Gap maintain a fairly constant elevation until approximately half a mile before Unicoi Gap. At this point it climbs briefly and then plunges very steeply all the way down to Ga 75/17. Even hiking down this slope with a pack puts considerable pressure on the hiker's knees, but ascending this part of the trail would be nothing short of a marathon climb. The 6.8-mile hike from Jack's Gap to Unicoi Gap takes about 5 hours walking time at a leisurely but steady pace. The trail crosses Ga 75/17 9.6 miles north of Helen.

Campsites on level ground are hard to find along most of these mountainous trails, although one area with some level sites is near the northern end of Jack's Knob Trail and is convenient to all three trails on Brasstown Bald. No water nearby, however. Another

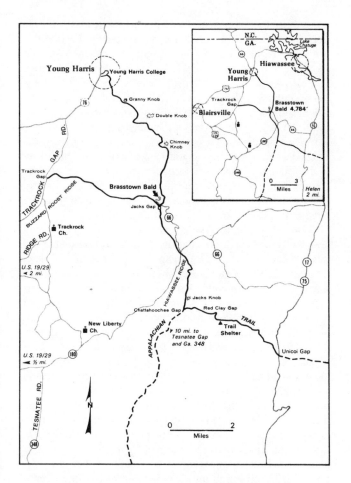

good possibility is the trail shelter and surrounding plateau located about halfway along the above-mentioned section of the Appalachian Trail. The heavy traffic on the Appalachian Trail has left the area adjacent to the shelter denuded of vegetation. It's really quite desolate looking, but concentrating campsites in one area helps the rest of the trail retain its wilderness character. A stream is located down the steep hill just behind the shelter.

Small gravel parking areas are located at Track Rock Gap, Jack's Gap, and Unicoi Gap to facilitate the parking of shuttle cars. A large parking lot near the top of Brasstown Bald serves the Visitors' Center located on the mountain's summit. It includes an observation deck, a 15-minute nature slide show, and a museum detailing Georgia's mountain history and natural resources. While of general interest to all visitors, the Center may be especially appreciated by waiting friends and relatives who have agreed to meet a hiker returning from a trip up the mountainside. The Visitors' Center is open 9:30–6 every day from May 1 through the first weekend in November. From mid-March to May 1 and from early November to mid-December, the Center is open weekends only, 10–5:30. The Center is closed mid-December through mid-March. The access road to the summit is currently open 24 hours a day, but if problems with vandalism reoccur, the Forest Service may close the road at night. Questions about the access road and Visitors' Center operation can be directed to the Visitors' Center, (404) 896-2556.

1979

The Chattooga. Dry!

by Tom Patterson

There was something almost surreal about the scene. First, there were the rainbow-hued variations on the basic uniforms—red, blue, lemon yellow, and orange life vests and shiny plastic helmets, all of roughly the same design—and the weird contrast they made with the pristine wilderness through which they moved, composed of the more muted, natural colors of wood, stone, water, and vegetation. Even more startling, though, were the sheer numbers of this strange, waterborne army. I had been resting for only five or ten minutes there on the west bank of the Chattooga, about a mile and a half upstream from Bull Sluice, as they call that bend in the river just north of the two bridges: the old rusted skeleton of the defunct one-lane bridge and the adjacent steel-and-concrete affair that now connects Georgia with South Carolina. But in that brief period I had already lost count of how many craft—to say nothing of their passengers—had gone by. No sooner would one group of boaters go sweeping past, lurching and whooping around the next downstream bend and out of my sight, than another cluster of rafts and canoes would appear from upstream, paddles slicing the swift current. Though I was standing right on the bank among some scrubby riverside plants and small saplings, and some of the troops were passing within only a few yards of me, not one of them seemed to notice my presence. I felt a little like an invisible resident of a bygone culture who had accidentally wandered out the wrong side of a rhododendron thicket into the twentieth century.

For some reason I never expect to see anybody else when I'm hiking. Once in the thick of the forest, I tend to forget, for the time being, about the strange civilization for which we've carved a place—a *big* place—out of the wilderness. When I'm hiking in vast woodlands at a good distance from any towns or highways, it might as well be 1822, as far as I'm concerned. These hordes of colorful river-runners had reminded me what era it *really* is.

Of course, had I given it much thought beforehand, I would have expected to see something like this. After all, I knew this was the most famous stretch of whitewater in the entire Southeast. After the Chattooga's ascent to international prominence with the release of *that* movie back in the first part of the decade, everybody and his sister wanted a chance to match wits with this river. Having grown up in South Georgia, though, where my only canoeing experiences were on the tranquil waters of the Oconee, some 50 miles downstream from the Lake Sinclair dam, I had never acquired a taste for whitewater. And by the time I was making occasional excursions up into the North Georgia mountains, I was always too busy hiking or exploring the back roads to discover the pleasures and perils of whitewater boating. Prior to this hike, my exposure to the Chattooga had been limited to crossing it on the US 76 and Ga 28 bridges, and I had never paused long enough at these crossings to notice how many boaters were passing along the river.

The US Forest Service staff at Walhalla, on the South Carolina side of the Chattooga, has recently begun keeping a tally of the number of people who ride down this wild river. According to their figures, more than 30,000 people did so last year, and 80 percent of these boaters made the trip during the period from mid-April to mid-September. Three outfitters—Southeastern Expeditions, Wild-water, Ltd., and the Nantahala Outdoor Center—pay a total of about $10,000 a year to the Forest Service for their rights to use the Chattooga. In addition to this fee, the outfitters are required to ensure that certain rigid safety standards—the wearing of helmets and life vests, for example—are strictly enforced. This increasing emphasis on river safety has paid off well in terms of the protection of human life. During the period from 1969 to 1974, when the popularity of boating here was rapidly accelerating and before the Forest Service had acquired rights to all the land along the Chattooga, about 20 people lost their lives in these treacherous waters. All of the victims were males between the ages of 16 and 29, and most were not wearing any form of life jacket. The majority were making single-boat trips, unaccompanied by another craft, and more than half of the victims had been drinking some form of alcohol either immediately before or during their final trips. The Forest Service now proudly reports that since beginning their program of river safety and management in 1975 there hasn't been a single death on the Chattooga—in spite of the fact that more and more people are traveling down the river each year.

It doesn't take much experience with whitewater boating to get some sense of how dangerous the Chattooga can be. All one needs to do is stand on the river's banks and observe the current near one of the more difficult sets of rapids. Since I had wandered up to Bull Sluice on the day of my hike a little too early to watch any rafts or canoes negotiating this incredible surge of water, it was farther upstream, at the base of Lion Mountain, that I encountered the first groups of rafters. They had put in farther north, at Earl's Ford, that morning. Here the water flowed fairly calmly along with only a few sets of minor rapids. Still, I was fascinated as I crouched Indian-style on the bank and watched raft after raft after canoe go shooting past me. It had never occurred to me that whitewater boating would make such an interesting spectator sport, but I could have stayed there watching all day. I could feel some fraction of the exhilaration experienced by the boaters, and I was, of course, thinking, "I've got to try this someday." For today, however, I had already chosen the landlubber's approach to the Chattooga and had set myself the task of completing before dark what should have been an overnight trip. I had at least eight more miles of trail to complete, and another six miles or so of walking on a secluded dirt road, before I would be finished. So I decided to get on with my hike.

Before beginning my walk, I had already discovered that hiking beside the Chattooga is not nearly as popular as boating on it. I had been unable to find anyone who had hiked the entire trail between Dick's Creek and the US 76 bridge. While eating breakfast early that morning in a café in Clayton, I had run into a friend who works for one of the rafting outfitters that make regular runs on the Chattooga, and had asked him about the trail. As many times as he had traveled down the river in a raft, he admitted that he'd never walked the Chattooga River Trail. I had also stopped in at the Tallulah Ranger District office, and no one there could tell me much about the trail's condition. Maxie Gates, one of the rangers there, had said that a Youth Conservation Corps work crew had just been dispatched to do some clearing and reblazing on the northern end of the trail a few minutes before I arrived at the office and that I might run into them before the day was over. But I wasn't able to find out anything more about the trail than what was obvious from the maps I'd already looked at.

Once I got underway, having left my car by the highway bridge, I quickly discovered that the first portion of the trail was not blazed. Except for perhaps two or three bits of plastic ribbon tied to trees along the way, there were no blazes all the way up to the place where I stopped to watch the boaters. To this point, the trail had stuck fairly close to the river's shore and had been easy to follow. About a half mile downstream it had merged with what I took to be an old logging road, and it was by this path that I'd reached the point at which I took my first break. Shortly after resuming my walk I got lost, however. The logging road had split into two separate tracks, one heading up a steep slope to my left and the other moving back in the direction of the river. I decided to take the low road. Soon, though, this branch of the path became increasingly tangled in underbrush and fallen tree trunks, until finally it disappeared altogether. Retracing my steps, I returned to the fork and tried the high road. Halfway up the slope this path too began to fade out, until I soon found myself in the midst of a large stand of rhododendron. After hacking my way through the slick green leaves and low branches for 15 minutes or so, I emerged where I had originally entered the thicket, sweating and panting as I looked at the logging road's path back downhill and downstream. It was then that I found the cryptic note. Written in washed-out ballpoint ink on an index card fastened with fishing line to a small maple sapling, it read:

If you've made it this far I admire
your stamina. But this is where
the trail ends.

           Good Luck!

I had to laugh. In all my years of hiking I had never encountered anything like this. I thought about my anonymous predecessor on this puzzling trail, trudging in disappointment back down toward the bridge three miles to the south, exhausted and done in, his hiking plans ruined by the confusing maze of old logging roads and thick underbrush. I lit a cigarette and contemplated my surroundings as I tried to decide what to do. There was no way I was going to turn back this soon. I wasn't about to ruin a perfect record of completing every hike I began. Also, I wasn't totally without faith in the Forest Service. If their maps showed a hiking trail here, then I figured there was a trail here—somewhere. And I was determined to find it. I crushed my cigarette and headed back downhill to the fork in the logging road. I made one more survey of the path's lower branch, following it into another thicket of rhododendron, which I explored until I was sure there was no trail there. Then I started backtracking. A few hundred feet past the place where I'd stopped to watch the rafters, I discovered another fork in the trail, which I had somehow overlooked when I passed this way the first time. Another branch of the network of old logging roads, this path led uphill along the lower slope of Lion Mountain. There were no blazes anywhere in sight, but I headed up this newly discovered path anyway. After 50 yards or so the trail began to level off, and as I rounded a bend, I spotted a swipe of bright blue paint on the trunk of a beech tree on my right. A little farther along I saw a diamond-shaped piece of aluminum painted white and nailed to another tree trunk. This was the trail, all right, and from this point on I had little trouble finding my way through the woods.

By the time I had finally picked up the trail again I was a considerable distance from the river. Earlier, when I had been nearer the bank, the rushing water had provided a steady, roaring background to the bird calls, the distant chain-saw growlings, and the other sounds one hears in the wilderness; but now it was so faint as to be almost inaudible. It would be another hour or so before I saw the river again.

Now on higher ground, I concentrated on keeping up a good pace and keeping my eyes open for whatever forms of wildlife I might encounter. Already I had noticed a plethora of rattlesnake orchids in full bloom all along the trail. There were also numerous clumps of those lovely little flowers known as Indian pipes. As on the previous day's short hike along the banks of the Coleman River, on the other side of Rabun County, I found plenty of different varieties of mushroom, including large clusters of the orange ones whose Latin name I've forgotten, but which my friend Melissa Tufts refers to as "chicken-in-the-woods," because their flavor when cooked is surprisingly similar to that of fowl. As for wildlife of the warm-blooded type, I saw little until much later in the day when I crested a hill just in time to catch a fleeting glimpse of the white tail of a full-grown doe as she disappeared into the forest, heading downhill toward the river.

It was quite late in the afternoon when I reached the three-way intersection where the Chattooga River Trail meets the Bartram Trail and the dirt road that runs from Sandy Ford out to Warwoman Road. Just a few minutes before that, I had come upon a particularly nice campsite on the bank of Rock Creek, which was crossed there by a quaint little wooden foot bridge like those found at several other creek crossings along the trail. The best way to do this trail, I thought as I stopped to eat a few almonds and dried apricots, would be to hike in from the north end of the trail late in the afternoon, set up camp here, and get an early start on a fairly leisurely hike downstream the next day.

Glancing at my watch, I saw that it was already 6 pm. There were only a couple of hours of daylight left, and though I knew I had almost reached the end of the trail I had set out to hike, I also knew that I had another six miles of walking on the dirt road out to the place where I planned to begin hitchhiking back to my car. As it turned out, this dirt road was a pleasant little addition to the hiking trail, winding as it does from the river through a couple of miles of woods and then through some lovely stretches of hilly farmland before coming out on the blacktop pavement of Warwoman Road. The weather, which had been unmercifully hot all day, was begin-

ning to improve as sunset approached, and there were large trees that provided plenty of shade along most of the dirt road. The day's reward finally came a couple of miles into the dirt-road portion of my hike, when, much to my surprise, I found a large thicket of blackberry bushes by the roadside. In the part of Georgia where I grew up, blackberry season is over by the middle of July at the latest. But here it was August in the northeastern mountains, and these bushes were loaded with fruit at the peak of ripeness. The berries practically leaped off the thorny branches into my hands, and I must confess that I pigged out thoroughly on the delicious little things before finally resuming my walk.

A few minutes after I reached Warwoman Road and began thumbing, a pickup truck pulled over and I climbed in. I hopped out of the pickup in Clayton and began walking back out US 76, sticking out my thumb every time a vehicle passed. My luck wasn't as good here as it had been on Warwoman Road, and by the time the sun went down, I had just about resigned myself to having to walk the entire remaining distance back to my car.

Any veteran hitchhiker will tell you how nearly impossible it is to thumb a ride at night, but just a few minutes before full darkness set in, a battered red Rambler with fishing rods sticking out the back windows stopped to pick me up. I was standing by a roadside park at the top of a steep hill, and as the old car slowed to a halt beside me, the engine sputtered and then shut off completely. There were three people in the front seat, and I mumbled something to them like, "Look's like y'all've been fishin'," as I opened the back door and moved the arsenal of fishing rods aside to make room for myself on the back seat. The car apparently had some battery or generator problem, because as soon as I shut the door behind me, the driver simply took his foot off the brake and we started coasting down the hill. As I took in the details of the car's interior—the shredded seat covers, the clumps of dried mud on the floor, the litter of crumpled tobacco packs, empty beer and soft-drink cans, a weathered tackle box, a bent-up processed-ham tin, stale bread crusts, and so on—I told the trio in the front seat that I was headed out to the river bridge.

The driver, a gaunt fellow in a plaid short-sleeved shirt and an old baseball cap, craned his literally red neck as he halfway turned and scrutinized me briefly, asking, "Ain't you one a'them that's got that raft business up the road here?" His companions—a heavyset black-haired woman who took up most of the front seat and an elderly bald-headed man wearing faded overalls and dangling his right arm out the window—both glanced back at me as if to confirm the driver's guess. By "raft business" I figured he meant Southeastern Expeditions, whose headquarters were a couple of miles or so ahead of us. I'm sure I looked like I'd spent the entire day on the river, so it was as good a guess as any. No, I told them, I knew one fellow who works there, but I didn't even live in these parts.

"You reckon they drink much beer over there?" the driver then asked me. I told him I didn't really know, but that they might. "Wonder if they'd let me have the cans?" he said. I asked him if he was saving aluminum cans to sell for recycling, and he said, "Naw, I need 'em for my hawgs." I wasn't sure what he was talking about—I had a brief mental picture of a bunch of hogs eating aluminum cans—but I let it pass.

The car had built up plenty of speed, and I heard the engine kick back into operation with a low rumble. The woman unscrewed the cap on a bottle of clear liquid that looked homemade, then took a drink and passed the bottle to the driver. He drank a shot and then offered me the bottle, which I gladly accepted. What better way, I figured, to top off my day's exertions than with a little taste of pure, illicit, mountain-made liquor? It was surprisingly smooth, with just the right hint of a burning in the throat and a sweet aftertaste on the tongue, and went down with just the right amount of kick to it. I passed the bottle on to the old man and settled back in the seat. When the driver said he'd be glad to go a mile or so out of his way and drop me off exactly where I'd left my car, I accepted that offer too.

Night had fallen by the time I reached the river, and I knew that all boat traffic had long since stopped for the day. The only passenger on the Chattooga tonight would be the reflection of the nearly full moon, shining as it rose in the sky and rode all the rapids simultaneously.

HIKING GUIDE

Chattooga River Trail

The Chattooga River Trail covers a distance of about ten miles on the Georgia side of the river between the US 76 Bridge on the south and the intersection with Dick's Creek Rd (also known as Sandy Ford Rd) on the north. Also at the north end, the trail meets the longer Bartram Trail, which can be combined with the Chattooga River Trail for a longer hike. To reach the southern end of the trail, take US 76 east from Clayton for about nine miles to the bridge. There is a dirt parking area on the left side of the road here, and the trail begins just beyond this open area. To reach the northern end of the trail, drive northeast from Clayton on Warwoman Rd for about six miles to Dick's Creek Rd, a dirt road that bears to the right off the paved road directly across from the Antioch United Methodist Church. You can't see the church from the road, but you should be able to see the pale blue United Methodist Church sign on the left side of the road here. Turn right on Dick's Creek Rd and continue for about a mile to the second bridge across the creek, on your left. Cross the creek here and continue, bearing left at the only fork on this stretch, for about five more miles until you come to a small wooden sign on the left side of the road indicating the crossing of the Bartram Trail.

If you walk just a few hundred feet along the Bartram Trail, on the left side of the road, you'll see the Chattooga River Trail heading off to the right. There are no signs marking this trail, but you should be able to recognize it by the combination of blue paint blazes and little white diamond-shaped metal reflectors nailed to some of the trees. The Bartram Trail at this point is marked by the same type of metal markers along with yellow blazes. If you decide to drive in on Dick's Creek Rd, you should know that this road is fairly rough and that it fords the creek in two places before reaching the trail crossing. If you're driving a pickup truck, jeep, or land rover, you'll have no trouble here, but my Honda made it across only one of the fords, and I had to turn back rather than cross the second, where the creek looked deep and swift enough either to trap my car in the mud or sweep it downstream toward the river.

As noted in the accompanying story, Dick's Creek Rd can be included as part of your hike, since it is relatively untrafficked and

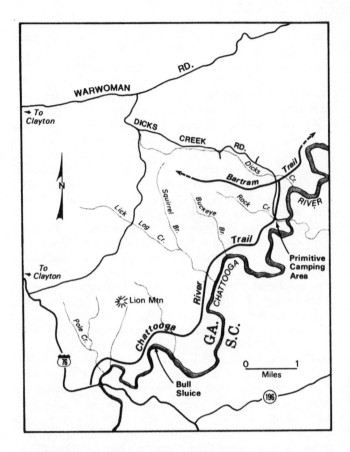

quite scenic, providing good views of some of the prettiest countryside I've seen anywhere in Northeast Georgia. It should be especially beautiful here when the leaves are changing in the fall.

There are no shelters nor designated camping areas on the Chattooga River Trail, but there are a number of places that have obviously been cleared and used a number of times for primitive camping. The best of these is the one at Rock Creek, about a mile south of the trail's beginning. If you're thinking of taking this hike, you might consider leaving a car near the intersection of Warwoman Rd and Dick's Creek Rd, leaving in midafternoon and hiking the dirt road all the way in, then joining the trail and stopping here to camp. You could easily walk the rest of the trail down to the bridge by late afternoon the following day, allowing plenty of time to stop and watch the boaters on the river, birdwatch, hunt wildflowers, or dawdle along the way.

The southernmost portion of the trail was inadequately marked when I hiked it in August. I informed the folks at the Tallulah Ranger District office of this problem later, and they told me it should be remedied before the end of the summer. But if you're hiking the trail from the south end to the north, don't be alarmed if you get momentarily lost. If you arrive at a makeshift campsite with a stone fire ring and a platform made of a partially destroyed Chattahoochee National Forest sign, you've missed that crucial left fork in the trail that's mentioned in the story—but not by far. All you'll have to do is retrace your steps for a little less than a quarter mile. The main thing to remember is that the first couple of trail miles are fairly close to the river bank, and after that the trail goes uphill and remains on high ground for some time before winding back down to the river.

1979

Standing Indian Area of the Appalachian Trail

The Appalachian Trail stretches 2,000 miles from Georgia to Maine. Eighty-three of the Trail's southernmost miles wind through the mountains of Northeast Georgia. Information and maps for this Georgia section can be obtained by contacting: 1) US Forest Service, Box 1437, Gainesville 30501; (404) 536-0541. Here you may obtain a waterproof strip map showing the trail and approximately five miles on either side of it, including roads, natural landmarks, location of trail shelters, and mileage. 2) Appalachian Trail Conference, Box 236, Harpers Ferry, West Virginia 25425. Source of *Guidebook to the Appalachian Trail in the Great Smokies, the Nantahalas and Georgia;* includes maps and detailed trail information in chapters covering several miles each. Also available at backpacking shops and larger bookstores.

A particularly scenic section of the Appalachian Trail is dominated by the 5,500-foot peak of Standing Indian Mountain. The Appalachian Trail (AT) runs along the mountaintops in Standing Indian's vicinity for 20 miles, while the walls of the valley below are laced with seven smaller foot trails that connect the AT with the valley floor. The AT is marked by white rectangular paint blazes on trees or rocks. The smaller side trails and also short trails to water sources are marked with similar blue blazes. With so many trails to choose from, hikers can combine them in various patterns to create routes for hikes that range from one to five days' walking time. For example:

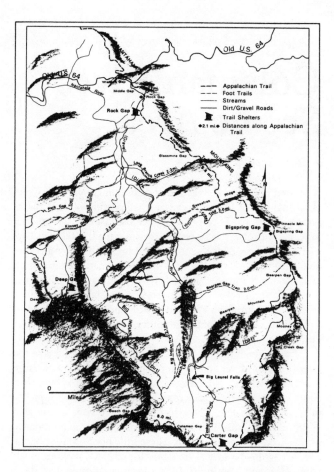

HIKING GUIDE*

Overnight Loop: (seven hours' walking time at easy-to-moderate pace). Take the scenic Kimsey Creek Trail from the right rear (southwest) corner of the camping area as it climbs gradually along the creek. Shortly before Deep Gap, the trail intersects and then climbs along a gravel road. At Deep Gap, follow the AT and its white blazes eastward up the mountain. The trail shelter is reached after about a three-hour climb. The AT does not cross directly over the peak of Standing Indian; rather, a sign points to the 0.1-mile cutoff to the top and its 360-degree vista. The Lower Trail Ridge path back to the campground descends from the AT 75 feet beyond (east of) this cutoff trail. It descends steeply in several places and enters the campground at space #23.

Appalachian Trail Four- or Five-Day Loop: Take Kimsey Creek Trail to the AT, and spend first night at Deep Gap shelter, then each succeeding night at the next two shelters. Then walk the 2.5 miles to Long Branch Trail, and descend 2.3 miles to the gravel road that leads to the campground. To make a five-day trip, continue from Big Spring shelter along the AT to the Rock Gap shelter, and the next day walk 1.3 miles back to the campground along the paved road.

Other combination routes can be devised by using the side trails to reach or leave the AT. Here are the mileages to each trail entrance from the fork in the road at the entrance to Standing Indian camping area: Long Branch Trail, 0.2 mile; Hurricane Creek Trail, 2.0 miles; Big Indian Trail, 3.2 miles; Bear Creek Trail, 3.6 miles (trail entrance very difficult to locate—ask park attendants); Beech Gap Trail, 4.6 miles; Big Laurel Falls—Timber Ridge Trail, 5 miles. Mooney Falls, audible from the road, is 5.7 miles from the starting point. All these trail entrances are marked by signs and the paths by blue blazes, but often the signs are torn down by vandals, and nothing but the 4 × 4-inch wooden post may remain to mark the spot.

Driving Directions: From the intersection of US 64 and US 441 in Franklin, drive west along US 64 for 13.6 miles, then turn left onto a well paved and graded road, which is old US 64 but not marked as such. After two miles, a wooden Forest Service sign marks the right-hand turnoff to the campground. Standing Indian Campground is open April 1 to December 1. Trailers up to 22 feet can be accommodated, but no electricity nor sewage hookups are available.

The Wayah Ranger Station and district Forest Service office are located 0.9 mile west of the intersection of US 441 and US 64. Open 8–4:30 Mon–Fri, they have free hiking maps for the Standing Indian area that are very detailed and most useful. The map can also be obtained by contacting: Wayah Ranger Station, Box 469, Franklin, North Carolina 28734; (704) 524-6441.

Coleman River Scenic Area

by Tom Patterson

Located in the northwest corner of Rabun County, the Coleman River Scenic Area is a small portion of the Chatta-hoochee National Forest that has been set aside as a memorial to R. C. Nicholson, who served as ranger for the Tallulah District of the national forest from 1912 until 1952. A mile-long hiking trail follows the east bank of the Coleman from the point where it flows into the Tallulah River upstream to where the trail ends in a thicket of rhododendron and fallen tree trunks. If you're looking for an afternoon of leisurely, scenic hiking in a place that isn't swarming with other nature lovers, this trail is ideal.

I made the hike on a hot afternoon, but the coolness of the river's rushing water and the ample shade provided by the large hemlock, hickory, oak, maple, and rhododendron trees on either side of the trail made for a comfortable walk with plenty of treats for the eye. There had been heavy rains in the area within the previous days, which had resulted in an abundance of mushrooms along the trail. These little nonflowering plants have always held a special attraction for me, and, without much effort, I found about 50 different species during the short course of my hike. Given the proper weather conditions, this trail would provide a fascinating field day for the mycologist on through the late fall. If you're not interested in mushrooms, there are plenty of trees, wildflowers, and memorable views of the river to keep you occupied. Several huge rock outcroppings jutting out over the narrow but turbulent river are good places to stop and relax, absorbing the wild splendor of this secluded forest. The uphill slope is in most places very gradual, so at no point is this a particularly strenuous hike. The return trip is, of course, downhill all the way.

The fishing in Coleman River is supposed to be quite good, so you could fish and hike the river for a day, then retire to the nearby Tallulah River campground to clean and cook your catch. The Forest Service sets a minimum size limit of 10 inches for rainbow and brown trout, and 8 inches for brook trout. Use artificial lures only.

To reach the trail, take Ga 197 north from Clarkesville to its intersection with US 76 on the northern end of Lake Burton. Turn right on 76 and follow it for about 2.5 miles to Persimmon Rd, a blacktop road turning north off the main highway. Watch for the Persimmon Volunteer Fire Department building on the left, a few hundred feet off the highway, and turn left there. (If you're coming from Clayton on US 76, this turnoff is about seven miles west of the city limits.) Follow Persimmon Rd for about four miles to a sharp right-hand bend in the road. Here a dirt road turns off to the left. A sign indicates the nearby presence of the Tallulah River campground.

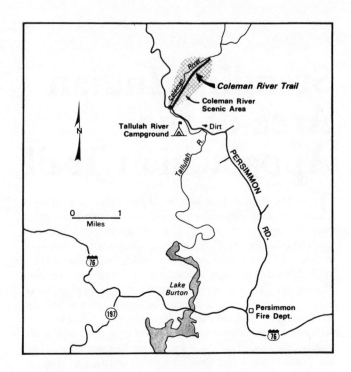

Turn left and follow the dirt road for about 1.5 miles along the Tallulah River to the Coleman River Bridge. A large sign east of the bridge lets you know this is the Scenic Area, and the trail begins immediately behind the sign.

Cloudland With Feeling

by John Earl

I'm almost ashamed to admit it but it was a New Yorker who told me about Cloudland Canyon. It all started one day in 1971 when I received a phone call from Robert Woodward, picture editor for Readers Digest Books, asking for a photograph of Cloudland for *Scenic Wonders of America*, published in 1973. I told him I did not know what or where Cloudland Canyon was, but that I would be most pleased to find out and take the picture he wanted. I got out a map and, sure enough, there it was way up in the northwest corner of the state. I thank Bob Woodward for that phone call because it led me to one of the nicest discoveries of my life.

Since that day in 1971 I have returned to the canyon again and again, in all seasons, in all types of weather. One night last winter, for example, I was sitting around complaining to myself about the weather when suddenly I found myself wondering what Cloudland would be like on a bleak day in mid-February. I got up about six o'clock the following morning, called John

Hall, a fine young photographer from Carrollton, and asked him if he would care to go with me to hike around in Cloudland Canyon that day. I heard a most emphatic "yes," and we agreed to meet in Rome in about an hour.

When I headed my station wagon up Interstate-75, the sky was completely overcast and the possibility that it would clear up later seemed remote. I picked John up in Rome, and by the time we reached LaFayette a light drizzle had begun to fall. As we turned onto Georgia route 143, smoke-like fog was beginning to stretch out in all directions. At the parking area, we were greeted by a damp, chilling wind, and all around us cold raindrops were dripping from the overhanging tree limbs. I had the feeling that it was going to be a marvelous day.

Donning rain gear, we put on our packs and set off on the Rimrock Trail. The trail drops off sharply and soon descends several flights of wooden stairs firmly secured to the canyon wall. At the bottom of the stairs we followed the fork which leads to the upper falls on Daniel Creek.

When viewed from the rim at the parking area, Cloudland Canyon looks like an inverted "Y." Daniel Creek leaps down the west canyon over two magnificent waterfalls and many beautiful rapids, while Bear Creek rushes and cascades down through the east canyon. They join each other where the two arms of the canyon meet to form Gulch Creek, which flows rapidly down through Sitton Gulch.

Cloudland Canyon is a part of Lookout Mountain. The altitude above sea level is 1980 feet. Breath-takingly beautiful, multi-colored sandstone walls are almost completely perpendicular. Rocks which form the rim are the result of erosion of the Appalachian Mountains into the Silurian Sea about 260 million years ago.

The rain had almost stopped as we passed many fine specimens of maple, oak, holly and tulip poplar trees. Some of these giants have succumbed to the bombardment of rain and gale-force winds that sometimes roar up the walls of the canyon. In spring and autumn the forest is a blaze of color, while during the summer months soft lush greens predominate. Rewards await those who are willing to brave the biting winds and damp soggy trails of winter. On wet, overcast days hundreds of beautiful lichen-covered tree trunks and boulders cast hues of bright green, white, yellow, blue and gray as far as the eye can see. During summer months this broad expanse of color is not nearly as visible due to the fullness of the leaves.

We stopped for a moment to admire a lovely clump of Christmas ferns growing on the rocky slope beside the trail. The sun suddenly broke through the thin layer of clouds, casting shafts of misty light and transforming the hardwood forest cove into a giant cathedral.

Unfortunately, all is not beauty. As we slowly made our way into the canyon, I noticed with sadness that far too much damage is being done by people who persist in taking short cuts by cutting across the switch-backs of the trail. This practice is not only dangerous and tiring, but causes irreparable damage to the forest floor. We also saw much evidence of littering along the way. I could fill my pack with trash on almost every trail I hike. If people are able to carry a candy bar and soft drink into the wilderness, why is it so difficult for them to bring back the empty can and paper wrapper?

My photography is based upon discovery and intuition, so each new hike into the wilderness becomes an exciting, different experience for me. Sometimes I spend hours on my hands and knees examining the many fantastic shapes and colors which exist only in the miniature world of lichens, mosses, very small flowers and tiny insects. There is so much joy to be gained by one who is willing to take the time to probe beyond the commonplace in nature. Tranquilizers can be left at home.

We soon arrived at the foot of the upper falls on Daniel Creek, and stood for a long time admiring the splendor of this magnificent 65-foot cataract plunging headlong into a deep and beautiful blue splash-pool at our feet. The great roar of falling, rushing water was broken only by the occasional "caw" of a crow somewhere further down the canyon.

The lichen-covered boulders caught the rays of the sun as it darted in and out of the clouds, shining with a luminescent whiteness which was almost blinding in its sheer beauty. These huge boulders, some of them more than 25 feet high, were hurled from the side of the canyon by an ancient avalanche of tremendous velocity and force. They now lounged like lazy sentinels along the banks of Daniel Creek. A shaft of sunlight suddenly penetrated the surface of the crystal-clear creek, and in so doing illuminated a rich green, moss-wrapped stone about a foot below the surface. Nature seemed to be switching its giant spotlights off and on.

We lingered at the falls for over two hours and after enjoying the lunch which John had brought along for us, we walked back up the trail to the point where it divides at the foot of the stairs. Taking the trail to the left, we now headed for the opposite rim of the canyon. Before long we came to a unique swinging bridge made of wood and suspended by steel cables. This splendid Himalayan-type structure swayed and creaked as we crossed over Daniel Creek in bright sunshine to the other side of the gorge. Now we were climbing steadily as the trail switched back and forth toward the opposite rim high above.

The view became more and more spectacular as we climbed up toward the rim of the north wall. Reaching the top, we found that the trail stayed very close to the edge of the high cliffs. At one point we looked back on a magnificent view of the upper falls and the canyon floor far below. We probably would not have noticed this particular view had it been summer. This was just one more reward which winter had to offer us.

Nothing excites me more than the dwarf, bonsai-like trees to be found growing on tops of cliffs or from the slits in canyon walls. The two most prominent trees which grow in such fashion along the rims of Cloudland Canyon are scrub pine (*Pinus virginiana*), and red cedar (*Juniperus virginiana*). The latter often assumes the shape of gleaming, twisted taffy. Beautiful clumps of reindeer moss (*Cladonia* lichen) were growing on the ground and shining like silver beneath these little bent and stunted trees. How these trees survive under such extreme weather conditions with little or no soil remains one of the marvels of nature. But, oh, how beautiful they are to behold!

Soon we reached a point where the trail turns suddenly away from the canyon so as to circumvent a small ravine, and we immediately found ourselves in a deciduous forest. The transition from one type of trees and shrubs to another was quite abrupt. Now we were passing dogwood (*Cornus florida*), rose-bay rhododendron (*Rhododendron maxium*), red oak (*Quercus rubra*), sassafras (*S. albidum*), which is an understory tree, and

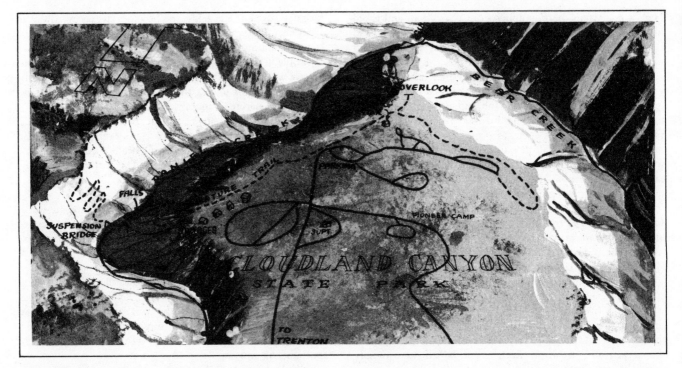

many other species which grow in a cove forest. Slate-colored juncos darted through the trees just above the ground in front of us. Before very long we again arrived at the canyon rim and continued on until the trail reached an end at the point of the canyon.

The setting sun cast bold, black shadows on the canyon walls as we made our way back toward the parking area, and I paused briefly to take one last photograph. Now and then a lone, squawking crow flew across the path in front of us and disappeared into the depths of the canyon below. The sky had been transformed from blue to deep gold by the time we got back to the car. We had walked about a total distance of three miles, and I was pleasantly tired, but also extremely glad that I had decided to come and walk in Cloudland Canyon on that particular day in February.

along the rim of the east canyon and ends in the forest near the tent and trailer camping area. Pamphlets for this lovely self-guided nature trail are available at the visitor center. Forty-two trees, shrubs and wildflowers have been marked along the trail, and this comprehensive and informative pamphlet allows one to make positive identifications of the flora in this exciting area. This trail is simply breath-taking in spring and autumn, but quite enjoyable during any season of the year.

Case Cavern, in the northwest section of the park, and reached only through Sitton Gulch, is not open to the public except by permit and only for organized groups with qualified leaders. A locked metal gate protects the entrance.

All reservations made through Park Superintendent, Cloudland Canyon State Park, Rising Fawn, GA 30338. Telephone: (404) 657-4050.

1976

HIKING GUIDE

Cloudland's Trails

Cloudland Canyon State Park is in Dade County about 20 miles northwest of LaFayette, off Georgia highway 143. It contains 1699 acres and the altitude above sea level is 1980 feet. Park hours are from 7 A.M. to 10 P.M.

The park contains a visitor center where concession items are available, an attractive picnic area, and two nature trails. The canyon trail, which begins just to the left of the visitor center, is divided into two sections. One arm of the trail leads to the upper falls on Daniel Creek, and the left arm crosses the canyon over a cable-supported swinging bridge just above the upper waterfall. On the other side of the gorge the trail climbs to the top, following the rim to the point of the canyon. Retrace your steps to the parking area by the same trail.

To the right of the visitor center Rimrock Nature Trail winds

Gilmer County's Rocky Mountain High

by Susan McDonald

We were puffing pretty heavily after the half-hour climb up the ridge toward Rocky Mountain, so it seemed a good idea to sit down and rest a minute while we admired the view from that height. Although the calendar said it was early winter already, the absence of leaves on the trees was the only clue that the season was so far advanced. The sun had been warm and bright for several days. Today it had beaten down through the empty tree branches with such strength that we had quickly peeled off our jackets during the first few minutes on the trail.

"I can't imagine ever having a better day to walk this trail," commented my hiking partner and sister, Karen, as she surveyed the mountainous horizon visible in a 180-degree panorama. "If we had come before the leaves fell," she continued, "I don't think we would have realized just how high we are. I think this trail must have been planned with winter hikers in mind."

I looked up from my map and agreed with her observation, silently remembering many summer hikes to mountain summits where the scenery had been limited to the thick green canopy above and below us.

Repositioning the map and briefly studying the ridge to the east, I snapped the compass cover closed and announced triumphantly to Karen, "Guess what. This ridge is the one the forest ranger told us to watch for, the Tennessee Valley Divide. All the rain falling east of us flows north into the Tennessee River and finally into the Mississippi, while the rain falling to the west flows down through Alabama and out into the Gulf at Mobile Bay."

"Hm-m-m," mused Karen, visibly unimpressed by the significance of her present geographical location. "Maybe we should be moving on," she decided, as she stood up and shouldered her rucksack.

We continued along the eastward curve around Rocky Mountain and passed through the gap to the mountain's north slope almost before we realized it. Constant exposure to the mountain's shadow here had given the terrain a decidedly different look. The soil was moist and covered with a thick layer of black spongy humus. Green patches of ferns dotted the slope, as well as several large boulders. Our feet, grown accustomed to wading through a six-inch carpet of dark brown oak leaves, were suddenly treading upon a golden yellow layer of recently fallen hickory leaves. After only about 15 minutes of walking, however, we moved onto the sunny ridge northwest of Rocky Mountain's summit and left the ferns and hickory forest behind as abruptly as we had entered it.

Circling below the summit of another unnamed mountain, we began the long gradual descent to Deep Gap. The downhill saunter was easy and pleasant, but I thought about how taxing the 800-foot rise in elevation would make a trip in the other direction. We found the last 200 to 300 yards of trail south of Deep Gap to be poorly marked by trail blazes, especially around several turns, but the sounds of traffic along Aska Road kept us moving in the right direction.

The trail entrance across the road was easy to locate, since the Forest Service had thoughtfully built some rustic log steps and handrail up the roadside embankment. The trail here skirts to the south of private property and then begins to climb up Green Mountain, traveling along the ridge just south of its crest.

The Forest Service had been doing some reforestation work and cutting along the mountain's summit, and at the top of the ridge we suddenly found ourselves on a newly built dirt road running northeast. Confused, we walked along it for about 75 feet, but then found another trail marker and the path leading off the road to the right.

Soon began the final descent toward Lake Blue Ridge and the last section of the trail, which follows the shoreline. Had we been planning to camp for the night, Karen and I both agreed that the lakeshore area would have been our choice.

The warm sun and slight breezes that day had lulled us into forgetting how short the daylight hours were this time of year. But as long, cold shadows began to darken the lakeshore, we knew that a chilly winter night was rapidly falling. Out came the jackets that had lain most of the day crumpled in our packs, and their warmth certainly felt good as we completed the last few turns in the trail. It had been an exceptionally warm and lovely early winter day, but now we were both thinking of a mug of coffee and a nice hot dinner to top off the chilly evening and a good day's hike.

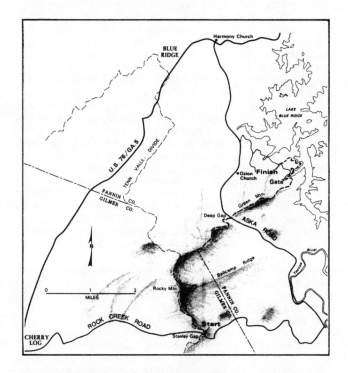

HIKING GUIDE

Rich Mountain Trail

The Rich Mountain Trail in Fannin and Gilmer Counties covers 11 miles, but it intersects a county road at mile seven, making two shorter hikes also possible. The difference in elevation from the trail's highest point (the gap between Rocky Mountain and Bellcamp Ridge) and its lowest point along the lake is 1300 feet. Hiking the trail from south to north takes advantage of this drop and gives the hiker long downhill stretches with only two short, but steep climbs. Going the other direction, however, the trail climbs slowly and steadily for the first eight miles, descending within that distance only once to cross Deep Gap.

The section from Stanley Gap to Deep Gap takes three to four hours, while the section from Deep Gap to the lake takes two to three hours. Water is scarce along most of the trail, since it travels primarily on top of the ridges. Many pretty campsites can be found along the lakeshore near the trail's end, however.

The trail is marked along its entire length by two-by-six-inch white metal strips nailed to trees. Unfortunately, many of the strips have rusted, which makes them hard to see against the tree trunks. At times, the trail markers are quite distantly spaced, but the path can usually be followed by watching for ax-cut blazes made in the trees alongside the trail or by looking for underbrush and tree trunks that were cleared out with chain saws during last summer's trail maintenance.

The Forest Service warns that winter hikers on Rich Mountain Trail should watch out for ice and slippery conditions along the trail's higher elevations, which may occur even on days when icy conditions are not evident in the town of Blue Ridge and at other lower elevations.

Driving Directions: To set up a two-car shuttle for the 11-mile hike, begin on US 76 just east of the town of Blue Ridge. Look for Harmony Church, and turn south off 76 onto Aska Road directly across the street from the church. Travel south on Aska Road 2.4 miles, and turn left onto a well graded gravel road. Continue along this road 0.8 mile, then turn left onto another gravel road. After 0.2 mile, the road forks. Take the right fork, and continue on 1.4 miles to a parking pull-off from which a jeep road leads off to the left. The hiking trail begins down this jeep road, but makes a right turn into the woods after about 50 feet.

To place the second shuttle car, return to Aska Road, and continue south 5.7 miles. Turn right onto a gravel road that is marked by a large wooden Forest Service sign saying "Rich Mountain Wildlife Management Area." Continue on this gravel road 4.1 miles to a jeep road leading off the main road to the right. This is the Stanley Gap Trail entrance, but park the car in the pull-off area about 50 yards farther along the road to avoid blocking the entrance. The jeep road narrows after about 0.2 mile and begins a steady climb that lasts about 45 minutes.

Stanley Gap can also be reached from US 76-Ga 5. The turnoff is 8.3 miles north of Ellijay's town square and 6.5 miles south of Blue Ridge. At the turn are signs for Rock Creek Church, Camp Potoka, and a large one for Rich Mountain Wildlife Management Area. From US 76-Ga 5, the trail entrance is 5.3 miles east along the road.

The trail crosses Deep Gap about 50 feet south of the gap's crest, which is located on Aska Road, 1.3 miles south of the signs for Ozion Church and the Baptist Assembly Grounds. The trail cuts through a parking pull-off on the right, which can be used for shuttle cars if only one section of the trail is to be hiked.

All gravel and dirt roads leading to the trail entrances are well graded and easily traveled by all but the largest luxury cars. The only section which might cause problems is the last 1.4 miles before the northern trail entrance. If the dirt road appears too muddy, the car can be parked somewhere before the turn-off, and hikers can walk the road back to their car.

1979

A Winter Hike on Blood Mountain

by Margaret Tucker

The Appalachian Trail leaps up Blood Mountain from Neels Gap as if its makers wanted to put the road behind them as fast as possible. The sounds of tires, car doors, and conversation fade as you and a few friends silently congratulate yourselves for having gotten out on a brisk winter day. Soon, silence is replaced by heavy breathing and you ask, not for the last time, "How far to the top?"

Your goal, the 4461 foot top of Blood Mountain, is the highest point on the Appalachian Trail (AT) in Georgia and the highest Georgia peak without a road to the top. Brasstown Bald, the highest, is topped by a Forest Service visitor center on a paved road. Rabun Bald, the second-highest, has a jeep road and fire tower.

From Neels Gap to Blood Mountain is only 2.1 miles, but you climb 1336 feet. The Appalachian Trail Conference *Guide* says, "The traverse of this Section does not involve undue exertion." I assure you it involves exertion. Whether or not it is undue is between you and your feet.

The trail winds through naked hardwoods. The big white oaks look deformed, limbs jutting out at odd angles. A winter trail through hardwoods is very different from its summer aspect, especially if you are lucky enough to be breaking trail through a light, fresh snow. Rocks stand out sharply. A large balanced rock to your left signals Flatrock Gap. You have climbed 327 feet in this first mile.

The next mile climbs about 1000 feet. Just beyond Flatrock beware of several slanted granite outcrops which can be icy and treacherous in freezing weather. At one switchback you have little choice but to cross the icy rock. One boy I know successfully made the turn only to slip and land in the trail below.

He did this inadvertently, but many people shortcut the switchbacks on purpose. Please don't! It's very damaging to the trail. From here to the top of Blood you can see bad erosion, often bare rock, where thoughtless hikers have gone straight up or down rather than take the switchbacks.

The trail is well marked with white blazes. Two blazes mean a turn ahead. The yellow marks you see on your left are boundary markers of the Chestatee Wildlife Management Area. Blue blazes indicate side trails.

The last half mile before the top is steep and rocky with lovely rhododendron thickets and mountain laurel. Now they are full of fat buds promising next summer's blooms. From the shelter of these thickets you step out into the full wind sweeping the rocky top. You'll be ready for a rest, but don't get chilled. The view makes you understand why these mountains are called the Blue Ridge. In clear weather you see 25,000 acres of wild land.

There's no water on the summit, so if you plan to stay overnight carry your own supply. On top is a two-room stone shelter with sturdy, hand-hewn beams. It's a good place to spend a winter night. The first room has a great stone fireplace, but there may or may not be shutters and a sound door to close out snow. Last fall the shelter was completely repaired, but it has been vandalized repeatedly. Litter has also been a problem, even though Georgia Tech students and the Sierra Club have sponsored clean-ups.

The floor is dirt and there are no bunks, so you'll need a groundcloth. You can hang your pack from one of the rafters. Watch and listen carefully before falling asleep. You may see a golden-footed mouse creeping out the rafter from his roof-corner home.

If you find the shelter occupied, which is a strong possibility, as Blood Mountain is one of the most popular sections of the AT in Georgia, you'll need a tarp or tent to rig outside. The ground is rocky, so you may want to use stones or trees for some of your tent lines. For winter camping on frozen ground you may want to invest in one of the mountaineering tents that do not require stakes.

Want a "secret hideaway" to sleep in? Explore the house-sized boulders beside the shelter. There are several overhangs with room for one or two people. A candle stub stuck on a small rock shelf will push back the darkness enough to make you feel secure in your half cave, but the shadows will be strong enough to remind you there was a time when men did not rule nature and she is still wild and strong enough to break into our shell of civilization.

The next day you have 8.3 miles to go to reach Woody Gap, but only one very short stretch as steep as the Blood Mountain ascent. Several hundred yards past the shelter the trail leaves the old road and goes abruptly left down a narrow path dropping gradually off the shoulder of the mountain. From here to Slaughter Gap the trail is newer, and has a more southerly exposure, making it a little drier. It is also less rocky than the trail up, a welcome change to the feet.

At Slaughter Gap (mile 3.2) you must make a left turn to continue on the AT. The blue-blazed path straight ahead leads 2.2 miles west to Lake Winfield Scott, a Forest Service recreation area.

Going toward Bird Gap you pass through old hardwoods with fewer understory trees and shrubs than before. There are many old white oaks, northern red oaks, and big chestnut stumps. Another .3 miles or about 15 minutes of walking brings you to the shoulder of Turkey Stamp Mountain (3770 feet) and an open, park-like woods. The trail climbs slightly, levels, and drops into a thicker forest with dogwood understory. (Make a mental note to return in the spring.) As you descend, you see Virginia pine, a welcome green touch after the bare hardwood trunks.

At Horsebone Gap (mile 4.4) there's a stand of straight-trunked tulip poplar and lots of level space for camping. Only .2 miles farther on is another good camping spot at the top of Gaddis Mountain.

This stretch of the trail is particularly blessed with wild-flowers during some seasons. There are two major wildflower seasons, early spring and late summer to fall. Here last fall I found the largest, most spectacular doll's eye plants I've ever seen. If you haven't encountered this uncommon and odd plant, I hope you will. It has a bright, fat red stem with a cluster of short red stalks at the top. On each stalk is a white berry with a black dot in the center—a doll's eye.

Leaving Gaddis Mountain (3545 feet) you find switch-backs on the rather steep descent to Jarrad Gap (3250 feet, mile 5). Nearing Jarrad Gap you'll notice signs of jeeps and several rock fireplaces built at camping spots. At the gap a dirt road crosses and signs have been put up reading "foot travel only."

A glance at the trail shows they aren't heeded by everyone. The road to the left comes from Waters Creek recreation area, crosses the gap, and continues northwest about a mile to Lake Winfield Scott.

About five minutes out of Jarrad Gap you'll find a spring on the left. It's good water. The trail climbs again to Burnett Field Mountain (3200 feet, mile 5.4). You're now more than half way between Blood Mountain and Woody Gap.

At Henry Gap (3100 feet, 6.3 miles) you may want to lean back against a tree, eat lunch, and look out over the frozen pasture on your right. It's a peaceful and abandoned place. The quiet is intense and rare.

Another mile will bring you to Miller Gap (3000 feet, mile 7.2) and a stand of tall white pines with their delicate five-bunched needles. This is also a good sheltered spot for lunch. Here a road leads right (west) about half a mile to the community of Quebec on Georgia highway 180.

Stay left along the steep side of a hill. The AT has been rerouted around some private property at Miller Gap, so the directions in the *AT Guide* which mention a house and pond are no longer correct. Reroutings are more frequent than re-printings of this handbook, by the way, so although it is very useful, it cannot always reflect the latest situation. You should keep a sharp eye out for the white blazes. If you lose them, backtrack to the last one and search out the turn you missed.

Going on you'll see rock outcrops on the right with lots of the evergreen Christmas fern growing among them. This fern is common in our area and easy to identify. The leaves are enlarged near the stem like the foot of a Christmas stocking. There are probably more scientific identifying marks, but that's easy to remember.

The trail continues to follow the steep hillside into the damp head of a cove. A small stream begins here. Around the next bend to the left the woods are dry again and the trees smaller. You cross another cove. I surprised a grouse in this cove once, and it, in turn, surprised me, shooting up on whirring wings.

This part of the AT is very new. Watch the blazes carefully. The trail crosses several old roads and travels them for varying distances. You will cross a stream and turn right on an old road. The turn is not well marked coming the opposite way, so some-one has jammed sticks in the ground and laid rocks across the road to indicate the turn. The pungent, woodsy smell here is a huge, dead red oak.

The old road ascends pretty sharply, then the trail turns right and is a narrow path for about ten minutes. It turns right again onto the old road. A small ditch across the road helps you spot another sharp left turn onto more new trail. Once more you turn left onto the old road, and again the turn is not well marked from the other direction.

The trail crosses a stream and climbs gradually away from it. The stream and a spring house lie below and to your right. The old road narrows and becomes drier after leaving the stream. Many storm-damaged trees lie across the trail for the next mile or two.

The path is less steep, but continues to climb. At mile 8.5 is a spring on the right. The big, shallow pool is circled by rocks to stand on while filling your canteen.

More rock outcrops on both sides and some slippery trail

signal a gradual descent. Good views to the left! At last—the rock lookout on Big Cedar Mountain (3737 feet, mile 9). It offers a view as rewarding as Blood Mountain, but different. It is both spectacular and intimate compared to the wide scope of Blood. The valley you are looking into feeds Waters Creek, part of the Chestatee system.

Cedars on the rock soften its harsh lines and add their incense to the air. Climb down to the next rock ledge and you can hear the river better. There are pretty cedars here on the edge. Cedars seem to love hardship. You'll find them growing on rock outcrops, trying to survive in a few inches of soil collected in a shallow rock basin.

You won't want to leave. In fact, some friends of mine who had planned this two-day hike in reverse, Woody Gap to Neels Gap, got to this point and spent the whole weekend. They came out on Sunday having walked only 3 miles. However, there's a mile and a half to Woody Gap and the sun is low. A bar of extra bittersweet chocolate saved for this point will make the last half hour of walking easier.

A few more moments bring you to Lunsford Gap where tulip poplars and pines form an attractive open stand. Leaving Lunsford, you ascend briefly, then begin the last 150-foot drop to Woody Gap (3150 feet, mile 10.4). You may spook deer on this stretch near dusk. The vegetation is thick, the trail narrow and rocky. Noises from the picnic area and highway at Woody Gap welcome you back to civilization.

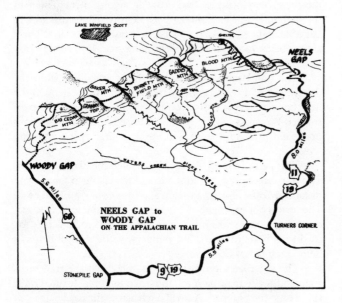

HIKING GUIDE

Neels Gap to Woody Gap

This hike along one of the most popular portions of the Appalachian Trail in Georgia extends 10.4 miles from Neels Gap in the north to Woody Gap in the south. At 4,461 feet atop Blood Mountain you look out over 25,000 acres of wild woodland.

The trail offers a variety of hikes. Neels Gap to Woody Gap, as outlined in the accompanying story, is a comfortable two-day trip with an overnight on Blood Mountain. The 2.1 mile climb up

Blood Mountain and return makes a solid one day trip or a leisurely overnight. Going south to north, the 1.4 mile hike from Woody Gap to Big Cedar Mountain is an easy day walk with as spectacular a view as the Blood Mountain Climb.

Allow plenty of time for these hikes. As a rule of thumb use two miles per hour plus one hour for each 1000 feet of elevataion gained. Be sure and notify someone of your whereabouts and when you plan to return.

There is adequate marking where the trail intersects with state highways at Neels Gap and Woody Gap. Cars can be parked nearby to set up a shuttle.

1974

One Day Walk to Ellicott's Rock

A short hike to the spot that marks the boundary of Georgia, South Carolina and North Carolina

by Margaret Tucker

Where's Ellicott's Rock?" my husband asked when I proposed a hike to it. "And who's Ellicott?" I thought I knew the answers (see box), so we began at 11:00 on a Sunday morning our first search for that elusive rock. Seven of us, my husband Skip and I, Butch Terry, Helen Johnston, Barbara Walmsley, and her children, David and Adrienne, stepped out of the car at Walhalla Fish Hatchery. David and Adrienne were off toward the creek with children's unfailing instinct to explore. We followed them across the bridge and onto the trail which climbed gently out of sight above the roaring creek.

The woods are moist along the East Fork and beds of soft green fern shone in the tree-filtered sun. Woods' magic took over my senses. Suddenly I noticed things—cool clay banks, the brilliant shine of galax leaves. It was good to be among green and growing things again. Hiking not only tones you up physically, puts you in touch with your body again, but it puts you in touch with the natural world. This relationship, like any human acquaintance, must be worked on, developed, given time and energy. Each trip into the outdoors produces new sights, renews old memories, and reforges and strengthens one's links with nature.

There are numerous interesting plants along this trail. In early June we saw the galax blooming—foot-long spikes with white flower clusters. In the fall you won't see the flowers, but the green leaves will have turned wine red or bronze. The trail has both true and false Solomon's seal, a plant with a zig-zag stem several feet long bearing alternately placed leaves. The true plant has its pale flowers and later dark berries along the stem while the false (just to confuse you) flowers and berries at the end of its stem. The largest Jack-in-the-pulpits I have ever seen, at least 2 feet high, were on this trail. Black-stemmed maidenhair fern grows here in graceful curves and spicy-smelling heart-leaf ginger is underfoot, hiding its purplish flower at soil level under its leaves.

As we walked on, we came to a cove where the roar of the East fork died. Neat, new stepping stones of concrete guided us over the small creek. "Is that cheating?" I asked myself. "Too easy?" Honestly, I prefer to take off my shoes and wade, or take my chances of wet feet by jumping from rock to rock. However, I think the primitive and the developed trails both have their places. This is an excellent trail for beginners and children. The many other creek crossings are also made easy by wooden bridges or half logs with cable hand holds. Footing is good, the grade is easy and the whole trail is designed and maintained with care.

Another of the beauties of this trail is that you can easily do it in one day without needing a heavy pack of equipment. You don't even need to carry water if you don't mind drinking from the many creeks and springs along the trail.

We continued down the east fork to a spot where a huge rock face carved over millenia by the water curved above our heads with water dripping over its face in two thousand places. I got thoroughly wet trying to catch a drop on my tongue. Ages ago this rock began to resist the urge of East fork to turn, bending the stream back. It still resists, but the stream has worn it into curves and polished it.

The two and a half miles we walked from the fish hatchery to the Chattooga follows an old Indian trail called Kusinunhi, Cherokee for "the trail to the Creek nation." This was a major trading trail from the middle Cherokee tribes in Virginia and North Carolina to the Creeks in Georgia. It passed a large Indian village called Canuga, or "blackberry patch," which stood on present day Indian Camp Creek near the fish hatchery. The Indian trail crossed the Chattooga just downstream of the East fork junction.

We reached the junction of the East fork and Chattooga in about an hour and fifteen minutes from our starting time. This is a great camping spot—level, sheltered with pines and tulip poplar, softened by pine needles. The water is quiet here as the fierce little East fork is swallowed by a much larger Chattooga, at this point deceptively slow. I wanted to stay here the rest of the day but couldn't decide which I'd rather have with me, a hammock or a trout fishing pole.

Backpacks stood against several trees while their owners ambled about or lay under the pines. Downstream several people were fishing. We didn't stay, however; today Ellicott's rock was our lunch destination. I almost wished we had no plans. It's nice sometimes to set out on a trail with no idea of where you want to stop or camp. Then you can respond to the lure of whatever charming place you find.

We continued over the level flood plain between red maples and through fern beds until my husband stopped short as a small garter snake slid across the trail. We caught it and offered it to the children to hold, but they were "only looking, thanks." We saw several snakes, all harmless, on this trip. David was surprised by a little ring-necked snake which was coiled

under the rock he picked up to skip on the water. If you encounter a snake on the trail, don't panic. He's usually on his way somewhere else. Let him pass. Don't try to catch him unless you know he's harmless and also know how to handle him correctly without hurting him.

While we were looking at the snake, Helen had disappeared over the hill. We heard her in the distance waiting for us, playing her soprano recorder, a flute-like instrument popular in the seventeenth century. This short pipe is always in her pack or pocket, along with a six-inch Buck knife. The combination says something about Helen, 17 and beautiful, with gentle eyes and glossy black hair to her waist, an accomplished musician with the recorder, guitar, or harmonica, she is also tough enough to backpack all day on bare feet or guide a raft of novices down the roughest whitewater of the Chattooga.

After about an hour of walking from the East fork junction, we came to the sign which the Forest Service has placed to indicate Ellicott's rock. On a small rock outcrop at the very edge of the water was Ellicott's marker. We picked our way down the steep bank to look at the inscription and ate lunch on the cold rocks. Then we headed back downstream to an island with a huge boulder on the upstream end.

The rocky beach here is also a good place to eat. The far side of the island hides a swimming hole and is screened enough for skinny dipping which some of us did. Those who preferred to stay dry and warm sunbathed on the beach while the children vied with each other in rock skipping and log walking on the big tree which had fallen across the channel between the beach and the island.

After an hour we started back. Along the way we stopped at a tempting sand bar where several of us napped, others waded and the kids built toad houses. We disturbed one more harmless snake and two trout fishermen, on our way out before reaching our car at 5:00. The two mile hike out from the East fork was only 45 minutes of actual walking. As we drove back to pick up our other car, I resolved to return in blackberry season. The road banks are loaded! This trail offers something to enjoy in every season and to all ages and levels of hiking experience.

HIKING GUIDE

Walk to Ellicott's Rock

The hike round trip to Ellicott's rock from Walhalla Fish Hatchery or from Burrell's Ford is 8 or 10 easy miles and makes a good one-day trip. To take advantage of the maximum downhill going, start at the fish hatchery and end at Burrell's Ford, if you have a shuttle car.

You will walk 2.5 miles down the north bank of the East fork to its junction with the Chattooga. Then follow the Chattooga, staying on the east bank, 2 miles to Ellicott's rock. Just before you reach the rock you will pass a huge tulip poplar about three feet in diameter on the right of the trail, then a small island in the river with a trailer truck-sized rock on its upstream end. A sign points down, where you will find Ellicott's rock at water level.

You can continue north up the trail to old Fowler Road and come out on Bull Pen Road 2.3 miles away, but the trail is not marked and it's easy to miss unless you're experienced.

Hiking back to the East fork is almost all downhill and fast. A log and cable bridge takes you over the East fork and onto the two mile trail to Burrell's Ford campground and FS road 708.

There are very few places where the trail leaves the East fork or the main Chattooga river. Sometimes it climbs the hillside and you walk level with the tops of the giant hemlocks in the creek gorge; often it's at river level, but all creek crossings are bridged and the trail is graded.

To shuttle: Drop one car at Burrell's Ford. From Georgia it's easily reached by taking Warwoman road out of Clayton 15.8 miles to state highway 28. Turn right at the town of Pine Mountain and go about 1½ miles to FS 646, an all-weather gravel road, well graded. Turn left and follow it 7.3 miles to the Chattooga river. Cross the bridge and leave one car. Drive out on FS 708 2.6 miles to S.C. 107. Turn left and go 1.5 miles to FS 68. Turn left and go 1.9 miles to the fish hatchery. This is a paved road, but steep and curvey.

1974

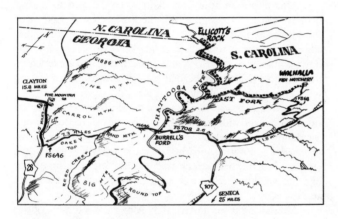

Where is Ellicott's Rock?

Major Andrew Ellicott was hired by Georgia Governor David Brydie Mitchell in 1810 to locate and mark the intersection of the 35th parallel and the Chattooga river so that the boundary of North Carolina and Georgia could be drawn west from that point, but when he returned, was dissatisfied with the payment he had gotten and refused to give his report to the state. The only direction he ever gave to the spot was that an island in the Chattooga helped locate it.

A team of commissioners from Georgia and North Carolina inscribed a rock in the general vicinity, "AD 1813, Lat 35, NCx GA." It has been called "Ellicott's rock" ever since. However, it is slightly north of the true 35th parallel, and is thought by many not to be Ellicott's at all. A survey party from North and South Carolina were working in the area immediately after Ellicott, and the rock dated 1813 is probably theirs, as Ellicott finished his work in 1812. Regardless, all subsequent attempts to mark the boundary of Georgia and North Carolina were unsuccessful and the exact boundary has never been accurately marked. In 1971 Governor Carter appointed a commission to recommend a solution to the problem and a new effort to mark the boundary will probably begin in the next few years.

See Rock City.
(Trust me.)

by Tom Patterson

It's always a bit puzzling to me why the northwestern corner of Georgia, which has some of the most interesting and relatively unspoiled natural areas in the Southeast, is usually overlooked by summer travelers who head for the mountains to escape the oppressive heat of dog days in the Southern lowlands. Every time I venture into the sparsely populated areas of northwestern Georgia—particularly Dade, Walker, and Chattooga Counties—I'm struck by this fact. Like most Georgians, I'm far more familiar with the Blue Ridge Mountains of northeastern Georgia than I am with the less-traveled territory to their west. So when I travel into the Valley-and-Ridge District, as the physiographers call it, I never have to look far to find new territory that makes for some fascinating exploration.

My most recent trip to this area took me up into Walker County, where I had planned to do some hiking on Pigeon Mountain, a 2000-foot-high plateau extending northeastward from the long, north-south ridge of Lookout Mountain. Together with adjacent Sand Mountain, these comprise the only portion of the Cumberland Plateau to extend into Georgia. This trip turned out to be one of the most rewarding hiking jaunts I've been on in a long time, giving me the opportunity to explore an interesting portion of forest and see some spectacular waterfalls, springs, and cave entrances, and allowing me to get a good look at some of the most unusual rock formations I've seen since my last trip to the Chiricahua Mountains of Arizona, about six years ago. After only two days on Pigeon Mountain, I was ready to nominate the place as one of those best-kept secrets in Georgia.

Until about five years ago Pigeon Mountain was privately owned, and access to it by the public was limited largely to a few hunting groups who had special permission to use the land. Since that time, however, the state of Georgia has been gradually buying up the land here under the Georgia Heritage Trust Program, set up in 1972 with the stated aim of forming "a framework for identification, protection, and preservation of cultural, natural, and recreational areas throughout the state." It doesn't take a visitor to Pigeon Mountain long to figure out why this area has been given such a high priority within the Heritage Trust Program. The mountain has all the distinguishing characteristics of its sister plateau, Lookout Mountain, but has fortunately escaped the fate of being developed into a commercial theme park, as has happened to the north end of Lookout Mountain. There are miles of underground caverns here, but there are no floodlights nor guided tours of these caves, and there is even a field of huge, weirdly-shaped boulders reminiscent of Lookout's "Rock City," but it's nestled in the midst of a dense woodland area on top of the plateau, accessible only by foot or by very rugged four-wheel-drive vehicles. The area is a veritable paradise for geologists and spelunkers, with over 75 cave entrances located at various points on the mountain. Ellison's Cave, with three entrances on Pigeon Mountain, ranks third in overall depth in the nation, and two of its pits are the first and second deepest, respectively, among caves throughout the entire world. One of these drops 510 feet, and the other 440 feet. About 13 miles of Ellison's Cave have been mapped, but all indications are that it is much more extensive than its explored area. It's likely, in fact, that the interior of Pigeon Mountain is one vast system of underground caverns and stream channels. Springs gush out of the mountain at many points with surprising force, flowing down into the surrounding valleys as good-sized creeks. Some readers may recall the period in early March of 1979 when Pigeon Mountain received a good deal of news coverage, after a group of amateur spelunkers from Georgia Southwestern College in Americus were trapped for hours in Anderson Cave, on the mountain's southwest slope, due to rising water in the wake of heavy rains. That near-disaster should underscore the fact that caving is a dangerous pastime, not to be embarked upon without expert guidance and the proper equipment. I kept this in mind when I got my first look into Ellison's Cave, contenting myself with a glimpse into the blackness from an opening about a mile off the loop trail that I hiked on the northern end of the mountain, and tossing a few small stones into it to hear what kind of echoes would come back. For the time being, I decided, I'd stick to above-ground hiking.

HIKING GUIDE

Pigeon Mountain

The first of these two hikes on Pigeon Mountain is on the Pocket Loop Trail, located in the vicinity of the steep-walled gorge bordering Pocket Branch, on the mountain's northwestern side. To reach the beginning of this trail, follow US 27 north to LaFayette, seat of Walker County. Turn left (west) on Ga 193 at the first traffic light in LaFayette as you approach from the south on US 27. Follow Ga 193 for 8 miles to the Gulf station on the right side of the road at Davis Crossroads. Turn left here, and follow a paved road for 2.7 miles until you pass Mount Hermon Baptist Church on the left and reach the hilltop just beyond the church. A paved road turns off to the left at this hilltop. Turn left here, and follow this road for a little over a mile, to beyond the point where the pavement ends. Shortly after passing a large sign on the left side that reads, "Pigeon Mountain Wildlife Management Area," you will reach a chainlink gate across the road. Park your vehicle near this gate where it won't block the road, and continue on foot beyond the gate, paralleling Pocket Branch on your right. You'll have no trouble recognizing (1) *Pocket Branch Falls* on your right as you emerge from the woods into an open clearing. After stopping to examine the falls, continue along the roadway, now only a narrow, twin-rutted jeep trail, until you reach a (2) *wooden shelter* on the right. Look for a blue sign nailed to a tree just to the right of this shelter: "South Pocket Trail," it reads, with an arrow directing you to the beginning of this 8-mile loop trail. A similar sign on the opposite side of the shelter points to the "North Pocket Trail," indicating that, since this is a loop trail, it's possible to hike it in either direction. I strongly recommend following the former, southward, course, however. Unless

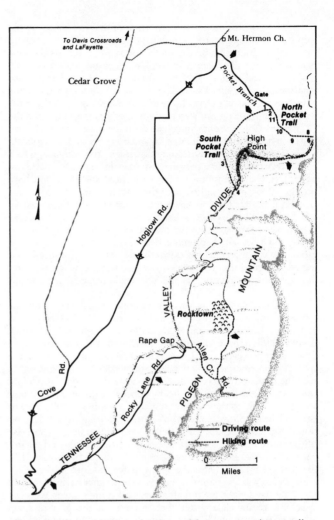

you've got masochistic tendencies and happen to enjoy grueling, uphill climbs, you'll find this route much more pleasant. Pick up the trail, then, at the shelter, and follow the blue-painted blazes on trees and rocks that mark the trail's course. When I hiked the Pocket Trail in early June, I found it to be in need of maintenance work. High weeds, fallen trees, and other natural obstacles made it difficult in places to discern the path's course on the ground, but the blue blazes were always there to indicate the correct route.

For its first 2 or 3 miles, the trail runs along the lower slopes of this portion of Pigeon Mountain, meandering gradually up and down before you begin the (3) *climb to the mountain's brow*, at which point the trail becomes markedly steeper. Upon reaching the (4) *relatively level mountaintop*, the trail bends to the left and follows the northwest rim of the mountain for a little less than a mile. At this point the trail follows, roughly, the line of the Tennessee Valley Divide. It will be well worth your while to stop at least once on this portion of the trail and take a few steps to the left of the track in order to get a good look at some of the odd rock formations clustered on the brow of the mountain here. Slim, natural sandstone pillars, deep crevasses, and other formations characterize this portion of the mountain, from which there is an excellent view of McLemore Cove (the low-lying valley to the west) and of Lookout Mountain on its far side. Be very careful here, though, as these are steep cliffs, and one unfortunate slip of the foot could make this the last view you'll ever see. The trail now follows the rim of the mountain to (5) *High Point*, Pigeon Mountain's appropriately named highest point, at 2329 feet; then it bends with the curve of the rim and continues within a few yards of this precipice for another mile or so. Most of this mountaintop portion of the trail lies along old jeep trails and logging roads, of which there is a complex network on Pigeon Mountain. Be careful to keep an eye out for the blue blazes, which will ensure that you haven't wandered off onto an unmarked road section. At the (6) *point where the trail leaves the old roadbed* and turns left, it's possible to make a side trip to one of the entrances to Ellison's Cave. If, instead of following the trail on the left, you continue on this jeep road for another mile, you'll find the (7) *Ellison's Cave entrance* immediately on the right side of the road in a deep hollow lined with huge, jagged boulders, and with a small, spring-fed trickle of water leading down into the entrance, which is just large enough for a person to squeeze through. Don't attempt to explore the cave unless you're a practiced spelunker and have brought along ropes, lights, and other caving gear.

Shortly after the trail leaves the old jeep road, turning sharply left, its course begins a (8) *gradual descent,* which becomes steeper as you move farther down the mountain. Once you reach this vicinity, you'll see why I recommended following the southern loop. Here, one is tempted to run down the mountain at top speed, taking advantage of the steep slope to save some time, whereas hiking in the opposite direction, up the hill, would make for a torturous climb.

As the trail nears the lower-lying slopes, you'll come upon the (9) *north fork of Pocket Branch,* which was dry when I hiked here in June. Near this area the trail emerges into a (10) *open field,* at which point you might have some difficulty in finding the next blazed tree. Once here, however, you'll be within a half mile of completing the trail. As you emerge into the field, simply continue straight across it in the direction you're facing as you leave the woods. You'll find the next blazed tree on the field's opposite side, at which point you'll also pick up the road upon which you initially walked up to the trail head. Shortly after you've passed through the field—no doubt you'll be hot, dirty, and thirsty—you'll find the best surprise of the entire hike: a (11) *natural spring* on the left side of the road, enclosed on two sides by stone slabs and traversed by another slab, like a small bridge. Thus, the spring is formed into a sort of icy bath, which was too tempting for me to resist after having hiked all day. I plunged right in, and afterwards filled my canteen with the delicious, crystal-clear water that flows from the ground here. Chances are that you'll want to do the same. Once you've had enough of this spring and its idyllic setting, simply continue along the roadway for another few hundred yards, and you'll soon find yourself back at the point where you began your hike.

The second selected hike on Pigeon Mountain is located farther south, on the mountaintop and in the vicinity of Rape Gap, at the eastern end of the gorge known as Anderson Gulf. Since it follows rough jeep roads rather than designated hiking trails for its entire length, it's also possible to drive the route if you've got a sturdy, four-wheel-drive jeep or a truck with oversized tires. Part of the route can even be driven with a family car. This route has been designed as a way of reaching Rocktown, the bizarre, 160-acre field of three-million-year-old sandstone boulders which is certainly one of Pigeon Mountain's most interesting features. As is the case with the Pocket Loop Trail, this hike is reached via the paved road turning south off Ga 193 from Davis Crossroads. Follow the same driving directions given for the first hike, turning left at Davis Crossroads and continuing past Mount Hermon Baptist Church. Instead of taking the first left turn beyond the church (2.7 miles from Ga 193), continue south on this road for 1.7 miles beyond that turnoff to Hogjowl Road, a paved road that turns off to the left. Turn left, and follow Hogjowl Road for 5.4 miles, bearing left at the point where this road merges with Cove Road. After about 1.5 miles the road begins climbing up Pigeon Mountain at the southern end of McLemore Cove. At 3.3 miles after merging with Cove Road, look for the large Pigeon Mountain Wildlife Management Area sign on the left, and turn left on the gravel road here. At about 1.5 miles beyond this turnoff, the road begins to get rough, and unless you have a particularly rugged vehicle, you may want to find a place to

pull your car off to the side of the road and walk the remaining 5 miles to Rocktown. At exactly 2 miles after turning onto this dirt road, take the left fork where it splits, and 2.4 miles later turn right onto Allen Creek Road, indicated by a wooden sign nailed to a tree at the intersection. Another sign on this same tree reads, "Hunting access road." From this point on, Allen Creek Road is much too rough for any but the most sturdy four-wheel-drive vehicles. After about a mile the road merges with the very rocky bed of Allen Creek, which is fairly dry at this point during most of the summer, and it follows the creek's course downhill. After only 1/10 mile, watch for a right-angle turnoff to the left from the creekbed. A small wooden sign on a tree trunk, easily obscured by thick foliage during the summer months, indicates that this is the route to Rocktown. Turn left here, and follow this road for 1.1 miles, watching carefully for another narrow jeep trail that turns off to the left; this intersection is marked by a piece of bright-blue plastic ribbon and another Rocktown sign nailed to a tree. Turn left here, and walk for about 20 yards, at which point the road forks. Take the left fork, and within another 50 yards you'll get your first glimpse of the sandstone formations that make up the area called Rocktown, which covers about 160 acres on this portion of Pigeon Mountain. There are no marked trails through Rocktown, but the undergrowth in this area is sparse, due to the fact that officials of the Game and Fish Division of the Georgia Department of Natural Resources did a "controlled burn" of this area in the spring of 1980, which got rid of most of the thick vegetation on the ground here. This makes it fairly easy to explore Rocktown to your heart's content. Be careful, however, not to lose your sense of direction during your explorations. It wouldn't be difficult to become totally lost within the surrealistic maze of oddly shaped boulders and outcroppings, many of which are bigger than houses. If you plan on camping during your visit to Pigeon Mountain, you'll find numerous clearings and natural shelters at Rocktown that would make ideal primitive campsites. If you plan to camp here, though, you should bring water with you, since it's about a mile from here to the nearest stream.

If you want to look at detailed topographical maps of the Pigeon Mountain area before embarking on either of these two hikes, these maps can be viewed at the Game and Fish Division's check station, located just off Ga 193 between LaFayette and the little community of Davis Crossroads, and thus directly on the way to the two hiking areas reviewed here. Watch for a dirt road turning off to the left at a sign that reads "Patton Rock Products," about five miles east of LaFayette on Ga 193. Turn left here, then immediately left again at the first opportunity, following a gravel road for about 1/4 mile to the Pigeon Mountain check station. If you wish to request further information about Pigeon Mountain by mail or phone before visiting the area, the mailing address is *Game and Fish Division, Georgia Department of Natural Resources, Rte 1, Armuchee, GA 30105; (404) 295-6041.*

Walks to Waterfalls

by Susan McDonald

Want to stretch your legs? See some scenery? Some foliage? Here are six walks to waterfalls that lead to some of the prettiest spots in the North Georgia mountains. All six of these hikes are located within the publicly owned lands of the Chattahoochee National Forest and were chosen not only for the beauty of the falls and landscape, but also to provide a variety of hiking experiences ranging from easy family outings to treks suitable for more seasoned hikers.

The hikes are listed in order of increasing difficulty, based on a combination of trail distance and strenuousness. The first two hikes do not need maps, since the trails are short and easy to follow. Getting lost should not be a problem on any of the other hikes either, since in most cases they stick close to the creek banks, making trails easy to locate and follow. In all cases, good walking footwear, not just Sunday strolling shoes, is recommended.

The first three hikes have picnic areas at or near the trail entrances. Primitive camping is allowed along all these trails, and many previously established campsites can be easily located and used again to avoid scarring up new spots. Camping is not allowed, however, within the developed picnic areas themselves, which are usually locked at night. Three of the hikes involve drives of two to 15 miles on winding gravel roads. All roads mentioned are well graded and drained.

A word of caution: Georgia's waterfalls are enticing and attractive enough to have lured 14 people to their deaths in recent years as they were climbing the deceptively slippery rocks around the falls. Excellent views of each of the six falls described here are possible from numerous positions that do not require hazardous climbs across wet or lichen-covered rocks. As long as observers treat the beauty and potential danger of each of these falls with respect, there won't be any prettier or more enjoyable places to hike in the North Georgia mountains.

Copies of a National Forest Service seven-page print-out entitled "Waterfalls in North Georgia" can be obtained free by contacting the U.S. Forest Service, Box 1437, Gainesville 30501; (404) 536-0541. Of uneven quality, the brochure provides confusing directions—or no directions at all—to some of the lesser known falls, and in addition, the reader is assumed to have a good knowledge of North Georgia geography. But for those with an explorer's temperament, the brochure could lead the way to some enjoyable outings.

HIKING GUIDE

Six North Georgia Waterfalls

Numbers mark the location of hikes to six North Georgia waterfalls, listed in order of the increasing difficulty of the hiking trails. It's no accident that five of the six falls are in the eastern part of the state. The western half of the region is much drier and a little less craggy, resulting in many fewer cascades.

1. Dukes Creek Falls: The falls at Dukes Creek are a Sunday-afternoon-for-the-family kind of place where kids run up and down the short, steeply switchbacked trail urging their puffing parents *please* to hurry up. It only takes about 15 minutes to walk down to the falls and 25 minutes to walk back up—scant labor, considering the loveliness of the falls below. A small stream, called Davis Creek, drizzles daintily over a 150-foot sheer granite cliff to intersect Dukes Creek as it tumbles over huge boulders and rock ledges for a horizontal distance of several hundred feet. Summer camp groups, outfitted in tennis shoes and bathing suits, oftentimes use a portion of the stream bed's slick rock surface as a water slide. At the second of its two rock staircases, the trail follows an old roadbed for 100 yards or so. If, when facing downhill, a right turn is made after the steps (instead of a left, which leads down to the falls), the old roadbed leads in 10 or 15 minutes to a ford along Dukes Creek. This is a quiet, pleasant place to enjoy one of the creek's more serene locations.

The trail begins at Dukes Creek Recreation Area, which is marked by a large wooden National Forest sign located on Richard Russell Scenic Highway (Ga. 348) 1.5 miles west of its junction with Ga. 356 near Helen.

2. High Shoals Falls: For sheer drama, High Shoals is pretty hard to beat among any of Georgia's waterfalls. But, as in the case of so many other natural beauties, the danger inherent in these magnificent falls has prompted the Forest Service to cage viewers at the two biggest cascades in small heavily-railed platforms which, however well intentioned and protective, still serve to lessen some of the awesome sensation which is a waterfall's principal attraction. Laying aside the pros and cons of protecting the public against itself, the falls are well worth the short, steep walk and rugged back-roads drive that it takes to reach them.

The trail entrance is on Forest Service Road 283, which turns east off Ga. 75 about nine miles north of Helen and nine miles south of Hiawassee. The turn is marked by a small sign saying "High Shoals Falls 2 mi." The road is steep, and at one point cars

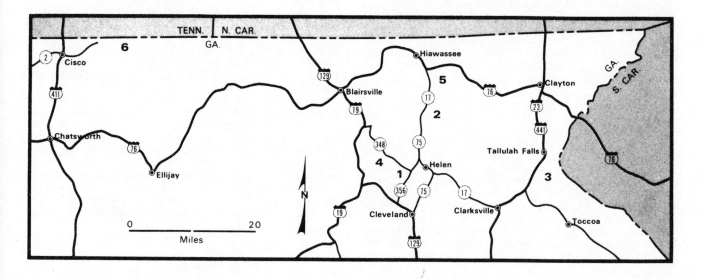

must ford a small creek about six inches deep and 20 feet wide. Most passenger cars, except those built very low to the ground, should be able to manage the road, however. The foot trail begins 1.5 miles after the turn off Ga. 75. There's no sign, but a small side road, primarily used as a parking pull-off, leads briefly into the woods at this point, and the trail goes down from the center of this fork. One-half mile farther along the road is a pleasant picnic area with tables by a stream. The falls trail is steep for about a quarter-mile, then levels out at the valley floor. The falls are downstream along the trail. About 25 minutes are needed to reach the first cascade and 15 minutes more to reach the second.

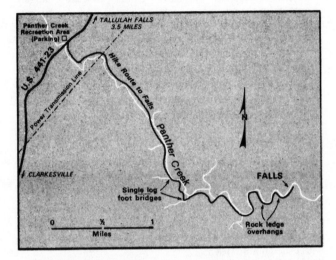

3. Panther Creek Falls: The wide, multiple cascades of the 80-foot-high Panther Creek Falls can be reached by walking a relatively easy four-mile trail that follows the creek down from U.S. 441 in Habersham County. The trail is dotted with huge white pines, some of whose trunks are over a yard in diameter. Granite ledges and overhangs not only enhance the scenery along the trail, but also provide rain shelters and a little rock-climbing variety to the trail's otherwise gentle slopes. The climbs will be no problem, however, for anyone able to handle a short stepladder. Hiking time should average about 2–2½ hours each way for the eight-mile round trip.

The trail entrance is directly across the road from Panther Creek Recreation area, which has picnic tables, barbeque pits, and a fresh-water pump. The recreation area is well marked by a big wooden Forest Service sign on U.S. 441 and 23 one mile north of Turnerville and three miles south of Tallulah Falls.

4. Raven Cliffs Falls: The three falls along this 3.5-mile trail are part of a proposed wilderness area in which the terrain bears strikingly little resemblance to that normally encountered in the North Georgia mountains. Tall granite cliffs form a stark backdrop along the creek's south bank that is softened by the narrow valley's dense patches of fern and laurel. Evergreens make up a high percentage of the forest, and mushrooms of unusual size and color are abundant during damp periods. Along the entire trail, Dodd Creek is one long rush of tumbling water as it drops from shoal to shoal between each of the major falls. The third waterfall, by far the most spectacular, crashes 50 feet straight down through a crack in the granite cliffs and then cascades rapidly downstream for about 75 yards. The section of the falls within the cliff can only be seen by climbing the mountain slope to the right as you face the falls.

The Raven Cliffs trail is more aptly described as a foot path than an actual trail. It receives only minimal maintenance from the Forest Service, so fallen trees, creek fords, and trail washouts are some of the obstacles to be overcome. The path is fainter than more heavily used trails, but should be easy to discern by observant hikers. The trail's several forks all appear to lead back to the main path

after a very short distance.

The trail begins at a parking pull-off (look for a small green mile signpost numbered 4) on Ga. 348, located 2.9 miles west of this road's intersection with Ga. 356. Follow the dirt road downstream about 100 yards until it divides into a three-pronged fork. Take the extreme right fork (really just a car turn-in for the adjacent camping spot), which narrows almost immediately into a footpath that climbs gently onto a terrace overlooking Dodd Creek. Follow this path upstream to the three falls, which are reached after about 10 minutes, 40 minutes, and two hours of walking time, respectively.

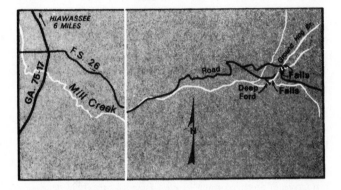

5. Mill Creek Falls: The falls on Mill Creek and its tributary, Ground Hog Branch, are really pretty ones. The only problem is that they are very hard to see through the leaves in the surrounding thick woods, so the best time to visit them will be after the leaves have dropped for the winter. The falls on Ground Hog Branch cascade gently on either side of the road for a total distance of 150 feet and (without leaves) can be viewed from the road or, with considerable difficulty clambering through the thick underbrush, from the creek bank below the road. The more spectacular 150-foot double falls on Mill Creek are much more trouble to reach and, to some people, may not be worth trudging along the steep and overgrown quarter-mile path to see.

To reach both falls, turn east (right, if proceeding north) off Ga. 75 onto Forest Service Road 26 about 2½ miles north of the point where Ga. 66 enters from the west. The turn is marked by a sign for Dyer's Trout Farm. Take the left fork at mile 1.1 from the turn, and continue on to an overgrown side road on the right at mile 2.1. This is the trail entrance for the Mill Creek Falls. Just continue on the main road to mile 2.3 to cross the falls at Ground Hog Branch. If the gate at mile 1.7 is closed, the car can be parked in the pull-off a few yards back and the next 0.4 mile walked on foot.

The side road at 2.1 miles is suitable only for jeeps and such, so it's best to walk from here along the old roadbeds that are in various stages of reverting back to forest. The trail heads toward and then follows Mill Creek for about 15 minutes of hiking time until it reaches a ford too deep to cross using stepping stones. Just before this deep ford, take the left fork, which soon climbs to a terrace 30 yards or so above the creek. The trail rapidly becomes very overgrown, with saplings of six to eight inches growing in the roadbed. In places the road washes out to the width of a narrow footpath along the steep bank. Watch and listen for the falls. There is no path down to them, so hikers must either view them from the trail (practically impossible before leaves drop) or descend the steep bank down to the creek's edge, where footing is uneven and steep. This trail—more like a raccoon path—is not a Sunday stroll under the trees, but rather an overland trek for those who enjoy picking their way through the woods.

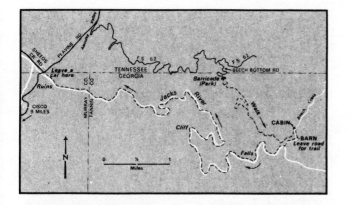

6. Jacks River Falls: This hike along the Jacks River in the Cohutta Wilderness was published as a separate hiking story in the Sept/Oct '75 issue of *Brown's Guide,* but the falls are so majestic and wild and the trail such a good one for early fall hiking that we could not resist including it in this collection of hikes to waterfalls. It is the most strenuous of the six hikes, requiring about seven hours for the 9½-mile trip. Although the distance can be covered in one day, an overnight hike is recommended to allow more leisure time for exploring the falls and other sites along the river. Because the trail fords the river 20 times after it passes the falls, the complete hike is suitable only for summer and warm-weather fall hiking. For a shorter, year-round alternative, hikers can simply turn around at the falls and retrace their route back to the trail entrance. An added bonus to this hike is the pretty 15-mile backwoods drive through the Alaculsy Valley before reaching the wilderness area. Here are the directions to the trail entrance and also information for setting up a two-car shuttle:

At Cisco, turn east off U.S. 411 onto Ga. 2 which, despite the warning sign that it's for four-wheel-drive vehicles only, is a fine gravel road navigable by any car. Stay right at the fork at mile 1.1, but take the left fork at mile 3.1. Again stay left at mile 7.8 where Ga. 2 makes a sharp right turn. This is Forest Service Road 302. At mile 8.6, the road crosses the Jacks River, which is the endpoint of the hiking trail and the spot at which to park the shuttle car. Continue straight along the road past the bridge for another 1.1 miles, and then turn sharply back to the right and uphill on F.S. Road 62. It's steep, but should be manageable by even big cars except perhaps after very heavy rains. Follow this road 4.7 miles, then bear right onto Beech Bottom Road (no sign). After 0.6 mile, the road is barricaded. Park so as not to block the entrance, and continue down this road on foot about two miles to a cabin on Beech Creek. Veer right at the cabin along a very rocky jeep road that crosses and then briefly follows the creek. Just before an old barn located 100 yards down this road is an unmarked trail to the right. Although it looks more like a washout from the road than a foot trail, it leads across the creek, through an old cherry orchard, across the creek again, and to the Jacks River. The Jacks River trail (marked with orange paint blazes) runs downstream along this bank and in only a few hundred yards meets the falls. The trail proper begins to climb the steep hillside above the falls, but the dry rocky ledges alongside the stream can be easily descended to view the powerful falls from the bottom. About a mile downstream from the falls occurs the first of the trail's 20 river crossings. The crossings, some diagonal and some perpendicular, are marked with orange metal diamonds on each bank. The ruins of an old mill are located just before the trail's end on the opposite bank of the river.

1978

The Magic of Rushing Water

by John Earl

There is a very special place in my heart for waterfalls. I have a driving compulsion to revisit the ones with which I am familiar, and constantly to seek out new ones wherever I travel.

Our Indian predecessors in North Georgia knew well the importance of running water and its relationship to man and his sense of well being. They held sacred the thousands of beautiful rivers and streams which once flowed wild and free throughout this beautiful land of ours. Today it is impossible to see and enjoy many of the waterfalls they knew and loved because of man's apparently insatiable desire to dam and destroy these free-running streams. How many of them are not there now, and how many will not be there in the future for our children to see, because they will lie buried beneath hundreds of feet of man-made lakes? Thus, I record on film waterfalls which now remain intact, in hopes of sharpening and increasing people's awareness of their importance.

I drove with John Hall, a friend and fellow photographer, to Rabun County recently to see four waterfalls that can all be visited in one day of combined hiking and automobile touring. As a young boy I spent many happy summers in this area visiting my grandparents, who owned the old Earl House, once a popular hotel in Clayton. Most of my days there were spent hiking the beautiful mountain woods.

Our first stop was at Lake Rabun and Minnehaha Falls. This lovely waterfall must surely have been a favorite spot of ancient Indians. It is located at the end of an easy trail of less than one-half mile which climbs gently back and forth through thick growths of mountain laurel and rhododendron, past large and stately hardwood trees. Quite suddenly Minnehaha comes into view, shining in the morning sunlight, framed by many low, overhanging rhododendron branches, cascading for more than 50 feet over dozens of moss-covered rock ledges.

I removed my shoes and waded knee-deep out into the icy water of the splash pool at its base in search of just the right angle for the photograph I wanted. A soft spray swept across my face. A wood thrush sang close by. Later, I sat on a large boulder which faces the falls. Bathed in warm sunlight, I closed my eyes and listened to the music of the rushing water.

About 11 A.M. we said good-by to Minnehaha and drove north toward Clayton. We were headed for a beautiful, somewhat smaller waterfall about three miles east of Clayton just opposite the Warwoman Dell Recreation Area on Warwoman Road. It is called Becky Branch Falls and is an old favorite of mine. I first discovered this falls over 40 years ago while hiking along an abandoned railroad bed that heads east from Clayton toward Charleston, South Carolina. Remnants of it are still evident today. It was never completed, but one can still find tunnels which were blasted through ridges in the eastern section of Rabun County.

We parked at a pull-out on the side of the road where a Bartram Trail sign has recently been erected. A loop trail about one-third mile long begins and ends at the pullout, and is moderately steep either way. At the top of this lovely circular trail a shaky wooden bridge crosses Becky Branch at the foot of the falls. This bridge serves as a marvelous vantage point from which to view and photograph the falls in all its delicate, plunging beauty. Becky Branch Falls is not spectacular as waterfalls go, but the loveliness of rushing white water and lush green forest combine to create a feeling of serenity and peaceful solitude.

We ate our lunch across the road from the falls at beautiful Warwoman Dell Recreation Area before continuing on our way toward two little-known waterfalls which are without a doubt two of Georgia's most beautiful.

We continued to drive east on Warwoman Road for about 10 miles. Immediately after this road crosses the Chattooga River, we turned left onto Forest Service Road 86. Although this gravel road is well maintained, it is rather narrow in places and twists and turns as it parallels first one bank and then the other of the Chattooga for several miles before beginning to climb steadily in the general direction of North Carolina. As we began to gain altitude, we noticed a change in the forest. The trees became larger as the slopes became steeper. After driving for about seven miles along this scenic road, we came to a pull-out on the right where a Forest Service sign points the way down a beautiful trail to Holcomb Creek Falls. The trail passes by many giant hemlock, tulip poplar, and white pine trees. The sheer magnificence of their size is overwhelming. The forest floor was carpeted with many lush ferns and mosses.

Soon we heard the roar of rushing water and almost immediately saw Holcomb Creek Falls. Sparkling rays of sunlight bounced back and forth in an interplay of flashing light between the many small and beautiful splash-pools which were formed over the years by the force of falling water. Ferns growing along the spray-covered ledges of this 200-foot waterfall glistened in the sunlight, reflecting emerald-green hues.

A wooden bridge crosses Holcomb Creek at the base of the falls and the trail goes on. We continued in quest of the fourth and final waterfall we were to visit that day. About an eighth of a mile further on, Ammons Creek Falls cascades wildly down the side of another high ridge, its foaming water churning and rushing along Ammons Creek to join with Holcomb Creek less than a half-mile away. Ammons Creek Falls is about two-thirds as high as Holcomb Creek Falls, but just as beautiful. The U.S. Forest Service has erected a banistered platform which affords the observer not only an excellent view of the falls itself, but from the opposite side an equally fine view of the cascades below the falls. I sat for awhile with my tired, aching feet dangling just below the surface of a clear pool at the base of the falls. A Carolina wren poured forth its beautiful song near by, and once in a while the tapping of a lone woodpecker added a perfect counterpoint percussion to this lovely serenade.

Rather reluctantly we packed our camera gear in our back packs and began retracing our steps down the trail. We walked

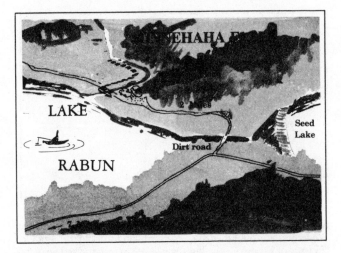

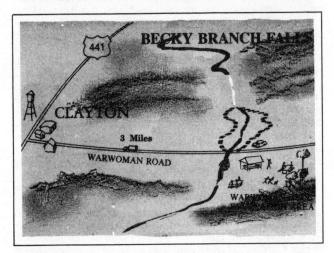

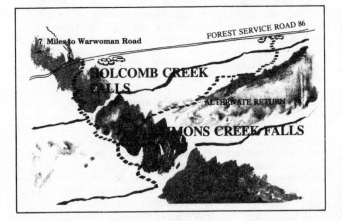

through woods comprised chiefly of large white pine and hemlock. Dwarf wild iris were growing in profusion along the trail, interspersed with bright yellow sun drops. Soon we were back to Forest Service Road 86, where a downhill walk of a little less than a mile brought us back to my station wagon and the completion of a fine day of viewing four of North Georgia's most beautiful waterfalls.

HIKING GUIDE

Four North Georgia Waterfalls

Minnehaha Falls: Minnehaha Falls is at Lake Rabun in Rabun County. Just north of Tallulah Falls on U.S. 441 look for one of several turn-offs on the left which point to Lake Rabun. Follow the Lake Rabun Road along the edge of the lake for approximately seven miles and turn left on a dirt road just below Seed Lake Dam. A Georgia Power Company sign will help identify this road. Follow this dirt road for about two miles and look for a Forest Service sign pointing the way to the falls at the trail head on the right-hand side of the road. Although the sign states that it is one-half mile to the falls, it is actually more like one-eighth of a mile. The grade is gradual and easy. A sign at the falls warns against climbing on them and is good advice. Return to U.S. 441 and continue north to Clayton.

Becky Branch Falls: At Clayton, turn right from U.S. 441 on to Warwoman Road, just south of the Heart of Rabun Motel. Drive east for three miles and look for a pull-off on the left-hand side of the road where a Bartram Trail sign has been erected. Take either entrance of the short loop trail to Becky Branch Falls. This ridge trail is quite steep but only about one-third mile in length round trip. Warwoman Dell Recreation Area directly across the road from the trail head is a delightful place to enjoy a picnic lunch.

Holcomb Creek Falls: Drive east on Warwoman Road for about ten miles. Immediately after crossing the Chattooga River, look for Forest Service Road 86. Turn left at this junction and continue on this gravel road for about seven miles to a pull-out on the right-hand side of the road where a Forest Service sign points the way to Holcomb Creek Falls, about one-half mile from the trail head at the parking pull-out.

Ammons Creek Falls: Continue on the same trail to Ammons Creek Falls, which is about one-third mile beyond Holcomb Creek Falls on the other side of a small ridge. Return by the same trail or take a right fork where a Forest Service sign indicates an alternate return to Road 86. This is a lovely trail which climbs gently upward for 1½ miles beside Holcomb Creek and then comes out on Road 86 one mile north of the trail head where one enters to go to the two falls. Turn left for the mile downhill walk back to the parking pull-out. Total distance of this hike is three miles.

Tim Homan Goes Public

A serious hiker tells some of his best secrets

by Whit Perry

During 15 months of walking, mostly alone, a young man named Tim Homan has hiked 349 miles of trails in North Georgia (80 trails in 26 counties) and has recorded his experiences in the form of short, straightforward trail guides in a book called *The Hiking Trails of North Georgia* (Peachtree Publishers).

Tim, who now lives in Gainesville, was born in Decatur, Illinois, and developed his interest in the outdoors at an early age. He had hardly started grammar school, he says, before he owned his first binoculars and his first bird-identification book. His early interest in naturalism, which was not shared by members of his family, was spurred when he discovered the works of John Muir. "He really captured my fancy," Tim says. "He was somebody who could put aside hunger, hardship, and loneliness to study nature. He seems to have total rapture. I admire him, and I also admire Edwin Way Teals, who took long car trips, getting out to study and photograph different natural areas and to write about the seasons."

Tim first saw North Georgia in 1972; he was in the Army, stationed at Fort Gordon in Augusta, and took a hitchhiking trip into the area. "I was awestruck," he says. "It's hard to imagine the difference between the sea of black mud in Central Illinois—miles and miles of it—and the cool, clear green waters of North Georgia. It was something I'd never seen before."

Upon his discharge from the Army, Tim decided to stay in Georgia, and he enrolled at the University of Georgia. He attended that institution for 3½ years but finally dropped out. He intended, he says, to become a writer. He had studied both forestry and English while at the university, and he considered the lack of a comprehensive guidebook to Georgia's trails to be a gap that he could fill. "There was really no good information from the U.S. Forest Service at that time," he says. At first, Tim wanted to cover all trails in the state, but he soon realized the magnitude of such an undertaking and narrowed the scope of his work to the tier of northern counties where most of the state's trails are located. "These trails are the most heavily used, the most frequently asked about, and, to the eyes of many, the most scenic," he says.

Tim is a self-taught and enthusiastic botanist, and as he and I walked the Panther Creek Trail, one of the trails covered in his book, he pointed out gaywings, bloodroot, crested dwarf iris, bluets, and other unusual flora. He often leads relatively large groups when he hikes these days, and he takes his responsibilities—keeping an eye on the youngsters and treating minor injuries—quite seriously. But he is especially cautious when he hikes alone, often passing up the pleasure of playing in a waterfall or some enjoyable but potentially dangerous activity. "If you suffer a fall when you're alone," he says, "you're in big trouble. Ideally, you should go with someone else, but I estimate that I did ninety-five percent of my hiking for the book alone. It's dangerous, but Daniel Boone, John Muir, and those people did it alone. I see nothing wrong with hiking alone, as long as you recognize the dangers and take the necessary precautions. Besides, you're likely to see more wildlife when you're alone."

One danger that Tim says some hikers overrate is poisonous snakes; he admits that they can be a problem, but he says, "I've never seen a single rattlesnake on my hikes. I have seen two copperheads off the trail, but both were totally docile." More dangerous, he feels, particularly when hiking without someone who can be sent for help, are insect stings and twisted ankles. Nor does he think that any of the larger wildlife that hikers are liable to meet on Georgia trails pose much danger. He says, "Three times, I've walked up on huge wild boars, but they just ran away from me up the trail. If they'd come my way,

I'd have headed for the nearest tree. As far as I can tell, they aren't dangerous unless you come between a sow and her piglets."

Other wildlife that Tim has seen while hiking trails in North Georgia include grouse ("If you're daydreaming," he says, "they can scare you when they rocket off the ground"), turkeys, beaver, woodchucks, skunks, and a bobcat.

Weather is an important factor in hiking safety, Tim says. "You just have to use common sense in deciding whether the weather is safe for a hike." And he feels that knowing what to take along on a hike and what to leave behind can make the difference between an enjoyable walk in the woods and an unhappy day or more of hard work. "I've seen hikers with cast-iron skillets, three-pound cans of spaghetti, libraries of books, even cans of dog food," he says. "Sometimes they'll have their gear spread out all over the trail; their packs are too heavy, and they're trying to figure out what to leave behind."

Tim Homan is a man who is comfortable with modern civilization—he is now employed by a finance company—but he hikes whenever he gets the chance. And although he often takes others on his hikes, he sometimes enjoys being alone. He says, "It's great to hike the status trails, such as the Appalachian Trail, and enjoy the campfire camaraderie, but I like to chuck it all aside sometimes and get some solitude. Some people say there's no place to get away from it all, and I guess that's true of over-utilized trails such as the Beech Bottom Trail in the Cohutta Wilderness and the Appalachian Trail, but you can still find plenty of solitude on many of the trails in Georgia, particularly the Bartram Trail and the loop trail from Springer Mountain to Slaughter Gap. I've walked the twenty-mile stretch of the Bartram from Warwoman Dell near Clayton to Georgia 28 three times, and I saw a total of only two other hikers."

While Tim realizes that publication of *The Hiking Trails of North Georgia* may diminish the quality of some of the trails by attracting more users than the trails can easily handle, he is optimistic that the benefits will outweigh any possible negative environmental impact. "I hope that more people can see and appreciate the true beauty of North Georgia," he says. "The more people who come to appreciate it, the more chance there is of preserving it."

Panther Creek and Raven Cliffs Trail

Homan rates these two hikes highly in his catalogue of the trails of North Georgia. He lists the five-mile Raven Cliffs Trail among the five best in North Georgia, and the Panther Creek Trail is among his top 10. To give readers a look at the format used in *The Hiking Trails of North Georgia,* we've included his guides to these two trails below. The guides are exactly as they appear in Homan's book. The maps are by cartographer Frank Drago.

Note. Two changes have been made in the Panther Creek Trail since Homan's book was written. The trail is now well blazed with blue paint. And the creek crossing, which is described below as consisting of "guy wires, rocks, and fallen trees," has been improved by the addition of a bridge made of logs and treated lumber built by Boy Scout Troop 650 of Cornelia.

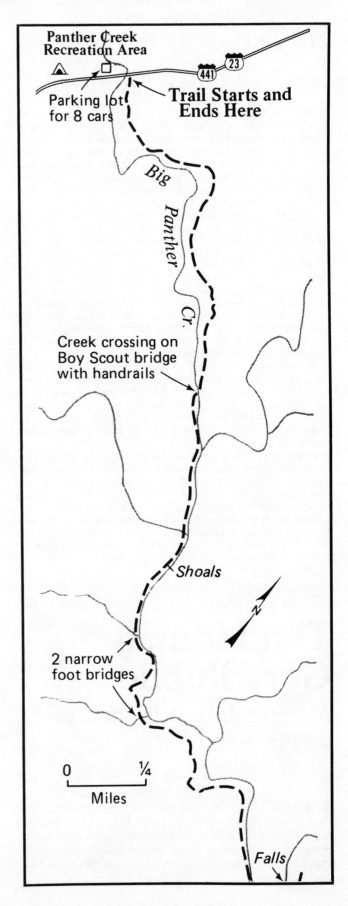

Panther Creek Recreation Area

Parking lot for 8 cars

Trail Starts and Ends Here

Big Panther Cr.

Creek crossing on Boy Scout bridge with handrails

Shoals

2 narrow foot bridges

0   ¼
Miles

Falls

HIKING GUIDE

Panther Creek Recreation Area
Chattooga Ranger District
Habersham County

PANTHER CREEK TRAIL *(approximately 4.0 miles one way to the large waterfall). Easy to Moderate to Falls; Moderate to Strenuous beyond. Not a good trail for those unsure of footing or afraid of heights.*

The trail, which follows Panther Creek downstream toward its confluence with the Tugaloo River, begins across the highway from the recreation area. To the left side of the Highway 441 bridge, follow the jeep trail or its offshoot path; both converge to form the main trail a short distance below. For approximately the first mile, the needle-cushioned path rises and dips, conforming to the creek-side topography. On this section of the path, you are usually within earshot of fast-flowing shoals and small cascades.

After the first few trail-crowding granite outcrops, the path crosses the stream at the first of the small signs guiding hikers to the falls. Guy wires, rocks and fallen trees help you negotiate the crossing. Beyond the crossing, the stream becomes calm, and the trail becomes sidewalk flat, at least for awhile.

Do not mistake the high shoals near the logged area for the waterfall; the waterfall, still a mile or more away past another group of path-narrowing outcrops, is much more impressive. The shoals and boulders are just extra bonuses along this highly scenic trail.

Not knowing what to expect, most people are astounded by the beauty, size and power of the waterfall, especially during the high water levels of winter and spring. The waterfall is really a series of falls, with a splashing slide in the middle. The trail winds along the upper falls on the outer edge of an immense outcropping and descends to the next protruding vantage point. From here the path becomes somewhat steep, sloping down to the bottom of the falls and the unusually large, enticing pool at its base.

The trail continues beyond the falls for nearly 2.0 more miles, but it becomes steeper, less defined and more dangerous as it heads toward its ending point at Davidson Creek. For the experienced hiker the scenery is well worth the effort: cliffs, huge boulders and more waterfalls make this portion of the stream one of the most scenic areas in Georgia.

Most of the typical mountain streamside plants abound along Panther Creek. Large white pine, hemlock and, below the falls, beech grow beside the stream.

Directions: Take U.S. 441 North through Clarkesville. Approximately 10.0 miles north of Clarkesville, past the small town of Hollywood, the Chattahoochee National Forest begins. A few hundred yards past the National Forest sign, Panther Creek Recreation Area is on the first paved road to the left. During the off-season the recreation area sign is removed and the gate is locked.

RAVEN CLIFFS TRAIL *(approximately 2.5 miles one way to the cliffs). Easy to Moderate to cliffs. The short paths leading up into the cliffs are Moderate to Strenuous.*

Beginning where Dodd Creek mingles its water and loses its name to Dukes Creek, this relatively unknown, 1,589-acre scenic area follows Dodd Creek and its valley back into the mountains, gradually widening as it moves up the watershed. Alternating between creek level and hillside, the gently sloping trail threads its way along the cascading stream, rarely leaving the sound of the rushing water.

Beside the path watch for the Fraser magnolia, a deciduous magnolia whose large leaves—10 to 12 inches long and 6 to 7 inches wide—emanate from the stem in a whorled arrangement; and watch for the sweet birch, whose twigs have the distinctive

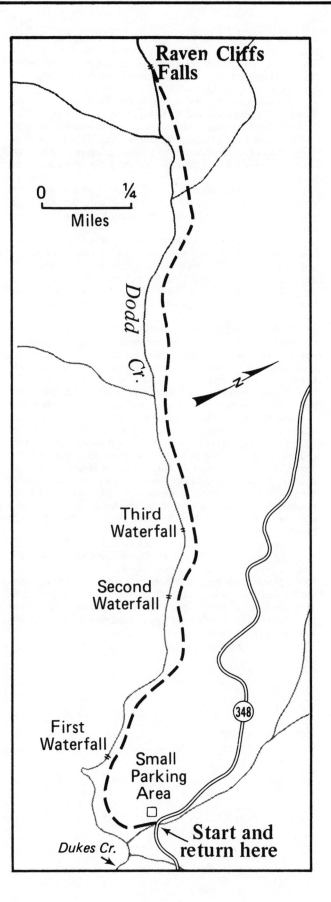

fragrance of wintergreen. During late May and early June, Vasey's trillium blooms underneath its characteristic three leaves. The flower, largest of the trillium species, is a rich carmine color. In late June, the luxuriant growths of rhododendron turn the stream borders into narrow swaths of white.

Trailside scenery builds its way to the climax of the cliffs and their falls, for within the first 1.5 miles, Dodd Creek has three other waterfalls. The first one is small; the second is over ten feet high and pours onto a conveniently placed boulder. The third is wide, 25 to 30 feet high, and drops into a large wading pool. Rock outcrops, the same color as the cliffs, dot the steep slopes above the path.

Even in summer the massive rockface is visible from a distance through the veil of trees. The cliff walls, some of them amazingly smooth, tower nearly 125 feet above creek level at their highest point.

The trail forks close to the base of the cliffs. One route rock-hops across the creek; the other stays on the right side of the stream and continues uphill to the top of the cliffs. It is here, beside the right fork, that the lower stage of Raven Cliffs Falls has knifed into the rock, splitting it in two. Called Raven Cliffs Grotto, this 40-foot waterspout is completely surrounded by cave-like walls, except for the narrow opening.

The path ascends a few yards farther and curls sharply to the left into a gap between cliff tops. Following a short, root-grabbing scramble to the top of the precipice, where the right fork ends, you gain exhilarating views of the upper falls to the right, the Dodd Creek valley below and mountain ridges to the left.

Across the creek the left fork (more narrow path than actual trail) skirts the bottom of the granite as it recedes into the mountain and meanders behind the cliffs, descending to one of the most dramatic scenes in Georgia. Above, the upper fall slides and splashes 75 feet and after a short rest plunges again, pouring down into the grotto. The enclosing walls impart a sense of enriching solitude.

Directions. Take Georgia 75 North through Helen to the Robertstown Community. At Robertstown Community turn left onto Georgia 356, crossing the Robertstown bridge over the Chattahoochee River. Continue on Georgia 356 for 2.3 miles, then turn right onto Richard B. Russell Scenic Highway (Georgia 348) North.

After traveling 1.7 miles on Richard B. Russell Scenic Highway, you will come to the sign for Dukes Creek Recreation Area. Proceed 1.3 miles past this sign to where the highway crosses Dukes Creek. Immediately beyond Dukes Creek there is a parking area to the left. From the parking area, walk downstream on the gravel road along the creek. Approximately 140 paces down the road a rivulet flows into the creek; cross the tiny stream, turn right and follow the trail to Dodd Creek.

1981

Alternative to Urbania

Finally, the first detailed walking guide to the 4000 acres of wilderness bordering Atlanta's Chattahoochee River.

by Tom Patterson

Let's say you're an outdoor enthusiast who, by some quirk of fate, happens to live in the midst of Georgia's capital and largest city. Or let's say you're a rural visitor to Atlanta who has already paid for two more nights in the Hilton or the Peachtree Plaza, and yet you find that you've had enough of skyscrapers, shopping malls, and expensive restaurants for one trip. Where can you turn to get away from it all without having to travel to the North Georgia mountains, Cumberland Island, the Okefenokee Swamp, or one of the other more distant portions of the state where the population density is blissfully low and there's still plenty of God's green earth to be explored, unblemished by the steel and concrete productions of modern human folly? Is there any escape from the urban frenzy that doesn't involve either using up a tank or two of precious gasoline or trespassing, at your own risk, on some millionaire's forested estate just beyond the urban fringe? Well, yes. And its name is Chattahoochee.

Not that the Chattahoochee River hasn't already been discovered by thousands of Atlantans and folks from all over the rest of Georgia. During the hotter parts of the year its waters are heavily trafficked by all manner of recreational craft, whose occupants can be seen and heard from the banks as they whoop it up along the popular five-mile run from the Morgan Falls dam downstream to the U.S. 41 bridge. But there is another way to see this river: by exploring on foot the wooded territory along its banks.

Not long ago this area was all under private ownership, and it seemed destined to go the way of the rest of North Atlanta: being developed into a maze of shopping centers, apartment complexes, condominiums, and asphalt thoroughfares. But during the early 1970s a coalition of state and local environmental organizations began an effort to protect this relatively undisturbed land and the river that flows through it. In 1972, after taking a canoe trip down this section of the Chattahoochee with members of the Georgia Natural Areas Council and the Bureau of Outdoor Recreation, then-Governor Jimmy Carter lent his support to this movement. Slightly under 1000 acres of this land were subsequently established as a state park before Carter left office in 1974. It was just last year that the National Park Service began buying other parcels of land along the Chattahoochee, in what was then left of its wild state. Together with the Chattahoochee River State Park, which has now been transferred to federal ownership, this land was set aside for preservation as a National Recreation Area.

At present the Chattahoochee River National Recreation Area (NRA) includes 12 separate parcels of land along a 48-mile stretch of the river between Lake Lanier and Atlanta's northern limits; together these parcels total some 4000 acres. As no comprehensive trail development nor maintenance program has yet been adopted for these areas, hiking opportunities at present are limited to old jeep trails and unblazed footpaths which the National Park Service inherited when it acquired the land. But this situation has its advantages for those who enjoy a few hours or days of solitary walking in the woods without running into dozens of other hikers. Since none of these trails has been officially designated or blazed, most of them are, at this point, little-used. They present a confusingly interwoven tangle to the pedestrian visitor who is unfamiliar with them. With an eye to clearing up this potential confusion and making it easier for Atlanta residents and visitors to explore this interesting natural area bordering the overly developed North Atlanta suburbs, I spent several days hiking the sections of the Chattahoochee National Recreation Area which border the capital city's limits this past summer, taking notes and marking topographical maps as I went along. Based on what I found, I designed the following hiking guides, selecting what I felt were the best of several alternative routes through each parcel. All of these are loop hikes, making it convenient to leave the car at a starting point, explore, and return to the starting point with a minimum of backtracking.

The maps, driving directions, and hike guides that follow are presented in west-to-east order. Not included here are several small sections of NRA land farther upstream—the Jones Bridge, Medlock Bridge, and Abbotts Bridge area—all located in the vicinity of Norcross and Duluth, as none of these is large enough to offer significant hiking opportunities. I have also omitted the Morgan Falls unit of the NRA, located upstream from the Morgan Falls dam between the Sope Creek and Big Creek units. Though there are several jeep trails that thread their ways through here, there is no convenient loop trail to be hiked here on the north shore of Bull Sluice Lake; neither are there any outstanding natural or cultural features such as the old ruins, scenic creeks, and large rock outcrops that can be found in the included hikes. The Bowmans Island unit of the Chattahoochee NRA, located in Forsyth County, just below the Buford Dam that holds back Lake Lanier, also falls outside the parameters of this hiking guide, which deals only with areas along the Chattahoochee in the immediate vicinity of Atlanta.

Hikers should allow about a half day to explore each of the NRA units included here, with the exception of Powers Ferry and Island Ford, each of which contains relatively short trail networks that can be walked in an hour or two. Camping in the Chattahoochee NRA is, unfortunately, against regulations at present, though staff naturalist Jerry Hightower says areas for camping may be set aside in the future, once the lengthy planning process for recreational development here is completed by National Park Service officials and approved by the Congress.

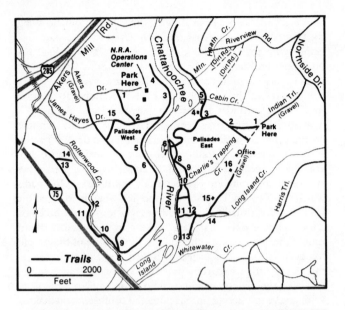

Trails

0   2000
Feet

HIKING GUIDE

PALISADES (East and West)

The Palisades area of the Chattahoochee NRA gets its name from the sheer, rocky cliffs that can be found on both sides of the river in this area, which lies along a major geological fault known as the Brevard Zone, extending from Virginia southwestward to Alabama and separating the more mountainous terrain on its north side from the lower-lying Piedmont region to the south.

To reach the Palisades East unit of the Chattahoochee NRA from downtown Atlanta, follow I-75 north for about six miles to the Mt. Paran Road exit. Leave the Interstate here, and turn right onto Mt. Paran Road from the stop sign at the bottom of the exit ramp. Follow Mt. Paran for about .4 mile to the second left turn, Harris Trail. Turn left on Harris Trail, and follow it for 1.5 miles to its intersection with Northside Drive. Turn left on Northside Drive, and continue for .6 mile to Indian Trail, which turns off to the left. Turn left again here, and follow Indian Trail for .4 mile to the point where the pavement gives way to a narrower gravel road marked by a red-and-white "DO NOT ENTER" sign. An iron bar gate, usually open during the daytime, separates the paved road from the gravel road here. Park on the right-hand side of the road, and begin your walk just inside the gate.

Palisades East hike: A *narrow trail* (1) leads off to the right of the gravel road just inside the gate. Follow this trail westward from here, above a deep ravine on your right. After a few minutes this path merges with a (2) *dirt road.* Bear right onto this road, and continue over rolling terrain for another few minutes to the (3) *point where the road splits,* one fork curving sharply back to your left, while the other continues almost straight ahead. If you continue along this roughly straight route you'll quickly reach a set of wooden steps leading downhill for a short distance to a (4) *wooden observation platform* which provides a good overlook of the river at the base of the hill. Several very narrow trails lead down into the woods from this platform, all of which are steep shortcuts to the river. The path on the right (north) side of the platform follows the contour of the hill for a few yards before heading straight down the hill, on a very steep grade, to the (5) *ruins of a stone house,* built here on the riverbank around the middle of the 19th century. A Confederate cannon battery was located near this house during the latter part of the Civil War. To complete the selected hiking loop, return to (3), uphill from the observation platform, and, approaching it from this angle, take the right-hand fork. Follow this dirt

road into the woods along relatively level terrain to the point where it narrows and loops back around to the left. Here you'll notice two narrower trails within a few yards of each other, both of which lead off to the right from the central path. Like those at the observation platform, these are simply steep shortcuts to the river. Stay on the wider path here, sharply looping left, after which the trail begins to move downhill, fording several small streams.

After a few minutes you'll reach a trail crossing, where three options are presented: a left turn, a path straight ahead, or a right turn. Turn left here, and walk through a shallow, rocky streambed that washes over the trail, heading downhill to the river's bank, just beyond which you'll see (6) *Beaver Island.* Turn left, and follow the bank, and you'll soon notice on your right a (7) *natural footbridge* composed of a big fallen hickory tree that spans the channel separating Beaver Island from the riverbank. Unless you have problems with your sense of balance, you can easily cross over to the island on this log. Once across you'll notice the charred remnants of campfires, indicating that this is one of the more popular areas in the Chattahoochee NRA for unauthorized camping. Between the island and the opposite bank of the river are numerous rock outcrops and smaller islands.

After exploring Beaver Island to your satisfaction, cross back to the riverbank, and continue in the direction in which you were headed before. After only a few yards you'll reach an (8) *fork in the trail.* The path leading to the right follows the riverbank, while the leftward trail leads past a (9) *7000-year-old Indian rock shelter,* located on the side of a steep hill to the left of the trail only a short distance beyond the fork. A narrow side trail leads off the main trail here and heads uphill to this manmade cave, carved into a mammoth, layered rock outcrop. Researchers from the Southeastern Archaeological Center in Tallahassee, Florida, have determined that this rock shelter, about 20 feet deep and 20 feet high at the top of its peaked ceiling, was made by Indians of the early Archaic period some 70 centuries ago. One of numerous rock shelters located along this portion of the Chattahoochee River, it was gradually enlarged to its present size by fires built under the stratified rock, which expanded with the heat and broke off, layer by layer. Charlie Poe, one of the archaeologists who have studied this site, says that it's virtually impossible to tell whether the shelter was a permanent dwelling or a seasonally occupied campsite for wandering hunters, due to the fact that its interior has been vandalized in recent years by curiosity-seekers who destroyed much of the archaeological information that might have been gained from the site.

From the rock shelter, return to the main trail, and continue to (10) *Charlies Trapping Creek,* traversed by a wooden footbridge. The trail that diverged toward the riverbank at point (8) intersects here with the suggested route and, on the other side of the creek, splits off again to the right, following the edge of the shore. In this case neither branch of the fork in the trail is recommended over the other. The left-leading path continues through the woods some 50 to 100 feet from the bank and eventually intersects once again with the shoreline route. Should you take the right fork and follow the bank, remain on this path until you cross a (11) *small stream* at the point where it empties into the river. As soon as you've crossed this stream, turn left onto a narrow path, and follow it back to its (12) *intersection with the eastern (left) branch* of the split in the trail on the south side of Charlies Trapping Creek. Upon reaching this intersection, turn right. If you took the left fork after crossing Charlies Trapping Creek, simply continue straight when you reach this intersection. From here the path bends gently to the left and soon splits again at another fork. The right branch of the fork leads to the (13) *bank of Long Island Creek,* only a few yards away. The route I've selected follows the left branch, which also approaches this same creek and bends to the left, paralleling the creek for a short distance. As you walk upstream along the northern bank of Long Island Creek, watch for a (14) *creosote post* about the size of a telephone pole laid across the creek to form a bridge. Shortly after passing this point, watch for a path leading uphill and to the left.

This portion of the route, known as Indian Ridge Trail, makes a steady and fairly steep climb to the top of this long, narrow ridge, after which it levels off before intersecting with the gravel road that leads back to your starting point. After passing a (15) *rest-room building* on your left, you'll arrive at a (16) *park maintenance shop,* at which point the trail merges with the gravel road. Continue along this road back to (1).

Driving directions to Palisades West. To reach the Palisades West unit of the Chattahoochee River NRA, follow I-75 north from downtown Atlanta to the Mt. Paran Road exit as indicated on the directions to Palisades East, above. After leaving I-75, turn left on Mt. Paran Road, and continue to the first traffic light at the intersection with Northside Parkway (U.S. 41). Turn right here, and follow Northside Parkway for 2.1 miles, across the Chattahoochee River, through one traffic light, and on to the second light, at the intersection with Akers Mill Road. Turn right on Akers Mill, and continue for 1.2 miles, crossing bridges over I-75 and Rottenwood Creek and passing the Palisades North apartment complex on the right. Almost immediately after passing the second of two driveways leading into this complex, turn right onto Akers Drive, a gravel road. Follow this road to its end, at a small parking area in front of the Chattahoochee NRA Operations Center, where National Park Service administrators have their offices. Park in this lot, and, to reach the starting point for this hike, backtrack for about 100 yards along Akers Drive until you see a dirt road, blocked to automobile traffic by a gate, leading into the woods on the left. Begin your hike here.

Palisades West hike: Hop over the (1) *gate,* and follow this dirt jeep trail, which heads downhill and southeastward toward the river. After a short distance you'll reach a (2) *T-intersection* with another dirt road, at which point you will be completing this loop. Turn left here, and follow the road down to the riverbank, where it intersects with a narrow path along the shoreline to the left and right. The leftward course heads upstream across (3) *Sandy Point,* a beach-like shoals area, and on past the NRA boundary. During high-water periods it's not possible to follow the trail past the (4) *rocky cliff* a short distance upstream from Sandy Point. Explore this upstream route if you've got the time and the inclination, but the selected route follows the downstream path, turning right when you reach the riverbank. The same types of cliffs and rock outcrops that you'd see on the upstream route can also be seen here. Follow the river southward around the (5) *sharp bend at Thornton Shoal,* near which you may have to scramble around some fallen trees. Shortly after rounding this bend, you'll come to an imposing section of (6) *rock outcrops* which may present a bit of difficulty. Heading uphill and around the tops of these outcrops, you'll find that the trail soon becomes tangled in a confusing maze of narrow, haphazard paths. Keeping in mind that your objective is to return to the riverbank by the quickest route possible, bear left at every opportunity in this trail network, keeping your course close to the water. You may have to do a little backtracking or bushwhacking in this area, but you'll be close enough to the river to avoid getting lost.

Once you've found your way back onto the path along the river's edge, continue downstream as the trail widens, near the next bend in the river, to the size of a jeep road. Soon you'll be in sight of the (7) *northern tip of Long Island.* After passing an intersection where a dirt road heads uphill to your right, continue to (8) *Rottenwood Creek,* at the point where it flows into the Chattahoochee. Future plans for the NRA call for emplacement of a footbridge across the creek here. Note the (9) *dirt road* heading uphill from the corner formed by the confluence of the creek and the river here. After a side trip up Rottenwood Creek to visit an old mill ruin, the route I've selected calls for returning to this point and following the road away from the river in order to complete the loop. For the moment, though, follow the path that leads upstream along the bank of Rottenwood Creek. If you happen to visit this area during the summer, as I did, you'll find numerous blackberry bushes laden

with ripe fruit along this section of trail. After walking about ¼ mile along the creekbank, you'll see a (10) *wide iron sewer pipe* which forms a bridge across the creek. Follow it to the other side, and turn right, continuing upstream. Watch the woods on your left side, noting the clearing for a (11) *power-line right-of-way.* Shortly after you come into sight of this treeless swath, you'll arrive at a fork in the path, the left branch of which heads uphill toward the clearing and the right branch of which continues along the creekbank. Take the right fork here, and follow the creek to the (12) *exposed section of sewer pipe* immediately to the right of the trail and at the edge of the creek. Here a dirt jeep trail splits off to the left, heading uphill along the side of a deep gulley in which the rusted carcass of an old station wagon rests upside down (a testament to the potential hazards of traveling too rapidly on roads like this one). Follow this road uphill and under the power lines as it bends to the right. After spending a short time on the west side of the power lines, the road crosses back under them to the east side, then heads downhill into a narrow valley and back up the hill on its other side. As you make this ascent, watch for a (13) *narrow trail leading down* into the woods on the right near the crest of this hill. Instead of remaining on the road, which leads out to Akers Mill Road, turn right on this path, and follow it downhill for 50 to 100 yards to Rottenwood Creek and the (14) *ruins of Akers Mill.* All that's left of this old gristmill, which operated during the mid-1800s, are portions of its stone walls, located on a particularly scenic portion of the creek.

From the mill site retrace your path to the (9) *dirt road* at the end of Rottenwood Creek. Turn left here, and head uphill and into the woods along this road. Bear right at the first fork in this road and left at the second. A short distance beyond the second the road begins to level off. At this point begin watching the terrain on your right for a low-lying area, on the opposite side of which is a hill that has been cleared of trees. Jutting up above the top of this hill you'll be able to see, from the road, a line of gray-roofed buildings. Watch for a narrow path leading off the road to the right here, and turn onto it. Follow this path across the low area and up the treeless hill to the edge of a (15) *abandoned and unfinished apartment complex.* According to Chattahoochee NRA naturalist Jerry Hightower, a real-estate developer began construction of these apartments during the early 1970s but ran into financial problems and never completed them. At present this property, which lies outside the NRA's boundary, is under the control of a federal court.

The trail cuts sharply back to the east at the southern edge of the cluster of uncompleted buildings, where a hand-painted sign nailed to a tree proclaims, "WARNING! TRAINED ATTACK DOGS ON DUTY 24 HOURS. KEEP OUT." When I arrived at this point, my curiosity got the better of me, and I made a shrill whistle to see if it would bring a canine response. When snarling, man-eating German Shepherds failed to come running after me, I proceeded to do a little harmless trespassing, wandering through the network of dirt roads overgrown with high weeds that winds among these modern yet rotting and dilapidated structures. It's an eerie place, a perfect setting for some kind of futuristic disaster movie about the effects of World War III on the suburban American landscape. From the warning sign the trail continues, heading due west to the point where it merges with the dirt road on which you began your hike at the (2) *T-intersection.* Upon reaching this junction, turn left, and head back through familiar territory to your starting point.

POWERS FERRY

To reach the Powers Ferry unit of the Chattahoochee NRA, follow the same driving directions given above for Palisades West, up to the point where Akers Drive turns right off Akers Mill Road. Instead of turning here, continue on Akers Mill Road, parallel to I-285 on your left, for another ½ mile to the intersection with Powers Ferry Road, which turns under the first I-285 overpass on your left. Turn left here, go under the overpass, and take an immediate right onto Interstate North Parkway. Follow this road for about ¼ mile to the Chattahoochee River bridge, and turn right into the dirt parking lot on the left immediately before the bridge. The trail begins at the opposite end of the parking lot.

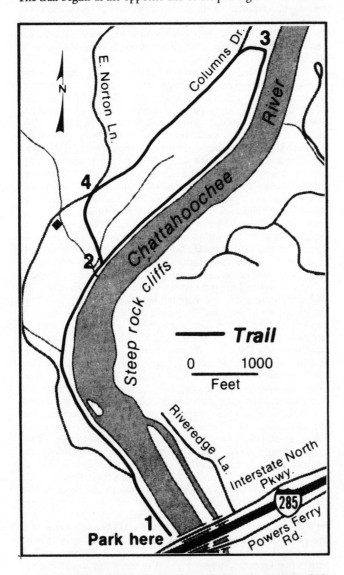

Powers Ferry hike: The trails in this area, consisting entirely of old dirt roads, are particularly popular with joggers from the surrounding suburbs, since the terrain is fairly level and the roads are free of obstacles. The trail follows a relatively straight course along the river for a little less than a mile before splitting into two branches that connect at the eastern boundary of this NRA unit, comprising a loop of about three miles in addition to the first near-mile.

Begin your walk at the (1) *northwest end of the parking lot,* following a dirt road that sticks fairly close to the river's bank. At several points along this section rock outcrops in the river to your right provide good spots for fishing or sunbathing. After passing a wide stretch of open fields that were once used as farmland and an old barn-like structure in the distance on your left near the edge of the woods, you'll cross a (2) *wooden footbridge* spanning a small creek. Just a few feet beyond this bridge is the point where the trail splits to form the southern end of its three-mile loop. Instead of turning onto the left fork here, continue on the road that runs alongside the river to the (3) *NRA boundary,* just beyond which you'll see the modern River Plantation apartments, with grass

planted all the way out to the riverbank. About 15 yards before reaching this boundary you'll notice another dirt road turning off to the left, beginning the northern end of the three-mile loop. Turn left here, and follow this road through a low-lying, marshy area where portions of the road are submerged in stagnant water that is littered with pieces of scrap lumber and discarded radial tires. From this point the road curves leftward and back to the south, forming the northern end of the loop. After rounding this curve, you'll be on a section of road that follows an underground oil pipeline owned by the Carolina Pipeline Company, as noted on several markers along this route. To your right the terrain builds gradually upward and is covered by thick growths of trees, primarily hardwoods, while on your left are small pines which surround a low-lying beaver swamp in the center of the loop. Much of this low ground was at one time farmland. About 1½ miles from the northern end of the loop you'll notice an intersection with another dirt road that leads up onto the high ground to your right, heading northward and connecting with the loop trail at Sope Creek (see point (8) on the Sope Creek unit hike, below). This is (4) *East Norton Lane.* After passing this intersection, the road begins to bend gradually to the left and, within another ¼ mile or so, crosses a creek to complete the loop just north of the (2) *wooden footbridge.* From this point retrace your steps along the road to the parking lot where you began your walk.

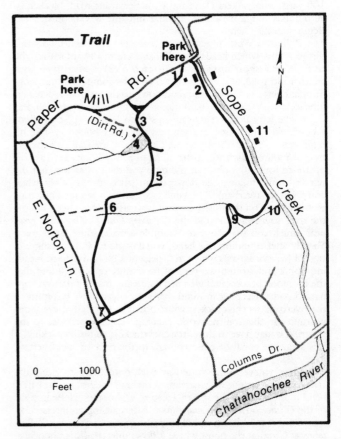

SOPE CREEK

To reach the Sope Creek unit of the Chattahoochee NRA, follow the driving directions for the Powers Ferry unit up to the point where Powers Ferry Road heads under the I-285 overpass. Instead of turning right here onto Interstate North Parkway, remain on Powers Ferry Road for 1.9 miles to the traffic light at Terrell Mill Road. Turn right here onto Terrell Mill, and follow it for 1.6 miles to a sharp leftward bend, where it intersects with Paper Mill Road. Turn right here, and follow Paper Mill Road for 1.5 miles to the concrete bridge spanning Sope Creek. Park on the right side of the road just before the bridge, and begin your walk from here.

Sope Creek hike: During the last half of the 19th century this part of Sope Creek was the location of the Marietta Paper Mill, one of this area's principal industries during that period. A number of stone buildings which lie in ruins along both sides of the creek south of the Paper Mill Road bridge were once part of this mill operation; they serve as reminders of a bygone period in this portion of what is now the North Atlanta suburbs. These ruins, crumbling and covered with vines, add a haunting quality to a creek that is already endowed with great natural beauty.

Begin your hike by crossing the (1) *narrow stream* that parallels Paper Mill Road and flows into Sope Creek at the western end of the bridge. Near this confluence is a (2) *ruined stone building,* the first of several remnants you'll see of the old Marietta Paper Mill. After crossing the stream and examining this structure, head west (upstream) for a few yards, and pick up the trail, which parallels the stream at this point. You'll soon pass another stone ruin on your left. From here the trail continues southwestward, crossing two other minor trails that lead back to Paper Mill Road before intersecting with a (3) *dirt road,* at which point the selected hiking route turns sharply to the left. Upon reaching this point, you'll notice, directly ahead, a (4) *small lake,* on the northern shore of which is an old, rotting boathouse. Follow the dirt road to the left, cross the earthen dam on the lake's northeast side, and continue, bearing right at the fork in the road, into the woods on the lake's south side. Soon you'll come to another (5) *road intersection,* where you'll notice a pile of brush, bent curtain rods, and other debris on your left. Turn right here, and continue along a winding stretch of road, on the left side of which the terrain slopes gently downward toward a small streambed. After a few hundred yards of curving road watch for a (6) *narrow path* turning off to the left. If you emerge from the woods into an open field overgrown with kudzu along the edges, then you've missed the turnoff onto this path. Should this happen, turn around, and retrace your steps for 60 to 70 yards, watching for the road's intersection with the path, this time on your right, where you'll see a few small pine saplings. Turn here, and follow this path into the woods to the south. After a few minutes you'll wander through a thick section of kudzu on the eastern boundary of the field to your right. Beyond the kudzu the path begins to head back into the woods and downhill toward a (7) *narrow stream.* If you were to continue across this stream, you would soon reach the trail's intersection with (8) *East Norton Lane,* a dirt road which connects to the south (left) with the loop portion of the Powers Ferry hike described above (see point 4) about 1½ miles distant. To complete the Sope Creek loop, however, watch for a path cutting off sharply to the left just before you reach the narrow stream at point (7). Turn left here, and follow this path along the stream to your right, which flows downhill toward Sope Creek. Between here and the creek you'll be roughly following the course of this stream, making only one major deviation, to circumvent a (9) *ravine,* at the bottom of which is another small stream that flows into the first. Just before reaching this ravine, the path heads uphill to your left and, at the northernmost end of the ravine, intersects with another path.

Upon reaching this intersection, turn back sharply to your right, heading downhill on the other side of the ravine. Soon the path merges with an old dirt road, at which point you'll need to bear right and continue downhill and across the stream you followed beginning at point (7). Continue along this road a very short distance until you reach Sope Creek at the point where it is crossed by a (10) *green pipe.* Turn left at the creek, and follow its western bank, lined by a path, back to your starting point at the bridge. About halfway between point (10) and point (1) watch for more (11) *stone ruins* on the opposite (eastern) bank of the creek. There are several points where you can cross the creek on rock outcrops in order to explore these ruins, and the creek is shallow enough that you can wade across in most places. The main building of the old

Marietta Paper Mill, larger than all the other stone ruins along the creek, is located at the point where a small, rocky stream flows into Sope Creek on its eastern side. A narrow strip of land on that side of the creek, including the land on which these ruins sit, is owned by the Chattahoochee River NRA, and there are trails leading back to the Paper Mill Road bridge on both sides of the creek from this point. From here, then, follow either bank of the creek back to your starting point.

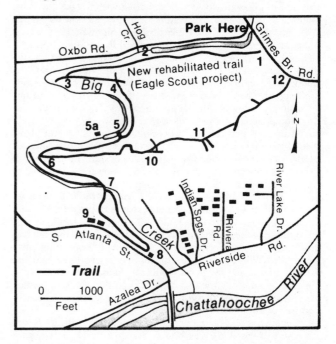

BIG CREEK

To reach the Big Creek unit of the Chattahoochee River NRA, follow the preceding driving directions to Sope Creek. When you reach the Paper Mill Road bridge spanning Sope Creek, cross it, and continue for 1.9 miles to the T-intersection with Johnson Ferry Road. Turn left on Johnson Ferry, and follow it for 1.1 miles to the traffic light at Lower Roswell Road. Turn right here, and follow Lower Roswell Road for three miles to the point where Willeo Road turns off to the right over a bridge and Lower Roswell bends to the left, its name changing at this point to Timber Ridge Road. Turn right here onto Willeo Road, and go across the bridge. At .9 mile after making this turn, you'll reach the Chattahoochee Nature Center, located in a clearly marked, rustic wood building beside a small pond on the left side of the road. If you have time, you might want to stop here for a look at the exhibits of native wildlife, including living specimens and others that have been stuffed and mounted by a taxidermist. Wildlife field guides and other publications which you might find useful on your walks along the Chattahoochee River can be purchased here. The Center is a nonprofit, educational organization, and it abuts the Chattahoochee River Park, which covers 770 acres along the river in this vicinity. A short nature trail makes a loop through the woods on the opposite side of Kingfisher Pond from the Center's headquarters, and a boardwalk winds its way through the river marsh across Willeo Road from the Center. Maps of the nature trail and boardwalk are available free at the Center.

Continue on Willeo Road for ½ mile past the Chattahoochee Nature Center to the point where Azalea Drive turns off to the right. Turn here, and follow Azalea for 1.7 miles, passing the Chattahoochee River Park's boat launch and picnic areas, to the intersection with Atlanta Road at the north end of the Chattahoochee River bridge (this is Roswell Road south of the river). Turn left here, and follow this road for one mile to the point where Oxbo Road turns off to the right just past an Otasco hardware store. Turn right, and follow Oxbo for 1.4 miles to its intersection with Grimes Bridge Road. Turn right here, immediately crossing a concrete bridge spanning Big Creek, and park along the right side of the road just on the other side of the bridge, near the starting point for this hike.

An alternative route to the Big Creek unit, if you're coming directly from downtown Atlanta and don't wish to take the scenic route via the Chattahoochee Nature Center, is to follow I-75 north to its intersection with the I-285 perimeter highway. Turn east on I-285, and drive to the third exit (Roswell Road-Sandy Springs), leaving the Interstate and turning left onto Roswell Road at the end of the exit ramp. Follow Roswell for about 7 miles to the Chattahoochee River bridge, crossing it and continuing for another mile to the point where Oxbo Road turns off to the right. From this point simply follow the directions in the preceding paragraph.

Big Creek hike: Big Creek, formerly known as Vickery Creek, played an important role in the development of 19th-century Roswell. The Ivy Woolen Mill, located along this creek during the mid-1800s, was one of the area's principal industries, and the dam which was built on the creek to provide a source of power for the mill (see point 5, below) is still standing, along with one of the old mill structures (see point 5a). During the Civil War the mill manufactured Confederate uniforms; therefore, it was targeted for destruction and burned by General William T. Sherman's Union troops when they marched through this area in 1864. Later, the mill was rebuilt and its name changed to Laurel Mills, operating until shortly after World War I, when the machines were dismantled and the mill shut down for good. South of the dam and mill site is Allenbrook, an old home that dates back to the 1840s and which was spared by Sherman's troops because its occupant was a Frenchman (see point 9, below).

Begin your hike on the southwest side of Grimes Bridge Road, just south of the Big Creek bridge. Watch for a (1) *narrow path* leading downhill into the woods on the right side of the road. Recently rehabilitated by a local Boy Scout troop, the portion of the trail between here and the old Ivy Woolen Mill dam is in good condition, cleared and well marked by red plastic ribbons on tree trunks along the route. The trail follows the creek along its southern bank through a section of forest which includes prominent specimens of bigleaf magnolia. After passing the (2) *confluence of Hog Creek,* which flows into Big Creek from its northern side, the path continues to an (3) *intersection with a dirt road* just east of the creek's sharpest bend. Turn left at this intersection, and follow the dirt road for a short distance to the point where a (4) *narrow trail* cuts off to the right, just opposite an intersecting dirt road that turns off to the left. Turn right onto this trail, and follow it south and west until you hear the roar of water, signaling the fact that you're approaching the dam. Watch for a downhill turnoff to the right; turn here, and follow this path to the (5) *old Ivy Woolen Mill dam.* During the summer months the section of rocky rapids below this dam is a popular spot for swimmers and sunbathers. A short distance downstream on the opposite side of the creek is the (5a) *only remaining mill building.*

Follow the dirt road that begins at the dam downstream along the edge of a steep ridge overlooking the creek, continuing to the point just above the next sharp bend in the creek, where another (6) *dirt road* intersects from the left. Later, after an excursion to the other side of the creek, you'll return to this point and turn onto that road, but for the moment bear right here, and continue around the bend and above the creek's bank. Soon the path heads downhill to the water's edge, at which point another twin-rutted road turns off to the right, following the creekbank upstream for a short distance and ending at the bend in the creek just downhill from point (6). Instead of turning right onto this road, bear left, and continue to the (7) *sewer pipe* that crosses Big Creek. A short loop trail on

the opposite side of the creek provides an opportunity to see some dramatic cliffs and rock outcrops, as well as the historic Allenbrook home. Cross the creek on the sewer pipe, and bear left on the opposite bank, following a narrow trail along the creek and through a meadow. After about 30 yards this trail bends sharply back to the right, away from the creek, and extends through the backyard of an (8) *deserted cinderblock house* and past a small outbuilding adjacent to it. From here it gradually ascends along a steep ridge overlooking the creek and the first portion of this loop.

Soon you'll reach a small clearing in which a battered, homemade bench and table are located; at this point you'll be only a few hundred feet behind the (9) *old Allenbrook home,* currently occupied by one of the Chattahoochee NRA park rangers. Built in the 1840s as an office and residence for the manager of the Ivy Woolen Mill, this two-story saltbox house is constructed of hand-molded clay bricks, its walls 18 inches thick and its interior characterized by brick fireplaces and heartpine floors and mantels. Théophile Roche, a French weaver who managed the Ivy Woolen Mill, lived in the house during the Civil War period, and when General Sherman's troops descended on this area on July 6, 1864, he hoisted the French flag in hopes of saving the house from destruction. The Union troops spared the house, but they took Roche into custody and sent him to the North for the duration of the war. During the 1930s the house was bought and restored by Barnett A. Bell, who named it Allenbrook.

As you wander through the clearing behind the house, watch for a narrow path cutting off to the right, and turn here, heading down over several layers of rock ledges below a sheer cliff that rises ever higher on your immediate right as you descend. Arriving at the base of this cliff, continue to bear right along the trail, and you'll soon return to the (7) *sewer pipe* on which you crossed the creek. Retrace your path to (6), and bear right at this intersection. Follow this dirt road for about 40 yards along a fairly straight and level course at the top of a ridge. Near a high point on the ridge the path curves sharply to the left and then gently back to the right, forming a half-circle before it straightens back up. Shortly after passing this curve, watch for (10) *two dirt roads* cutting off to the left within a few feet of each other and then joining at their far ends. Turn left here; then turn right at the point where the two roads join, following a dirt jeep trail along the southern edge of an open field. This road continues straight for about 30 yards, with the field on your left and a pine forest on your right, until it reaches the (11) *eastern edge of the field.* Here the trail splits into a three-pronged fork. Take the leftmost (and least defined) of the three paths from this point, heading back into the woods and to the northeast. From here you'll pass two more intersections before completing your hike. Bear left at the first of these, then right at the second, and continue on through an old dumping ground near the eastern NRA boundary before coming out on (12) *Grimes Bridge Road.* When you reach the road, turn left, and walk back to your starting point near the Big Creek bridge, about 20 or 30 yards to the north.

ISLAND FORD

To reach the Island Ford unit of the Chattahoochee NRA, follow the preceding directions to the Big Creek unit up to the point where Azalea Drive intersects with Atlanta Road at the northern end of the Chattahoochee River bridge. Coming from Azalea, turn right here, and cross the bridge, watching for the first left turn south of the bridge. Turn left here onto Roberts Drive, and follow it for 1.5 miles to the point where a dirt road cuts off into the woods to the left. A white cement marker at this intersection designates this dirt road as Island Ferry Road. Turn left here; then bear right at the first intersection, and park your car in the area where the road bends sharply back to the right. You'll notice here on the left side of the road a fence with a gate that is blocked to automobile traffic by a pile of broken cement gutters and other debris, marking the starting point for this hike.

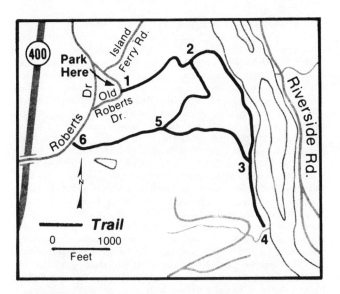

Trail

0   1000

Feet

Island Ford hike: Smaller than most of the other Chattahoochee NRA units included in this hiking guide, Island Ford is used primarily during the warmer months by swimmers and sunbathers, who are attracted by this scenic section of the Chattahoochee River, shallow enough to get across by wading and walking on the numerous rock outcrops and small islands that punctuate the river. When I walked the area this past summer, I encountered about 100 young people along the river, each of whom had staked out a territory among the rocks and shallows. The recommended loop trail shown on the accompanying map is shorter than the others included in this guide, and it can be hiked nonstop in about an hour. But if you're going to visit Island Ford, you'll probably want to stop and spend some time along the riverbank here. The crowds of North Atlanta youngsters who populate this area in the summer will probably have thinned out by early October, and if your timing is right, you may even find you've got the entire area to yourself.

Begin your hike at the aforementioned (1) *gate,* and head downhill along a path through the woods. Near the base of this hill the trail intersects a (2) *dirt road.* Turn left on this road, and follow it as it bends back to the right and soon reaches the river's shore. From here the path follows the riverbank upstream past several outcrops and natural rock shelters. When the path begins to bend slightly to the right and away from the river, watch for a (3) *wide path* that cuts off sharply to the right, heading up a steep hill. If, instead of turning here, you were to continue on the lower path, you would ford a small stream and return to the riverbank within a short distance, continuing upstream until you'd reach the NRA boundary, at which point the trail crosses a stream on a (4) *wooden bridge.* On the opposite side of the stream is a red-and-white "NO TRESPASSING" sign that also carries the large letters "ABA." Beyond this point are the grounds of the Atlanta Baptist Assembly. National Park Service officials are currently negotiating with the owners of this property to purchase it for inclusion in the Island Ford unit of the NRA. For the time being, however, it's Baptists only beyond this point. Unless you want to follow the river up to the NRA boundary, then, turn onto the uphill road at point (3). Judging from the way the earth has been torn up and the roots of adjacent trees exposed, this path has been used in the not-too-distant past to test the fortitude of four-wheel-drive vehicles. Follow it up a fairly steep grade to the (5) *crest of the hill,* at which point the path intersects with a southward-lying portion of the same road you joined at point (2). Bear left here, and follow this road through the woods and back out to (6) *Roberts Drive* at Hunters Glen apartment complex. Turn right at Roberts Drive, and continue for a short distance to the first dirt road intersecting from the right, turning here to return to your starting point.

Additional Information

If you would like more information on the Chattahoochee River National Recreation Area, call (404) 952-4419.

1980

Wild Places in the Big City

Four hikes in or near Atlanta

by Laurie O'Brien

Wilderness, while not quite a state of mind, is where you find it. And you may be surprised to find more of it in and around Atlanta than you ever thought possible. Here are four hikes that are easy to take whether you live in or near Atlanta, or are just visiting. None of the walks is more than a few minutes from Interstate 285, the loop highway that circles the city, and none requires arduous back-road driving. What's more, these hikes offer a variety of outdoor walking experiences, from hill climbs to paved trails, from historic ruins to fast-running streams.

The faint hum of city traffic may ring in your ears as you walk, but there's no mistaking the familiar feeling of hitting the trail: pine needles beneath your feet, blue sky overhead, a far-reaching vista laid out before you after a good climb. The Palisades, Sope Creek, Kennesaw Mountain, and Fernbank Forest await you. Come on along.

HIKING GUIDE

THE PALISADES: Soon to be a full-fledged state park, the Palisades, located at the end of Indian Trail Road near the perimeter, provides plenty of natural scenery, an invigorating but not severely taxing hike, and the rewards of winding your way down to the banks of the Chattahoochee River as a destination.

My husband, Mark, dog Alice, and I tried this trail, a wide, tree-strewn avenue that dipped gently down through the trees. We followed it as far as we dared, coming finally to a not-so-tiny tributary of the river which someone had decided could be crossed by means of two fat telephone poles thrown across the water. We explored alternative routes, but this seemed the only way to go, and while we all had fun playing around with the idea, in the last analysis, only Alice was brave (or foolish) enough to make the crossing. Satisfied that we had had a good walk anyway, we turned back, figuring that as refinements are completed for this park, a real bridge of some sort may show up one day.

The park property is located right up against a residential area, and as yet does not provide much in the way of parking. Although the soft hum of traffic is within earshot, the open space provides a pleasant retreat, complete with good views of the hills to the northwest.

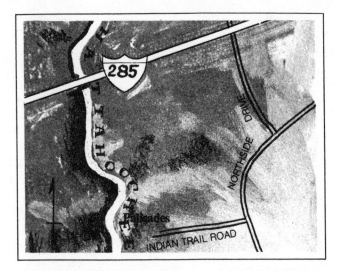

To reach the Palisades, go south from I-285 on Northside Drive, then turn west on Indian Trail Road. The Chattahoochee River State Park entrance is at the end of the road.

KENNESAW MOUNTAIN: With 15 miles of marked trails traversing Big Kennesaw, Little Kennesaw, Pigeon Hill, and Cheatham Hill, Kennesaw Mountain National Battlefield Park provides some of the best real hiking in the Atlanta area.

The park lies along a ridge just to the west of Marietta and is easily reached from I-75. Take the Kennesaw exit, and follow the signs to the visitor center. You can leave your car here, get a map from the ranger inside, and even see a brief slide show that will give you a feel for the area.

My dog Alice and I started up the trail toward Big Kennesaw, passing a couple of college kids on their way down, a man with a very small boy, a young photographer with a very large tripod, and a pregnant woman. None described the trail as particularly difficult, and all said it was a good hike.

We found the trail wide and easy to follow, but while Alice didn't find the going at all tough, after a long sedentary winter I found that a few stretches left me breathing pretty hard. We followed the trail up the side of the mountain and around the switchbacks, passing the original earthworks where General Joseph E. Johnston's Confederate troops dug in for one of the last defenses of Atlanta against the invading forces of Major General William T. Sherman.

At several points along the trail there are overlooks with particularly good views of Marietta and the valley below, views one usually gets only after longer and much more arduous climbs.

SOPE CREEK: When you're looking for a place to get away from it all, what could be better than an easy-to-reach woods complete with a fast-running creek and several historic ruins? The area around Sope Creek and Paper Mill Road just north of Atlanta in east Cobb County may be just what you're after, especially if you like your hiking easy and your efforts visually rewarding.

To begin your trek, go north on Roswell Road to Johnson's Ferry, then west on Paper Mill Road until you come to the bridge over Sope Creek (just beyond Atlanta Country Club Estates). The road forms a sharp right angle and doesn't have much of a shoulder, so you'll have to look for a place to leave your car. When you walk back to the bridge, you can see a path leading down to the water. Head this way and you'll come upon the ruins before you know it. And while there is no real hiking trail per se, you can spend a pleasant afternoon scrambling around the many ruined and crumbling walls and foundations that remain on the banks of the creek.

We tried Sope Creek on a sunny Sunday, my dog Alice and I, one of us looking for a little scenery, the other just for a good place to run. We both found what we were after, although only one of us had a dip in the waters of Sope Creek.

The ruins that stretch out along the creek include the shell of a Confederate paper mill built in 1854 which manufactured newsprint, wrapping paper, and stationery, and an old flour mill. The mills were burned by Federal troops in 1864, rebuilt after the war, burned in 1870, rebuilt a year later, and operated until 1902. They are in various stages of disrepair, but you can climb their stairs and peer through arched stone windows at the rushing water below. The ruins lie along a fairly steep bank, but the land flattens out along the water's edge and allows a hiker room to pick a pathway.

FERNBANK FOREST: Fernbank is a forest with visiting hours—to be precise, from 2 to 5 every afternoon except Saturday, when it is open from 10 until 5. The 65 acres of what is billed as "relatively undisturbed forest" is just that, a lush, quiet enclave within the hustle and bustle of DeKalb County.

We tackled Fernbank Forest on a crisp Sunday afternoon, a friend and her two sons, aged eight and six. Our preparations for

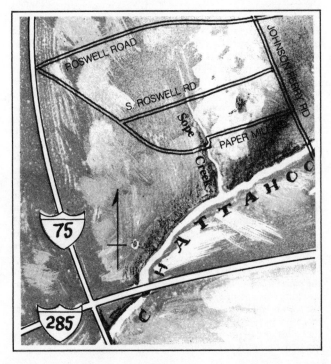

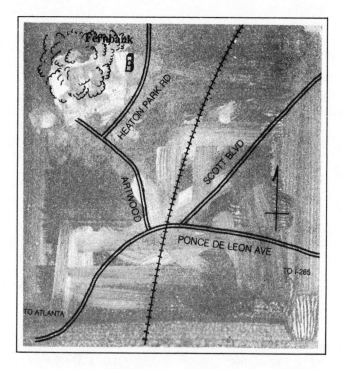

this expedition had been minimal, but the minute we hit the trail, it became apparent that the forest was an excellent choice for a place to take small people on their first hike.

Jed and Paul ran eagerly down the hard-surfaced trails, which extend for one and a half miles. Signs indicating the kinds of trees immediately caught their attention, and the leafy underbrush was just the place to look for trolls. Tree trunks that had been cut in a particular manner became "thrones" to the boys, and each tried out a number of seats.

Grownups, too, can enjoy Fernbank Forest, especially if they pick up a copy of the seasonal guide sheet, available at the entrance, which offers descriptive information about the forest for the current season. The walking is easy, and it is virtually impossible to get lost, thanks to the broad trails and the sign-in system in effect.

If you do have small children in tow, it may prove to be difficult to leave Fernbank without a tour of the museum and a trip to the planetarium. The museum houses a varied collection of exhibits—everything from a real space capsule to a forest diorama complete with bears and snakes. The planetarium, offering a dramatic view of the universe, is a popular way to learn about the stars and planets.

Fernbank Forest is reached by going east from Peachtree Street or west from I-285 on Ponce de Leon Avenue and turning north on Artwood Road. Take a right on Heaton Park Road, and the main entrance will be on your left.

1978

Trailblazing With Neal Wickham

by Tom Patterson

The first thing that caught my eye that chilly January morning as I steered my car into the roadside park near the tall television tower off state highway 85W south of Warm Springs was Neal Wickham's bright-red hiking hat, which he wears to make sure no hunter ever mistakes him for a deer. I brought the car to a halt near one of the concrete picnic tables only a few yards from the foundation of a demolished barn that had once been part of Franklin D. Roosevelt's farm, and Neal strolled up to greet me as I began unloading our hiking gear from the back seat.

Neal, who operates an outdoor-equipment shop in nearby Columbus, introduced his dog Brownie, then offered a critical appraisal of my backpack, hiking boots, and a few of the other accouterments I was carrying. An experienced outdoorsman and an authority on hiking gear, he wanted to make sure I was sufficiently prepared for my planned 25-mile overnight excursion along what is known as Section West of the Pine Mountain Trail. Clad in brown hunting pants, a darker brown wool shirt, hiking boots, and a heavyweight parka, Neal carried no backpack nor other extraneous equipment. He planned to hike only the first few miles of the trail, along a section which at that time had only been partially cleared and flagged with colored ribbons prior to final marking with small blue paint blazes on tree trunks.

I had met Neal for the first time the previous afternoon at his shop, Wickham's Outdoor World, where we had spent a couple of hours reviewing topographical maps of the Pine Mountain Valley area and discussing the development of the trail by the Pine Mountain Trail Association. Among the association's 80 members, Neal is by all indications the most intrepidly active. During our conversation, he had offered to hike this first section, along the west end of the trail, since it was not yet fully marked. "I don't want you to miss that part, though," he had said. "It's one of the prettiest areas on the whole trip, as beautiful as any place you'll find on the Appalachian Trail." It had become quickly apparent that Neal takes a great deal of pride in this trail, of which he has been the chief planner and organizer. During the course of the next two days hiking the trail, I would see that he had every reason to be proud. There is a subtle art to designing and building a mountain hiking trail, and the evidence of Neal's work on the Pine Mountain Trail's Section West indicates that he is a master of this art.

"You lead the way," Neal said to me once I had strapped on my pack and we had made our way past the television tower to the trail's beginning. We set off on the downhill slope toward Wolfden Creek and within minutes found ourselves in the midst of lush, junglelike thickets of rhododendron, mountain laurel, and native azalea along the banks of the narrow creek whose flow of clear water was accentuated at points by small waterfalls spilling over into well shaded pools. The trail wound back and forth across the creek, and as we crossed below one of the falls, planting our feet on strategically placed stones near the remnants of an old moonshine still, Neal said, "You oughta come back and hike through here around the second week in April, when everything's in bloom and these trees are really thick. It'll be just like a tropical rain forest." Though we would see more of this type of vegetation within the next 24 miles, nowhere else would we find such thick growths of it nor would we see anything else to compare with the small, rocky waterfalls along

22 miles without his entertaining and almost non-stop commentary. Once we reached this point, however, Neal changed Wolfden Creek.

Portions of the Pine Mountain Trail consist of horse trails and paths that were blazed by Boy Scout troops from nearby towns prior to formation of the trail association some three and a half years ago. They provide an interesting contrast to the sections designed and built by the association. The latter are easily recognizable by the single, small, regularly shaped blue blaze appearing on tree trunks along their course. The Boy Scout trail blazes are usually larger and more sloppily painted, and the horse trails are marked with red or yellow.

We joined the first of these inherited trail sections as we left Wolfden Creek near Cascade Falls, the area's largest waterfall. In general, the Boy Scout and horse trails are noticeably inferior to the association's newer sections, indicating that the builders of these older trails perhaps neglected to scout the surrounding areas for better alternative routes. These older sections often pass along the bottoms of ridges for hundreds of yards with little variation in their slope, then suddenly make sharp turns up steep hills, so that hikers are forced into unnecessarily strenuous climbs. In most such cases, a slight rerouting would make for an easier, more scenic, hike. The newer sections, designed and built by association members and volunteers, indicate more careful planning.

As Neal Wickham will testify, there's a great deal more to building a hiking trail than simply moving through the woods from one point to another, clearing a path, and painting a few tree trunks along the way. Neal has spent well over half his weekends since the Pine Mountain Trail Association was formed leading volunteer work crews in scouting the area and blazing new sections of this trail. He and other association members have even found themselves involved in state politics as a result of their efforts to develop the Pine Mountain Trail. Since most of the land the trail traverses is owned by the state, all plans for routing it must be approved by the Georgia Department of Natural Resources. But so far the DNR has been reluctant to allow the association to reroute any preexisting trails in the area.

Department officials point out that the older trails in F. D. Roosevelt State Park were built at a time when the state was doing no landscape planning inside state parks. Between that time and 1975, when the Pine Mountain Trail Association was formed, however, the DNR adopted stricter land-management practices. State Parks interpreter Dennis Lovell, who has represented the DNR in several meetings with Neal and other association members, has said that "in many cases Neal's ideas don't fit in with our land-management plan for the park." Even though Neal and others have volunteered their own time to work on the trail, Lovell says the DNR has been "reluctant to use unsupervised volunteer labor" on state-owned land. He adds that portions of the trail may still be rerouted and that DNR's 1979 budget includes funds for trail improvements in the park.

That first day out on the trail, we soon passed the unmarked "rain forest" area that Neal had wanted to show me. His original plan had been to leave me and hike back to his car once we reached the first crossing of Georgia 190, about three miles past our starting point, leaving me to hike the remaining

his mind. "You're making history," he said, pointing out that I would be the first hiker to walk the entire length of Section West in one trip. Neal had put too much of himself into this trail to miss out on an opportunity to be on the first expedition to hike the whole thing. If I didn't mind, he said, he'd like to hike with me to my planned campsite on the other side of Dowdell Knob. Since he hadn't brought a sleeping bag, he said he'd hike out to the highway, hitchhike back to his car, then meet me early the next morning for the walk to the trail's western end, at Callaway Gardens. Fine, we agreed. And that's exactly what Neal did.

Shortly after sunrise the following morning, as I sat by the campfire over a second cup of coffee, I heard a good-natured howl from uphill, in the direction of the highway that follows the crest of Pine Mountain's ridge. Looking up, I could see Neal's familiar red hat through the bare gray branches and brown leaves. I returned the howl, and Neal's little brown dog came bounding through the carpet of dried leaves just a few steps ahead of her master. Within minutes, we had everything packed up, had drowned the coals of the fire, and were back on the trail. Neal warned that rain had been forecast for the afternoon, and the sky did seem a bit cloudy. But by noon the sky had cleared to a deep shade of turquoise, and the weather had warmed up so much that it felt like early spring. There wasn't a cloud in sight.

Midafternoon found us gazing out over the spectacular view of Callaway Gardens to the west. As we neared our destination, I wished for another 12 or 15 miles of trail like that we had just walked. I am sure that Neal Wickham was wishing for at least that. If he and the other members of the Pine Mountain Trail Association get their way, this trail will someday stretch from our exit point at the Gardens northeastward along the Fall Line for almost 150 miles to the Oconee National Forest. And Neal will surely be among the first to hike its entire length.

HIKING GUIDE*

Pine Mountain Trail

Section West of the Pine Mountain Trail, winding along near the ridge of Pine Mountain for 25 miles between Callaway Gardens on the west and the WJSP-TV tower on the east, is now open all the way. The entire Pine Mountain Trail as proposed will extend well over 100 miles beyond the TV tower northeastward to Rock Eagle in the Oconee National Forest, but only a few very short sections of that eastern portion of the trail have been opened to date. Section West, however, provides one of the best two-day hikes to be had south of the Great Smoky Mountains, as well as numerous possible shorter expeditions. To hike the entire trail, one can begin at either end and expect roughly the same amount of uphill and downhill grades. To reach the beginning of the westward route at WJSP-TV headquarters, take Georgia highway 85W to the TV tower, about four miles south of Warm Springs and just a few hundred yards north of the intersection with Georgia highway 190. The eastward route begins at the gateway to Franklin D. Roosevelt State Park, near the Callaway Gardens Country Store, where Georgia 190 intersects U.S. 27, less than three miles south of the town of Pine Mountain.

Since the trail follows a course very close to that of Georgia 190, which runs along the ridge of Pine Mountain and crosses this

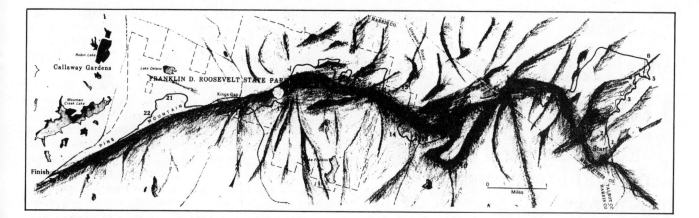

highway a number of times, shorter hikes can be easily planned. A good all-day hike might be planned from either end of the trail to Dowdell Knob, which can be reached by car, and which is very near the halfway point of the 25-mile course.

1. Eastern end of trail at WJSP-TV tower and roadside park. This is the site of Franklin D. Roosevelt's old farm, which has been torn down. Trail begins a few hundred feet behind TV tower. The tower can be seen from a great distance and makes for a good landmark by which to mark your progress along the trail. **2.** Beaver dam and old lake bed immediately east of trail. **3.** Ruins of moonshine still, consisting only of a few old barrel hoops and rusted pipes beside the creek bed. **4.** Series of small waterfalls along Wolfden Creek. This area is thick with mountain laurel, rhododendron, and native azalea, and promises to be especially beautiful in the early spring. **5.** Cascade Falls and overlook from Wolfden rock cliffs. This is the steepest waterfall in the area. A short walk upstream reveals a quaint old stone dam. The barbecue grill atop the rock cliffs was one of FDR's favorite picnic spots. From this point the trail joins a slightly older Boy Scout trail for several miles. **6.** Trail turns abruptly west and crosses stream over a log bridge. Pay close attention here, as another trail continues straight ahead and eventually loops back to Wolfden rock cliffs. Both trails are marked with blue blazes. Also be careful crossing the creek. The narrow log bridge was nearly rotten when we crossed in January, but the creek is narrow enough so that another crossing can be easily found if necessary. **7.** This section of trail will eventually be rerouted from the currently used Boy Scout trail. Blazes on trees here are sloppy and unnecessarily conspicuous, as if a herd of drunken house painters had been turned loose with blue paint. This was not the work of the Pine Mountain Trail Association.

8. Ruins of old stone park-ranger cottage. **9.** Inconsistent blazing on trees along this section of old Boy Scout trail, as if the scouts used so much paint on #7 (above) that they had very little left at this point. Trail may be a bit difficult to follow in this area. Watch for terracing and other signs of previous farming activity. **10.** Dowdell Knob. The newer Pine Mountain Trail, more expertly blazed by PMT Association members, splits off from the Boy Scout trail about 100 yards west of the knob. Another barbecue grill used by FDR is located at the tip of the knob, marked with a plaque that has been defaced by graffiti. This peak provides probably the best view of the entire valley, but is unfortunately marred by tons of disgusting litter. **11.** Site of Air Force B-25 crash in the early 1950s. The plane, en route from Florida's Eglin Air Force Base to Andrews AFB in Washington, D.C., crashed here during a heavy storm, killing five passengers. The only remaining indications of the crash are depressions in the ground north of the trail. Neal Wickham keeps a few fragments of the wreck, which he found while blazing this section of the trail, in a cigar box at his Outdoor World equipment shop in Columbus. **12.** Good campsite in a narrow hollow, with spring water piped through a plastic hose. Good spot to refill can-

teens. **13.** Trail crosses dirt road to Hines Gap. This is the approximate halfway point of the 25-mile trail. **14.** Scenic overlook from large rock. Side trail from rock leads down into adjacent hollow 100 yards or so to one of the best campsites along the entire trail—three stone-walled terraces, each large enough for a tent, built by Life Scout Matt Lowe (BSA Troop 1, Columbus) for an Eagle Scout project. A short distance downhill from the terraces is a small spring, and further downhill are the remains of another moonshine still. Legend has it that a wagonload of gold was mysteriously lost in the area to the south of here, near Lake Franklin, during the early 1800s. **15.** Mountain Top Inn, a rustic hotel owned and operated by Mercer University, is located here, a short (¾-mile) distance off the trail for anyone who might wish to sleep indoors in the midst of the hike. **16.** Pine Mountain Trail joins older horse trail (yellow blazes along with the familiar PMT blue) in this area. PMT Association members would like to reroute this section in order to provide for better campsites and more gradual slopes along the trail, but the Georgia Department of Natural Resources has so far refused to grant them permission to do so. **17.** Trail passes through reforested farmland, last tilled during the 1920s. Terracing in this area is obvious. Beautiful hickory forest, bisected by a narrow clearwater stream, is an excellent spot for camping. **18.** Trail merges with remains of early-19th-century stagecoach road to King's Gap just before crossing Georgia 354 and continues to follow this old road for a few hundred feet on the highway's other side. **19.** Pumphouse at spring-water stream. Not a bad campsite for those who don't mind sleeping near the highway. **20.** Trail passes FDR State Park headquarters, water tower, and tourist cabins. **21.** Trail passes along dry lake beds maintained during the late 1930s as fish hatcheries. According to one version of the story, these were abandoned on the orders of President Roosevelt after a reporter published the news that the President was using Civilian Conservation Corps workers for pet projects on his own property.

22. Trail crosses spring-water stream in the midst of a thicket of native azaleas, one of the most beautiful spots on the trail during the early spring when the plants are in bloom. **23.** Overlook at Georgia 190 crossing provides excellent view of Callaway Gardens to the northwest. **24.** Trail joins old quarry road just below crest of Pine Mountain ridge. Note rock outcroppings here, which give support to the view that this ridge and Oak Mountain (two miles to the south) were once part of a single mountain that split apart due to geological disturbances below the earth's surface millions of years ago. **25.** Western end of trail at FDR Park entrance and Callaway Gardens Country Store. If you're finishing your hike here and would like to eat in the Country Store restaurant, plan to arrive by 3 p.m. or after 5 p.m., as the restaurant is closed between those hours. Parking lot here is a good place to leave a car during an overnight hike.

1979

William Bartram Double Take

"But I'm sure that lake wasn't here. And I remember more mosquitoes."

by Tom Patterson

The sky over Clark Hill Lake had been threatening rain all morning and into the afternoon. A hurricane off the Gulf Coast was spinning a dense web of clouds all over the Southeast that morning, and, before beginning my roughly 15-mile walk along this section of the Bartram Trail, I had stood on the Clark Hill Dam that connects Georgia with South Carolina and watched these clouds rolling and streaming over the 40-mile-long reservoir here on the Savannah River, feeling almost certain that I would need my poncho before the day was over. By midafternoon, however, the misty clouds that had overhung the lake had burned off. About halfway into the day's hike I emerged from the woods under a clear, blue sky in a wide clearing near a large inlet on the lake's shore. This open area was rectangularly shaped and extended inland for at least 150 yards. In the distance, at the clearing's opposite end, I could see several pale shapes that appeared to be a cluster of buildings. One of the U.S. Army Corps of Engineers employees with whom I had discussed the trail that morning, Assistant Resource Manager J. E. Collette, had mentioned to me that at one point the trail would cross an unpaved landing strip used by crop-dusting planes for a Corps-sponsored mosquito-eradication program in the area, and I figured this must be it. There were no planes and no other people in sight, so I decided to leave the trail for a few minutes and walk up to that far end of the runway for a closer look.

As I neared the area, I made out the forms of two huge, cylindrical tanks, painted silver and held about five feet off the ground by a metal scaffolding framework. Up close, I could easily read the 5000 GAL. marks on each tank. A thick piece of metal pipe connected the two tanks, and at its center was a shutoff valve to which was attached an orange rubber hose about ten feet long and snaking over the sandy ground here, its other end chopped off and not hooked to anything. Directly above the hose, between the two tanks, was a painted, wooden sign, stenciled upon which, in bold letters, was the warning, "DANGER: LARVICIDING MATERIALS." I figured this must be where the planes loaded up with the chemical which they sprayed over low-lying wet areas around the lake to kill off the mosquito larvae that breed there. Standing in front of the two silver cylinders, I took in the whole little compound, which also contained three small pre-fab aluminum sheds and a small

shelter that covered what looked like some kind of fuel pump. In the weeds nearby, among clusters of bright yellow wildflowers, was another sign in the same style as the one between the two tanks of poison. This one read, "NO SMOKING WITHIN 50 FEET."

By this time I had noticed a vague chemical odor subtly but steadily hanging in the air over this place, and I was wondering just exactly what was in those tanks. What were the effects of this chemical, I wondered, on other insect populations in the area, and on the next step up in the food chain—the local bird population? My eyes wandered back out over the grassy runway and focused on one of the bluebird houses that stood on wooden posts on both sides of the airstrip. About three quarters of the way down the landing field, toward the lake, was a low, marshy area—the kind of place where mosquitoes breed and where sandpipers and other shorebirds like to feed. Taking one last glance around this little chemical outpost hidden in the woods, I noticed another detail—a small, silver adhesive-paper sign stuck like a bumper sticker to one of the large chemical tanks. "U.S. GOVERNMENT PROPERTY/NO TRESPASSING," it chastised me. On that note, I made my way back to the trail, which skirted the nearby marsh and continued on toward Keg Creek, the southernmost portion of Clark Hill Lake, where this segment of the Bartram Trail ends. I was thinking, for the moment at least, about William Bartram, and speculating silently about what he might think if he could somehow leap across the two centuries from his assigned place in American history to spend a few days venturing through what we have made of the landscape that he was one of the first white men to explore. I wondered especially how Bartram, by no means an opponent of technology and progress, would feel about our civilization's attempted manipulation of the natural environment, as evidenced by the mosquito-control program and, in a larger sense, by this huge, man-made lake itself.

Bartram, the explorer, botanist, and illustrator whose journeys through southeastern North America in the late 18th century have become legend, would find the entire Savannah River Valley much changed from his days of travel in these parts. In those days, this territory was familiar only to the wildlife and the native American tribes that occupied it. In the spring of 1776, while journeying northward from the Savannah's confluence with the Little River to its intersection with the Broad River—the area now occupied by Clark Hill Lake—Bartram wrote in his journal of "the wild country now almost depopulated, vast forests, expansive plains, and detached groves." He rhapsodized over the brilliant azaleas in full bloom on the surrounding hillsides, so brightly colored that "We are alarmed with the apprehension of the hill being set on fire." The portion of the valley he thus describes was entirely, and more or less permanently, flooded about 30 years ago, when the Corps of Engineers built their massive hydroelectric dam just below the Little River.

The natural beauty of the area now on the shore of the lake is still roughly intact, as is apparent to any hiker who spends a day or two exploring this section of the Bartram Trail. When routing this portion of their trail, the Bartram Trail Society followed the hills and low-lying areas along the shore, as near as they could come to the naturalist's actual path. The area has never been densely populated, and, although there has been

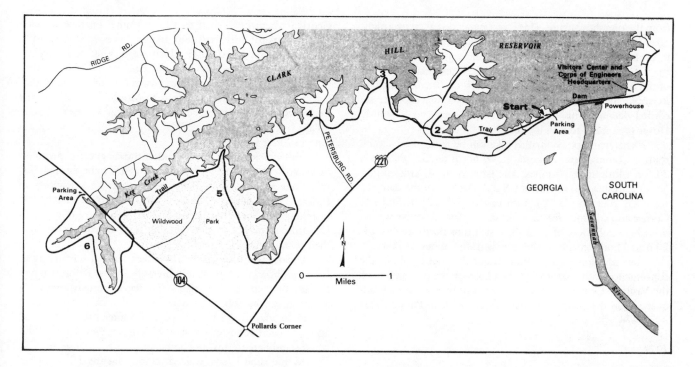

considerable timber-cutting in the vicinity during this century, many of the plant species which Bartram catalogued on his travels can still be seen growing in profusion. Shortleaf and loblolly pine are apparently the most abundant species of tree here, but there are also oak, hickory, yellow poplar, sycamore, sweetgum, sassafras, and persimmon trees in fairly large numbers. Bamboo shoots can be seen growing in some of the wetter, more low-lying areas of the woods. The trail seems designed to take in as wide a variety of terrain as possible, winding back and forth at irregular intervals from the lake's shore to the denser sections of woods, covering hills as well as marshy areas.

One of two roughly equivalent sections of the Bartram Trail on Clark Hill Lake, this path follows a tributary of the Little River near its intersection with the Savannah River, just upstream from the dam, extending for about 15 miles to the vicinity of Keg Creek near where it is crossed by Georgia 104. The trail begins on the Georgia side of the dam and is well marked with yellow blazes on adjacent trees. It was late summer when I hiked the trail, and I found it slightly overgrown in places. But this should present no problem in late fall, when the underbrush won't be nearly as thick. The path crosses several roads as it meanders through the woods, and, just before the third such crossing west of the dam, it passes through an old cemetery for Confederate soldiers (**Point 1** on the hiking map). Here a group of weathered tombstones emerges from a thick carpet of green tendrils in the shade of a large cedar tree wrapped in arm-thick muscadine vines. Each headstone bears the name of a dead soldier, his rank and regiment, and, finally, the initials C.S.A. There are no dates on the stones and no recorded hopes that the Civil War veterans would rest in peace.

At **Point 2** a spur trail splits off from the Bartram Trail and heads north for a little over a mile, ending at the tip of this peninsula at Lake Springs Park, where a picnic area and boat ramp are located. If you choose to include this spur trail as part of your hike, add another two to three miles to the approximately 15 miles of this Bartram Trail section. The grass landing strip used by larviciding planes is located in the vicinity of **Point 3.** Upon reaching this area, the trail crosses the runway near the lake's shore, extending into the woods on the opposite side and turning sharply left. Here it parallels the landing strip on its west side for about 150 yards, sloping gently downhill toward a low, marshy area that extends almost all the way across the runway. Here the trail turns sharply back to the left (east) and recrosses the airstrip. Upon reaching the woods on that side, it turns back to the right, following what appears to be a barely defined jeep trail between the marsh and the woods' edge, and turns once again to the right after crossing the marsh. For the second time, it heads back into the wooded area on the west side and again becomes easy to follow. This is the trickiest section on the entire trail, and it could stand to be a bit more carefully marked.

One of two designated camping areas along the trail is located at **Point 4,** in the area known as Petersburg Road campground, named for an old road used during the Revolutionary War period, when Bartram traveled through the area. Traces of this road can still be seen between here and U.S. 221. Another camping area is located in Wildwood Park at **Point 5,** along with another picnic area. Corps of Engineers' regulations limit camping along the trail to these two areas, but these regulations are not strictly enforced. Careful campers who avoid littering or unsafe fire practices will, in all likelihood, be left alone if they choose to camp discreetly in remote areas outside these designated locations. The trail ends near **Point 6,** where Georgia 104 crosses the Keg Creek portion of the lake. Don't be surprised to find several acres of the forest south of the highway stripped of most of their trees, as the larger pines were harvested from the woods here a little over a year ago.

The trail can, of course, be hiked in the opposite direction from the one shown here. This is recommended as an overnight hike, so that you can allow for a leisurely pace and ample time to explore the varied types of terrain and vegetation along the trail's course. It's always recommended, when hiking sections of the Bartram Trail, to take along a copy of *Travels of William Bartram,* the journals in which the 18th-century explorer recorded details of his journeys over 200 years ago. A sturdy Dover paperback edition is available.

The starting point for this hike can be reached by several routes: Coming from Augusta, travel north on Ga 104 or Ga 28 for a little over 20 miles. The latter highway crosses into South Carolina and intersects US 221 just east of the dam. To reach the trail via Ga 104, turn east on US 221 at Pollard's Corner and continue for six miles to the dam. Another way to drive here is by way of Ga 150, which runs northeast from I-20 near Thomson and reaches the dam after about 22 miles.

Any additional information about the trail or about the conveniences available at Clark Hill Lake can be obtained from the Visitors' Center and U.S. Army Corps of Engineers' headquarters on the South Carolina side of the dam. Phone (803) 333-2476.

1979

Augusta's Bartram Trail

William Bartram, the 18th century naturalist and explorer used Augusta as the jumping off point for three of his famous southeastern journeys. This hike retraces his path around one of Georgia's most historic cities.

by Carol Carstarphen

It is morning and I am walking. It is one of those misty days when horizons are muted and time seems to lose its importance. It is a day for reflecting. Days like this I have spent lost in the green of a forest, studying nature's many faces. But today I am outside a city, and walking toward it. All around me are the creations of man, barely softened by nature's reclaiming hand.

My walk is a proposed section of the Bartram Trail, along the Augusta Canal, down the levee by the Savannah River, and through the oldest surviving sections of the town itself. The trail is named for the great American naturalist, William Bartram, who passed through Augusta several times between 1773 and 1776. Bartram used the frontier town as a departure point for three different excursions into the wild, unknown parts of

Georgia where he wished to gather plants. First he traveled with a party of surveyors and Indians who were measuring lands northwest of Augusta which were being ceded by the Indians. Another trip took him up the Savannah River Valley through Rabun County and into North Carolina. Still another led him along the Fall Line Trail to Mobile and back. In his *Travels,* Bartram remembered, "The village of Augusta, situated on a rich and fertile plain. . . ." Nearby was ". . . the most magnificent forest I had ever seen."

Walking along the sandy road of the canal bank, my mind drifts farther back, to the time when DeSoto came through this valley. We are not far from the place where he kidnapped an Indian Queen, who said she would take him to the gold he was searching for. She saved herself and her people from the death DeSoto had dealt others by leading him far from her village, then escaping in the night.

DeSoto was here four hundred years ago. I start trying to count up how many times my lifespan that is. Before I figure that up, I remember the remains of Indian cultures nearby. Only a mile upstream from the where I started walking are artifacts of people who lived here as long as seventeen thousand years ago. My head is fairly spinning with antiquities. I feel as if I could stand here in this spot and exist in any time I wish.

By the time I have walked to the MacKay House, I am with Col. Elijah Clarke's revolutionaries. During the American Revolution Fort Augusta changed hands bloodlessly several times as first one side, then the other would gain advantage in other battles. In truth, many Augustans were reluctant revolutionaries. But when the battle finally did come, it was as mean and cruel as any. Col. Browne, the British commander, had occupied the Mackay House. Besieged by Clarke, wounded, and without water, he was so desperate that he had his men save and drink their urine. When Browne's reinforcements arrived, Clarke had to withdraw, leaving 28 of his men who were too severely wounded to be moved. Thirteen of these Browne hung from the stairwell at the Mackay House. The rest were tortured to death by Indians, allies of the British. The house, escaping Clarke's inaccurate artillery fire, still stands. Restored with careful attention to historical detail, it is a state-owned museum.

Following the revolution, Augusta continued to be an important transportation center because of its riverside location. But the coming of the railroad age threatened its economic security. Col. Henry C. Cumming is credited with the idea that improved Augusta's prospects. It was the building of a 9 mile long canal. It was built in 1846 and 1847 not just for transportation, but to offer a source of power to attract industry. The idea was so successful that the canal was enlarged thirty years later.

In the five years following the original canal's construction, the population of Augusta more than doubled. An interesting part of the population influx were the workers who came to enlarge the canal. Some of these were Irish and Chinese. Present-day Augusta has a community called Dublin, and a proliferation of Chinese restaurants. These are but the obvious evidences of two peoples who have contributed to the growth of Augusta.

Today I have walked from the outskirts of the city to its insides. I have traveled in my mind through its history, with visible reminders to key on almost everywhere I go. What next? For that I turn to Don Pendergrast, who with his wife Phyllis and my husband Bruce, has been my walking companion. Don is the ranger for the Augusta Canal Park. The park, when it is developed, will include the portion of the canal and levee which are a part of our trail. But before the park is completed, a land exchange must take place between the city, which owns the canal now, and the state, which will own the park. Things appear to be moving toward a smooth transition, but it may be some time before the exchange is finalized.

Don and Phyllis already use the area for their personal recreation in another way that is projected for the park. They canoe on both the river and canal. Don says that the canal is for quiet drifting and watching the wood ducks. The river is a little more exciting, though he complains that there is only one really good rapid. Add the cyclists we met, and you have proof of a really versatile recreation area.

Walking this trail is much different from driving to the mountains, then plunging into an all out hike. For one thing, the walking is much easier, inviting the very young and the elderly as well as the average hiking enthusiast. Then too, it is convenient to a large population, but offers the restfulness of the countryside. It is interesting, having beautiful scenic areas (especially around the lock and dam and the aqueduct on the canal). It has history to tell in its landmarks. To me, it has most of all a quality of intimacy, and closeness, to be appreciated on a small scale, not as a panorama. When I walk like this, I begin to gain a sense of perspective, a feeling for my place in time.

HIKING GUIDE

Augusta's Bartram Trail

This map traces an urban hike through historically interesting parts of Augusta. You'll see terrain that DeSoto explored in 1539 and pass buildings and monuments that date back to prerevolutionary times. The walk follows the Augusta Canal, completed in 1847, and the levee along the Savannah River. The complete trail is some 10.5 miles (one way) but may be taken in sections for shorter excursions.

If you plan to walk down the canal and levee, leave transportation at St. Paul's Church (Sixth and Reynolds) near the river. To walk the length of the canal, leave a vehicle at Thirteenth Street and Walton Way. Alternative parking places for shorter walks are the water works on the Goodrich Street Extension, and the vicinity of Goodrich Street and Broad. Don't drive all the way up the Goodrich Street Extension to the lock and dam unless you want to face the possibility of backing up over a mile to turn around.

To get to the upper end of the canal, go north on Washington Road. Go under I-20. At the traffic signal, turn right onto the access road. Take the first left. You are now on Stephens Creek Road. Cross a railroad and pass a pond on your left. Take the next right. At this turn, you should be 3.1 miles from the traffic signal. Go one mile to the end of this road. Walk down to the canal and cross it on the dam and gatehouse walkway.

There are no markers on this trail. Just follow the canal bank, the levee, and the city streets as marked on the map.

Use caution around the canal machinery and high places.

The Goodrich Street Extension which follows the canal is good for biking. The canal and adjacent portion of the Savannah River offer canoeing. Here are some of the highlights of the sights along the trail:

1 Lock and dam. Gates here control the amount of water flowing into the canal.
2 State champion multi-branched loblolly pine. Unmarked, it is the big pine opposite the quarry.
3 Warren Lake. You can't see it, but listen for the waterfowl.
4 Squatters' shacks and fishing camps.
5 Water works pumping station. Victorian trim on a graceful brick

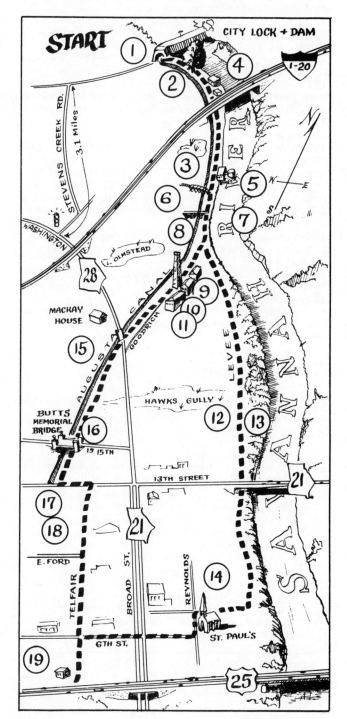

building is overpowered by modern additions.

6 Seaboard Coastline Railroad. Because of the railroads' competition with with Augusta's river traffic, the canal was built to attract industry.

7 "Akey Duck." This local corruption of the word "aqueduct" refers to a canal improvement built by the Works Progress Administration in 1940. A large spillway and set of gates lead to two manmade waterfalls, which rival the beauty of natural falls.

8 "Augusta's Scenic Landfill." Area of the old city dump. Expect litter. Good example of a bad use for a floodplain.

9 Ruins of the silk mill. It is in the process of being torn down. Early colonists hoped that Georgia's main industry would be silk production. This building predated the canal.

10 Augusta Powder Works chimney. The only remnant of the building complex which supplied most of the gunpowder for the Confederacy. The chimney is now a confederate monument.

11 Graniteville Sibley Mill and King Mill. These buildings were designed in the same style as the powder works.

12 Hawks Gully. Part of the canal flows back to the river here, after picking up some urban runoff. On this creek was a skirmish between American revolutionaries and Indian allies of the British.

13 Since the building of the levee, the river bottom lands have returned to forest.

14 Oglethorpe Park lies on the riverside of the levee, St. Paul's Church on the town side. Buried by the levee is the site of Ft. Augusta. The fort was built in 1736 as a garrison to protect and regulate traders. The church was erected in 1750. This is the fourth building on the site. The church yard is of particular interest. William Few, signer of the Constitution, is buried in front of the church.

15 The Mackay House. Built prior to 1750, this house served as a trading post and home. It was the site of a battle during the revolutionary war.

16 The Butts Memorial Bridge is listed in the National Register of Historic Places, as is the Canal itself. It is named for a hero of the Titanic disaster.

17 The main level of the canal ends at thirteenth street. Here, too, is the home of George Walton, signer of the Declaration of Independence.

18 Georgia Historical Commission's Bartram marker. In the park on East Ford Street.

19 Telfair Street Historic District.

1975

William Bartram and the Bartram Trail

William Bartram was the son of John Bartram, who was the King's Botanist in the American Colonies. Between 1773 and 1776 the younger Bartram traveled nearly 1000 miles in Georgia alone. He also went to North and South Carolina, Alabama and Florida. His *Travels* was a source of inspiration to scientists and poets of his time. It has been edited and reissued several times and is still a prime reference source for the botanist, the ethnologist and the historical geographer. Several Bartram societies are working on trails in different states. The possibility exists for a network of trails commemorating the Bartrams and providing recreational hiking throughout much of the southeast.

Savannah's Barometer

What a few birds think of some old rice fields is a pretty good guide to the environmental weather of the whole coast.

by Tom Patterson

The great blue heron stood motionless among the three-foot-high cut-grass on the edge of the canal, looking like a prize-winning entry in a taxidermy contest, his long, slender neck straight as the blades of grass and his spearlike beak tilted slightly upwards. As we watched him from the cab of the idling Dodge Power Wagon pickup truck about 10 yards away, I expressed surprise that he hadn't flown when we approached, and Pat Young, who was behind the steering wheel, said, "He thinks he's camouflaged."

I pushed my glasses down on my nose and peered over the top of their rims at the large wading bird. From this nearsighted perspective he seemed to blend in with the tall shoots of marsh grass that surrounded him, but I figured anyone with reasonably good vision would have no trouble sighting him. Removing my glasses completely, I put binoculars to my eyes and regarded the heron through the magnifying lenses. The blue-gray of the feathers on his back and neck matched the color, as filtered through the morning's humid haze, of the tall Continental Can Company paper mill in the distance behind him, on the west side of the Savannah River. My gaze moved from the perfect circle of the bird's gold eye to the strobe lights flashing in a slowly regular pulse near the top of the distant monolithic industrial structure, where small, white smoke plumes rose in meaningless signals. To the right of this building I could see four huge framelike structures that looked like rocket-launching devices or giant space-age cannons of some sort, but were in fact the cranes used for unloading big ships at the container yard of the Georgia Ports Authority.

"Keep watching the banks of the canal, and you'll see some alligators," Pat said as she eased off on the clutch so that the truck resumed its forward motion along the narrow dirt road. "There're some really big ones out here. Real monsters. Dave Goeke, the refuge manager, saw one that was about twelve feet long in the canal last year."

The big heron was out of our sight now, hidden behind the tall clusters of plume grass, dog fennel, and cut-grass that grew so prolifically along the edges of the freshwater diversion canal, designed and built by the U.S. Army Corps of Engineers to provide a constant source of upstream fresh water to the network of waterfowl-management pools here on the 26,555-acre Savannah National Wildlife Refuge. The pools, each about an acre in size, are the nearly-200-year-old remnants of dike-protected rice fields left over from a period when rice plantations covered much of the coastal marsh area from Georgetown, South Carolina, south to Brunswick.

Glancing back at the road behind us, I saw the heron take to the air, rising slowly from the top of the vegetation as he headed out over one of these pools. His bluish neck was curved now in an S shape, and his spindly legs hung downward as his gray wings beat the air in their sluggish but peculiarly graceful way. His image gradually receded to that of a small, dark fleck against the cloudless backdrop of blue sky.

Pat wasn't watching the heron now; rather, she was scanning the marshy landscape ahead as she guided the big four-wheel-drive vehicle along the bumpy road that followed the top of an old rice dike near the southeastern border of the refuge. An experienced ornithologist, Pat is accustomed to seeing great blues, which are common in these parts. She knows the birds of Savannah National Wildlife Refuge well, having spent the past two years working as an outdoor recreation planner for the U.S. Fish and Wildlife Service, which manages the refuge. Prior to her current job, the 35-year-old bird watcher taught environmental education at the Savannah Science Museum, a job which also brought her out to the refuge on occasion.

I had met Pat for the first time the previous afternoon at her office in the Savannah Federal Building, and we had arranged to meet again this morning here at the refuge, just inside the South Carolina border. In keeping with her promise to show me around the area, she was now giving me a preview of the proposed scenic wildlife drive through the southernmost portion, a project she had been helping to plan for several months now. I saw several large earth-moving machines, which were being used to restore eroded parts of the old dike system for this vehicular trail.

"Some of these dikes are below the present river level," Pat said. "We've got to get 'em raised. We've had nine- and ten-foot tides in here, and some of the dikes are only about seven feet high." Water levels in the individual pools, she told me, are controlled through the use of wooden gates, or "rice trunks," of the same basic design as those used in rice-plantation days. These simply built gates can be raised during incoming tides to flood the pools or when the tide recedes to drain them—both processes which take several days to complete.

As we passed one of the drained pools adjacent to a partially restored dike, Pat pointed out several ancient cypress stumps that had been exposed by the drainage, saying, "Look how huge those stumps are. They're left over from the days before rice cultivation started here. Originally, you know, this whole area was a mixture of freshwater marsh and swamp that was full of big cypress and tupelo trees. Without these dikes the area would revert back to freshwater marsh again. Those stumps are *several* hundred years old, and since they're covered with water most of the time, they just never rot. Back in the old days they used that same kind of wood to build the rice trunks. Now we build 'em out of creosoted wood."

Gesturing toward the old rice fields on either side of the road, some of which were now heavily clotted with tenacious growths of cut-grass, she said, "When you see the extent of these fields and consider the fact that slaves had to hand-clear all this land, it just boggles the mind." The portion of the refuge that consists primarily of the restored rice pools, she noted, occupies about 3000 acres. "Once the land was cleared, I'm told, it took three slaves working all day long just to till one acre."

The old rice pools now used by the Fish and Wildlife Service as waterfowl-management areas had all been part of a pre-Civil War plantation known as Laurel Hill. The proposed scenic road through the south end of the refuge, thus, has been termed "Laurel Hill Scenic Wildlife Drive." At the beginning of our tour of this route, Pat had shown me the remnants of an old brick wall, just across U.S. 17 from the refuge headquarters buildings, and explained that this had been part of the plantation's winnowing house, where the rice crop was sifted and separated from the shafts. Nearby, on one of the highest patches of ground in the area, was a grove of gnarled oak trees behind which the plantation house had once stood. The wildlife drive, Pat told me, would be supplemented with interpretive displays and other information about life on an early-19th-century rice plantation in the Savannah River delta.

I was interested to learn that the Fish and Wildlife Service was now promoting the refuge's value as a historical relic, especially in light of some information I had run across the day before in an archaeological study that Pat kept in her office. According to this report, many of the old plantation structures on the refuge had still been standing as late as 1940, but that year the federal government had them demolished under a program entitled "Raze Old Undesirable Structures."

This archaeological study also provided me with some good information about much earlier periods in the history of this area, which has been used by humans in various ways for more than 5000 years. The refuge area was the scene of intense prehistoric occupation, with Paleo Indians living here as early as 7000 B.C. Shell mounds left by the Indians of the Middle and Late Archaic periods offer conclusive proof that the area was, to some degree, settled during the period from 5000 to 1000 B.C. Though these early occupants were primarily hunting and gathering tribes, the white settlers and their slaves of the early plantation era were not the first to farm this land. Maize agriculture was introduced to the Indians in this area about 750 years before the arrival of Europeans. But for the most part the remains of prehistoric civilization are now well concealed beneath the cut-grass and the muck at the bottom of the old pools remaining from the era of rice cultivation, which, in the great tradition of European civilization, left a much more indelible mark on the land.

A bird's-eye view of the refuge shows the full extent of this vast network of rice fields which dominated the area's agriculture a century and a half ago. Just a few miles upstream from where Pat and I were traveling in the government truck, the river splits into three channels, like the prongs of a southward-pointing pitchfork. The westernmost of these channels is known as Front River, with the central and eastern channels referred to as Middle and Back Rivers respectively. The refuge boundaries cover both the Back and Middle Rivers, and extend all the way to the eastern bank of Front River, which is used as a shipping channel for the Savannah port.

An aerial photo which I had seen in Pat's office shows the crisscross pattern of old rice-field dikes covering almost the entire area of the refuge south of the three-pronged fork in the river, like a grid overlaying the whole thing, with each square representing a rice pool. The course of the Corps of Engineers' freshwater diversion canal could also be seen in this bird's-eye photo, threading its way at regular angles for nine miles through this grid pattern on the east side of Back River. North of the canal, the crisscross scheme fades out into the green overgrowth of Argente Swamp, which covers the northern end of the refuge. At one time this grid pattern could also be seen on the west bank of Front River, but it is now obscured and covered over by a much more recent layer of human development—the industrial landscape of the Savannah port area.

"This refuge is a sort of environmental barometer for the whole Savannah area," Pat said as she steered the truck around a bend in the road, headed directly back toward U.S. 17 now. "As you can see, we're nestled pretty close to a lot of heavy industry, so we're naturally concerned about water quality. It's a precarious situation."

Among the industrial concerns located directly across Front River from the refuge and within the next mile or so downstream are a sugar refinery, two paper mills, the Savannah Electric Power Company generating plant, several chemical plants, a small oil refinery owned by Amoco, a manufacturer of asphalt roofing, a factory where gypsum wallboard is made, and a building-products manufacturing plant owned by Certain Teed Products, Inc.

"By monitoring bird populations in the refuge," Pat continued, "we can get a good idea of the water quality. Birds tend to be relatively sensitive to environmental changes. If you begin losing species in an area like this, then you know something's wrong."

The truck slowed to a halt as the road intersected U.S. 17, which traverses the refuge near its south end. A big pulpwood truck loaded down with pine-tree trunks passed in front of us, heading probably toward one of the paper mills on the Georgia side of the river.

We crossed to the other side of the highway, where Pat got out briefly and unlocked a steel cable gate leading onto a continuation of the road and dike system. This stretch of road north of the highway, she explained, is closed to all traffic except government vehicles, though it's open to foot travel by anyone. When she drove through the gateway, I hopped out of the truck and went back to refasten the lock, then got back into the cab.

As we moved along this road, overgrown with weeds and punctuated by little dirt mounds that I took to be fire-ant beds, I noted that the terrain here was much the same as that south of the highway. The absence of heavy equipment and drained pools, however, indicated this area was not presently undergoing major repairs such as those underway in the scenic drive vicinity.

This part of the refuge also seemed more open, without as many of the little wooded islands of high ground, known as hardwood hammocks, so prevalent near the dirt road south of here. In the distance ahead we could see the ragged gray-green tree line of the swamp that covers the relatively inaccessible northern portion of the refuge.

We took note of a pair of blue-winged teal swimming

along the surface of a pond to our left, laden with lilypads and lotus pods on long, thin stalks, and Pat picked up the conversation about the refuge's precarious environmental circumstances. Water pollution, she said, has been a major problem at various times along this portion of the Savannah River.

The truck rolled past a group of three elderly black men fishing off the dike at the roadside. We exchanged waves as our truck passed, and Pat said, "Six years ago you couldn't eat the fish in this refuge, 'cause the water was so polluted. Now the water's been cleaned up incredibly due to the enforcement of new federal water-quality regulations. We monitor the fish here for contamination, and unless they're relatively free of it, we don't allow any fishing."

Despite stringent federal regulations pressuring manufacturers to be more careful in disposing of wastes, Pat noted, industrial pollution still presents problems for the refuge and its wildlife. As an example she cited two industrial spills that have affected the refuge within the last year and a half. Curious to know more, I asked her for details.

"In late July of last year a big quantity of asphalt was accidentally dumped into the river not far downstream from the refuge," she said. "This happened when some outflow pipes at Certain Teed Products failed to work right. As it happened, the tide was coming in, so the stuff was pushed up into the Back River, and a lot of it got into the refuge. It was a real mess to clean up, but of course the company had to pay for it. The marsh grass had to be cut over about a seven-mile area and bagged out. A lot of the snakes and alligators in the refuge were pretty thoroughly coated with asphalt, and we had a massive die-off of fiddler crabs as a result of the spill. We still haven't been able to determine the effects on the food chain."

"Now, you say there were two spills?" I asked.

"Right. No sooner had we begun to recover from the first spill than a Russian freighter spilled a bunch of crude oil downriver, and again an incoming tide washed it up into the refuge. This was in early October of '78, so soon after the first incident that we couldn't cut the grass in the refuge. The oil wasn't quite as bad as the asphalt, though—not as thick and mucky. Over a period of weeks it washed out of the refuge naturally."

She paused to watch a distant bird of prey circling in the sky, identifying it as a marsh hawk by the distinct white spot just above its tail. Then she said, "In some ways the public is lucky that the material from these spills went to the refuge. Otherwise, if the tide had been going out when they occurred, it would have gone out to the ocean and been carried down along the entire coastline for miles south of here. This just illustrates the fact that our proximity to heavy industry means that we've got to be extremely alert, because the industrial concerns around here have a pretty haphazard manner of notification about spills and other pollution problems. There's going to be a new oil refinery built downstream soon, and we don't really know yet how that's going to affect us here."

Construction will begin this spring on the refinery, which is being built by Hamilton Brothers Petroleum Company. It will be located not directly on the river, but very near, only two and a half miles west of the Georgia Ports Authority, right across the river from the refuge.

I had been curious to know more about the Army Corps of Engineers' freshwater diversion canal which runs through the wildlife-management area of the refuge, and I asked Pat if this had anything to do with offsetting the possible effects of industrial pollution downriver.

"No," she said. "The canal is supposed to guarantee that the water in the refuge doesn't become too salty." If the salt content in the primarily freshwater environment of the refuge were to increase significantly, she explained, certain changes in the wildlife habitat would automatically follow. Since one of the refuge's main functions is to provide a haven for wintering ducks, and since ducks require freshwater plant species for food, the possibility of increasing water salinity would threaten the management program here.

Thus, a few years ago when the Corps of Engineers was drawing up plans for constructing a tidal gate to draw ocean water up into Back River, they had to take this factor into consideration. The purpose of the Corps' plan was to force more water into the major shipping channel that is Front River and, by means of that natural dredging operation, keep the channel deep and clear enough to accommodate the large ships that use it. By trapping more incoming ocean water in Back River, the Corps reasoned, they could accomplish this. But since the refuge derives its water supply from Back River, the proposed tide gate would bring great amounts of salt water into the refuge. So the Corps included in its plans a provision for building this canal through the refuge, by means of which fresh water could be diverted from farther upstream, on what is known as Little Back River, to maintain the established habitat. The project was approved and, over the course of about four years, finally completed, at a cost of about $2.5 million.

Now, however, Pat says, "The canal isn't doing what it's supposed to do. As it turns out, the salt water has backed up farther than the Corps of Engineers anticipated, and it's getting into the refuge by way of the diversion canal that was supposed to guarantee us a constant supply of fresh water." A good example, I noted, of the old adage about the best-laid plans of mice and men.

We were now threading our way along a very poorly maintained section of the road that followed one long stretch of dike. We had just crossed the northernmost end of the diversion canal when Pat cast a studious eye toward a couple of large birds hovering over a wooded area to our left. An old, dilapidated fire lookout tower emerged from the trees in that area, which looked to be about 50 yards or so from the road.

"Are those eagles?" she asked.

I quickly removed my glasses and peered through my binoculars. "I can't tell yet," I said as I adjusted the focus. The sunlight was shining directly through the birds' large outspread wings, making the color pattern a bit difficult to distinguish. "They look more like hawks to me."

Without taking her eyes off the birds, Pat said, "They could well be bald eagles. There's a pair of them that nest up in the swamp, and a lot of the time you can see them around this old fire tower and in—" She hesitated for a moment, then said, "No, of course not. Those aren't eagles. See the dark feathers on top of the head? They're ospreys. Of course."

One of the birds then lit in the top of a tree, and through my binoculars I picked out the distinguishing marks, particularly on the head. "Yeah, you're right," I said.

Pat continued to watch the pair of birds and said, "Eagles

and ospreys are both making a comeback all along the coast here. We've had that pair of bald eagles I was telling you about here on the refuge for four or five years now, and we've known where their nest was for a couple of years. We don't like to be too specific in talking about exactly where the nest is, though, for fear that it'll be interfered with. Two years ago a golden eagle was shot just over in Hardeeville, west of here, and no one's been prosecuted for it yet. We've even seen a helicopter out here buzzing right over the treetops in the area of the swamp near where that nest is, as if somebody was looking for it. So you can understand why we want to keep its location fairly secret."

She watched one osprey dive from the treetop and said, "This brings us back again to the issue of water quality. Twenty or 25 years ago there were eagles and ospreys all along the coast. They nested on Pinkney, Wassaw, and Hilton Head islands. But they had virtually disappeared by the 1960s. All the DDT and chlorinated hydrocarbons and other industrial chemicals in the water were picked up by the wildlife which these birds depend on for food, and this in turn was affecting the birds' eggs. As their hatching success decreases, the birds'll move on to some other place where the environment's more favorable to their survival. So when you see these birds returning to the area, it has to mean better water quality."

Pat had stopped the truck, and I was scanning the sky around the old tower in hopes of catching my first glimpse of a bald eagle. But she put the truck back in gear, and we began to roll again. Within minutes we had reached the northernmost end of the refuge road system, near the bank of Vernezobre Creek on the edge of the huge second-growth cypress and tupelo swamp. Here we got out and walked along a raised pathway—originally part of the system of dikes, but now completely surrounded by large trees—which extends for about a mile back into the swamp. Pat said this was her favorite section in the entire refuge for birdwatching, noting that she had seen prothonotary warblers' nests in this area during the spring.

We didn't linger here long, though. Pat had an appointment to keep back at her office in Savannah, so we walked back to the truck and got in, turning around and heading back toward the highway. As we passed the old fire tower again, I watched the sky for the eagles, but again I didn't sight them.

Pat had returned to the subject of the refuge's value as an "environmental barometer." Steering the truck over one of the rice trunks, she was saying, "We're watchdogs, I guess you could say. We're going to be constantly out here to monitor the effects of industry on birds, fish, and other wildlife. Adverse publicity by the Fish and Wildlife Service encourages the industries to be more careful. If nobody raised a stink when we have problems like these oil spills, the industries would never clean up. But there's finally beginning to be some talk about what's to be done in case of an oil fire in the water. There had been no such talk prior to these recent spills.

"At this point, though, the Ports Authority is totally unprepared for major oil fires. They need a lot of special equipment, like these vacuum trucks that can suck spilled oil off the water's surface, but they've said in the past that the cost of these provisions for industrial disaster prevention is prohibitive." She looked out over the landscape of marsh and old rice pools

through which we were driving and said, "You know, it may be that we can't afford *not* to have these things."

HIKING GUIDE

Savannah National Wildlife Refuge

Savannah National Wildlife Refuge is one of the best spots along the Southeastern Coast for bird watching, providing food and breeding grounds for over 200 avian species. Three basic bird habitats can be found within the refuge—freshwater marsh, hardwood hammocks (small, slightly elevated land areas overgrown with oaks and other hardwood trees), and swamp containing a mixture of cypress and tupelo trees.

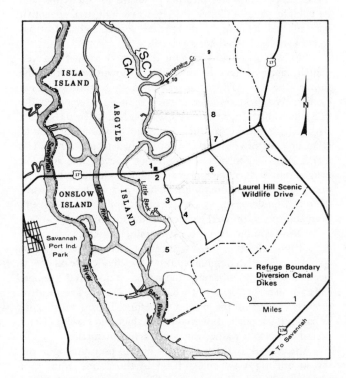

The largest portion of the refuge—Argente Swamp, which covers the entire northern three-fourths of the land area—is accessible only by boat. This hiking guide, therefore, deals with the 3000-acre wildlife-management area on the southern end, which can be best seen on foot. This portion of the refuge contains just slightly under 40 miles of dikes and jeep roads that can be used as hiking trails.

With the exception of the uncompleted "Laurel Hill Scenic Wildlife Drive" south of U.S. 17, all of the refuge roads are closed to vehicles other than official U.S. government trucks and jeeps, so hikers need not worry about frequent disturbances from automobile traffic on these roads.

Rather than plan a particular route for this hike, I have simply indicated on the accompanying map all the roads and dikes that can be walked. There is no real point in attempting to hike the entire 40 miles. It's best simply to plan for an early-morning arrival at the refuge, then pick out several sections of the road and dike system to hike on over the course of the day. The refuge is open from sunrise until a half hour after sunset, and if you're hoping for a good day of birding, plan to spend this entire period there, as the birds tend to be more active during the early-morning and late-afternoon hours.

(1) *Refuge headquarters,* a good place to leave your car while out walking the area. (2) *Site of Laurel Hill Plantation house,* where "Laurel Hill Scenic Wildlife Drive" begins; only one brick wall, part of the old rice-winnowing house, remains here as a relic of the plantation era. (3) *Old slave graveyard* on west side of road, containing four tombstones placed here during the early 1800s. (4) *Remains of old cistern,* used during plantation days, on east side of road; hardwood forest in this area is good habitat for warblers and other songbirds; another special feature of this area is the presence of the large-leaved Chinese parasol trees. (5) *Suggested birdwalk* along dikes surrounding these pools, through a combination of marsh and hardwood habitats. (6) *Nesting boxes for wood ducks* on posts in this pool. (7) *Entrance to restricted road area,* closed to public vehicles, but open to hikers, bird watchers, and fishermen; roads are located on either side of freshwater diversion canal; a recommended walk is along the road on the east side to point 9, as the western road does not cross the canal at its westward right angle, one mile north of U.S. 17. (8) *Management pool* where the uncommon whistling swan has been seen in winter during previous years. (9) *Tupelo Trail,* just under a mile long, which offers the only opportunity in the refuge for walking into the swamp habitat; large second-growth cypress and tupelo trees on either side of path, plus a few even larger first-growth trees; good habitat for warblers, sparrows, and woodpeckers; prothonotary warbler nests here during spring; outdoor-recreation planner Pat Young says this part of the refuge alone is worth a trip here. (10) *Old fire lookout tower,* in the vicinity of which can often be seen a pair of bald eagles that nest in the swamp a few miles away, as well as osprey and several kinds of hawk; don't attempt to climb this tower, as it is badly deteriorated and could come tumbling down any time.

If you're inexperienced as a bird watcher, don't let this fact discourage you from trying this hike. Birds are by no means the only attraction. Other wildlife that can be found here are deer, mink, otter, rice rats, bobcat, wild hogs, marsh rabbit, alligator, and several kinds of snakes, including the cottonmouth, mud snake, rainbow snake, brown water snake, and banded water snake. Among the fish that can be caught in the pools here are bass, carp, eel, garfish, and large blowfish. Fishing is allowed from March 15 till October 25.

Even if you don't have much experience as a bird watcher, you'll be missing one of the most important aspects of this place if you don't pay special attention to the birds. It is advisable to bring a bird field guide (*Birds of North America: A Guide to Field Identification,* is the best one for beginners) and a pair of binoculars. A list of all 224 species that have been sighted in the refuge since 1935 is available from Fish and Wildlife Service, Savannah NWR Complex, Box 8487, Savannah 31412. Enclose a self-addressed stamped envelope. If you need additional information, call this office at (912) 944-4415.

To reach Savannah National Wildlife Refuge from Savannah, take U.S. 17A northeast across the Savannah River and into South Carolina. Ten miles out of Savannah watch for an overpass ahead, and take the last left turn before reaching the overpass. This connecting road will lead to U.S. 17, where you turn left and continue for one mile to the refuge headquarters, on the right side of the road.

1979

Hiking Georgia's Coastal Isles

Wilderness hiking on Georgia's coastal islands can truly be heaven, but until recently the islands were just about as hard to reach. The National Park Service has now opened Cumberland Island, with 13 or so miles of awesome oak and palmetto forest and duned beach, to visitors. Easily accessible, Cumberland should amply satisfy the appetite of most outdoor lovers.

But for those who can't stand the sight of another *Homo sapiens* in their wilderness, nearly deserted spots still exist and are open to hikers on the National Wildlife Refuge islands of Wassaw, Blackbeard, and Wolf. Private boat transportation must be arranged to reach these islands and it's usually expensive, but you'll have a greater probability of being alone in paradise here than almost anywhere in Georgia. Wildlife information and background material for these three islands is available from: Savannah National Wildlife Refuge Complex, Box 8487, Savannah, GA 91412, (912) 944-4415.

A word about conditions. Warm weather on the coast, regardless of the season, hatches insect eggs and brings out mosquitoes and other pests. Repellent is strongly recommended. Sun protection (hat and/or lotion) is another must, particularly during the very hot summer. Ideal hiking seasons are early spring and late fall. Winter, which is rarely very cold, is also enjoyable if you are properly dressed.

HIKING GUIDE

Cumberland: Cumberland Island National Seashore. Simply, beautiful. Day visitors may take self-guided walk to Carnegie mansion ruins or explore independently. Miles of trails fill the island's northern half. Maps are given to each visitor during orientation at the island's tiny nature museum, where a good film on marshland ecology is shown on request. Three primitive campgrounds open for 40 people, camp with restrooms and electricity accommodates 40 more. No food nor supplies available, no fires; only portable stoves permitted out of developed camp. No pets, bikes nor vehicles allowed on the ferry, which departs from St. Marys. Early reservations suggested, especially for campers. Call (912) 882-4335 between 10 AM and 2 PM, Monday–Friday.

Wolf Island: Wolf Island, although predominantly covered by salt marsh, has a wide three-mile beach that is seldom visited. No docking facilities, so boats must be beached. Boat launch or transportation (sail or motor) can be arranged through Blackbeard Cove Marina, located just north of Ridgeville, Box 1064, Darien 31305; (912) 437-4878.

Wilderness Southeast runs nature trips in several coastal areas. All equipment and food are provided, plus guides trained to understand and love the wilderness. This is an especially good way to experience the coastal wilderness if you're not ready to go it alone.

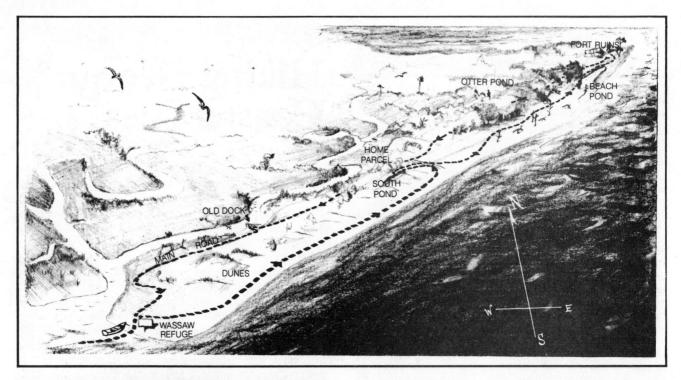

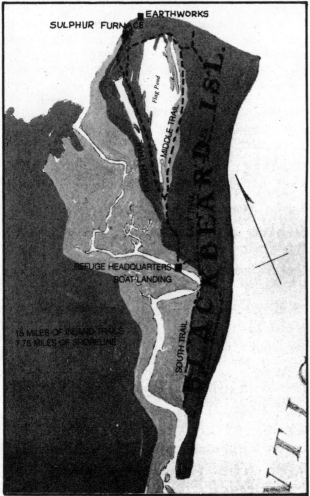

Custom-designed trips can also be arranged. Details from Wilderness Southeast, 711-VC Sandtown Rd., Savannah 31410; (912) 897-5108.

Wassaw: Wassaw Island is the least spoiled, most natural island on the southern Atlantic coast, since it was never heavily farmed and its forests were left uncut. Ten miles of trail, beginning at the island's south end, loop up the beach and the turn inland to return along the interior jeep roads. Wassaw is open for day use only and camping is no longer permitted, thanks to those who could not remember to pick up their litter.

The closest boat ramp is Montgomery Landing in southern Chatham County. From Abercorn Extension, go east on Montgomery Crossroads and turn left onto Whitfield Ave after 1½ miles. Continue on Whitfield (veering right at the fork) for about three miles. Turn left onto Bell St, which ends at the ramp. It's an 11-mile trip. When anchoring your boat, remember the seven-foot tidal change every six hours.

Boat services to Wassaw are offered by:

Capt. Helmey, Rte 2, Box 307, Wilmington Island; (912) 897-2478.

Wilderness Southeast, 711-VC Sandtown Rd., Savannah 31410; (912) 897-5108.

Blackbeard: Blackbeard Island has nine miles of beach and 15 miles of inland jeep trails that provide some beautiful hiking. Southern trail loop passes through the newly designated wilderness area of mixed pine and hardwood forest, while northern trails enter climax live oak and palmetto forest. North and south shores of North Pond have large bird rookeries. The sulfur furnace on the island's northern tip is rumored to be the crematorium for the government quarantine hospital operating on the island in the late 1800s. The path to the furnace and fort almost loses itself in the boggy underbrush, which is ideal habitat for snakes. Pond fishing Mar 15–Oct 25. Only youth and conservation groups are allowed to camp; permit required from Refuge Complex office. Boat launch or 20-mile round-trip ferry service available from:

Benny Ammons, Fisherman's Lodge, Shellman Bluff; (912) 832-4671. Mailing address: Townsend 31331. Coast Guard-approved.

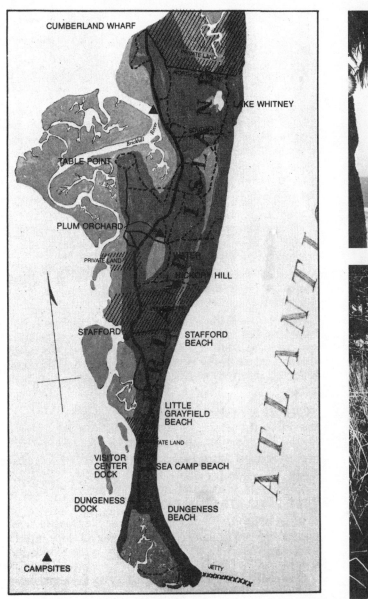

Kip's Fishing Camp, Shellman Bluff; (912) 832-5162.
Reservations suggested for both ferries.

1978

Canoeing Trips

CONTENTS

INTRODUCTION

Whether you paddle, row, sail, or just drift with the current, a boat is a great way to get away. The fantasy of losing yourself on the water, if only temporarily removing yourself from the universal flow of time, has wide appeal.

Brown's Guide canoeing writer Reece Turrentine recognized the diverse uses of the canoe—running whitewater rivers, lazily floating a calm stream, crossing lakes, exploring dense coves or narrow creeks, or touring swamps. He also acknowledged that canoeing pleasure depends on a combination of the skill of the boater, the kind of water to be negotiated, and the proper design of the boat.

Efficient canoeing begins with having the right type of craft. Propelling through whitewater requires speed and maneuverability; therefore, one needs an ABS fiberglass (both wood and aluminum types can be trashed on rocks) canoe with a rounded or U-shaped hull and a curve along the bow-to-stern axis.

In calm water, the V-shaped hull glides smoothly straight ahead, acting as a keel and providing stability. This type of canoe has a relatively flat bottom, with little curvature between bow and stern.

Touring canoes are a compromise between whitewater and flatwater designs, since touring canoeists often encounter a variety of water conditions. Touring canoes have shallow, V-shaped hulls, some curvature from bow to stern and cargo space for gear.

Canoes also vary in length from 13 to 17 feet, and again, one's choice depends on the most frequent use. If one plans trips alone, the shorter boats are the best design for solo paddling.

The weight of the boat material may also be a factor; the lightest boat material is Kevlar, a high quality fiberglass fabric developed for use by NASA. Wood canoes are also light, but are more expensive and require more maintenance than the other materials.

Turrentine's canoe trips are adventure stories. They take him to places where neither man's feet nor his machines can go, such as the "upper, upper Hooch" (a wild section of Jasus Creek, which flows into the Chattahoochee River above Helen). Yet he gives every detail someone would need to make the identical trip: precisely where to put in and take the boat out of the water, what hazards one encounters along the route, water gauge data, distances by miles and time, portages, and an indication of the difficulty of the run, so experts won't get bored and beginners won't get in over their ability. Canoe trips also include what scenery and highlights to expect, campgrounds and accommodations near the route, and, of course, detailed maps.

Turrentine's guide to the Tallulah River and its five impounded lakes (Seed, Burton, Rabun, Tallulah and Tugalo) outlines the history of how the once-"terrible" Tallulah was tamed in 1913. He recalled that the four miles below the then-awesome falls had attracted tourists from across the country to its "scenic wonders." Yet his article doesn't dwell on the past. It chronicles a 36-mile trip that he says "offers an exciting and unusual type of canoeing experience," even though it is nothing like what was possible 100 years ago.

Some 5,000 miles of waterways are navigable by canoe in Georgia, according to estimates, and *Brown's Guide* writers covered a range of different trips. The secret joys of rivers are almost routinely discovered and shared with readers, a passable tunnel on the Etowah, for instance, or a primeval cypress forest hidden near Darien.

Canoeing stories often share the technique of running a particular series of rapids and give a mile-by-mile account of a river, including how to avoid the familiar "scrunch" of rocks in shallow sections. Once Turrentine even analyzed how paddling reflects one's personality, in the manner of an amateur psychologist, with tongue firmly in cheek.

Reports on canoe trips also catch the folklore of the region, including some of its colorful characters. For example, when Turrentine set off to canoe the Apalachee, he stopped in Bethlehem, where he discovered "a charming little town with a cracker-barrel store and a famous old covered bridge south of town." In the text, he slipped in this story:

"'My old mules hated that bridge worse than they hated each other,' one old-timer said as we sat chatting around the general store. 'They'd go through it, but they hated them walls. They'd lean away from them towards the center until they'd be leaning flat up against one another, like a couple of lovers. Once through it, they'd bite and bray at each other like always. But they sho leaned on one another through the bridge!'"

These canoe trips interpret the state's geography in a personal way. For example, Turrentine acutely observes that the Altamaha not only carries more water than any other river in the state but it also washes the topsoil of middle Georgia into the delta, making the farmers' loss the shrimp fishermen's gain.

Turrentine obviously loves life afloat and communicates the excitement and inspiration he gets from his trips. In one story, he writes: "It was wilderness at its peak, full of raw contrasts, full of design and pattern. The whole scene renewed my spirits." He also admits mistakes he made, so others can try for a perfect experience. He shares stories he picked up from people whose lives are tied to the rivers he is exploring and quietly advocates conservation and considerate manners, without being preachy.

Surely the state's best known canoe trip—one that annually attracts visitors from all over the world to Stephen Foster State Park—is through the Okefenokee Swamp, with all its menace and gloom, magic and majesty. Turrentine, a native of Thomasville, canoed the swamp with veteran Dick Dumbleton and recorded their dramatic encounters with the permanent residents of this wilderness—alligators, egrets and herons, cottonmouth moccasins, racoons.

Canoe paddlers of all levels who want more information about this form of outdoor recreation can subscribe to a national magazine (Canoe, 131 East Murray St., Fort Wayne, Indiana 46803) or join any of the state canoeing clubs (Atlanta Whitewater Club, the Chattahoochee Chapter of the Sierra Club or the Georgia Canoeing Association).

J.W.E.

Whitewater 101

How to Shoot the rapids in one not-so-easy lesson

by Reece Turrentine

The dark rock that lay directly ahead of my canoe looked like the shiny back of a hippopotamus. I had just enough time to reach my paddle far out over my canoe's gunwhales, plant it deep in the water, and sweep in with a strong draw stroke. It was just enough. My canoe grazed the rock, sending scraping vibrations across the bottom of the canoe, up my knees and thighs, and through my body. I glanced back, concerned that Guy might have trouble with this one. He looked awkward in a borrowed life-vest that was too small for him. He didn't look comfortable in a canoe yet. And I felt very uncomfortable about having him on this whitewater river. The current was drifting his canoe toward a broadside collision with that dark rock. He hit it with a glancing blow.

"Lean toward the rock, not away from it," I yelled as he sideswiped the rock, almost tipping over.

"Yeah, I know," he replied as he slipped off the rock, just in time to avoid being capsized.

"No, you don't know," I yelled back at him. "You said you didn't know. Why won't you listen to a suggestion or two?"

"I'm coming along OK," he said. "Go on, and stay ahead of me."

I muttered under my breath and glided out of the eddy where I had been waiting for him. Guy was going to do it, but he was going to do it "his way."

Even though we were still in the beginning stretches of Cooper Creek, it was obvious that we were in for a busy day. Cooper Creek was turning out to be a fast, downhill run of whitewater—the kind of river on which you must keep your eyes riveted just ahead of the canoe, watching for submerged rocks. Because the current was so fast, we'd have only an instant to take evasive action, or we'd be swimming. This kind of canoeing was not unusual for eight of us on this trip; we were experienced whitewater canoeists. But with Guy, it was different. This was only his third time in a canoe, and his first time soloing a canoe in fast, mountain whitewater. I kept looking back to see how he was doing. He was struggling, but, as he said, he was "coming along."

Guy Hutchison, a close friend of mine from Atlanta, and I have hunted, fished, hiked, and vacationed together for years. Recently, I had talked to him about going on some canoe trips with me.

"Naw," he said, "I'll leave that whitewater stuff to you fellas. I'll fish those mountain streams, and let ya'll canoe them."

"You don't have to give up fishing," I replied. "Just start canoeing some with us. As much as you've handled fishing boats, you won't have any trouble."

"But those canoes are something else," he replied.

"So? You too old to try something new?" I replied. I knew that would get him.

As he paused to think up a retort to blast me with, I took the opportunity to give him a little of the speech that I've given many times to folks hesitant about canoeing. I tried to explain that it takes no special kind of skill to handle a canoe. Some people think you have to have the balance and agility of a tight-rope walker to control a canoe. It's just not so. All it takes is a couple of weekends on a calm lake to get the feel of it, then a couple of runs on a moderately fast river, preferably with an organized canoe clinic like most of the outfitters offer. With this preparation, you're ready to start canoeing.

"I've never known you to balk at trying something different," I said to him.

"I've fished most of those streams you fellas canoe," Guy replied with a knowing smile.

I knew he was right about that. Guy is second to none when it comes to fly fishing. I've been with him on many trips, and the little bit I know about fly fishing, he taught me. Guy knows the currents, eddies, chutes, and channels of the streams he fishes, and he knows how to cast a fly into a current that'll carry it right to the mouth of a hungry trout.

Seeing him struggling back there with the canoe, I almost wished he were fishing now, instead of canoeing. But it was too late for that. I had finally talked him into canoeing. He had made a couple of trips with me on calmer rivers, but now he was on a whitewater trip. I was afraid it was a little more than he was ready to handle.

I pulled into another eddy to wait for him and to offer a suggestion or two.

"Go on," he called. "Don't wait for me. I'm coming along." He had that determined set to his jaw. With his chin extended, and his lips pressed tight, he appeared to be in deep thought, pondering the matters at hand. He was working on it.

For the next mile, the river was like a downhill raceway. Shiny-backed hippos were everywhere. I didn't have much time to check on Guy. He was lagging behind, and sometimes he would be out of sight, back around the last curve. I'd pause a moment until I saw the nose of his blue canoe rounding the curve. His strokes were short and jabby, mostly rudder-type action and backwater strokes. As he swung the paddle from one side of the canoe to the other, he'd send a high arch of water spraying off the paddle into the air across the river, creating his own type of rhythmical water show. Although his strokes were hardly the textbook type, they were effective and powerful. Guy was getting the job done and creating his own art form while doing it. He was coming along.

Around the next curve, I saw the rest of the group. They had beached out and were standing on a large boulder in the middle of the river. As I approached, I began to hear the reason why they had stopped even before I could see it. The deeper pitch of heavy water was increasing. It sounded like someone had started blowing a tuba in the midst of a lot of trumpets. A waterfall lay ahead. I joined the others on the rock.

"What have we here?" Guy asked as he slid his canoe onto the rock. We all stood there, studying the tricky drop and currents beyond.

"Ya'll gonna run that?" he asked.

"Probably," I replied. "But that doesn't mean you have to run it. You can always portage around it, you know."

"Are you going to run it?" he asked, poking me with his elbow. I turned around to see his face.

"Now, don't start that, Guy," I said. "We've done stuff like this before. You don't have to do everything we do—not on your first trip."

"I want to watch ya'll," he said grinning. "I think maybe I can make it."

That grin was the same expression I had seen on a memorable night thirty years earlier. That night, Onie, who was then my bride of only a few months, had already gone to bed, when Guy knocked on the door of our little one-room garage apartment near the Emory University campus.

"Open the door," he called from the outside.

"It's late, Guy," I called back. "We've already gone to bed."

"Open up," he insisted. "I want you to meet someone."

He knew that to open the door, we had to get up and fold up our hide-a-bed, which blocked the door. But we got up, folded up the bed, and opened the door. Guy introduced us to his date, and we cooked them some eggs for a midnight snack. While sitting at the table, I casually tossed a paper towel over my shoulder into the trash basket.

"Get up," he said.

"What do you mean?" I asked.

"Just get up, and let me sit there," he insisted. As he sat down, he wadded up a paper towel and tossed it over his shoulder into the trash basket.

"That's one to one," he said.

"Get up," I said.

Three hours later, the score was in the hundreds, and the apartment was in shambles. Joyce, his date, later said that if she had not had Onie to talk with that night, she would have walked out and would never have spoken to Guy again. But she didn't walk out. She dated him again, and again, and finally married him. A foursome of friendship that has spanned decades began that night. Over the years, we have frequently knocked on each others' doors, helped each others' kids grow to adults, and traveled together to distant places of the world.

Now, standing at this waterfall, I saw that same grin again.

"It's up to you, Guy," I said. "You can try it if you want."

The waterfall was about five feet from top to bottom and was about as wide as a canoe is long. The drop was straight down, and thirty feet beyond the waterfall a car-sized boulder sat right in the middle of the current, receiving the full force of the water pouring over the fall. If Guy made it over the fall, he would have a space just twice the length of his canoe to turn sharply to the right to miss the boulder. It looked like a good place for an accident.

Eight of us ran the waterfall and collided with the boulder beyond it with varying degrees of severity. Each of us, however,

managed to stay upright and dry. Guy got in his canoe, lined it up at the top of the fall, shot over the edge, and glanced off the rock. He seemed to have everything under control, but he relaxed a little too soon. Before he knew it, the current swept him back against the rock and sucked the canoe out from under him. He came up laughing.

"I thought I had it," he yelled as he sputtered to the surface. "What happened?"

"You did have it," I called back. "You just quit before you were through."

"I believe I could make it if I did it again," he said.

"There are probably more downstream you can try if you want," I replied.

"But I shouldn't have turned over there," he insisted.

"Don't worry about it," I said. "It's no big thing. Everybody who canoes turns over. It's how you recover that counts, and you've done fine. Let's get your gear together."

I had finally delivered my little speech, and he had listened. He was ready for more action downstream. He was geared up, and I wasn't surprised. Canoeing affects people that way.

Guy pulled out ahead of me this time, raring to go. I watched him paddle as he twisted and turned through the maze of rapids and rocks downstream. In spite of his struggling strokes, he was moving the canoe. He knew the currents and where the canoe ought to be, and he was putting it there—and having a ball doing it. He had the fever.

"Try a draw stroke like this, Guy," I called to him as I demonstrated. "It'll slide the canoe sideways without having to turn it around every rock."

"Yeah, I know," he replied as he kept on digging.

CANOEING GUIDE

Cooper Creek

General Information: Cooper Creek flows from the base of the dam on Lake Winfield Scott, a little jewel of a lake nestled in the North Georgia mountains. The dam is 14.5 miles south of Blairsville on Ga 180. From its beginning, Cooper Creek twists and flows out of the mountains for 15 miles before it joins the Toccoa River along Ga 60. The creek runs through three federally protected areas: the Chattahoochee National Forest, and two areas within the forest, Cooper Creek Game Management Area and Cooper Creek Scenic Area. Cooper Creek has long been a popular trout-fishing stream. With higher water levels, it could become one of Georgia's most popular canoeing streams as well.

The first four miles of Cooper Creek are too narrow and shallow to canoe, and the final four miles flow mostly through flat, privately owned farmland. The seven-mile stretch in between, however, is as challenging a run of Class II whitewater as Georgia has to offer. The average gradient of Cooper Creek is a steep 40 + feet per mile, which puts it in the "gradient class" with such mighty rivers as the Chattooga Section IV (45 feet per mile) and Alabama's Little River Canyon (31 feet per mile). However, because Cooper Creek has a smaller watershed area and a lower level of water, it is less difficult to canoe than either of these rivers (Cooper Creek is within the Class II–III difficulty range). Nevertheless, the creek is a steep little stream that requires experience and skill to negotiate.

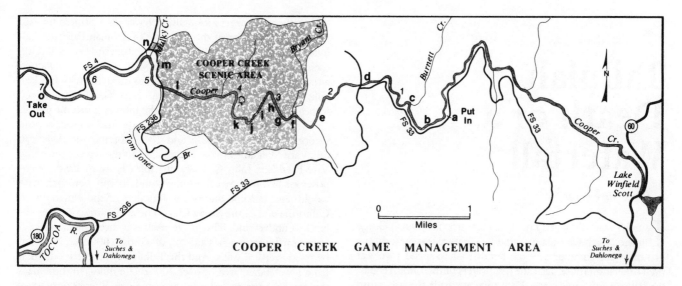

COOPER CREEK GAME MANAGEMENT AREA

There are two waterfalls, one drops five feet and the other eight feet, which are good Class III runs. A long slide of twisting channels and barrier rocks, which descends more than five feet, is, in high water, a Class III run as well.

Low water level has been the most serious barrier to canoeing Cooper Creek. But if meteorologists are correct in saying our 2½-year drought has been broken, streams like Cooper Creek may once again offer challenging canoeing.

Shuttle: To reach the put-in on Cooper Creek, drive north out of Dahlonega for nine miles on US 19/Ga 60 to the point where the two roads separate. Bear left on Ga 60, and drive seven miles to Suches, and turn right (north) on Ga 180. Drive north on Ga 180 for 4.4 miles to Lake Winfield Scott Recreation Area, where Blood Mountain Trading Post is located on the left. Turn left down the road that runs to the right (north) of the store. This is Forest Service Road 33. Drive on FS 33 for five miles. An access path leading down to the edge of the creek branches off FS 33 at the five-mile point. Limited but adequate parking space is provided at this put-in.

To reach the take-out, drive west from the put-in on FS 33 for 1.4 miles to an intersection. (If you turn right at this intersection and drive .1 mile, you will come to the Bryant Creek Road Bridge. The bridge offers a good view of the river and could serve as an alternate put-in, which would shorten the canoe trip by 1.7 miles.) To reach the take-out, turn left at the intersection and continue on FS 33 for 3.5 miles to where it meets FS 236. Turn right (north) on FS 236 and drive for 2.3 miles to the Cooper Creek Scenic Area and the Tom Jones Creek Bridge over Cooper Creek. Drive over the bridge and continue for .5 mile through the campground area. Turn left (west) on FS 4. Drive another .5 mile to Mulky Creek Campground, which runs along Cooper Creek. Signs in the campground indicate where shuttle cars may be parked without interfering with campsites. Reverse these directions to return to put-in.

Water Level: Cooper Creek does not have a water gauge, and the dam on Lake Winfield Scott does not regularly release water into the creek. Water level of the creek is determined by rainfall and natural overflow from Lake Winfield Scott.

Distances: The total distance of this trip on Cooper Creek is seven miles from put-in to take-out.

Hazards: Cooper Creek is not for beginners. Although the creek does not have a high volume of water, it does present numerous twists, ledges, and shoals which require skill and care to negotiate. Some of the chutes run close to the banks and under limbs. The canoeist must be able to maintain control of his canoe while duck-ing under limbs and plowing through bushes. Both vertical waterfalls on this section can approach a Class III level of difficulty in moderate water, and both have obstructive boulders at their bases. These waterfalls are located at mileage points 2.9 and 3 on the map, and are five feet and eight feet high, respectively. The slide at mileage point 3.7 is difficult to portage around due to heavy undergrowth along the banks, but with normal waterflow, it is canoeable. You must portage over a fallen tree at mile point 2.3, and around a logjam at mile point 3.5. Most other deadfalls can be run under or over, but are tricky in the fast current. Emergency exits from the river can be made easily along the first 1.5 miles and the last 2.2 miles of this seven-mile run. These sections are bordered by forest service roads. But the section from mile 1.5 to 4.8 presents difficult exits from the river because there are no roads in the immediate vicinity.

Map Guide: Numbers on our map indicate river mileage. Letters locate points of interest and check points on river.

    a. Put-in (mile 0).
    b. Deadfalls, canoeable only in high water (mile .2).
    c. Burnett Creek enters on right (mile .7).
    d. Bryant Creek Rd Bridge crosses Cooper Creek (mile 1.7).
    e. Portage over big tree (mile 2.3).
    f. Long shoals with overhanging limbs (mile 2.7).
    g. Stop and scout 5' waterfall. Tree blocks right chute. We ran left chute (mile 2.9).
    h. Stop and scout 8' waterfall. Class II slide on right or Class III drop over center (mile 3).
    i. Heavy rapids with multiple twists and turns (mile 3.3).
    j. Portage around logjam (mile 3.5).
    k. Class III slide, with submerged rock at bottom of slide (mile 3.7).
    l. Cooper Creek Scenic Area parking lot at Tom Jones Creek Bridge (mile 4.8).
    m. Cooper Creek Campground (mile 5).
    n. Mulky Creek enters on right (mile 5.2).
    o. Take-out at Mulky Gap Campground (mile 7).

Additional Maps: The Mulky Gap Quadrangle (7.5 minute series), a USGS topographic map, covers this seven-mile section of Cooper Creek from put-in to take-out. It can be obtained from the Department of Natural Resources, Map Sales, Fourth Floor, Agriculture Bldg., 19 Martin Luther King, Jr., Drive, Atlanta 30334.

1982.

Tallulah Death of a Waterfall

by Reece Turrentine

I was 10 years old when I made my first stop at Tallulah Gorge in the North Georgia mountains. We were traveling on the first of several summer trips our family took to spend a week at the Dickerson House, near the headwaters of the Little Tennessee River north of Clayton. Each time we made the trip, stops at Mrs. Gussie Harvey's store, perched on the rim of Tallulah Gorge, were a ritual. Because of these trips, Tallulah Gorge became more than just a place on the map to me. It became part of my experience of growing up. Stops there had a special meaning for me. I'm not sure why. It could have been because I had never seen a similar canyon, and I was really impressed. Or it could have been that the stop at Tallulah Gorge meant we were finally in the mountains, just a short distance from the place where I'd spend a week climbing hills, swinging on vines, and riding Moo, the gentle cow who lived on the Dickersons' farm. Few years have passed during my life when I haven't found myself traveling US 441 for some reason and approaching Mrs. Harvey's store overlooking Tallulah Gorge. I always stop at the same place, get out, and look at the gorge. For a long time, I assumed that one of the ribbonlike waterfalls visible tumbling into the gorge from the distant rim was Tallulah Falls. I'm sure other tourists assume the same. But they're wrong.

Until the turn of the 20th century, Tallulah Falls and Tallulah Gorge were relatively unchanged by man. Formed by the mighty Tallulah River, which joined the Chattooga River just beyond the canyon, it was protected from outsiders by the rugged mountain terrain. For centuries only the Cherokee Indians inhabited the area, and few whites penetrated the wilderness. The few white hunters and traders who wandered through the area told stories about the gorge and its thundering waters, but little was known about it. Even the Cherokees seldom ventured into the gorge, believing it to be inhabited by a strange race of "little people," who were alleged to live in the nooks and crannies of the cliffs overlooking the falls. The Cherokees also believed that one of the caves in the gorge was the entrance to the Happy Hunting Grounds, and if an Indian ever entered it, he would never return.

After the Cherokees were driven out in 1819, white adventurers began to explore the region. Unhindered by the Indians' fears about the gorge, they probed its depths. When they returned to civilization, they said that they understood the Indians' awe and the wonder that they had felt about the falls and the gorge. Within a year of the Cherokees' departure, spectacular accounts were circulated concerning this natural wonder in the northeast Georgia mountains. Newspapers printed the stories, and knowledge of the existence of Tallulah Falls and Tallulah Gorge spread like a prairie fire. Tourists began forging their ways through the mountains to see this curiosity of nature, although great stamina was required to make the trip. Clarkesville was the closest point where pack horses could be obtained to begin the 12-mile trek through the mountains to the gorge.

Interest in Tallulah Falls and Gorge had spread beyond Georgia. During the 1830s and 1840s foreign and American dignitaries began to make pilgrimages to the region, including Vice-President John C. Calhoun; John Howard Payne, composer of "Home, Sweet Home"; and Joseph LeConte, who would later become one of the founders of the University of California and of the Sierra Club. The area's attraction was not hard to understand. The gorge itself is a three-mile-long gash in the earth that reaches a depth of almost 1000 feet, bordered by rocky, vertical walls. And the Tallulah River carries drainoff from a watershed area of over 200 square miles. In those days this mighty river roared into the gorge over a series of spectacular cataracts, creating a continuous thunderlike sound that echoed through the gorge, day and night.

At the head of the gorge, the bed of the Tallulah River became suddenly narrow, creating a swift current heading toward the first falls. This narrow bed was named Indian Arrow Rapids by the tourists. The first of the great falls over which the Tallulah poured into the gorge was named Ladore, then came the 76-foot-high Tempesta Falls, then the 96-foot Hurricane Falls. The fourth of the great falls was named Oseana. Next was Bridal Veil Falls, with a drop of 17 feet. And last was Sweet Sixteen Falls, with a 16-foot drop. Beyond the falls, deep in the canyon, was a great bend in the river called Horseshoe Bend, from which visitors liked to gaze upward to guess the height of the towering cliffs. Many streams and creeks poured over the canyon rim into the gorge below, and were given appropriate names—no one knows exactly by whom. Everything was named. The pool at the bottom of Ladore Falls was named Hawthorne Pool, in memory of a man who fell to his death there. A natural water slide on the side of the gorge was named Hank's Sliding Place, in memory of a native of the region who slipped and fell more than 100 feet into the raging river below—and lived to tell about it. The thundering waters beneath an overhanging rock reminded someone of the voice of Satan, so that rock was named Devil's Pulpit, probably the most popular tourist site at the gorge, then and now. An outcropping that reminded someone of a profile was given the name Witch's Head and was a popular spot for photographers in the 19th century.

As tourists grew impatient with making the long trek in from Clarkesville and with having to camp at the gorge, inns began to be built nearer the attraction. Although the Civil War interrupted tourism for a while, lodges right on the rim of the gorge were in operation soon after the end of that conflict. Fine hotels were built, able to accommodate as many as 300 guests. Tallulah Gorge became a mecca for summer vacationers, offering cool temperatures, spectacular views, and accommodations for rich and poor. Georgians were proud of Tallulah Gorge, whose natural attractions had been made available to the public without damage to those attractions.

The editor of the *Atlanta News* said in 1905 that "Every foot of the scenery which surrounds Tallulah is superior to that of Niagara, and the state should buy that magnificent domain of scenery and make it the most beautiful park and reservation this side of Yellowstone." The mention of Niagara Falls in the piece was not accidental. Business interests had long had their eyes on the Niagara River, desiring to divert its flow in order to generate electric power. Business interests were also eyeing the Tallulah River, with the same idea in mind. Colonel John H. Estill, editor of the *Savannah Morning News,* wrote in 1906, "To commercialism there is nothing beautiful except the machine that grinds out dollars, unless it possibly be the power that actuates the machine. Imagine Bridal Veil Falls sawing logs, or majestic Tempesta ginning cotton. Think of Horseshoe Bend as a mill site, and the magnificent cliff across the rim covered with patent-medicine signs. There is only one Tallulah, and if it is spoiled, the loss will be immeasurable."

In 1905, the state legislature made an effort to buy the land around Tallulah Gorge to preserve it, but that body could not come up with the $100,000 needed to make the purchase. Three years later the Georgia Power Company was organized by E. Elmer Smith of York, Pennsylvania, and Eugene Ashley of Glen Falls, New York, and in 1909 these two men made a trip to explore Tallulah Falls. They were impressed with what they saw and obtained the $108,960 necessary to purchase the strategic tract of land around the head of the gorge. By late in 1910 they had completed the necessary contracts with construction companies to build dams, tunnels, and power plants along the Tallulah River and in the gorge.

Efforts were made to rescue the river and gorge from development. In the first large environmental battle in the state's history, a group of citizens led by the widow of Confederate General James Longstreet appealed to officials of Rabun County, to the state legislature, to the governor, to the Georgia Supreme Court, and even to President Taft. But it was too late. Work on Tallulah Dam began.

Throngs of people came to the gorge area to watch this remarkable engineering feat. But more came in 1912 to view Tallulah Falls for the last time. The editor of *The Toccoa Record* wrote, "The men and women with sentiment have taken their last look at the falls as they loved them. Both Georgia and the United States had a chance to save this unparalleled natural wonder, but we've waited too late."

In September of 1913, with the dam at the head of the gorge completed and the river diverted through its powerhouses, electricity flowed for the first time over the wires to Atlanta—to run the city's trolley cars. The "terrible" Tallulah River, as the Cherokees had called it, had been tamed and reduced to a trickle, dripping through Tallulah Gorge.

The decline of Tallulah Gorge as a tourist attraction was rapid after the dam was completed. Many of the hotels closed. Others were burned in a fire that almost destroyed the little town of Tallulah Falls, which had sprung up to serve the tourists, in 1922. In 1924, US 441 was built, bypassing the town.

The moaning of the wind is the only sound that comes from the gorge now, although the place has enjoyed a few brief moments of notoriety recently: Karl Wallenda walked on a wire strung across the gorge in 1970, and a few scenes from the movie *Deliverance* were shot in the canyon in 1972. These events followed the filming of the real classic, however: *The Great Locomotive Chase,* by Walt Disney.

The dripping waterfalls I saw as a boy from Mrs. Gussie's store were not Tallulah Falls. They were just some of the many streams and creeks that pour over the canyon's rim during wet seasons. The real falls disappeared when the river was dammed. I've canoed what is left of the Tallulah River. It is enjoyable. I've also canoed the lakes created by the dams on the Tallulah River. They are beautiful mountain lakes, with recreational areas and campgrounds that attract many people. But I never got to see Tallulah Falls. Neither will my children. And neither will their children. Like so much else in nature that has disappeared, the Tallulah Falls are extinct.

CANOEING GUIDE

Tallulah River and its Lakes

Before 1900, the most famous river in northeast Georgia was not the Chattooga, now so well known because most of the movie *Deliverance* was filmed there. The Tallulah River brought early tourists from across the country to view its scenic wonders. From its mile-high beginnings on the southwest slopes of Standing Indian Mountain in North Carolina, it bounded southward through the North Georgia mountains, falling more than 4700 feet during the 46-mile journey to its confluence with the Chattooga beyond the end of Tallulah Gorge, at the South Carolina border. Its last four miles, beginning at the falls, were the most spectacular. Over these falls, the river plunged downward a total of 600 feet in less than a mile.

But in 1912, after Georgia's first great environmental controversy, the Tallulah Dam was built at the head of the gorge. The "terrible" Tallulah River was tamed ("Tallulah" is a Cherokee word for "terrible"), and its awesome falls were reduced to a trickle. In the years that followed, four other dams were built on the Tallulah River, creating a chain of impounded lakes in northeast Georgia: Burton, Seed (Nacoochee), Rabun, Tallulah, and Tugalo.

What remains of the once terrible Tallulah River? That was the question that sent Dave Gale, owner of the Wildewood Shop in Helen, and I on a canoeing expedition to the Tallulah River area—to explore the old riverbed and canoe what's left of its waters. After canoeing and exploring the 36-mile Georgia section of the river, we found that although the Tallulah is nothing like it was 100 years ago, it offers an exciting and unusual type of canoeing experience. This guide provides instructions for canoeing 31.5 miles of the Tallulah, including its scenic impounded lakes and sections of the river where Class I–IV rapids provide hints of what the river once was. This run can be divided into six parts or done as one long trip. Either way, canoeing the lakes and river sections of the Tallulah offers a rare opportunity to view the mountains from the scenic lakes, run the rapids of what's left of the Tallulah, and pay tribute to what was once one of the mightiest rivers in Georgia.

Although the first 10 miles of the Tallulah are uncanoeable, driving beside it is worth the time if only for the spectacular mountain scenery. Forest Service Rd 70, reached by driving four miles north on Persimmon Rd from US 76, eight miles west of Clayton, runs parallel to the river and crosses it several times as it winds high into the mountains, passing Tate Branch Recreation Area, three miles above the put in for Section One (see below); the village of Tate City; and crossing the North Carolina border.

SECTION 1:
THE UPPER TALLULAH RIVER

General Information: This section begins 10 miles from the source of the Tallulah River and offers five miles of Class I–III whitewater paddling on a relatively untouched area of the river that runs beside the Coleman River Wildlife Management Area of the Chattahoochee National Forest and two miles of paddling on the backwaters of Lake Burton (miles 0–7 on our map).

Shuttle: The take out for this stretch is on US 76, 9.2 miles west of Clayton on Jones Bridge over the Tallulah River finger of Lake Burton. The best take-out point is not at Jones Bridge itself, but .2 mile up Vickers Rd, which starts at the northwest corner of the bridge, at the trash container by the side of the road. A little slough here allows easier access to the river than do the steep banks at the bridge. After leaving the shuttle car in the parking area at the northwest corner of the bridge, proceed to the put in by driving 1.2 miles east (toward Clayton) on US 76 to paved Persimmon Rd at the Persimmon-Tallulah fire station. turn left (north) onto Persimmon Rd, and drive four miles. Turn left (west) onto Forest Service Rd 70, and drive 1.3 miles to the Tallulah River Recreation Area's campground. Put in either at the campground or just up the road at the Coleman River bridge.

Distance: The river distance of this stretch is seven miles: five miles through whitewater, and two miles on a lake.

Hazards: Class II & III rapids dot this stretch after heavy rains and during wet seasons. If you use the Coleman River bridge as a put in, scout the rapid just downstream, which offers a healthy chute with a tight twist against the left bank. Watch for a nice ledge at mile .5, rockgarden rapids at mile 1, nice shoals at mile two, a tight turn under a bridge at mile three, a portage over a wooden bridge at mile four, and fast current under Plum Orchard Rd bridge at mile 4.3. The banks here are private property, so nonstop canoeing is suggested in order to avoid confrontations with property owners, which could be hazardous to your health.

Water Levels: Check the water gauge at the Plum Orchard Rd bridge (mile 4.3). It is located about 50 yards downstream on the right (west) bank. To reach it, drive 1.8 miles on Persimmon Rd from the point where it leaves US 76. Turn left (west) onto Plum Orchard Rd at Welburn's Grocery Store, and drive 1.1 miles to the bridge. This bridge can also serve as an alternate take out if you do not wish to paddle the two-mile Lake Burton backwater section.

SECTION 2: LAKE BURTON

General Information: Lake Burton, the largest of the five reservoir lakes covered in this guide, impounds almost 10 miles of the Tallulah River in its 2775 acres. It's a many-fingered mountain lake with 62 miles of shoreline. This lake serves as a holding lake, controlling the water flow to the lakes below it. It's a favorite spot for fishermen, impounded in 1919 upon the completion of Burton Dam, named after the town of Burton, which once occupied the site on which the lake now stands. This guide describes a 4.5-mile paddle down the lake's main Tallulah River channel, from the Jones Bridge put in to the Murry Cove take out, the nearest public landing to Burton Dam (miles 7–11.5 on our map).

Shuttle: Use the Section 1 take out (see above) as the put in for this section. To reach the take out, drive east on US 76 from Jones Bridge for 2.2 miles, and turn right (south) onto paved Charlie Mountain Rd. Follow this road for 3.5 miles, and turn right onto paved Bridge Creek Rd. Drive .3 mile, and turn right onto Murry Cove Rd (has a dirt surface) across from Wood's grocery store. Proceed to the public boat ramp at the edge of the lake.

Hazards: Lake Burton is a large lake, and canoeists must be alert for rapidly rising winds and thunderstorms. Paddling near the banks is recommended here. Life vests should be worn at all times. Canoeists must be careful to follow our map carefully on this lake in order to avoid taking a wrong turn into one of its dead-end

fingers. The trip from Jones Bridge to Murry Cove Landing is in a generally southerly direction until you turn eastward into Murry Cove (mile 11.5 on our map). Using our map and a compass will keep the paddler from winding up where his shuttle car is not.

Water Levels: All the lakes in this system are maintained at high water levels during spring and summer and are lowered during fall and winter. Lake Burton is sometimes lowered as much as 15–17 feet, depending on the water demand downstream.

SECTION 3: SEED LAKE
(ALSO CALLED NACOOCHEE LAKE)

General Information: Seed Lake offers a canoeing experience that is entirely different from that offered by Lake Burton. Lake Burton's wide and many-fingered layout provides breathtaking views of distant mountains. Seed Lake, on the other hand, is tight and narrow and follows the original bed of the Tallulah River quite closely. Seed Lake is 4.5 miles long and is impounded by the 75-foot-high Nacoochee Dam, completed in 1926. The lake has a 13-mile shoreline. Our guide carries the canoeist on a 3.5-mile trip from the put in at the base of Burton Dam (mile 12.7) to the Seed Lake public boat ramp on Lake Rabun Rd (mile 16.2), which runs parallel to this series of lakes along their northern shores.

Shuttle: Put in for this 3.5-mile trip on Seed Lake is at the base of Burton Dam (mile 12.7 on our map). To reach it, take Murry Cove Rd to its intersection with Bridge Creek Rd, turn right, and drive 1.6 miles to Lake Rabun Rd. Turn right (west), and drive .5 mile to the bridge over the Tallulah River at the base of Burton Dam. Access roads to the base of the dam are available along both sides of the river. The best access road is on the east side of the river, leading to a shallow put in with adequate space for parking. To drop a shuttle car at the take out, return to Lake Rabun Rd, turn left (east), and drive 3.6 miles along the lake to a sign identifying Seed Lake Boat Launch, just off the road at the lake's edge (mile 16.2).

Hazards: None, but exercise normal caution if sudden winds or thunderstorms come up, and don't land on private property on the lake's developed shoreline without permission.

SECTION 4: LAKE RABUN

General Information: Lake Rabun is the most popular recreation area among the five lakes covered in this guide. Houses and cottages were built on its shores as early as the 1930s, and today its 25-mile shoreline is dotted with homes. But the Georgia Power Company, which owns the shoreline and leases land for homes, limits development, so you won't find sprawling motel complexes here. This eight-mile trip (miles 17.4 to 25.4 on our map) is winding and scenic, offering a stop at the popular Rabun Beach Recreation Area and Campground (mile 18.5 on our map).

Shuttle: Put in for Lake Rabun is at the base of the dam on Seed Lake at the Nacoochee Park Recreation Area (mile 17.4 on our map), located just off Lake Rabun Rd. The Nacoochee Park Recreation Area offers picnic tables and restrooms. The take out is at the top of the Mathis Dam on Lake Rabun (mile 25.4 on our map). To reach it from the put in, drive six miles east on Lake Rabun Rd. Turn right onto a dirt road about 200 feet before you reach a paved road (old US 441) that crosses the river, and drive one mile to the take out, a public boat ramp at Mathis Dam (mile 25.4 on our map). If you don't want to canoe the entire length of Lake Rabun, an alternate take-out point is at Hall's Boat House in the little town of Lake Rabun (mile 24.5 on our map).

SECTION 5:
TALLULAH RIVER AND TALLULAH LAKE

General Information: The special feature of this 5.5-mile stretch is that it follows for four miles the original bed of the Tallulah River,

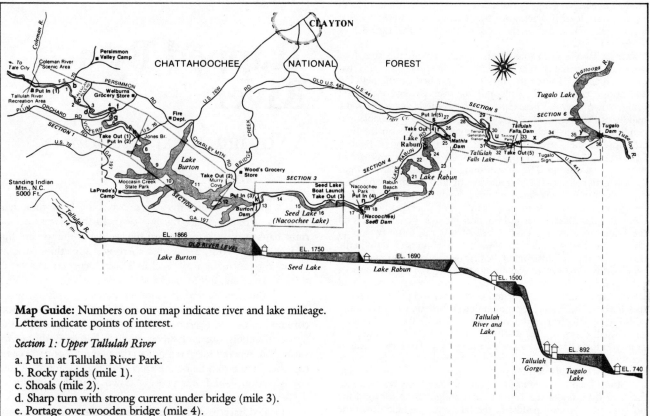

Map Guide: Numbers on our map indicate river and lake mileage. Letters indicate points of interest.

Section 1: Upper Tallulah River

a. Put in at Tallulah River Park.
b. Rocky rapids (mile 1).
c. Shoals (mile 2).
d. Sharp turn with strong current under bridge (mile 3).
e. Portage over wooden bridge (mile 4).
f. Plum Orchard Rd, bridge with gauge (mile 4.3).
g. Backwaters of Lake Burton (mile 5).
h. Take out on Vickers Rd beside Jones Bridge (mile 7).

Section 2: Lake Burton

h. Put in on Vickers Rd beside Jones Bridge (mile 7).
i. Take out at Murry Cove Landing (mile 11.5).
j. Burton Dam (mile 12.7).

Section 3: Seed Lake

k. Put in at base of Burton Dam (mile 12.7).
l. Take out at Seed Lake Boat Launch (mile 16.2).
m. Dam on Seed Lake (mile 17.4).

Section 4: Lake Rabun

n. Put in at base of dam on Seed Lake (mile 17.4).
o. Rabun Beach Recreation Area (mile 18.5).

p. Hall's Boat House on Lake Rabun (mile 24.5).
q. Take out at top of Mathis Dam (mile 25.4).
r. Mathis Dam (mile 25.4).

Section 5: Tallulah River and Lake

s. Put in at Tallulah River bridge (mile 26.5).
t. Loop in river, with Class II & III shoals (miles 29–30).
u. Terrora Generating Plant, with Class IV rapids (mile 30.8).
v. Tallulah Lake take out (mile 32).
w. Tallulah Dam at the top of Tallulah Gorge (mile 32.3).

Section 6: Tallulah Gorge and Tugalo Lake

x. Tallulah Gorge (mile 33).
y. West fork of Tugalo Lake (miles 34–35).
z. Put in and take-out at Tugalo Dam (mile 36).

offering significant rapids. The final 1½ miles are on a lake complete with waterfalls and mountain streams trickling along its banks. This small lake, only 63 acres, is impounded by Tallulah Dam, which is 130 feet tall. It was the first dam to be built on the Tallulah River, completed in 1912. Its construction on the rim of Tallulah Gorge cut off most of the water for Tallulah Falls.

Shuttle: The take out for this stretch is in Terrora Park, behind the Terrora Visitors Center off US 441 at Tallulah Dam. Leave a shuttle car in the public parking area by the lake near the fishing pier, located just upriver from the public swimming area. The take-out point is at the wooden dock that runs under the fishing pier designed for handicapped people. To reach the put in, leave Terrora Park on the one-way exit road, turn left onto old US 441, and drive four miles to the put-in bridge (mile 26.5 on our map). The road that leads across the river to the Terrora Generating Station .8 mile beyond Terrora Park and a bridge over the Tallulah River .9 mile beyond the park are good places from which to scout the rapids in this section. At 1.6 miles into the shuttle old 441 joins the current US 441 for about 100 yards (turn left at this intersection). Stay on old 441, which leaves the new road at the signs pointing to Lake Rabun. The put in, located one mile downstream from Mathis Dam, at the junction of the Tallulah River and Tiger Creek, is steep. Best access is at the northwest corner of the bridge.

Water Levels: No gauge is available on this section of the Tallulah River. Water level is determined by the amount of water released from Mathis Dam and by the amount of rain in the Tiger Creek watershed.

Hazards: Two sets of major rapids are found along this stretch of the river. Beginning at mile 29 on our map is ½ mile of rapids that can reach Class III intensity (they begin just beyond the new US 441 bridge, continue along a loop in the river, and end at the next bridge downstream). These rapids can be scouted from rocks in the middle of the river, and several run options may be available, depending on water levels. The most dangerous rapids on the river are those at the Terrora Generating Station, just above Tallulah Lake (mile 30.8 on our map). These rapids should be approached with extreme caution. The current under the bridge near the right bank is extremely swift and leads directly into the first dangerous drop. Even if you have observed these rapids from the bridge during the shuttle, it is wise to view them again before deciding to run them. In high water, the first drop, near the right bank just beyond the bridge, is a curling Class IV rapid that can easily swamp an open canoe. Don't paddle idly down the river and get caught in the flow of this rapid. Capsizing in the first rapid allows you practically no recovery time before you are washed into the jagged rocks of the second rapid. Most of the rocks in these rapids were blasted into the river during construction of the dam and powerhouse, so they have not been there long enough to be smoothed by the water (this is especially true of the third rapid). The fourth rapid is actually a small concrete dam where a run through the spillway positions you for a drop over a five-foot ledge! Careful maneuvering is necessary here to keep the canoe away from the right edge against the bank, where jagged rocks protrude from the water. Just beyond the rapids, keep to the left of the flow of water being released into the river from under the Terrora Generating Station. Beyond the powerplant is an easy paddle to the take out, one mile down the lake. If the water level is high, don't hesitate to portage these rapids.

Distance: Total canoeing distance of this section is 5½ miles (miles 26.5–32 on our map).

SECTION 6:
TALLULAH GORGE AND LAKE TUGALO

General Information: The last two miles of canoeable waters on the Tallulah River are in Tallulah Gorge, paddling on the west finger of Lake Tugalo. Tugalo Dam, constructed in 1922, impounded the waters of the Tallulah River at its juncture with the Chattooga River, forming the two fingers of Lake Tugalo. I canoed this section as a four-mile round trip, using the same point as put in and take out. The special appeal of this trip is that it allows the canoeist to view the many small, active waterfalls around the edge of the west finger of the lake and to view the towering cliffs of the gorge from below.

Shuttle: This trip begins and ends at the top of Tugalo Dam. To reach this dam, drive 1.8 miles south from Terrora Park on US 441 to a sign pointing to Tugalo Dam. Turn left at the sign, and drive 2.5 miles to Tugalo Village, a company town owned by the Georgia Power Company. Drive through the village to the end of the paved road, where the road forks onto two dirt tracks. Take the left fork, following the signs, and drive 1.5 miles to the base of Tugalo Dam. Take the left fork at the bottom of the dam, and drive up the road to the dam's top. At the end of the road is the steep bank used as a put-in point.

Hazards: This lake is deep, cold, and isolated, with no development along its banks. Life vests should be worn at all times. Rocks around waterfalls are slippery, requiring extreme caution while climbing on them. Avoid getting too close to the water released from the power station at the head of the lake.

1982

Trapped By a River

A voyage of exploration

by Reece Turrentine

I was so busy guiding my canoe down the brisk mountain creek, I didn't notice the line of rocks that started on the right bank and angled in toward the middle of the stream. But as I got closer to it, I saw that there was something strange about this formation of rocks. There were no chutes in the wall large enough for a canoe to pass through or run over. Instead, the river filtered through hundreds of small openings. Then I noticed another identical line of the football-sized rocks coming out from the left bank. I stopped paddling and tried to figure this thing out and survey the whole scene. About fifty yards from where I sat in my canoe, the two rows of rocks came together in the middle of the river to form a giant V-shaped configuration, and I was floating down toward the point of the V.

I called back to my canoeing companions, Steve Higgins, a whitewater guide for Southeastern Expeditions on the Chattooga River near Clayton, and Dana LaChance, the owner of Appalachian Adventures Shop in Dahlonega. Steve was far enough upstream that he had time to find a small hole in the wall and squeeze his shallow draft kayak through it into deeper water. But Dana was too close behind me in her canoe. She and I had no place to go except straight down the middle of the V where the rock walls were converging on us. We were in no danger, but both of us were intrigued.

It had all happened just as it was supposed to happen. We ran out of water space just as we were supposed to. The old device still worked perfectly. We had been caught in the snare of an ancient Indian fish trap. We sat in our canoes, firmly grounded in the narrow end of the trap—just like a couple of fish. As we looked back upstream from where we sat, we could see that the contraption was still intact. Over time, the rocks that the Indians had laid had taken on the natural shades and tones of the river rocks, camouflaging the old rig, which would work today about as well as it did a hundred years ago.

Had we been fish in the river, we would have headed downstream inside the V just like we did today in our canoes. Indians, perhaps a dozen or so, would have spread out across the river at the wide opening of the V. Then they would have waded downstream in the knee-deep water, herding the fish down toward the inside point of the trap. The rock walls extend about a foot above the surface of the river during normal water levels, which would prevent the fish from swimming over it. The fish would continue to retreat downstream as the Indians advanced, until finally all the fish were herded together in the inside point of the V-trap. There, the Indians would simply scoop them up with hand nets, or allow them to swim through a small opening at the end of the V where the fish would fall into large baskets made of woven vines or split canes.

Steve, having escaped the trap, came paddling back upstream to view our predicament. We all sat there for a while just laughing and looking. Dana and I could do nothing except get out of our canoes, step down the rocks at the end of the trap, and drag our canoes until we were again back in the river channel. We thoroughly enjoyed the whole adventure. Here we were, with our supposedly sophisticated equipment and know-how, and we had been out-witted and out-maneuvered by a primitive contrivance devised by what some have called an uncivilized culture.

I've never named my canoe. It gets too many bumps and scrapes for a painted name to last very long. But if I did name it, I think I know what I would paint on its bow. On the bookplate of one of Francis Bacon's works is an engraving of a small ship sailing through the Pillars of Hercules toward an uncharted sea. Painted on the bow of the vessel is a proud and defiant name: *More Beyond*. I like the idea expressed in that name. Beyond every rapid and around every river bend, there's more beyond. The rivers have all been mapped and charted now, but I haven't seen them. And I want to, because there's always more beyond.

Granted, I don't come upon experiences as intriguing as Indian fish traps on every river I canoe. But something is always happening. Not long ago, drifting down a slow section of a mountain river, I heard this unusual "cracking" sound up the mountainside. After a moment of silence, I heard the cracking and popping again. I peered up among the trees trying to locate the source of the strange sound. Then, with an almost explosive discharge, I saw a large boulder crashing down the slope of the mountain. It had finally abandoned its place on the hillside and splashed in a fury of spray into the edge of the river. In a moment, it was all over. Another boulder had found its place among the rocks that have been falling throughout the eons. I guess it was no big deal. But the big deal to me was in the fact that I was there to see it happen. I was an eyewitness to a natural change in the face of the earth.

Through the years, I've had to portage canoes, gear, and myself over the countless tree falls I have encountered on the rivers I canoe. One of these days, I know it's going to happen: I'm going to be there when that cosmic event occurs, and a tree will finally sway and crash into the river, leaving a hole in the sky for other trees to grow and fill.

As Steve, Dana, and I paddled on downstream towards the take-out, we took a lunch break on a large boulder in the river. During such lunch stops, I always stretch my legs by wading around in the shallows of the eddies behind the rocks. I'm still looking for something: a perfectly round little stone—round and smooth like a silver dollar. I've picked up thousands that were "almost." Many I've been tempted to keep. But they weren't exact. So I curl my forefinger around it and pitch it out across the water, hoping to break my own record at stone-skipping across the surface. But one of these days I'll reach down for one of those thin, round, smooth little rocks, and it'll be my silver dollar. That one I'll put in my pocket.

CANOEING GUIDE

Mountaintown Creek

General Information: Mountaintown Creek, located about four miles west of Ellijay in Gilmer County, offers both Class I and Class II whitewater. It is a tributary of the larger Coosawattee River, the main feeder stream of Carters Lake. Mountaintown Creek is formed by four little streams that flow off the southern slopes of Cohutta Mountain, and it becomes canoeable as it passes under the Ga 282 bridge west of Ellijay. The beginning of the canoe run is not very scenic; the creek is bordered by a used car lot, streamside dwellings, and the muddy shore of a private campground under construction at the put-in. But a couple of hundred yards downstream, the creek enters the primitive and untouched wilderness of the Coosawattee Wildlife Management Area. From that point on, canoeists experience a crescendo of paddling excitement. The width of the stream at the put-in expands from 20 feet to 40 or 50 feet. The slight gradient-descent at the put-in steadily grows to a brisk twenty to thirty feet per mile, increasing both the number and speed of the rapids. Particularly noticeable is the increase of the size of the mid-stream rocks. At the beginning, the shoals squeeze through little rocks about the size of footballs. Later on, however, in the Management Area, canoeists twist through rapids created by car-sized boulders. Scenic beauty increases as paddlers are carried down the stream into areas of high rock outcroppings and oak and hickory forests.

After 5.7 miles of maneuvering down the crisp current of Mountaintown Creek, canoeists break out into the larger Coosawattee River, which offers a couple of more miles of interesting Class I & II rapids before flowing into the quiet backwaters of Carters Lake.

Some canoeists may consider the final three miles of paddling to the take-out to be anticlimactic. I think of them as being merely different. I like to paddle, whether it's on whitewater or flat water. The three-mile paddle down the backwaters of Carters Lake adds some interesting variety to the trip. It gives canoeists a chance to examine the rugged and wooded shoreline of this small, but extremely deep lake in the North Georgia mountains. Such a natural shoreline is a refreshing contrast to the overly developed banks that border too many rivers in the Southeast. And paddling this flat water also gives you a chance to work on those oft-neglected forward power strokes. As you paddle, you can think about the house-sized boulders that now lay silently deep beneath the surface. Carters Lake has silenced what once was some of the wildest and most powerful whitewater in the Southeast which flowed through this section of the Coosawattee River. It was the Coosawattee River that inspired James Dickey to write the gruesome but exciting book *Deliverance*, which was later made into a movie (the movie used the Chattooga River in Northeast Georgia for the river scenes).

Shuttle: Our point of reference for the shuttle is in Ellijay, at the intersection of Ga 285/52 and US 76 (a Dairy Queen sits at the intersection). To get to the take-out to leave the shuttle car, drive west from Ellijay on Ga 282 for seven miles to the signs pointing the direction to Ridgeway Public Use Area on Carters Lake (3.5 miles out of Ellijay on Ga 282, you will cross the put-in bridge over Mountaintown Creek.) Turn left at the signs for Ridgeway Park, and drive on this dirt road (which will become paved after a few miles) for 3.8 miles to the boat ramp at the take-out. After leaving

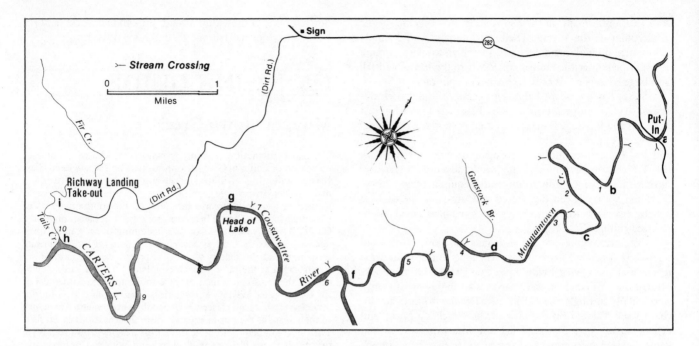

the shuttle car in the parking lot above the boat ramp, return to Ga 282, turn right (east), and drive 3.5 miles back to the put-in bridge at Mountaintown Creek.

The put-in is located on the northeast corner of the bridge—property owned by Mr. Roy Abercrombie, also owner and operator of the business at the southwest corner of the bridge, Roy's Used Cars & Trucks. Mr. Abercrombie is willing for *Brown's Guide* canoeists to use his property as a put-in. At the time of our trip, he was constructing a campground along the creek, and he requests that canoeists see him before embarking on the trip so he can direct them where to park their cars so they won't interfere with construction activity.

Distances: The total distance of this trip is 10 miles: 5.7 miles on Mountaintown Creek, 1.5 miles on the Coosawattee River, and 2.8 miles on Carters Lake. The gradient of Mountaintown Creek is a rapid 25 feet per mile. All you need to do is steer and use turning strokes. Take your time, stop frequently, and enjoy the scenery. The mile and a half down the Coosawattee River also requires little forward paddling. Save your power strokes for Carters Lake. You'll need them.

Hazards: We encountered no deadfalls on our trip. But on a small creek like Mountaintown, seasonal rains or flash floods could wash such hazards into it overnight—so be on the alert for them. Although at normal water levels, Mountaintown Creek has only Class I & II rapids, higher water levels could increase some of the rapids in the lower stretches to Class III, which require scouting and study to navigate successfully.

When you reach Carters Lake, you will need to adjust to a new set of hazards, so keep your life vests on. Carters Lake is a narrow and extremely deep mountain lake, and its shores are high and steep. Watch for power boats and water skiers, which may zoom around curves where you are paddling. Remember to control your canoe so the bow strikes the waves from power-boat wakes at least to a quarter degree. If your canoe is hit broadside by a heavy wave from a power-boat wake, you will be swamped before you know it.

I might list an additional hazard—a hazard to your health. On our trip, at the point where the current of the Coosawattee River diminished, and where the wind was blowing up the lake, a hundred-foot-wide barrier of trash, gunk, styrofoam, bottles,

limbs, and one greasy innertube stretched all the way across the lake. It may have been an unusual occurrence caused by a rare combination of current and winds conditions. It made paddling almost impossible, and breathing very unpleasant.

Another hazard is the very real possibility of missing the take-out. You can't see it from the main channel of the lake. While paddling down the 2.8 mile stretch of Carter's Lake, hug the right shore. At the end of the second long westward channel of the lake is the hidden cove leading to the boat ramp take-out. Watch for concrete picnic tables high up on the right bank of the lake shore just before you reach the cove.

Water Levels: Mountaintown Creek is normally canoeable from January through July. Water levels at other times depend on the amount of rain in the area. There is no water gauge on Mountaintown Creek, so you will have to depend on levels given by area residents, which are usually given in terms of "high, low, or medium."

Author's note: The exact location of the Indian Fish trap written about in the story is not indicated on the map. *Brown's Guide* canoeists will come upon the trap when they canoe the creek. They will see it, enjoy it, and leave it unmolested. Giving its exact location might tempt vandals to walk into it and disturb a very rare and valuable archaeological relic.

Map Guide and Index: Numbers indicate river miles. Letters locate points of interest.

- a. Put-in at northeast corner of Ga 282 bridge (Roy's Used Car Lot is on the southwest corner).
- b. Scenic rock outcroppings (mile 1).
- c. Class II rapids down southwestern stretch of river (mile 2.5).
- d. More Class II rapids (mile 3.5 to 4).
- e. Noticeable increase in gradient and river speed (from mile 4.5).
- f. Junction of Mountaintown Creek with Coosawattee River (mile 5.7).
- g. Beginning of Carters Lake backwater (mile 7.3).
- h. Cove on right leading to take-out (mile 10).
- i. Take-out at Ridgeway Public Use Area boat ramp.

1982

Mr. Allison's River

It's the old irresistible force, immovable object routine

by Reece Turrentine

Charles Allison was standing high on the riverbank, just beyond the first curve, his feet spread and his arms folded across his chest. The paddlers in the first three canoes were bunched together beneath him, close to the bank. The two other canoes ahead of me were heading over to join them. I was the last to leave the put in for this Tesnatee Creek run, and so I had just rounded the first curve, expecting to see the canoes all lined up single file, heading downstream. Instead, when their bright blue, red, and yellow colors caught my eye, they were all up against the bank or heading there, with Allison standing above them.

"Uh-oh," I thought. "A landowner."

I knew we were in an area where confrontations had been reported between canoeists and property owners. Perhaps I should have warned my friends that this could happen before they decided to run this stream. I paddled over quickly to join them.

"—and my grandfather owns all the land on the other side of this creek, way on down," the man on the bank was saying, pointing across the creek, as I slid my canoe in with the rest of them. He was a young man, apparently in his mid-twenties. He had a kind face, but a firm voice. "—and we'd rather you not stop to fish, or get out to camp, or anything like that," he continued. As group leader, I decided it was time to let our intentions be known.

"Sir," I began, intending to sound respectful, "we don't intend to trespass on your property. These folks are serious canoeists, and we just want to canoe the creek."

"Well, we've had trouble lately with groups like yours," he replied. "We just don't want a lot of folks in here. It messes up the creek and the banks."

I wanted to press on and inform him that we not only take out our own litter, but a lot of other people's, too. But he was turning to go.

"Since you're here, it's OK this time," he said, "but just canoe straight on through if you will." With that, he was gone. And I thought we'd better go, too. At least he hadn't asked us to leave. So I motioned to the others, and we backed away from the shore and into the current, still hoping to enjoy a sunny day trip on the scenic Tesnatee Creek.

On the first straight stretch of our run was a rapid known as the Trash Pile. Here, flat rocks stretch all the way across the

river, creating a natural damlike barrier. While there are sheer drops near the left bank, the rocks near the right bank slant gradually downriver, creating a long slide that ends in a healthy chute. Although the slide is bumpy, once momentum is achieved, the ride on down through the chute and through the waves at the bottom is speedy.

What's at the bottom of the chute on its left side gives the rapid its name. The force of the chute pouring into the big pool below causes a large and sluggish eddy, like a whirlpool, on the left. Sticks and limbs and trash bob around in this slow-motion eddy for a long time before finally being released to float downstream. The eddy is no fun to play in, but the slide and chute are. My group had a ball bumping down the slide and being catapulted through the chute.

As the group played, I beached my canoe on the rocks at the top of the rapids to step out and watch them. Glass tinkled around my feet; I looked down and saw a broken beer bottle I had almost stepped on. I picked up the biggest fragments and hurled them into the bushes on the bank.

"Come on, Reece," one of the men in my group called to me as he dragged his canoe back up the rocks for another run down the slide. "Are you going to make this run or just stand there on the rocks all day?"

"Go ahead and run it," I called back. "I'll be right behind you."

I had something on my mind. That exchange on the bank with the landowner, who I later learned was named Charles Allison, had put a damper on the day for me. I couldn't seem to shake my sad feeling. As we moved downriver, through the twists and drops of rapids, I'd forget it for a while, but then, on the smooth stretches, I'd go back to thinking about him—standing on the bank, looking down on the canoeists. He clearly had been unhappy with our presence on the creek, and I was unhappy with the way we'd left things. Could I have been more convincing? Should I have stayed longer and gone into the whole matter of canoeing and property rights? It's a big issue with no easy answers. I wanted to know him better, and I wanted him to know me better.

Frankly, I was displeased with the idea that he even thought that I could be associated with anything that bordered on misuse or abuse of rivers and land. I just didn't like being lumped in with other groups he had "had trouble lately with"—especially after all the years I've spent promoting land and water conservation.

During my 30 years of canoeing, I've developed a relationship with rivers that goes deeper than using them for recreation. Oh, I have plenty of fun on them, but through the years, they've grown to be something far more than just playthings. Some of my more practical friends jokingly accuse me of going a little too far in humanizing rivers. But rivers *do* seem almost human to me. They come the closest of all inanimate objects to reflecting my moods. Always restless and in motion, and resembling man's life cycle, they begin in small places and grow through stages of turbulence and tranquility. They're shyly restrained when dammed and held back; then they leap forward when released. And through it all they make their ways persistently toward eternity in some distant sea.

Through the years, I've paddled rivers, camped by rivers, bathed in them, watched their moods, and listened to their murmurings. I've felt the caress of their gentleness, and at other times the sting of their anger. I've heard them whisper and sing and shout. And they've made me sing and shout, as well as whisper many a prayer on their sandbars at night. Camped alone on some riverbank at night, as the flames of the campfire burn down to glowing embers, magic moments come for me, when I sense the serene harmony of all this. The steady flow of the river, the sturdy but delicate plant growth along the banks, the amazing array of creatures that call in the night: all so full of energy and harmony that I want to reach out and claim kinship with the wholeness. But at other times I feel as if I'm more of an intruder than a kinsman. So all I can do is pray: "God, let it stay like this forever." I imagine every outdoorsman has felt these emotions and has expressed similar hopes. I didn't need Mr. Allison to caution me about protecting the water and land.

We continued on our trip down the Tesnatee without major mishaps or accidents. The rapids were numerous and exciting, though bumpy from lack of water. Although some in the group commented on what a great run it would be if there were more water, few of them complained about anything. The sky was too clear, the trees too tall, and the springs bubbling out of the rocks on the shore were too inviting for anyone to complain. As we approached the take out, everyone was pleasantly tired and in good spirits.

Everyone, that is, except me. I was downright aggravated at myself for not being able to shake off my feelings about my brief meeting with Mr. Allison. I had been thinking about it all day, and I knew I couldn't let it go. I knew now that I felt so strongly about it, I would have to seek him out again and confront him and let him know who I am—and find out who he is.

The unpaved driveway turned off Towns Creek Road and quickly assumed the appearance of a tunnel covered by the dense forest. I approached the first house. Two weeks had passed since our run, and now I was back to see Mr. A. I was a little wary, not certain of what to expect. A young man with a baby in his arms came across the yard toward me. He introduced himself as Lloyd Allison, Charles' younger brother. He introduced me to their mother. After a few words, Lloyd said that his brother Charles lived just down the road, where he is rebuilding the old homestead. As we drove down the winding road, the signs of many years of life and work around the place were visible on each side: old garden tools, an old equipment shed, and the house that Charles Allison is rebuilding for his family.

"Charles and his wife are expecting a baby any day now," Lloyd told me. "They are living in that mobile home there behind the house until he finishes rebuilding it."

As we drove between the old house and the mobile home, Charles Allison came out onto the front-door platform of the trailer. Lloyd and I got out of the car, and he told his brother that I had returned to talk to them.

"Yeah, I remember you," Allison said as we approached. I could see his pregnant wife lying on the sofa just inside the trailer's door.

"I hear you're gonna be a father any time now," I said, hoping to get us off to a friendly start.

"Yeah, we're just kinda waiting for things to happen most any time," he said. His shirt was open at the top, and his jeans were spotted with sawdust from his construction work around the old house. Beyond the house, I could see the overhanging trees on Tesnatee Creek and the place on the bank where Charles Allison had stopped us.

"I guess you folks thought I came down on you pretty hard," Allison said.

"Well, Mr. Allison, we just wanted you to know we weren't trying to trespass on your property," I said. "We just came up to canoe the creek."

"Every time I hear anybody down on the creek nowadays, I go down to see who it is," he explained.

"What do you men think of people canoeing rivers and creeks and that kind of thing?" I asked them both.

"Well," Lloyd began, "it's an OK thing to do, I guess. We're outdoors types ourselves. We grew up in these woods, hunting in the fall and swimming and fishing in the creek in spring and summer. I know every rock and pothole on that creek. We used to walk barefooted all the way down it when we were kids."

"But you don't want canoeists coming on Tesnatee Creek, do you?" I asked him pointedly.

"It's not that we don't want them, exactly," Charles Allison said. "It'd be fine if folks would come in and just leave things alone, and leave it like they find it. But the trouble is, you can't control it any more. We used to have just fishermen and the sportsman types come on the creek, and we didn't have trouble with them. But nowadays you got all kinds of folks coming in here, and you can't control it any more."

"You mean canoeists?" I asked.

"Some of them are in canoes," he replied, "and some in rafts and tubes and all kinds of floats. Some of them are rowdy, beer-drinking crowds that really mess things up. I had to go down there not long ago and stop a crowd from throwing beer bottles up against the rocks just to see them bust in the river."

"Did you ask them to leave?"

"Well," he began thoughtfully, "you can't come down on folks like that too forceful. You never know when that kind will come back and set fire to your place just to get back at you."

"We don't want trouble with anybody," Lloyd said. "But we gotta take care of the Tesnee Creek. This has been our land since Grandpa bought it years ago from the old Courtney estate. We were born and raised on it, and we don't want to leave it. We thought of leaving it, like all boys do when they grow up and want to move on. And we could have found jobs away from here that paid more and offered more. But we decided we didn't want to leave these mountains and the creek. Mama and Daddy are living in the house down there by the road, I'm living in the house up yonder," he said, pointing through the trees, "and Charles is rebuilding the old home place for his family. We want our children to grow up here like we did, so they can swim and fish and hunt like we did. So they can walk barefooted down the creek like we did. But you can't walk barefooted down a creek that's full of beer bottles."

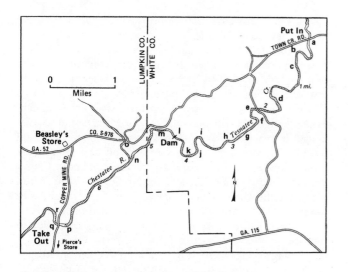

CANOEING GUIDE

Tesnatee Creek

General Information: Tesnatee Creek (called "Tesnee" by area residents) is a whitewater mountain stream that offers the canoeist 6.8 miles of unspoiled beauty and technical challenge. A tributary of its better-known neighbor, the Chestatee River, Tesnatee Creek bounces out of the hills of White County to begin its short but active life. After about six miles it becomes canoeable where it's joined by Town Creek, at the Town Creek Rd bridge, 3.6 miles west of Cleveland. After Town Creek bridge it begins to drop at a rate of from 20 to 40 feet per mile. This steep gradient creates numerous Class I and II rapids, with some (the Trash Pile and Capitol Steps Rapids) approaching a mild Class III in high water. Although they're not particularly dangerous, these rapids are of the shelf type rather than the chute type (except for the chute at the end of the Trash Pile): bouncy and scrapey, inviting a sideways tumble with accompanying bumps and bruises. Inexperienced canoeists should walk down these sections; experienced canoeists can bump down them, exercising caution to avoid being swept sideways.

The quiet stretches between the rapids allow the canoeist time to enjoy the mountain scenery of dense forests, high rock faces, and mountain laurel. Tesnatee Creek remains largely unaffected by man. The one major exception is the dramatic intrusion of the old DuGoss Dam at mile 4.3. The eerie appearance of the old dam, with its gutted tower rising against the mountainous background, has caused local residents to name this stretch of the Tesnatee "Hobbit Land," after J. R. R. Tolkien's creatures of Middle Earth (one wishes that some little spying elf would come out of his hiding place to lend a hand with the arduous portage required around this 10-foot dam and the 20-foot waterfall just below it). The dam and waterfall are not runnable, and the portage is steep, but it's worth it. Standing under that waterfall refreshes both body and soul.

The canoeist on the Tesnatee can have the added treat of seeing some of the Chestatee River's main attractions. Upon paddling into the Chestatee River (at mile 5.3), he or she is treated to a dramatic view of Grindle Shoals (sometimes called Chestatee Falls) some 300 yards upstream. The canoeist can paddle, pole, or tow—whatever his or her skill permits—up for a closer look at this spectacular, 75-foot cascade. Then, after a 1.6-mile paddle on the Chestatee, the take out (above or below the famed Copper Mine Rapids at the new Copper Mine Rd bridge) is reached.

Water Levels: Water level is the most crucial concern when considering a run on the Tesnatee. The creek has no water gauge, so the canoeist must check the Chestatee River gauge on the Ga 52 bridge, 3.8 miles east of Dahlonega. Don't be fooled by the old gauge station you'll see 100 yards or so upstream: there's no gauge there. The active gauge is on the bridge itself, on the upstream side of the western-most concrete piling. You'll have to wade the river from the east bank to be able to read it. Access from the west bank under the bridge is blocked by a barbed-wire fence. High-powered binoculars might make a reading possible from the east bank, but the water-level markings are likely to be covered by debris; so go ahead, and get wet early, since you must get a reading from this gauge. When we waded across, the water came up to our seats. The gauge read 0.60—extremely low, and far below the recommended level for running the Tesnatee. Minimum acceptable level for canoeing the Tesnatee causes a reading of at least 1.5 at the Chestatee gauge; the ideal level is 3.

Shuttle: If the Chestatee River gauge on Ga 52 indicates sufficient water for a Tesnatee run, drive east on 52 from the Chestatee bridge for 3.6 miles, past its junction with Ga 115, to the point where 52 and 115 divide at Pierce's General Merchandise Store. Turn sharply left on Copper Mine Rd here, and drive 1.9 miles to New Copper Mine bridge over the Chestatee River. If you do *not* want to run Copper Mine Rapids (see "Hazards," below), take the access road to the take out *before* you cross the bridge; it leads to the left at the southwest corner of the bridge, where you'll find ample parking space as well as the old copper-mine shaft, which warrants a visit. If you choose to run the healthy Class III Copper Mine Rapids, use the access road beyond the bridge, .7 mile up the hill and to your left. This road will take you .6 mile back down to the north bank of the river below Copper Mine Rapids.

After dropping your shuttle vehicle, drive 1.3 miles north from the Copper Mine Rd bridge to where Ga 52 joins the old Cleveland-Dahlonega Rd (County Rd S-976) at Mrs. Beasley's store. Turn right here, and drive .9 mile to the point where the pavement ends at Grindle Bridge over the Chestatee River. After crossing the bridge, turn right onto a dirt road, and drive 2.7 miles to where it meets Town Creek Rd (paved, and still County Rd S-976). Bear right onto the paved road, and drive .5 mile to the put in at Town Creek Rd bridge.

The put in is moderately strenuous with limited space. Unload vehicles at the northwest corner of the bridge, but do not leave them there. Leave this private road, and leave vehicles on the shoulder of Town Creek Rd. The only path to the river begins in the bushes at the northwest corner of the bridge, where the metal guardrail joins the concrete bridge.

Hazards: Most of the rapids on the Tesnatee are Class I and II, with few complications. The shelflike construction of the Trash Pile and Capitol Steps Rapids create shallow conditions at almost any water level. Canoes may turn sideways, resulting in a bruising tumble. The inexperienced are advised to portage or to walk their canoes down these rapids. The portage around DuGoss Dam and Falls is steep. Watch for broken glass on rocks at the lower end of the portage.

The famed Copper Mine Rapids at the take out on the Chestatee are substantial Class III rapids and should be scouted carefully. Normally, the best run is just to the left of the large boulder in the middle of the river at the top of the rapids. Varying water levels, however, will make other routes possible.

Distances: The total length of this Tesnatee-Chestatee run is 6.8 miles. But sightseeing, portages, and scouting will make this a full-day run. Shuttle mileage is 5.4 miles.

Alternate put ins for shorter runs are at the Ausbury Mill Rd bridge and at Old Cleveland-Dahlonega Rd.

Maps: US Geological Survey topo maps of both the Cleveland and Dahlonega quadrangles, which include this run, are available, but they are of 1951 vintage and do not show roads and bridges around the Copper Mine Rd bridge. Topo maps can be obtained from the Georgia Geologic Survey, 19 Martin Luther King Jr Dr, Atlanta 30334; (404) 656-3214.

Index to Map: Numbers indicate river mileage.

a. Put in at Town Creek bridge.
b. First noteworthy shoals (mile .5).
c. The Trash Pile at mile .8. Enter at far right, then edge back to center.
d. Capitol Steps Rapids (Moody Shoals) at mile 1.7.
e. Ausbury Mill Rd bridge.
f. Class I shoals continue past bridge to this point.
g. Flat stretch to mile 3 at entrance of Shoal Creek on left.
h. Shoals just beyond mile 3.
i. Good Class II shoals. Enter at left, and cut across to right.
j. Scenic loop to mile 4 (power line at mile 4).
k. Backwaters of DuGoss Dam begin.
l. DuGoss Dam and Falls. Portage required down right (north) bank, down path next to old tower; launch at foot of waterfall.
m. Old Cleveland-Dahlonega Rd parallels river (mile 4.5); good access.
n. Junction with Chestatee River (mile 5.3).
o. Chestatee Falls (Grindle Shoals) visible upstream on Chestatee River.
p. Small wooden dam.
q. Take out above Copper Mine Rapids.
r. Take out below Copper Mine Rapids.

1981

The Surprise of Lookout Creek

When the water's down, you don't have to be

by Reece Turrentine

For me, Lookout Creek is literally an unexpected river, a delightful surprise that I came upon while in the extreme northwestern corner of Georgia to scout and canoe the west fork of the famed Little River. A low water level rendered the Little River impassable. So, after spending several fruitless hours scouting other familiar rivers in the area, all with water levels too low for canoeing, I was ready to call it quits and head for home. Then I crossed a bridge bearing a sign that says, "Lookout Creek." I glanced over the bridge rail at the waters below. What I saw made me stop my car, walk back to the bridge, and take a closer look. Passing beneath me was a briskly flowing and substantial stream. Immediately, questions popped into mind. Why is this creek full while others are all but dry? Where does the stream come from, and where does it go? Does it have whitewater or calm water—or both? Is it canoeable? A few inquiries at a nearby little town with the lyrical name of

Rising Fawn answered most of my questions and introduced me to a new canoeable friend.

Lookout Creek runs through Lookout Valley, along the base of Lookout Mountain. It begins just across the state line near the little town of Valley Head, Alabama, and flows northeastward, slicing across the extreme northwestern corner of Georgia, then into Tennessee, where it empties into the mighty Tennessee River at the base of Lookout Mountain in Chattanooga. It weaves its way through Georgia for 30 miles, in and out of wilderness areas and pastureland, offering the canoeist briskly flowing flat waters and a moderate number of Class I shoals. Scenery varies dramatically during the nine-mile run covered in this guide: at one moment you'll pass through heavy forests, the next through open pastureland that offers impressive views of Lookout Mountain, your constant companion to the east.

Strange things seem to happen in this corner of Georgia, an area of canyons and caverns. Although the headwaters of Lookout Creek are scarcely a mile from the headwaters of the Little River, these two neighboring rivers flow in opposite directions. The former flows north, placidly winding through Lookout Valley. The latter flows south, roaring violently down the spine of the mountain. The explanation: although born in the same neighborhood, the streams belong to different watersheds. Lookout Creek belongs to the Tennessee Valley watershed, and the Little River to the Coosa Valley watershed. This fact also explains why Lookout Creek can maintain its water level: it's filled by water running off the western slopes of the entire Lookout Mountain plateau, while its rocky-bottomed neighbor up on the mountain, fed by a smaller watershed, can quickly run dry.

CANOEING GUIDE

Lookout Creek

Lookout Creek is located in the northwestern tip of Georgia. It flows northeastward through Lookout Valley in Dade County, parallel to the Georgia sections of I-59, US 11, and the Alabama Great Southern Railroad. Larry Longshore, a canoeing friend of mine who lives nearby, canoed the nine-mile section between Rising Fawn and Trenton with me.

Directions: Highways that lead to the northwestern tip of Georgia are scarce and curvy. Leave I-75 at the Ga 136 exit, 5 miles north of Calhoun. Drive west on 136 for 55 miles to Trenton. You will cross the take-out bridge as you enter Trenton. Turn left onto US 11 South in Trenton, and drive 7.5 miles to Rising Fawn. Turn left (east) on Furnace Road in Rising Fawn (at Mac's Gun and Tackle Shop), and drive .3 mile to the put-in bridge.

Shuttle: The take-out bridge is on Ga 136, .7 mile east of where 136 meets US 11 in Trenton. The best take-out spot, however, is not at the bridge itself, but down a dirt road that runs south along the west side of the creek for .2 mile to a good access point above an old mill dam. Leave your shuttle car here.

To reach the put in, return to Trenton on 136, turn south (left) on US 11, and drive 7.5 miles to Rising Fawn. Turn left (east) on Furnace Road at Mac's Gun and Tackle Shop, and drive .3 mile to the put-in bridge. Best access to the river is at the northwest corner of the bridge: follow a narrow path to the creek's edge. Respect private property on the southeast corner of the bridge.

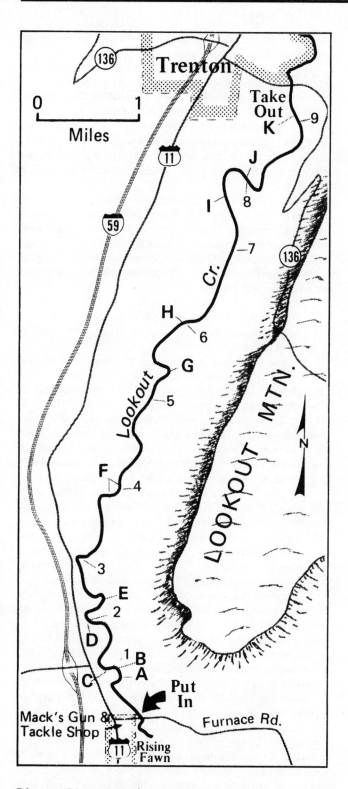

Distance: River mileage from the put in to the take out is 9 miles (the entire length of Lookout Creek in Georgia is 30 miles). This 9-mile stretch can be canoed in a leisurely 4 hours, plus an hour for lunch.

Hazards: The shoals on Lookout Creek are not hazardous. None exceed Class I or II. Fallen trees may, however, present a problem in the swift current. Local canoeists run Lookout Creek frequently and generally do a good job of keeping passageways through tree-

falls open. (Wouldn't it be nice if all canoeists carried a small saw or hatchet for such purposes?) Although this stream is safe for families with children, canoeists should, as always, wear life vests and keep valuables in waterproof containers that are tied down.

Water levels: Lookout Creek has no water gauges. The creek is usually runnable except in periods of extreme drought. It's fed by numerous streams on the western slopes of Lookout Mountain, and it makes an ideal summer canoeing stream for those visiting the mountain country of northwestern Georgia.

Accommodations: Cloudland Canyon State Park offers cottages, camping, and breathtaking views of several canyons. It's located 7 miles east of Trenton on Ga 136. Thirteen miles north of Trenton on US 11 or I-59 is the tourist area around Lookout Mountain, near Rock City, where numerous motels and restaurants are located.

Map Guide: Numbers on our map indicate river mileage; letters identify points of interest.

a. High rock outcroppings and small cave, about 10 feet below the top of the ledge.
b. Railroad trestle over creek (1 mile from put in).
c. Small shoals.
d. Allison Creek enters on left (2 miles from put in).
e. Interesting old iron bridge crosses creek, possibly homemade, with concrete-filled oil drums for foundation and iron pipes for runners.
f. Nice rapids. Run to the left of the island. Notice old mill foundations and limestone outcroppings.
g. Power lines cross creek.
h. Railroad trestle crosses creek. Watch for fallen tree in rapids just below trestle.
i. Nice shoals just before Turners Creek enters on left.
j. Creek bends to the southeast; good view of Cloudland Canyon State Park on top of mountain. The little mound in the pasture on the right is a training mound for hang-gliding students.
k. Take out on left, just above old mill dam.

1981

The Dark Eye of God

And just when you thought you were out of sight

by Reece Turrentine

When canoeists talk among themselves about the Etowah River, opinions are strong and contradictory. Some say, "Canoe the river, but stay out of the tunnel. It's too dark and unpredictable." But others disagree. They say, "When you canoe the Etowah, don't miss the tunnel. It's the experience of a lifetime." Canoe the tunnel! Don't canoe the tunnel! What tunnel? Whoever heard of canoeing a tunnel, anyway? After hearing the argument one time too many, I knew that it was time to go to the Etowah.

I stopped by Don Otey's Buckhorn Mountain Shop in Gainesville to ask him about the river. Otey, with his associate Bob Sehlinger, wrote *Southern Georgia Canoeing* and *Northern Georgia Canoeing,* so I was sure he'd be able to help me. "Yeah, I've been through it," he said. "When do you want to go?" And the next morning, Don and I were paddling down the warming waters of the Etowah River just south of Dahlonega. My wet suit kept my body warm enough, but the thought of that tunnel sent a chill of expectation through my mind. I couldn't imagine what it would be like to canoe almost a quarter of a mile through an old gold-mine tunnel.

Dahlonega is in gold country, and the Etowah River runs right through the heart of it. So we watched the shores of the river as we paddled: you never can tell when rain might uncover some hitherto hidden nugget. Gold mining in Georgia was no joke in 1828, when the nation's first gold rush brought thousands of miners, and those who preyed on them, to the state, and, really, it's no joke now. Even though the major mining companies have gone, serious prospectors can still be found in the remote valleys and river bends.

Don and I drifted through gentle pools and ran over shoals for several miles without much conversation. It occurred to me that I wasn't canoeing this river as I have others. Usually, my eyes scan ahead, looking for possible danger. Or else I watch the scenery, study rock formations, and stay alert for wildlife. But on the Etowah my gaze was diverted down, over the gunwale of the canoe, scanning the bottom of the river. Gold fever had me, mildly, in its grip. I bumped into rocks I should have seen and even bumped embarrassingly into Don's canoe. I knew that finding any gold was unlikely, but I also knew that it was possible.

"There it is," Don called from ahead. I thought he'd found a nugget, but when I looked up and saw what he was pointing at, I forgot about gold. Recessed in a deep gully on the shore was a giant black hole in the hillside: the Etowah Tunnel. As if it were a mouth in the mountain, it swallowed water from the river. We weren't ready to risk entering that gaping mouth unexplored, so we edged toward it cautiously and prepared to explore the entrance on foot. The tunnel's entrance bore patches of moss and the stains of old age: it's been there for nearly 50 years.

On the day before our trip, we'd visited Charles Davis, a real-estate broker at Arcadian Properties in Marietta, to learn something about the history of the Etowah Tunnel. "My grandfather helped dig that tunnel when he was a little boy," he'd said. The shelves in his office were lined with Indian relics and mining paraphernalia, collected during his family's many years of involvement in land and mining in the Georgia mountains. "The old Etowah Mining Company blasted that tunnel through the mountain back in the 1930s," he continued. "Actually, it was not dug as a mine itself, but as a water tunnel to divert the river through the mountain and dry up one mile of the river for mining. They blasted the tunnel, but they had to bore the air shafts."

"What air shafts?" I asked.

"The vertical shafts from the top of the mountain down to the ceiling of the tunnel below," he explained. "They had to dig them to provide fresh air in the tunnel for the workers. It was quite an engineering feat for those days."

As Don and I studied the entrance to the tunnel, it became obvious that not much water was pouring into it. That didn't bother us, however: if you're going to canoe the Etowah Tunnel, it's better to have too little water than too much. Attempting a run through it in high water would be disastrous in that tight space, and the prospect seemed dangerous enough without high waters. The relatively low waters meant that the first criterion for determining the runnability of the tunnel had been met.

Beyond the few feet that were illuminated by the light at the entrance, the tunnel was utterly dark, except for the tiny splotch of brightness at the distant exit at the other end of the tunnel. Seeing that light at the far end meant that the second important criterion had been met: it was unlikely that any trees or other large debris that might block our way had washed into the seven-foot-high tunnel.

"Ready to try it?" I asked Don.

"Well, at least it's not dangerous at this low water level," he replied. "We might have to do some dragging, but we ought to get through all right."

We got back into our canoes, and I held back as Don drifted into the entrance. I watched him pole with his paddle through some loose gravel at the beginning; then suddenly he was swallowed by the tunnel's darkness. I gave him a few moments to get well ahead of me, and then I too plunged into the tunnel. I shoved through the gravel, and then everything went black. My canoe lurched and jerked; the current was swift but shallow, and only a few yards from the entrance I ground to a stop. Frankly, I was relieved. I needed a few minutes to accustom my eyes to the darkness. I could see Don and his canoe silhouetted against the light from the far end. I called ahead to him, but my words were lost, reflected by the walls of the tunnel until they were nothing but incomprehensible reverberations. Even after my shouts died, the noise made by the water inside the tunnel was deafening: no heavy rapids are inside the shaft, only a couple of small ledges, but the sounds of the water running over these was magnified, as my voice had been.

Over the water sounds, I could hear Don's canoe bumping and thumping on the rocks ahead, so I knew that I faced a stop-and-go ride. I put my paddle to work: pushing, braking, prying, and dragging. I welcomed the times when I ground to a halt on the bottom of the channel. They allowed me a few moments to take in the sights and sounds that surrounded me. My canoe has taken me to some strange places, but this place topped them all.

I had made it through about half of the tunnel when I noticed that the roar of the water was getting louder; some kind of turbulence was just ahead of me. Nothing to do but get ready for it. I spread my knees, flattened my paddle in the water as a brace, and prepared for whatever was about to happen. My canoe lurched forward and dropped out from under me. My heart skipped a beat, but the crisis was over almost before it started. The little ledge I'd just gone over couldn't have been more than a foot high, but it had sounded as loud as Niagara

HIGHLANDS

Falls. Then, before my nerves (and stomach) had had time to settle, I encountered another surprise: a beam of light shot down on me from above. I noticed it first on the bow of the canoe, and then it was on me. I felt as if I had suddenly been exposed by some questioning searchlight aimed by God and asking me, "What are you doing down there?" I jabbed my paddle into the bottom to stop my canoe and looked up. A vertical shaft four feet wide passed through the earth above me to the mountaintop over 100 feet above the tunnel. At its end, I could see blue sky. I had found one of the air shafts that Mr. Davis had told us about. Looking through it, I felt as if I were looking up from the center of the earth.

Two weeks after my run, I returned to the tunnel and climbed the ridge through which it runs to search for the air shaft. I wanted to look through it from the top. Malcolm Lewis, director of nearby Blackburn Park, accompanied me to the entrance, where I used a compass to determine the direction of the tunnel. After I determined its heading, we climbed the ridge and hiked across it on a line that we assumed was directly above the tunnel. The climb was steep and tough, but our efforts were rewarded: we found that gaping hole in the ground. I chose a small tree with a good root system at the edge of the shaft and planted my foot firmly among the roots. After testing to make sure that the roots would hold my weight, I gradually swung my body out over the open shaft. A steady updraft of cold air blew in my face as I gazed down into the darkness, hearing the river's distant roar before I could see its waters. Then, as my eyes adjusted to the dark, I saw the river flowing through the tunnel far below. I was looking down on the place from which I had looked up just two weeks before. I felt as if I were looking at myself in a different time, in a different world.

But that experience was still in the future. At the moment, I was down in the tunnel, looking up, wondering if I would ever be up there looking down. And I had to finish my trip under the mountain.

I could see Don breaking out into the light at the exit, so I knew that I'd meet no major obstacles before I was through. After a few small drops and bumps, I, too, moved into the light at the exit, then out of the tunnel. I beached my canoe beside Don's. "That's something else," was all I could say.

"I don't know anything like it for canoeists," Don replied.

We paddled the remainder of our trip down the Etowah mechanically, preoccupied with our private thoughts about that incredible tunnel. Charles Davis had told us, as we sat in his Marietta office on the day before our trip, that the tunnel project was not as productive as the old mining company had hoped. Little gold was found. That's too bad; a lot of effort and dreams went into the tunnel. But that was the way of life in those days: wild dreams, extravagant efforts, and colossal failures.

Although few people may ever see the Etowah Tunnel, it will be there, carved out of solid rock. It's a time tunnel, waiting for some adventuresome canoeist, who, if conditions are just right, will take a fantastic voyage back in time, through the center of the earth.

CANOEING GUIDE

Upper Etowah River

General Information: I'm surprised that canoeists don't flock to the upper section of the Etowah River. Local residents canoe it, as do students from North Georgia College in Dahlonega. But canoeists from the rest of the state don't come here. It offers canoeists a potpourri of river and wilderness experiences: whitewater (numerous Class I, II, and III rapids), deep-blue holes for swimming or fishing, a waterfall, easy access from the highway and good shuttle roads, an old mine tunnel, and perhaps even some gold dust to help defray expenses. It is an ideal river for beginning canoeists, families, and organized groups who want to run a brisk mountain river and also be close to the scenic and historical attractions in the Dahlonega area.

The 12-mile section described in this guide can be run in a day of steady paddling. But what's the hurry? Take time to explore the waterfall and the tunnel. If you want to take two days for your run, you can stop at Castleberry Bridge and camp at nearby Blackburn Park, which has developed campsites, including water and electric hookups. The park's manager, Malcolm Lewis, is a fine canoeist and is anxious to provide accommodations and activities geared to canoeists. More comfortable accommodations are available in Dahlonega, only seven miles north on Ga 9E.

The name "Etowah" comes from the Cherokee word *Etawa* or *Itawa*. The early settlers in the area turned that into "hightower," a familiar name in these parts. Nearby are the Hightower community and a famous old Indian trail called the Hightower Trail. Many older people here refer to the river as the Hightower River.

Shuttle: If you plan to canoe this 12-mile run in one day, drive south from the bridge over the Etowah on US 19 for 7.2 miles. Turn left at the intersection of US 19 and GA 136, and continue on 136 for 5.2 miles to the take-out bridge over the Etowah River. Best access to the river is on the south side of the bridge.

If you plan a two-day trip and you want to camp at Blackburn Park, leave the river at the Castleberry Bridge, and drive east on Castleberry Bridge Rd to where it meets Ga 9E in the tiny ghost town of Auraria. Turn right here, and travel 1.3 miles south on 9E to the park's entrance. To leave a shuttle car at the Castleberry Bridge, drive 3.5 miles north on US 19 from the put-in bridge to 19's intersection with Ga 9E. Turn right here, and drive 5 miles south on 9E to Auraria and Castleberry Bridge Rd, the only road that branches from 9E in town. Drive .9 mile west to the Castleberry Bridge take out.

Water Levels: Check the water level at the put in before you leave your shuttle car. The water-level gauge that used to be on US 19 at the put-in bridge is gone, so you'll have to check the bridge pilings. On the day we ran the Etowah, the water was brushing over the top of the square concrete foot of the bridge piling nearest the north bank, a little lower than the ideal level for this trip. Someone has painted a red line just above the foot of the piling; it's visible from the north shore, under the bridge. If the water is above that red line, the water levels at the waterfall and tunnel will be dangerously high.

Hazards: For the most part, the rapids on the Etowah are mild or moderate. Several features on the river are, however, potentially hazardous. The first potential hazard is Chuck Shoals (.3 mile downstream from the put-in bridge). High water could make the run through these shoals a complicated one. Enter the shoals from the left, and move toward the main chute in the middle.

The waterfall 1½ miles from the put-in bridge can also be dangerous. These falls are jagged and steep; they should be por-

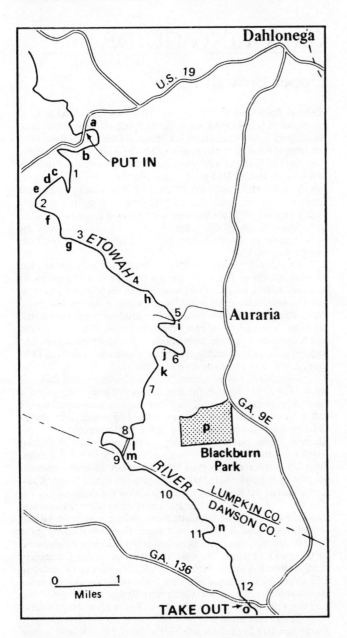

great care. This is definitely not a canoe's natural habitat, and unexpected difficulties are likely. If you feel any doubts about conditions in the tunnel or about your ability, stay out of the tunnel, and follow the main channel around it.

Distance: This guide covers just over 12 miles from the put-in bridge on US 19 to the take-out bridge on Ga 136. Although the distance does not seem excessive for a one-day trip, seeing the waterfalls, the tunnel, and other scenic attractions takes time. I advise taking two days and camping at Blackburn Park.

Camping: Excellent camping is available at Blackburn Park, 1.3 miles south of Auraria off Ga 9E. Also available here are swimming in a lake with a sandy beach, fishing, hiking, archery, a nature museum, and rental equipment for gold panning. The park has primitive group campsites and campsites with water and power hookups.

Map Guide: Numbers on the map indicate river mileage. Letters represent the following points.

(a). Put-in bridge on US 19.
(b). Chuck Shoals.
(c). Shoals just above waterfalls.
(d). Dangerous 10-foot falls.
(e). More shoals below falls.
(f). Shoals with small ledge.
(g). Scenic waterfalls on right bank.
(h). Moderate, twisting rapids.
(i). Castleberry Bridge.
(j). Moderate rapids.
(k). More shoals.
(l). Tunnel entrance on left bank.
(m). Tunnel exit.
(n). Scenic cliffs.
(o). Take-out bridge on Ga 136.
(p). Blackburn Park.

1981

Short Ride On a Long River

A canoeing guide to what we've got left of the Coosawattee

by Gary DeBacher, with Reece Turrentine

The Coosawattee River was once as fine a whitewater stream as the Chattooga. In fact, canoeing insiders believe that James Dickey's novel, *Deliverance*, the film of which was shot on the Chattooga, was actually written more with the Coosawattee in mind than that other wild North Georgia river. In 1974, however, the Army Corps of Engineers' construction of Carters Dam left only the upper reaches of the river of interest to canoeists.

taged. Land on the rocks near the right bank, observe the falls, take pictures, have a picnic, and then portage over or around the rocks to the right.

Another hazard is, of course, the old mine tunnel. This tunnel is only about seven feet in diameter, and it's about ⅕ of a mile long. The distant exit opening, visible from the entrance, is a key factor in determining the safety of running the tunnel. If the exit light is not clear and bright, don't enter the tunnel: stumps or trash may be lodged inside. Water level should be low: just enough to float a canoe. You might scrape bottom and have to push your canoe along (be careful of slippery footing), but that's better than being trapped against the low roof of the tunnel by high water. A fallen tree has washed across the gully leading to the tunnel entrance, which may restrict water flow into the tunnel except during flood conditions. The tunnel is quite dark, but a flashlight is of questionable value. In most circumstances, it's best to let your eyes get used to the dark. If you have to get out and walk, slide your feet along the bottom with extreme caution. You'll be feeling your way in the dark. Whether you paddle or walk, however, calculate each move with

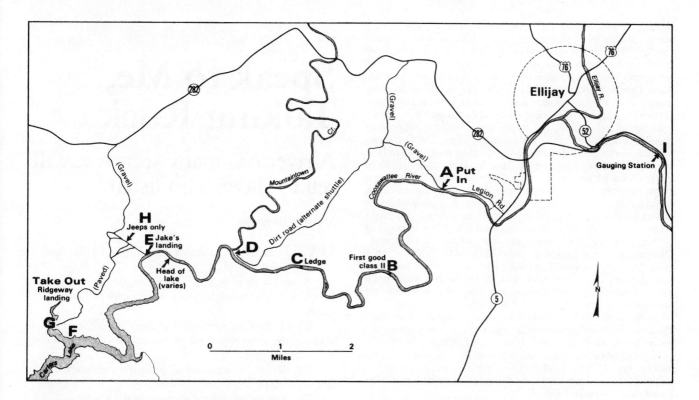

In September of 1979, Gary DeBacher, who is active in the Georgia Canoeing Association, canoed the shortened Coosawattee and found it an enjoyable stream with Class II rapids separated by stretches of easy slackwater. "Since I had previously canoed the stream in 1976," he says, "the only new signs of civilization on the canoeable parts are a second-home development and a riverside park near the beginning of the run. Later on, about three and one half miles into the run, the scenery gets a lot better, largely of a wilderness character all the way down to the lake. Take it easy on this section, since it's easy to find yourself at the lake before you've had your fill of the river."

DeBacher warns that the point where the moving water ends and the lake impounded by Carters Dam begins "can vary by as much as three quarters of a mile, depending on variations in the lake's level, so some of the landmarks you'll be looking for around the take out may look somewhat different than expected." Here is Gary DeBacher's guide to the Coosawattee.

CANOEING GUIDE

General Information: The Cartecay and Ellijay Rivers meet in the town of Ellijay to form the Coosawattee, one of the largest rivers in the North Georgia mountains. Once out of town, the river turns west through the southern Cohuttas, carving downward more than 500 feet in 22 miles through a spectacular gorge and emerging through a narrow breach into what geologists call the Great Valley. The highest earth-fill dam east of the Mississippi now fills that breach, and Carters Lake has inundated more than half the river, including the biggest rapids and the highest cliffs. But a fine run of intermediate difficulty remains on the upper section, past forested bluffs, and it is as yet little affected by development. Even the lake

is free of marinas and second homes, since the U.S. government owns the land around it right back to the ridgetops. Because of the open nature of this river, affording wide views of the surrounding forest, it is most scenic in April, when the trees are leafing out, and in October during the fall color display. Although the river gradient is almost 30 feet per mile in places, the rapids do not exceed Class II and are separated by easy flat sections which allow paddlers to relax and enjoy the scenery.

The run described spans 12.5 miles from Legion Road southwest of Ellijay to Ridgeway boat ramp, down on the lake. Under most conditions, you're better off paddling tandem, to share the burden of four miles of lake paddling facing prevailing winds. Rafters may find the lake paddling too much to handle, but they can still make the run if they have a friend to help them out on the lake with a powerboat.

Put In and Take Out: To find the put in, first locate the Ga 5 bridge over the Coosawattee south of Ellijay. On the north side of the bridge, turn west on Legion Rd and drive about a mile to where the road comes right to the river's edge **(A)**. Please be considerate of the folks in the house just upstream. You can also put in a couple of miles upstream at the Gilmer County Park, just south of the intersection of Ga 5 and Ga 282.

To reach the take out, go back out Legion Rd to Ga 5, up to Ga 282, and west about 8 miles, watching for a large sign directing you to the Ridgeway access area. The road to Ridgeway will turn from gravel to packed dirt. Some ruts and slick spots may worry you, but stick with it—you will soon come to good blacktop and signs directing you to the boat ramp **(G)**.

Our map shows two other roads that are the best ways to go if you wish to take out early and avoid paddling the lake. Leading from Legion Rd to the junction **(D)** of Mountaintown Creek and the Coosawattee, before Carters Lake, is a long, sinuous dirt road which, except after rain, can often be negotiated by determined drivers in ordinary cars. You'll miss the last two miles of river, but you may gain enough time to run Mountaintown Creek the same day. The other road, **(H)**, for which you must watch carefully when driving toward Ridgeway boat ramp, is for jeeps only, but you could leave your shuttle car at the top of the road. The ¾-mile portage is easy by Canadian standards. This road leads to Jake's Landing (E), right at the head of the lake. If you do leave your shuttle car here, walk down the bank and take a good look at the stream and falls, so you can recognize them from the river later on.

Water Levels: With a watershed area of more than 240 square miles at the put in, the Coosawattee carries a lot of water at any season of the year. But through some quirk of local geology, the rapids are quite broad and shallow, and summertime paddlers will need to allow extra time to pick their way down the ledges. The Coosawattee gauge on Legion Rd had been ripped out by floods the last time we checked, but the gauge on the Cartecay (I) about a mile east of Ellijay on Ga 52 isn't too far out of the way. Watch for the metal gauge structure, and climb down the bank to read the scale on a concrete block set right at the water's edge. A reading of 2.0 is minimum for a comfortable Coosawattee run, although you might get by with less. As the reading rises above 2.5, the waves begin to get heavy, and above 3.0, less experienced paddlers should stay off.

Distance: From the Legion Rd put in to the head of the lake is 8.5 miles. Depending on wind and water level, this can take from 2 to 5 hours of paddling time. Allow another 1½ hours to cover the 4 miles on the lake to the Ridgeway boat ramp (G). Note that you must paddle a little way up Tails Creek inlet (F) to find the boat ramp. Be careful not to miss the inlet when coming down the lake.

Hazards: To broach or swamp in high water on a big, wide river always poses rescue problems. Have extra flotation gear in your canoe, wear your life jacket, and if you do end up swimming, remember not to try to stand until you're in the calm water next to shore. If your foot gets caught on a snag in fast water, you may be forced under, life jacket and all.

This wide, open river and the lake face right into the prevailing winds. Check the wind prediction on the weather forecast, and hope for "light and variable." As soon as you reach the reservoir, marked either by slack water or, if the lake is down, by muddy banks and dead trees, watch for a small creek on the right bank, with a waterfall and an unusual poplar which fell across the stream and then proceeded to grow three new trunks from its side. Jake's Landing is on the upstream side of the creek, and it's about ¾ mile up the hill to the dirt jeep road (see above). On weekends in summer months, one or two patrol boats cruise the lake and may offer assistance to wind-stranded paddlers. If you don't scowl at the other powerboaters, they may also offer help. If you opt to buck the winds, try to trim your boat with the bow a little lower than the stern.

Powerboat wakes should be no hazard to anyone who can handle Class II rapids, but for added security, kneel for stability, and keep your life jacket on.

Rapids: The first good Class II rapids (B), about 3½ miles from the put in, are run right of center and have a sneak crosscurrent at the bottom which can strip the boat out from under you. After passing a large island, the river turns west, and you'll come to a 3½-foot ledge (C). The best run is near the right bank. The other rapids are easily scouted from the boat, but in low water, expect a lot of picky maneuvering, and in high water, bring your bailer and your low brace.

Map Guide:

(A) Put in on Legion Road
(B) First good Class II rapids
(C) 3½-foot ledge
(D) Mouth of Mountaintown Creek (optional take out)
(E) Optional take out at Jake's Landing, to avoid lake paddle
(F) Mouth of Tails Creek. Watch for it, or you'll miss your take out.
(G) Take-out boat ramp up Tails Creek, or Ridgeway landing
(H) Possible road for portaging lake
(I) Gauge on the Cartecay

1980

Speak to Me, Talking Rock

A river has many secrets it will tell to those who listen

by Reece Turrentine

"We must be close to Cedar Cliffs," I called back to Dick.

"Couple-a more bends," he grunted, timing a stern stroke to send us neatly through a chute in the rapids of Talking Rock Creek.

Up till then his estimates had been perfect, so I started scanning the steep river banks for the cliffs we'd been waiting to see all morning.

The day before, while scouting the river, we had heard the story of Cedar Cliffs from Mr. Low.

The sign on one side of the road in the hamlet of Talking Rock read "Low's Pulp Wood." The sign on the other side was for "Low's General Store." Through the middle of town ran Talking Rock Creek.

"I think Mr. Low's the man to talk to, don't you?" I asked Dick.

We found him inside the general store sitting at a rustic check-out counter and surrounded by shelves that held everything from pins to plows.

"What can I do for you, gentlemen?" he asked, barely glancing up from his ledger as we walked toward him.

We introduced ourselves as he rang up a purchase for a customer.

"We'd like to know more about Talking Rock Creek," I said.

Though our introductions had rated little interest, this request created an immediate reaction.

"Yeah?" he responded, turning in our direction. "What do you want to know about it?"

"To begin with," I said, "can you tell us where it got its name?"

Mr. Low leaned forward, and for the next 30 minutes, except when he rang up sales, we had each other's undivided attention.

A tribe of Indians, he told us, once lived on the creek right across from Cedar Cliffs. The braves would gather on the edge of the creek to dance and shout up questions to the overhanging rocks. They asked where to hunt, how to avoid floods, whether or not to go to war. The cliffs, the Indians thought, gave back echoes—became talking rocks—faithfully answering important questions in the life of the tribe.

"There are other stories about how Talking Rock Creek got its name," he said, "but that's the most accepted. I got it from my father and he got it from folks further back.

"Dad," he said, his voice lowering and faltering, "was a rural mail carrier on and around this creek for 42 years. He walked it, crossed it, was around and behind it, but he had never been all the way down it in a boat. So when he was 70 years old, I put him in a raft with me to make the trip. Just below Cedar Cliffs, the raft punctured and we had to walk out." Mr. Low recalled the memory with a smile, but the smile quickly faded. When he spoke next, it was with great difficulty.

His father, he said, had been killed a few days before. "Dad still insisted on driving around in his little pickup. A few days ago a big truck hit him just as he turned up on the bridge over Talking Rock Creek."

Dick and I apologized for bringing up a topic so full of memories and recent sorrow, but Mr. Low didn't seem to object to that. Talking Rock is a part of his life. To avoid conversation about the creek would be to avoid conversation about living. And living has been going on around this creek for a long time. But it was an awesome thought, as we discussed it later, that one man's life could be so bound up with a river as to be born near it, live on it, work by it, and then tragically—yet, somehow appropriately—die on it. In this sense all creeks and rivers should bear the name "Talking Rock." All of them could talk of the lives and loves and losses of the generations who lived and died along their banks.

We speed over creeks and rivers on modern bridges and seldom give them a glance or a thought. Why, even that day I had belittled Talking Rock Creek from highway 156 bridge. "Doesn't look like much from here, does it?" I said. I should have known better. Like most people, creeks don't reveal themselves much at points of public viewing. You have to go back into their interior and their history to discover what they are really like.

The fast-flowing water of Talking Rock brought my mind back to the present. As we drew closer to Cedar Cliffs, we passed through a good set of rapids without a bump or a scrape. I felt better, and without looking back or asking, I could tell that Dick felt better, too. That morning we had run into trouble immediately, hanging up on a boulder not 200 yards from our put-in, and after that we had too many bumps and scrapes for experienced canoeists.

"Talk to me, Dick, talk to me," I had encouraged him. "We're doing something wrong."

I had said "we" hoping to share the blame, but I knew better. Dick Dumbleton was practically born in a canoe. It was the only transportation he had at Forest Ranger School in Wanakah, New York, near the Canadian border. That was the way they went to town, to church, or to the trading post. And in the 25 years since then, as a forester for Georgia Craft Corporation, he has kept his skills intact.

The problem was that the two of us had never been in a canoe together. What's more, it had been years since I had canoed from the bow. I felt uncomfortable with the different view and different feel.

"Which is your best side?" Dick called out.

"The right," I yelled back.

"Then stay on that side in the whitewater and pry and draw stroke from there," he advised. "Then I'll know what you're going to do. I can call you strokes you need to make."

That worked fine. From then on we ran into no more trouble.

"We should be at the cliffs any minute," Dick told me. "When we get there, we'll have to be sure and look for Mr. Priest's rock."

I laughed to myself, thinking back to the day before when we had ended up in Mr. Priest's store looking for a Coke and some creek talk.

We found Mr. Priest sitting on the edge of a drink crate with a couple of old mountain dogs snoozing at his feet.

"Where'd the name 'Talking Rock' come from, Mr. Priest?" I had asked.

"Well," he drawled as he shifted his weight on the crate, "word is that some folks once found an old rock in the creek with some Indian writing on it. They got somebody to translate it and it said, 'Turn me over.' So they turned it over and found some more writing on the other side. That said: 'Now turn me back over so I can make a fool outa somebody else.'" He rocked back on the crate and he laughed, and we laughed with him. The old dogs didn't even budge. I guess they were accustomed to laughter around that place.

"That's rough country back yonder," he asserted as he thumb-pointed back over his shoulder through the store, across the field, back through mountains towards the creek. "I used to haul logs with a mule team across that creek when I was a boy," he recalled. "They paid me a dollar a day. Said that made for easy bookkeeping."

I figured we must be in the vicinity of his thumbpoint right now as we moved through the canyon-like cliffs along the creek. It was rugged wilderness, all right. Far different from my superficial bridge view the day before. The canyon walls all but blotted out the sun's rays. And under the clefts of the overhanging rocks were great blocks of ice still untouched by the warmth of this early spring day.

As we rounded a bend, I saw a distinct break in the tree line on the high ridge above. As we came closer, we caught glimpses through the trees of massive rock outcroppings. Then the trees slid by like a great parting curtain, and there in full view was Cedar Cliffs. Long ledges and shelves overlapped their way up to a height of what must have been 70 or 80 feet. Crevices and caves darkened its surface. Its face looked old and weatherworn. We pulled in by a sandbar to view Talking Rock's main attraction.

This was to be our lunch stop, so Dick unfolded his little camper seat. Dave Gale, who, canoeing solo, was the third member of our party, found a rock to sit on and I located a leaning tree that provided perfect viewing. Then we were quiet for a while, eating our lunches and watching the river run past the cliffs. I don't know what the others were thinking, but I could almost picture in my mind Mr. Low's Indian camp with its tepees and camp fires. We were probably eating right on the spot where the ceremonial dances took place and the calls went up to the echoing cliffs above.

My imagination was almost hearing ancient tomtoms when Dave broke the spell with a dream-shattering question: "I wonder if those Indians back then were like some politicians today?"

My visions were busted, so I took the bait and asked, "What do you mean?"

"Well," he said, "some old chiefs probably stacked the deck before the dance, and had a brave hidden in a cave up there who'd be sure and call back the right echoes!"

We chuckled and agreed it was possible. If they played practical jokes by writing on both sides of rocks for fools, they probably stacked the deck at the talking rock, too. In any case, I'm sure their tribal life wasn't all the romantic legend my day-dreams had imagined.

"I'll bring some of my groups on this creek," said Dave, who closed the doors of a successful contracting business in Atlanta to move to Helen and open an outfitting and guide service called the Wildewood Shop. "But I'll make it an over-night trip, unless all of them are experienced canoeists. This is too hard a push for beginners in one day. Besides," he continued with common sense, "why all the rush? People who push for 14 hiking miles a day ought to go for seven, and enjoy it. Instead of canoeing 20 miles a day, they should go for 10, and get something out of it. Why, on this creek, any kind of delay could catch you in the dark. And this is no creek to get caught on in the dark!"

"Amen!" I replied, inserting a little professional terminology, "and we'd better get started ourselves."

I was reluctant to leave Cedar Cliffs. With a little more time I believe I could've really heard those distant tom-toms and legendary echoes from the cliffs. But the more exciting rapids lay before us.

I felt a real exhilaration as we shoved the canoes back into the swift current. The creek was more like a friend now instead of an alien wilderness. We had gotten to know it. We had probed its history, met its people, run its currents, and seen a little of its beauty. And also there was the exhilaration of the companionship—really getting to know people. On such a trip you don't just share a river, you share yourself. You meet on a common ground where titles, stations, and professions don't count. Pretenses are lost among the rapids, and you are accepted as an equal.

Exhilaration is not quite the word. Inspiration is more like it. At least, a canoeing trip contains the necessary ingredients to inspire me: a touch of the visionary to quicken the mind and stir the imagination with such shadowy sounds as ancient tom-toms and echoing cliffs, but balanced with rugged realism, common sense, good humor, and down-to-earth companionship with real people. When I can get that all together, I'm inspired. And that explains the bone-weary but contented sigh that accompanied me to bed late that night. But it also explains why, just before cutting out the light, I went back to the map—to pick out another river, in another place, for another day.

CANOEING GUIDE

General Information: Talking Rock Creek is a beautiful mountain stream deeply etched into the canyon-like foothills of the Cohutta and Blue Ridge Mountains of North Georgia, just northwest of Jasper. Generally running northwest, it empties into the reservoir

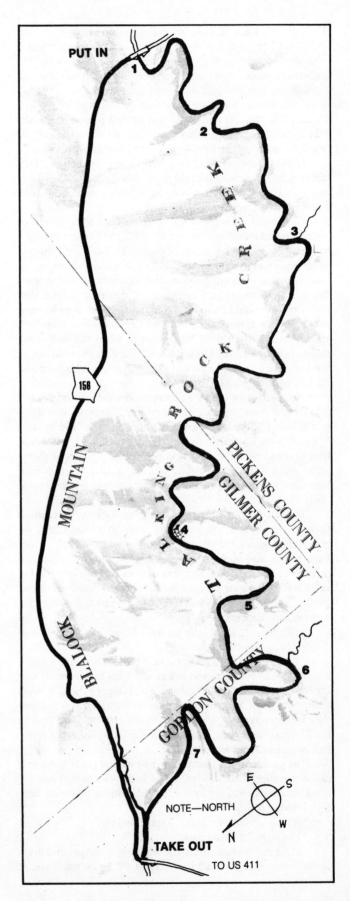

just below Carter's Lake Dam. Wild and remote wilderness. High cliffs and primitive mountain scenery.

Type of River: Clear mountain stream with class I to II rapids advancing to possible IIIs on the last half. (See map guide for locations.)

Shuttle: Put-in and take-out about nine highway miles apart on Georgia 156. Put-in bridge about two miles north of Blaine, Georgia, and take-out bridge where creek runs into reservoir below Carter's Lake Dam. Dirt road on southeast of put-in leads to creek's edge, but should be portaged when muddy. Paved road to creek's edge at take-out bridge.

Water Level: Only water gauge on creek is 4½ miles downstream. You'll need topo maps to find access roads to gauge, but Talking Rock is canoeable under a wide range of conditions. If water is within banks at put-in bridge, it should be safe. A gauge reading of two feet is ideal. Much below that, rapids become fuzzy and require precise paddling. If above three-foot reading, expect most smaller rapids to be washed out but a wild ride on the larger ones. (Only for experienced canoeists.)

Distance: Creek distance from bridge to bridge is 15 miles. Steady paddling by experienced canoeists makes a six-hour trip feasible. A raft trip should take about 10 hours, and a tube float trip would take two days.

Hazards: The most serious hazard would be trying to push daylight hours. This is extremely rugged country with few access roads. (See map guide.) ALL canoeists should be equipped with compass and overnight survival gear. Life-vests should be worn, not just carried along. Expect possible headwinds during the last three miles, cutting into travel time considerably. Expect possible Class III rapids beyond Cedar Cliffs (see map). This creek is too long and tricky for beginners unless accompanied by experienced canoeists.

Map Information: *Miles 0–3:* Action begins just beyond put-in bridge with class II chute near right bank (1). A half-mile downstream you approach a bushy gravel island that squeezes water towards both banks. We ran right side, hugging the island. Two miles downstream, look for Scarecrow Cliffs on right, first of the many cliff formations that border creek (2).

Miles 3–5: Only water gauge (3) is 4½ miles downstream where Scarecrow Creek enters Talking Rock on the left. (Remember, two feet is ideal, above three feet is wild.) There is an exit road at water gauge near old cabin (the only cabin on creek). Good idea to check travel time at this point. If it's taken over two hours to reach this point, you're too slow for a one-day run. It's doubtful you'll make it before dark.

Miles 5–7: Pleasant section of Class I and II rapids, most of them straightforward and fun. Good section to view scenery and cliffs. Many beautiful fishing holes if this is two-day run.

Miles 7–9: Cedar Cliffs are at mile 8. This is a must stop. Ideal for lunch or overnight camp. Use extreme caution climbing cliffs. This is no place for injuries. Exit road from cliff area at this point long and twisting. Bad place to have to leave; the real fun is yet to come.

Miles 9–11: Area of Class II and possibly III rapids. About a mile beyond Cedar Cliffs, watch for rocky island which constricts stream into powerful chute with haystack rapids close to left bank. Scout this on foot and make your plans. This is fun, though tricky. More strong rapids just beyond it, leading to another good chute near right bank (5). Occasional jeep trails seen during this stretch, but may not lead anywhere useful.

Miles 11–15: Raccoon Branch Falls enters creek on left (6). Class II rapids taper down to Class I, then fizzle out altogether by mile 13. You're in the backwaters of the reservoir and paddling will be deadwater until take-out bridge just downstream. So, just dig in and practice your J stroke.

1977

Dave Gale's Secret River

You've heard of the Hooch? The upper Hooch? Well, say hello to the upper, *upper* Hooch!

by Reece Turrentine

Dave's old shake-rattle-and-roll truck was grinding away. It strained at the hills and creaked at the curves. We had left the little town of Helen far below us and were climbing high into the mountains. The Chattahoochee River was visible out my window, but I caught only a glimpse of it now and then, far below the roadbed.

This part of the Chattahoochee was new to me. Canoeing the section below Helen is old hat. But the section above Helen? I didn't believe it could be done.

"It's my favorite section of the river if you can catch the water right," Dave had said earlier. "I don't take charter groups on it. It's too tight and unpredictable. Besides, I kind of like to save it for myself. But you got to see this and run it." So now we were heading up into the mountains.

"How far up are we going for our put in?" I yelled to Dave above the rattles.

"Well, I'm kind of thinking about that," he replied, glancing at his watch. "You got anything to eat in that old canoe case of yours?"

"You hungry already?" I asked, recalling his notable appetite.

"No, I'm thinking about something else," he explained. "How would you like to make this an all-day run and go way back into the mountains? We're getting an early start and the water looks right. We can do it if you got anything in that old box we can eat for lunch."

I reached down and found the handle of the old, scratched-up, olive-drab, World War II ammo box I've been dragging around for 10 years. It's beaten and dented, but still watertight. I flipped the lid; pushed aside a knife, a compass, and other assorted paraphernalia; and came up with two little cans of stew beef, some containers of cheese crackers, and some crushed Granola bars. Lunch was covered.

"What'll it be like?" I asked.

"Narrow, bumpy and fast. We'll be coming down the mountain," Dave laughed.

"Let's go do it," I replied. As Dave shifted into low gear, I braced for more punishment from the truck as we headed farther up into the mountains.

"We can put in at a little bridge on Jasus Creek and canoe down to where it joins the Chattahoochee," Dave explained as, while still driving, he opened his door to spit out a chaw of tobacco. Dave Gale is a strange one—a Citadel graduate and a former army officer with a master's degree from Georgia Tech in civil engineering. He gave up a million-dollar contracting business several years ago to head for the hills. Now he's an outfitter and canoe guide, and a man I like to canoe with as often as I can.

As Dave slammed the door, the ashtray lid on the dash fell off. He didn't even notice it. I left it on the floor with all the other junk. Soon a little one-lane bridge came into view, and I got my first look at Jasus Creek.

"We gonna canoe that?" I asked in disbelief. Dave just smiled. The entire creek bed was scarcely 12 feet wide, and the little ribbon of water in it raced around a large boulder and then disappeared completely into some underbrush below.

"That's fast, tight stuff," I commented skeptically.

"That's the point," Dave said, bounding from the truck. "It'll show us what kind of canoeists we are. Let's get to it." We unloaded the canoes and slid them to the water's edge.

"You go first," I suggested. "This is your country."

"Well, give me plenty of room to get ahead," he instructed. "I don't want you bashing me from behind when I get stuck. And we'll probably get stuck."

With that observation he planted one foot solidly in the center of his canoe and, with hands on gunnels, used the other foot to push off from the bank and into the swift current. Dropping to his knees, he swung deftly around the boulder downstream, leaned over, and disappeared into the underbrush and out of sight. Beyond those bushes you couldn't see anything. Blindly I pushed off, fell to my knees, swung around the boulder, and ducked for the bushes, holding on to my hat. The bushes occupied me for only a second and proved to be a guarded gateway to an almost fairyland scene. I broke out into a dark, primeval forest, where autumn-golden trees formed a tunnel for the creek that ran down through the mountains. Although the sun was bright and the fall colors brilliant, everything seemed dark. The sun couldn't reach us. It was beautifully eerie, and I was glad to broach a rock and take it all in.

But this was no time for aesthetics. I had my work cut out for me. Although there was no massive volume of water to deal with, what water there was was fast and furious. Rocks and drops were everywhere. As Dave said, we were coming down the mountain. I glimpsed him poling off a rock. Just as he broke free, I grounded to a halt on my own rock. Hunching off, I set my alignment for another battering-ram drive through more bushes. These knocked my hat off and out of the canoe, and I had time for only one paddle scoop to come up with it. Then I jabbed my paddle back in the water just in time to line up for a three-foot falls which was already under my bow. I dropped cleanly through, then down a series of shallow but fast ledges, under more trees, and through some more bushes. I was beginning to wonder how long my luck would last. I was not satisfied with my canoeing control. So far, I had gotten through all right, but many of my choices were poor, decisions late, and strokes inept. At the bottom of a drop just ahead was a boulder with a big blue smudge on it. Some canoeist had left his mark. In spite of my efforts otherwise, I smacked it a glancing blow and left my bright red among the fall colors. A few more mistakes like that and I'd get dumped.

My old canoe has gotten me into and out of many breathtaking places. Handled properly, it will admit you to some amazing sights and sounds. It will take you where neither man's feet nor his machines can go. But only if it's handled right. The dents and the bumps on its hull are reminders of the times I haven't handled it right. You can almost tell when it's going to happen, like a lovers' quarrel when two people pick at each other until one finally says, "Okay, you do that to me and I'll do this to you." And over you go. Once separated, you both go flailing away helplessly down the river. We both have scars from such times.

Soon we emerged from the trees, and a series of bumpy cascades slid us out of Jasus Creek and into the Chattahoochee River. The scene we came upon stopped us cold.

"Not many folks ever see this," Dave said as I slid my canoe into the little eddy next to his. Dave's face was lifted upward, and he was gazing all around. The view we beheld was one that excited every sense. The whole scene was framed in autumn gold. Even the bottom of our little eddy pool was covered with golden leaves. Jasus Creek bounded in from the left, and from the right high overhead a silken waterfall sprayed down into the river. We were in the bright sun now, and out of the tunneled creek. The river's descent looked like a giant staircase dropping into the distance. Its water danced with a silver lucency. This was not whitewater; it was silver water. It was wilderness at its peak, full of raw contrasts, full of design and pattern. The whole scene renewed my spirits.

"That really looks like 'pick-or-pay' downstream," I commented, turning my attention to the task ahead.

"That's the name of this game," Dave laughed back, "and this is what I call canoeing." With that, we shoved out into the strong current heading for the bucking broncos below. Soon our canoes were jumping, bumping, listing, and twisting. Dave was right: this was canoeing at its best. It wasn't the big waters of a Chattooga or Nantahala, but this run was tight, tense, and kept you busy every second. Paddling was by instinct. You didn't have time to think about what strokes to use. Your arms just had to react—reaching out and over and back, prying, drawing, digging, and sweeping. There was little time for finesse: brute force was needed to make the canoe do what it had to do. We used all the strokes we knew, and then some.

Near where Jasus Creek merges with the Chattahoochee, we had stopped for lunch and rested awhile, and now I was feeling better. My strokes were stronger, and my decisions quicker. The canoe responded instantly with clean turns and easy lineups. I dropped through slots, slid over shelves, and slipped past boulders with impressive precision. I felt almost detached as I observed and enjoyed every minute of the following hours.

This run had now become one of those rare times when everything seemed to get together. As in a well tuned engine, everything clicked just right, just at the right time. I began to feel a marvelous harmony between myself and my canoe. And, beyond that, I felt us both blending with the force of the river under us, the rocks around us, and the mountains above. There was a distinct rhythm to everything, and we were a part of it, moving through it and blending with it. Perhaps Sidney Lanier had felt this rhythm when he sat beside the river and heard the harmony that he called "The Song of the Chattahoochee." To "run the rapids and leap the falls" was like music, and I was not only hearing it, I was doing it as if I were a part of the river. I admit that I was under its spell. The silver water with its golden frame of foliage, the wind and the roar, the danger and the exertion, all of these had my nerve endings on tiptoe. Hour after hour it continued. Occasionally I would glance up from the river to see some golden hardwood standing like a giant against the mountain. "God, look at that," I'd whisper under my breath, but that was foolish. He didn't have to be alerted. He had made it.

Soon we bounded out of the mountains into more level terrain. The highway leading into Helen joined the river.

"I don't blame you for keeping this jewel to yourself," I said to Dave as I pulled up beside him. "I want to repeat this someday."

"Well, I'm not being selfish," he replied, smiling. "It's just that most of my charter groups aren't experienced enough for this kind of water, and besides, very rarely can this stretch be run at all. You've almost got to hit it on the morning after a night's rain. But if it rains too much, it's lethal. Too little and you're grounded. We're just lucky to have caught it just right today. Be glad you made it this time," he laughed. "You probably won't get to run it again." I smiled at this little joke, but I didn't like the idea of it. There had to be another time, somehow, someday.

Oh, I doubt if it would be just like this run. This had been a rare experience, when all the ingredients happened to come together at the right time. The weather, the water, the colors, the whole combination was almost too good to be recaptured ever again. Some experiences once offered just aren't offered again. I should be satisfied.

But I'll stay in touch with the water gauge at the bridge in Helen, and there are weather forecasts and temperature predictions. So I'll wait and read and listen. And someday things will begin to match up again. Then I'll reach for the phone: "Operator, I'm calling Mr. Dave Gale in Helen, Georgia. . . ."

CANOEING GUIDE

Upper, Upper Chattahoochee

General Information: This section above Helen is a tight, difficult, and rapidly descending mountain river. It should be run by experts only. Water levels vary almost hourly and usually can be run only after a night's rain.

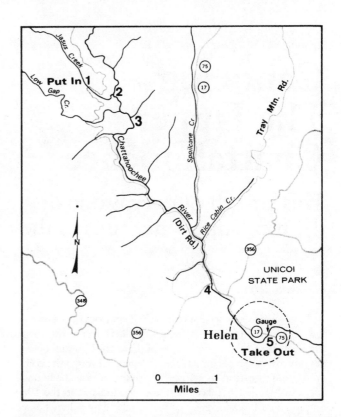

Put In: Go north out of Helen on Ga 75 for approximately 1.5 miles, turn left on Ga 356, cross the bridge, then immediately turn back right on dirt road on west side of river. Follow this road past ranger station (3.5 miles) and on to where the road crosses Jasus Creek. Put in here.

Take Out: In Helen, at parking area across street from Wildewood Shop.

Hazards: This upper stretch is extremely rocky and tight. Prepare for much scraping and many bumpy drops. Overhanging bushes on Jasus Creek can be treacherous in high water. Drops and ledges are so numerous that scouting is all but impossible. Experienced canoeists can run them *if* water level is safe. Otherwise, don't even try it.

Gauge: Water-level gauge on northwest corner of bridge in downtown Helen. Water level at time of our run was 1.2. Ideal would be 1.5. Over that, conditions could become dangerous. Under 1.2 would result in being grounded.

Distances: From put in on Jasus Creek to junction with Chattahoochee River is 1 mile (approximately 2 hours). From this point to take out at Helen is 7 miles (approximately 4 hours). Total is 8 miles and approximately 6 hours for the entire run.

Guide to Map Numbers:
1. Put in at Jasus Creek Bridge.
2. Junction with Chattahoochee River.
3. Old log bridge (must be portaged).
4. Ga 356 bridge.
5. Take out in Helen.

1980

Canoeing The Upper Chattahoochee

This stretch of river is one of the top white water runs in the state

by Claude Terry

Some rivers seem destined for excitement from their first discovery. With such rivers time only adds luster to the image and incidents to the legends. One of these, the Chattahoochee, has served as the basis for its share of legends through the years. Within our historical knowledge, the river served as the boundary between the Cherokee and the Creek Indians; in the 19th century, the Chattahoochee was immortalized by Sidney Lanier and became the site for gold hunting activities; it was used by locals to transport their goods (particularly moonshine) to market.

Today, the upper river, above Lake Lanier, is probably the runner-up to the Chattooga as the best white water canoeing

river in the state. It is this section of river that this story is about.

The best canoeing section (class III) of the river lies between highway 255 bridge, east of Cleveland and Duncan bridge (map). The area is hilly to low mountainous, and the watershed is adequate to allow year-round canoeing and kayaking. Rafting is also good most of the year. The Georgia Canoeing Association has someone running the river most weekends of the year.

A gauge is located 300 yards north of the 115 bridge on the east side of the river. It's important to check this marker before beginning a run. A minimum level for a comfortable run is 1.6 feet: an optimum level for open boats is about 2.5 feet and at levels above 3 feet extreme caution should be exercised. Novices and intermediates should stay off above this level.

Put your boat in the water at the highway 255 bridge (map). This is rather precipitous, being entirely on the highway right-of-way. The owner of the northwest quarter of the intersection takes a dim view of canoeists parking along the road. I have parked for years on the southwest quadrant side. Some time ago, I returned from running shuttle to find the residents from the other side, armed with garden tools, shooing my Boy Scouts back into the scout bus. Their offense? Picking up litter while we ran shuttle. Best to leave these people alone and carefully park on the other side.

Now, let's go down river.

Below the put-in you encounter mild rapids for about three miles. At three miles, you will see a sloping granite outcrop on your right, with a still pool in front. *Please note that this, and all other significant rapids on this section of the river, are preceded by a grey granite outcropping on the right.* The granite ledge which dams the pool is the upper end of Smith Island. You should run the east (left) side of the island, keeping close to the island, all the way down. In particular, slow the boat above the last drop and watch the twisting current. Many novice and intermediate tandem canoes spill here. Smith Island by the way is a possible lunch or overnight camping spot.

A mile and one-half of moderate rapids brings you to the 115 bridge, and Mrs. Wyches' store. This charming lady, with her indefatigable good humor and sly country hustle, is a character worthy of a *Foxfire* story. I always buy something just to get into a conversation with her.

The 4.5 miles of river to this point can be run by novice-intermediate paddlers. Below this point, intermediate and advanced paddlers will be happy, but beginners can get some spills and bumps. In the next 3.5 miles the river drops 93 feet with the gradient unevenly distributed.

Three hundred yards downstream from 115 there is a ledge which is best run on the extreme left. Buck Shoals starts immediately after the left turn. This shoals is best run on the left side, staying left until you pass the end of the island. Below the island the best passage bends right. There you will encounter a nice sliding drop and several smaller rapids down to a pool with a sandbar. We have traditionally lunched on the sandbar. There is an extensive amount of second home development being done in the area, so, who knows, maybe next week there will be a house on the sandbar!

Wintertime on the River

Contrary to the opinion of many, winter canoeing is fantastic. The water is generally high and southern temperatures are mild. We wear wet suit pants (scuba divers neoprene rubber suits) and wet suit vests or woolen sweaters under a coated nylon jacket.

About four years ago Payson and Aurelia Kennedy, Ross Wilson, Frank Hatfield and I went to this stretch of the upper Chattahoochee and found it frozen over except for one small channel down the center. We decided to go anyway since the water was high. At Buck Shoals I knocked a two inch hole in my new kayak which rapidly began to swamp. We discovered then that it is very difficult to get out of the current across ice. Finally, after floundering down a couple of rapids, I was able to reach the side. It had begun snowing. We built a fire to dry the boat for tapeing and opening several cans of chili, we placed them in the edge of the fire. As we sat on logs watching the chili bubble, drinking hot chocolate and bouillon from thermos bottles there was a moment when we all stopped talking and just grinned at each other through the snowflakes. I finally broke the spell by saying, "Most people would consider this insanity, yet it's a totally beautiful, exciting day." There was instant agreement; I still recall that day as one of my great canoeing adventures.

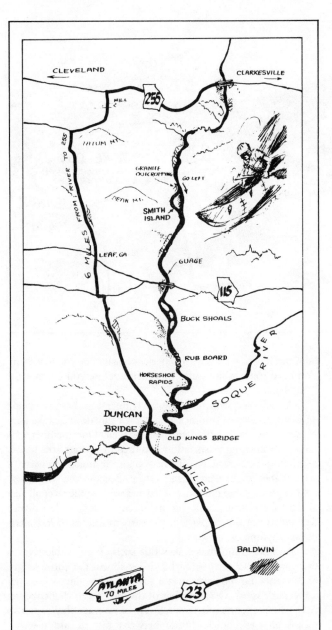

The Upper Chattahoochee

The portion of the upper Chattahoochee described here winds through the hills of north Georgia between White and Habersham counties.

To reach the takeout point where you will set up a shuttle, drive north on I-85, take highway 365 past Gainesville, then U.S. 23. About 7.5 miles beyond Lula and about one mile before Baldwin you will pass a restaurant on the left. At the top of the next hill the road with the small concrete island on the left leads directly to the river.

You will leave a vehicle at this point and continue on to highway 255 where you can enter the river. Note the gauge near the highway 115 bridge. This marker should be checked before beginning any trip. Author Claude Terry specifies acceptable water levels in the accompanying story.

There is another set of shoals below this point, with larger (about 2 foot) drops. This series is entered on the right, the current followed left around a boulder. There is then, a quick drop to the right with a tight left countermove at which point you are above Three Foot Ledge. You may want to land on the right and scout this one. There is a "cheat" on the right or a good run slanting off left. A note of caution: the ledge creates a small hydraulic or "keeper" at high water levels.

There are really two more sets of shoals; the first, Rub Board, merely requires picking your way over a series of parallel ledges. Horseshoe Shoals appears similar but you must work to the left side of the stream since Horseshoe Rapid is encountered at that side. Again, the grey granite face above warns of the rapids, and a further identifying mark is the sandbar to the left of the rapid. Horseshoe Rapid is entered from the left, slants right across the river behind the main ledge, then spills over two shallow drops to unite with Soque river.

Below this point here, there are only small rapids to the takeout. Just above the takeout, there is an example of the river at work. The inside of the bend is rapidly eroding away down the center, cutting off an island.

Please remember your courtesies when you use this or other rivers. Respect landowner's rights, and don't litter. And remember, well prepared winter canoeing is great.

1974

Nantahala River Run

This Nantahala River run is only eight quick miles from start to finish, but what it lacks in distance it makes up for in action. Once you put in the water, there's hardly a place to catch your breath.

by Claude Terry

During last year's Nantahala canoe race I watched as a 240-pound insurance salesman pumped up an inflatable kayak that belonged in a swimming pool. Within a few minutes he had stuffed himself inside it and had set off down river at his appointed starting time. I could not tell where stomach ended and kayak began. Good-hearted soul that he was, he bounced through the first rapid, negotiating it, if not in style at least right-side-up and with a certain infectious enthusiasm that made me cheer him on. I watched him disappear around the bend and left shaking my head and wishing him well. Half an

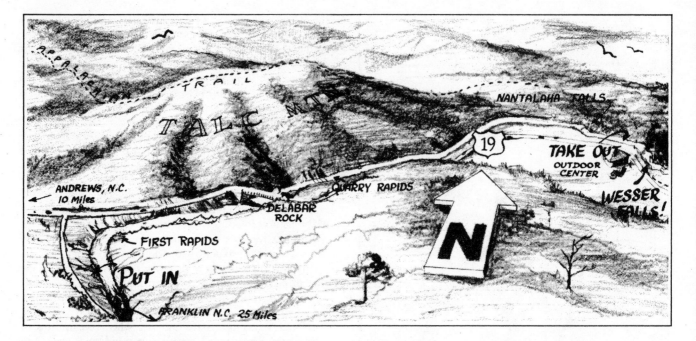

hour later I walked into the little grocery store at the Nantahala outdoor Center and there was my friend, downing a pint carton of chocolate milk. I couldn't resist. "You were on the river a few minutes ago," I questioned him. "Too much for that little boat," he chuckled. "Got to get me something else. Couldn't control the thing at all."

To me that little episode said a lot about the river and about the people who enjoy it. The Nantahala is a good time river. And it's popular. If you run it, you'll probably have company, all types of company from bikini-clad lovelies to wet-suited olympic types. But this river is a powerful force. It must be treated with respect or it will extract its own special type of retribution.

The Nantahala rates as one of the top recreational canoeing streams in the southeast. Randy Carter in his book *Canoeing White Water* calls it, "the most delightful canoeing river of all."

The river has a lot of things going for it. For one thing, it's only eight miles long and can be canoed in an hour under race conditions or three hours in a leisurely, "play in the rapids" fashion. You can make the trip twice in one day.

The water drops 33 feet per mile. That's plenty steep. If you didn't know the river, it might even be a little frightening. But the fact is that the water moves in a continuous downhill flow rather than in a series of dramatic rapids punctuating long stretches of calmer water. This aspect of the Nantahala means that there is some element of danger inherent in canoeing it. If you are a good swimmer and not afraid of the water and observe basic safety rules, there is little personal hazard. But for your boat, that's another thing altogether. A water filled canoe is extremely difficult to control in this stream, mainly because there are so few calm pools where you can stop, empty your boat, collect your wits and take a fresh start. Once you are in the water, business really picks up. Many boats have been lost

here and it was not always inexperienced canoers who lost them. You need some white water experience before you attempt the Nantahala.

An icy cold stream, the water temperature hovers around 45 degrees, even in summer. A spill on a July day will take your breath away. It can be dangerous as well. One member of a Georgia Canoeing Association trip died of a heart attack after a spill into the Nantahala. The reason for the attack was partially attributable to the water temperature. Because the water is so cold anytime, large numbers of hardy souls use the river all year around for rafting, canoeing and even tubing. A skin diver's wet suit is not out of place in the early mornings or late afternoons anytime of the year.

Another thing that makes this such an enjoyable river is that highway 19 runs parallel to it for almost the entire length of the canoeing run. That means that canoeing almost becomes a spectator sport. One member of the family can challenge the river while other members watch. This convenient highway also means an easy, quick shuttle between put in and take-out points. Along the river there are numerous vantage points for good photographs. If you are spectating rather than canoeing you can go right down to the water level at the first rapids and at Nantahala falls (see map) and watch canoeists almost eyeball to eyeball as they battle whitewater with skill and concentration. This is very exciting in itself and provides subject matter for some excellent photographs.

Of course you have to take the bad with the good. The Nantahala is a controlled stream, meaning that the flow of water is regulated by the Nantahala Power Company a subsidiary of TVA. Often the power company doesn't generate on Sundays and that means no water for canoeing. It's always a good idea to call in advance to check on this. The Nantahala Outdoor Center (704) 488-6470 is a good number to call for information on water levels.

CANOEING GUIDE

The Nantahala River is north of the Georgia state line and runs parallel to highway 19 near Andrews, N.C. This canoe trail is about eight miles long and can be paddled in one to three hours depending on the pace you want to set. Put in at the power house just across the bridge (turn off of highway 19 which parallels the river). The take-out is just below Nantahala Falls on the highway side. Scout the first rapid (about .6 mile from where you turn to put in there is a wide shoulder with picnic tables). Approach this rapid on the right side. If you have an open canoe you will probably need to pull out and bail at the end of this stretch. A full, wallowing craft is too difficult to handle and there will be more waves to come. This rapid is typical of the Nantahala—not too much difficult maneuvering but an almost constant bouncy, exciting ride. Most open boaters will find a bailer (a plastic bleach or milk jug with the bottom cut out) an essential piece of equipment on this run, particularly if they don't want to be always stopping and dumping the water from the canoe. Another helpful hint—move the bowman back behind the front seat to raise the bow and reduce the amount of water taken in.

Also scout Quarry Rapid (3.5 miles from the put-in by the side of Three Sisters Mountain) and Nantahala Falls which is not quite so ominous as it sounds since its not really a waterfall. You should enter Nantahala Falls on the railroad side of the river and move diagonally to exit at the right center.

Warning: *Wesser Falls beyond Nantahala Falls is dangerous and should not be run under any circumstances. Take out after Nantahala Falls.*

1975

Spring White Water

A canoeing guide to one of Georgia's prettiest and most varied streams

by Claude Terry

How else can I describe the Toccoa? For my money it's Georgia's prettiest white water stream. I first became aware of the Toccoa's canoeing potential five years ago as a result of a suggestion in *Burmeister's Canoeing Guide* (now out of print). On my first trip I put my boat in at Cooper creek (map) and followed it to join the river. That stretch was punctuated with plenty of stops to lift my canoe over trees.

The stream's first couple miles provide a startling contrast between undisturbed river banks and those touched by the hand. In apparent efforts to squeeze a little more yield from flood plains, some farmers have cleaned to the edge of the water,

removing vegetation which holds the soil. The consequence is that the banks are rapidly eroding, dumping silt and any remaining vegetation into the water. The Soil Conservation Service in their information to farmers should stress leaving 25 to 50 feet of vegetation along the banks.

The Toccoa offers a variety of interesting forms of vegetation for each season: early spring brings bluets in the moss, then azalea, laurel, and all around Deep Hole campground, wild strawberries. In late spring abundant rhododendron garnishes the banks. Summer offers the richness of mature hardwood stands in full leaf. When autumn comes the hardwoods take on an incredible glow. Alternate leaf dogwood and deciduous holly sport their bright red berries right on into winter. Where upper story trees provide enough shade, galax carpets the banks, the waxy leaves dark green until December, then thriving as coppery as a penny for the winter months. This plant is gathered for use as a background for floral displays, which has led to its near extinction in some areas.

The most beautiful section of the Toccoa lies behind Toonowee Mountain (map). Small rapids, hemlocks trailing in the water and the beautifully clear stream itself combine to saturate the senses.

Curiously the Toccoa has been so forgiving of error that my canoeing companions and I have avoided any spectacular spills. But the possibility is there. On my last trip the head of the best rapid was blocked by a giant hemlock which lay with its root system pointing upstream; a smaller tree was enmeshed at right angles. We ducked the root mass, which was twisted under the trunk upraised in an eddy, to examine this beautiful but dangerous giant. Laurel still grew from the root mass. I could foresee a good winter rain lifting the massive corpse and completely blocking the rapids below it with its trunk and stiff spring limbs.

Signs of beaver and muskrat are obvious along the river banks below the bridge. With no natural enemies to contain

---

Spring Canoeing Tips

Spring water is undoubtedly the best water in the Southeast. Big rivers are *big* and small streams are canoeable. Enjoy the abundant water, but do it with an eye to the variability of the weather. Warm days of early spring are seductive and beguiling. However when the sun drops behind the ridges you may chill even in a wet suit. Even on beautiful spring days wear or carry wet suit gear or woolen clothing and a windproof (usually nylon) jacket. Otherwise you'll risk hypothermia.

Expect rain in north Georgia on short notice. Carry a complete set of dry clothes in a tested container; take a poncho or ripstop tarp and waterproof matches. A candle or firestarter is not a luxury either.

Run only with experienced boaters. Early spring high water is no time to have inexperienced, ill-equipped friends initiated into survival swimming. All safety procedures become very important such as making sure a non-boater knows your put-in and take-out points.

them, they run riot. Their slides, leading from bottom land cornpatches to the water, intercept the bank at 20-foot intervals. The fragile soil has yielded to the repeated friction of wet bodies and some slides are worn a foot or more deep. Erosion damage to the banks has resulted in some areas.

One November day I ran the stretch of rapids above Shallowford Bridge (map) with Bill and Anabelle Close who probably use it more and know it better than anyone else. We were part way down the rapids when we spotted a magnificent buck lying on an island; he had been dead several days. The hunter's arrow which had killed him still protruded from his side. We had a similar find a year later below Dicks Creek on the Chattooga. Hunters should note that deer run for islands when hurt.

There it is then: a beautiful river scarcely larger than a mountain trout stream, growing into placid, full-bodied maturity. When you know the Toccoa's many ways, you will appreciate it as one of the most interesting and beautiful rivers in the Southeast.

CANOEING GUIDE

Toccoa River

The Toccoa in the middle of north Georgia offers a variety of canoeing experiences. All of the rapids can be run, and the stream is an excellent beginning white water challenge for canoeists who have paddled flat water streams before. There is usually enough water to canoe throughout the year. A gauge (5) reading of 2.5 is good canoeing; 3.5 to 4.0 is high but okay for experienced boaters.

There are eight miles of canoeing (figure about 2½ to 3 miles per hour) from the road curve put-in (1) to Dial Bridge; putting in at Deep Hole campground (2) adds one-half mile, or entering at Coopers creek (3) adds two miles more. (I must note that I've never found Deep Hole campground open.) From Dial Bridge to the bottom of the last rapid above Lake Blue Ridge (6) is 1½ miles.

The most beautiful and exciting section of the Toccoa lies behind Toonowee Mountain (4). The rapids here can be anticipated by observing Rock Creek entering on the left. Then, in the next bend a large rock juts far in from the left bank. The following bend has a broad flood plain on the right (good camp site), and the next bend conceals the rapids. They build up into excitement, culminating in a right turn down a series of two-foot drops which you may want to scout. I've seen several boats spill carelessly running a place other than the notch in left center. Throughout this section you may need to stop to bail if the water is high. (Don't go at over 3.5 on the gauge.) This section behind Toonowee is a nice place to stop for lunch if you started late.

Just beyond where the mountain drops away, the terrain levels out and the next couple of miles wind through a more civilized area with fields and pastures bordering the river. This mild terrain continues with the river running class II rapids down to the Dial Bridge.

Dial Bridge makes a logical place to stop for anyone interested in a short trip. Or it's a good put-in for the next section which extends to the backwaters of Blue Ridge Lake. This section continues to be pastoral—a good trip for a lazy day. It lacks the wilderness beauty of the upper stretch but compensates with the bucolic pleasures of pasture and field. Just above Shallowford Bridge there is a stretch of rapids which at most water levels is run best on the left.

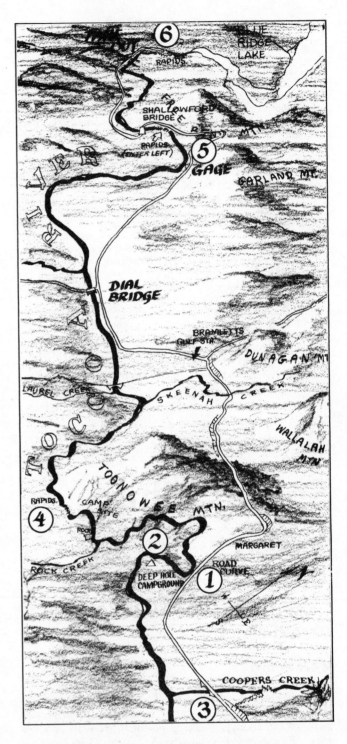

Below Shallowford there is a good rapid (6). The impending white water can be heard as you approach. It can be recognized by the rip-rapped road shoulder on the left. It is best to scout this section on your first trip. After the rapids below Shallowford Bridge the river slows and broadens into Lake Blue Ridge.

1975

Canoeing The Chestatee

by Claude Terry

Moonshining is not a dead art in Georgia. I tell this story with some hesitancy, lest "revenuers" take up canoeing and canoeists be mistaken for agents of the Federal Government. Still, it did happen on the Chestatee River. The river was green, fast and dancing. We had run the introductory rapids, and were working our way through a series of hemlock-lined ledges, a staircase set in stone and carpeted with water. The sudden barking of a dog seemed out of place here, but lost foxhounds and beagles out for rabbits do show up along rivers. We were quiet, savoring the wildness of the Chestatee and the physical pleasure of stretching muscles stressed too little during city life. The fact we were quiet probably acted in our favor, as we slid by the area where the dog was barking. A small stream entered just below, and I was surprised by the rich odor of fermented mash. Someone had drained their distillery wastes down the stream! It all suddenly fit together, and we slipped silently away downstream.

This is just one example of the rare and endangered forms of mountain life to be found along the Chestatee River.

Born in the rock faces of Blood Mountain, the Chestatee cascades out of the Chattahoochee National Forest as one of Georgia's best trout streams. From Turner's Corner to Ga. Highway 52 the river is one of the best canoeing streams in the state. Although the small watershed limits the river's use to winter, spring and rainy periods in the summer, the beauty makes it well worth the effort involved in planning a trip for "when it rains." Individual preferences for water levels also come into play here, since some people may not mind dragging their boat over shallow ledges, etc. The scenery is excellent, particularly in spring and early summer. Azaleas and dogwoods in April, laurel in May and rhododendron in early June provide small splashes of color against the rich magnificence of the white pines and hemlocks.

The first six miles or so from Turner's Corner is down a green-lined tunnel, with no real rapids of note, but plenty of beauty. The first really decent rapid is a ledge with an "s" turn (1). There follows a series of moderate rapids, with abrupt turns in the river revealing steep banks covered with white pines. The next rapid (not shown on the map) is just above the lunch spot, and is preceded by an old white pine covered in "old man's beard" lichen. This runs best on the left.

Lunch is on the rocks by the pool below the rapid, and there is a possible emergency exit from the river on the west side. The walk out to a paved road is about two miles. The activity of beavers is obvious in the lunch area, and it appears to be a place where deer come to the river to drink. Last Easter we were on the Chestatee (in rain of course) and we ate lunch under a rock shelter about 100 yards upstream of the normal lunch stop. There's really nothing like leaning your back against a rock, and watching rain erase the morning's deer tracks from the sand as you get your hands and mouth orange and blue from Easter egg dye.

Below the lunch spot the action begins in earnest. Round the curve, and there is a slide (2) best run on the right. Look back up this valley from the bottom for one of the better views in Georgia. Around another curve, and you are into the gorge (3). This is about three hundred yards of good rapids which are a solid class III stretch at 3.0 ft. on the gauge. These rapids come complete with a vulture tree. This spring we ran the gorge while two vultures sat in a tree on the right side, peering after us with obvious hope. On the same trip we saw a Cooper's hawk, an owl of undetermined pedigree, and an osprey. The only other osprey I've seen in North Georgia were a pair on the Chattooga River last summer. Numerous kingfishers, woodducks, and a little green heron added to our pleasure that day.

Below the gorge there are minor rapids with a pasture on the left signalling the entrance to Tree Rapid. In the pool at the bottom of the rapid is an enormous tree, moved in lock, stock and roots. Below Tree Rapid, more moderate rapids lead to the Staircase (5) which is quite demanding in low water, and could be dangerous in really high water (over 4 ft. on the gauge). Numerous switches from one side of the river to the other are required. Below Staircase are a few easy rapids down to Garnet Bridge. One-half mile below Garnet Bridge is Woolsey's Folly (6) (also coming to be known as the Grouch's Rapid). This rapid has eaten many more canoes than such a ledge should. I once saw Clyde Woolsey with a new canoeist in the bow miss in this one, and the newcomer found herself perched five feet up on the rock as the stern (and Clyde) sank slowly into the river.

Below the rapid you find the only house currently along this stretch of the Chestatee and a sign saying "NO CANOEING." Best to leave this disagreeable person to his own unhappiness and use the right side of the river which is owned by a presumably nicer guy. From here to Grindle Bridge is one and one-half miles of moderate rapids.

Chestatee Water Gauge

The water level gauge at the Chestatee is located about 150 yards upstream from the Highway 52 bridge. It's always advisable to check the gauge before setting out as the river levels of 1.5 ft. are runnable but draggy. Three feet is a good level but uncommon. A level of 4.0 ft. would probably be great for intermediate and advanced kayakists, but high for open boats. Above 4.0 ft. everyone should beware. I must rush to say the four foot level is a projection since I have never been on the river at over 3.3 ft. I surely would like to catch it higher. I ran the Chestatee in the spring with a small party at 3.3 ft. We moved quickly since it was storming. The run from Tate Bridge to Grindle Bridge took an hour and forty minutes. This same section at normal water levels generally takes intermediate canoeists about six hours.

There is a severe danger point below Grindle Bridge. Chestatee Falls are one of the prettiest cascades in Georgia, falling about 40 ft. in a series of leaps. They also would be unforgiving of any canoeist unwary enough to enter them. I once encountered a couple in a banged-up canoe (whose isn't?) laden with camping gear passing under the Grindle Bridge. They were headed down-river, with the waterfall one hundred yards around the curve below them. They were blissfully unaware it was there. They took my suggestion and exited the river.

Most trips on this stretch of the Chestatee end at Grindle. The portage for the falls is atrocious. Steep banks and laurel thickets make canoe carrying impossible. If you choose to go on to the Highway 52 bridge, it is better to leave the river at Grindle Bridge and re-enter at Copper Mines (7). This requires that you spot a car to shuttle canoes the two miles or so down river.

Copper Mines (7) rapid must be one of the most photogenic rapids around. At 3.0 ft., the rapid can be run at a variety of places with the right side most technically demanding. The center sluice is awesome to the unitiated, but straightforward.

The river at this point has been swollen by the addition of Tesnatee Creek, and is runnable more of the year. Two miles below Copper Mines there is a significant rapid (8) marked by a pile of blasted rock on the left about a quarter mile below a creek on the left. Land and scout this one. You may want to line or carry. Otherwise this stretch is class I to II. Another mile brings you to Georgia Highway 52 bridge.

The shuttle for the upper section is ten miles of new road. I learned this route from a local gentleman who was nice enough to shuttle me back to the top after our shuttle car was found to be without keys.

This river deserves your attention in spring and rainy summer weather. It also deserves state attention and protection. Any help in getting the Chestatee state protection would be appreciated. Remember, rainy days are Chestatee canoeing days.

CANOEING GUIDE

(From Turner's Corner to the Highway 52 Bridge.)

Begin at Turner's Corner near where Highways 19 and 9 cross the river. (Tate Bridge makes a good put-in for a shorter trip.) The first six or so miles of this trip is down a tree-lined tunnel with no real rapids of note but plenty of beauty. The first significant rapid (1) is a ledge with an "s" turn. The current enters on the left, moves right, then runs back quickly to the left and spills into a pool. The next rapid (not designated on the map) is just above the lunch spot. It's preceded by an old white pine covered in "old man's beard" lichen. Run this one on the left. Lunch is below the rapid on rocks by a pool. Here, there is a possible emergency exit on the west side of the river; the walk out to a paved road is about two miles. Below the lunch spot the action begins in earnest. Around the curve there is a slide (2) best run on the right. Around another curve and you are into the gorge (3) and about 300 yards of good rapids. At 3.0 ft. on the gauge these rapids are a solid class III. Below the gorge there are minor rapids with a pasture on the left signalling the entrance to Tree Rapid (4). This starts as a shoal at the top, usually run on the left, leading into a chute on the right which piles into a

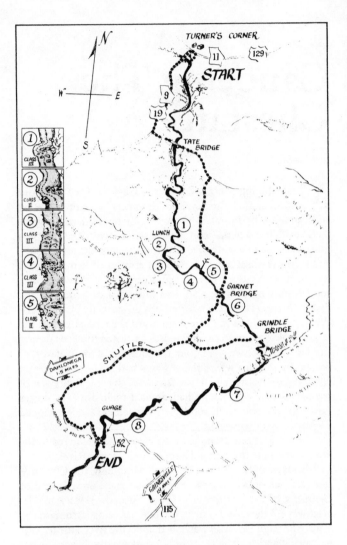

rock at the bottom. In the pool at the bottom is an enormous tree moved in lock, stock and roots. Below Tree Rapid more moderate rapids lead to the Staircase (5) which is quite demanding in low water and could be dangerous in really high water (over 4 ft. on the gauge). Numerous switches from one side of the river to the other are required. One-half mile below Garnet Bridge is Woolsey's Folly (6). Run this entering extreme left and moving right, then hard left down the chute. Take out at Grindle Bridge. Forty foot Chestatee Falls around the next bend is impassable. Many canoeists choose to end their trip here. The portage around Chestatee Falls is difficult if not impossible. To continue the trip below Grindle Bridge, leave the river at the bridge and re-enter at Copper Mines (7). Copper Mines Rapid can be run at a variety of places with the right side the most technically demanding. The center sluice is awesome but straightforward. Two miles below Copper Mines is a significant rapid (8) recognizable by a pile of blasted rock on the left about a quarter mile below a creek which enters on the left. Land and scout. You may want to line or portage. Otherwise this last stretch is class I to II. Shuttle Note: If you plan to run the section of the river below Grindle Bridge, spot a car at the bridge to shuttle canoes from there to the re-entry point at Copper Mines (7). Canoeing Times: At normal water levels, intermediate canoeists should allow about six hours to canoe between Tate Bridge and Grindle Bridge.

1974

A Different Kind of Beauty

Not everybody who looks at the Alcovy River sees the same thing.

by Margaret Osborne

When I invited Mary to float the Alcovy with me, she said, "I'd love to get out, but . . . well, to tell you the truth . . ." Again she hesitated. I wondered what she was struggling to say. "I guess the reason I'm not sure I want to go is, I heard it's flat and ugly." The condemnation in her voice surprised me. I didn't ask her who said it. It didn't matter. I didn't argue. It would have been useless.

That judgment "flat and ugly" could have come from any of half a dozen "whitewater freaks" I know. Don't misunderstand, I'm a whitewater freak myself (some of my best friends are), but that doesn't mean I write off all water that isn't falling vertically as "flat and ugly." There are reasons for running "hair," the foaming Class IV and V rapids, but there are equally valid reasons for canoeing a flatwater stream.

For one thing, tranquillity is as pleasant an experience as thrills, if that's what you need. A little of both adds richness to your soul. If you don't eat steak and potatoes every night, why should your outdoor experiences be set in one pattern? Take a chance! You've heard it's flat and ugly? Go see for yourself with open eyes and an equally open mind.

My mind was open enough, but I was having a little trouble with my eyes on a recent early Sunday morning as I picked up my friend Charlie and arrived at Betty Terry's to load up two canoes. As Charlie and Butch Terry loaded the boats, Betty and I planned the trip—at this point our planning only extended to where to get a cup of coffee.

Over coffee we talked about why we suffered through early-morning rising, canoe loading, etc., for this sport and about what made a river pretty or ugly. It's true that some types of beauty seem easier to appreciate than others. The Lochsa River in Idaho after snow melt in the Rockies is hypnotic with continuous rapids. The full moon rising over LaDore Canyon on the Green River in Colorado is breathtaking. The beauty of these rivers is stark and overpowering. In such company maybe the Alcovy is "flat and ugly." Or is its beauty perhaps just different?

Yes, it's a more intimate, subtle beauty. The river is small, gently winding, with an easy current and swamps on both sides. Unless you do something very stupid, it won't drown you with tricky currents or freeze you into hypothermia. Is it then deserving of your respect and admiration? Your interest? Again, yes. If you take the time to know it, you'll be rewarded.

This Piedmont river offers an interesting and unusual combination of geologic and natural characteristics, blending some features of the mountains and the coast. It's dead flat for miles, then tumbles into Lake Jackson over a half mile set of shoals ending in a river-wide falls. Here are unusual combinations of plants—water-loving tupelo trees with swollen bases, usually thought of as coastal plain trees, in the same stretch of river with the pink-blooming mountain laurel of the north. It's a crazy, mixed-up little river, and I like it. There's always some surprise in store for you on the Alcovy.

It was a sunny late morning when we arrived at the put-in for a leisurely one-day float. Two fishermen on the bank weren't having much luck. We soon knew just how they felt. Our wildlife watching was frustrated again and again by a noisy kingfisher who spotted us on the first mile and proceeded to do his duty by warning every living thing on the next seven miles of our approach. Busybody! I wished dire fates at him—owls at midnight. Hawks in his sky. Snakes in his favorite tree.

He teased me by flying just far enough ahead to be out of camera range. First he scared up two big ducks. They flew away downstream, skimming the water and squawking in protest. Then there was a mysterious loud splash—too loud to be the kingfisher, though he dived into the water ahead of us often, doing his fishing. All afternoon we floated downriver, an orderly parade, two canoes preceded by an angry kingfisher, preceded by two increasingly badgered ducks, preceded by mysterious loud splashes, sometimes in sets of two or three. We were puzzled. Snakes? Beaver? Fat frogs? We debated the mystery and resolved to find out.

We became stealthy. Butch, who at 16 doesn't know how to be quiet, especially when paddling with his mother, was relegated to the rear. Charlie and I did a quiet glide in the other canoe. No talking. We tried the old North Woods guide trick of not lifting the paddle from the water, but turning the blade parallel to the boat and sculling it back into stroking position. (The flatter the blade, the less noise.) The quieter we became, the more we realized how noisy we had been. We could finally hear every rustle in the woods. It was a revelation. A wasp overhead sounded like an airplane as he hovered near his nest. A fish jumped and we jumped.

Charlie pointed silently ahead and I saw an odd brown shape on a log at the next bend. Slowly I got out my 200-mm telephoto lens, attached it, and focused on three dinner-plate-sized turtles just before they tumbled, splat, splat, splat, into the safety of the water. Mystery solved—cooters—the shyest of turtles.

The next mystery was, what warned them? The kingfisher had given up. He quit promptly at 5:05 and flew overhead, presumably home to dinner. Could it have been the glint of sun off our canoe so far away? It's hard to believe they heard us over the normal river sounds after we started our quiet stalk. I'll never think of turtles as slow and dull-witted again. These could

take care of themselves. As a matter of fact, turtles have been taking care of themselves on this planet a lot longer than we have. They and the river swamps like the Alcovy have been here through long ages.

As you float the Alcovy, looking at the tall, thin river cane, which not only fed the bison 200 years ago, but served the Indian as an arrow shaft, you realize that the river swamps are one of the few places you can go in the Southeast and see the landscape looking much the same as the Indians saw it. An Indian today would be bewildered by our cities, and most of our countryside as well, with its ever-present pavement and power lines, but he would still be at home in the river swamps.

These swamps are a refuge for all kinds of animals today—deer, duck, turkey, raccoon, and beaver. The beaver, the one animal which perhaps did more than any other to open up America to settlement, as its fur lured trappers farther and farther into the wilderness, was nearly destroyed in the process, but is coming back strong, at least in Georgia.

On the Alcovy we saw the most intriguing beaver cut I'd ever encountered. We climbed out of our boats to pull over a "blowdown," a large pine felled across the stream by the undercutting action of water on the outside of a bend. On the bank lay seven firewood-length pieces of log, neatly chiseled at each end. Usually a beaver will cut a tree down, then strip the whole trunk of bark without further cutting. Why had he cut them into lengths? Looking at the end of the line of logs, I suddenly understood. The tree still hung, its tip two feet off the ground, its tip inextricably twined in its neighbor. The beaver had chewed the base through, and in falling, it hit the other tree and caught. The persistent beaver had chewed through again, and the equally persistent tree, with its top still caught, merely swung into a more nearly vertical position. This game had gone on for seven cuts before the beaver gave up.

We sat down by the beaver tree to have lunch. In the middle of my kippered herring, I discovered that the canteen was in the canoe. Taking a shortcut back to the boat, I slid down the steep bank onto a little muddy beach at water's edge. Surprise! I was mired in mud up to my knees. I jerked my leg up to climb out and nearly dislocated both knee and ankle joints. The mud had a tremendous hold. Slowly I worked my leg out, amazed at the suction of the mud. My next step mired me up again.

The mud was making strange sucking and slurping noises which drew attention. Butch's head appeared over the bank. "You've got to do something to increase the surface tension," he said. "Here, lay this stick on the mud and step on it." I tried, but although the foot on the stick didn't sink, the other one was still caught. By now the stream of loud advice, exhortation, and instruction from Butch had called the others. They snickered, then laughed, then guffawed. I glared at them. It's hard to be indignant when you have no dignity, but I faked it. They subsided into giggles. I was a mess. When I got out and looked at myself, I too was reduced to giggles.

I remembered a similar experience with sand on a desert river in Utah. At the side of the river a hot spring flowed in over a sandbar, making a shallow, loose, "quicksand." These are called "whales' bellies" out West and they're fun. The holding power of the sand is so great that you can stand ankle deep in them and lean over to a 45-degree angle without falling. I stood in the whale's belly and swayed in a circle, arms wide. Others joined me and we had imaginary boxing matches, falling backwards in slow motion, ducking sideways with our feet securely held.

When I had retrieved my dignity and my canteen, I stood drinking and silently assessing the Alcovy. "Flat and ugly" echoed in my ears. I looked around. Much of the beauty would be missed by someone barging swiftly downstream in search of whitewater. I remembered a warm, rainy summer morning on the Alcovy years ago when raindrops beaded every one of literally millions of tiny spider webs in the trees. Ugly?

I remembered an October trip when the reds, purples, and yellows of the hardwoods were reflected in the still water. Not ugly.

I thought of young David Woodward's first encounter with a baby snapping turtle on the Alcovy. He kept running his fingers over the elaborately sculptured little shell. Definitely not ugly.

I thought of the old mill by the river that I knew we would soon reach, its aged planks and simple, functional lines. I remembered the beautiful shoals dropping to Lake Jackson just below the takeout. Too broad and shallow to canoe most of the year, but a great place for a picnic or for children to wade.

I decided that "ugly" was a state of mind that affected one's vision, leading perhaps to permanent blindness. The only effective prevention is to train your eyes to look *at* what a river offers, not *for* one particular item you have selected as the only value. I looked toward the river where the canoe lay swaying in the current. What would we find downstream? I wouldn't guess. I would wait and be surprised.

CANOEING GUIDE

Alcovy River

The put-in for this nine-mile, five-hour run is on Georgia 213 just south of Covington. Unload on the west side of the river and put in on the downstream side of the bridge. There's an old road here to carry the canoes down, but it's been blocked off so cars can't get down it. You'll have to park your car on the shoulder. To run the 15-minute shuttle, backtrack .7 miles to the intersection of Ga. 213 and Ga. 36. Turn left on 36 and go 6.9 miles to Newton Factory Bridge Road. It's marked and paved. Turn left on it and go 1 mile to an old iron bridge. This is the takeout, which is easiest on the west side above the bridge. Park well off the road, as the local sheriff checks regularly.

Look at the little shoals above the bridge. This is the only rapid on the run. However, this half-mile rapid gets bigger below the bridge. There's a trail down the west side of the river that offers

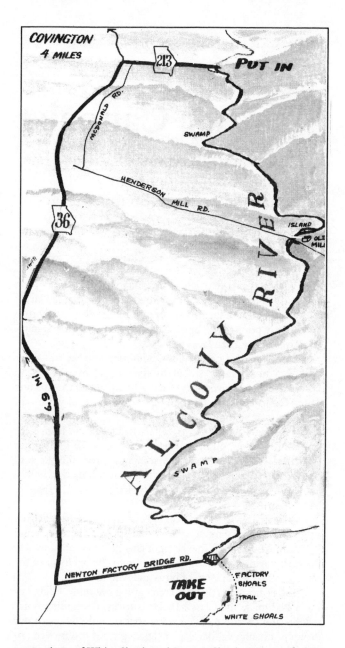

great views of White Shoals and Factory Shoals (can you find the traces of the old factory?)

For a visit by car to the old mill that is on the river halfway down, shuttle back to the put in on the west side. From the iron bridge, drive .6 miles to a left turn onto McDonald Road. Follow McDonald 2.5 miles to a left onto Henderson Mill Road. Two miles will bring you to the old mill. After a look, turn right onto Dixie Road before the bridge and follow Dixie 1.5 miles to a right turn onto Big Woods. It takes you .9 miles back to Ga. 213. Turn left and go .8 miles to the put in.

1976

The Foul Weather Canoeist

It was raining. Everyone was tired. The rapids had been harder than we expected. And we had 35 miles to go. *How did I get myself into this?*

by Margaret Osborne

"Didn't you say this float was suitable for *children?*" John Bittner asked me incredulously. He sounded tired. So was I. We'd just spent two hours scouting, then partly running, partly portaging a huge, dangerous rapid on the Ocmulgee River below Lake Jackson.

Embarrassed, I only nodded, admitting that the trip so far had been much more strenuous than I had expected—and slower. We'd gone five miles of the 20 I'd planned for this first day of a two-day trip. It was 3:30 and we were all worn out. Worse, it started raining.

The stretch of the Ocmulgee we had taken on, from Lake Jackson to Macon, 40 miles, was reputed to be easy. I had not run this stretch before, but the first 25 miles from the put in to Dames Ferry had been described to me as mostly flat, with a few Class II shoals, not counting the long Class III rapid we had just struggled down.

The last 15 miles from Dames Ferry to Macon I knew from a previous run to be moderately swift, with frequent Class I and II ledges, easy enough for the right channel to be obvious. On the earlier trip I had been impressed with the wildness of the river, and had seen plenty of birds and wildlife.

Today, however, things weren't going smoothly. High, fast water had made the Class I-II shoals tricky, demanding quick reflexes and precise paddle strokes that several novices in our group just hadn't yet developed. The big rapid had proved unusually hard to scout, as islands blocked the view of the main channel from both banks. Running the far right channel was impossible because of a sheer five-foot drop. Since the rapid was extremely long and the trees thick, portaging was awful. We resorted to having the experienced paddlers run their canoes down, then walk back for other canoes.

Finally, at the bottom of the rapid, I looked over the group as everyone pulled out raingear. There were 22 people including me—17 adults, mostly married couples, plus three teenagers and two children. I knew only two of them well, having met the others for the first time at the put in.

I was trying to figure out what the others would want to do from this point. It was obvious we'd never make it to the camping spot I had planned for tonight. It was doubtful if we'd be able to make up the lost time tomorrow, and our cars, except for one, were in Macon, 35 miles farther downstream. Would the experienced members of the group want to paddle until dark today and complete the trip with another hard day tomorrow? Could the novices keep up? Would tomorrow's shoals be too difficult for them? Would ill tempers begin to show if the rain continued?

I suddenly realized I'd been foolish to organize a trip for strangers on a river I'd never paddled. While I was confident we'd all get off the river safely, I knew that for the Juhlins and their friend and daughter, this could become a frightening experience rather than a pleasant float. They had had one spill and swim already, plus a tiring portage. I didn't know exactly what lay ahead, although I knew this was the only big rapid on the river. Even a small shoal might upset them. With the weather getting cool, they didn't need another swim. We'd have to go on cautiously, as we had so far.

As I led off downstream in my kayak, I realized I had a headache. Why? I was worried, sure that people weren't having a good time, afraid someone would be hurt. I felt responsible for everything from the water level to the weather, but I couldn't do anything about those problems, including how the others felt. As I heard Melanie Brookman and Jim Brown laughing in the rain, I realized whether each person enjoyed the trip or hated it was entirely up to him or her. All I could control was my own attitude.

I relaxed and lay back on the deck of my kayak, letting the rain pepper my face. I remembered my summer as a lifeguard at a hometown pool. Rainy afternoons had been my delight because no one came to the pool. It became my private world.

If you go out in the rain while everyone else is hiding by the fire, you'll have a unique experience. I did while walking along the usually crowded Palisades of the Chattahoochee River in Atlanta one rainy Christmas afternoon. I threw a thick wool cape over me and walked for hours, seeing no one, hearing only the rushing river and the rain in the trees. Not a bird twittered. Silence. I could have been in the North Woods. The rain gave me a wilderness for one afternoon in the middle of a city.

Today, however, I wanted to see some animals, and the rain was making that unlikely. The Ocmulgee usually has osprey, kingfishers, lots of turtles, and deer, if you're lucky. So far our only deer sighting had been while driving shuttle, when a large doe leaped out in front of us. On the river sharp-eyed Jim had spotted one water snake. Everything else seemed to have holed up. The high water had even covered up all traces of muskrat or beaver except a few well-chewed sticks that washed by.

About four o'clock we floated past several miles of low banks forming the first sandy beaches we had seen all day. A few scattered trees and the grass sure looked inviting. I began to think longingly of a warm cosy camp with a fire, because it was still raining.

Stacy Lang loaned me her rain jacket. She and her mother Eileen were warm because they were working hard to push their Blue Hole canoe along on the flat water. My downriver-model kayak was making things too easy for me.

About six o'clock the Georgia 83 bridge appeared ahead. Here the Juhlins had left their car. Bless 'em, they volunteered to drive to Macon and get one of our other cars so we wouldn't be faced with a 28-mile paddle on Sunday. The next bridge was only four miles downstream, and wouldn't give us much of a trip for the next day, so we asked them to drop a car for us at Dames Ferry, 12 miles farther. With the trip shortened, we wouldn't have to push and could camp early.

It was none too soon. Everyone seemed tired, and the continuing rain was depressing. The Hodges family were still going strong, but Carolyn confessed, as she passed out candy to revive the rest of us, that they had gone square dancing until late the previous night, then gotten up at 5 a.m. to drive from Clarkesville to meet us.

We began to look earnestly for a camp site. Around us were only swampy woods. The river had flooded the weekend before, and every low spot was soggy. Finally I spotted a small hill and paddled to shore. It looked as if the hill top might be level and dry. I pulled my kayak in to the bank and hooked the grab loop over a stump. Pulling myself up the muddy, slippery bank by hanging on to bushes, I knew we'd never get our gear up this hill. Besides, the top, although dry, was a thicket of brush and poison ivy. I retreated.

Jim scouted the next hill, with no better luck. We paddled on for almost an hour, trying and rejecting a dozen spots. My dreams of a warm fire were being crowded out by nightmares about mud and poison ivy. Everywhere we looked there were three or four feet of steep muddy bank between us and firm ground.

Once I paddled up a little tributary creek, hoping to find a gentle slope where we could unload easily. The creek was even steeper than the main river bank, but my discouragement was lifted by the sight of a well-used otter slide. At least someone knew how to enjoy mud.

Finally we spotted Tyler Island. Surely there would be a place to land. At the moment all I wanted out of life was to be dry and inside a sleeping bag. Jeff Viehmayer jumped ashore; others followed. By the time I got to the island, they were walking slowly back to the canoes. "Full of poison ivy," someone muttered.

Then we heard John call from upstream. He had paddled around the back of the island and found a rocky ledge leading ashore—our bridge over the sea of mud! Behind the trees was a clearing with plenty of room. John was our hero. In ten minutes he and Mac had a big fire going. Suddenly we were all moving with energy again. I passed around cups of double strong, sweet hot tea and spirits revived. With tents and tarps up we all relaxed, anticipating supper.

I had packed light, carrying no luxuries, because I hadn't camped from this particular kayak before and didn't know how it would handle with a load in the back. Consequently, I was eating freeze-dried food. After I offered around samples of my dinner, which were politely declined by all, I was treated to some real food by the Hodges and Bittners.

Tom Hodges brought out chunks of Vermont cheddar for an appetizer. While I munched, I watched Steve Herskovitz retrieve from the coals a foil-wrapped stew that had been cooking for half an hour or more. Mary Bittner replaced the stew with a Dutch oven full of sliced apples, brown sugar, and cinnamon. Again, coals were raked over the goodies. Mary said she hoped there wasn't too much water in the apples. She was worried? I

wasn't. I could tell from the way their eyes were riveted on the fire that the others weren't either. If it turned out half as good as it smelled it would be wonderful. I couldn't believe it when Steve asked if anyone wanted cake for dessert. He was ready to bake one in the coals, but we were stuffed.

I decided that night that my camping style was missing a certain flair. Compared to spiced apples freshly baked in the fire, an instant freeze-dried pudding tastes sick. Maybe I'll get a Dutch oven.

As I drifted off to sleep, a breeze lifted the raindrops off the surrounding trees and sent the swiftest of showers across my tarp. Then all was still except for the soft steps of someone banking the fire for tomorrow.

I wondered what tomorrow would bring. Would it still be raining? Would the portage of the dam at Juliette be as long and hard as this morning's at the big rapid? Would the car be waiting at Dames Ferry? It suddenly didn't matter. We'd work it out, regardless. We were strangers no longer. The hardships and discomforts of the day had created confidence in each other and a sense of responsibility to the whole group. We were pulling together. At some point during the day or evening, almost every person had done something to help another or to benefit the whole group. This had worked a magic. Although the trip itself was physically uncomfortable, I found that I was thoroughly enjoying it. There's no adventure like getting to know other people, especially if a river brings you together.

CANOEING GUIDE

Ocmulgee River

From just below Lake Jackson to Macon, the Ocmulgee runs over 40 miles. It's a good three-day trip, and can be broken into approximately equal parts by camping the first night below Ga. 83 bridge and the second night below Dames Ferry bridge. Much of the east side of the river is publicly owned land in the Oconee National Forest and Piedmont Wildlife Management Area.

While on the stretch from Ga. 16 to Ga. 83, be careful not to leave your canoe beached at the water line. A sudden release of water from Lloyd Shoals dam can abruptly raise the water level.

The river is almost completely undeveloped, except for the towns of Juliette and East Juliette on the river. From the river all that can be seen of the towns are the tops of a few buildings. Just below the highway bridge at Juliette is an old dam, completely across the river. Approach with extreme caution, as the water spills over the top. Land on the west side at the old factory for a portage. You have your choice of an arduous lift of the canoes over several concrete walls down to the base of the dam or an equally arduous but simpler walk around the abandoned buildings, following the railroad tracks and ducking under the last building.

Besides the dam at Juliette, the only other danger point is the big rapid about four river miles below the put in. Scout this carefully. The waterfall in the chute between the right bank and an island could be run by an experienced decked boater. Experienced canoeists could eddy out just above the fall and carry around it or run the main channel between the two islands if there's enough water. The main channel is a long Class III shoal that can be run almost anywhere. Scout it from the island off the left bank. One three-foot ledge about a mile above Dames Ferry and a similar one

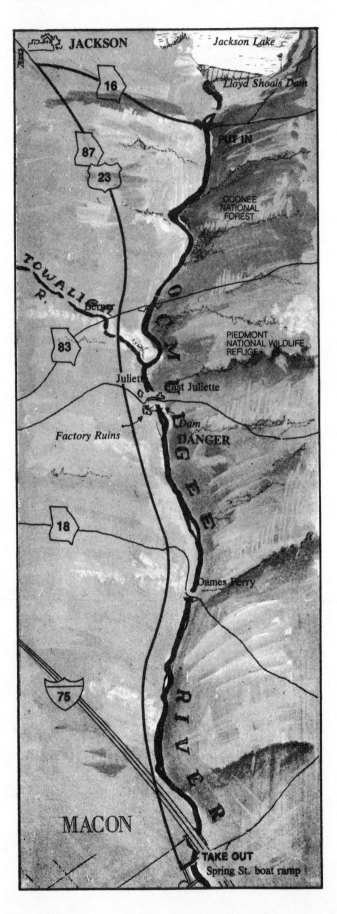

just downstream of the bridge, both Class II, could be tricky in high water.

To shuttle: Unload below Lloyd Shoals dam and take Ga. 16 west to Jackson, where you turn south on Ga. 87. Follow 87, which parallels the river, all the way into Macon, where it turns left and crosses the river. One way, the shuttle is 44 miles. If you're running one of the shorter stretches, you'll still find it easiest to use Ga. 87 as your shuttle road, but the distances will be less.

For a shorter trip, either one day or overnight, take your pick of the following. From Ga. 16 to Ga. 83 is nearly 13 miles. On to the bridge in Juliette is another four miles. Farther downstream to Dames Ferry and the Ga. 18 bridge is 8½ miles. On to Ga. 87 bridge in Macon is another 15 miles. At Ga. 16 the easiest put in is off a paved road that runs north along the east side of the river. At Ga. 83 you can drive practically to the water on the east side. At Juliette there is good access on the west side at the dam. At Ga. 18 a dirt road on the east side is a good walking path, but too rough for cars. Park on the shoulder. In Macon the Spring Street boat ramp on the east bank downstream of the U.S. 23 and Ga. 87 bridge offers plenty of parking.

1976

Ti-laggi, You Fickle River, You

It'll excite you, exasperate you, entice you, infuriate you, and only reluctantly let you go. A canoeing adventure.

by Reece G. Turrentine

The Towaliga has interested me for years. Most folks see the river only at its most dramatic point, where it crosses the Fall Line at High Falls State Park in northwest Monroe County. After it pours over the dam where it once provided water power for old mills and powerhouses, it goes crashing over the falls in a thunder of foam and spray.

But my attention was attracted to the stretch of river below the falls. What was it like, where did it go, and was it canoeable?* Different people gave me different answers: definite *yeses,* emphatic *noes,* and in-between *maybes.* I was to discover they all had been right. For canoeists, the Towaliga both invites and forbids, it rewards and punishes.

Burns Willis and I dipped our paddles into the Towaliga for the first time in the grey overcast of a Saturday morning. It

---

* One thing other than its canoeability has always interested me about the Towaliga: How does one pronounce it? The generally accepted pronunciation is *towel* (like "bath towel") and *aggie* (as in "Maggie"). The natives along the river, however, leave out a vowel and make it simply *Ti-laggi.*

felt good to be in a canoe with Burns again. It helps to have a close friend as a partner. You need to canoe with someone with whom you can be irritated on one curve, and laughing on the next. Burns, a Methodist minister, is that kind of friend. Years of shared experiences, agreements, and irritations have produced that friendship.

Burns had been good-naturedly apprehensive from the first moment he answered my phone call.

"Burns," I had said.

"No," he interrupted. "I can't do it."

He always starts like that so he can blame me when things turn sour, as they did in the middle of the Okefenokee Swamp a few years back when we got caught in an ice storm. But I knew he'd go.

The opening few miles were kind. The Towaliga gently lets the canoeist in on her many moods. We settled into the rhythmic pattern of paddling we had developed on many previous trips. Burns with his good strong stroke and good eye for the river in the bow, and me in the back.

With more water the first rocky shoals we came to would be moderate whitewater runs, but we had to scrape and scratch, bump and thud to get through. The shoals became more numerous and the shallow water was a problem. We had to portage one set, because the water just spread into nothing.

For the first of many times that day I thought back to the conversations I had had with folks along the river when I was trying to decide whether or not to canoe it. "It's too shallow, too rocky," park ranger Letson at High Falls had told me. "Too many trees blocking the way. We don't have the water we used to have."

"I hope there aren't many of these," I said to Burns as we hefted our boat over the rocks. He didn't comment.

A little further down river we began to notice another side of the Towaliga's personality: sand bars. At first we tried to predict where the deep "run" of the river would be. Normally, it follows the outside of the bend, but the Towaliga isn't normal. Sometimes the run is on the outside, next, on the inside. Then it'll divide and go on both sides. Next, straight down the middle. This made for constant chatter: "Go to the left," Burns said. "But the outside is to the right," I countered. "Never mind, go to the left."

Sometimes he was right, sometimes I was. We had quite a few "I-told-you-sos." I think Burns recognized its unpredictability before I did. I kept trying to figure out a pattern; he realized there was none. We had to keep a sharp eye out and guess. Since he was in the bow, I followed his eyesight—at times, with misgivings. A carefully arranged hierarchy of command doesn't work too well on the Towaliga. Canoeing it needs to be a joint effort.

In two hours I spotted Flat Bridge, a sight I had visited two days earlier while scouting the river. It's an old one-lane bridge in the back country on a twisting road. And what a swimming hole! When I was there on my motorcycle, a half dozen naked, brown-skinned boys were taking turns swinging on a rope far out over the river. Their shouts made me want to join them.

"Any of you boys ever canoe this river?" I called out.

"Naw, we only swim in it," was the answer.

I left them to their swimming and looked around for myself. The view from the bridge helped me decide to canoe the Towaliga. The shoals I saw were shallow, but I spotted a run through the rocks next to one of the bridge pilings and made a mental note of its location.

Now in the canoe I heard Burns call out, "We can't get through those shoals under the bridge."

"Yes we can," I replied in a superior tone. "I see a run through them."

I headed for the spot I had scouted from above and we skimmed right through. He was impressed, and I didn't reveal my secret.

About fifty yards down from the bridge, Burns said: "Look at that big catfish caught in the shallows." His fin and tail were visible, wriggling for deeper water. As we got closer, Burns' voice changed pitch: "That fish isn't caught in shallow waters. He's caught in a snake's mouth!" A large moccasin had him fast, and was making his way towards shore. We watched with anxious fascination.

Once the snake was at the shoreline, he inched out of the water, exposing the whole fish. He held him there, until the fish stopped squirming. Then off into the woods with his breakfast, dinner, and supper in his mouth. It was an awesome sight.

We later commented on the fact that neither of us thought about killing the snake. At other times we would have, but here it seemed inappropriate. We had been allowed spectator privileges to a normal process in the wilderness. We simply observed this rare sight.

We caught sight of the Georgia highway 42 bridge, our lunch stop, at exactly noon. We slid up beside a sand bar and unpacked a can of Spam, Vienna sausages and hot Cokes.

"Where's Mr. Pitt with his barbecue?" asked Burns.

"Afraid I didn't make plans for that," I replied. "Didn't know our schedule."

"That's no excuse. With a little planning we could be eating fresh barbecue instead of this stuff."

I didn't even bother to reply.

Burns' needling brought back to mind a little barbecue shed on highway 42 that I had passed while inspecting the river. "Pitt Bar-B-Que," the sign said. A misspelling, I thought to myself until I sought out the owner and met Mr. Pitt himself.

"Of course, you can canoe it," he assured me. "Let me know when you plan to be at the bridge and I'll bring you a fine barbecue plate for dinner."

I was glad I had taken the advice about the river and regretted as much as Burns did that I hadn't taken him up on the offer of a good lunch.

The lunch break didn't revive us as much as we expected, and we were beginning to feel tired when the river's next mood became evident.

We entered a primeval wilderness, with no signs of civilization whatsoever. Massive fallen trees intertwined from both sides of the banks. Around each bend it looked as if our passage would be blocked. Actually, we portaged only twice, but the Towaliga kept us guessing right up to the last minute. Some trees we could go around, some over, others under. Some boughs were so close to the water the canoe had to go under and we had to go over.

A couple of hours later we glided under Georgia highway 83 bridge, the only hint of civilization during this part of the run. It was here during my scouting expedition that I had met Mr. Thomas. I was huddling under a big oak tree during a rainstorm, when his friendly voice called from the porch: "Come on up here and wait out the rain!" My enjoyable visit with him lasted long after the rain stopped. "Folks canoe it now and then. The Treadwell boys from Forsyth ran it last week. Sorry you got caught in this rain. But it was just right for my turnips." His hospitality and pride for his turnips made me even appreciate the rain. I splashed into Forsyth to look up Mr. Treadwell, who owns the Ford dealership. "Definitely run it. I went with the boys last week and it's beautiful. Hard in places, but worth it."

Around a couple of bends beyond the highway 83 bridge and we were back to primeval wilderness. It was really getting tough now. How we longed for some deep water, to get one full paddle stroke. But with each stroke our paddles would crunch in the sand, jolt our back muscles and rattle our teeth. This stretch was as hard as any part of the trip, but we still averaged about two and a half miles an hour.

One old area resident had told me, "The river's like a fickle woman, always making promises, but not delivering, hinting at one thing but then changing her mind. She'll excite you, then exasperate you, entice you, then infuriate you."

The Towaliga seemed almost to reach out after us. I'm sure our fatigue had something to do with this illusion. There were times the massive fallen trees seemed like giant webs blocking our path. As we inched through its branches, we almost expected the giant creature that spun it to reach out and "get" us. We were tireder than we realized. It's a tough trip, but never boring.

As the day wore on, we realized our mood had changed, too. We began to fit in with the river instead of fighting it. We accepted its surprises. I ceased trying to figure it out, pattern its current, match its obstacles, overrun its barriers. We stopped trying to compete with it, and instead submitted to it. The Towaliga was not a challenge to be overcome. It was an experience to be absorbed.

This mood of submission, coupled with sheer weariness, carried us down the final hours in relative silence. Burns all but whispered the directions, and I steered like a robot.

The end came suddenly. We went under the U.S. highway 23 bridge, under a railroad trestle, around a few more bends, and we saw the wide expanse of the Ocmulgee ahead. "We'll finally have some deep water!" I sighed. This brought a moment of mild enthusiasm. But the fickle waters of the Towaliga must have affected the Ocmulgee at that point. The deep water was beautiful, but the wind was contrary and there was no aiding current. Then it was almost as if she reached down river to us one more time, to give us a departing touch of her contrary ways.

The mouth of the Towaliga was still in sight when we ground to our most crunching halt. We sat still in disbelief. There were no sand bars, trees, stumps or anything. But we were pinned down, and no maneuver could free us. I climbed into the bow with Burns and we slid free. We glimpsed our captor as we drifted off: an old piece of steel frame from a sunken bridge. We laughed at the absurdity of the thing. "It must have come from the Towaliga years ago," I laughed.

Driving home that night, my arms still wanted to paddle instead of steer. Around each curve in the road I expected to see fallen trees and great sand bars. My aching body fell into bed that night and I said to my wife: "Never again. It's insanity to subject yourself to such agony. Never again!"

My bones still ached when I rolled over to cut off the alarm the next morning. I stumbled out to get the paper in the pre-dawn light. It had rained during the night. As we sat at breakfast, I asked her, "Did you know it rained last night?" She didn't. Then, I was surprised at my own next question. I couldn't believe it. But I was saying it: "I wonder if it rained at High Falls." "Why?" she asked with growing suspicion. "Well," I stammered, "maybe the Towaliga's up." She stared with disbelief. "Are you serious?"

I didn't say anymore about it, and haven't since. But there's an old stump I spotted as we passed under the last bridge. It stuck about six inches out of the water. I'm watching that stump every time I cross that bridge. And in February and March, when the rains come and the water reaches the top of that stump, I'm reaching for the phone. "Burns?" I'll say. "No, not me," he'll reply. But he will. And so will I.

CANOEING GUIDE

Towaliga River

The Towaliga is one of the choice wilderness rivers of Middle Georgia. It is small, twisting, and obstructed with shoals, sand bars, and fallen trees. But great for canoeing. The current is good and the scenery is wild and up close. You can run the entire length (20 miles) from High Falls to where it empties into the Ocmulgee River in one full day. Or you can divide it into any number of shorter runs, as indicated on the map. The four bridges that cross it are about five miles apart, and ideally located for easy shuttle.

Each segment has its own character; shoals and trees dominate the first half, sand bars and fallen trees the last.

The water level is important. Two or three inches of water spilling over the dam at High Falls means great canoeing. This much water usually comes during late winter and early spring. Less than that, you'd better prepare for scrapes, bumps, and sore muscles.

Your put in is at High Falls State Park (1 on map) at the lower campground. If this section of the campground is closed (from Nov. to April), you can put in at the parking area at the old powerhouse. You'll want to see this and hear of its history, anyway. To get to these points, follow the road that leads beside and behind the High Falls Restaurant (a must for a meal!) This leads to both the powerhouse and campground, right on the river.

The first leg from High Falls (1) to Flat Shoals bridge (2) is about five miles. You've got mild rapids and shoals here that could get interesting with higher water. A few cabins dot the banks, but they disappear in time. At Flat Shoals Bridge, don't miss the great swimming hole on the left as you approach the bridge. You can run the shoals that stretch under the bridge by hugging the right side of the right bridge abutment.

From Flat Shoals Bridge to the Georgia highway 42 bridge (Forsyth-Jackson Road, 3 on the map) is another four or five miles.

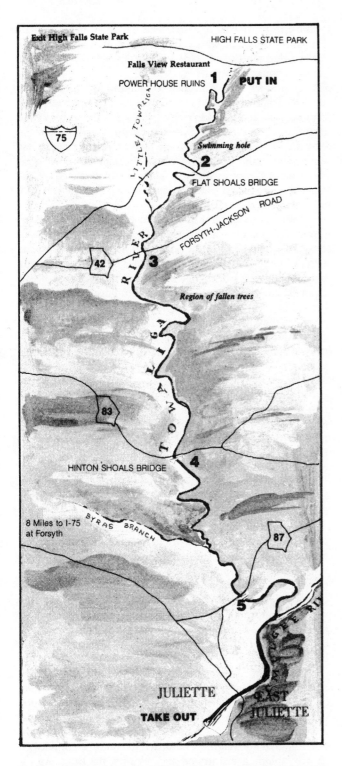

Banks are high around this bridge on 42, so scout ahead if this is to be your take out.

The stretch between 42 bridge and 83 bridge (between 3 and 4 on map) becomes more desolate. You enter primeval wilderness with great fallen trees creating your biggest obstacles. You just have to work your way through them. From highway 83 bridge to the Ocmulgee is primitive. You may want to take out at highway 87 or continue on to the Ocmulgee and down it a couple of miles to

Juliette. The Ocmulgee seems like the ocean compared to the Towaliga.

One word of caution about Juliette. The Ocmulgee pours over the dam, so use caution approaching it. Just before you reach the dam, there's a little slough off to the right—a good take out point right on the road.

1976

Scrunch!

Every canoeist has heard it, that shoulder-humping sound when boat hits rock. The thing about the Broad is that it gives you a choice of SCRUNCHING or not

by Reece Turrentine

"Well, are we going to paddle upstream, and see it?" I asked once more. We had discussed it earlier, but now the time of decision had come. The canoes were in the water, and we were in the canoes. We couldn't put it off any longer.

"I just hate the thought of paddling upstream for a quarter of a mile," Owen complained. "We'll be worn out before we start." I couldn't disagree with that. I didn't look forward to an upstream paddle, especially since all of us were soloing. But I replied half-heartedly, "Mr. Parham said that in his younger days they used to pole their flat-bottom boats and race up to it."

We were talking about a place upstream that had intrigued me since hearing about it the day before. I had stopped by Mr. Parham's house on the river bank near the put-in bridge. He had been sitting on the porch surrounded by a bunch of children and grandchildren. As I drove up and told him of my interest in the river, his eyes lit up. He replied, "Well, I've lived on its banks all my life. There are a lot of interesting things on it. Take the Devil's Pulpit, for example." And then he went on to describe this large rock overhang with caves and cliffs. Being a minister, my curiosity was immediately ignited.

"Where'd it get that name?" I inquired.

"Nobody seems to know that," he replied. "It's just always been a place where strange things went on. Folks have always been kinda leery of it." Then he went on to recount some of the mystery and intrigue that had surrounded the "Devil's Pulpit" through the years. Once a band of escaped slaves hid out there. Then a Civil War deserter holed up in the cave with the slaves. He became a shoemaker, selling shoes to the local residents and using the slaves as his secret salesmen. Nobody ever saw him, but they bought his shoes. They say he was mean and evil, and would shoot any intruder on the spot.

As we continued to debate the upstream paddle, Jan entered the conversation. "Why not wait till your next trip? You're gonna want to run this river again soon, and you can put in at the next bridge up, make a two-day run of it, and see it on the way down." That made sense and settled the question. After all, Jan was the professional of the group. He operates his outdoor center known as "Blue Ridge River Touring" a few miles from the river in Danielsville, and has been on this river many times. We took his advice, saved the Devil's Pulpit for another day, and slid our canoes out into the steady current of the Broad River.

Though full of intriguing history, it was the present we were interested in right now. Foreboding mysteries may hover over its past, but it's a fun river now.

"Why, sometimes there are so many folks camped under the bridge," laughed Billy Martin at his Riverside Fish House restaurant, "that you can't unroll another sleeping bag. A lot of them are students from Athens, but a lot of families come, too. It's close to Atlanta, Augusta, and Athens. Folks come here rather than travel up into the mountains. And you got all kinds of rapids at each spot. It's fun for experts and beginners. And this pretty weather's gonna really bring 'em out."

He was right about that. We shared the put in with several groups. Right behind us were two couples in canoes, and grandma and grandpa with a bunch of grandchildren in a big rubber raft. The weather and river were bringing 'em out.

As the bridge disappeared around the curve, we heard our first sound of the coming excitement ahead of us. The roar of the rapids. No matter how many rivers you've run or how many rapids you've raced, that sound has an effect all its own. It always stirs the blood a bit and quickens the heartbeat. Even calm water foreshadows their presence. Deep water, backed up, means something's blocking it up ahead, usually shoals, rocks, and rapids. When you hear them long before you see them, you think it may just be the wind in the trees. But as the faint sound grows louder, it takes on an unmistakable roar. So you adjust your knee pads, glance around to be sure everything is tied in securely, and get ready for the fun.

"Flat Shoals ahead," Jan called back to us. "We'll stop and scout these and check on the optional runs." It was a favorite stopping place. Large flat boulders stretched across the river, with the current being squeezed between them. It was too inviting to pass by, so we slid our canoes in beside the largest flat rock and got out to scout the rapids.

"I usually like to run that chute on the far left right up against the bank," Jan said. "But that log jammed over there recently, and it makes the approach pretty tight. This one right next to our rock is probably the best one today. Let me see how it runs." With that, Jan was back in his canoe, shoved it at an angle upstream until the current caught its bow, and swung it down towards the run of the rapid. He shot the chute cleanly and swiftly. Once through, his body arched far over the side, as he reached with a high brace stroke and dug his paddle into the calm eddy water beside the rapid. Using his body as the pivot, he smoothly swung the bow into the eddy, allowing the current to swing the stern behind him. With one expert stroke the whole canoe glided into the eddy and up to the rock where we were standing.

"That's just plain beautiful," Owen sighed to me. And it was. It looked more like ballet than paddling. Jan Fortune had told me that canoeing had always been his first love. So after a stretch in college at Athens, he and his wife decided to try to make a business out of doing what he loved most. With such skill he's bound to make it.

"I wonder what happened to grandma and grandpa and the grandchildren behind us?" Owen asked. They had put in right after us and we hadn't seen them since. But as we looked upstream, there they came around the bend. And it was obvious why they were so slow. They were playing. As their canoes and raft rounded the bend, you could see high arches of spray shooting out from each canoe. Their laughter echoed up and down the river walls. It was the age-old game of paddle splashing, a favorite river sport.

"We'll probably end up like that before the day is over," Owen smiled at me with a devilish grin.

"Yeah, and you'll be the one to start it," I shot back at him. I know him too well. Owen Williams lives on the edge of laughter. His bushy beard, muddy boots, and messy pickup hardly identify him as the minister of the Methodist church in Roberta. But his genuine love for people and joy of life do. Young people follow him around like his old trailer and its fleet of canoes. His canoes are special, memorial canoes given in memory of young people who died in his town. Names like "Johnny Wright" and "Mary Ann" are painted on them in large letters, and the bow decks carry shiny little brass memorial plaques with inscriptions such as, "This canoe is given to this youth ministry in memory of Johnny Wright by . . ." Though the canoes are meant for fun and laughter, those little plaques add a note of touching sentiment. Reading them makes it easier to think of the deeper meaning of the great outdoors and the beauty of God's nature.

"We can't stay here all day," Jan warned. "We've got rapids to run." So we slid our canoes into the current and down the chute, and on to the shoals below.

The tree line and the drop along the shore now gave definite indications of a good downhill run ahead. The back of my neck gave off the little sting of exhilaration that always comes just before such a run. And it was a good one. The pace was rapid and the choices plentiful. The smooth-bottom whitewater canoes responded to every touch, gliding through Vs, over shelves, bending and blending with the currents. I felt my face reflecting my choices: a smug smile when the choice was right, and the familiar frown when the "scrunch" of the bottom was heard.

Soloing increased our margin of error somewhat. The canoes rode high and seemed to bounce on top of the water. But on one twisting turn I misread the current, and the midsection slid sideways onto a rock. The rushing water lapped dangerously close to the canoe's edge, threatening to spill over the side. I shifted my weight forward, and the canoe windmilled on its axis, spinning me around and releasing me back into the rapid. Down the chute I went—backwards!

"What are those pipes sticking out of those rocks up there, Jan?" Owen called out. Before Jan could reply, I butted in. "Mr. Cornwell's great-grandfather ran a ferry across here," I answered smugly.

"I asked Jan!" Owen snorted with friendly contempt. "You don't live around here."

"No, but Mr. Cornwell's lived on this river all his life," I shot back, seeing a rare opportunity to get the upper hand on Owen. "I tried to get you to come up with me yesterday and talk to some of the folks that live around here, but no, you were too busy."

Through his bushy beard, I could see his devilish grin. "I was about the Father's business," he said with a superior tone. I didn't even bother to reply.

I enjoy talking with the folks on the rivers almost as much as I do canoeing them. They all love to talk about "their" river when I inquire with genuine interest. Their bits of history and local color give me an added dimension when I enter the river. I respect it more. I feel as though I take some of their love for it with me as I look for rocks and old roads and decaying ruins that have played so important a part in so many lives. Those old landmarks occupied the river long before modern canoes came along. Rocks that now provide shoals for canoe enthusiasts once held pilings for ancient bridges, or fish traps, or bygone ferrys. To run them so quickly without at least an awareness of their bygone importance seems a little disrespectful.

"Let's stop for lunch," Owen called out.

"Stop again?" I replied. "We'll never finish this run." What started out to be a serious canoe run had become a stop-and-go fun-time. Carefully planned schedules had fallen victim to the mood of the day and the carefree leisure of the others on the river.

"My sardines are getting hot," Owen retorted. "There's a perfect place ahead." So we slid onto one of the massive boulders in mid-river and settled down to our favorite canoeing cuisine: sardines and saltines.

"Where does the pipeline cross the river, Jan?" I asked, remembering another one of Mr. Cornwell's yarns.

"Just around the curve," he replied. "Why?"

"Well, according to Mr. Cornwell, that was THE spot on the river years ago. It was the location of the famous 'Still House,' a stagecoach inn which was an overnight stop for aristocrats traveling from the Carolinas to Georgia. They called it the Still House because next to it was a government-operated still. They say it used to be the best stop on the line. Until recent years you could still see the old stone wall along the river bank, but the pipeline throughway erased every bit of evidence."

With lunch over, and back on the river, we rounded the curve, and the pipeline throughway came into view. It was like a giant gash across the land, with no trees, only clay hills on each side of the river. Mr. Cornwell was right. There wasn't the slightest evidence of the Still House. I couldn't even imagine it in my mind. But I could imagine, looking up a little service road that ran down the throughway to the river's edge, that at any moment it might come into view: the cloud of dust and the pounding horses, racing the stagecoach down the hill on its scheduled run.

In the few remaining miles, we took advantage of Jan's company and the ideal conditions of the Broad River for instruction and practice. Just below the pipeline crossing is a healthy waterfall on the right of an island. Jan had run it before, but warned against it because of the water level. The chutes to the left were fun enough.

We spent the last hour within sight of the take-out bridge, running and rerunning rapids, practicing various strokes, and generally having a ball.

After an easy take out and shuttle, Owen and I were back at the put-in bridge, sinking our teeth into some of Billy Martin's fresh catfish at his Riverside Fish House, and making our plans for a return to the Broad River.

"I knew you'd want to come back," Mr. Martin laughed. "Most folks do."

"We have to," I smiled back at him. "We've got to make that upper run that comes by the Devil's Pulpit. I have an idea it'll just fit Owen."

CANOEING GUIDE

Map Information: *Mile 0-1* No particular fast action in this first mile. Swift, deep water with plenty of fishing holes. Overhanging limbs and swift current could cause trouble if fishing too close to shore.

Mile 1-2 Around sharp bend in river to right is Flat Shoals (A), first good white water. Stop and scout and stretch on inviting rocks. Fast chute against left bank may be blocked by recent drift limbs. Several optional runs through these shoals.

Mile 2-3 After Parham's Deep Water, one of the deepest pools on the river, you come to Scarbrough Shoals (B). Watch for ferry pipes sticking out of mid-river rocks. This is location of off-river beaver ponds, ferry crossing, and possible old bridge debris. Class I and II rapids here.

Mile 3-4 Our lunch stop (C) on these rocks near left bank and old road entrance. Unsightly pipeline throughway gashes through forests around bend. This was site of famous but now extinct "Still House" (see text).

Mile 4-5 Below pipeline throughway is Brown's Shoals. A must stop to scout waterfall on right (D) of mid-river island. Unless you're an expert, use chutes to left of island, which should be scouted, too. If you choose to run the waterfall, take the right side of the island. The water will pass over the ledge in three well-defined places. We chose the left drop, about 15 feet from the left shore. This would rate the mildest class III, and that only because the drop is four to five feet. The approach is flat water and simple to make. Aim for the slight dip in the very center of the drop. The ride is more of a slide and is the most fun of any on the river. Below Brown's Shoals notice Skull Creek entering river on right. Human skulls of Indians or slaves found along this creek bed.

Mile 5-Take Out Class I and II rapids in and around Compton's Shoals (E). Fun place to practice runs and reruns within sight of take-out bridge. Since you're already wet, continue downstream past bridge to island (and good take-out point). Take a flying swing on the rope at this favorite swimming hole.

General Information: The Broad is a wide river in the Northeast Georgia foothills, 20 miles northeast of Athens. Its north and middle forks join with the Hudson River just southwest of Royston, and thus supplied with a great volume of water, it continues southeast until it enters the Clark Hill Reservoir on the South Carolina border.

Type of River: Clear, mountain-type river with Class I and II rapids, shoals, and shelves. There are possible class IIIs in high water. Ideal for the intermediate-range paddler. Rapids usually offer two or more runs, so paddlers can choose according to their skills. This same quality also makes the Broad an excellent teaching river.

Put In and Take Out: Put in on state highway 281 five miles south

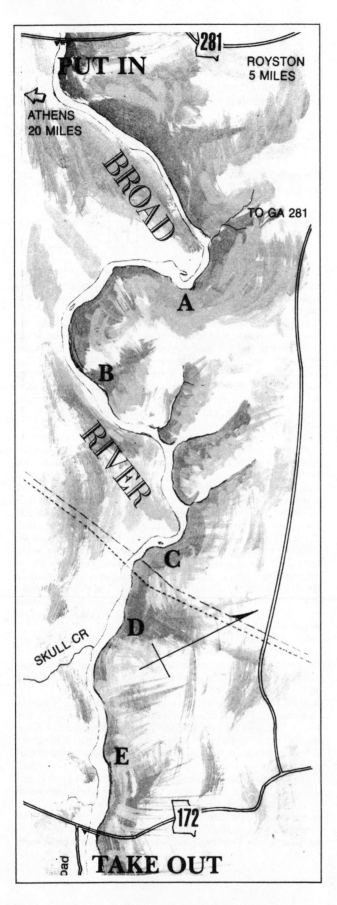

of Royston. Northeast corner of bridge has large dirt parking area. Road leads down to river's edge for unloading, but only if ground is dry. Suggest leaving vehicles parked in large area in case rain turns road into impassable mud slide. Take out is on Georgia 172. Good dirt road parallels river on southeast side, offering several optional take-out points below bridge.

Shuttle: Easy and short. Paved county road parallels river to north (see highway map) between Georgia highways 281 and 172.

Water Level: No water gauge on this stretch, but just below take-out bridge on the upstream side are the old remaining foundation blocks of a covered bridge. Unless water is flowing over the tops of these, river should be safe.

Distance: River distance from bridge 281 to 172 is about 5½ miles, making this an easy afternoon's run, allowing time for drifting, fishing, and picnicking. Trip can be doubled by using put-in bridge on U.S. 29, extending it to a 10-mile run.

Hazards: Serious problems could arise from failure to scout the few more advanced rapids on this stretch. Though mostly class I and II, there are several optional runs approaching III. Don't allow the leisurely nature of the river to drift you suddenly into the currents of these stronger rapids and waterfalls (see map for location).

1977

Wham!

Rapids that'll blow you out of the water

by Reece Turrentine

The bow shot out over the edge of the waterfall. For a moment it hesitated; then it tilted down and plunged like an arrow toward the foaming fury at the foot of the falls. I shivered as I saw the front quarter of my canoe disappear into the boiling water of the hydraulic. Water poured in over the bow and the gunwales. I don't know why I hadn't expected it. I had already watched two kayaks disappear like submarines into that hydraulic. What chance did I have in an open canoe? And I couldn't say I hadn't been warned.

"I just don't take open boats on Potato Creek," Jim McDaniels had told me earlier on the day of our trip. "In fact, I won't rent out my canoes for that creek. It's just too unpredictable. I'd rather stick with the Flint River. A few local men kayak Potato Creek now and then, but they're good, and the water's got to be right."

I had listened with respect to his warnings. I've known Jim and Margie McDaniels for several years, and I've stopped occasionally at their Flint River Outdoor Center to chat and admire the progress of their riverside outpost. But for several years I've also been curious about nearby Potato Creek. And, finally, my curiosity made me stop and scout a spot on that creek that looks like the edge of the world, downstream from the US 36 bridge. The first time I scouted Potato Creek, I thought: "Impossible. Too little water to canoe it." The next time I scouted the same section, several months later, I thought: "Impossible. Too much water." But in the back of my mind I kept wondering if it would be possible to catch Potato Creek with the water just right. My search for the answer to that question had brought me to see Jim.

On the bright winter morning of our run, Richard Rogers, who works at an outfitters called Macon Outdoors, and I had strapped my canoe and his kayak onto our cars and headed for the Flint River Outdoor Center. The usual warm hospitality and hot coffee awaited us as we pulled in. We sat around for a while, chatting, catching up on the local news, and looking over Jim's newest equipment. Then I broached my question.

"Tell me what you know about Potato Creek," I began cautiously. Immediately, his mood changed.

"We don't do too much over there," he said skeptically. "If the water's down, you're dragging bottom all the way. If it's up, it can be a killer, with rapids approaching Class Five and runnable only by experts in decked boats." Respecting his caution, yet still anxious to know more about Potato Creek, I pressed my question.

"But suppose you hit it between the extremes. I mean, after a moderate rain, like yesterday, but before it floods."

"Well," he drawled hesitantly, "I haven't checked it lately, and I've never been on some sections of it."

"Why don't we make a short run down to the big rapids, and scout them below the Georgia 74 bridge," I suggested quickly. "We can always take out if it's not right." This one-step-at-a-time approach and the brilliant winter day must have struck just the right note in Jim. He asked Margie if she could keep the store for a while, and we were off. It wasn't long before we were gliding down the initial section of Potato Creek below the US 19 bridge, toward the unknown.

Although our planned run was practically within the Thomaston city limits, we left all signs of civilization behind as we rounded the first curves. The first mile of our run was serene and silent: no hint of violence here. I felt a little foolish, all decked out in my life vest, wet suit, and helmet. We were all armed to the teeth, but there was no sign of an enemy.

As we passed the Hannah's Mill Road bridge, we heard the first rumblings of rough waters. We approached cautiously as we neared the rapids, but they turned out to be moderate: a good chance to flex our muscles and practice some strokes that we might need downstream.

"How does the water look to you?" I called over to Jim as we finished our run through the rapids.

"I can't tell," he replied. "I haven't run this section before, and I won't know until we get to the Georgia 74 bridge. There's a makeshift gauge someone has painted on a bridge piling. We'll check it out there."

It wasn't long before the bows of our boats grated onto the shore under the Georgia 74 bridge, and we got out to study the gauge: someone had spray-painted marks a foot apart on the bridge piling.

"You need inch markings on this creek," Jim observed. "Two or three inches either way makes the difference between dragging your boat and busting your boat. But while we are here, we might as well paddle down to the big rapids and see

what they look like. We can always paddle back up here if we want to and take out."

The current was almost gone now. The creek had that dammed-up look, that telltale stillness that always portends rocks or dams or something else downstream holding the water back. It's usually the stillness before the storm.

A few strokes beyond the bridge, we came within sight of what looked like the edge of the world. A spray mist lay heavily across the creek ahead, and wet, gray boulders dotted the horizon. Then I heard it: a faint rumble that grew to a thunderous roar as we paddled. I could see several swirls of water where the creek was squeezed into channels between rocks and then disappeared over the edge of a 20-foot waterfall.

As the current increased, we beached our canoes and followed a well-worn path down the shore. We had to find out how to get around what lay ahead. As we walked, we spoke very little. We were too busy studying and analyzing the contorted twists, turns, and drops in the slanted slice of earth that makes up this part of Potato Creek's bed.

The three of us separated; each wanted to get his own view of the threat before us. I sat for a while on a boulder on the shore, eyeing the powerful swirl of current that carried the main body of the creek over that killer of a waterfall. It would have to be avoided. Though the lesser channels that I could see were poorly defined, there was one that broke off and down over a lower waterfall on the east side of the creek. It looked runnable. But rocks and boulders seemed to have been placed to preclude running an alternate channel without sideswiping them.

When we got back together, Jim opened the conversation. "If we can run this left side, then to the middle, and back down there to the left," he said, pointing, "that secondary current will take us over the east waterfall and on down the rapids below. There are three waterfalls similar to this one, and also a long, steep run of fast, bumpy rapids. But I think the water level is right. If you want me to, I'll go first in my kayak. Y'all hike on down below the east falls and be ready for me with a throw rope, just in case."

I was anxious to see how his kayak would behave running over the waterfall. I was concerned about a rock that sat right at the top of the falls. Much of the water pouring over the edge seemed to be washing right into that rock, but Jim felt that he could turn sharply enough to avoid it.

Richard and I were ready at the foot of the falls when we saw Jim and his kayak enter the rapids upstream. His run through the drops and ledges was clean, with twists and turns made just at the right time to avoid the powerful current that threatened to sweep him over the dangerous falls on the west side. Soon he was beyond that danger, but he quickly faced new ones. Speeding over the rocks on his approach to the falls below which we waited, he rounded the final curve with a high brace, struggling for position to miss that rock at the top of the falls. But the water was too powerful. It sucked him right into the rock. He tilted dangerously for a moment, but he kept his balance, escaped the rock, and plummeted over the falls and into the foaming fury below. His kayak dove and disappeared completely. Only his head and shoulders were visible above the spume and spray. Then he and his kayak popped up, and he eddied safely onto the opposite shore. We clapped and shouted as he held his paddle high in a gesture of victory. Our applause, however, was somewhat constrained. We knew that we still had to face what he had survived.

Richard's run, also in a kayak, was almost identical to Jim's. He, too, was swept into the rock at the top of the falls, then catapulted over the edge. He almost capsized. Then it was my turn. I felt less confident than ever. The thought of fighting that turn, broaching into that rock, and facing a spill at the top of those falls grew less and less inviting. I could see why Jim had advised using decked kayaks on this creek.

I studied the falls, looking for an alternate route. I noticed a slot on the far side of the rock that looked more straight-forward than the route that Jim and Richard had tried. I decided to try that one.

My run through the upper rapids was like riding a bronco. My heavy canoe was hard to control. The current trying to force me toward the main falls was frightening, and my speed over the slippery rocks made proper stroking impossible. I resorted to anything that worked. I jabbed, poked, pried, and prayed. I did anything I could think of to make my reluctant canoe move into the weaker flow that led away from the bigger falls. I finally managed it, but I found myself heading straight for that rock at the top of the east falls. If I hit it, I would capsize.

Stretching to reach an eddy, I broke out of the current to catch my breath and align myself for the final plunge. Then I was back in the current. With one well-timed stroke, I aimed my canoe for my planned point of entry.

The bow of my canoe shot out into the air over the edge of the waterfall. The boat seemed to drop out from under me as it tilted downward and plunged toward the boiling foam of the hydraulic. Suddenly, half of my canoe disappeared under the water; water was pouring in over the bow and the sides. Reaching forward to brace and dig for water, I plowed deep with the paddle, and the canoe popped up and out of the hydraulic, sending me downstream still upright. But as I felt icy water around my knees and thighs, I knew I wasn't out of trouble yet. My canoe was half full of water, and I knew that that shifting ballast could capsize me quicker than the rapids. Kneeling low, I stretched for the haven of a nearby eddy. I skidded into it and slid safely onto a rock. I was too tired to hold my paddle up in victory, and I wasn't sure that it was time for such a gesture. Those falls had almost sunk me, and I wasn't through yet. I started to bail.

The next two waterfalls buried my bow again, and I spent more time bailing. Then came the grande finale: a long, fast, quarter-mile drop, with rapids as tight and torrential as any I've ever run.

An hour later, wet and exhausted, we slid up onto the sand beneath the take-out bridge. The late afternoon sun was low, and the air was cold.

"There's more of the same just below this bridge," Jim said.

"Yeah, I've seen them before," I replied. "Let's save that for another day." I started to unload my gear. We'd done enough for one day. Besides, to run the next rapids meant either a take out and a long portage back up to the Georgia 36 bridge, or an eight-mile run to the next bridge. We had neither the time nor the energy. But there'll be another day, when, after some rest and some rain, the water will be right and the sun will be bright. And we'll peel off again into Potato Creek.

CANOEING GUIDE

Potato Creek

General Information: Expert whitewater enthusiasts will find plenty of action on this short but heavy whitewater section of Potato Creek. Although practically within the city limits of Thomaston, it has all the qualities of a wilderness river.

The creek is very dangerous. Local residents are hesitant to give it much publicity for fear that ill-equipped and inexperienced canoeists will flock to it as they did to the Chattooga after *Deliverance* was filmed there. Flint River Outdoor Center will not rent canoes for use on Potato Creek. Only canoeists who have had numerous and successful encounters with Class III & IV rapids should even attempt it.

Shuttle: To drop a shuttle car at the take-out bridge, drive 3 miles west out of Thomaston on Ga 36 to the bridge over Potato Creek. There is enough room to park one car at the northwest corner of the bridge. The long, rocky road at the southeast corner is suitable only for 4-wheel-drive vehicles. Keep off the land on the bridge's southwest corner: it's private and posted.

After dropping your shuttle car, proceed to the put-in bridge by returning to Thomaston via Ga 36; then travel 1.9 miles north on US 19 to the put-in bridge. Follow the dirt road on the southeast corner of the bridge to the second brick pumping station at the creek's edge.

Distance: The distance from the put-in bridge (at US 19) to the take-out bridge (at Ga 36) is 6 miles. Plenty of time should be allowed for thorough scouting and studying of the rapids, especially the mile-long stretch below the Ga 74 bridge.

Hazards: This stretch of Potato Creek contains several sections of powerful and dangerous rapids. High water would cause several falls and ledges to approach Class V. Moderate water levels would confront the canoeist with Class III & IV rapids. Therefore, only groups of at least 3 should attempt this run, so that help will be available if necessary. Equipment should include life vests, helmets, wet suits in cold weather, and safety lines. A support team should wait for each canoeist below the heavy ledges and falls with safety ropes in case of trouble. (Scouting all of these rapids before running them is essential. The rapids below the Ga 74 bridge must be scouted from both banks. Beach your canoe on the west [right] bank, well above the rapids, and walk down for a look at the falls, which must be avoided at all costs. Then ferry your canoe to the east [left] bank to scout all rapids downstream, studying currents carefully and planning your run along the east bank.) The degree of danger on this creek increases rapidly with the slightest rise in water level. No runs should be attempted without thorough knowledge of current water levels.

Water Levels: Water level is the key to the runnability and safety of Potato Creek. The secret is to run it a day after a *moderate* rain in the watershed area (around Barnesville and Zebulon). If there's been no rain, forget it: it will be too shallow. If there's been heavy or prolonged rain in the area, avoid it: it will be too rough. There are some makeshift markers on the piling under the Ga 74 bridge (visible from the west bank). These spray-painted markers are not very helpful, however, since they measure feet only: more detail is needed to judge the runnability of Potato Creek. When we ran it, the water level was at the one-foot marker. Six more inches would have put the level above the square base pad of the bridge piling.

Don't trust this makeshift gauge. Walk a short distance below the Ga 74 bridge, and scout the shoals for yourself.

Additional helpful water-level information is available at the gauge on the Flint River at the Ga 36 bridge (5 miles west of the Potato Creek bridge). The Flint River gauge read 8.8 on the day we ran Potato Creek. Remember, however, that Potato Creek has a much faster runoff of water than the Flint River, so high water on the Flint does not necessarily mean correspondingly high water on Potato Creek.

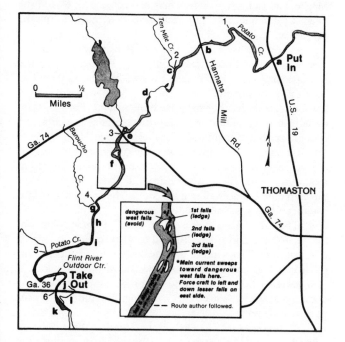

*Map Guide: Numbers on our map indicate river mileage. Letters indicate the landmarks and points of interest listed below.
a. Put-in bridge on US 19.
b. Hannah's Mill Rd bridge.
c. Ten Mile Creek enters on right. The moderate rapids below the bridge are best run near the left (east) bank.
d. End of moderate-rapids area. Pump house on left.
e. Ga 74 bridge.
f. Heaviest rapids area (see map insert for details).
g. Baroucho Creek enters on right at end of rapids.
h. A few moderate shoals.
i. Homes on left bank.
j. Take-out bridge at Ga 36.
k. Extremely dangerous rapids below Ga 36 bridge.
l. Rough dirt road leading through woods to rapids below Ga 36 bridge. Scout road and rapids before running.

1981

This Time, Through!

The Apalachee *had* to be good.

by Reece Turrentine

The roar of the rapids ahead had a different sound than the others back upstream. This one had a bass note to it. Like the diapason pedal of a great pipe organ, you felt it as well as heard it. And around the next bend we'd see it. We were beginning to wonder if the bank fishermen back upstream had been right.

"How far you fellows going?" one had called to me and Ronnie Wills, an old canoeing buddy from Macon, as he reeled in to let us pass.

"Down to 441 Bridge, we hope," I'd replied.

"Then y'all will have some gosh-awful totin' to do around them shoals at Price Mill," he'd warned. "Them rocks will tear you and your boats up."

"We're gonna look at them real careful," I assured him.

"Ain't no matter of being careful. It's a matter of taking out and carrying," he replied, smiling at his partner.

Maybe he was right. But, as a rule, noncanoeists have little conception of what a canoe can do. They think in terms of flat bottoms and johnboats. But give a canoe a drop of water and a needle's eye, and it can do some amazing things. But then again, maybe he was right. If he was, it wouldn't be the first time I'd been stymied by the Apalachee.

A year ago, I'd tried to run it. I had put in farther upstream around Bethlehem—a perfect setting for the Christmas issue of *Brown's Guide,* I had thought. I had discovered a charming little town with a cracker-barrel store and a famous old covered bridge south of town.

"My old mules hated that bridge worse than they hated each other," one old-timer had said, as we sat chatting around the general store. "They'd go through it, but they hated them walls. They'd lean away from them towards the center until they'd be leaning flat up against one another, like a couple of lovers. Once through it, they'd bite and bray at each other like always. But they sho leaned on one another through that bridge."

On that trip, I'd met a lot of people and heard a lot of folklore, but I'd learned the hard way that it was not a good stretch to canoe. The local advice had not helped much. It had been as contradictory as usual:

"It's about six miles through there," one local resident had said.

"Naw, it's fifteen if it's a mile," another replied.

One fellow who had been sitting quietly spoke up: "Well, at the rate a canoe goes, I 'spect it's farther than that."

"Sure you can canoe it," one had said.

"You'll never make it," another warned. "Too many fallen trees." I'd wished I had listened to him. A friend and I tried that stretch the next day and spent more time out of the canoes than in them. It was one log jam after another. We hauled and pulled and scraped for five hours. Our sleek canoes were turned into battering rams! We gave up that section as a lost cause, but I didn't give up the Apalachee. I knew there had to be a good, canoeable section somewhere on that river.

I had been seeing the Apalachee for years from 441 Bridge, as we whizzed over it on the way to Athens for football games. It looked good. It had to be good. I was determined to try it again.

So a few weeks ago I loaded my old motorcycle with gear and headed back to really search it out. This time, I went to the little town of North High Shoals. And that's where I met Gaynor Bracewell.

"Sure you can canoe it," he said with gusto. "It's got some tough spots, but canoes can make it. In fact any of *Brown's Guide's* readers can use my place for a put in."

The "my place" he referred to is a recreational center called the Paradise Falls Club he's built among the ruins of the once-famous High Shoals Manufacturing Company—an old, pre-Civil War wool and cotton mill. It was reputed then to be the most modern mill of its type in the South. The old turbines are still visible and in amazingly good condition. Bracewell's guided tour revealed his knowledge and extreme pride in his place.

"I discovered this place years ago, when I was a student at the University of Georgia," Bracewell explained. "We came down here one night for a hayride, and I told them then that one day I'd own it. Twenty years later, I came back for a class reunion and brought my wife over here to see it. To my surprise, there were 'for sale' signs all around. I went back to Florida, sold my housing development business, and came back up here and bought it. I run it now as a recreational center for young people."

"Is that what all the screaming is about out in the shoals?" I inquired.

"Yeah, they're getting ready for the 'King of the Slide' contest I'm putting on next week. The boys have to slide down the chute standing up, make a 360-degree turn, and then make a perfect dive into the pool below."

"What about the girls?" I asked.

"We'll have a bikini contest for them at the same time," he explained. It sounded like great fun.

"Georgia history has neglected this place," Bracewell continued. "For example, this land was once the only free and independent kingdom in North America. Elijah Clark took this land between the Apalachee and Oconee Rivers from the Indians and designated it as the 'Free and Independent Kingdom of Trans-Oconee.' Federal troops came in and gave it back to the Indians, but for a while it was a kingdom. And on that beach over there," he explained, pointing across the river, "Elijah Clark's son fought a duel with a Senator William H. Crawford from Georgia in 1802. They'd gotten into a political feud

and challenged each other to a duel. They crossed the river so they'd be out of U.S. territory and shot it out. The senator got off the first shot but missed. Then, according to the code of honor, he stood at attention to receive Clark's shot. He crossed his arm over his chest, and Clark's shot hit his hand and the bullet stopped in the pistol butt. It would've gone straight in his heart. It shattered his hand, but saved his life. It happened right on that beach over there. I use it as a campground now. Maybe y'all can camp there when you come back to run the river." I assured him we'd be back. I was determined to run the Apalachee.

So now we were back, and almost halfway through the stretch, and it was not a disappointment. Here the Apalachee was open and clear. What fallen trees we had encountered had been easily maneuvered out of the way. Some we went over; a few we went under; but most we went around. The rapids up to now had been fun and frequent. Nothing big, but just enough to make the run active and interesting.

But now, at the halfway point, the current had stopped. It was an obvious backup from what we were hearing from around the bend: the noise of Price Mill Shoals. Could we get through them? Bracewell said we could. The fishermen said we couldn't. Others had advised we shouldn't.

"They do sound hefty, don't they?" Ronnie Wills observed. Ronnie and I have listened to such sounds on many a river together. That kind of roar makes you stop paddling. An old iron bridge frame came into view, and we paused to look at it. Then I found another good reason to add to the delay. I detoured to the left bank to get a reading from the government gauge I had spotted.

"Two-point-one," I called out to Ronnie. "Write it down, while I get out of these bushes." I pushed back out into the river, got turned around, and continued toward the old bridge frame and its accompanying thunder.

"Something happens down there," Ronnie called to me, as we approached the upper rocks. "The bottom sho drops outa the river over something." I grunted in agreement and picked out a spot on the upper rocks on which to beach out and explore.

"I don't see anything so gosh-awful; do you?" I inquired.

"Not at all," Ronnie replied. "In higher water some of those drops could be boateaters, but they're not now."

"We've been through a lot worse," I stated.

"Many times," Ronnie agreed. "Unless there's something here we don't see."

So we decided to look some more, studying in silence.

The river was wide at this point, and there was a lot of water pouring over a lot of rocks in a lot of places. Most of the runs we ruled out; there wasn't enough water. But the run left of center in the river looked uncomplicated.

"There's a tricky little curl we have to watch as we drop into that first slot," Ronnie warned.

"Yeah, and then just pick our way on down and through that next big chute down yonder," I pointed. That one worried me a little. We couldn't really see it, but it couldn't be much. The whitewater shot straight out from it.

"Go ahead," I suggested to Ronnie. "I might try that first drop at a little different angle and brace over into the left run."

We both had our ideas and plans and had studied them carefully. We got one more good look at our marker rock and started sloshing back to our canoes.

Once in them, we had to bump our way through the rocks to get to the deep channel leading to the main run. The swift current grabbed Ronnie's bow and swung it out into the run. We didn't have but a few feet before the first falls. Ronnie shot out into the current and disappeared around the big boulder. I gave him a second or two to clear the first drop and then pushed out from behind the boulder into the current myself. I glanced over the falls and saw Ronnie clean and upright, sailing towards the chutes below. Then my attention and my canoe headed for the falls. A quick draw stroke gave me the different angle I wanted, and down I went. My bow parted the foam below me and leaped up clear and clean. I jockeyed for position for the rapids still ahead. Rocks were everywhere, but they were not unmanageable. The canoe bucked but held steady. The last strong chute was as we had imagined: strong but straightforward. I shot through it, then tried to impress Ronnie with an eddy turn equally as efficient as I had seen him execute. My canoe slid up beside his.

"Nothing to it," he said casually.

"Not at all," I replied.

"Let's stop and eat," he suggested.

"And rest?" I inquired. But he didn't reply.

We munched our lunch and looked back up at the shoals.

"That's great fun," Ronnie sighed.

"Especially when you make it through," I replied.

"Yeah, but we didn't have any real trouble with 'em, in spite of what those fishermen said."

"Yeah, they didn't know what they were talking about," I commented.

"Bank fishermen usually don't know much about rivers, anyhow," Ronnie continued.

Our cocky conversation ended about the time our dinner did, and soon we were back in our canoes.

The second half of the Apalachee was like the first: stretches of active shoals and stretches of quiet. A drizzle pelted the surface and brought a quiet calm over everything. It grew into a steady but light rain. The water was still now, and everything serene. It seemed to fit our mood, as we parallel-paddled and shared the contentment of the day's closing hours.

Part of my contentment came from finally having made it on the Apalachee. I'll admit those bank fishermen had me a little worried for a while. But that's part of the game. You just never know until you get in a canoe, push off from shore, and head for those hidden sights and sounds downstream.

CANOEING GUIDE

Apalachee River

General Information: The Apalachee River is part of the Oconee river system. It begins in the hills west of Winder and flows southeast, becoming the western boundary of the Oconee National Forest and finally emptying into the Oconee at the National Forest's southern end.

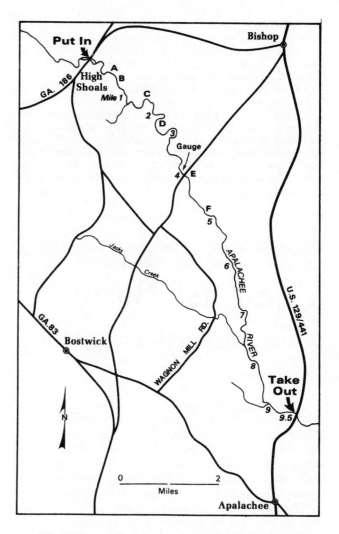

The section covered in the map and guide is the 9.5-mile stretch between North High Shoals Bridge (on Ga 186) and US 441. Longer runs are possible, but it's inadvisable to begin much above the US 78 Bridge, northeast of Ga 186—it's too narrow and tangled. If you run below the 441 Bridge, the riverbed widens somewhat, but is still secluded and scenic.

Put in and Take Out: Put in is at North High Shoals, which is 16 miles southwest of Athens.

Take out is at US 441 Bridge. Roads lead down from both northwest and southeast corners of the bridge.

Water Levels: A government gauge is located about 300 yards upstream (north bank) from a new bridge at Price Mill Shoals. Gauge is in bushes near silver weather tube. Path to gauge offers good opportunity to view rapids and study dangers. Gauge reading for our trip was 2.1. Much over this might require a portage of Price Mill Shoals.

It's also advisable to check with manager at Paradise Club regarding river levels. They have a private gauge there, with normal reading about 3.0. Higher water will change the character of this river and its rapids drastically.

Distance: From put in to take out, it's 9.5 river miles. We made it in a leisurely run of a little less than five hours, but we took an hour for lunch and scouting Price Mill Shoals.

Hazards: No serious hazards before Price Mill Shoals (at mile 4). Beginning rapids are clean and straightforward. Price Mill Shoals must be scouted carefully and possibly portaged. When canoeing, watch for gauge on left bank as old bridge frame comes into view.

Check the gauge. If over 2.1, consider portage down left bank. If under, try run directly downstream from left bridge foundation.

Another hazard is at mile 5. An excellent chute is blocked by a fallen tree. You have to bump down to the left of it. A good chain saw or a flood is needed to open this up.

Map Guide: (Numbers represent miles; letters represent rapids): **Mile 1–4:** (a) Class I rapids; (b) fallen trees; (c) small shelf; (d) rapids. **Mile 4:** (e) Price Mill Shoals, with Class II to possible Class III between old and new bridge. **Mile 5:** (f) Chute blocked by fallen tree. Bump down to left of main run. **Mile 5–9:** Steady current with frequent shoals and trees. Excellent scenery. *Caution: if continuing below US 441 Bridge, scout shoals between highway and railroad bridges. They are about 200 yards upstream from the railroad bridge. These can get rough.*

1979

The Last Bang

Flat Shoals Creek ain't all flat

by Reece Turrentine

I'd fallen into a trance, but the gurgling sounds downstream brought me out of it. Those gurgles raised my hopes; I needed a little whitewater excitement to put some zest into this trip. All day I had been anticipating the rapids which were rumored to be on this creek. After all, the very name, Flat Shoals Creek, implied rapids, or shelves, or chutes, or *something*. But I had been hearing the sound of gurgling waters all morning, and so far it had signified nothing but water pouring over fallen trees, or tributary creeks spilling into the stream, or swirls around isolated rocks. I was beginning to think that Flat Shoals Creek should have been named just "Flat Creek."

I'd come to Flat Shoals Creek to satisfy a long-standing curiosity about it. But first, for guidance, I'd called West Georgia's "Mr. Outdoors," Neil Wickham, owner of Wickham's Outdoor World in Columbus. He's an outfitter and a canoeist, and I knew he would know something about it.

"I think you'll like it," he told me over the phone. "Be at my place Thursday morning at nine o'clock, and we'll run it and see."

On Thursday morning at nine o'clock I was at his place, and so was he, and he'd brought along a couple of his buddies, Lewis McClure and Howard Johnson, to make the trip with us. After strapping his Blue Hole canoe to the top of his vintage station wagon, we headed north on I-185.

What should have been a 30-minute drive from Columbus to the put in turned out to be a two-hour exploration of all the slick, muddy roads in Troup and Harris counties. Explorer that he is, Neil thought that we might find a shortcut for the shuttle run on these back roads, but after smearing our vehicles with layers of mud, we decided to stay on the pavement.

When we finally arrived at the put-in bridge, the view of the creek was not very impressive. In fact, the whole scene was downright depressing. The weather had turned foul and foggy, and the creek looked dull and drab: all the earmarks of the beginning of a dreary day.

"I hope it gets better than this," I called over to Neil as I slipped my canoe into the lazy current. Either he didn't hear me, or he was too busy getting his canoe launched, because he didn't answer. So I paddled on ahead to see for myself what lay around the first curve.

Our first mile on the creek did little to improve my outlook. A big, sprawling pasture dominated the scene along the right bank, and little scrubby trees defaced the bank on the left: hardly what one would call a wild and scenic landscape. I paddled along aimlessly, allowing my mind to wander back home to all the work I had left undone and to the many constructive ways in which I could have used this day.

That's why those gurgles had excited me, but they turned out to be just what I expected: water bubbling around another fallen tree. A long limb bobbed up and down as it was caught and then released by the current. It made a splash each time it hit the water, like some strange, long-necked serpent pecking for food. I glided by it, studying its rhythmic motion in detail. Granted, it wasn't really worth all that attention, but it was about the only thing of interest on the river up to that point. Past the tree, I continued to cruise, not really looking at nor listening to anything in particular.

Then Neil's voice punctured my disinterest. "Just look at that oak, Lewis," I heard him call from his canoe behind me. I turned to look in the direction in which he was pointing. Up in the woods was a magnificent monster of a tree. Battle-scarred, yet strong and sturdy, it dominated its immediate area. I swept my eyes through the woods all around it. I spotted gum, poplar, maple, sycamore, hickory, just to name a few, and suddenly I realized that the feel of the creek had changed: it was taking on the look of a true wilderness river, with deep forests on each side, the trees resplendent in their fall colors. My spirits quickened, and I began to take a lively interest in where I was and what I was doing.

Then things began to happen, or, rather, I began to notice the things that had been happening around me. Three wood ducks catapulted into the air downstream, stretching for altitude and distance, and disappeared over the treetops. A kingfisher chattered and darted from side to side, swooping low, then up to where his feet found a limb, just at the apex of his ascent. And as we rounded a curve, a hawk leaped into the air far downstream, screaming his disapproval of our intrusion.

Although the wild creatures voiced their opinions to the contrary, I didn't feel as if we were intruders. As my canoe glided through what seemed to have turned from a dull creek into a colorful carpet of floating leaves, I felt that we were a natural part of the scene. A sensation of quiet delight came over me. The dreary mood of those early miles was left far behind. I no longer thought about rapids or shoals or whitewater excitement. The tranquility of traveling such a meandering creek, with its wild and varied sights and sounds, was suddenly satisfaction enough. The morning's drizzle had stopped, and an invigorating chill freshened the air. But it was not yet cold enough to retard the activity of the hornets buzzing around a trophy-sized hornets' nest which I spotted in the limbs overhead. I sat motionless in my canoe as I glided beneath the nest: I certainly didn't want them annoyed at me.

Then, from around a curve ahead, came that sound again: bubbling water. "Another fallen tree, no doubt," I decided. We were by now approaching the final mile of our planned run, and so far I hadn't seen any rock foundations which would suggest the possibility of shoals. But as I rounded the curve, I beheld a most amazing spectacle: the creek suddenly spread out to at least three times its normal width, and its smooth surface had broken into jagged fractures of rocks and boulders and ledges and shoals as far as I could see.

"This has to be Flat Shoals," Neil called from the canoe behind me. "I knew it had to be here somewhere."

Before us were dozens of possible runs. I headed toward the chute nearest me. The tranquility of our leisure paddling was over: the creek was all action now, a solid mile of twisting and turning, jabbing and bracing, shoving and shaking—anything to get through its tight maze of rocks and ledges. The currents and channels changed every few feet, requiring instant decisions and reflexes.

During the first half mile I didn't even take time to check behind me for the other canoes, but I knew they were there. Above the roar of the water, I could hear Neil yelling instructions to Lewis. And I could hear Howard's aluminum canoe crunching and scraping over the rocks and ledges. I was scratching over them, too, but my ABS plastic canoe was just not so noisy about it.

In higher water, this last mile would be a run of tight, twisting speed. But in low water, while it certainly was tight and twisting, we scraped bottom too often to get up much momentum.

As our take-out bridge came into sight, so did the last chute of the rapids. By the size of its standing waves, I could tell that Flat Shoals Creek had saved its biggest blast for last, like a giant exclamation point. This last rapid was a long chute with a big boulder right in the middle of its bottom. I hugged the side of the chute, dug in like mad, and barely skimmed the boulder. Once through, I got into the eddy behind the big rock to wait for the others. Howard came through next in his aluminum canoe. He broached the boulder by running into it sideways and tilted just enough to take on water, but he recovered well enough to slide off the rock and begin paddling toward the take out, just a stone's throw away, without bailing. And then came Neil and Lewis, careening down the chute and missing the boulder, but striking Howard a sharp blow in the stern, which shifted all the water in his canoe back toward the stern, lifting his bow out of the water. While we dissolved into laughter, Howard sat solemn-faced and disbelieving, sinking like the *Titanic*, a final touch that made the day complete. A canoe trip just isn't a canoe trip unless somebody gets wet.

Flat Shoals Creek offers the canoeist a poetic adventure of many moods. It's romantic at first, but the last stanza is totally uncharacteristic of romantic poetry: it ends with a healthy exclamation point.

CANOEING GUIDE*

Flat Shoals Creek

General Information. Between Columbus and LaGrange the Chattahoochee River draws water running off the western slopes of the Pine Mountain area via many creeks and streams. Flat Shoals Creek is one of these. Cutting across the bottom of Troup County, it ends in the Chattahoochee impoundment called Lake Harding, some six miles below West Point, near the Alabama line. We canoed the 10-mile stretch starting at the Ga 219 bridge (7 miles south of LaGrange), continuing under the Ga 18 bridge, and on to the take out at the Ga 103 bridge (3 miles south of the Ga 103 & 18 exit off I-85).

Shuttle. To drop a shuttle car at the take-out bridge, drive approximately 3 miles south on Ga 103 from the West Point exit off I-85. (Access to the river here is on the bridge's northwest corner, down an extremely rocky dirt road. We chose to portage rather than risk driving it.) To reach the put in, drive back north on Ga 103 to where it intersects with Ga 18. Turn right (east), and drive 6.4 miles to the Jones's Crossroads intersection with Ga 219. Turn left (north) on Ga 219, and drive 2.4 miles to the Ga 219 bridge put in. Access to the river is on the bridge's northwest corner, down a poor road.

Hazards. There are no special hazards on this run. The final mile consists of continuous Class I and II rapids which could get rougher in high water. The first 9 miles have a few fallen trees which could present hazards in higher water. Life vests should be worn at all times.

Water Levels. There is no water gauge on Flat Shoals Creek. You might, however, want to use this makeshift suggestion. Directly under the take-out bridge on Ga 103, in the middle of the creek, is a large pile of rocks. If the water level is near the top of this pile, it should be sufficient for a good run. A level 6 or 8 inches below the top of the pile means a passable but shallow run.

Camping. The banks of Flat Shoals Creek are mostly private property requiring prior permission for camping. Sandbars do exist if the water level is low enough; they're more numerous in the last 5 miles (below the Ga 18 bridge). You might want to use the campground at nearby Roosevelt State Park at Pine Mountain.

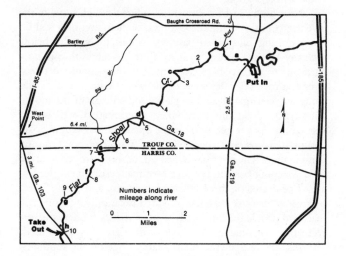

Map Guide: The numbers on our map indicate river mileage.
(a). Open pasture on right for the first mile.
(b). Mouth of Mud Creek at mile one.
(c). Fallen trees here, but someone has cut passages through some of them.
(d). Ga 18 bridge at halfway mark (mile 5).
(e). Big Branch enters on the right.
(f). Massive stone foundations. Possibly an old covered bridge.
(g). Beginning of the mile-long rapids.
(h). Last chute at take out.

1981

The Flint, Now!*

Test your canoeing skills on this liquid treasure in middle Georgia.

by Claude Terry

Take a river labeled "Georgia's Number One Scenic River" by the Natural Areas Council, add the spice of three controversial dams which will drown this river valley, cap that off with the fact that this stream offers the best whitewater canoeing in middle Georgia and you can only be talking about Georgia's unique Flint River. Fishermen float and hike the river, canoeists drift down the easy stretches or risk boat and limb in Yellow Jacket Shoals, and hunters prowl the adjacent forests in large numbers to stalk the plentiful deer.

The landscape along the Flint is enormously varied and the visual aspect is good.

Near highway 18 the river meanders through some of the loveliest country in middle Georgia, with rolling hills and fat cattle grazing blue-green pastures. About three miles below highway 18 the country changes, Pine Mountain throws up a barricade to the river's passage, and resulting conflict between river and rock provides some of the most exciting scenic vistas along any Georgia river. The plants and animals of the mountains occur along this river valley, intermingled with coastal vegetation. As a result, you can see Spanish moss hanging over mountain laurel and rhododendron, a strange but beautiful combination. The river has walled off, or more properly, carved off a sweeping bend in the Pine Mountain escarpment, leaving a cove protected on three sides by mountains, and on the fourth by river. This river cove has provided isolation for plants, animals and people for thousands of years. Today it offers the best recreation potential in the middle of the state, if properly used.

Just above Spewrell Bluff, a large ridge on the southwest side of the river, the Flint offers a series of shoaly rapids, of no real consequence, but enough to pep up an otherwise placid run. (This is the site for the first and most controversial Flint

River dam proposed by the Corps of Engineers.) A county park opposite Spewrell bluff affords a take-out point for the upper trip, a place to enter the river for the lower stretch, or a picnicing and viewing point for the auto traveler. From Spewrell bluff to highway 36 the river continues its good manners, with little gradient and no significant rapids.

Canoeist and rafters desiring an easy trip can get on the Flint at highway 18 and paddle down Spewrell bluff park (14 miles) or on to highway 36 (21 miles). Those desiring more adventure should read on!

At highway 36 bridge the river appears swift but smooth, a tempting place for an easy Sunday float. Don't you believe it! Around the first bend you begin to encounter a building series of rapids, climaxing in the twisting drop at the bottom of Yellow Jacket Shoals.

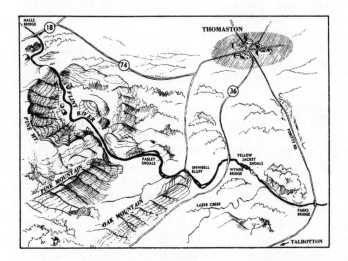

At high water (10 feet or greater on the highway 36 gauge) these rapids can build up some *heavy* water, with large waves, big holes and a better than even chance to swamp an open canoe. At about 10 to 11 feet the river can be run by decked boats and rafts manned by *competent* experienced paddlers.

At high levels, even these paddlers would probably be endangered. This spring, I paddled the river at 11 ft. and found the section from highways 18 to 36 okay for experienced open boaters, and the Yellow Jacket section okay for kayakers and rafters of moderate experience. However, we saw pieces of several flat-bottomed boats and canoes, and a local resident along the side informed me that 10 canoes and one life had been lost in the last couple of weeks on this stretch of river. To those of us with heavy water experience, the river would be class III at these high levels. However, to the area boaters who normally run flat rivers this tricky section could be hairy indeed! At lower water levels (about 8 feet) the river offers intricate maneuvering and long, steep drops down narrow chutes. Minimum levels have not been established since the gauge is new but are probably about 7 feet. Take out for this run is at Pobiddy (Talbotton) road. The Yellow Jacket Shoals stretch with medium flow requires about 3 hours running time, a comfortable afternoon run.

I doubt if there is another river in the world where tupelo trees form part of the obstacles in a rapid, where Spanish moss drips onto mountain laurel, where water and rock have combined to give such a beautiful sweep to the travelers vision.

To casually inundate such a treasure with the dam that the Corps of Engineers proposes would seem incomprehensible, particularly in a region where such mountain beauty is rare. Yet the proposal to build Spewrell bluff dam and a reregulating dam is still pushed by the Corps, some state officials, and various economic interests. But *not* by those whose land will be inundated. There is much local opposition by the young landowners who will be flooded out, and by sportsmen.

It now appears that the benefits in flood control and power production are negligible, and it is apparent that recreational benefits of a lake must be weighed against lost benefits of a unique river corridor. Lakes silt out in 50 to 200 years, leaving mud flats. Rivers just keep on "rollin' along"—at least until man in his infinite wisdom intervenes.

Georgians have a choice of a long narrow pool which will soon (is 100 years really very long?) be a mud flat or the infinite river. See the Flint River now, and let your children and grandchildren see it.

1981

This section of the river naturally divides itself into several different trips. From highway 18 to Spewrell Bluff (about 14 miles, 6 hours) is an easy trip with no significant rapids. From Spewrell Bluff to highway 36 (7 miles, 3 hours) is more of the same. From highway 36 to Pobiddy (Talbotton) Road it's a different story. Just around the bend is Yellow Jacket Shoals. At 10 feet or more on the highway 36 gauge these rapids can build up some heavy water with a better than even chance of swamping an open canoe.

Beginning boaters should remember that different water levels completely change the personality of a river. At 11 feet the sections above highway 36 will require more skill.

Creatures of the Night

Part of the pleasure of canoeing the Hudson River is not canoeing it.

by Reece Turrentine

This time, we did it just right: we hit just the right sandbar at just the right time—a combination that's hard to pull off. Too often, canoeists on an overnight trip will paddle too long the first day, looking for that just-right sandbar to camp on. Eventually, however, they find themselves pitching tents and cooking supper in the dark. At other times they'll stop too early and settle for a camping place that's less than ideal. Then, the next morning, they'll kick and cuss themselves as they pass the perfect places that would have been theirs if they had paddled a little farther. But that's part of the game. When you're on a river for the first time, you just never know what's ahead.

But this time we were sure that we'd made just the right choice, and I should have known then that such good fortune was a good sign for the evening that was ahead of us.

I look forward to camping overnight on a river as much as I do to canoeing it. You have to do more than just paddle to get the feel of a river. You have to spend time with it, sit beside it, listen to it, hear its night sounds, and greet it at the morning's first light. That way, you feel a part of the wilderness, rather than just paddling through it. Since my last few river trips had been short runs, I was ready to camp. Gene Willis, a buddy of mine from Macon, was with me. We had loaded our canoes that morning and set out for a leisurely two days on a stretch of the Hudson River near Commerce. We drifted, fished a little, and observed the nice sandbars that dot the upper stretch of the Hudson. But as the afternoon wore on, I noticed that the sandbars were becoming rare. I was beginning to get a little worried that we might end up fumbling around in the dark, trying to camp on some high bluff in the woods. Then, precisely at 4:30, right on my "three-hours-before-dark" deadline (the time by which I like to have chosen a camping place), we came upon what seemed like the perfect place. We congratulated each other on our superb timing, although we both knew that finding the place was due to pure luck. We slid our canoes into the little natural harbor at the end of the sandbar and started to explore our home for the night.

We walked carefully over the sand, observing and identifying the tracks of many species of animals that covered its virgin surface; the sandbar was obviously a favorite haunt of the animals in the area. We knew that we'd be upsetting the private habitat of a lot of birds and beasts that night.

We busied ourselves with unloading our gear, pitching our tents, and building a fire. While we waited for the flames to die into hot coals, we worked our fly rods around the edge of the sandbar and out into the main current of the river. No action here; so we soon transferred our energies from fishing to the camp stew, which we prepared and cooked with love and meticulous care. We were soon leaning back on our inverted canoes, with our bottoms planted deeply into contoured depressions that our wiggling had made in the sand, gorging ourselves with stew. We finished just about the time the sun was finishing its day's trek across the sky. Content and stuffed with stew, we moved a little closer to the fire and enjoyed some hot coffee that helped to temper the noticeable chill of the late afternoon air. We didn't know it, but it was almost show time—time for the first feature in an evening of wilderness entertainment.

The first feature was presented by the ducks. They came from around a curve in the river, banking low and with landing gear down, ready for a landing and a night's roost under the overhanging willows on the shore. Just before they touched down, they spotted us, and they had a sudden change of plans which resulted in a whirring of beating wings as they frantically tried to regain flying speed. Retracting their legs, they shot on down the river, crying an alarm that must have alerted every bird and beast for miles around. The commotion brought a curious hawk over to spy us out. Circling above us, he uttered a scream of protest that made us feel downright unwanted.

Next came the buzzards. "He just needs a bath, that's all," Gene called up to them, apparently referring to the fact that I had been unwilling to bathe in the chilly water that day. I just told him to shut up or he'd scare away all the animals. The buzzards soon flapped away to look for other roosting grounds for the night.

"Shhh, listen," Gene ordered. Although the sky was still light, the trees of the forest on the river's banks were now silhouettes. Something was moving among the silhouettes, and we peered across the river. The movement was at several places among the bushes on the bank. Whatever was moving was also making soft clucking sounds. Surely, there were no chickens in this wilderness. And quail and doves don't make those noises.

"Turkeys," Gene whispered. "That's what they are, wild turkeys over there. They are probably coming to the river to drink before roosting."

"Watch that rock leading down into the river," I suggested, pointing across the stream. "That's a good place for them to drink." We sat, motionless, peering across the darkening river at the rock, but they never appeared. They just kept moving through the bushes, clucking softly as if in subdued conversation about our presence. Eventually the scratching and clucking ceased; they must have retreated farther back into the woods.

"We've really messed things up for a bunch of creatures," Gene said. He was right, but we'd only be disturbing them for one night. They'd get over it tomorrow.

"KAPLOSH!" The report came from somewhere downstream.

"What in the world was that?" Gene asked.

"It sounds as if somebody dropped a big boulder into the water," I answered, knowing that that was impossible. But how could I explain the sound, or the ripples that I'd noticed fanning out about 50 yards downstream?

"Jumping fish don't make that kind of splash," Gene commented. "That had too deep a sound."

"Beavers!" I announced excitedly. "Look at that rock across from the splash. How do you like the size of those dudes?" Two big beavers lumbered around on the rock. And we could see telltale wakes of others that were swimming in the river. The section just downstream was full of them.

"KAPLOSH!" Another one hit the water.

"There's still enough light," I said to Gene as I headed for a canoe. "Let's paddle down there and see what's going on." Both of us got into one canoe so that we'd have enough paddle power for the return trip upstream.

"KAPLOSH! KAPLOSH!" One popped the water right up against the side of the canoe, startling us with noise and spray.

"Boy, are they mad at us," Gene laughed. And he was right. We had really intruded into their world, and they were an-

nouncing their displeasure in no uncertain terms, sounding an alarm to alert the whole beaver kingdom.

The beavers create all of their furor with their big, flat, paddle-sized tails. They lift them out of the water, then pound them down sharply, making a sound and causing a splash not unlike those caused by a cannonball dive. Our beavers were really putting on a show.

We paddled back upstream to our sandbar camp in almost total darkness. The flickering campfire was our only beacon. Once we were safely back, the splashing from downstream ceased, and we settled down to enjoy the fire and some hot coffee. Before long our conversation began to lag and our eyelids to sag. After securing the food, we retired to our tents, thankful for warm sleeping bags on a chilly night.

I was about to doze off when, "KAPLOSH!": another beaver let his opinion of us be known right beside our sandbar. I pointed my high-powered flashlight out of the tent door toward the water's edge. Shining flashlights will often rouse beavers on a river at night, but our beavers must have been splashed out; I couldn't stir up any more.

I zipped my tent up and snuggled down in my sleeping bag to enjoy what is usually the finale to the river's nocturnal symphony: the distant songs of the whippoorwills. I listened awhile, but I dropped off to sleep before the coda of their moonlight sonata. It must have been close to eleven, and I didn't expect any further sounds from out of the night.

But in the wee hours I was startled awake by a gunshot somewhere in the woods. It was past three. Who would be hunting at this time of night? Poachers? Illegal deer hunters? Rabbit hunters? I could hear an old hound baying in the distance, but that sound came from the opposite direction. The idea of big guns in the dark worried me. Then another shot echoed through the night from the same direction as the first. I opened my tent flap and swept the sandbar with the strong beam of my flashlight. Nothing had been disturbed. There was no movement on the river. I waited, and then the gun reported again. Then I let go a sigh of relief; I realized what I had been hearing: one of those automatic shooting machines. Timed and activated by compressed air, they're designed to sound like guns. They keep animals out of farm gardens. I was annoyed at the disturbance at three in the morning, but I was also relieved that no stray high-powered shell was about to crash into our campground. The sound was harmless enough, just man's version of the beavers' "KAPLOSH," trying to keep intruders out. I zipped up my tent and soon dropped off into a sound sleep.

CANOEING GUIDE

Hudson River

General Information: The Hudson River begins in the hills of northern Banks County and flows southeastward through the county, skirting the town of Homer and eventually forming the county line between Franklin and Madison counties. Finally, it joins the Broad River just below the US 29 bridge.

Canoeists on the Hudson River will be challenged not by its difficulty, but rather by its diversity. The upper sections have

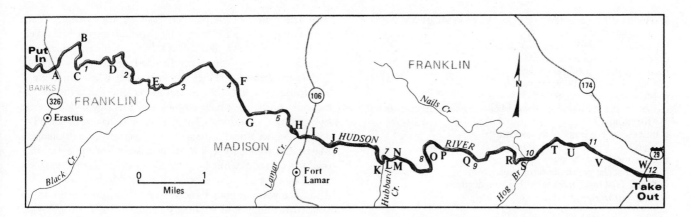

stretches of outstanding beauty, but the canoeist has to work to see them. The river's scenic treasures are guarded by treefalls, narrow channels, and crisscrossed drifting logs. A few of these have to be portaged, but others are loose enough that they can be negotiated.

Whether a canoeist should attempt the upper sections of this river, above the Ga 326 bridge, depends not only on his physical stamina, but also on his philosophy of canoeing wilderness rivers. If he wants the comfort of open channels and wide waters, the upper parts of the Hudson should be avoided. But the canoeist with a sense of adventure, who enjoys not only pioneering but also trail-blazing through the twists and turns of nature's mazes, will be rewarded by this river's beauty as far upstream as the Ga 59 bridge. In this guide, however, I will describe only the 12-mile section between the Ga 326 bridge, located 8.7 miles northeast of Commerce, and the US 29 bridge, located 8 miles northeast of Danielsville.

Shuttle: To reach the put-in bridge, drive 8.7 miles northeast of Commerce on Ga 326 to the bridge across the Hudson. Access to the water is at the northwest corner of the bridge (park under the bridge).

To reach the take-out bridge, drive north on Ga 326 for 2.1 miles from the put in, to where it meets Ga 164. Turn right (east) on 164, and drive 3.7 miles to where it ends at Ga 106. Turn left (north) on 106, and drive 2.1 miles to where it intersects Ga 51. Turn right (east) on 51, and drive 1.5 miles to the little village of Sandy Cross, where you'll bear right (southeast) onto Ga 174 and drive 4.4 miles to where it meets US 29. Turn right (south) on 29, and drive down the hill (.2 mile) to the take-out bridge. Leave your car at either southern corner of the bridge. This is a high bridge, and take out is rough. You have a choice: either use the short but extremely steep path that leads directly down to the water from the bridge's southeast corner, or use the longer but easier path that enters the woods at the end of the guardrail on the bridge's south-west corner. This path leads to an old stone bridge foundation about 50 yards upstream from the bridge.

Water Levels: The gauge that was once at the bridge over the Hudson in Homer is no longer there. Residents of Homer claim that it was not replaced when the new bridge was completed last year. The lack of gauges is a growing problem on our state's rivers. Through neglect and vandalism, dependable gauges are becoming a rarity. Many of those that still exist have been knocked out of position and can no longer be trusted. If I didn't detest defacement, I'd paint my own gauges on bridge pilings around the state.

Fortunately, the water level on the Hudson River remains fairly stable, except during drought. It can be canoed during most months. A substitute level indicator is on the Ga 326 put-in bridge. Under the bridge, between the two concrete pilings that enter the water near the north bank, is an old steel piling that sticks out of the water. On the day of our run the water level was 13 inches from the top of that piling, and we had no problem with low water.

If the water is stained and covers this old piling and nears the top of the river's banks, and if it moves in rushing currents, the river may be approaching flood conditions. All the sandbars would then be covered, and the river could be dangerous.

Distances: From the put in at the Ga 326 bridge to the take out at the US 29 bridge is 12 river miles. With steady paddling and limited stops, the run can be done in one full day. But why rush? This is an ideal two-day trip; taking two days will allow plenty of time to portage treefalls, scout rapids, explore sandbars, and camp overnight on that strand of sand at mile 7.

An additional 3 miles can be added to this trip by using the next bridge upstream from Ga 326 on Hebron Church Rd as the put in. This is called the Wright's Mill Lower Bridge. To reach it, drive north from the Ga 326 bridge for 2.1 miles. Turn left (west) on Ga 164, and drive 1.5 miles to Hebron Church Rd (watch for Hebron Presbyterian Church sign, with arrow). Turn left (south), and drive 1.5 miles to the bridge. This added three miles of river is arduous, with several treefalls to negotiate, and the put in is difficult.

Hazards: Treefalls constitute the major hazards on the first three miles of this run. The swift currents in and around the treefalls can suck a canoe under if you don't anticipate your turns and watch the currents carefully. Also, be aware of all limbs that you plan to go under or that you might be forced to grab to help pull you through obstructions. We saw enough water moccasins stretched lazily on limbs to warrant mentioning them as hazards.

The shoals begin at about mile 5.5, just above the Ga 106 bridge. The early ones are small and harmless. The rapids that are fun begin at about mile 7.3, just beyond the sandbar where we camped. They grow in number and intensity all the way to the take out. Though moderate and uncomplicated, some could approach Class II or more in high water (especially those at mile 9); these require scouting and caution.

Accommodations: Motels are available at the Commerce exit off I-85. Four miles north of the take-out bridge on US 29 is Victoria Bryant State Park in Franklin Springs, with campsites for tents and trailers.

Index to Map: Numbers on our map indicate river mileage. The letters locate and identify points of interest and navigational aids.

a. Put-in bridge on Ga 326.
b. Good sandbar campsites or lunch stop.
c. Beaver dam on right; trashy stumps and limbs in river.
d. Granite outcropping on right; sandbar campsite.
e. Black Creek enters on right. Twisting and trashy section.
f. Open area with good cruising. Many beaver holes in banks.
g. Major turn to the east, just past small power line over river.
h. Sandbar campsite on right just before island. First rocky shoals.
i. Ga 106 bridge at mile 5.6.
j. Shoals at mile 6.

k. Hubbard Creek enters on right. Small sandbars are possible campsites.
l. Our campsite on large sandbar at mile 7.
m. Power line crosses river. Many beaver slides.
n. Shoals just beyond power line.
o. Class II shoals (100 yards) at mile 8.
p. More shoals to mile 9.
q. Good Class II rapids just above islands at mile 9. Islands are ideal for camping.
r. Interesting big boulder in stream.
s. Nails Creek enters on left at mile 10.
t. More moderate shoals.
u. More shoals; granite outcroppings.
v. Scenic final mile; trees provide a tunnel effect.
w. Take-out bridge at US 29.

1981

Water Therapy

The canoe paddle as Rorschach test. Or, don't analyze my stroke.

by Reece Turrentine

My back was breaking, my arms aching, my shoulders cramping, and my body and mind were sinking fast. I was just plain sick and tired of trying to paddle my canoe—which is uncharacteristic. Usually, I can paddle hour after hour, day after day, and love every minute of it. But this wasn't paddling. This was punishment. These last few miles were about to ruin a perfect day.

We couldn't have asked for a better beginning that morning: a short shuttle, a simple put in, and a perfect departure. All the ingredients were there to provide that special pleasure that a canoeist feels when he is "back in the saddle again" and moving into the deep woods to see and hear the sights and sounds that he loves so well. The paddle felt good, and the strokes were beginning to fall into that rhythmic cadence of motion—rest, stroke; rest, stroke—that makes one feel he's in time and tune with the heartbeat of the natural world around him.

I love to paddle. Not to get somewhere, but just to paddle. To me, it's not just a means of propulsion; it's a pleasure. I like the motion, the exercise, the response of the canoe to every little twist of the blade and sweep of the stroke. The paddle and the way it's used are so intensely personal. It's interesting to watch someone else handle a paddle. I've seen shy girls pick up a paddle as if it were made of crystal, hesitant to get it wet or to disturb the water. And I've seen blustering boys seize it with fury, squeeze it in an iron grip, and flail away at the water in a frenzy. And I've seen the pros lift it like a baton and conduct a symphony of grace and motion. Paddling must reflect certain personality traits of the paddler. Take me, for example. When I'm soloing (which I usually am), I paddle almost exclusively on the left side of my canoe. And I don't use the traditional and orthodox J-stroke. I finish my forward stroke with a lazy pry against the gunwale. (Does that mean that when I'm alone, I lean toward the left, the less traditional and less orthodox direction?) But when I have a bowsman, I usually paddle on the right, using the traditional J-stroke. (Could that mean when I'm with someone, I tend to be a more conservative traditionalist?) Maybe I'm trying to seek a balance, a kind of middle-of-the-road fence straddle. But I expect all of this is sheer baloney.

Canoeing does not lend itself to self-analysis; it's for fun. And once you get your basic strokes down, go ahead and do your own thing. And in these opening miles, I was enjoying my own thing: paddling for the fun of it, with my lazy little pry stroke and all. Unfortunately, my fun was not about to last.

But it did last a while longer. There were the rapids, and they were good ones. They gave plenty of time to play and practice all those special strokes that sweep you into chutes and draw you into eddies. And this river had it all, rough waters and calm. I just knew that we had found a real gem in the Little River of Putnam County.

Then things began to happen. First the water began to give out. The river widened into a flat, sandy bottom. Only inches of water rippled over the sand flats. We had to push and shove our way down. We gave up searching for channels; now we searched for enough inches of water to keep us afloat. Paddling became impossible. Each stroke died at its birth, as the blade ground to a halt on the sandy bottom. Each stroke was a jarring, tooth-rattling battle with the bottom. And my paddle—that finely designed instrument of propulsion—was being misused as a crowbar, a shovel, a scoop, and a battering ram. I was about ready to get out of the canoe, grab the bow line, and drag the canoe mule-style to the take out.

Then an idea popped into my mind, an old idea from my canoeing past. In fact it was so old that my mind wanted to reject it and leave well enough alone. But the idea persisted: poling. I had experimented with it years ago with only limited success. But I had tried it enough to know that it added a different dimension to canoeing. Standing in the canoe, you drive yourself forward, backward, and sideways by using a 10- to 12-foot pole, pushing and pulling against the bottom. It's almost a forgotten art today, but long ago the Indians, voyageurs, and pioneers honed it to a fine art. In their skilled hands, with their fine senses of balance and control, they performed feats outstanding enough to be passed down to us in the sagas of river travel. They used their skill to go upstream and down.

These ancient river masters could drive their craft upstream, against the current, with remarkable effectiveness. Even formidable rapids could not stop them: they were climbed. Like leaping salmon, they shoved up the shoals, played the eddies, and slid beside racing downstream chutes.

But those pioneers of American poling were not on my mind just now. I was just trying to relieve my aching back and get three miles downstream to the take out, and I thought that poling just might be the way to do it.

I scanned the treefalls along the banks, looking for a limb that might be trimmed down to become a 10-foot pole. When

I spotted it, I rummaged through my duffel bag for my little collapsible saber-toothed saw. A few sweeps with the saw across the limb freed it from the tree, and soon I was trimming it with my knife.

"What's all that for?" my companion called back from downstream, eyeing my activities suspiciously.

"I'm going to try poling down this mess," I replied, trying to sound matter-of-fact.

"Ha!" he laughed skeptically. "I'll wait for you at the take out."

I didn't reply, but his attitude egged me on. Now I was determined to give it my best. Which, at best, would probably be pretty poor.

I stood up and assumed what I thought to be a classic poling stance, but my opening probes were unsteady and unproductive. Holding the pole horizontally as if I were a high-wire walker, I gave my canoe the old rocker test. I stood at its center with my feet spread wide and rocked the canoe violently until the water almost spilled in over the gunwales. This test reminds you how much a canoe can stand and how stable it is. It helped me to re-establish my balance and my confidence in being able to stand without tipping over. Then I resumed poling.

Little by little, from some distant brain lobe, I began to recall the feel and technique. I began to put my weight onto the pole, and soon the canoe was moving through the shallows. Just to see if I could do it, I attempted a 180-degree turn and poled a little upstream. Not too bad. Then I headed back into the downstream current, gaining feel and speed. When I caught up with my companion, who was still crunching along with his paddle, I made an effort to appear as professionally smooth and casual as possible.

"I'm gonna have to brush up on this," I said with a smirk as I zipped past him. Just to show off, I executed another 180-degree turn, stopped in midcurrent, and waited for him to catch up, then peeled off and poled on downstream. I turned my head to call a final word back to him, and almost lost my balance as I scraped a rock. It would have served me right if I'd tipped over, but it also would have spoiled the effect of my final word: "I'll be waiting for *you* at the take out."

CANOEING GUIDE

Little River in Putnam County

General Information: Putnam County's Little River passes through the wilderness of the Oconee National Forest for the first 5.5 miles of this 12.2-mile run. During the remaining 6.7 miles, the national forest continues on the right bank, with relatively undeveloped private land on the left bank, so the entire run has a definite wilderness feel.

Although the Little River actually begins in southern Walton County, about 20 miles northwest of the put-in bridge on Ga 300, it doesn't become dependably canoeable until it passes under Ga 300, 6 miles northwest of Eatonton.

The nature of this river is inconsistent. At times the canoeist will be busy threading his way through treefalls and rapids. Then,

around the next curve, he can slide up onto his canoe seat and leisurely stroke his way through the still waters. Except for a few stretches, the Little River takes on a different character each time it flows under a bridge. Treefalls occur during the first 3.5 miles, between the put-in bridge and Martin's Mill Rd. The heaviest concentration of rapids lies between the Martin's Mill Rd bridge and the Ga 16 bridge. These exciting shoals begin at about mile 5.3. Then, at mile 5.6, a large pyramid-shaped boulder sits on the right bank: the place to tighten your life vest, lash your equipment securely, and drop to your knees. Around the next curve begins a half mile of continuous Class II rapids, bouncing and twisting shoals that will give the canoeist a good workout. Just before reaching Ga 16 bridge, you may have to portage (depending on water level) a blockage created by a collapsed railroad trestle. The next 2.5-mile section, between Ga 16 and the Glenwood Springs Rd bridge, includes scattered treefalls and stumps and isolated shoals.

The visual treat of this run is at the Glenwood Springs Rd bridge: the old, 30-foot-high electric power dam. Local folks say that this structure wasn't used long as a generating plant, and it hasn't been used for that purpose for 75 years. About 30 years ago vandals blew a hole in its east end, so water no longer backs up behind it. Portage not required here.

In the final 2.7-mile stretch, between the Glenwood Springs Rd bridge and the US 129 take-out bridge, the river spreads out and becomes quite shallow, with channels all but hidden along the banks. According to city officials, the town of Eatonton pumps over ¾ million gallons of water for drinking daily from the Little River (the pumping station is at mile 5.8, just above the heavy rapids, with a spillout station at the end of the rapids). If the river is low, as it was on our run, effects of this removal of water will be most apparent during the final 2.7 miles of this run; beware of very shallow water. But at normal water levels, this stretch should present no problems.

Just before the take-out bridge on US 129, you'll pass under an arched bridge at mile 12. This old bridge is part of a little loop road off US 129. Enjoy examining its design, and be thankful that you don't have to lug your canoes up to that thing.

Shuttle: The take-out bridge is on US 129, 5.3 miles south of Eatonton. The access road is on the northwest corner. To reach the put in, drive 5.2 miles north on 129 from the take out to the courthouse square in Eatonton. Turn left (west) onto Ga 16 here, drive .6 mile, and turn right onto Ga 213. Drive 5.5 miles on 213 to where Ga 300 joins it just before the bridge over Indian Creek. Continue about 100 yards beyond the bridge, bear left where Ga 300 leaves 213, and drive .5 mile to the put-in bridge. The access road is on the far side of the bridge on the right (southwest) corner. Drive a short distance into the woods on this road to an excellent put-in spot near a parking area.

Distances: River mileage from the Ga 300 bridge to the US 129 bridge is 12.2 miles. You should be able to average about 2 miles per hour. Plan at least a long, one-day trip. I suggest a two-day trip, which will allow you to enjoy the scenery.

Water Levels: The Little River has no water-level gauge, so this makeshift suggestion will have to do. At the put-in bridge are 11 steps, made of railroad crossties that lead down to the water's edge. The water level for our run came up to the bottom of the last step, and our run was a little shallow.

Hazards: Three types of hazards threaten a canoeist on the Little River: treefalls, rapids, and the dam. Although treefalls exist along the entire run, most are in the 3.5-mile section between the put-in bridge and the Martin's Mill Rd bridge. Be especially careful on curves, where the water is swift: currents often sweep canoes broadside into these treefalls. So watch your currents, anticipate your moves, and please don't grab limbs carelessly during snake season: anytime except winter. The first mild (Class I) shoals are encountered at .5 mile into the run and get no rougher during the first 3.5 miles. Watch the unexpected narrow chute and twist at the drop at

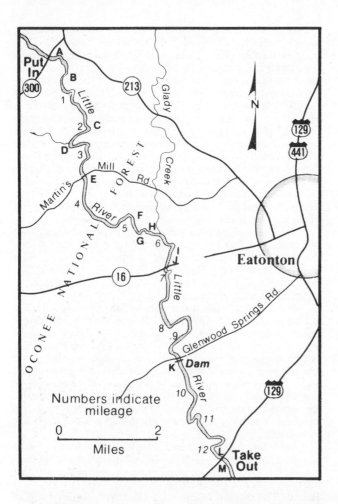

Numbers indicate
mileage

0 _____ 2

Miles

tered was right of center, to the right of the island at mile 5.8. If you are in a party with several canoes, give each canoe plenty of space for this run to avoid unnecessary spills. These rapids should be run only by canoeists of at least moderate skill and experience. Beware that collapsed railroad trestle at mile 6.7: if water level is sufficiently high to paddle across this blockage, watch for old spikes and sharp edges of steel girders just below the surface. It's better to portage here, as we did. The old electric power dam at mile 9.4 at the Glenwood Springs Rd bridge is interesting to look at and to canoe. The rapids that run under the right side of the bridge are challenging, and they flow against the bottom of the old dam. Once through the rapids, you must execute a left turn quickly, continue across the face of the dam, then make a quick right turn through the hole in the east side of the dam.

Alternate Trip: If you have only one day or want to avoid the major area of treefalls, I suggest using the Martin's Mill Rd bridge as your put in. The run would be reduced to 8.7 miles. To reach the Martin's Mill Rd bridge, drive .6 mile west on Ga 16 from the square in Eatonton, and turn right (north) onto Ga 213. Drive 1.4 miles north on 213, and turn left onto Martin's Mill Rd. Drive 3.5 miles on Martin's Mill Rd to the put-in bridge. Access to the river is via a road on the right just before the bridge.

Index to Map: Numbers on our map indicate river mileage. Letters indicate points of interest. **(a).** Put-in bridge on Ga 300. **(b).** First small shoals at mile .5. **(c).** More shoals at mile 2, with tight chute. **(d).** Mild shoals at mile 2.7. **(e).** Martin's Mill Rd bridge (mile 3.5). Beginning of heavier rapids. **(f).** Shoals at mile 5.3. **(g).** Big, pyramid-shaped rock on right bank at curve. Rapids just ahead. **(h).** Half mile of continuous Class II rapids start here and continue to mouth of Glady Creek at mile 6. **(i).** Old collapsed railroad trestle. Possible portage on left side if water is low. **(j).** Ga 16 bridge at mile 6.9, followed by somewhat flat and cluttered water for the next 2.5 miles. **(k).** Glenwood Springs Rd bridge and old dam. Exciting rapids under right side of bridge, requiring sharp left turn out of current that runs into bottom of dam. Continue across the face of the dam to chute running through it on the east side. **(l).** High, arched bridge just before take-out bridge. **(m).** Take-out bridge on US 129.

1981

mile 2; it will wake up a sleepy paddler. The substantial Class II rapids begin at mile 5.5. The best run at the water level we encoun-

Swamp Fever

Not usually fatal, though victims should be isolated in a canoe and quarantined in the Okefenokee.

by Reece Turrentine

Through the smear of the windshield wipers, we saw the entrance gate with the sign: "Stephen Foster State Park." I announced our arrival to the crowd in the van, but most of them couldn't have cared less. Their mood pretty well matched the scene outside: dismal and overcast. They sat expressionless, half-staring through the rain-streaked windows. The jovial mood that had accompanied our predawn departure from Macon had long ago been dissolved by the rain. Some of us who'd been here before weren't surprised by the swamp's changeable weather, but the first-timers were obviously skeptical about the whole affair.

After checking in at the park office we headed for the campground. We'd spend the night in the park and head into the swamp tomorrow for a two-day stay. "Not much way to start a canoe trip, is it?" one of my companions remarked as we pulled into our campsites. I tried to ignore the question and started unloading the van.

"Hey, Reece, what about that 'inspiring, uplifting experience' you said we'd get here?" smirked another voice.

"Come on, guys, give it a little time," I replied in mild agitation. "We haven't even been here thirty minutes. We've got three days ahead of us. And who knows, even you might find it by then."

"Yeah, if I don't find pneumonia first," he mumbled under his breath.

I sometimes wonder why I keep bringing groups to the Okefenokee. Changeable weather is characteristic there, and there's always groaning and moaning. But every year or so I get hit by swamp fever, and the only cure is to head south. So here I was again with another group from my church, heading them into the "Land of Trembling Earth."

I'll admit, the Okefenokee does have a feeling of menace and gloom about it. I got that feeling as a child growing up in Thomasville. Down the street from my boyhood home lived Vereen Bell, author of the best-seller *Swamp Water*. They made it into a movie that sent a shiver across our little town. There were two scenes I would remember for life: the old skull perched on the post, and the strike by a cottonmouth on Walter Brennan's cheek. It's a wonder I ever went near that swamp.

But with the passing of the years, facts replaced fiction, and I ventured nearer. Once I entered it I was captured by its magic. I've been bringing groups here ever since, hoping they would endure its moods, plow through its trails, and discover some of its secrets.

"Is everybody set up, with their gear stored?" I called out cheerily across the campsites. "We want to canoe out to Billy's Island and show you some old graves and things. It'll be a good warm up for tomorrow." Their spirits seemed a little brighter since the rain had stopped. But the fog was still pretty thick. On such a gloomy day, the eerie tales about Billy's Island would probably put "the glooms" back on them. After all, the violent sagas of old Chief Billy Bowlegs and his Seminole raiding parties against the settlers might not come across as particularly "inspiring and uplifting." Nor would an account of the 300 troops sent in as retaliation. They pursued him deep into the swamp, but he got away, and the troops got lost. (After the Indians left, a lusty little lumbering town grew up on Billy's Island, which became headquarters of a rampant lumber-cutting expedition whose indiscriminate methods were as violent as the little town. That project didn't succeed either.) The swamp is strange and tricky. Most of man's invasions of it have been frustrated and defeated by the swamp itself. "Ain't nobody gonna tame or take that swamp," a swamp-edge resident told me once. "The swamp won't let them. It'll be good to you if you respect it. But try to mess with it, and it'll get you."

We arrived at Billy's Island and beached our canoes at the little public landing site; then we wandered quietly up to see the old graveyard. We strained to read the tombstone markers through the high fence. (Can you believe it? They've fenced in the graveyard—because of vandals! In the swamp, no less!) Then we followed the graveyard trail deeper into the island and viewed the old rusty rails and cast-iron fragments of its bygone days. The group really seemed interested in it all, until it started to drizzle again. That sent some of them scurrying for their canoes to head back for the park. During the return trip they didn't even bother to fish nor to look for alligators; they just seemed bent on beating the rain. The rest of us followed reluctantly in their wake. Hopes of anything resembling "an inspiring and uplifting experience" seemed shot at this point.

Then I heard something. Or at least I thought I heard it. It was faint and distant, and it rolled in on the moaning of the wind.

"Did you hear anything, Dick?" I called back to his canoe. If anyone is instinctively tuned to wild sounds, it's Dick Dumbleton. And his knowledge and experience of the swamp are deep and dependable. If there had been a sound, he would have heard it.

"Hear what?" he inquired.

"A sandhill crane," I replied excitedly. "I thought I heard one call." Dick feathered his paddle and listened attentively for a moment; no one spoke.

"I'm afraid you're just hoping," he said as he resumed paddling. I guessed he was right. I was a little overanxious for something to salvage a dreary first day. And for the group to hear that call, and possibly even see that rare crane, would've been a real plus. Once on the endangered-species list, the Florida sandhill cranes present a sight and sound few people ever experience. I remember when I first heard one call. It was years ago on my first trip across the swamp. That passionate, staccato cry shattered the swamp's silence and jerked my head around to scan the horizon. I didn't see it, but that sound left no mistake in my mind that it belonged to a creature of royal rarity. Years later, I had an actual sighting. We were canoeing one of the many "prairies," when that haunting cry pierced the air. And from a lone cypress, far across the prairie, he rose. His long legs folded straight out behind and his neck stretched straight like a spear, he soared off toward some distant throne.

Now, if only this group could see one or even just hear one on this trip. But they are usually deep in the swamp. Maybe we'd see one tomorrow, or perhaps the next day.

Back at the campground we secured our canoes for the night and headed to our campsites and supper. The rain had stopped, but the air was still muggy, and the damp wood on the campfire smoked more than it burned. We made an effort to sit around the campfire for a while, but most of the folks wanted to turn in early, so they headed for their tents. There had been some little bandit-faced raccoons sneaking among the shadows beyond our camp since dark, and I knew they'd steal us clean if the food wasn't secured; so I gathered the boxes up and stored them safely in the van. With a few remaining camp chores done, I headed for my tent and zipped in for the night. Settled snugly in my old sleeping bag, I didn't much care how the others felt at that point. I felt supremely contented and soon was fast asleep.

Next morning the campfire crackled cheerily, though still somewhat reluctantly, and heads popped out of tents at the smell of the fresh coffee brewing. "We'd better go easy on the coffee," I warned. I hated to mention it, since the day seemed to be beginning well. The rain had gone, and I didn't want to be the cause of any early groaning. But facts are facts about the effects of coffee. "Remember, we'll be confined to our canoes most all day today. You can't be hopping outa your canoes to go to the bathroom. There's not much solid ground out there. Most of the ground is floating muck, and you'll just sink down in it." There were a few groans, but most of them seemed anxious to get started.

So we broke camp, packed our canoes, and headed down that fog-covered canal. As the familiar buildings of the park dropped behind us, I sensed the group's hesitancy: the deep interior of the swamp carried a certain dreadfulness about it.

A little marker arrow labeled "Red Canoe Trail" appeared ahead; it stood at the entrance of a waterway that was noticeably smaller than the canals around the state park and defiantly pointed northeast, into the heart of the swamp. Once you turn onto one of these marked canoe trails, you're through playing around in the park; you're headed for some serious paddling and exploration.

Before starting down the trail we regrouped and laid down some ground rules. We had decided that since Dick Dumbleton, the most experienced canoeist-outdoorsman in my church, knows the trails best, he and his partner would lead the way. My partner and I would stay near the back of the group to bring up the rear. We offered some brief paddling suggestions for the novices in the group, since good control is important on these winding, narrow waterways. But they were only casually interested in lectures and demonstrations; so we just started out.

The first few hundred yards were covered slowly. The folks were superficially occupied with this and that, fooling with their gear and chattering noisily. As expected, however, it wasn't

long before the complaints started. "Hey, Reece, this water's moving," one fellow growled. "I thought the swamp was still-water. We're paddling against a current."

Though not a serious problem, it was a fact. We were actually paddling up the infant headwaters of the Suwannee River, which originates deep in the Okefenokee. It and the St. Marys are the two big rivers born in the swamp. All the water in the swamp moves: it slides languidly across the earth, eventually flowing to the Gulf of Mexico via the Suwannee, or to the Atlantic via the St. Marys.

"Just try to keep your strokes smooth and your canoe straight," I suggested. But although you can talk canoeing all day, it takes some experience to get that "feel," and that wasn't happening now.

"You're not paddling right," a bowsman yelled at his partner.

"Change to the other side," another complained from farther up the line.

"Back up! Back up!" one girl screamed as she and the canoe's bow wound up in the bushes on the bank. "You've got me in here where I'll bet there are a thousand snakes."

Though the group paddled slowly, the hours passed, and we moved deeper into the swamp, where its real nature began showing. The trail now took on the appearance of a tunnel, with the giant cypress trees reaching their moss-laden limbs far out over the canal. Though clean, the water appears to be black because the swamp's black peat bottom allows a view of only a few inches beneath the surface. And now there were also the alligators, as black as the water; we were seeing them with regularity. Sinister creatures, they range from a few feet in length to monsters. With cold, unblinking eyes they watched our caravan glide by. They were quiet and docile now, but during mating season, their night-piercing bellows and violent mating battles keep the swamp awake and aquiver. Such prehistoric savagery reminds one quickly that he's a visitor here: an outsider from another world coming as a guest to observe and respect this wilderness.

By midafternoon we were nearing Big Water, our camp area for the night. There are some islands in the swamp firm enough for campsites, but on this trail nights are spent on platforms measuring only 28 feet by 20 feet, but built on stilts and safely above the water's edge. It'd be close quarters.

After reaching the Big Water camping platform near Big Water Lake and unloading our canoes, we stretched our legs, set up the kitchen, and put on the stew. After supper we sat around listening to the evening sounds, talking softly, and watching the silhouetted cypress trees disappear into the dark sky. Soon the chorus of frogs began its evening concert. Complete with soprano, alto, tenor, and bass voices, this chorus had some undesignated midranges also. The hiss of the Coleman lantern added a familiar sound, always a peaceful reminder of evening time around a camp. Its circle of light enclosed us in our own little private world, dimming the reality of the vast, alien wilderness beyond our platform. Suddenly, a pattering sound brought someone's flashlight beam over the edge of the circle. A curious raccoon blinked at the light. A slight splash across the canal swung the beam in that direction, and two red eyes shone through the marsh grass. A 'gator was curiously observing the goings-on. His presence brought a few whines from some, but we assured them the height of the platform would keep him in his habitat and off of ours.

"I guess we'll miss seeing 'Old One Eye,'" Dick Dumbleton commented.

"Who's One Eye?" one of the girls asked with slight suspicion.

"Aw, he's an old 'gator," he drawled as he leaned back in his little homemade camp seat to relight his pipe. I smiled to myself, knowing this was the signal for another of his famous camp yarns. "He always stayed around the other platform up at Big Water," he continued. "He lay right down at the edge of it, never bothering anybody, but watching everything. Word had it that years ago, while poking at him with a stick, someone poked one of his eyes out. Ever since then, he's been there waiting and watching with that one eye, looking everybody over. He's a big dude, ten or twelve feet long, but he won't hurt anybody. He's just waiting for one person. And if he ever sees him he's gonna give him a new name, 'Ole One Leg.'" It was good to hear the group chuckle. We sipped hot coffee and continued the soft talk until yawns began to spread around the group. One by one, they got up to unroll their sleeping bags. It'd be shoulder-to-shoulder sleeping, but nobody really minded: we were glad to be high, dry, and safe. A few quips and jokes continued after the light was out, but soon the platform was quiet, and most were asleep.

I lay awake to listen to the night sounds a little longer. There were distant splashes and rustles among the reeds. An owl hooted and was answered by another miles away. Something whimpered in the distance and fluttered in the darkness. The symphony soon lulled me to sleep.

The next thing I was aware of was the smell of fresh coffee: Dick was standing over the stove in the early light of dawn. I slid out of my bag and gingerly stepped over and around the sleeping mummies. "I was gonna fix coffee this morning," I whispered to him.

"Yeah, I've heard that before," he answered.

Dick and I sipped our first cup and watched the bundles of sleeping mounds begin to stir.

"Let's go fishing," Stan said before his eyes opened. Stan Harrell is our associate minister at the church and a never-say-die fisherman.

"Oh shut up, Stan, and go back to sleep," a voice called from deep in a sleeping bag.

The morning was beautiful and clear, and after breakfast most of us piled into our canoes and headed back up to fish Big Water Lake. Lynn, my canoeing partner, agreed to paddle so that I could fly-fish. Though not a fisherman, she's an ardent nature lover and enjoys drifting near the banks to explore the little nooks and crannies—perfect drifting for fly-fishing.

"Good morning," she said to the cypress knees, as if they were the little people they so resemble. She can make apparent, even to my sluggish eyes, the shapes of elephants, hippos, and other images she instantly sees in the gnarled roots and twisted trunks along the bank. It's a good thing we were studying nature: the fish sure weren't biting. Lynn is a staff member at my church, and I felt that I could confide in her some of the misgivings I was having about this trip.

"Do you think this is a bust for them?" I asked as I reeled in my line.

"Try over there," she suggested, ignoring my question. I couldn't help but smile as I stood up for one more cast. She wanted me to catch a fish as badly as I did, and it surely was a fishy looking place.

Then it happened—not where I had cast, not even on the water, but in the sky, over the treetops. It was that sound again: the staccato cry of a sandhill crane. And it was close, real close.

"There!" Lynn whispered urgently. "Right up there over our trees." Through the trees I saw them, two of them, heading our way. My head bobbed for a better view through the trees. But they accommodated my desires and broke out into the clearing over the lake, so that we had a clean, clear view of both of them. The bright morning sky encircled them with a silvery lucency. And to top it all, they crowned the golden moment with another haunting call.

Then they were gone, as quickly as they had come. Lynn and I looked at each other, wanting to say some unsayable something, but our mouths were frozen in open grins, and we simultaneously burst into exuberant laughter. Nothing needed to be said.

"Did y'all see them?" I called to the next canoe down the lake.

"Yeah," they shouted back. "We saw them." The buzz and chatter from the other canoes told me that their occupants were as excited as we were. We paddled back to camp, content that such an experience had been shared.

For me, the trip was complete. That sighting had provided me with a mental image I could always recall on command, simply by closing my eyes and remembering. Big Water would be a place I'd always remember. "I may have a bonus for you," Lynn had said cautiously. "I was jumping around so much I'm not sure. But I may have gotten a picture of them."

"That'd be something," was all I could say.

We soon left Big Water to begin our day's journey back to Stephen Foster Park. Special permission allowed us to circle through the spacious brightness of Floyd's Prairie, a meadow-like expanse of sedge and sunshine. Life was stirring everywhere here. A gentle wind brought the swishing sounds of the white egrets' wings as they rose from the sedge. A great blue heron hopped from his lone cypress perch to spread his wings and soar in search of another. The 'gators even put on a show: they climbed up to their mud banks to bask in the sun. The whole mood of the swamp had changed. No longer sinister and menacing, it moved with brightness and serenity. It was obvious a new mood had permeated the group, too. They were alert and responsive to the sights and sounds around them. They were calling things by name and asking questions concerning objects they would have ignored earlier. Even their paddling was more natural and easy, allowing their attention to range beyond the canoes.

What had happened to them? Were they viewing the swamp with different eyes because the day was prettier or because the weather was better? No! Now they were laughing about yesterday's bad weather, canoeing into bushes, and paddling against the current. Instead of gloomy cypress forests, one described our surroundings as "ancient abandoned cathedrals." That's some change.

But I've seen this happen before. In fact, it almost always happens. And the reason for the change was simple: they gave the swamp time—time to get to them and to speak to them. For three days the swamp had bombarded them with an on-slaught of life—birth and death, peace and terror, gloom and glory—and each person was bound to be affected by something sooner or later. Given time, some moment, some sight, some sound, some creature will make the swamp visitor stop and look and listen.

CANOEING GUIDE*

Okefenokee

General Information: This wilderness is more than a magnificent wildlife refuge; it is a haven for sightseers, students, artists, naturalists, photographers, fishermen, and especially for canoeists who want to probe its deep interior, where few people are privileged to go. (Entry to the swamp is limited by a strict system of reservations and permits.) The swamp encompasses an area of 435,000 acres, most of which is under the control and protection of the Okefenokee National Wildlife Refuge. The name "Okefenokee" is a derivative of a Choctaw Indian word meaning "quivering earth." The swamp is actually a vast peat bog filling a huge saucer-shaped depression that was once part of the Atlantic Ocean floor. This bed of peat ranges in depth from a few feet to more than 20 feet in places. As gases build up in the peat, they often surface—this is called a blowup—creating instant islands overnight. The ground is so unstable that it trembles when stepped on, hence "quivering earth."

Over 225 species of birds have been identified in the swamp, as well as 42 species of mammals, 58 species of reptiles, 32 species of amphibians, and 34 species of fish. The alligator population is now past the 10,000 mark within the Okefenokee.

Canoe Trails: Canoeing into the swamp allows a person to experience the swamp, rather just see it. Thirteen canoe trips on carefully marked trails are available to groups of up to 20 persons. Permits and reservations for such trips are required. These are available from Refuge Manager, Okefenokee National Wildlife Refuge, Box 177, Waycross 31501. Complete maps and descriptions of conditions in the swamp will be sent to group leaders upon granting of reservations.

Put Ins and Take Outs: There are three approved entrance-exit sites for canoe trips into and across the swamp. Two are reached from the eastern side of the swamp: Kingfisher Landing, located 13 miles north of Folkston off US 1; and Suwannee Canal Recreation Area, at Camp Cornelia, located 10 miles south of Folkston off Ga 121 (also listed as Ga 23).

The one approved entrance-exit site reached from the western side of the swamp is at the Stephen Foster State Park, located on Jones' Island, almost in the center of the swamp. It's reached by driving 18 miles northeast from Fargo along Ga 177, which parallels the Suwannee River.

Shuttle: This is a pain. Unless advance arrangements can be made to have someone do it for you, the shuttle for a trip crossing the swamp—this is the normal practice—involves long miles and long hours. You can sometimes enter and exit at the same site: a few such trips are approved by the refuge manager, but those taking such trips miss the experience of actually crossing the swamp.

Hazards: None, other than those which exist in any extremely wild and primitive area. Though snakes, alligators, and insects abound in the swamp, few people are ever harmed if the fauna is left unmolested. Detailed safety requirements are listed in the materials sent you along with your permit. This material also includes complete information on needed equipment, likely weather, camping requirements, and everything else you'll need to know.

Time and Distances: Designated canoe trips vary from a 12-mile, two-day trip to a 55-mile, 6-day trip. Following is a list of the possible trips available:

Kingfisher–Maul Hammock–Big Water-Stephen Foster: 3 days (31 miles).

Kingfisher-Bluff Lake-Floyd's Island-Stephen Foster (via Floyd's Prairie): 3 days (24 miles).

Kingfisher-Bluff Lake-Floyd's Island-Stephen Foster (via Suwannee Canal Run): 3 days (27 miles).

Suwannee Canal–Cedar Hammock–Suwannee Canal: 2 days (12 miles).

Suwannee Canal–Suwannee Canal Run-Stephen Foster: 2 days (17 miles).

Suwannee Canal–Cedar Hammock–Floyd's Island-Stephen Foster (via Floyd's Prairie): 3 days (24 miles).

Suwannee Canal–Cedar Hammock–Floyd's Island-Stephen Foster (via Suwannee Canal Run): 3 days (27 miles).

Stephen Foster-Cravens Hammock-Stephen Foster: 2 days (18 miles).

Suwannee Canal–Cedar Hammock–Floyd's Island-Suwannee Canal: 3 days (29 miles).

Suwannee Canal–Cedar Hammock–Floyd's Island-Bluff Lake-Kingfisher: 4 days (32 miles).

Kingfisher–Maul Hammock–Big Water-Floyd's Island-Bluff Lake-Kingfisher: 5 days (43 miles).

Kingfisher–Bluff Lake–Kingfisher: 2 days (15 miles).

Kingfisher–Maul Hammock–Big Water–Stephen Foster–Floyd's Island–Bluff Lake-Kingfisher: 6 days (55 miles).

1980

Ebenezer's Promise

This is Ebenezer, isn't it?

by Reece Turrentine

As I PADDLED DOWN the initial mile of Ebenezer Creek, I examined the creek's banks and the surrounding scenery like a pawn broker evaluating a piece of merchandise brought in by a suspicious-looking customer. After all, when the General Assembly declares a river to be a "Wild and Scenic River," you expect it to be something special, like a Stradivarius violin, or a Steuben glass, or a Bowie knife. Georgia's other "Wild and Scenic Rivers" are special. The Jacks River in the Cohutta National Wilderness Area, the Conasauga River in the same area, and the famed Chattooga River in Rabun County all have cascading waterfalls, thundering rapids, and crystal-clear mountain pools. But Ebenezer Creek? It was pretty enough. But each of the creeks and rivers I canoe seems beautiful in its own way. But after all the plaudits I had been hearing about Ebenezer Creek, I was expecting something exceptional. So far, I was disappointed. This beginning section was bushy, swampy, and full of treefalls. I was beginning to think I had been led to expect too much from what I had heard from others about this little tributary of the Savannah River.

"There's really nothing quite like it in Georgia," Dr. Charles Wharton had told me. This noted ecologist, a staff member of the Institute of Ecology at the University of Georgia, wrote about the unusual ecosystem of Ebenezer Creek in his book, *The Natural Environments of Georgia*.

"Oh yes," Julie Weddle had added. "The Department of Natural Resources came here and did all kinds of preliminary studies on the creek." This attractive, young editor and publisher of the *Springfield Press* was all excited about her "home creek" receiving all these special honors. "They were supposed to publish their findings and present it to the General Assembly for approval as a 'Wild and Scenic River.' I'm not sure whether it was ever actually approved or not."

"It was approved all right," Tim Cash had informed me. Cash was one of the Department of Natural Resources officials who did much of the study on the creek. "I was standing right there when the governor signed it into law. It's an officially designated 'Wild and Scenic River.' But that's not all. Ebenezer Creek has also been declared a 'National Natural Landmark,' a 'State of Georgia Natural Area,' and a 'Heritage Trust Hallmark Site.'"

I was relating all these high-sounding names to my fellow traveler, Guy Hutchinson, as we approached the second treefall that blocked our passage. We performed a balancing act standing on the dead tree as we hauled our loaded canoe across it.

"You sure you got the right creek?" Guy asked as we slid off the tree back into the canoe.

I knew I wasn't mistaken about the location of the creek, but I was beginning to suspect that some political shenanigans had gone on somewhere in pushing this stream for scenic-river status. Not that it really mattered. So, what if the county fathers wanted a bit of local publicity, and put a bill through the legislature to give a title to a little creek that really didn't have much to offer? No harm done, really. Except that right now we were trying to canoe the thing, and around every narrow curve the bushes along the banks were trying to jerk us out of the canoe.

"'Wild and Sinister' would be more like it," I said to Guy.

"Well, it was your idea to put-in way up here in the swamps," he reminded me. And he was right. I wanted to canoe the entire length of Ebenezer Creek, from "Old Ebenezer" to "New Ebenezer," just like some of the region's earliest settlers, the Salzburgers, did back in 1734. The Salzburgers were a group of Protestant dissidents who came to the Savannah colony after being exiled from predominantly Catholic Salzburg, Austria. They soon left Savannah and migrated 30 miles up the Savannah River and nine miles up Ebenezer Creek, to establish their settlement. But they didn't stay up the creek long. After much sickness and hardships, they requested and obtained permission from General James Oglethorpe, who was in charge of the colony, to abandon this swamp settlement and move down to the mouth of Ebenezer Creek on the Savannah River. Here, at "New Ebenezer," the two hundred Salzburgers built their town and raised their families. Today, a restored cabin that occupies a place next to the Salzburg Museum shows the type of dwellings they built. The old cemetery across the road has numerous graves bearing the names of the settlers and their descendants, and the "Jerusalem Church," built in 1767, still maintains an active membership of around 450. It is the oldest continuously used building in Georgia.

Although the Salzburgers and the early settlers of the area were mostly farmers, they considered farming to be a necessity rather than a calling. During off seasons, the settlers turned to marketing timber to supplement their incomes. Ebenezer Creek swamp had great stands of cypress, water tupelo, and yellow pine, which the settlers harvested every year. During these harvests, the Salzburgers looked more like ranchers than farmers. Like Western ranchers, who had cattle drives, these settlers had log drives. They would cut the cypress and tupelo trees, drag them through the swamp on oxen-pulled timber carts that had wheels seven feet high or more. Workers stacked the logs on the banks of Ebenezer Creek to dry. When the logs had dried and the water had risen to a high level, they would roll the cut trees into the creek, tie two or three logs together to form a raft, and float them down the creek. While in the creek, they had to keep the rafts small and manageable in order to navigate the tight curves and small channels. Workers would ride the rafts, guiding them with long poling staffs, keeping them moving downstream and off the banks. Once they reached the Savannah River, they would increase the size of the rafts by adding on more logs and joining them to the rafts of other settlers, until a large flotilla of log rafts began drifting down the river to a startled Savannah. This somewhat romantic period of rafting stretched over 150 years, from the time Georgia was settled until the 1900s, when rail and highway transportation made log rafting obsolete.

"Don't you wonder how those Salzburgers got the rafts down this creek?" I asked Guy, as bushes squeaked against the side of the canoe. "And here we are struggling to get a little canoe down this stream."

"Maybe we ought to be poling instead of paddling," he said.

As we approached the Long Bridge area, the creek began to open up. It had a well-defined channel and wider banks. Just beyond Long Bridge, we came to a place known as Alligator Gardens, where the creek widened even more. And, sure enough, we saw the telltale wake of two gators, rippling the surface as they glided out from the bank towards the center of the stream. As we came into their view, they submerged like a couple of submarines on a secret mission, leaving nothing but bubbles floating on the surface.

Around the next curve we came upon an unusually large cypress trunk, at least four or five feet in diameter. I told Guy about a story I had read about one of the residents of the area, Mr. Ernest Gnann. Gnann and his wife were on a fishing trip on this stretch back in 1940 when they were caught in a violent thunderstorm. They found shelter from the storm by standing inside the hollow trunk of a cypress tree until the storm passed. "She has left me now and gone to her blessed reward," wrote Gnann in his memoirs, "and the old cypress stump now lies slanted in the creek. But I can still see the place in the old tree where we stood together that day of the storm."

The creek had widened to such a point that Guy, who had been paddling in the bow seat, put down his paddle and started working his fly rod. I paddled him slowly down the creek as he lashed the line out, dropping the fly deftly in choice spots along both banks.

We rounded several more curves, and the landscape changed abruptly. The water in the creek spread out into a dark, placid lake where a forest of 100-foot-high water tupelo trees rose from the surface like columns in a Greek temple.

"Just look at that," Guy said, trying to watch the scene downstream and handle his fly rod at the same time.

We continued to glide deeper into the lake forest. The landscape exhibited a clean uniformity. All the tupelos were about the same size, each with a swollen buttress about three feet in diameter, and each with a strange counterclockwise twist to its root system. They looked as if someone had planted them by hand, spacing them about 12 to 15 feet apart. Little underbush clouded the lake, and the trees were separated only by the mirror-like surface of the water, which hugged each tree trunk tightly, reflecting its image across the dark water. Guy reeled in his line and laid his fly rod in a slanted position across his lap. As the canoe glided in under the trees, he took off his old fishing hat, and, bending his head backwards, surveyed the tall trees from their trunks all the way up to their tops. Only near the top did branches extend outward, mingling with the branches of neighboring trees. These mingling branches created a thin roof that covered the lake and allowed the light to enter on filtered sunbeams. I stopped paddling and let the canoe drift slowly forward, using a slight skull-stroke so as not to disturb the glass-like surface of the water. A woodpecker interrupted the silence with his staccato rapping on a tree somewhere. The sound re-verberated from everywhere, making it difficult to determine his location. His echo slowly decayed, and everything was quiet again.

"This place is like a cathedral," Guy said.

The canoe was not moving at all now. It sat still in the water like a drifting log, with scarcely a ripple reaching out from its hull. A slight breeze rustled through the tops of the trees, causing an undulating wave to move across the leafy ceiling of the swamp and the beams of sunlight to dance about from one tree trunk to another. The stir brought me back. I moved my paddle and stroked gently through the water. Guy removed his fly rod from his lap and placed it on the floor of the canoe. He picked up his paddle and started stroking in rhythm with me. The canoe moved slowly out of the tupelo forest and back into the channel of the creek. Soon we were cruising downstream, toward the take-out. A few fishing cottages dotted the shores along the bank.

Ebenezer Creek has little in common with its scenic-river cousins to the north. The Jacks, Conasauga, and Chattooga Rivers bound out of mountain valleys with noisy exuberance. But Ebenezer Creek makes one thing clear: wild rapids and ragged rocks are not the only things that make a river "wild and scenic."

CANOEING GUIDE

Ebenezer Creek

General Information: Ebenezer Creek is a tributary of the Savannah River that begins four miles southeast of Springfield in Effingham County at the conjunction of Runs Branch and Little Ebenezer Creek. From that point, it flows westward for 9.5 miles until it empties into the Savannah River. The first two miles of the creek twist through narrow channels and through heavy underbrush. The last 7.5 miles flow through more open areas bordered by numerous elongated lakes.

Ebenezer Creek is one of four rivers in Georgia that have been declared by the General Assembly to be "Wild and Scenic Rivers." According to the Georgia Scenic Rivers Act of 1969, a "Wild and Scenic River" has "valuable scenic, recreational, or natural characteristics which should be preserved for the benefit and enjoyment of present and future generations." The other such rivers in Georgia are: the Jacks River, the Conasauga River, and the Chattooga River—all well known whitewater rivers in the north Georgia mountains. In contrast, Ebenezer Creek is a short, flat-water stream with an elevation of only fifteen feet above sea level. But what it lacks in gradient and length, it makes up for in environmental significance and historical value.

Environmental Significance: In 1978, the Georgia Department of Natural Resources published *The Natural Environments of Georgia*, by Dr. Charles H. Wharton, noted ecologist and staff member at the Institute of Ecology at the University of Georgia. In the work, Dr. Wharton describes Ebenezer Creek as "Georgia's best example of a 'backwater stream eco-system.'"

Such an eco-system occurs when the water level of a major river rises to where it backs water up the channel of one of its smaller tributary streams. This action is similar to what occurs in coastal marsh areas when the rising tide backs water up the creeks and streams around the marshes. Then, as the tide recedes, the little streams and creeks around the marshes rush to empty themselves, acting as though they were tributaries, or feeder streams, flowing

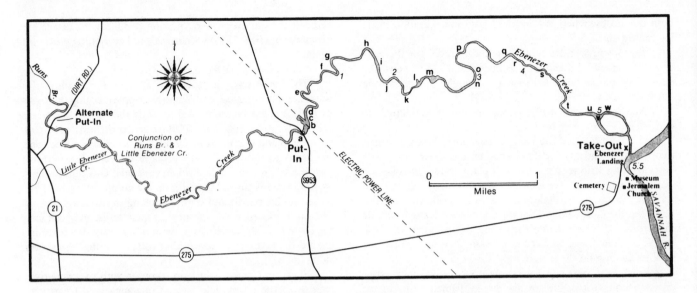

into the sea and supplying it with water. While the Savannah River/Ebenezer Creek eco-system is not a tidewater phenomenon, the Savannah River has an effect on Ebenezer Creek similar to the effect the sea has on marsh streams. When the Savannah River rises, due to rains and seasonal floods, it blocks the flow of its tributary, Ebenezer Creek, and actually backs water up the creek for five or six miles. This occurs several times a year, and over the centuries has created an eco-system of vast swamps, elongated lakes, and water levels that can fluctuate as much as eight feet.

No one knows for sure just what caused this backwater system on Ebenezer Creek. Some say that long ago the west bank of the Savannah River eroded near the Ebenezer Creek area, which allowed the river to flood the creek and create a broad basen swamp. Others say it's related to sea level changes. About 25,000 years ago, the sea started rising again (as it still is) and created a condition in which the Savannah River traps the water up Ebenezer Creek. Either way, Ebenezer Creek produces plant growth and land-water relationships seldom seen on most river systems.

Most dramatic of Ebenezer Creek's scenic curiosities are the large stands of water tupelo and bald cypress trees that display greatly enlarged buttresses. Ecologists suggest that this swelling is a way that the trees adapt to being underwater for long periods of time, which restricts their oxygen supply. By swelling, a tree provides itself with an increased surface area for oxygen intake, as well as a broader base for stability in the swampy, soft ground where they grow.

Also of environmental importance is the wide variety of wildlife the area supports. American alligators inhabit the swamp in substantial numbers, and striped bass spawn here.

Ebenezer Creek can be canoed at many water levels. Actually, the varying water levels enhance the scenic value of the creek. At high water, the canoeist can take side trips in and among the trees of the water tupelo forests, and up the sloughs and elongated lakes of the creek's lower section. At low water, the canoeist has a well-defined channel to follow, and a good view of the strange swelling and counterclockwise twisting of the buttresses of the trees.

Historical Value: It was around Ebenezer Creek that the Salzburgers, a small band of Protestant dissidents from Salzburg, Austria, settled in Georgia in 1734. Soon after arriving, the Salzburgers left the Savannah colony and migrated up the Savannah River and nine miles up Ebenezer Creek to establish their first settlement, now known as "Old Ebenezer." They stayed at that location only two years. Because of swamp fever and many other hardships, they moved down the creek to its mouth on the Savannah River to build their permanent town, called "New Ebenezer," which in time

would grow to a population of 1600. No landmarks remain of Old Ebenezer, but part of New Ebenezer has been preserved. The old cemetery bears the graves of many of the original settlers. The Salzburg Museum displays early relics of the settlers and is open to the public. The church here, built in 1767, was occupied by the British troops during most of the Revolutionary War, and was used as a hospital, a horse stable, and a place to preserve meat. To this day, the clean, white walls of the sanctuary are slightly stained in spots where grease and salt from meat saturated the brick beneath the plaster. The church still supports an active congregation, some of whom are descendants of the original Salzburgers. The "Jerusalem Church," as it is called, is the oldest continuously functioning building in Georgia.

Distance: The canoe trip covered in this guide is a 5.5-mile paddle from Long Bridge Landing to Ebenezer Landing at the mouth of the creek on the Savannah River. This is the most scenic and canoeable section of the creek and is the section designated "wild and scenic." (For longer runs, see "Alternate Trips," below). This 5.5-mile trip can be paddled in about three hours. But don't depend on any current to increase your speed. But why hurry? It would be more enjoyable to take six hours to fish the deep holes, study the flora and fauna, and enjoy this wilderness scenery.

Shuttle: To reach the take-out, travel south from Springfield on Ga 21 for 4.1 miles to Ga 275. Turn left (east) on Ga 275 and drive 5.5 miles to the end of this paved road on the bank of the Savannah River. At the end of the road, a dirt access leads off to the left and down to the river's edge at Ebenezer Landing. The parking area is large; remember to put your fee for use of the landing in the yellow box. After leaving the shuttle car at the take-out, return to the paved road (Ga 275), and drive back west for 3.2 miles to the first paved intersection. Turn right (north) onto Country Road S953, and drive 1.2 miles to Long Bridge over the creek. Immediately before the bridge, a dirt access road branches off and leads down to the creek, where you can park near the ramp that will serve as your put-in.

Hazards: This trip on Ebenezer Creek is a gentle journey suited for families and novice canoeists. Just remember to practice the usual precautions that apply to all wilderness river trips: wear lifevests while canoeing, watch for snakes on overhanging limbs, respect private property, and don't annoy the alligators. This creek is not particularly suited for swimming. It would be wise to carry a compass and follow a map. During periods of high water, there is little or no noticeable current to follow, and it's easy to take a wrong turn up a slough or lake. In low water levels, watch the trash on the surface. It usually flows down the main channel of the creek.

Water Levels: Canoeing on Ebenezer Creek is possible any month of the year, even though the water level can fluctuate as much as eight feet, depending on the water level of the Savannah River. High water levels do not present any particular danger, and the water seldom gets so low that canoeing is impossible.

Area Accommodations: There are no motels or public campgrounds in the vicinity of Ebenezer Creek. The nearest accommodations are south, near Savannah. Call the Savannah Convention and Visitors Bureau and ask for the motels in Garden City on old US 17.

Alternate Trip: If you don't mind deadfalls and extremely confined canoeing conditions in narrow channels, you can extend this trip by four miles and make it an overnight excursion as we did. The put-in for this trip is at Log Landing. You reach this put-in by returning from the take-out at Ebenezer Landing on Ga 257, back to Ga 21. Turn right (north, towards Springfield) on Ga 21, and drive one mile (just past the bridge over Little Ebenezer Creek) to a dirt road leading off to the right. Notice a historical marker regarding "Old Ebenezer Town" at this junction. Turn right (east) on this dirt road, and drive 5 miles (crossing the new concrete bridge over Runs Branch) to a picnic and swimming area on the left side of this road. A put-in here on Runs Branch is one mile upstream from the conjunction with Little Ebenezer Creek, which is the beginning of Ebenezer Creek.

Note: Most maps now list Run Branch as "Ebenezer Creek." The locals and most older maps, however, indicate that Ebenezer Creek does not begin until this narrow stream joins the Little Ebenezer Creek further downstream.

Map Guide: Numbers on our map indicate creek mileage. Letters indicate points of interest.

a. Put-in at Long Bridge Landing on County Road S953.
b. Savannah Electric Company power line crosses creek (mile .1).
c. Area known as "Alligator Gardens" (mile .15).
d. Long, wide stretch known as "Kramer Sea" (mile .2).
e. Hollow cypress log at end of western slough where Mr. & Mrs. Gnann sought shelter from the rain (mile .5).
f. Good fish "drop" at foot of black cypress at sharp bend in creek (mile .8).
g. Submerged pine logs at "Bevens Landing" on horseshoe curve in narrows could be hazardous in low water (mile 1.2).
h. Narrows with overhanging branches as you approach elevated Rahn Landings (mile 1.6).
i. Large lake area, autumn foliage should be spectacular (mile 1.7).
j. Half-Moon Landing on right with fishing cabins (mile 1.9).
k. Fork in Creek, canoeist's preference (mile 2.2).
l. Old fish trap near Weitman Landing (mile 2.4).
m. Cut through possible in high water to avoid horseshoe curve ahead. Otherwise stay left in channel (mile 2.5).
n. Creek gets larger and deeper (mile 2.9).
o. First tupelo gum swamp (mile 3).
p. Buntz Landing on left. Easy access out (mile 3.3).
q. Large cypress swamp on north side. Site of unsolved murder of a black man in 1915. (mile 3.9).
r. Large tupelo forest. Outstanding scenery (mile 4).
s. Exposed pilings from old logging narrow-gauged railroad (mile 4.2).
t. Thirty-foot "High Bluff" on right (mile 4.6).
u. Pilings from Old Savannah-Augusta Road, one of earliest in Georgia (mile 4.9).
v. Creek forks, stay left (mile 5).
w. Pilings from old "log boom" (mile 5.1).
x. Take-out on right bank in the Savannah River (mile 5.5).

1982

Canoeing Georgia's Toe

The St. Marys, 175 miles of wild, beautiful river.

by Reece Turrentine

If you look at a state map, you can't miss Georgia's toe. It's the little crook in the southeast corner formed by the St. Marys River. Somewhere near Ellicott's Mound in the Okefenokee Swamp, the river begins as a slight current of swamp water. The current flows westward for a while, then southward as it develops into a river, then east, then a long stretch north, and finally eastward again to the sea. Between those four major directions are thousands of curves and twisting bends. It's only 65 miles from its source to its mouth, by straight line. But canoeing its curves will take you 175 miles through its swamplike beginnings, along glistening sand beaches, to the tidal waters of the coast. It's been there for eons, like a giant twisted sea serpent, with its neck and head poised to strike at the sea.

"We call it 'the River of a Thousand Bends,'" Burt Rutkin said as we paddled toward his Canoe Outpost at the bridge on U.S. 1.

"Is that an official name?" I asked.

"Not really," he replied. "Judy and I made it up because it fit so well. But it's catching on. Now we're looking for a good Indian name that means that. You know, like 'Nantahala' means 'Land of the Noonday Sun,' and 'Okefenokee' means 'Land of Trembling Earth.' There oughta be a good Creek Indian name for 'River of a Thousand Bends.' And it would just have to be musical and romantic and all of that."

Though the river was low from lack of rain, I noticed recent high-water marks on the bank.

"It's the tide," Burt advised me.

"But we're seventy-five miles from the coast," I replied. "Does salt water come in this far?"

"Not salt water," he explained. "But the tidal effect does. It pushes the river up. Salt water may get in ten or fifteen miles sometimes, but that's all. And notice something else—though the tide is coming in now, the river current still flows toward the sea."

I had to stop paddling and reflect on this a few minutes. I sensed the powerful forces of nature working under me, each one performing its own function. The incoming tide didn't reverse the river flow, but appeared to lift the current above it, permitting the river to keep on its way to the sea. And our little canoe sat on top of it all, being moved by earth, moon, and sea.

But Burt didn't need my philosophical musings. He needed my paddle. So I dug in again. The tea-colored water gurgled around the paddle blades, and we glided forward briskly.

"This water is the same color as the swamp's," I observed, remembering previous canoe trips through the Okefenokee. "Is it because of the same tannic acid that's in the swamp water?"

"Mostly," Burt said. "But it picks up some more chemicals from palmetto roots and sand bottoms and the like. And that's what made this water so famous."

"What do you mean 'famous?'" I asked. Burt stopped paddling this time and turned to face me.

"Why, old sailing vessels used to detour hundreds of miles off course to fill their drinking kegs with St. Marys' water," he stated emphatically. "Things like that shouldn't be forgotten. Today, only fishermen and canoeists are interested in the St. Marys. But one hundred years ago, it was known all over the world for its pure, healthful water. People didn't know the chemistry of it, but they knew it would last for months. One old sea captain claimed its water kept fresh and unsoured for two years. It was just one of those things known back then to the old, hearty race of men who manned the sailing vessels, and it was handed down from generation to generation until it was known by that class of men all over the civilized world."

I had stopped paddling by now.

"They even hauled it to Fernandina," Burt continued, "and sold it to the sailing ships for a penny a gallon for drinking water. Years ago, Jacksonville once thought of pumping St. Marys' water forty miles for drinking purposes, but gave up the idea."

It probably wouldn't have worked. Pumps, pipes, and canals don't work too well in this area. Other similar attempts have been made, but given up. In the late 1800s, Captain Harry Jackson, a prominent Atlantan, attempted the biggest construction snafu of the century. He wanted to drain the Okefenokee Swamp into the St. Marys River by digging a ten-mile canal across the ridge that runs under U.S. 1 and 23. That way, he figured, he could get to the timber in the swamp. He hired engineers to study it. They said it would work.

"They won't ever do it," said an old black resident who lived on the edge of the swamp. "The swamp has some strange ways, and it don't give up its secrets easily." But they started digging anyhow, and soon they discovered the water ran toward the swamp instead of away from it toward the river. Fearing they'd drain the river into the swamp instead of vice versa, they abandoned the plan. You can read and hear all about "Jackson's Folly" at the Okefenokee National Wildlife Refuge on U.S. 1 and 23.

The river was showing definite tidal effects as we canoed around Trader's Hill, one of the few points of public access to the river. The old deck pilings and ruins were the only visible evidence of a once-thriving trading post and county seat. Established in 1700, it was defended by a stockade garrison of U.S. soldiers during the Indian wars. Many of the original pioneers are buried in the cemetery behind the ruins of the old church.

"This was the head of navigation for the St. Marys," Burt remarked. We got out and walked around the attractive recreational center built by the county. "Let me show you something few get to see anymore," Burt said, heading back for the canoe.

We paddled downstream for a half mile or so, and turned the canoe toward a small opening on the left bank. After following a little winding canal, we broke out into a hidden lake. "Have you ever seen cypress trees like that?" he asked. I sat looking without reply. I hadn't.

"This is the only stand of primeval cypresses left in the area. The logging companies got the others in the swamp and on the river. But they missed this little hidden lake," he said, smiling.

The giant sentinels all but surrounded the lake. Their lofty tops swayed in the breeze, but their enormous trunks protected the lake from the slightest ripple. We sat in a motionless and silent world. Each giant was surrounded by its own army of guard-like cypress knees, extensions of its own root system, bending upward for air and nourishment. This little hidden Shangri-la was so still and untouched, I hated even to touch the water with my paddle. But we had to leave, so we eased out with as little wake as possible.

Back out on the river, our silent world was ruptured by the sound of paddles banging aluminum sides. Voices were chattering as 12 canoes appeared rounding the curve, digging in upstream.

"That's the Project Big Step group," Burt remarked. "I heard they were on the river."

"Where y'all headed?" I called out.

"To the Gulf of Mexico," one called back, without missing a stroke.

"Hold up a minute, let's talk," I insisted, not wanting to miss this story.

They were 10 youthful offenders, given the choice of 30 days in the juvenile detention home or 30 days under the custody of two Outward Bound officials on a river trip.

"I wish I'd gone to the home," one said jokingly, glad to have a minute's rest. They had put in four days before at Fort Clinch on the coast, were canoeing upstream to Trader's Hill, where they'd jog the 10 miles to the Okefenokee Recreational Area, canoe through the swamp to the Suwannee River, and on to the Gulf. It was an endurance test for 30 days of outdoor wilderness training, including a two-day solo survival expedition for each one.

"It's tough," said Jim McCullough, the Outward Bound leader. "But most come out of it better people than when they went in. This group's having a ball."

We wished them good luck and watched as they dug in for their upstream journey. I was glad to have the current with us as we headed downstream.

Around a few more bends, a bright yellow canoe appeared, beached on a sandbar.

"That's my canoe," Burt said. "We've caught up with my wife Judy and her friend." Judy and Lisa Kent sat smiling at us as we beached beside their canoe. After the introductions, we all sat down to eat and share our various lunches. River eating is not like it used to be. They had all kinds of exotic packaged delights. I still stick pretty much to sardines and saltines.

Judy and Burt used to operate a Computer Service Bureau in Miami. She was a professional soloist with the Miami Civic Choral Association. "I just couldn't take the computers anymore," Burt explained. "I was beginning to feel like one."

"And I just wasn't cut out for the confinement of a music career," Judy added. "I felt like I was living with blinders on."

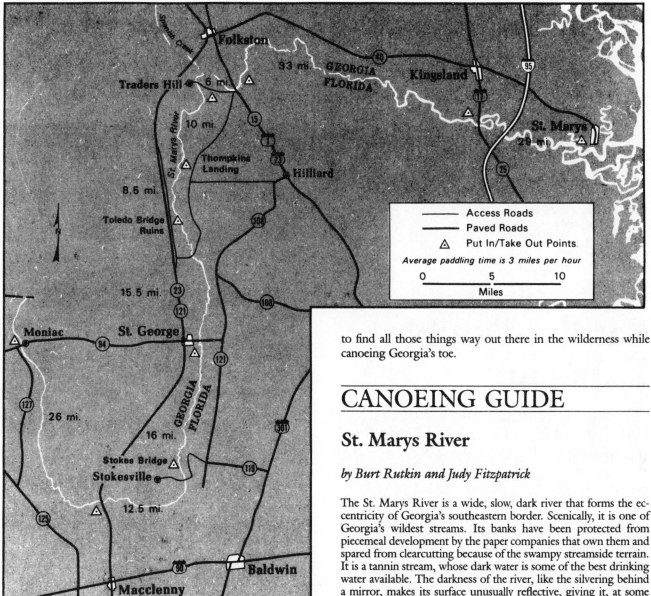

Judy's friend Lisa Kent is an artist, just having finished an art show in Waycross.

"We left it all and came to the river," Burt said. "Making the break was hard, but once we made it, we had it made. Canoeing business is great on the St. Marys. We keep a full schedule all year round."

"What a mixture," I thought, as we headed downstream toward the takeout at the Outpost. Here were the genius of a computer expert, the trained voice of a soprano, and the hands of an artist—all blended now in the art of canoeing the wilderness. But they all seemed to fit it like a glove. They were honest and authentic people, with their blinders off, becoming a part of the very nature that endowed them with such rich gifts.

The "River of a Thousand Bends" had a surprise at every bend: a discovery, an encounter, a revelation. I hadn't expected

to find all those things way out there in the wilderness while canoeing Georgia's toe.

CANOEING GUIDE

St. Marys River

by Burt Rutkin and Judy Fitzpatrick

The St. Marys River is a wide, slow, dark river that forms the eccentricity of Georgia's southeastern border. Scenically, it is one of Georgia's wildest streams. Its banks have been protected from piecemeal development by the paper companies that own them and spared from clearcutting because of the swampy streamside terrain. It is a tannin stream, whose dark water is some of the best drinking water available. The darkness of the river, like the silvering behind a mirror, makes its surface unusually reflective, giving it, at some hours of the day, a quality of beautiful unreality. Its upper reaches, down as far as Folkston, are lined with intermittent pure-white beaches and display all of the wildlife—palmetto, cypress, armadillos, Florida bobcats, bears, vultures, coons, screech and hoot owls, kingfishers, and ospreys—plus the moody landscape that characterize the adjoining expanse of the Okefenokee Swamp. Its scenery will give pleasure to all canoers, unless they demand white water. The St. Marys is hardly stirred by a ripple, and its width, leisurely pace, and frequent restful beaches make it ideal for the beginner. Another advantage for the novice is the proximity of parallel highways on both sides of the river, far enough away not to intrude, but near enough to provide a possible hike out for canoeists who have met mishap or have overextended themselves.

The St. Marys' length from its swampy headwaters to the mouth near the town of St. Marys can be divided into three distinct sections. 1). Above St. George, it is a small stream, and though these are some of its most beautiful and mysterious regions, they are also some of the most difficult and, occasionally, dangerous. The river is deathly slow here when low, and swift when high. Hazards on this stretch include occasional downed trees, which do not entirely cross the stream, and overhanging hornets' nests. Not recommended for the beginner. Below McClenny, a wider current allows more maneuverability and more stable water. 2). From Stokes Bridge to the U.S. 1 bridge below Folkston, the St. Marys is wider—from 15 to 20 yards wider—but still bears most of the wonder and intimacy it had upstream. Picnic or camp on the white beaches in the bends, and explore several of the interesting tributaries, especially Cypress Lake and Spanish Creek. 3). Below Folkston, the beaches are replaced by high, sandy bluffs, and your progress will be increasingly determined by the level and direction of the tides, whose influence you may begin to feel as far upstream as the U.S. 1 bridge. After U.S. 17, the water becomes decidedly brackish, and the banks give way to wide expanses of tidal salt marsh.

Although the St. Marys is a docile stream, be sure to tie your belongings into the canoe. Once they sink in the tannin-stained water, even to a shallow depth, they are likely to be invisible and, hence, lost beyond recovery.

1979

Satilla: Double Exposure

"I thought about the solitude of that first day and how I had lured Sam with the prospect of good fishing."

by John Moll

At 5:30 on Saturday morning Sam McClesky and I stood on the U.S. 301 bridge and looked down at the Satilla River. The night was black—no moon, and the stars were still shining brilliantly. The road was deserted. The only sound we heard was the soft murmur of the river. As our eyes adjusted to the dark and the first light of dawn began to shine in the east, we watched a faint mist form and rise quickly from the black water.

"What do you think, Sam?" I asked.

"I think I'm ready to be on the river," he answered.

In the predawn light we slid our boat into the water and paddled out into the main current. The river was flowing fast, surprisingly fast for this flat swampy country, so we immediately relaxed a little, reassured that we would have no trouble completing the 24-mile trip by Sunday evening. We unpacked fishing rods and began to cast toward the bank, paddling only to avoid submerged logs.

I was happy just being on the water, but for Sam's sake I hoped the fish would bite. For canoeing Sam favors white water. "Flat water," he made it clear when I asked him along on this trip, "doesn't excite me." I had lured him to the Satilla with a promise that he would catch enough bass to feed us.

Soon we found ourselves drifting through the middle of a deep cypress swamp. The dark-brown water was so heavily stained that we could not see much more than one foot down into it. Off to each side were tangles of cypress knees and fallen trees. A dedicated fisherman could spend days exploring a single mile of this river, but with only two days to cover 24 miles, we fished the most likely spots and floated on.

As we fished, we began to see more clearly that this was truly an undisturbed wilderness. There was almost no litter washed into the river and none on the banks. It was pristine and magnificent. As we rounded each corner, we startled small flocks of ducks and egrets. Occasionally a hawk would sail overhead, inspecting us. But the fish inspected us not at all. We tried everything we knew: plastic worms, spinner baits, spoons, plugs—they refused it all. We spent the day that way paddling, drifting, enjoying the sun as the day warmed up, fishing and not catching fish.

Around two o'clock we began looking for Big Satilla Creek (some folks call it Little Satilla River), which flows into the river about the halfway point of our trip. "Be nice to see that creek about now," Sam muttered, searching through his tackle box for the magic trinket that would produce supper.

He was beginning to feel anxious, and I shared the feeling. We were sure we had traveled a lot of river miles, and the swampy sections of the Satilla are so full of backwaters and sloughs that we could have passed the stream without knowing it. Yet we had to be sure we had come far enough so that we could complete the journey the next day. Then we saw a large stream coming in from the left, its flow heavy enough to match the main river. "Big Satilla Creek," we said together.

Soon after we passed the confluence of the river and the creek, we came to a long white sand beach on the left side. No need for discussion: this was camp. Setting up camp took only a few minutes, and we both settled in for a quick nap to recover from our early start. I crawled into the tent, but Sam just lay out on the beach in the sun. Around five o'clock the chill had returned to the air, and we got up to make dinner. A half hour of furious fishing activity yielded only one embarrassingly small bass. If fresh fish tops the camping menu, then hot chicken gumbo soup on a cold night outdoors runs a mighty close second. By the time we finished cleaning up, the temperature was back in the low thirties and a slender crescent moon hung briefly in the sky, then set. We built a roaring fire and just enjoyed being there, far away from the rest of the world.

Sam and I met through our mutual interest in whitewater, and we've been friends a long time. We talked of past trips and all the good times our two families have spent in the North Georgia mountains—and how different this was. Memories floated through my mind for a few silent moments before we turned in. I was glad to be able to sit on that bend in the river that night. I said as much aloud, and Sam nodded his agreement in the glow of the fire.

We weren't long in the water the next morning before I realized that the character of the river had changed from the day before. It was much wider and slower. Although there were still some swampy sections, the banks were mostly dry. In this flat country we were surprised to see a 30-foot bluff with a soft sand face descending steeply into the water. We saw large white egrets and one stately blue heron. We passed a private fish camp with rental boats tied up on the left shore and met several fishermen in small powerboats on the now wide, sluggish river.

At four o'clock we rounded a curve and saw the railroad. We maneuvered between the pilings, the only navigational hazard on the river, and a mild one. By the time we lugged our gear out from under the U.S. 84 bridge along the right-of-way (we respected the "Posted" signs on a convenient boat ramp), it was nearly five, and getting cold and dark. Sam lost a coin toss and was thus chosen to get a ride to the car. He was picked up almost immediately.

While he was gone, I stood on the U.S. 84 bridge and watched the sun set on a different river than I had first seen through the mists the day before. I thought about the solitude of that first day. I worried about how I had lured Sam, the original hard-core white-water buff, into his first flat-water trip with the prospect of good fishing. I wondered how he felt when we failed to catch anything decent. But then we had talked of a return trip with our wives and daughters. He couldn't have thought it was *all* bad.

The chill had returned to the air, and the same thin crescent moon hung low on the horizon when Sam returned and pulled off next to the bridge. As we loaded the equipment, I remembered some of the things I had read about the river. Early settlers had called it the "Great" Satilla River and I thought I would try that one out on Sam. "I'll have to put this down as a fine trip on a great river," I told him as we pulled away from the bridge.

When white-water fanatic Sam said, "I've got to go along with that," I knew it *was* a great river.

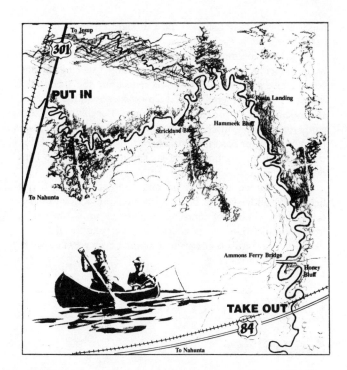

Satilla: Double Exposure*

"I didn't study its history, interview its people or pinpoint its features; this was canoeing for canoeing's sake."

by Reece Turrentine

Are you kinda out of sorts with things in general? You may need a good dose of a tonic I discovered recently called "Satilla." Are business pressures crowding in? Let me recommend a tranquilizer named "Satilla." But I warn you, it's habit forming. You and your mate been at odds lately? Go to the marriage counselor named "Satilla." No charge. Maybe you just need a day off to regroup and rethink some things, get it all together again. Try a little resort I know of called "Satilla." Relaxation, reconciliation, recuperation, or just reflection—there's no better place for it than the winding black ribbon of South Georgia water called the Satilla River.

I had dreaded the long drive to the coast for a church meeting, but many of our meetings are held at St. Simons, and as minister of the Riverside Methodist Church in Macon, I was

scheduled to go. For years I've been crossing the Satilla River just north of Waycross. A mere glimpse of those pure white sand bars at the bridge enticed me. There were always cars at the bridge, but I never had time to stop. Before this last trip, I made an impulsive decision: I'd strap "Ol' Wood and Canvas" to the car top and leave a few hours early. A brief encounter with the Satilla would be better than none.

As my canoe slid into the waters, it took only a couple of strong pumps with the paddle for me to be gliding into its current and on downstream toward those glistening sand bars. My paddle moved only slightly thereafter, just to keep me lined up and moving forward. This was no marathon. It was a drift trip, just to soak up some sun and listen to some silence.

I guess that silence is the reason canoeing so gratifies the senses. It is a noiseless activity, which allows you to hear the sounds of wind and water and occasional wildlife. In that silence, the other senses are heightened by simple things—the touch of a wooden paddle and the sense of propelling oneself across water, the taste of ordinary food made delicious by the surroundings. On a river an RC and a Moon Pie become a banquet, and saltines and sardines become a feast.

The Satilla River is one of the last remaining wild rivers in Georgia. My one mistake of the trip was allowing myself only a few hours instead of a few days. This river should be camped on. The glistening, pure white sand bars were made for tents, a glowing campfire, a pot of coffee, and a snug bedroll.

I left my footprints on most of the sand bars. I couldn't resist stopping to stretch and stroll. I didn't see many human footprints, but plenty of wild critters had been there before. After each stroll I'd reenter my canoe to paddle a few strokes and drift. The only human sound I heard was my own sighing now and then, just relaxing and letting the muscles go.

I even got reacquainted with my old canoe. I took time to look at her, think about her, remember some experiences we've had together. Lately I suspect she'd thought I'd just been using her.

Will you permit a little confession? In the last year I've been canoeing for the purpose of writing canoeing stories. Now, I love to write and I love to canoe, and the assignment makes a beautiful blend. But I'd almost forgotten the pleasure of canoeing just for the sheer pleasure of it. For this trip I didn't study river history, interview people who live on its banks, pinpoint features, or record special characteristics. In fact, I didn't even take along my little water-soaked notebook where I jot down my notes.

As it turned out, that offhand approach to the Satilla helped me understand it better. This river provides an opportunity for the kind of canoeing none of us should get away from—simple, relaxing, done for the pure pleasure of the experience. The Satilla is not white water, not even very fast water, but it is healing water.

CANOEING GUIDE

Satilla River

by John Moll

In General: The Satilla is a beautiful black-water river in Southeast Georgia. It flows briskly through swamps and lowlands from its headwaters near Waycross to the Atlantic Ocean near Jekyll Island. This river offers over 150 canoeable miles of scenic wilderness.
Put in and take out: Numerous runs are available. We ran from U.S. 301 about 20 miles south of Jesup to U.S. 84 about 10 miles east of Nahunta. To set up shuttle, travel south from the U.S. 301 bridge to Nahunta and turn left to head east on U.S. 84.
Water level: This river holds its level well, so having enough water to paddle is no problem. Relatively high water makes it easier to avoid sand bars, but usually slows down the fishing.
Distance: This section was 25 miles, a good two-day trip. U.S. geological maps will show you numerous access points, so that you can choose a run of any length. Figure to make 10–15 miles per day if you take time to enjoy the river.
Hazards: All along the way mild maneuvering is required to avoid fallen trees and sand bars. At the take out, the pilings of the railroad bridge are closely spaced but easy to avoid.

1978

The Folks around Wrens and Keysville have

A Love Affair with a River

by Reece Turrentine

The ice crunched as we slid the canoe into the edge of the creek. The thermometer back at Padgett's Grocery in Keysville had registered 15 degrees, the coldest day of the year so far. "Has your canoe ever made like an ice-breaker before?" quipped my partner. "Not by choice," I replied as I settled into the back seat. Of course you don't pick such days. But if you are there, standing on the edge of the river all ready to go, you don't back out just because the weather turns cold. If you've got enough clothes, you go. We had, so we were going.

A gentle push from shore and a couple of deep strokes with the paddle sent us gliding out of the ice into the swift, swollen currents of the creek. My canoe has a glide like no other canoe I've ever paddled. I notice it anew each time I start a trip. It's an old wood and canvas, long, sleek, and thin. It knifes through the water effortlessly, responding to the slightest paddle movement. I'm sure I'm prejudiced, but it sure seemed in top form this morning.

I can't say the same for it the day before, bouncing and pouncing all over the top of the car. Those gusty winds had given me some anxious moments. A canoe is never at its best when it's inverted on top of a car, though. Now it was in its element: gliding out into the waters for which it was made, blending in with the dark, swollen currents of Brier Creek.

But why Brier Creek? I stumbled on it, by pure serendipity. I was thumbing through an old Georgia history book and found a paragraph about early efforts to improve Georgia's waterways. Back in 1817 money was appropriated to improve five *major* waterways in the state: the Chattahoochee, the Flint, the Altamaha, the Savannah, and . . . Brier Creek! The other four I could easily consider "major," but what and where was Brier Creek?

I had a dim recollection from school days about a famous "Battle of Brier Creek." The history book refreshed my memory about this battle, fought during the Revolutionary War in 1779, where the British scored a major victory against a regiment of Georgia patriots on the point of land formed by the junction of Brier Creek and the Savannah River.

After that, however, Brier Creek recedes into the dim pages of history. It emerges again in 1817, with the river improvement project. Brier Creek became a major transportation and settlement center in early Georgia history when families moved north from Savannah up the river and branched off at the creek, settling inland along its banks.

"But who knows anything about it now?" I thought to myself. I looked on the map for nearby towns. Wrens, Keysville. I didn't have to look further. "Hurdle will know!" I said aloud to myself.

Bill Hurdle, an old college roommate, has been a close friend for almost 30 years. He served the Methodist churches in both Wrens and Keysville right after college. I even went over there and preached for him years ago. After years of traveling across the state for visits, we're together in Macon now, so I simply dialed the phone across town.

"Hurdle, you remember anything about Brier Creek?"

"I sure do," he replied emphatically. "I remember how attached everybody was to that little creek. It's like they had it in their veins."

"You want to canoe it with me?" I asked. That's all it took. The date and time were set.

We were now on it, and it was cold but sunny. We'd left the Keysville Bridge about 9:30 am, and in less than 30 minutes, just beyond the railroad trestle, we encountered the problem we'd been warned about. The creek was flooded and at times was pouring out of its banks, spreading into the woods. We'd have to employ some ingenious detective methods if we were to stay in the creek and not spend our time paddling into dead ends.

Yet to me, part of the delight of a creek like this is the sheer joy of exploring and discovering and working your way through something. Unless you're actually traveling somewhere, it's more interesting than open-river canoeing, and it's a good substitute for winter whitewatering. You stay busy. Instead of looking for the rocks, Vs, and eddies of mountain streams, you watch for limbs, stumps, and the deep currents of the creek run. When you're working your way through flooded woods like this, you learn to look for certain signs of the creek. Ofttimes, the fastest current will reveal the creek's course, but if it's really flooded, water pours everywhere and the current's all through the woods. Then you might look up at the trees for a clue. An open path in the sky or trees leaning towards each other, forming an inverted V or tunnel effect, often reveal the creek course.

Making correct choices brings satisfaction. Wrong choices mean backtracking and looking again. You may turn into an area that looks completely blocked ahead, but when you get there, you can usually work your way through. The brisk current calls for quick scanning and quick decisions. You'll have to use your hands, heads, arms, and paddles to get around, under, and over the branches and bushes you'll be swept through. Heavy clothing will protect you from sharp-pointed holly leaves and scraping, scratching twigs. Wear gloves, and a hat other than a knitted stocking cap. We had to backpaddle three times to retrieve mine left hanging on snags and limbs.

A word of caution: don't canoe this creek (or others like it) during snake season. They say that in the summer a moccasin is staked out on every limb. Save this sort of trip for winter and early spring.

By 10:15, we were out of the wooded area into a river-like creek with well defined banks. It was pleasant traveling. At 10:45 we faced our first of only two portages because of a fallen tree, the work of Mr. Beaver, directly across the creek with no way around it. We were ready to stretch our legs anyhow, so we didn't mind. The portage was easy and the walk did our cold feet good.

"What's that noise?" Bill asked abruptly. I heard it too, way off in the distance: a sharp, deep-throated boom. Guns. It was the reason we'd decided to put in at the Keysville Bridge rather than further upstream as originally planned. Yesterday, I had stopped at Minnie's Truck Stop below the U.S. 1 bridge to inquire about the creek in that area. Several local residents were sitting around chatting and drinking coffee. One old gentleman, overhearing my inquiries, offered: "That stretch you're asking about is on Fort Gordon property. They won't let you on government land."

"Aw yes they will," countered another fellow, "that's a public waterway."

"Well, maybe so," replied another, "but they got Sam in there the other day."

"But he was hunting," chimed in another, "and the game warden got him."

The dispute went on and I was enjoying listening. Then "Uncle Bill" spoke up. He'd been sitting silently, sipping his soup. "Well, all of you are forgetting something else," he said philosophically, wiping his beard. "Several times a week they shoot them big guns over that creek. Legal or not, I wouldn't want to be on that creek with them shells whistling over my head."

That statement settled it for me. We started further downcreek. Now, listening to those booms in the distance, I was pleased with my decision. Even miles away, they sounded ominous. They'd be with us all day, punctuating and intruding into the silent sounds of the wilderness.

By 11, we were back in the canoe, refreshed from our legstretch. We were still in a fairly open section, enjoying the brisk pace of the current and the sights and sounds around us. Soon I saw the pond race on the left, just as Hubert Padgett had said, a clean-cut little canal heading on up through the woods. "When you get to the pond race, you'll be about half way to Farmer's Bridge," (our take-out point). "If you have time," he continued, "it's a nice hike of about a half mile through the woods to the old Chamber's Mill. Folks used to gather there all the time in the old days, just to sit around and talk. But there's nobody there anymore." There was a hint of sadness in his voice, sadness over a land and time that seemed to be disappearing, in spite of his efforts to preserve it. "I fought 'em all the way to the courthouse about that pollution business," he said emphatically. "They weren't going to dirty up my stream!"

Hubert Padgett deals only in declarative statements. He doesn't hem and haw. He's ready to wage war against those who would destroy the land and the creek. "You'd better warn your readers to respect this area if they're gonna come here," he said emphatically.

I replied emphatically, "Why, that's what *Brown's Guide* is all about. You don't have to worry about its readers."

"Well, that's fine, then. We'll be glad to have them. But the other kind will get in trouble!"

I'd seen what he meant earlier as we drove by part of his land. Signs on the posts said "Trespassers will be shot!" Yet there's a softness in his voice when he talks about the creek and the land. "I was born around Keysville," he said in gentle tones. "I went off, taught school for a while, and had some excellent job offers." He paused a moment, then said: "I would have left Keysville long ago, had it not been for Brier Creek." He was silent after that.

What Hurdle had said about folks having that creek "in their veins" began to make sense. I had heard the same thing said in different words the day before, from "Uncle Bill" at Minnie's Truck Stop, for instance: "It's the only clean stream left in Georgia. I hate for folks to find out about it." Or Mr. Hubert Barrow of Wrens: "I've got the best sucker hole in Georgia staked out on the stream. I've had it for years." Or Mr. Howard Reeves, with whom we'd talked about the creek around the warm fire in his house outside Wrens: "Our old homestead was down on Brier Creek. My father used to be a steeltrapper on that creek in the early nineteen hundreds. He'd

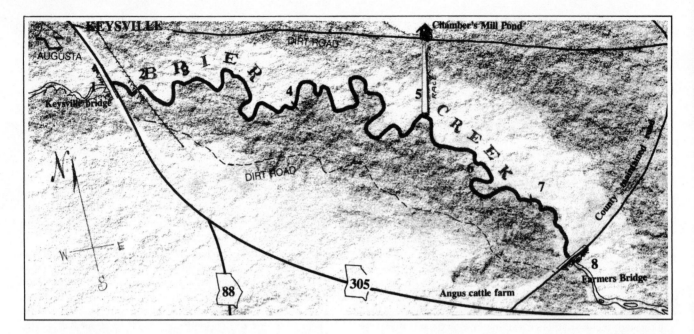

trap muskrat, mink, bobcat, and some possum and coon. I still see signs of them down around Boggy Gut marsh." A lot of the folks around Wrens and Keysville are tied to the land because of Brier Creek.

In the early afternoon we faced our next portage around another tree, flat out across the creek. The current was gentle here, so we slid up parallel to the tree, got out, and eased the canoe over. Not a procedure recommended in swift current. It's always risky to get crosscurrent in a canoe, especially if your canoe has much of a keel to it. Sometimes I think my old wood and canvas has a "centerboard" instead of a keel. That makes it tough in tight turns, but a thing of beauty and a joy forever in open water.

"Let's eat some lunch before we go on," suggested Hurdle, who lives with food in the back of his mind. I don't object to the idea either. So we cleared a small area on the bank and started a twig fire. Soon, the most magnificent aroma filled the air: frozen Vienna sausage roasting over a small blaze. The taste was even better, as was the warmth on cold feet. In fact, the whole occasion was just about perfect.

"Do you remember Sister Bessie?" Bill asked with a mouth full of sausage sandwich. She used to attend one of his churches around here, but she was also one of the true-to-life characters Erskine Caldwell used in his famous novel *Tobacco Road*. Caldwell was from Wrens, and the real Tobacco Road is a few miles north of Keysville. Many readers don't appreciate what they consider the unfair portrayal he gave the people of this area. Sister Bessie, if you remember the book, was the woman preacher who marries the 17-year-old boy because "the Lord told her to." In the book she would run around the church with a cap pistol "shooting the devil" before she preached. I never heard the real-life Sister Bessie preach nor saw her running around the church "shooting the devil," but when she came to church, she always had her Bible with her and tightly tied to it with rubber bands a little silver cap pistol. She was a beautiful poet as well as a very gifted musician.

"We can't sit here all day thawing Vienna sausage," I said, gathering up our trash and watering down the little fire. In a few minutes we were back in the creek. We came to another couple of overflows, but we could figure out the creek bed by the leaning trees and opening in the sky. At 2:30, we emerged from the last little patch of woods to come into view of Farmer's Bridge. We were right on schedule.

The canoe dripped water on the car for a few miles as we drove towards home. Soon the wind dried it out and erased all the remnants of Brier Creek. That is, except that part of it that continues to flow in our minds. Neither wind nor time can erase that. It's the kind of little creek that's been "flowing in the veins" of people for many years around the Augusta area. Even back in early Georgia history, it was reaching out to people and making them say: "I'd have left these parts long ago . . . had it not been for Brier Creek."

CANOEING GUIDE

Brier Creek

The canoeing distance on Brier Creek from the Keysville Bridge to Farmer's Bridge is about eight miles. An average canoe team should make this trip in four to five hours. Flooded water conditions will require longer, allowing for time to backtrack from wrong turns, out of the main creek run. With normal water levels, you should have a well defined creek bed to follow, with obstructions of nothing more than fallen trees and overhanging branches.

Soon after you leave Keysville Bridge (1) you will come to the railroad trestle (2). It was just beyond this point that we encountered our first flooded overflow in the woods (3). Once back out of the woods, the creek followed a well defined course for about two miles, then we encountered our first portage around a fallen tree (4). With lower water, you should be able to go under this tree. Of course, others will appear then which we did not have to encounter.

For the next two miles, the creek stays well within its banks, having the character of a small river. Checkpoint (5) is the mill race entering the creek from the left. This would be a fine place to stretch your legs and enjoy a half-mile hike up through the woods to Chamber's Mill Pond. About a mile beyond the mill race, we confronted our next large flooded area (6). Trees leaning towards one another revealed the creek run and we were able to navigate through this area without wrong turns. Another mile down, we faced our only other portage, a large tree fallen across the creek (7). This should cause no problems at normal water level.

From this point on, we were in and out of small flooded areas, but with good current signs, until we reached Farmer's Bridge. **Shuttle** for this trip is easy. From Keysville (located on Ga. 88, 20 miles south of Augusta), you cross the Keysville Bridge over Brier Creek just at the south edge of town. After traveling a half mile south on Ga. 88, you bear to the left onto Ga. 305, following this road for about four miles. You will then see an Angus Cattle farm sign on the left. Just beyond the sign, you turn left onto a county-maintained road, following this for two miles until you come to Farmer's Bridge. There are two sections to this bridge. Go to the far end of the second bridge, then follow the road to the left down to the creek's edge. There's plenty of open, dry area for parking.

The quality of water in Brier Creek is excellent, being well fed from many pure springs from the Fort Gordon area. Though there are no rapids or shoals on the creek, it maintains a brisk current. Sweeping curves can take you into branches and overhanging trees unless you are alert and vigorous in your paddling.

The stretch below Farmer's Bridge opens up into more river-like surroundings. Several fine overnight trips could be planned in the area of U.S. 25 bridge on down to the creek's junction with the Savannah River. Gary DeBarker, exploration chairman for the Georgia Canoeing Association, reports there's been a lot of logging downstream near the Savannah River. Shallow water could make this area difficult to negotiate.

If you want a little more activity and variety than you find in flat river canoeing, but are not yet ready to brave the cold of mountain whitewater runs, Brier Creek is made to order. The scenery is remote and primitive, and the creek keeps you alert and busy. If you show a genuine interest and appreciation for Brier Creek, the folks around there will bend over backwards to accommodate you in every way.

1977

A River of Memories

When you go canoeing alone, you're not always by yourself

by Reece Turrentine

I could've sworn the river felt familiar as I dug my paddle into its waters. Could it be possible that a river has a feel that it retains over the years? Nonsense, of course. Water is water. It was my imagination. But then, my imagination was going to give me trouble all day.

It all started the week before when my wife, Onie, said: "Reece, I'm going to Thomasville Monday to see Mama and Daddy. Could you go with me? I hate to make that long drive by myself."

I don't like her going alone either, but I didn't see how I could make the trip. "I wish you'd wait," I said, "but if you must go, I want you back before dark." I sounded pretty firm. But so did she.

"How can I when it's three hours one way, no matter how I go?"

I got out the maps to search for back roads that would cut the time.

That's when it happened. When I look at a map, I see two things: the black, red, and gray lines of the highways; and the thin blue lines of the rivers. As I surveyed the landscape between Macon and Thomasville, I saw something that had a strange effect on me. It was a name from out of the past, a name running along one of those little blue lines around Thomasville: the Ochlockonee River. That name brought back memories that hadn't surfaced for years. Thomasville was *my* hometown, too. And to every Huck Finn and Tom Sawyer from Thomasville, that old Ochlockonee had been "our" river. As kids, we fished on it, swam in it, and camped by it. But most of all, it was on that river—33 years ago—I discovered canoeing. I was one of a noisy bunch of boy scouts who took a two-week trip down the Ochlockonee, on into Florida. I remember how the mosquitoes bit, and how the scoutmaster fussed at all the noise we made, but that's when it started, my long love affair with a canoe.

"When did you say you were going to Thomasville, honey? I've got an idea."

The idea was, that she could drop me off on the bridge going into town. While she had a visit with her folks, I could make a short trip down the Ochlockonee, just for old times' sake. She could pick me up at another bridge in the afternoon and we could head home.

"You mean you're going all by yourself?" She knew the cautions against solo canoeing.

"Well, it's a short trip," I said. "And the Ochlockonee doesn't have many hazards."

But then she countered with some bothersome logic: "How do you know? You haven't been on that river in 30 years."

She had a point. But I had a rebuttal: "I'll call Talbot, he'll know."

Talbot Nunnally was one of the old river gang still living in Thomasville. His voice on the other end of the phone said: "Sure, we still go on it. We fish it often. It's still pretty much the same." Then he recalled some of the old items of interest: the Confederate Bridge, the mysterious old cable nobody can explain, the open meadows through which the river meanders at times. "I'll ride out tomorrow," he offered, "and check on the water level and call you back." His return call settled it.

Early Monday morning the car was humming towards Thomasville. Onie and I were inside and another member of the family was on top; Old Wood and Canvas, firmly tied to the canoe rack, was pointing the way to the Ochlockonee. I could even imagine that it sensed the excitement of the occasion, that after 30 years it would take me back to my home river.

It was about 10 o'clock when I read the sign on the bridge: The Ochlockonee River. Of course, this bridge was not our bridge. This was a new one, all bright and white and concrete. Our bridge was off to the side, abandoned and unused now. The old Confederate Bridge. It had all the history and the memories.

Onie helped me unload, she took some pictures, then she was off to town. I watched the car as it disappeared around the curve.

Everything was quiet. For the first time, I paused to look carefully at the brackish waters of the old river. They were dark, but fairly clear. Recent rains had not muddied them too much. A few yards upstream an old oak spread its limb out over the dark waters. "Could that be the same old tree?" I said to myself. We used to dive in the river around here from limbs like that. No, that tree's too small. But then again, things look larger when you are young.

I looked up at the rusted girders of the Confederate Bridge. Even though the new bridge was bright and modern, it couldn't touch the Confederate for romance and history. On one of those old girders, a man once hanged himself. The case was surrounded with mystery and intrigue. As kids we used to sit wide-eyed and spellbound as grownups told about that legend of death and terror.

Most parents didn't want us swimming out here. They said there were deep holes around the old bridge that would suck a person under and never let him go. Still, we used to sneak out on our bicycles. The show-offs in the crowd would flirt with death by jumping off the bridge, right into those terrible holes. The rest of us would wait breathlessly, to see if they would come up. They always did.

"Well, enough daydreaming," as I snapped back to the present. "It's time to get started," I said to the canoe. I gave it a gentle shove, and it slid me out into the river. I picked up my paddle, and ceremoniously dug it into the waters. I still say it had a familiar feel to it. I think I got its message: "Welcome back."

I soon settled into a more realistic mood and rhythmic strokes. The first curve took me out of sight of the bridge and into the remote interior of my sentimental journey.

The Ochlockonee is a scenic little river with a lot of variety to keep things interesting. Recent winds had laid a blanket of colored leaves on its surface. Those leaves were going to prove to be a big help to me in a little while. For I soon left the clearly defined banks, and the river spread out into a wide forest-filled lake. "Which way to go?" I thought. I paddled a bit out into the middle of the tree stand. No, that's not it. So I returned to my point of entry. Then I saw it. The carpet of leaves was spread out motionless across the tree-filled lake. Motionless, except in one spot. Over near the left bank, the leaves moved along with the almost imperceptible current of the channel. That moving carpet led me through the forest-lake, and into the river again. That's one good thing about river travel. There's almost always a current. At times its waters may spread out into lakes, but the main current is still there, if you can just find it. Floating objects help. Leaves, sticks, debris, anything that will show a current drift. Stay with that and you'll avoid a lot of backtracking. I was soon back between the banks.

I had felt completely alone so far. So the noises back in the woods surprised me. "Hmm," was my only audible sound, which is a big disadvantage to solo canoeing. It's not conducive to good conversation. Normally, spoken words would've asked, "I wonder what that is? Is it a cow, or fisherman, or maybe a deer?" It was the last possibility that made me think a bit further. It was deer season and I remembered so-called deer hunters who have shot cows, dogs, people, and goats, anything that moves. And I was moving. It'd be just like some idiot to think I was a deer, out for an afternoon swim down the middle of the river. I wished for some clothing of that bright survival orange. Maybe a jacket, since my old quilted one was dark. I'd also be glad to have a cap, gloves, pants, socks, and underwear to match. I didn't have any of them, so I just started whistling. That didn't last too long, though.

"Hmm," came another of my solo conversations. It was the old railroad trestle. Time for the first stop. I had wasted some time wandering around in that wooded lake back there, so I couldn't take long. But I had to climb up on that railroad track so I could catch sight of the buildings of Dawes Silica Mine. My father had worked at Dawes during the war years as a bookkeeper. I used to go up there, borrow an old rod and reel from the office, and fish in a lake behind the office. I can see him now, strolling out of the office one day with the plant manager. "Here, son, give me that rod and let me show you how to catch a fish." The manager, a friend of Dad's, smiled at the absurdity. Dad just wasn't a sportsman. He always had on his coat and tie. But he was a lot of fun. He took the rod, drew back, and let it go with a mighty cast. And I mean he let it go. He let everything go—the plug, line, rod and reel—right in the middle of the lake. "Damn, Turrentine," the manager yelled, "you threw away my rod and reel." I just knew Dad was going to get fired on the spot. But it was so typical, the manager broke into riotous laughter. I joined in with them, relieved his job was still secure.

A distant train whistle jolted me back to the present. I had to get off the tracks and back in the canoe. I had spent far longer than I'd realized.

About half a mile from the trestle, the old U.S. 19 bridge came into view. I could hear the traffic crossing it, with the tires slapping the old tar joints on the concrete. I remembered the many times our old car crossed this bridge, carrying Dad to work everyday. On the days mother needed the car, I would drive Dad out. I had just gotten my driver's license. I'm sure the sound waves are still echoing around this bridge somewhere: "Slow this thing down, son. You're driving too fast. This old car just won't take it." I was pretty rough on it. The old war-time synthetic recaps wouldn't take more than 35 mph. Neither would the rest of the car. It carried the extra strain during those days with Dad's secretary in the back seat. She was rather stout, to put it mildly. The old roof leaked over the back seat, and on rainy days she'd sit back there with a face as gloomy as the day—with her umbrella open. It was one of those cold rainy mornings Dad had his first hint of heart trouble. But it would take 20 more years before his stubborn heart would finally give out.

As the river left the bridge behind, it drifted through a beautiful little section of small trees and sandbars. I enjoyed its serenity.

"There's the old cable!" I said out loud. I was tired of hearing just "Hmms." As I slid under it, I held on for a few minutes. What could it have been? An old ferry cable? The remnants of an old swinging bridge? An ancient trot line? Nobody seems to know. It's just always been there, stretching from shore to shore.

After a short distance, the river broke out into the opening of a power-line clearing and without the protection of the trees, the wind was fierce. I struggled to keep my heading. I was in the solo kneeling position, but the bow was still swinging around. I moved to the center, but I still couldn't control it. Finally, I crawled all the way up into the bow, paddled hard, and let the stern swing as it would. I controlled the direction pretty well, but it was tough traveling. After a few turns, the river headed back into the woods. Was I glad! I was resting a few moments when I saw more trouble ahead. A logjam was blocking the way. The river banks were narrow and the current was stronger and swirling. This is about the only type of hazard that could give anyone trouble on the Ochlockonee. I bumped, scraped, and twisted my way through. By then I was tired. The last half mile had worked on me. I rested and looked over the map, trying to get a location and the remaining distance. The verdict was clear. I was way behind schedule and had made too many stops, recalling too many memories. Though this was a "sentimental journey," I had a schedule to meet and it was obvious I wasn't going to make it on time.

I reached under the seat and pulled out a little piece of equipment which I make a rule of carrying on solo trips—just for emergencies: my little one-horsepower "Mighty Mite" outboard. I dropped it over the side, clamped it to the gunwale, gave the rope a pull, and it jumped to life. The distance from old U.S. 19 to U.S. 84 bridge is about five miles. During this stretch the river has fewer logjams and obstructions, and even, once in a while, gives you a little straightaway. I glided along enjoying the rest and making up for lost time.

Lost time? I can hardly call it that. The sentimental detours and nostalgic images had been enjoyable company. That's the reason I'd come in the first place.

After a couple of miles, I stored my little outboard and resumed my paddling. It was good to have the silence around me again. Splashing sounds directed my eyes to a large flock of ducks ahead, neck-stretching it out of there. Wildlife abounds on this river. It's always been a hunting and fishing favorite.

For the next hour, I glided through the twisting turns of the little Ochlockonee. I say "little," because it's not a big river like the Flint or Ocmulgee. It alternately narrows and widens. On down this stretch, a wide meadow appeared on both sides, an interesting change from the forest-lined banks.

I wanted to make one more little detour, but I kept on paddling. If I kept up this pace, I'd get to the bridge right on schedule. I had wanted to take a brief hike up into the woods along this bank. I wondered if there were any remnants of the old boy scout camp. The times we had there, kicking the cans, "stealing the bacon," commanding spit-ball wars, and bandaging cuts and bruises. Back up there in the woods, under one of those tall South Georgia pines, I had sat with my head all bandaged. I looked like a war casualty. Actually, the only battle I had been waging was with the scout test called the Knife and Hatchet, which I had just failed. In chopping a block of wood,

I turned the blade of the hatchet around so I could hammer it in two. On the upswing, I hit the wrong block of wood! So I wrapped my kerchief around my head and went looking for the scoutmaster. I had to wait in line. I was sure the bandage would qualify me for the "First Aid" merit badge, but he wasn't impressed at all. He sat me down under a tree.

While thinking about all this foolishness, the Cairo bridge came into view. I was a little ahead of schedule. I guess I had enjoyed the "Mighty Mite" a little too long. I slid up next to the shore, unloaded the canoe and took a few pictures. I walked over to the river's edge.

Yes, it was on this spot under this bridge where I had met a canoe, three decades before. A lot of water had gone under this bridge since then. A lot of things had changed. The bridge above me could speed me to places just down the road that had no resemblance whatever to things of the past. But flowing under the bridge, hidden among the trees, the little Ochlockonee flows about the same as it did many years ago. Rivers aren't very impressed with all the changing fads and fashions the days bring. Rivers don't listen much to the days. They listen more to the years.

The horn honked. Onie was right on the dot. She took a few more pictures, helped me load up, and in minutes we were on our way.

"Well, how was the trip?" she asked excitedly.

"Real fine," I replied. But that was certainly an understatement. I tried again: "It was one of the most meaningful experiences I ever had." But that sounded too canned.

Before I could try again, she said: "I sure was relieved to see you waiting at the bridge when I drove up. I was a little worried about you on the river. How'd you get along? I mean by yourself and all?"

There was a pause, and then I said: "Well, to tell you the truth, I really wasn't by myself."

"You mean there were others on the river, too?"

"Yes," I hesitated. "there was that bunch of kids back on the Confederate Bridge, jumping into the water holes; and that crowd of noisy scouts banging canoes and supplies around, loading up for a trip into Florida; and then there was this man, trying to fish—with a coat and tie on . . ."

CANOEING GUIDE

Ochlockonee River

If you're in Southwest Georgia for a few hours or days, try canoeing the Ochlockonee River. It's twisting and straight, narrow and wide, surrounded by dense forests and wide-open meadows affording plenty of variety and interest. The current is good, and the scenery is wild. Six bridges and trestles cross it around the Thomasville area, providing easy put-ins and take-outs for any length of trip. You can extend it into days or even weeks if you like. Weaving southwest from Thomasville, it flows down into the big waters of Lake Talquin west of Tallahassee. Then, it continues through the wilderness of northern Florida until it empties into Apalachee Bay on the Gulf of Mexico.

As with most rivers, the water varies with the rainfall. But the Ochlockonee usually maintains a good deep channel. A call to the

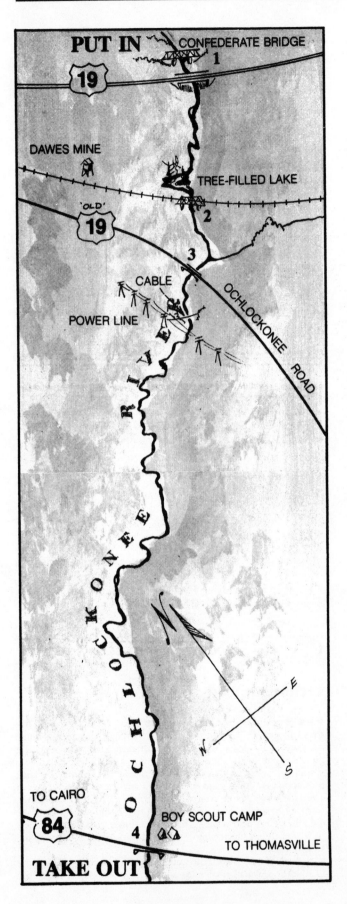

Thomas County Forest Service can give you important current information.

The put-in point (1) on the map is about six miles north of Thomasville, on the new U.S. 19 (don't confuse this with the old 19, known as the Ochlockonee Road) that by-passes Thomasville to the east. Take-out for my trip was on U.S. 84 (4) about seven miles west of Thomasville, better known as the Cairo Road. The river distance between these two bridges is about eight miles, providing a good three- to four-hour run with medium paddling. Shuttle between the bridges is easy.

As for points of interest along the way: be sure to take a good look at the old Confederate Bridge, lying unused next to the new U.S. 19 bridge. The first leg of the river, from the Confederate Bridge to the railroad trestle (2), is about a mile. In this stretch the river opens out into a tree-filled lake. Keep the left bank in sight, and you'll follow the main run of the river through this lake.

The second leg, (2) to (3), is from the railroad trestle to old U.S. 19, about a half mile. It's just beyond this bridge you'll see the old cable stretching across the river. After the cable, you break out into the open of a powerline right-of-way. From this point on, the river twists and turns, following a fairly well marked channel. Soon you'll come upon meadows surrounding the river, providing interesting contrast for travel. This last stretch, (3) to (4), about five miles, goes from the old U.S. 19 to U.S. 84. The only hazards you should encounter are occasional debris pile-ups, and swirling waters where the riverbank narrows. I know of no rapids or shoals on the Ochlockonee.

Every mile of the Ochlockonee is not a pleasant memory. On much of the river, particularly the last half of the section I canoed, fallen logs and brush piles inhibit canoe travel, trap litter and generally detract from the beauty of the landscape. There is a movement alive in Thomasville to clear the river of these obstructions. A little work with a power saw would do a job which would be a service to all Georgians.

1977

The Ogeechee Affair

Gentle. Surprising. Unforgettable.

by Reece Turrentine

What's this thing I've got going with the Ogeechee River? Memories of it will lie gentle on my mind until I am forced to get up bodily, load up my old canoe, and go make another run on it. The attraction certainly doesn't come from any whitewater thrills (although, right after heavy spring rains, the extreme upper section does offer whitewater). No, the attraction the Ogeechee has for me is not its thrills, nor its water stained brown by tannic acid, but rather its character. There is something solid and authentic about it.

For example, the Ogeechee is uniquely stubborn about its identity. Unlike many other rivers in our state which flow into other rivers and lose their names to bigger names or larger lakes, the Ogeechee is the Ogeechee from beginning to end. Ogeechee waters trickle at its very beginning, way up in Greene County, and they remain Ogeechee waters for 245 miles, until they merge with the brine of the Atlantic Ocean. This makes the Ogeechee the longest uninterrupted river in Georgia retaining its original name and character for its entire length.

Another character trait of the Ogeechee is that although its name may remain the same, it's a river of infinite variety and surprises. It may not be a thriller, but it's an entertainer of the first order. On one stretch you will be drifting through swampy cypress forests, and on the next between sandy bluff banks. For a while you can drift straight and lazy, then around a curve you will be scrambling for your paddles, working like mad as the current squeezes your canoe through the narrow, twisting channels of fallen trees. Here, you have got to be on your toes, or, more properly, on your knees. Watch those swift currents flowing under fallen trees. They will suck a canoe right out from under you.

Another rare character trait of the Ogeechee is that it provides clean fun—literally. Natives call its tannic-acid waters the cleanest in the state, and they just may be right. The Ogeechee flows through no major towns, is used by few industries for dumping wastes, and has no dams to clog its natural flow.

Twenty-one of us canoed the 22-mile stretch described in the following guide. Once again, memories of the Ogeechee are lying gently on my mind. I'm sure they will take me back again and again.

CANOEING GUIDE

Ogeechee River

This material pertains to 21 miles of the Ogeechee, from the bridge at Millen south to Lane's Bridge (listed as Lone Bridge on topo maps).

General Information: Although similar in some ways to other rivers of the Coastal Plain, the Ogeechee has some unique features. It's more like three rivers in one. First, some parts of the extreme upper section, between Jewel and Louisville, can offer some exciting whitewater runs, but *only* immediately following heavy spring rains. This upper section is usually considered uncanoeable. The middle section, south of Millen, resembles other Coastal Plain rivers in some ways, but it offers far more variety than other rivers in the area. Wide, long stretches alternate with tight, twisting curves. There are tree jams through this section, but we did not have to portage, managing to squeeze under, over, or around them all. Of course, you may find yourself having to portage, depending on the water level at the time of your run. The third nature of the Ogeechee is seen as it approaches the coast below Savannah. Here, it becomes wide and marshy, with its flow totally determined by the tides. Tides and inland lag times must be calculated before canoeing the coastal regions.

Shuttle: To get to the take-out bridge (Lane's Bridge) to drop your shuttle car, locate the intersection of US 301 and Ga 17 on the map (11 miles northeast of Statesboro). From this intersection, proceed three miles northwest on Ga 17 to a paved road leading off to the left. Take-out bridge is one mile down this road. Leaving your shuttle car at the bridge, return to Ga 17, and continue on to Millen. Go south out of Millen on US 25 for one mile to the put-in bridge.

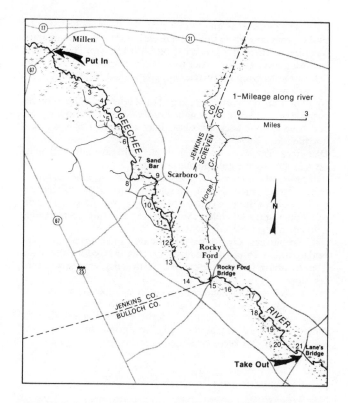

The road to the water's edge is on the west, or upstream, side of the bridge.

Water Levels: There is no usable water-level gauge on this section of the Ogeechee. There are remnants of an old marker at the gauge station at the Scarboro Bridge ruins (notice I said "ruins"; there is no bridge crossing here, although one is shown on some old maps). On the downstream side of this old concrete gauge station, however, is an old steel door. The day we canoed the Ogeechee, the water level was right up to the bottom of this old steel door. It might pay you to check this as you pass through Scarboro on the shuttle run. Water level is very erratic on the Ogeechee, and a level much below the bottom of the steel door might expose some more sandbars suitable for camping, but it also might necessitate some portages over fallen trees and other obstructions. While you're at the Scarboro Landing, fill your canteens from the gushing artesian well in the bushes behind the gauge station.

Hazards: The open, smooth stretches of the Ogeechee are safe and free of hazards. But watch those narrow, twisting sections you'll suddenly come upon. Broadsiding a fallen tree in swift current can capsize a canoe quicker than rapids. Anticipate your entrance through narrow passages well upstream, and be lined up straight as you squeeze through or around obstacles. And when taking curves, favor the inside corner. The current wants to push you to the outside, and lazy paddling here can have you in the bushes along the right bank before you know it, grabbing for your hats and glasses. Don't grab those overhead limbs. Swift current will sweep the canoe right out from under you, either capsizing it or leaving you playing Tarzan on the limbs. "Anticipation" is the word for early setups through and around these narrow places. It's great fun, and it's good practice for canoe control.

Another caution: Be reasonably watchful for snakes, especially going through limbs and trees. Snakes are on the Ogeechee. We saw plenty, but were bothered by none. They are fascinating to observe, but they're no fun to grab for if you mistake one for a limb.

Camping: There are no authorized campgrounds along this stretch of the Ogeechee, but some sandbars and riverside areas are available for small groups of overnight canoeists. Sandbars are best if water level exposes enough of them. But drive a stick into the sand at the waterline to check the river's rise or fall before you go to bed. A fast-rising level will have your tents floating before dawn: no fun. Permission to camp on private property should be obtained from the landowners.

For what it's worth, we camped on a beautiful sandbar on the esat side of the river, a few hundred yards above Scarboro Landing. You have to look back up a little inlet to see it, but it is worth watching for.

Distances: The river mileage from put in to take out is 21 miles (as indicated by the mileage numbers on our map). Depending on water level, the river's flow is normally about two miles per hour. In calculating canoeing time, be sure to consider the different canoeing skills of those in your party, time you'll spend exploring the many interesting side inlets along the way, and time spent dealing with any mishaps which might occur.

On our first day, we traveled the nine miles from the Millen bridge on US 25 to the sandbar where we camped for the night. The remaining 12 miles we covered the next day, with several brief rest stops.

With a topo map and compass, it's easy to keep up with your location on the river at all times, noting the direction of long, straight stretches and identifying turns and side creeks. But for those not inclined to play the navigator's game, just lie back and enjoy the trip. But keep paddling.

1980

The Lure of the Alapaha

You know about whitewater canoeing—now it's time to try black water

by Margaret Tucker

The bobcat never looked up as I floated by with motionless paddle, holding my breath. He crouched over a tiny waterfall on a tributary stream and its noise masked any sounds from my canoe. He crouched as any cat would, but he was bigger, with tufted ears and the mottled tan coat of his kind. He dabbed twice in the water with his paw, whether to catch something or at his reflection, I don't know, for my canoe drifted past and I knew it would be useless to paddle back upstream.

I had enjoyed this one rare glimpse of a bobcat at his morning toilette. What right had I to barge upstream again with noisy paddle strokes and scare the shy animal to satisfy my own curiosity? We humans trample thoughtlessly enough on most of nature most of the time. One of the points of a river trip is to be patient, float with the rhythm and speed of the current,

and recapture some of the ancient harmonies of body and soul with the natural world. In search of that experience, I had come with a party of friends to the Alapaha River for a weekend float.

The Alapaha is a river to take at its own pace, to savor, to dream upon, because it is more mysterious and like a poem than the fierce whitewater rivers of the hills, which demand your conscious attention every second and challenge your muscles, nerves, and reflexes. The Alapaha challenges your imagination.

Its waters are nearly black, but reflect every leaf that hangs above them. Ancient tupelo trees with roots twisted into fantastic shapes line its banks. They seem to have the potential to become animated, to move those face-like shapes, perhaps to speak. On the day of our trip grey, overcast skies enhanced the sense of mystery. I wondered if the rest of the group was feeling the same spell of the river. I knew that Betty Terry, who was paddling bow with me, was as fascinated by the trees as I because she kept turning and pointing out one after another, urging me to take pictures, but it was too dark to make the shots effective.

Behind me were Rodger Losier with several of his Boy Scout co-leaders, while two canoes and one kayak of 12-year-old scouts from Rodger's troop had long ago disappeared downstream. We knew that the river held few dangers and the boys were experienced canoeists, so no one worried. Also up ahead were Betty's teenagers, Mike and Denise, and my friends Mark and Trish.

We paddled quietly, occasionally losing sight of each other around the bends in the river. Rodger was in an 18-foot, sleek canoe, made for flat water cruising with a narrow beam and sharply pointed bow. It wouldn't turn without a struggle, but it was effortlessly fast. Betty and I wallowed along in our 16-foot broad-beamed whitewater model as Rodger and his partner breezed by.

But they weren't in a hurry. Leisurely flatwater cruises are Rodger's special delight, and he had been trying for years to get me interested in what he considers "real canoeing," while I insisted on building whitewater boats, fighting rapids, running "heavy" water, and racing in slalom competitions. "Well, Maggie," he grinned, "like this river?" He was asking a rhetorical question, savoring his triumph. He could see I was hooked.

The Alapaha is a wild river, remote and undeveloped, running through a hunting preserve and a former wildlife management area. The current is slow and easy, suitable for beginners, although in early spring after a rain it could be swift. The twisting course of the river keeps a new scene in front of you all the time and makes wildlife observation easy if you're quiet. The water is clean and, so far, the banks are unlittered.

Coming around a sharp bend, we found Mark and Trish pulled up to shore, waiting. "Go on," Mark said, "we're going to stay back by ourselves and try for some good pictures. I had a big water snake in focus a little while ago and two of the kids came around the corner, racing." Obviously not everyone was under the spell of quiet and mystery. Well, there are other spells, and boisterous joy is not to be denied.

Later in the afternoon we had further occasion for uproarious fun. As we rounded a bend, we saw a huge pile of suds floating into the river from a tiny stream on the east side. At first I thought someone just upstream on the creek had dumpled laundry waste into the water. The suds were two feet thick! We beached our boats and scrambled to the creek. All the foam was coming from a little fall only four feet high that had carved a nearly vertical miniature gorge in the limestone rock of the river bank. From the fall to the river was only 25 to 30 yards. I wondered how many thousands of years that little trickle of water had worked to move its tiny falls this far back from the riverbank where it had originally tumbled into the much bigger Alapaha. However small, it was making a big noise and a prodigious pile of foam. Rodger explained that the foam was natural, caused by the tannin in the water, which is also what gives it its dark color.

One of the kids pushed a canoe across the mouth of the creek, blocking the foam and forcing it to pile up. Then they began to dare each other to jump in at the waterfall and swim under the foam to the canoe. Michael finally took the dare on the condition that we move the canoe if he came up and couldn't breathe in the foam, which was now a good three feet deep. He lowered himself into the foam, took a couple of deep breaths, and was gone. Then we saw the foam heaving, looking like a giant bubble bath. It rose, first toward the other side of the creek. It looked hilarious, but I was getting concerned. He emerged, choking more with laughter than with water and wearing a thick hat of suds. "I came up twice and couldn't tell where I was!" he spluttered.

Since it was late afternoon, and we were as relaxed as turtles in the sun, the Terrys and I, with Mark and Trish, soon decided to camp. Rodger and the scouts pushed on, looking for a bigger sandbar downstream. I walked away from the river, into the lush longleaf pines. Beautiful big cones lay on the ground, some a foot long and perfectly shaped. Soon I had collected a dozen. Piled in a straw basket, they make beautiful natural fireplace decorations. When I was a child in a house with four fireplaces, we collected pine cones and soaked them in chemical salts to make colored flames.

Pine cones on the ground I consider fair booty for the treasure hunter. I don't believe in digging wild plants or adopting captured wildlife, but shells, driftwood, sticks whittled by beavers, water-worn rocks, last year's birds' nests—my house is full of them. Nor do I hesitate to harvest wild persimmons in the fall, cattail shoots in the spring, day lilies in the summer, and sassafras roots anytime of the year. None of these is in any danger of disappearing, at least at the moment.

When it got too dark to search for pine cones, we built a fire and cooked our supper. Maybe it was because I was tired from the week before and the pressures of several deadlines at work, but nothing went right for me in spite of the clear, mild night and a blessing of stars. My backpacking stove was flaring up, I picked up a frying pan whose handle had been in the fire, and when I had fixed myself a nice hot cup of mocha coffee for after dinner, I put down my Sierra cup, turned around, and promptly stepped back into it. In a snit, I retreated into the dark alone and watched the others silhouetted against the flames. Tranquillity gradually returned to my annoyed spirit, soothed by the quiet sounds of the river and the soft, cool sand.

The white sandbars are one of the Alapaha's greatest assets. They alternate with grey limestone banks which are covered with green mosses. The sand is not tan as on many rivers; it's sugar-pure and startlingly white against the dark water. The sandbars record the local goings-on. Here a raccoon washed his dinner, there a bird landed. The soft sand makes a great bed and we indulged in noontime naps both days. After lunch on Sunday I stretched out only to have a handful of warm sand poured on my middle by Mark. In a minute Mike and Denise joined him and they industriously covered me up to the neck. It felt good. I kept laughing and causing minor earthquakes in their work.

When, using me as a base, they had finished a sand lady sculpture with two huge, slightly out-of-line breasts, I was convulsed with giggles and ruined the whole thing.

Returning to the canoes, we drifted downstream. Soon an unfamiliar sound broke the quiet. A rapid? It proved to be a limestone ledge across the river, about three feet high at the low water level that weekend. Imbedded in it were big pink nodules of chert whose smoothness contrasted with the rough surface of the limestone. It was not a difficult ledge for even moderately experienced paddlers to run in an open canoe, but beginners might have a spill on this or one of two or three others in the weekend float. Michael and Denise ran it first, not going straight down the right-hand chute, but finding a small passage through the swollen trunks of the tupelos, making an eddy turn behind one tree, and easing the canoe between more tangled roots. This "tree rapid" was more exciting than the ledge.

The few small rapids make an interesting contrast to the predominant flatwater of the trip, and they provide a few moments of suspense. The greatest thrills of the Alapaha, however, are the wild animals. The bobcat was our most unusual sighting, but we also saw a lizard and two of the kids got a glimpse of a four-foot alligator. It was our encounter with the rattlesnake, however, that was the most exciting, and briefly dangerous.

We had stopped at Ga. 187 bridge to swim and lie in the sun on the big sandbar and discovered a cable swing suspended from the bridge. We soon put it to use, swinging far out over the river and dropping off. Mark was swinging head down and doing somersaults off the bar when I heard him yell, "Hey, look at this snake!" We all ran to the water's edge to look. Mark was still suspended upside down, helplessly swinging with the slow momentum of a pendulum. Directly under him a three-foot snake was slowly making its way upstream. I could see that it was colored rather brightly, but it was too far away to make out the pattern, or the shape of the head, much less check for face pits, the characteristics of a poisonous snake. Because it was in the water, I assumed that it was either a harmless water snake or a cottonmouth (water moccasin). Those are the snakes you will commonly find in coastal plain streams, although I have seen an occasional copperhead in the water. This snake was patterned on the back, whereas cottonmouths are dark, so I said, "I think it's harmless," and walked upstream along the bank, hoping for a closer look.

A local fisherman solved the identification problem decisively. "It's a rattlesnake," he said, reaching for his son's .22 rifle.

It was, indeed, and I felt quite foolish for not recognizing the obvious. When he said it, suddenly the markings were obvious to me. I knew that rattlesnakes were common in the area. In fact, the evening before, when we were all spreading our sleeping bags, Mark had asked me, "What kind of snakes do you find around here?"

"Rattlesnakes," I had replied without hesitation, looking at the dense palmettos beyond our clearing, "lots of big nasty ones."

It was too much reliance on textbook learning that had thrown me. "At home in the palmetto flatwoods and dry pinelands," says Conant's classic *Field Guide to Reptiles and Amphibians,* describing the Eastern diamondback rattlesnake. Since they aren't *supposed* to be swimming blithely upstream in the middle of the river, my mind had refused to consider what my eyes would have instantly recognized on dry land as a rattlesnake. Instead, I was vainly trying to pigeonhole that snake in one of the "waterloving" categories, and it just wouldn't compute.

I think it's a common mistake, and often costly, to rely too much on the rules in the out-of-doors. They are useful in the majority of cases but it's easy to forget that exceptions are also the rule in nature. This snake episode reminded me to keep my mind flexible and trust my own observations. After all, one of the endless fascinations of the wild is that it is varied and exceptional. If we were never surprised on a mountain or a river by an out-of-season bird, an unusual plant, or a sudden rainstorm, we'd probably all stay home.

1976

Down Upon the Suwannee

If Stephen Foster had only seen the river what a song he might have written

by Dick Murlless

The Suwannee River is one of the most famous rivers in the world, thanks to a man who never saw it, Stephen Foster. Its name conjures up images of a long, lazy, romantic stream flowing through an idyllic countryside of quiet beauty and contented people. This much is true, but there's even more.

Some say the Suwannee River starts deep in the heart of the Okefenokee Swamp. There the dark swamp waters flow so slowly that you have to check the underwater stems of the weeds to see which way the water moves. For me, the river starts as it emerges from the Okefenokee Swamp, flowing over the Suwannee River Sill. The sill is a long, low earthen dam, constructed in the late 1950s to hold water in the swamp during droughts. It forms a distinct boundary between the slow-moving swamp waters and the faster-flowing river with its solid

banks. But don't get the idea that the Suwannee is zipping along, for its current is usually about one mile an hour.

For several miles below the sill, the river is swampy with low banks, frequently covered with water. There is little or no high ground and the broad flood plain is covered with cypress trees. The river here is much like the nearby Okefenokee. Many tupelo (gum) trees line the banks. The Ogeechee lime tupelo is the most common with its long, red fruits in the fall. During low water you can see the strange root formations at the base of these trees. Fantasies of a wild gnome forest could not appear more strange.

We put our canoes in the river at Griffis' landing about 2 miles below the sill. The Griffis family has for years guided famous naturalists and fishermen through the Okefenokee area. The river was narrow and twisting, and the main channel was easy to follow by searching for the cut with the strongest current. During high water the current sweeps through the cypress-gum forest, cutting across the bends in the river and finding the shortest path. Then many alternate routes become visible and the main channel can be hard to follow.

After two miles on the river (at river mile 4) we passed Cumbis Camp, a popular area used for camping and fishing. The high ground of this natural bluff is often littered with garbage which we attempt to burn or remove. It is sad to say that every time I return to this spot it is again covered with trash.

As we paddled along, the river became somewhat wider and soon we could see the first hint of a low river bank. Along these banks grow sawtooth palmetto and pine forest, a good indication of high ground not often flooded. Occasionally a part of the river swamp extends back into the higher ground, creating a slough. It is in these fingers of swamp that fish find food and protection from predators.

Below Rives Landing at river mile 10, we passed into an area where large cypress still grow. These particular trees have very large bases (up to 7 feet in diameter) and often the base is hollow. One tree below Fargo is large enough to hold five adults standing inside the trunk! Another tree has a hole completely through the base. It looks large enough to canoe through, but my repeated attempts to do so have failed. These large cypress wait like mighty sentries, standing watch along the river's bank.

At the concrete bridge near Fargo we stopped briefly to dispose of our collected garbage and for a cold soft drink purchased from a nearby gas station. Many people like to swim here, but, having cut my foot, I would not advise it. Just downstream are many excellent sand beaches and more stately cypress.

At river mile 16 we came to the first high bluff on the Suwannee, just as the stream turns to the left. We pulled our canoes onto the right bank and walked a short distance up the road to meet the owner, Mrs. Sarah Touchton. I always plan to spend at least an hour visiting with Mrs. Touchton, and listening to her stories about life along the river on her farm. Her memory is remarkable, and I hope that I can have as keen a mind and spirit as she does when I'm 83. She talks of home remedies, quilting with friends and fishing parties she has cooked for. She still quilts today, and she enjoys a chance to sit and talk with interested visitors. A sign at her landing shows

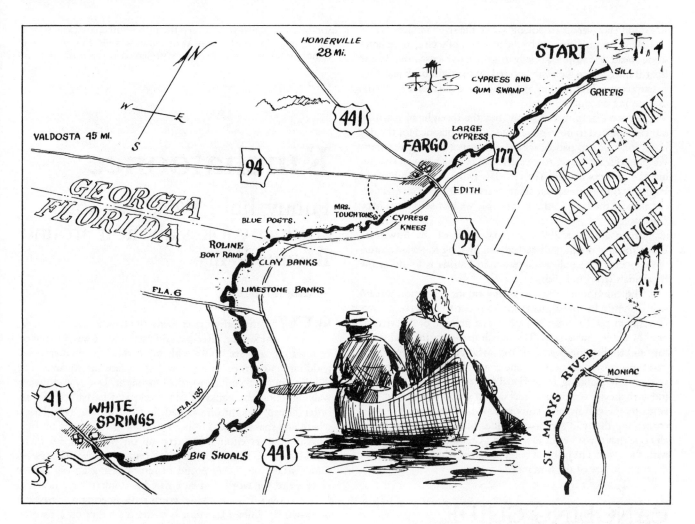

the high water mark of the April 1973 flood, some 13 feet above the high bluff. This record flood closed the bridges of I-75, but her house escaped any damage. The landing has an excellent, clean campsite and plenty of level ground. We spent the night there listening to barred and screech owls breaking the sound of silence along the river.

An early start the next day gave us plenty of time for wild-life watching and swimming. The long, white sand beaches were beautiful for mile after mile. We finally stopped for some exploring and to cool off in the clean, clear water. The dark brown waters of the Suwannee swirled around us, making our hands an orange color. It was like swimming in a giant, moving tea bath.

These waters are stained brown by organic acids leached from the decaying leaves in the river swamps. The tannic and humic acids give the water an interesting taste, too. When canoeing, you will notice that many bubbles are created by the motion of your paddle. These bubbles are also a result of the dissolved organics which act as natural foaming agents.

The Suwannee is seldom used below Mrs. Touchton's, so we had a wild river all to ourselves. Once we stood quietly on a sand bar and watched while two deer cautiously approached the river and then plunged in to swim across.

The river is home to many different varieties of wild crea-tures. On one trip our canoeing party rounded a bend to find an eight foot alligator trapped by the current against a hanging branch. We pushed the body loose and dragged it to shore for inspection. Our best guess was that a bullet had done him in. Someone didn't like alligators, even if they are an endangered species. Trying to make the best of it, one companion took the jaw, complete with a very impressive set of teeth, and all in perfect condition. This momento now hangs on the wall of the waiting room in his dentist office.

As we moved further along, the river banks became higher and the cypress-gum forest declined to a narrow zone along the steep banks. It seemed strange to see cypress trees clinging to the sandy slopes beside the river. Live oak and pine began to dominate the forest gallery.

We followed a kingfisher downstream to the state line. Two blue posts with a cross bar indicated this landmark on the right bank. About two miles into Florida, the left bank became a steep, hard mud wall, five or ten feet high. After a rainstorm I have seen small creeks form waterfalls flowing over these banks to seek the river. We held our canoes against a north-facing wall and enjoyed the plants which prefer this cool moist habitat. Beautiful growths of ferns, mosses and liverworts covered sec-tions of these banks. Occasionally the underlying layers of limestone and clay were seen poking above the river surface.

We continued, excited by the prospect of seeing more limestone ahead. We stopped briefly to stretch our legs at the Roline Boat Ramp, which we easily spotted on the right bank just after a sharp curve. This landing is a public area suitable for a picnic or camping overnight.

We were getting tired now, but the thought of reaching our cars spurred us on. The seventeen miles planned for the day was a long way to paddle with the river not moving very fast. We passed some large, rusty steel towers which are all that remain of Turners Bridge. Then the last two miles brought us to Highway 6 Bridge and our shuttle cars. We greeted several fishermen near the bridge, the first people we had seen since Mrs. Touchton's.

There are over 200 additional miles of the Suwannee River, most of it still undisturbed and inviting to the adventurous canoeist. The only white water in Florida is found at the Big Shoals (river mile 56).

The Suwannee River is an important recreation stream which should be given protection in order to preserve its outstanding natural character. Only three percent of the river is now in public ownership. The remainder is controlled by private and timber company holdings, who generally have done a good job of stewardship. At one time the federal government was actively planning for national protection of the river, but today money is scarce and federal help seems to be remote. It is up to the private and corporate owners to make plans for conserving the wild and scenic values of this river. We should all hope that the states of Florida and Georgia will work closely with the owners to bring about a program which will maintain the high quality of the Suwannee.

CANOEING GUIDE

Upper Suwannee River

The section of river described here starts at river mile 2, two miles below the Suwannee River Sill, and goes to river mile 33.5 at Florida Highway 6. In moderate to high water this is a moderately difficult two-day trip. However, the character of the river changes markedly with different water levels. During low water in late fall or winter the trip should be shortened unless you wish to paddle hard all day long. Fargo to Roline Landing would make a more leisurely trip. During high water many landmarks are hard or impossible to see and sometimes even the high bluffs are underwater.

For longer trip you can put canoes in the water at Stephen Foster State Park and paddle to the sill. A short, 150 foot, portage later you are in the Suwannee River. However, you must have written permission from the Okefenokee National Wildlife Refuge, P.O. Box 117, Waycross, Ga. 31501, to cross the sill.

Many canoeists like to continue beyond Highway 6 to enjoy the Big Shoals. These rapids change dramatically as the water level varies, and often are impassible with a loaded canoe. The best plan is to portage all your gear around the shoals, using a dirt road which parallels the left bank for ¼mile. Then shoot the rapids all you like in an empty canoe, wearing your life preserver.

All of the land along the described section of the river is privately owned except Roline Landing. Remember that the river banks are private property and the owners' rights should be re-

spected. It is up to you to keep the places you enjoy clean so that others may also enjoy them. Poor campers could ruin the opportunity for the Suwannee to become preserved as a recreational river.

1975

Kinchafoonee

Funny, huh? Well, just don't crack any jokes about it around Ronnie Wills

by Reece Turrentine

"Why, the earliest river memory I have is about the Kinchafoonee," Ronnie said excitedly. "I was a barefoot boy, setting out set hooks with my daddy." Ronnie stopped paddling and turned in his bow seat to face me squarely. He didn't want me to miss a word. "One night, Daddy and I were walking along the banks of this creek, and he barked out an order: 'Keep ya light on the path in front of you, boy. That's where any snakes'll be. No need to shine it out in the bushes. Anything smart enough to creep up on you from out there would've done gotcha by now.'" Ronnie laughed hard as he told his tale, obviously proud of remembering an old family story word for word. I'm sure that his children have heard it over and over. It's a heritage worth remembering and passing on down the line: a barefoot boy and his father on a river at night, together. Too few have such moments to remember.

Some weeks before Ronnie shared his memory with me, I had casually mentioned to a group of folks my plans to canoe the Kinchafoonee Creek near Albany. Ronnie had interrupted me. "I've got to go with you on that one," he'd said emphatically. "That's my creek." His tone was greedily possessive, and he went on to explain that his childhood home was near the banks of the Kinchafoonee and that he had grown up swimming and fishing and playing in that creek. "I can tell you all about it," he said with pride.

Of course, I was delighted to have him along. Ronnie Wills and I have paddled rivers together for years. From the raging whitewaters of North Georgia to the sleepy still waters of South Georgia, we've had adventures about which our families have heard again and again. But on this trip my relationship with Ronnie would be different than on our previous runs. On other rivers, we've shared adventures as equals. But on the Kinchafoonee, I would be the guest, and Ronnie would be the host. The Kinchafoonee is *his* creek.

On the day of our run, Ronnie sat in the bow of my canoe as we slid away from the put in. We had a long 18 miles ahead of us, but his strokes fell into rhythm with mine, and we covered the opening miles quickly. His usual powerful strokes seemed to have an added drive: the excitement of being back on his boyhood creek, perhaps.

I've seen Ronnie Wills excited on rivers before. I've heard him shout as he tore skillfully through whitewater fury, and I've heard him laugh while recalling the many delights of running rivers in open boats. But on the Kinchafoonee, as I'd expected, his behavior was different. He acted like a little boy again. He seemed to see ordinary river scenes as extraordinary. "I think I remember this spot," he said, far more often than seemed within the capabilities of human memory. And sometimes he said ridiculous things, as when he identified a flock of ducks as "direct descendants of those from my boyhood hunts."

"Come on, Ronnie," I laughed. "You're losing control." But the laughs were good-humored.

We stopped several times to explore the sprawling sandbars that dot the Kinchafoonee. We also explored the bordering woods, which are full of intriguing plant life; neither of us could identify some of it. At times I wished that I had left Ronnie behind and brought a naturalist, who could identify and label some of the plants at which I could only gaze in wonder and ignorance. And when we got to the sections of the river where limestone outcroppings punctuate its banks, how I wished for a geologist; he probably could have told the story of creation that was described in those stratified rocks. But neither of us is a naturalist or a geologist; we could only guess at identifications and meanings.

But I was glad that Ronnie was along, because he brought something to the trip that was more important than scientific knowledge: a love of and feel for a river that can come only to one born and raised near its banks.

We spotted one sandbar that was too inviting to resist, so we stopped for lunch. We beached the canoe, and I rummaged around in my old canoe bag for some grub. Ronnie just stood there, looking at the sandbar. As I stood up, he stretched out his arm, blocking my way.

"Before you tromp up the place with your big feet, just look at all those animal tracks," he said. And he was right. The sandbar was honeycombed with the tracks of cats and coons, birds and beavers.

"This must be convention headquarters for the county's wildlife," I observed.

"Wouldn't you love to camp across the river," Ronnie mused, "and be here at dawn, propped on your elbows in your tent, and just watch all the activity that goes on here?"

I glanced across the river and saw nothing but thick underbrush. "It'd take a bulldozer to clear out a spot for a tent over there," I replied. But Ronnie didn't even hear me. I could almost hear the wheels turning in his head. He'll be back here someday, with a bulldozer if necessary. And I'll probably be with him.

Bulldozers have already made their marks along the Kinchafoonee. The natural beauty of this stream increases on its lower stretches, but so do the numbers of cabins and houses on its shores. As it nears Albany, fine homes line the banks. But the banks are nicely kept, and the creek is surprisingly free of litter. Others love the Kinchafoonee, too.

"One of these days—" Ronnie began, looking up at a neat little cabin on the shore. The explosion of a flock of ducks downstream terminated his sentence. But I know what he was thinking.

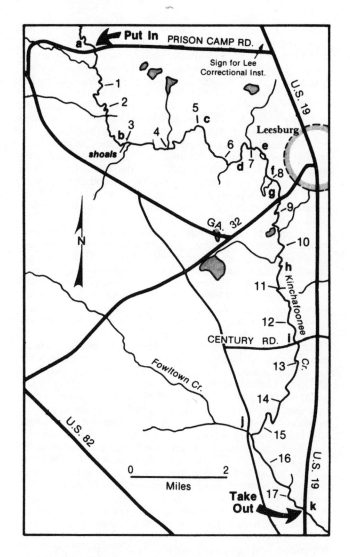

CANOEING GUIDE

Kinchafoonee Creek

General Information. I wouldn't say the folks around Albany have tried to keep the Kinchafoonee under wraps; it's just that they have always been a little protective about their creek. Almost hidden among the trees, and winding through remote wilderness, it is usually upstaged by its more famous neighbor, the mighty Flint River. But that's just fine with Albanians. "Let the big Flint take the heavy traffic," they say, "and leave little Kinchafoonee alone."

It's easy to understand why they have such protective affection for this creek. In sharp contrast to the garbage-dump look of the Flint, the Kinchafoonee is clean, sparkling, and scenic. Even around Albany, where homes have been built along its shores, the Kinchafoonee is neat and litter-free. Although folks around Albany have canoed, fished, camped on, and played in the Kinchafoonee for years, its reputation is only now beginning to spread. Anyone who is willing to protect its beauty and respect its quiet mood will be rewarded with one of the most enjoyable canoeing experiences available in the state.

The Kinchafoonee begins in the gentle hills of Marion County, grows in size and volume as it flows south into Webster County, becomes canoeable as it passes just southwest of Plains, and becomes a major waterway with limestone banks before it finally empties into the Flint River at Albany. Although local fishermen report navigable waters well north of Plains, this canoeing guide can report only on the section that I have canoed: from Prison Camp Rd to the US 19 bridge in Albany, a distance of 17.5 river miles.

The opening miles of the run are shallow and swampy, with frequent tree falls. Sandbars are abundant and should remain usable for camping in most water levels (except extreme flood stage).

The first 10 miles or so are wild and remote, with little development along the banks. The woods are full of large cypress, oak, magnolia, and catalpa trees; the blooms of the last two types should provide quite a view in the spring. Wildlife is abundant, with many flocks of wild ducks (wood ducks, ringnecks, and mallards). They entertained us all day on our run, startling us around almost every bend.

Beyond the Ga 32 bridge (8½ miles into the run) the creek widens and deepens. Beautiful limestone banks appear with increasing frequency, always dripping with water through abundant growths of maidenhair ferns. Although this section is more beautiful to the eye, it is also more intensively developed, with cabins and houses growing in density until they completely line the banks as you approach the Albany area. But this development does not prevent the creek from being one of the most beautiful waterways available to canoeists in South Georgia.

Shuttle: Drop your shuttle car at the access road on the southeast end of the take-out bridge on US 19, which is ½ mile north of the US 19 Bypass loop north of Albany. Then drive 7 miles north on US 19 to Leesburg and 2.5 miles farther to Prison Camp Rd, a paved road on the left that's marked by a sign: "Lee Correctional Institute." Turn left (west) here, and drive 4 more miles to the put-in bridge (called "New Hollis Bridge," but there's no sign saying so). Access road to the water is on the bridge's northwest corner.

To set up a shuttle for an alternate 9-mile canoe run from the Ga 32 bridge to the US 19 bridge, drive north on US 19 to the "Leesburg City Limits" sign. Turn left on Ga 32 here, and drive one mile to the put-in bridge. Access to the river is at the northwest corner of the bridge.

Water Levels: The Kinchafoonee has no water-level gauge. On the day that we canoed it, the water was about a foot below the horizontal cross brace on the midcreek steel girder of the US 19 take-out bridge—a good level for our trip.

Hazards: Kinchafoonee Creek presents no serious hazards, although the few scattered shoals could offer excitement in high water. Also, high water could create swift washings under limestone overhangs at the banks.

Distance: Our trip from the put-in bridge on Prison Camp Rd to the take-out bridge on US 19 was 17½ miles. Canoeing time was 5 hours (with steady paddling). The current is good in the creek's upper stretches, but it slows considerably during the last 4 miles.

Camping: Camping should be restricted to sandbars, which are plentiful. Most bordering land is privately owned.

Map Guide: Numbers on our map indicate river mileage; letters indicate points of interest.

a. Put-in bridge ("New Hollis Bridge" on Prison Camp Rd).
b. Small shoals (depending on water level).
c. High banks on left; river becomes wider and deeper here.
d. Limestone outcroppings.
e. Power line crosses creek.
f. Take the left channel here to save about a mile of paddling.
g. Ga 32 bridge.
h. More limestone cliffs; also maidenhair ferns.
i. Century Rd bridge.
j. Fowlton Creek enters Kinchafoonee via a 3-foot waterfall.
k. Take-out bridge at US 19.

1981

░░░░░░░░░░░░░░░░░░░░░░░░░░░░░░

See Cypress City

All you do is catch an incoming tide, canoe for three hours, and slosh through a thousand yards of swamp

by Reece Turrentine

The red ribbon marker was not hard to spot. It hung limply from a tree limb that extended out over the bank of Big Buzzard Creek, the twisting little waterway through which we passed to reach Lewis Island. The ribbon marker pointed the way to the next phase of our adventure. It marked our point of entry onto the island itself, where, on foot, we followed similar ribbons into the deep interior of the island's swamp. The ribbons marked the only way to reach the area of the big cypress trees which was our goal.

I knew from the start that it would not be an easy trip. It would require some difficult paddling against possibly strong headwinds, which can come up suddenly on open stretches of the Altamaha, and I would have to take into account changing tides that affect this portion of the river. Then, to get to the trees, we'd have to hike a quarter mile into the island, tromping through the slush and muck of a swamp. But I had to see those trees. Ever since I'd first heard of their existence years ago, I'd felt compelled to go in there someday and see them for myself. "They're giants," someone had told me. "And there are no more like them—anywhere!"

Behind the limb with the red ribbon, the bushes along the island's edge parted to form a small opening. As we walked on the island, the suspicions I had felt during the days we had spent on the Altamaha River were confirmed: this is a strange and different world. Even the mud on this coastal island is different: your foot doesn't just sink in; it is swallowed up, almost devoured by the mud, which rushes in to cover the foot with a sinister aggressiveness. You can pull your foot out of the mud, all right, but you'll usually have to pull your foot out of your shoe first. (Actually, this mud is of the highest quality in both texture and richness of nutrients. It comes downstream, rich topsoil and clay stripped from thousands of Middle Georgia farms. It is filtered through hundreds of miles of the Altamaha's tributaries. During its trip, the grains of sand are filtered out, and the pure mud is deposited, soft as chocolate pudding, in the marshes and around the islands of the river's delta.)

Stepping out of the mud and onto a more solid area of the island's bank, David Edwards, manager of the Altamaha State Waterfowl Management Area, who had joined us for the Lewis Island portion of our trip down the Altamaha, called our attention to the plant growth around our feet. He is an expert on all of the plant and animal life of the area. Leaning over, he cupped some of the little plants in his hands.

"This rare little plant is called Asiatic day flower," he explained. "Nobody knows exactly how it got to this continent, but we do know that it is carried and scattered by ducks and geese and other waterfowl. They love to eat it. A few patches have been found growing around some beaver ponds in the inland Piedmont area, but it is mostly found in little patches like these around the coastal islands."

"Tell me again what you call it," I said. My interest was piqued by the plant's rarity.

"Asiatic day flower," he repeated. "*Aneilema keisak* is the botanical name."

Lewis Island has been described by naturalists as Georgia's best outdoor classroom. They say that the island is a living laboratory both for students and advanced scientists, who ponder the wonders of its elaborate and delicate ecology. The island supports many rare birds, plants, and other water life, some of which is found in no other location.

Lewis Island is eight miles long and contains 6000 acres. It's inaccessible, forbidding, infested with snakes and gators: a wilderness wonderland. Today, it is probably more like the wild swamp that the Indians roamed than it has been for 300 years. During the early 1700s, white men's loud weapons killed or scared off the island's buffalo and elk. In 1721, 100 Scottish Highlanders came down from the Carolinas to build Fort King George near what is now Darien, and they used the giant tidewater cypress trees from Lewis Island to construct the fort. Then, during the 1800s, logging crews spread throughout the coastal swamps, stripping them clean of their extensive forests of cypress and other hardwoods. The Altamaha River, which runs through these swamps, became the major artery for transporting the giant trees to the sawmills in Darien on the coast. The river was heavily trafficked by great log rafts and paddlewheel steamboats, carrying passengers and supplies to the inland ports of Macon and Dublin. The swamp on Lewis Island, like other swamps on the coast, was shaken by this activity. Hunters all but annihilated the swamp's vast alligator population to satisfy the demand for belts, shoes, and bags made from alligator hide. Even when the construction of modern highways curtailed much of the activity on the river during the 1920s and '30s, unrestrained logging and hunting in the area continued, lasting well into the 1960s.

In 1974, the state of Georgia, urged on by environmentalists, purchased Lewis Island from the Georgia Pacific Corporation for what is said to have been about half its commercial worth. And now, the wildlife is returning. In the northern half of the island (where giant oaks and other hardwoods, rather than cypress, pierce the sky) birds are returning: ibis, swallowtail kites, and even bald eagles are finding a home here. And in the deep recesses of the island, where dozens of streams and creeks flow freely and unpolluted, small snails are appearing and are attracting a rare resident: the limkin, the majestic crane that devours snails, is finally returning after an absence of two centuries.

"Our giant cypress trees are safe now," Manager Edwards said. "And since the state owns and protects this land, the gators are returning, too. We run a regular check on the alligator population, and it is holding healthy and steady," he said proudly. "Someday, we hope to have an elevated boardwalk, like they have in the Okefenokee Swamp, here on Lewis Island, leading into the cypress-tree area."

A boardwalk sounded like a good idea as we trudged through the muck of the swamp, with only the red-ribbon blazes to mark our way in to the trees. We were fortunate that our hike was being made during a dry season; the muck didn't cover our feet. "Sometimes when you come in here," Edwards explained, "you're hiking through swamp water up to your knees and above." We ducked and twisted through the swamp, going over and under the roots, limbs, and vines. We paused at each ribbon blaze so that we could spot the next one. Then we trudged on behind Edwards in single file, into the deep recesses of the island.

Sooner than I expected, Edwards announced, "There's one of the cypress trees up there, ahead of us." Following his point and looking through the underbrush, I saw what looked like a big brown streak painted against the backdrop of the swamp. It was a tree trunk so big that it seemed alien to the growth around it. To approach its base, we had to weave in and around the many knees of its extensive root system. Four men would have been needed to reach around its trunk. Peering up from its base, I saw that this towering giant rose far above the roof of the swamp, leaving the other trees to their lower realms, while it ruled at an altitude all its own.

Moving on through the swamp, we soon spotted another cypress, about the same size and height as the first, and then another one in the distance. The fourth one we came upon was the biggest we had seen yet. The swamp growth had folded back from it, and it commanded a large space all its own.

The size of these trees is impressive enough. But I felt an added sense of wonder, knowing that I was standing in an area that is just a tiny remnant of what once was the widespread kingdom of these giants. This is the only known grove of these tidewater virgin gum cypress trees in Georgia. Once, whole forests of them, some as old as 1300 years, stood sentinel over the river swamps of the state's coastal plain.

"There are only about fifty or so healthy cypress trees left in this grove," Edwards informed us. "And the only reason they are here is simply because the cable that the logging companies used to drag out trees was too short to reach them." He went on to explain how the loggers would run a tram deep into the swamps, with a 1000-foot cable that would reach out on each side to drag the cut cypress trees through the swamp and into the river, to float down to the sawmills in Darien. "These trees were too deep in the swamp for the thousand-foot cable to reach them. So they were left," Edwards explained.

"That must have been some undertaking," I commented.

"Oh, those trees would shake the island when they fell," he replied. "And then when they lashed that cable to them and drug them through the swamp, it must have been like a huge tank, ripping and tearing away everything in their paths."

"These swamps must have been slashed to pieces by such operations," I said.

"Yep," he replied, "it must've been pretty bad." Then, looking up at the giant tree under which we were standing, Edwards added, "And with a little more cable, they would have gotten these, too. But they're safe now," he concluded.

Luck and location may be part of the reason these cypress trees have survived. But they have confronted and survived threats as formidable as man's cables: centuries of storms, floods, lightning, disease, and fire. While I lingered, gazing up at the trees, I began to feel a little philosophical, pondering the trees' qualities that have helped them to survive, and might aid us, too: inner strength, rootage, and heredity—and a healthy dose of privacy.

Both time and tide prompted us to conclude our visit to the trees and begin our journey out of the swamp. As we were leaving, I spotted another giant tree, different from the rest. Instead of having a long, perfectly straight trunk, it was deformed by a massive tumorlike growth around its base.

"What caused that?" I asked Edwards.

"Oh, any number of things could have done it," he replied. "It could have been an old disease, or perhaps an injury when it was a young sapling. It could have been struck by a floating object during a flood, or been stepped on by a large animal or reptile. Or, maybe an Indian did it," he added with a smile as he walked on ahead.

"Well," I thought to myself, "injury or not, it's still standing. It survived as well as the rest of them." and perhaps that injury, whatever caused it, might even have helped a little. No Indian would have selected that twisted grain for canoe material. And only long, straight timbers were used to construct Fort King George. And the early loggers probably would have suspected some kind of inner decay and left it alone, even if their cables could have reached it. There is no sure way to know.

But this we can know: nature, as it sometimes does, somehow compensated for the injury, strengthened the blemish. The tree sent out more roots and climbed right on up through the roof of the swamp. Scars and all, it's still standing there among the others—a survivor of the centuries.

CANOEING GUIDE

Lower Altamaha River

The Altamaha is the largest river in Georgia, with a colorful history, indeed. It is also more ecologically sensitive, commercially valuable, and politically controversial than any other river in the state. Any effort to tamper with it in any way is liable to be opposed by historians, environmentalists, archaeologists, botanists, sportsmen, and politicians from all over the state, and with reason. Botanists still search for the elusive *Franklinia alatamaha*, a plant discovered in the area and named by naturalist William Bartram in 1790 (it has never been seen there, or anywhere else in the wild since, and the only extant plants are descendants of Bartram's cuttings). Archaeologists work to protect the more than 1000 Indian sites in the area, where pottery fragments can be found on the bluffs beside the river. Historians consider the river and the area near it to be a microcosm of 400 years of history: the Spanish Mission era of the 16th century; the battles among the Indians, the French, the Spanish, and the English for control of the area during the 17th century; the Colonial and Revolutionary eras of the 18th century; and the 19th century, when plantation life, riverboats, and log rafts characterized the river and its environs. Foresters plead for protection of the few remaining giant trees in the area. They have been sought after since the great swamp cypress were cut to build Fort King George in 1721. Later, the area's hardwoods were used to build America's most famous fighting ship: the *USS Constitution*. Naturalists claim that the Altamaha River and its basin provide Georgia with its most concentrated and variegated outdoor environment, supporting wildlife and marine life unequalled by any other area in the state. Coastal environmentalists and commercial fishermen monitor river conditions carefully. A very delicate ecological balance must be maintained here to make sure that Georgia's normally abundant fishing and shrimping grounds, in and near the river's delta, are protected.

Industrial corporations also have a big stake in what happens along the Altamaha River. IT and T's Rayonier plant at Jesup is the world's largest cellulose manufacturer. Georgia Power Company's Plant Hatch, beside the river near Baxley, is Georgia's only nuclear power plant. Other corporations, such as Georgia Pacific, St. Regis, Union Camp, and Brunswick Pulp and Paper, have substantial landholdings along the Altamaha.

With so many interests demanding so much from the Altamaha, one would think it would be a hodgepodge of activity and change. But thanks to farsighted political and community leaders, cooperative industries, and efficient wildlife management, the Altamaha River retains much of its wilderness quality. Most of the bordering land below the Altamaha Park Fish Camp is already owned by the state, including the 6000-acre Lewis Island tract bordering the river's north bank, and most of the river's islands are now under the protective management of the Altamaha State Waterfowl Management Area. And on the upper stretch (from Jesup to the Altamaha Park Fish Camp) the state owns a 100-yard-wide strip of land on each shore; these strips, donated by Rayonier, act as buffer zones.

The entire stretch from Jesup to Darien is being considered for the establishment of a river park for public recreation and education. The guide below covers 13.7 miles, including a side trip to Lewis Island, the location of Georgia's last stand of rare virgin cypress trees.

General Description: Although this area of the Altamaha River offers many possible types of canoe trips, I chose to make the straight run from Altamaha Park Fish Camp to Darien's city dock, via the Altamaha (10.5 miles), the Rifle Cut (1.5 miles), Darien Creek (1 mile), and the Darien River to the take-out ramp (.7 mile)—a total of 13.7 river miles. The detour up Big Buzzard Creek to the Lewis Island area adds another two miles.

We put in at the Altamaha Park Fish Camp at high tide, early enough to allow us to explore a lake called Alligator Congress (mile .8), where we saw many gator tracks but no gators. We stopped at Wesley Horn (mile 6), at the site of a floating cabin, illegally attached to land by a boardwalk (on state-owned land, as here, floating houses are allowed only rope moorings). The shore behind the cabin would make a suitable campsite. We selected a shack at a site downstream, however, nearer Big Buzzard Creek, as our campground. This loggers' shack of 19th-century vintage sits on the south bank of the main river channel at mile 7.5, about 400 yards below the fork of the Altamaha and South Branch (mile 7.2). To find the shack, hug the right bank of the main channel below the fork, and look carefully for it (its aging lumber blends so well with the forest that it's easy to overlook).

While at the old loggers' cabin, we met David Edwards, manager of the Altamaha State Waterfowl Management Area, who came up to give us a guided tour of Lewis Island's grove of rare cypress trees. To reach this grove, we traveled .7 mile downstream from the cabin to Big Buzzard Creek on the left (north) side of the Altamaha at mile 8.2. One mile up Big Buzzard Creek is a slight clearing in the forest on the right (east) bank. This is the remains of an old canal dug to get dirt to build the tramway just to its right. Just 1/10 mile farther up Big Buzzard Creek is a second tramway and canal (both are indicated on the Sterling Quadrant topo map). These trams were built to move cut trees to Big Buzzard Creek. Just beyond the second tramway, the Georgia Department of Natural Resources keeps a red ribbon marker tied to a tree along the right bank, the only marked entrance point to the cypress grove. From here, hike 1000 yards or so due north into the swamp to reach the tree area. This is a very wild area, with no paths—only red-ribbon blazes on trees every 20 or 30 yards. Stop at each blaze, and don't continue until you spot the next one. Don't wander off aimlessly. The cypress trees are scattered throughout the grove area. Spend some time looking at them, but don't lose your sense of direction or contact with the red-ribbon blazes. If you get lost, head southeastward (don't forget a compass on this trip). This should bring you to the old tram ditch, which you can follow south to Big Buzzard Creek. Remember, your canoes are just to the west of the ditch. Visitors to the tree area should be equipped with sturdy shoes; walking may be through ankle- or knee-deep swamp.

To continue to Darien, retrace your route out of Big Buzzard Creek to the Altamaha River. Once back on the Altamaha, keep to the left (north) side of the river, past Cottonbox Island (at mile 9) and on to the large entrance to Lewis Creek at mile 9.8. At this point, you must begin looking for the most critical checkpoint on the trip to Darien: less than a mile ahead, on the left bank at the big curve, is the entrance to the Rifle Cut. This 1.3-mile straight-as-an-arrow canal, running on an east-west axis, will save three miles of river travel. Cut near the turn of the century for the purpose of diverting the Altamaha River to Darien, it was never widened as planned. It has remained a scenic little 20-foot-wide canal flowing through a tunnel of trees. From the point at which Lewis Creek enters the Altamaha (mile 9.8) you can see in the distance a slight V in the treeline on the left bank near Piney Island; this is the entrance to the Rifle Cut (hug the left bank of the river, and look carefully). Once you've paddled through the Rifle Cut, the channel bends slightly to the right before entering Darien Creek. Turn left (north) into Darien Creek, which runs under I-95; you are now about a mile from the take-out. Bear right (south) at the confluence of Cathead Creek on the left (the stream now becomes Darien River), and continue around the curve to Darien's city dock and the take-out ramp.

An Alternate One-Day Lewis Island Trip

Those who wish to canoe to the cypress grove in one day can try the following trip. Put in at Darien's city dock at the earliest possible low tide (in daylight). Using the current caused by the incoming tide, paddle up the Darien River for .7 mile, then 1.2 miles on Darien Creek, 1.3 miles through the Rifle Cut, then 2.5 miles up the Altamaha River, and right onto Big Buzzard for a mile to the red-ribbon marker on the tree at the entrance point near the tram ditch that leads to the trees. The canoeing should take 3–4 hours, leaving a couple of hours to see the trees before returning to Darien.

Hazards: Canoeing the Altamaha requires special skills and precautions. Despite its beauty, this river is potentially dangerous, presenting perils not usually faced by canoeists. Only experienced canoeists who are also skilled outdoorsmen and strong swimmers should attempt this trip. The primary hazards are big water, ocean tides, sudden winds or storms, shortage of campsites, mazes of misleading channels, and an abundance of wildlife, including snakes and insects.

The Georgia Department of Natural Resources administers the Lewis Island Natural Area, and folks there are more than anxious to have interested people visit it. Nevertheless, they make several requests. Let them know about when you plan to enter the grove and when you plan to come out. They suggest that at least one canoe in a party carry a small gas outboard motor in case of unexpected storms or tide changes. Carry a detailed map and a compass at all times.

Big waters: This is the largest river in Georgia, with a flow comparable to that of the Nile. It is the center of the largest river system on the Eastern Seaboard south of Chesapeake Bay. These waters are deep and powerful; they should not be entered without careful planning and preparation.

Tides: The stretch from the Altamaha Park Fish Camp to the coast is strongly influenced by ocean tides. They affect water levels and direction of flow. Canoeing downstream on this section must be done on an outgoing tide. Sustained progress against the tidal flow is impossible, so the entire trip must be calculated with careful attention to tidal tables (each tide lasts about 6 hours). Remember: the printed tidal tables for the whole Brunswick area are based on measurements taken at a point on the coast called the Outer Bar. The time between when the tide is a certain depth at that point and when that depth occurs at your location must be calculated. For example, the "lag time" at Darien's city dock is plus 1 hour, 15 minutes. The "lag time" for the Altamaha Park Fish Camp is 4 hours. If you plan a lengthy trip downriver from the Altamaha Park Fish Camp, put in at high tide at the boat ramp.

Sudden winds and storms: Unexpected weather changes are common in coastal areas. This river becomes quite wide on the lower stretches, as much as 1200 feet, and the paddler should be extra cautious about watching for storms and taking necessary action before they are upon him. The frontal winds of an ordinary summer thunderstorm are of an extremely high velocity. Coastal squalls can suddenly develop out of a clear sky. If bad weather is approaching, head for the nearest leeward (downwind) bit of land, and nestle in among the overhanging trees or, preferably, get to shore. If you are caught in open water by high winds, head into the wind and waves. Do not let the wind blow the canoe into a sideways, or broaching, attitude against the waves; this will result in a capsize (life vests should be worn at all times). If you should capsize, stay with your canoe—it will float—and dog paddle yourself and your canoe to the nearest shore.

Scarce campsites: Unlike the upper section of the Altamaha, where many sandbars await campers, in this lower stretch from the Altamaha Park Fish Camp to Darien sandbars are nonexistent (this is due to the constant ebb and flow of the tides). Camping is on bluffs along the bank. When selecting a possible campsite, be sure the ground is not damp from a recent high tide (this section of the river rises 5–6 feet at high tide). Topo maps indicate campgrounds along some banks, but don't depend on those being maintained.

The 13.7 miles covered in this guide constitute too long a run with too many unpredictables to be considered a one-day trip. Plan to take two days. I suggest camping at mile 7.5, at the old loggers' shack on right, stay on the right side of the main channel, and watch for the shack about 400 yards below the fork. The cabin site has space for two or three tents, and the cabin has a dry floor. When tying canoes for the night, remember to leave enough slack in the lines to accommodate the rise and fall of the tide. Better still, drag canoes out of the water. This old shack is said to have been used by the early log rafters as a place to wait for the tide to come in. The state now owns the shack and Chambers Island, the land on which it sits.

Misleading channels: As the Altamaha River nears the coast, it divides into branches, creeks, and cuts. Getting lost in the marshes and swamps of the river's last 5 miles is unnecessary, but it's very likely if certain precautions are not taken. It is important to let folks at the Altamaha State Waterfowl Management Area know when you mean to take this trip and when you plan to get off the river. Carry our map or a topo map and a compass, and use them carefully.

Wildlife: If proper equipment is used and precautions are adhered to, the extensive wildlife of the area will be one of the most enjoyable features of this trip. Snakes, alligators, raccoons, bobcats, and other large critters are plentiful in the swamps of the Altamaha. During snake season, look before you grab limbs or step onto stumps along the banks. All well equipped sportsmen should carry snakebite kits. Don't poke or shoot at any wildlife. Just watch them.

Shuttle: This shuttle guide begins at the take-out ramp at Darien's city dock (Darien is 17 miles north of Brunswick on US 17). Turn west onto Broad St at the north end of the US 17 bridge over the Darien River, drive one block, turn left (south) onto Screven St,

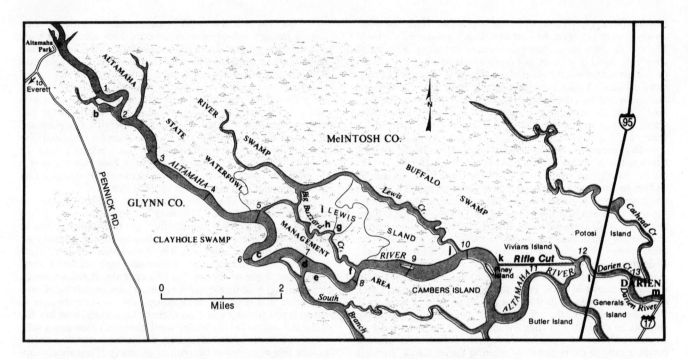

and follow it to the river's edge. Park the shuttle car well away from the ramp.

To reach the put in, drive back up to US 17, turn right (south) onto Broad St, drive over the bridge, and continue on 17 for 4.7 miles to its intersection with Ga 99. Turn right (west) onto 99, and drive 6.9 miles to Sterling, where 99 intersects US 341. Turn right (north) onto 341, and drive 9.6 miles to Everett, just beyond the RR overpass. Turn right at the Altamaha Fish Camp sign (across from the Union 76 station). Follow a paved road for 3.3 miles. Drive under the RR trestle to the put-in ramp. Ample parking is available.

Water levels: Water level for this stretch of the Altamaha is obtained from the gauging station at Doctortown, near Jesup. Readings are given daily in the *Savannah Morning News* and are announced over WLOP (1370-AM) and WIFC (105.5-FM) at 20 minutes, 35 minutes, and 50 minutes after each hour.

Although gauge readings are a help in knowing the overall condition of the river and will warn if the river is approaching flood stage (10 feet or more), river readings are less important for this 13.7-mile stretch from Altamaha Park Fish Camp to Darien than they are on most rivers. Here, the tide is the critical force, both in terms of water levels and direction of flow. It is imperative that you be aware of tidal tables and the current state of the river.

Distances: The river mileage from the Altamaha Park Fish Camp to Darien's city dock (via the Rifle Cut, Darien Creek, and the Darien River) is 13.7 miles. Unfortunately, the mileage markers placed on the river by the Army Corps of Engineers, which are still on its upper reaches, no longer exist on the stretch from the Altamaha Park Fish Camp to Darien (we have, however, noted these mileages on our map).

Maps: The area from Altamaha Park Fish Camp to Darien's city dock is included in four topo maps: the Cox, Sterling, Darien, and Ridgeville quadrants.

Map guide: Numbers on our map indicate river mileage. Letters locate points of interest.

a. Put in at Altamaha Park Fish Camp.
b. Alligator Congress Lake.
c. Wesley Horn, with floating cabin.
d. Fork of South Branch.
e. Campsite at old loggers' shack.
f. Entrance to Big Buzzard Creek.
g. Tram canals.
h. Red ribbon, marking entrance to cypress trees.
i. Area of virgin cypress trees.
j. Entrance to Lewis Creek.
k. Entrance to the Rifle Cut.
l. I-95 bridge.
m. Take out at Darien's city dock.

1982

River Picnic

A summertime float trip on peaceful Whitewater creek

by Margaret Tucker

Whitewater Creek isn't—whitewater, that is. It's blackwater, mysterious, and absolutely flat. This tributary of the Flint is the prettiest, most peaceful little swamp river you'll find. Exactly right for a lazy day's float, for a big old-fashioned picnic, for taking all the kids and the dog along.

It's also one of the few rivers you can go to with excellent public access for both your put in (at Whitewater Creek State Park) and your take out (on the Flint River). No slipping with your loaded canoe down a near-vertical road embankment, no getting stuck in the mud on some rutted cow path, no private property to cross, no poison ivy to wade through. Heck, it's not even a challenge to get in. We didn't even get wet feet launching the canoes when my husband Skip and I, with friends Ruth Gershon, Doug Woodward, and Harriet and Charlie Landau set out for a day's float in 3 canoes overloaded with an amazing assortment of food.

I had billed this trip as a floating picnic, so we were all bringing some goodies. I thought I had the *piece de resistance* with my home-baked bisquits and real, farm cured country ham from a secret source known to my agriculture-teacher father. When we put in at noon, Charlie had already ravaged the bologna sandwiches, but everyone else was waiting for the mossy bank, the shady oak, and the picnic in the grand style.

The creek is an enchanting place. It winds so much that even if there are more than three canoes in your party, you won't see but one or two of them. The swamp is shady with big swollen-based gums, water oaks, red maples—thick with Spanish moss. Bird songs echo through the quiet. A hollow "plop" sounds as a turtle reluctantly slides from his sunning spot into the dark water to escape you, the threatening intruder.

Isn't it tiresome to always be the enemy? The birds fly, the deer flee in panic. Of course, if you stand *absolutely* still, deer frequently come back for another look, being more curious than any animal except possibly cows. But a canoe will bring you closer to wild animals than almost any other transportation, including feet. If you just drift you can come right up to many animals. I've drifted along behind mama ducks and their fledglings and been practically nose to nose with beaver. I'll never forget a young woodcock who happily foraged on a muddy bank while I floated only feet away.

This day, however, my sneaking wasn't up to par. As Skip and I bore in on a fat, sleeping water snake, hoping for a good picture even without a telephoto lens, he awoke and was gone, didn't even splash. They're hard to sneak up on when you want to. On land they can actually feel you coming through vibrations. I don't know what warned this one.

We drifted on downstream, getting hungry and looking for that ideal picnic spot. It wasn't easy. The river was in flood and water stretched back into the trees as far as we could see. (Although most rivers in flood are very dangerous, Whitewater Creek and this stretch of the Flint are safe even in flood stage.) We had seen only one dry spot since the put in, a small clearing and bank on the south, but a lady and her dog seemed to be enjoying the tranquility there and we hesitated to disturb them. She was the only person we saw.

Finally, almost to the junction with the Flint, we saw a bank on the south side. We pulled the canoes up and were about to jump out, when a huge pig came over the bank. In a second we were faced with a dozen pigs, curious about this novelty in their drinking spot. Done out of our picnic spot by the pigs, we retreated into the flooded swamp and tied the canoes three abreast between two tupelo gums for our picnic.

Ever spread a table cloth in the bottom of a Grumman? It didn't affect the taste of fried chicken, country ham, deviled eggs, and banana bread at all.

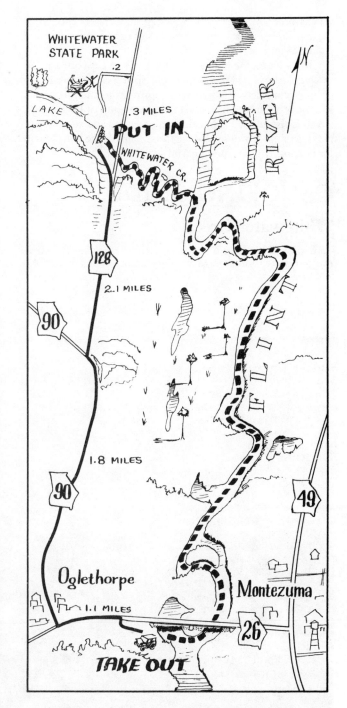

After lunch we switched the beginners to the stern paddling position, which is where most of the work is done in flatwater, to learn the J-stroke. Ruth made a few circles at first, but soon caught up. Once out of the swamp and on the broad, smooth water of the Flint, it didn't matter if we went in circles, as there were no obstacles. The Flint is a pleasant change from the smaller river. Where Whitewater Creek was almost a tunnel with trees arched overhead, and an occasional limb to duck under or scrape across, we now had acres and acres of open water. Although the Flint looks sluggish, it moves enough to make paddling almost unnecessary. I stretched out in the sun and let Skip steer.

We spotted the highway bridge before we expected it. To reach the car we had to go under one span then around the tip of an island a few hundred yards upstream to the other span and the boat ramp. The island marks the mouth of Buck Creek, which is also runnable, but that's another day and another picnic. There's plenty of time along the swamps of the Flint system for floating, fishing, sunning, and swimming.

CANOEING GUIDE

Whitewater Creek

To Set Up Your Auto Shuttle: Leave one car at the Flint River bridge between Montezuma and Oglethorpe on highway 26-49-90. There's a public boat ramp and parking on the west side of the river just downstream of the bridge. Drive southwest 1.1 miles into Oglethorpe and turn right (north) on Georgia 90. Follow it 1.8 miles north to Georgia 128, which bends right. Georgia 128 will lead you another 2.1 miles to the Whitewater Creek bridge just downstream from the state park where you'll start this easy float trip down Whitewater Creek and the Flint River. Allow about 5 hours, including lunch, for the leisurely 8 mile trip.

If you want to enjoy a shady picnic or set up a camp before you begin, then cross Whitewater Creek and turn left .3 mile beyond the bridge and left again .2 mile farther to enter the park. There are good camp sites beside the lake, a put-in path below the dam that forms Whitewater Pond, and picnic tables under the trees.

If you intend only to canoe the stream, you'll find it more convenient to turn left .1 mile before crossing the creek and put in on the south side of the creek below the dam. It looks like this road only leads into the Baptist churchyard, but there's a state park launching site a few yards farther.

1975

APPENDIX

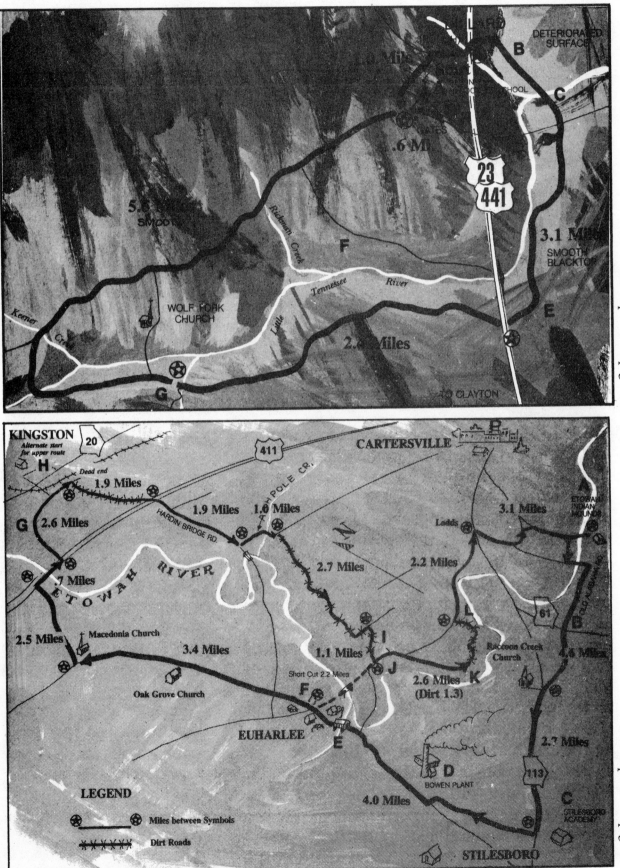

*This map refers to page 25.

*This map refers to page 31.

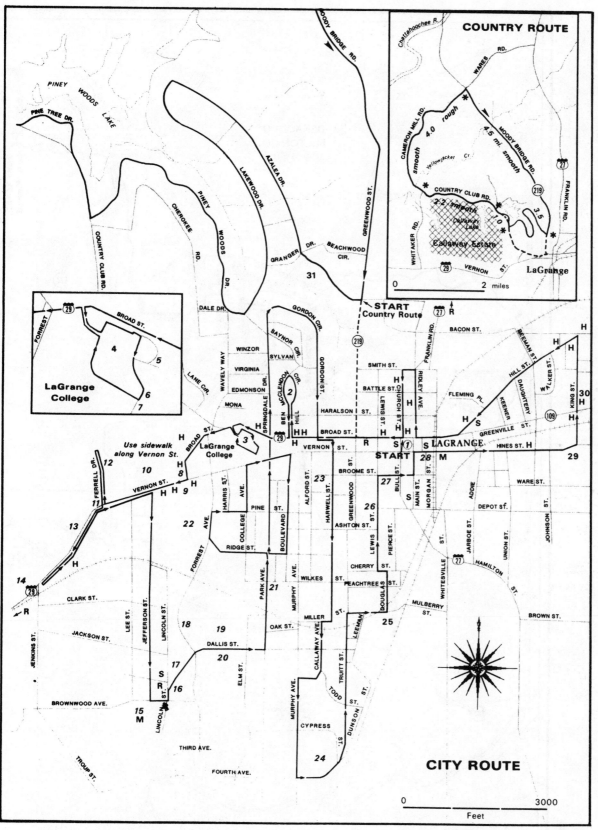

COUNTRY ROUTE

CITY ROUTE

This map refers to page 53.

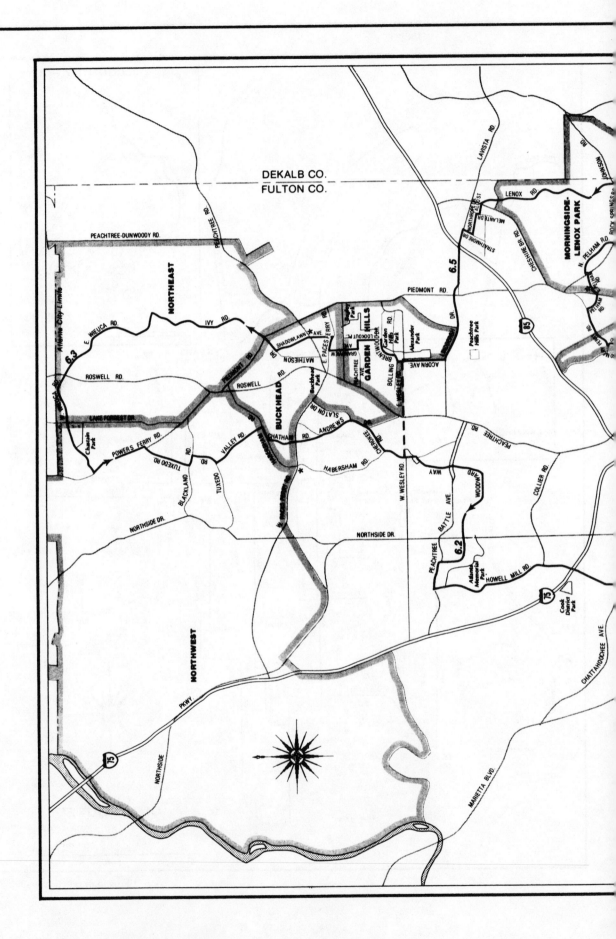

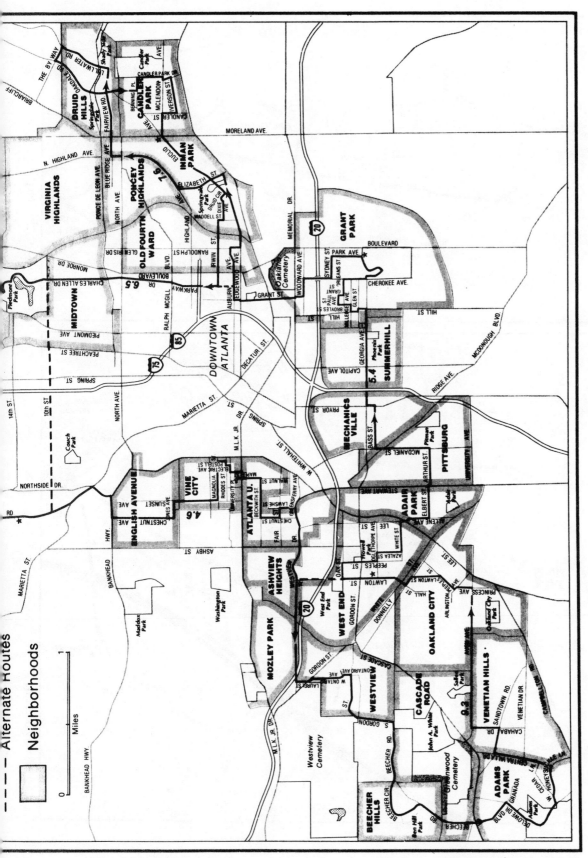

This map refers to page 43.

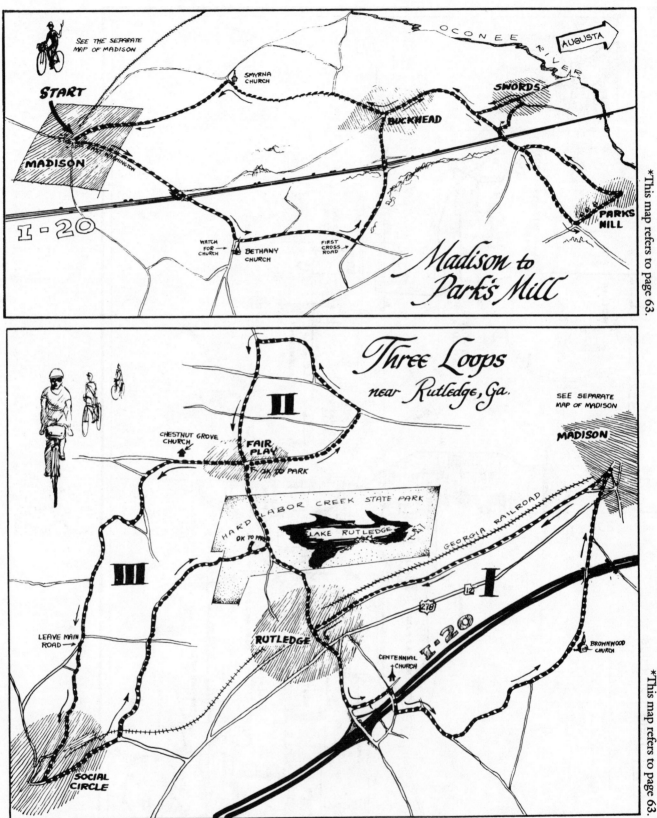

SEE THE SEPARATE MAP OF MADISON

START

SMYRNA CHURCH

OCONEE RIVER

AUGUSTA

SWORDS

BUCKHEAD

MADISON

EAST WASHINGTON

PARKS MILL

I-20

WATCH FOR CHURCH

BETHANY CHURCH

FIRST CROSS ROAD

Madison to Park's Mill

*This map refers to page 63.

Three Loops
near Rutledge, Ga.

II

CHESTNUT GROVE CHURCH

FAIR PLAY

OK TO PARK

SEE SEPARATE MAP OF MADISON

MADISON

HARD LABOR CREEK STATE PARK

LAKE RUTLEDGE

GEORGIA RAILROAD

III

OK TO PARK

I

12

278

I-20

LEAVE MAIN ROAD

RUTLEDGE

CENTENNIAL CHURCH

BROWNWOOD CHURCH

SOCIAL CIRCLE

*This map refers to page 63.

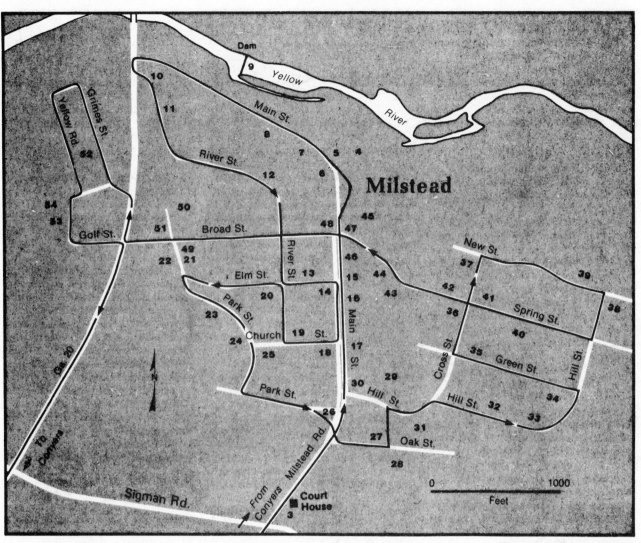

*This map refers to page 65.

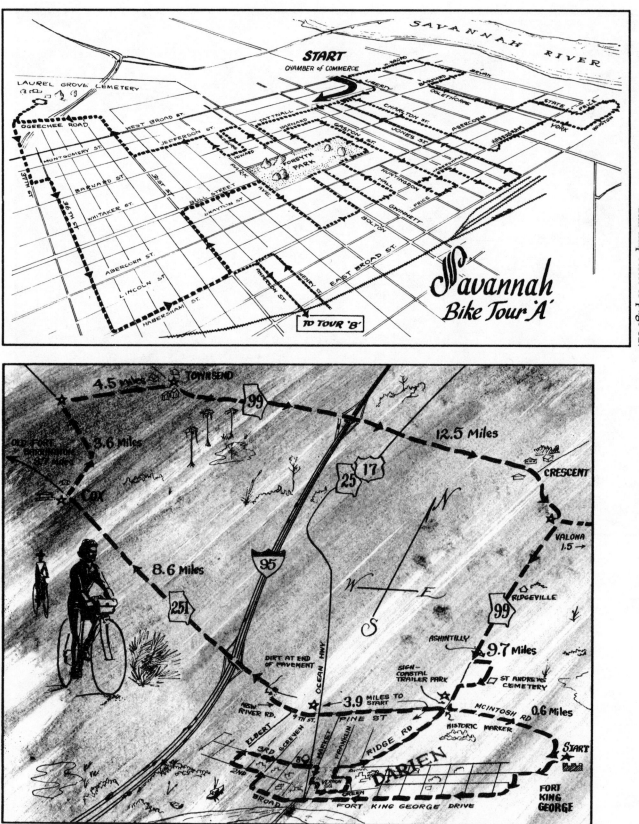

*This map refers to page 82.

*This map refers to page 86.

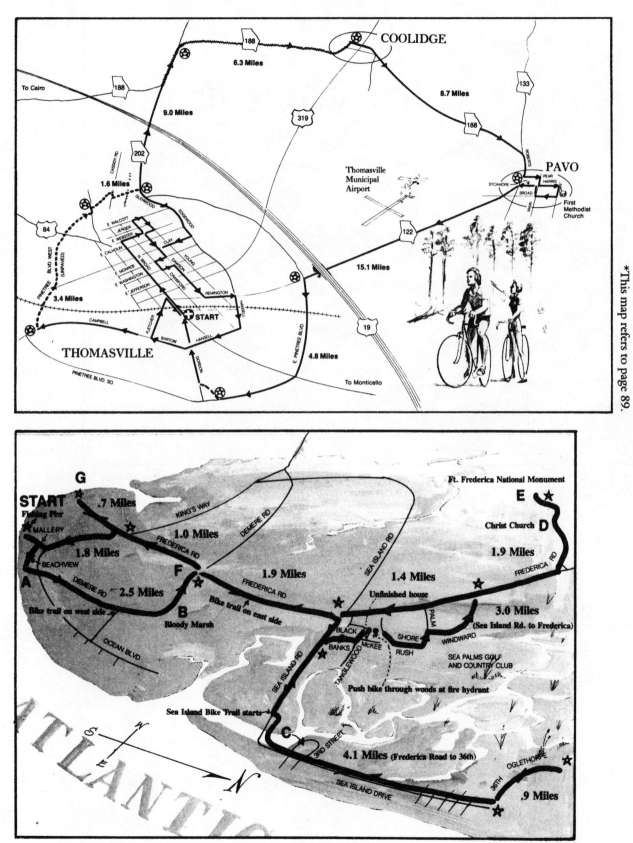

*This map refers to page 89.

*This map refers to page 92.

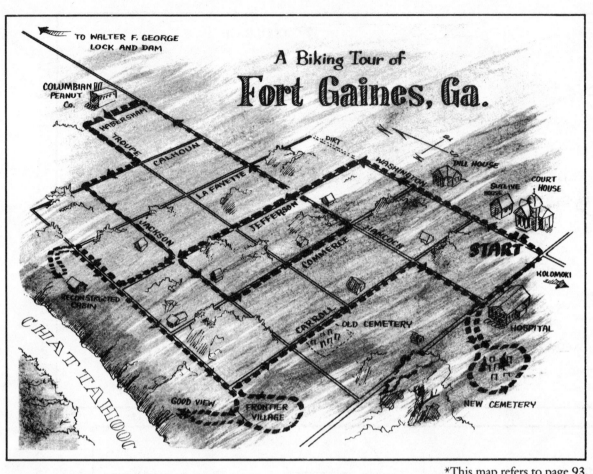

*This map refers to page 93.

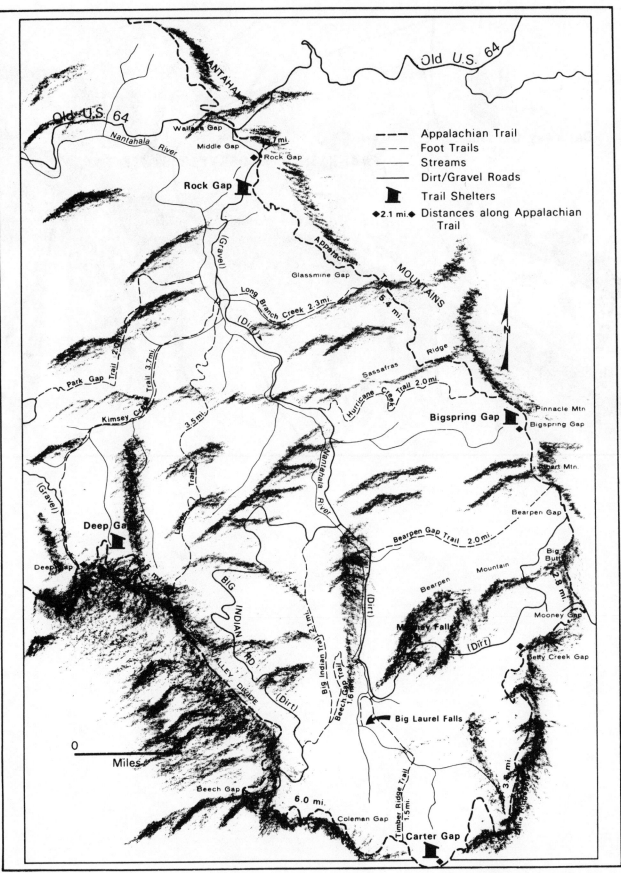

Old U.S. 64

NANTAHALA

Old U.S. 64

Nantahala River

Wallace Gap

Middle Gap

.7 mi.

Rock Gap

Rock Gap

Appalachian Trail

Glassmine Gap

MOUNTAINS

5.4 mi.

Long Branch Creek 2.3 mi.

(Gravel)

(Dirt)

Ridge

Sassafras

Park Gap Trail 2.0 mi.

Kimsey Cr Trail 3.7 mi.

Hurricane Creek Trail 2.0 mi.

Bigspring Gap

Pinnacle Mtn

3.5 mi.

Bigspring Gap

Standing Indian Trail

Nantahala River

Hart Mtn.

Bearpen Gap

(Gravel)

Deep Gap

Bearpen Gap Trail 2.0 mi.

Big Butt

Mooney Gap

Deep Gap

2.8 mi.

BIG INDIAN RD.

Bearpen Mountain

Mooney Falls

(Dirt)

NANTAHALA VALLEY DIVIDE

(Dirt)

Betty Creek Gap

Timber Ridge Trail 2.1 mi.

Beech Gap Trail 1.6 mi.

Big Laurel Falls

0

Miles

Beech Gap

Timber Ridge Trail 1.5 mi.

3.5 mi.

6.0 mi.

Coleman Gap

Carter Gap

Appalachian Trail ----

Foot Trails - - -

Streams ——

Dirt/Gravel Roads ——

Trail Shelters

◆2.1 mi.◆ Distances along Appalachian Trail

N

*This map refers to page 113.

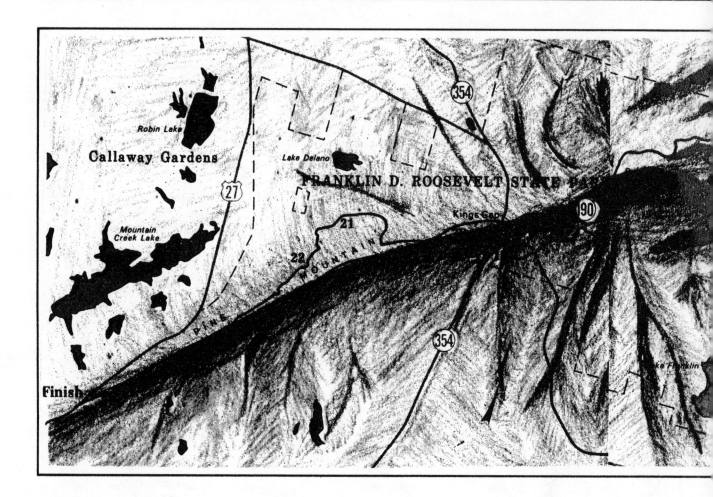

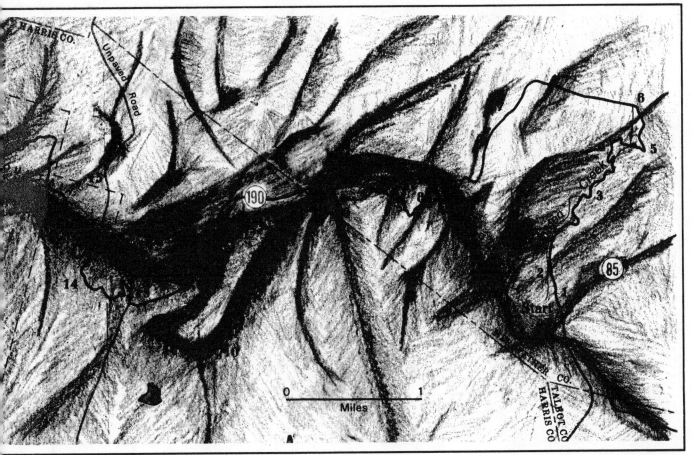

*This map refers to page 142.

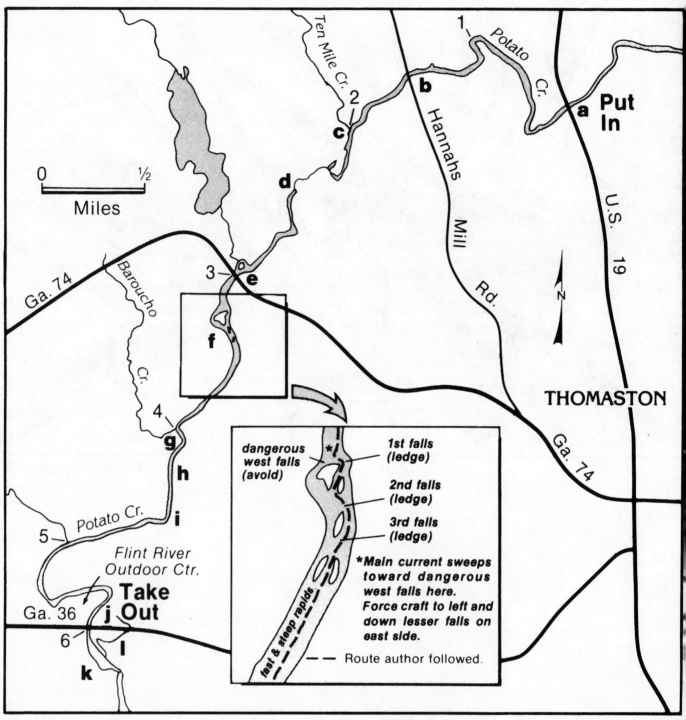

1

Potato Cr.

b

a Put In

Ten Mile Cr. 2

Hannahs Mill Rd.

c

U.S. 19

d

N

0 ½

Miles

THOMASTON

Ga. 74

Baroucho Cr.

3

e

f

Ga. 74

4

g

h

dangerous west falls (avoid)

1st falls (ledge)

2nd falls (ledge)

3rd falls (ledge)

i

Potato Cr.

5

*Main current sweeps toward dangerous west falls here. Force craft to left and down lesser falls on east side.

Flint River Outdoor Ctr.

Take Out

Ga. 36

j

6

l

k

fast & steep rapids

— — — Route author followed.

*This map refers to page 207.

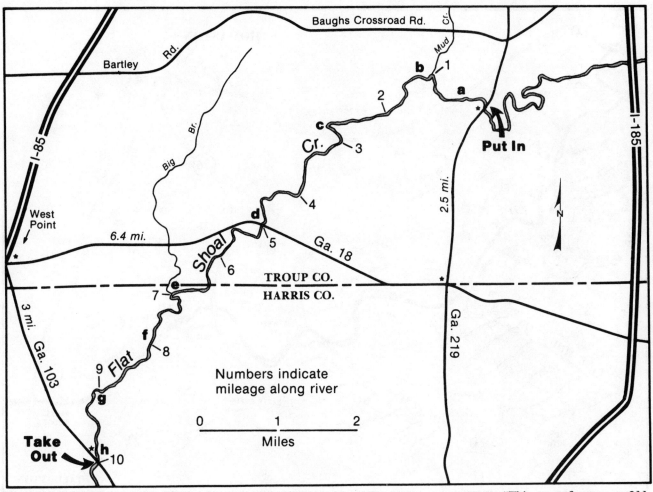

Baughs Crossroad Rd.

Bartley Rd.

Big Br.

I-85

I-185

West Point

6.4 mi.

Shoal

Flat

3 mi. Ga. 103

Cr.

Ga. 18

Ga. 219

2.5 mi.

Mud Cr.

Put In

b 1

2

c 3

4

d

5

e 6

7

f 8

9

g

Take Out

h 10

a

TROUP CO.
HARRIS CO.

N

Numbers indicate
mileage along river

0   1   2
Miles

*This map refers to page 211.

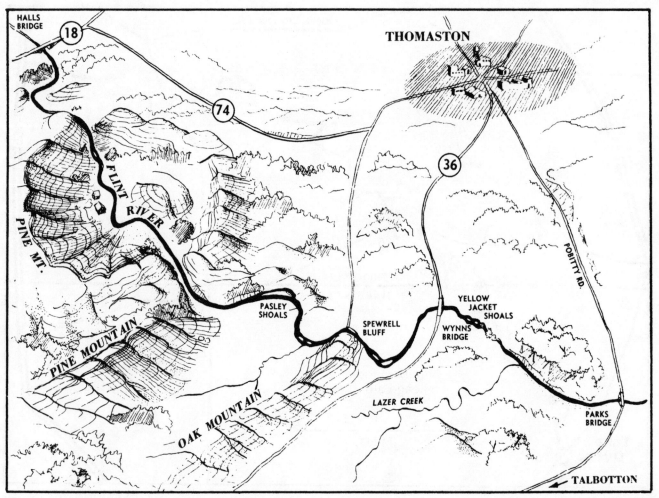

HALLS BRIDGE

18

THOMASTON

74

36

PINE MT.

FLINT RIVER

PINE MOUNTAIN

OAK MOUNTAIN

PASLEY SHOALS

SPEWRELL BLUFF

LAZER CREEK

WYNNS BRIDGE

YELLOW JACKET SHOALS

POBITTY RD.

PARKS BRIDGE

TALBOTTON

*This map refers to page 212.

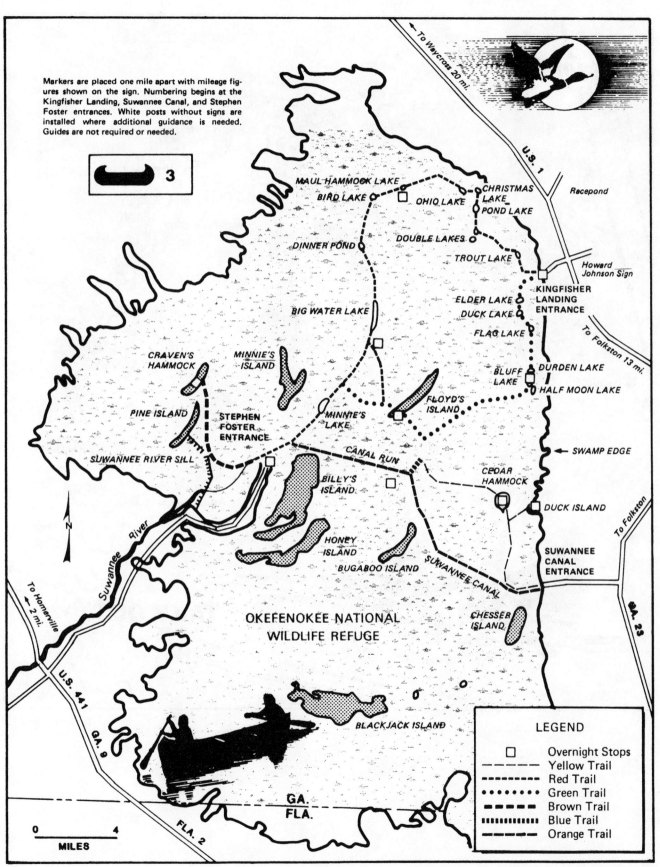

Markers are placed one mile apart with mileage figures shown on the sign. Numbering begins at the Kingfisher Landing, Suwannee Canal, and Stephen Foster entrances. White posts without signs are installed where additional guidance is needed. Guides are not required or needed.

3

To Waycross 20 mi.

U.S. 1

Racepond

MAUL HAMMOCK LAKE

BIRD LAKE

OHIO LAKE

CHRISTMAS LAKE

POND LAKE

DINNER POND

DOUBLE LAKES

TROUT LAKE

Howard Johnson Sign

KINGFISHER LANDING ENTRANCE

BIG WATER LAKE

ELDER LAKE

DUCK LAKE

FLAG LAKE

To Folkston 13 mi.

CRAVEN'S HAMMOCK

MINNIE'S ISLAND

BLUFF LAKE

DURDEN LAKE

HALF MOON LAKE

PINE ISLAND

STEPHEN FOSTER ENTRANCE

MINNIE'S LAKE

FLOYD'S ISLAND

SWAMP EDGE

SUWANNEE RIVER SILL

CANAL RUN

CEDAR HAMMOCK

To Folkston

N

Suwannee River

BILLY'S ISLAND

DUCK ISLAND

SUWANNEE CANAL ENTRANCE

To Homerville 2 mi.

HONEY ISLAND

BUGABOO ISLAND

SUWANNEE CANAL

GA. 23

U.S. 441

GA. 9

OKEFENOKEE NATIONAL WILDLIFE REFUGE

CHESSER ISLAND

BLACKJACK ISLAND

GA. FLA.

FLA. 2

0   4
MILES

LEGEND

☐   Overnight Stops
— — —   Yellow Trail
- - - - -   Red Trail
· · · · ·   Green Trail
– – – –   Brown Trail
▮▮▮▮▮   Blue Trail
— —   Orange Trail

*This map refers to page 223.

To Jesup

301

PUT IN

SATILLA Strickland Bluff Hammeek Bluff Rosin Landing

To Nahunta

RIVER

Ammons Ferry Bridge

Honey Bluff

TAKE OUT

84

To Nahunta

*This map refers to page 231.

INDEX